Microsoft®

Excel

Visual Basic®
for Applications
Reference

Microsoft
PRESS

PUBLISHED BY
Microsoft Press
A Division of Microsoft Corporation
One Microsoft Way
Redmond, Washington 98052-6399

Library of Congress Cataloging-in-Publication Data
Microsoft Excel visual basic for applications reference / Microsoft
    Corporation.
        p.   cm.
    ISBN 1-55615-624-3
    1. Microsoft Visual BASIC.   2. Microsoft Excel (Computer file)
    I. Microsoft Corporation.
    QA76.73.B3M543   1993
    005.369--dc20   93-36466
                                                               CIP

Printed and bound in the United States of America.

1 2 3 4 5 6 7 8 9 FFG 9 8 7 6 5 4

Distributed to the book trade in Canada by Macmillan of Canada, a division of Canada Publishing Corporation.

A CIP catalogue record for this book is available from the British Library.

Microsoft Press books are available through booksellers and distributors worldwide. For further information about international editions, contact your local Microsoft Corporation office. Or contact Microsoft Press International directly at fax (206) 936-7329.

Introduction

This manual is an alphabetic reference for the Visual Basic™ Programming System, Applications Edition, as implemented in Microsoft® Excel. The reference contains topics for all functions, methods, objects, properties, and statements in the language, and is essentially identical to the information contained in the online Visual Basic for Applications Reference Help.

Where to Find Information About Visual Basic

Your Microsoft Excel package includes the following four sources of information about Visual Basic:

- The *Microsoft Excel Visual Basic for Applications User's Guide* teaches you how to record, run, and edit macros; how to create and enter user-defined functions; and how to program in Visual Basic so that you can write your own macros or even create complete applications.

- The main Microsoft Excel Help file provides general online Help about macros (what they are and how to record and run them).

- Examples and Demos are lessons within online Microsoft Excel Help that show you how to perform common macro tasks.

- The online Visual Basic for Applications Reference (the information that is duplicated in this manual) is a detailed reference for Visual Basic functions, statements, methods, properties, and objects.

You can also order *Microsoft Excel Visual Basic for Applications Step by Step,* a self-paced tutorial with timesaving examples on disk that makes learning Visual Basic in Microsoft Excel easier. To place a credit card order, call 615-793-5090, or call toll-free 800-MS-PRESS. Please be sure to have your reference code FXL ready for faster order processing. CompuServe members can also order through the Microsoft Press Electronic Book Store by typing **GO MSP**.

Using the Visual Basic Reference

The *Microsoft Excel Visual Basic for Applications Reference* provides information about all the keywords in the Visual Basic language. A *keyword* is a word or symbol that is recognized as part of the Visual Basic programming language. Statements, functions, objects, properties, and methods are examples of keywords. Even if you do not yet know what these words mean, or much about Visual Basic code, you'll find the *Microsoft Excel Visual Basic for Applications Reference* useful as you explore the Visual Basic language.

The *Microsoft Excel Visual Basic for Applications Reference* uses a template to describe its keywords. The items that make up the template are shown in the following table. The topic for a given keyword rarely contains all the items.

Heading in the topic	Information provided about the keyword
Title (not labeled)	The keyword whose topic you are reading.
Applies To	A list of the objects to which the method or property applies. Appears only in descriptions of methods and properties.
Description	What the keyword is, does, or returns.
Syntax	The *syntax* of the keyword—the arguments to the keyword in the correct order.
Elements	A description of the elements in the syntax, including whether those elements are optional or required and what values they can take.
Remarks	Miscellaneous information about the keyword, its usage, or its syntax.
See Also	A list of topics related to the keyword.
Example	Sample code containing the keyword.

Within the Syntax and Elements sections, items that you must type (the keywords themselves, for example) are **bold**. Placeholders for the items that you must specify (objects, for example) are *italic*. Other placeholders (arguments, for example) are *italic* and **bold**.

Using Online Help

You can access the online Visual Basic Reference Help in one of the following four ways:

- In a Visual Basic module, select a property, statement, or other keyword, and then (in Microsoft Excel for Windows™) press F1 to get context-sensitive Help. In Microsoft Excel for the Apple® Macintosh®, press COMMAND+SHIFT+QUESTION MARK.

- In Microsoft Excel for Windows, choose the Contents command from the Help menu; in Microsoft Excel for the Macintosh, choose Microsoft Excel Help from the Help menu (which is the ? menu) or the Window menu. Click the "Programming with Visual Basic" topic.

- In the Help window, choose the Search button, and then search for a specific topic or Visual Basic term.
- From the View menu, choose the Object Browser command, and then choose the Help button (appears as a question mark) for information about an object, method, property, or function.

Document Conventions

Visual Basic uses the following typographic conventions.

Convention	Description
Sub, **If**, **ChDir**, **Print**, **True**, **Debug**	Words in bold with initial letter capitalized indicate language-specific keywords.
setup	Words you are instructed to type appear in bold.
object, *varname*, *arglist*	Italic, lowercase letters indicate placeholders for information you supply.
pathname, ***filenumber***	Bold, italic, and lowercase letters indicate placeholders for arguments where you can use either positional or named-argument syntax.
[*expressionlist*]	In syntax, items inside square brackets are optional.
{**While** | **Until**}	In syntax, braces and a vertical bar indicate a mandatory choice between two or more items. You must choose one of the items unless all of the items also are enclosed in square brackets. For example: [{**This** | **OrThat**}]
VBA.INI, ESC, ENTER	Words in all capital letters indicate file names, keys, and key sequences.

Convention	Description
ALT+F1, CTRL+R	A plus sign (+) between key names indicates a combination of keys. For example, ALT+F1 means to hold down the ALT key while pressing the F1 key.
' This is a comment.	An apostrophe (') introduces code comments
MyVar = "This is an " & _ example" & _ "of how to continue code"	SPACE+UNDERSCORE continues a line of code.

& Operator

Description	Used to force string concatenation of two expressions.
Syntax	*result = expression1* **&** *expression2* °
Elements	The **&** operator syntax has these parts:

Part	Description
result	Any numeric variable.
expression1	Any expression.
expression2	Any expression.

Remarks Whenever an *expression* is not a string, it is converted to a **String** variant. The data type of *result* is **String** if both expressions are **String** expressions; otherwise, *result* is a **String** variant. If both expressions are **Null**, *result* is also **Null**. However, if only one *expression* is a **Null**, that expression is treated as a zero-length string when concatenated with the other expression. Any expression that is **Empty** is also treated as a zero-length string.

See Also Operator Precedence.

Example This example uses the **&** operator to force string concatenation.

```
MyStr = "Hello" & " World"          ' Returns "Hello World".
MyStr = "Check " & 123 & " Check"   ' Returns "Check 123 Check".
```

* Operator

Description	Used to multiply two numbers.
Syntax	*result = number1 ∗ number2*
Elements	The ∗ operator syntax has these parts:

Part	Description
result	Any numeric variable.
number1	Any numeric expression.
number2	Any numeric expression.

Remarks The data type of *result* is usually the same as that of the most precise expression. The order of precision, from least to most precise, is **Integer**, **Long**, **Single**, **Double**, **Currency**. The following are exceptions to this order:

- When multiplication involves a **Single** and a **Long**, the data type of *result* is converted to a **Double**.
- When the data type of *result* is a **Long**, **Single**, or **Date** variant that overflows its legal range, *result* is converted to a **Variant** containing a **Double**.
- When the data type of *result* is an **Integer** variant that overflows its legal range, *result* is converted to a **Long** variant.

If one or both expressions are **Null** expressions, *result* is a **Null**. If an expression is **Empty**, it is treated as if it were 0.

See Also   Operator Precedence.

Example   This example uses the * operator to multiply two numbers.

```
MyValue = 2 * 2              ' Returns 4.
MyValue = 459.35 * 334.90        ' Returns 153836.315.
```

+ Operator

Description   Used to sum two numbers.

Syntax   *result = expression1+expression2*

Elements   The + operator syntax has these parts:

Part	Description
result	Any numeric variable.
expression1	Any expression.
expression2	Any expression.

Remarks   Although you can also use the **+** operator to concatenate two character strings, you should use the **&** operator for concatenation to eliminate ambiguity and provide self-documenting code.

When you use the **+** operator, you may not be able to determine whether addition or string concatenation will occur. If at least one expression is not a **Variant**, the following rules apply:

If	Then
Both expressions are numeric data types (**Boolean**, **Integer**, **Long**, **Single**, **Double**, **Date** or **Currency**)	Add.
Both expressions are **String**	Concatenate.
One expression is a numeric data type and the other is any **Variant** (except a **Null**)	Add.
One expression is a **String** and the other is any **Variant** (except a **Null**)	Concatenate.
One expression is an **Empty Variant**	Return the remaining expression unchanged as *result*.
One expression is a numeric data type and the other is a **String**	A `Type mismatch` error occurs.
Either expression is a **Null**	*result* is a **Null.**

If both expressions are **Variant** expressions, the underlying type of the expressions determines the behavior of the **+** operator in the following way:

If	Then
Both **Variant** expressions are numeric	Add.
Both **Variant** expressions are strings	Concatenate.
One **Variant** expression is numeric and the other is a string	Add.

For simple arithmetic addition involving only expressions of numeric data types, the data type of *result* is usually the same as that of the most precise expression. The order of precision, from least to most precise, is **Integer**, **Long**, **Single**, **Double**, and **Currency**. The following are exceptions to this order:

- When a **Single** and a **Long** are added together, the data type of *result* is converted to a **Double**.
- When the data type of *result* is a **Long**, **Single**, or **Date** variant that overflows its legal range, *result* is converted to a **Double** variant.
- When the data type of *result* is an **Integer** variant that overflows its legal range, *result* is converted to a **Long** variant.
- When a **Date** is added to any other data type, the data type of *result* is always a **Date**.

If one or both expressions are **Null** expressions, *result* is a **Null**. If both expressions are **Empty**, *result* is an **Integer**. However, if only one expression is **Empty**, the other expression is returned unchanged as *result*.

See Also   Operator Precedence.

Example   This example uses the **+** operator to sum numbers. The **+** operator can also be used to concatenate strings but to eliminate ambiguity, you should use the **&** operator instead.

```
MyNumber = 2 + 2              ' Returns 4.
MyNumber = 4257.04 + 98112    ' Returns 102369.04.
Var1 = "34" : Var2 = 6        ' Initialize variables.
MyNumber = Var1 + Var2        ' Returns 40.
Var1 = "34" : Var2 = "6"      ' Initialize variables.
MyNumber = Var1 + Var2        ' Returns "346" (string concatenation).
```

- Operator

Description   Used to find the difference between two numbers or to indicate the negative value of a numeric expression.

Syntax 1   *result = number1-number2*

Syntax 2   *-number*

Elements   The - operator syntax has these parts:

Part	Description
result	Any numeric variable.
number	Any numeric expression.
number1	Any numeric expression.
number2	Any numeric expression.

Remarks   In Syntax 1, the - operator is the arithmetic subtraction operator used to find the difference between two numbers. In Syntax 2, the - operator is used as the unary negation operator to indicate the negative value of an expression.

The data type of *result* is usually the same as that of the most precise expression. The order of precision, from least to most precise, is **Integer**, **Long**, **Single**, **Double**, **Currency**. The following are exceptions to this order:

- When subtraction involves a **Single** and a **Long**, the data type of *result* is converted to a **Double**.
- When the data type of *result* is a **Long**, **Single**, or **Date** variant that overflows its legal range, *result* is converted to a **Variant** containing a **Double**.
- When the data type of *result* is an **Integer** variant that overflows its legal range, *result* is converted to a **Long** variant.
- When subtraction involves a **Date** and any other data type, the data type of *result* is a **Date**.
- When subtraction involves two **Date** expressions, the data type of *result* is **Double**.

If one or both expressions are **Null** expressions, *result* is a **Null**. If an expression is **Empty**, it is treated as if it were 0.

See Also

Operator Precedence.

Example

This example uses the - operator to calculate the difference between two numbers.

```
MyResult = 4 - 2              ' Returns 2.
MyResult = 459.35 - 334.90        ' Returns 124.45.
```

/ Operator

Description

Used to divide two numbers and return a floating-point result.

Syntax

result = number1/number2

Elements

The / operator syntax has these parts:

Part	Description
result	Any numeric variable.
number1	Any numeric expression.
number2	Any numeric expression.

Remarks

The data type of *result* is usually a **Double** or a **Double** variant. The following are exceptions to this rule:

- When both expressions are **Integer** or **Single** expressions, *result* is a **Single** unless it overflows its legal range; in which case, an error occurs.

- When both expressions are **Integer** or **Single** variants, *result* is a **Single** variant unless it overflows its legal range; in which case, *result* is a **Variant** containing a **Double**.

If one or both expressions are **Null** expressions, *result* is a **Null**. Any expression that is **Empty** is treated as 0.

See Also

Operator Precedence.

Example

This example uses the **/** operator to perform floating-point division.

```
MyValue = 10 / 4 ' Returns 2.5.
MyValue = 10 / 3 ' Returns 3.333333.
```

\ Operator

Description

Used to divide two numbers and return an integer result.

Syntax

result = *number1**number2*

Elements

The \ operator syntax has these parts:

Part	Description
result	Any numeric variable.
number1	Any numeric expression.
number2	Any numeric expression.

Remarks

Before division is performed, the numeric expressions are rounded to **Integer** or **Long** expressions.

Usually, the data type of *result* is an **Integer**, **Integer** variant, **Long**, or **Long** variant, regardless of whether or not *result* is a whole number. Any fractional portion is truncated. However, if any expression is a **Null**, *result* is also a **Null**. Any expression that is **Empty** is treated as 0.

See Also

Operator Precedence.

Example   This example uses the \ operator to perform integer division.

```
MyValue = 11 \ 4 ' Returns 2.
MyValue = 9 \ 3 ' Returns 3.
MyValue = 100 \ 3    ' Returns 33.
```

^ Operator

Description   Used to raise a number to the power of an exponent.

Syntax   *result = number^exponent*

Elements   The ^ operator syntax has these parts:

Part	Description
result	Any numeric variable.
number	Any numeric expression.
exponent	Any numeric expression.

Remarks   *Number* can be negative only if *exponent* is an integer value. When more than one exponentiation is performed in a single expression, the ^ operator is evaluated as it is encountered from left to right.

Usually, the data type of *result* is a **Double** or a **Variant** containing a **Double**. However, if either *number* or *exponent* is a **Null** expression, *result* is also a **Null**.

See Also   Operator Precedence.

Example   This example uses the ^ operator to raise a number to the power of an exponent.

```
MyValue = 2 ^ 2      ' Returns 4.
MyValue = 3 ^ 3 ^ 3      ' Returns 19683.
MyValue = (-5) ^ 3      ' Returns -125.
```

Abs Function

Description   Returns the absolute value of a number.

Syntax   **Abs**(*number*)

Elements   The *number* argument can be any valid numeric expression. If *number* contains no valid data, **Null** is returned; if it is an uninitialized variable, **Empty** is returned.

Remarks   The absolute value of a number is its unsigned magnitude. For example, ABS(-1) and ABS(1) both return 1.

See Also   **Sgn** Function.

Example   This example uses the **Abs** function to compute the absolute value of a number.

```
MyNumber = Abs(50.3)      ' Returns 50.3.
MyNumber = Abs(-50.3)     ' Returns 50.3.
```

Accelerator Property

Applies To   Button, Buttons, CheckBox, CheckBoxes, DrawingObjects, GroupBox, GroupBoxes, Label, Labels, OptionButton, OptionButtons.

Description   Returns or sets the keyboard accelerator character for the control. Read-write.

Syntax   *object*.**Accelerator**

Elements   *object*
                        Required. The object to which this property applies.

Remarks   Each control has one accelerator character which the user can press in combination with the ALT key to activate a control while a dialog is running.

The first text character of the control that matches the first accelerator text character will be underlined. The comparison for underlining is case-sensitive, but case is not considered when a key is pressed.

On the Apple Macintosh, the accelerator character is only underlined when the **CommandUnderlines** property is **True**. If this property is **False**, the accelerator character is preserved, but it is not underlined.

If the accelerator key doesn't match any text in the control, the accelerator is non-functional.

Example   This example sets the button text and accelerator key for button four.

```
With DialogSheets(1).Buttons(4)
    .Text = "Press Me"
    .Accelerator = "P"
End With
```

Activate Method

Applies To   Chart, ChartObject, DialogSheet, MenuBar, Module, OLEObject, Pane, Range, Window, Workbook, Worksheet.

Description   Activates the object, as shown in the following table.

Object	Description
Chart, ChartObject	Makes this chart the active chart.
DialogSheet, Module, Worksheet	Makes this sheet the active sheet. Equivalent to clicking the tab.
MenuBar	Activates the menu bar. There are certain restrictions on which menu bars you can activate at certain times. See the Remarks section for details.
OLEObject	Activates the object.
Pane	Activates the pane. If the pane is not in the active window, the window that the pane belongs to will also be activated.
Range	Activates a single cell, which must be inside the current selection. To select a range of cells, use the **Select** method.
Window	Brings the window to the front of the z-order. This will not run any Auto_Activate or Auto_Deactivate macros that might be attached to the workbook (use the **RunAutoMacros** method to run those macros).
Workbook	Activates the first window associated with the workbook. This will not run any Auto_Activate or Auto_Deactivate macros that might be attached to the workbook (use the **RunAutoMacros** method to run those macros).

Syntax   *object*.**Activate**

Elements   *object*
         Required. The object to activate.

Remarks   When you activate a built-in menu bar, you can display only a menu bar
appropriate for the object. For example, if you try to display a chart menu bar for a
worksheet or macro sheet, this method returns an error and interrupts the current
macro.

Activating a custom menu bar disables automatic menu bar switching when
different types of documents are selected. For example, if a custom menu bar is
displayed and you switch to a chart, the two chart menus are not displayed (they
would be if you were using the built-in menu bars). Automatic menu bar switching
is reenabled when a built-in menu bar is displayed.

See Also   **RunAutoMacros** Method, **Select** Method.

Examples   This example activates the window for BOOK4.XLS. If there are multiple windows
open, it activates BOOK4.XLS:1.

```
Workbooks("BOOK4.XLS").Activate
```

This example selects cells A1 through C3, and then makes cell B2 the active cell.

```
Range("A1:C3").Select
Range("B2").Activate
```

ActivateMicrosoftApp Method

Applies To   Application.

Description   Activates a Microsoft application. If the application is already running, this method
activates the running application. If the application is not running, this method starts
a new instance of the application.

Syntax   *object*.**ActivateMicrosoftApp**(*index*)

Elements   The **ActivateMicrosoftApp** method has the following object qualifier and named
arguments:

object
Required. The Application object.

index
Required. Specifies the Microsoft application to activate (one of
xlMicrosoftWord, **xlMicrosoftPowerPoint**, **xlMicrosoftMail**,
xlMicrosoftAccess, **xlMicrosoftFoxPro**, **xlMicrosoftProject**, or
xlMicrosoftSchedulePlus).

See Also   **AppActivate** Statement, **Shell** Function.

Example	This example starts and activates Microsoft® Word.

```
Application.ActivateMicrosoftApp xlMicrosoftWord
```

ActivateNext Method

Applies To	Window.
Description	Activates the next window by moving it to the front of the window z-order and sending the specified window to the back of the z-order.
Syntax	*object*.**ActivateNext**
Elements	*object* Required. The Window object.
See Also	**ActivatePrevious** Method, **Next** Property.
Example	This example activates the next window and sends window three to the back of the z-order.

```
Windows(3).ActivateNext
```

ActivatePrevious Method

Applies To	Window.
Description	Activates the previous window by moving it to the front of the window z-order and sending the specified window to the back of the z-order.
Syntax	*object*.**ActivatePrevious**
Elements	*object* Required. The Window object.
See Also	**ActivateNext** Method, **Previous** Property.
Example	This example activates the previous window and sends window three to the back of the z-order.

```
Windows(3).ActivatePrevious
```

ActiveCell Property

Applies To   Application, Window.

Description   Returns the active cell of the active window (the window on top). Read-only. The active cell is a Range object.

Syntax   *object*.**ActiveCell**

Elements   *object*
                     Optional for Application, required for Window. The object to which this property applies.

Remarks   Be careful to distinguish between the active cell and the selection. The active cell is a single cell inside the current selection. The selection may contain more than one cell, but only one is the active cell.

                     The following expressions all return the active cell, and are all equivalent:

```
ActiveCell
Application.ActiveCell
ActiveWindow.ActiveCell
Application.ActiveWindow.ActiveCell
```

Examples   This example sets the variable currentSelection to refer to the active cell, and then sets the value of the active cell to 42.

```
Set currentSelection = Application.ActiveCell
currentSelection.Value = 42
```

                     This example toggles italic formatting on text in the active cell.

```
With ActiveCell
    .Font.Italic = Not (.Font.Italic)
End With
```

ActiveChart Property

Applies To   Application, Window, Workbook.

Description   Returns the currently active Chart (either an embedded chart or a chart sheet). An embedded chart is considered active when it is either selected or activated. When no chart is active, this property returns **Nothing**. Read-only.

Syntax	*object*.**ActiveChart**
Elements	*object* Optional for Application, required for Window and Workbook. The object to which this property applies.
Example	This example turns on the legend for the active chart.

```
ActiveChart.HasLegend = True
```

ActiveDialog Property

Applies To	Application.
Description	Returns the topmost currently running DialogSheet. If there is no running dialog, this property returns **Nothing**. Note that the active dialog is not necessarily the active sheet. Read-only.
Syntax	*object*.**ActiveDialog**
Elements	*object* Optional. The Application object.
Example	This example hides the active dialog sheet.

```
ActiveDialog.Hide cancel:=True
```

ActiveMenuBar Property

Applies To	Application.
Description	Returns or sets the active MenuBar. Read-write.
Syntax	*object*.**ActiveMenuBar**
Elements	*object* Optional. The Application object.
Example	This example sets the variable currentMenuBar to the active menu bar.

```
Set currentMenuBar = Application.ActiveMenuBar
MsgBox "The active menu bar is " & currentMenuBar.Caption
```

ActivePane Property

Applies To   Window.

Description   The active Pane of the window. Read-only.

Syntax   *object*.**ActivePane**

Elements   *object*
                         Required. The Window object.

Remarks   This property applies only to worksheets and macro sheets.

                      This property returns a Pane object. You must use the **Index** property to obtain the
                      index of the active pane.

Example   This example activates the next pane for the active window.

```
With ActiveWindow
    i = .ActivePane.Index
    If i = .Panes.Count Then
        .Panes(1).Activate
    Else
        .Panes(i+1).Activate
    End If
End With
```

ActivePrinter Property

Applies To   Application.

Description   Returns or sets the name of the active printer. Read-write. The name is a string.

Syntax   *object*.**ActivePrinter**

Elements   *object*
                         Optional. The Application object.

Remarks   This property cannot be set on the Apple Macintosh.

Example   This example displays the name of the active printer.

```
MsgBox "The name of the active printer is " & Application.ActivePrinter
```

ActiveSheet Property

Applies To	Application, Window, Workbook.
Description	Returns the active sheet (the sheet on top) of the active workbook. Returns **Nothing** if no sheet is active. Read-only.

The object type returned by the **ActiveSheet** property depends on the active sheet, as shown in the following list.

Active sheet	Object type returned
Worksheet	Worksheet
Visual Basic module	Module
Chart	Chart
Dialog sheet	DialogSheet

Syntax	*object*.**ActiveSheet**
Elements	*object* Optional for Application, required for Window and Worksheet. The object to which this property applies.
Remarks	If a workbook appears in more than one window, the **ActiveSheet** property may be different in different windows.
See Also	**Activate** Method, **Select** Method.
Example	This example displays the name of the active sheet.

```
activeSheetName = Application.ActiveSheet.Name
MsgBox "The name of the active sheet is " & activeSheetName
```

ActiveWindow Property

Applies To	Application.
Description	Returns the active Window (the window on top). Read-only. Returns **Nothing** if no windows are open.

Syntax	*object*.**ActiveWindow**
Elements	*object*
	Optional. The Application object.
See Also	**Activate** Method, **Select** Method.
Example	This example displays the name of the active window.

```
Set currentWindow = Application.ActiveWindow
MsgBox "The name of the active window is " & currentWindow.Caption
```

ActiveWorkbook Property

Applies To	Application.
Description	Returns the Workbook in the active window (the window on top). Read-only. Returns **Nothing** if no windows are open or if the active window is the info window or the clipboard window.
Syntax	*object*.**ActiveWorkbook**
Elements	*object*
	Optional. The Application object.
Example	This example displays the name of the active workbook.

```
Set currentBook = Application.ActiveWorkbook
MsgBox "The name of the active workbook is " & currentBook.Name
```

Add Method (AddIns Collection)

Applies To	AddIns.
Description	Adds a new add-in file to the list of add-ins. Returns a new AddIn object.
Syntax	*object*.**Add(***fileName, copyFile***)**
Elements	The **Add** method has the following object qualifier and named arguments:

object
> Required. The AddIns object.

fileName
> Required. The name of the file containing the add-in you wish to add to the list in the add-in manager.

copyFile
> Optional. Ignored if the add-in file is on a hard disk. If **True** and the add-in is on removable media (a floppy disk or CD-ROM), the add-in will be copied to your hard disk. If **False**, the add-in will remain on the removable media. If this argument is omitted, Microsoft Excel displays a dialog box and asks you to choose.

Remarks
This method does not install the new add-in. You must set the **Installed** property to install the add-in.

See Also
Installed Property.

Example
This example adds the Solver add-in, and then installs it by setting its **Installed** property to **True.**

```
Set solverAddIn = AddIns.Add("C:\EXCEL\LIBRARY\SOLVER\SOLVER.XLA")
solverAddIn.Installed = True
```

Add Method (Arcs and Lines)

Applies To
Arcs, Lines.

Description
Creates a new arc or line.

Syntax
object.**Add**(*x1, y1, x2, y2*)

Elements
The **Add** method has the following object qualifier and named arguments:

object
> Required. The Arc or Line object.

x1, y1
> Required. Specifies the position of the first coordinate of the object, in points (1/72 inch) relative to the top left of A1 or the upper left of the chart.

x2, y2
> Required. Specifies the position of the second coordinate of the object, in points relative to the top left of A1 or the upper left of the chart.

See Also
Add Method (Drawing Objects), **Add** Method (Drawings Collections), **Add** Method (DropDowns Collection), **Duplicate** Method.

Example
This example creates a new line with the arrowhead pointing to the upper left. Note the order of the points -- the arrowhead points to the second coordinate.

```
With ActiveSheet.Lines.Add(80, 80, 10, 10)
    .ArrowHeadStyle = xlOpen
    .Border.LineStyle = xlDot
End With
```

Add Method (Charts Collection)

Applies To   Charts.

Description   Creates a new chart. Returns a Chart object.

Syntax   *object*.**Add**(*before, after, count*)

Elements   The **Add** method has the following object qualifier and named arguments:

object
> Required. The Charts object.

before
> Optional. Specifies the sheet before which the new sheet is added.

after
> Optional. Specifies the sheet after which the new sheet is added.

count
> Optional. The number of sheets to add. If omitted, the default is one.

Remarks   If *before* and *after* are omitted, the new chart is inserted before the active sheet.

Example   This example creates a new chart and inserts it before the active sheet.

```
ActiveWorkbook.Charts.Add
```

Add Method (DialogSheets Collection)

Applies To   DialogSheets.

Description   Creates a new dialog sheet. Returns a DialogSheet object.

Syntax   *object*.**Add**(*before, after, count*)

Elements   The **Add** method has the following object qualifier and named arguments:

object
> Required. The DialogSheets object.

before
> Optional. Specifies the sheet before which the new sheet is added.

after
> Optional. Specifies the sheet after which the new sheet is added.

count
> Optional. The number of sheets to add. If omitted, the default is one.

Remarks   If *before* and *after* are omitted, the new sheet is inserted before the active sheet.

example, **Rectangles.Add** creates a new rectangle; **Ovals.Add** creates a new oval.

Syntax   *object*.**Add**(*left, top, width, height*)

Elements   The **Add** method has the following object qualifier and named arguments:

object
> Required. The object to which this method applies.

left, top
> Required. Specifies the initial coordinates of the new object, in points (1/72 inch), relative to the top left corner of cell A1 on a worksheet, or to the upper left corner of a chart.

width, height
> Required. Specifies the initial size of the new object, in points (1/72 inch).

See Also   **Add** Method (Arcs and Lines), **Add** Method (Drawings Collection), **Add** Method (DropDowns Collection), **Duplicate** Method.

Example   This example adds a new oval.

```
ActiveSheet.Ovals.Add 0,0,72,72
```

Add Method (Drawing Objects)

Applies To   Buttons, ChartObjects, CheckBoxes, EditBoxes, GroupBoxes, Labels, ListBoxes, OptionButtons, Ovals, Pictures, Rectangles, ScrollBars, Spinners, TextBoxes.

Description   Creates a new drawing object using coordinates specified in points (1/72 inch).

The type of the object depends on the collection on which you call Add. For

Add Method (Drawings Collection)

Applies To	Drawings.
Description	Creates a new drawing using the first two vertices of the polygon as coordinates relative to A1 or the upper left corner of the chart. Additional vertices can be added to the first two vertices using the **AddVertex** method.
Syntax	*object*.**Add**(*x1, y1, x2, y2, closed*)
Elements	The **Add** method has the following object qualifier and named arguments:

object
> Required. The Drawings object.

x1, y1
> Required. Specifies the position of the first coordinate of the polygon, in points (1/72 inch) relative to the top left of cell A1 or the upper left of the chart.

x2, y2
> Required. Specifies the position of the second coordinate of the polygon, in points relative to the top left of cell A1 or the upper left of the chart.

closed
> Required. If **True**, the new drawing is closed and the last vertex is always connected to the first vertex. If **False**, the drawing is open and the last vertex is not connected to the first vertex.

See Also	**Add** Method (Arcs and Lines), **Add** Method (DropDowns Collection), **AddVertex** Method, **Reshape** Method, **Vertices** Property.
Example	This example creates a new open trapezoid.

```
With ActiveSheet.Drawings.Add(100, 100, 200, 100, False)
    .AddVertex 180, 200
    .AddVertex 80, 200
    .Border.Weight = xlMedium
End With
```

Add Method (DropDowns Collection)

Applies To	DropDowns.
Description	Creates a new drop-down list box using rectangular coordinates specified in points (1/72 inch).
Syntax	*object*.**Add**(*left, top, width, height, editable*)

Elements	The **Add** method has the following object qualifier and named arguments:

object
>Required. The DropDowns object.

left, top, width, height
>Required. Specifies the width, height, and initial coordinates of the upper left corner of the object, in points relative to the top left of cell A1 or the upper left of the chart.

editable
>Optional. **True** if the drop-down list box can be edited. If this argument is **False** or omitted, the contents of the list-box editing region can be changed only by selecting from the list.

See Also	**Add** Method (Arcs and Lines), **Add** Method (Drawing Objects), **Add** Method (Drawings Collection), **Duplicate** Method.
Example	This example creates an editable drop-down list box.

```
With ActiveSheet.DropDowns.Add(10, 10, 120, 18)
    .DropDownLines = 10
```

End WithExample	This example creates a new dialog sheet and inserts it before the active sheet.

```
ActiveWorkbook.DialogSheets.Add
```

Add Method (MenuBars Collection)

Applies To	MenuBars.
Description	Creates a new menu bar. Returns a MenuBar object.
Syntax	*object*.**Add**(*name*)
Elements	The **Add** method has the following object qualifier and named arguments:

object
>Required. The MenuBars object.

name
>Optional. The name for the new menu bar.

Remarks	The name of the menu bar is the same as its caption.
Example	This example creates a new menu bar.

```
Set newMenuBar = MenuBars.Add
```

Add Method (MenuItems Collection)

Applies To   MenuItems.

Description   Adds a new menu item to the specified menu. Can also be used to restore one of Microsoft Excel's built-in menu items which has been deleted. Returns a MenuItem object.

Syntax   *object*.**Add**(*caption, onAction, shortcutKey, before, restore*)

Elements   The **Add** method has the following object qualifier and named arguments:

object
Required. The MenuItems object.

caption
Required. The text of the menu item (sets the initial value of the **Caption** property for the new menu item). Use an ampersand (&) before the command underline. Use a single hyphen ("-") for the caption to create a separator bar.

onAction
Optional. An initial value for the **OnAction** property of the new object.

shortcutKey
Optional. Used only on the Apple Macintosh. Specifies the shortcut key for the menu item as text.

before
Optional. Specifies the menu item before which the new item will be added. Can be either a number (1 to insert at the top of the menu, for example) or a caption of another, existing menu item (in the language of the macro, without the ampersand), or a reference to the menu item.

restore
Optional. If **True**, Microsoft Excel will restore the previously deleted built-in menu item named *caption*. If **False** or omitted, Microsoft Excel will add a new menu item.

See Also   **Checked** Property, **Enabled** Property, **OnAction** Property.

Example   This example adds a new menu item to the top of the Help menu on each menu bar.

```
For Each mb in MenuBars
    mb.Menus("Help").MenuItems.Add _
        caption:="Read Me First", _
        onAction:="Read_Me_First", _
        before:=1
Next
```

Add Method (Menus Collection)

Applies To   Menus.

Description   Adds a new menu. Can also be used to restore one of Microsoft Excel's built-in menus which has been deleted. Returns a Menu object.

Syntax   *object*.**Add**(*caption, before, restore*)

Elements   The **Add** method has the following object qualifier and named arguments:

object
  Required. The Menus object.

caption
  Required. The text of the menu (sets the initial value of the **Caption** property for the new menu). Use an ampersand (&) before the command underline.

before
  Optional. Specifies the menu before which the new menu will be added. Can be either a number (one to insert at the beginning of the menu bar, for example) or a caption of another, existing menu (in the language of the macro, without the ampersand), or a reference to the menu. If this argument is omitted, the new menu is added to the left of the Window menu.

restore
  Optional. If **True**, Microsoft Excel will restore the previously deleted built-in menu named *caption*. If **False** or omitted, Microsoft Excel will add a new menu.

Remarks   On the Apple Macintosh, this method returns an error if there is not enough room to create the new menu. You should always check the return value to ensure that the new menu was added successfully.

In Microsoft Windows, the menu bar will wrap if necessary to fit the new menu.

You cannot create a new shortcut menu; you can only modify a built-in shortcut menu.

Example   This example adds a new menu to the worksheet menu bar.

```
MenuBars(xlWorksheet).Menus.Add caption:="More Help"
```

Add Method (Modules Collection)

Applies To   Modules.

Description   Creates a new Visual Basic module.

Syntax   *object*.**Add**(*before, after, count*)

Elements   The **Add** method has the following object qualifier and named arguments:

object
> Required. The Modules object.

before
> Optional. Specifies the sheet before which the new module is added.

after
> Optional. Specifies the sheet after which the new module is added.

count
> Optional. The number of sheets to add. If omitted, the default is one.

Remarks   If *before* and *after* are omitted, the module is inserted before the active sheet.

Example   This example inserts a new module before the active sheet.

```
ActiveWorkbook.Modules.Add
```

Add Method (Names Collection)

Applies To   Names.

Description   Defines a new name. Returns a Name object.

Syntax   *object*.**Add**(*name, refersTo, visible, macroType, shortcutKey, category, nameLocal, refersToLocal, categoryLocal, refersToR1C1, refersToR1C1Local*)

Elements

The **Add** method has the following object qualifier and named arguments:

object
Required. The Names object.

name
Required (unless ***nameLocal*** is specified). The text to use as the name (in the language of the macro). Names cannot include spaces, and cannot look like cell references.

refersTo
Required (unless one of the other ***refersTo*** arguments is specified). Describes what the name refers to (in the language of the macro, using A1-style notation).

visible
Optional. If **True** or omitted, Microsoft Excel defines the name normally. If **False**, the name is defined as a hidden name (it does not appear in the Define Name, Paste Name, or Goto dialog boxes).

macroType
Optional. Specifies the macro type, as shown in the following list.

Value	Meaning
1	User-defined function (function procedure)
2	Macro (also known as sub procedure)
3 or omitted	None (that is, the name does not refer to a user-defined function or macro)

shortcutKey
Optional. Specifies the macro shortcut key. Must be a single letter, such as "z" or "Z". Applies only for command macros.

category
Specifies the category of the macro or function if ***macroType*** is 1 or 2. The category is used in the function wizard. Existing categories can be referred to by number (starting at one), or by name (in the language of the macro). Microsoft Excel creates a new category if the specified category does not already exist.

nameLocal
Required if ***name*** is not specified. The text to use as the name (in the language of the user). Names cannot include spaces, and cannot look like cell references.

refersToLocal
Required (unless one of the other ***refersTo*** arguments is specified). Describes what the name refers to (in the language of the user, using A1-style notation).

categoryLocal
Required if ***category*** is not specified. Text identifying the category of a custom function in the language of the user.

refersToR1C1

Required (unless one of the other **refersTo** arguments is specified). Describes what the name refers to (in the language of the macro, using R1C1-style notation).

refersToR1C1Local

Required (unless one of the other **refersTo** arguments is specified). Describes what the name refers to (in the language of the user, using R1C1-style notation).

Example   This example defines a new name for A1:D3.

```
ActiveWorkbook.Names.Add _
    name:="tempRange", _
    refersToR1C1:="=Sheet1!R1C1:R3C4"
```

Add Method (OLEObjects Collection)

Applies To   OLEObjects.

Description   Adds a new OLE object to the current sheet.

Syntax   *object*.**Add**(*classType, fileName, link, displayAsIcon, iconFileName, iconIndex, iconLabel*)

Elements   The **Add** method has the following object qualifier and named arguments:

object

Required. The OLEObjects collection.

classType

Optional (you must specify either *classType* or *fileName*). A string containing the OLE long classname for the object that is to be created. If *classType* is specified, *fileName* and *link* are ignored.

fileName

Optional (you must specify either *classType* or *fileName*). A string specifying the file from which the OLE object is to be created.

link

Optional. **True** if the new OLE object based on *fileName* should be linked to that file. If it is not linked, the file is created as a copy of the file. **False** if omitted.

displayAsIcon

Optional. **True** if the new OLE object is displayed as an icon, or as its regular picture. If **True**, the *iconFileName* and *iconIndex* can be used to specify an icon.

iconFileName

Optional. A string that specifies the file that contains the icon to be displayed. This is used only if *displayAsIcon* is **True**. If not specified or the file contains no icons, the default icon for the OLE Class is used.

iconIndex

Optional. The number of the icon within the *iconFileName*. This is used only if *displayAsIcon* is **True** and *iconFileName* refers to a valid file containing icons. If an icon with the given index does not exist in the file specified in *iconFileName*, the the first one in the file is used.

iconLabel

Optional. A string specifying a label to display beneath the icon. This is used only if *displayAsIcon* is **True**. If this argument is omitted or the string is empty (""), then no caption is displayed.

Example

This example adds a new OLE object.

```
ActiveSheet.OLEObjects.Add fileName:="README.DOC"
```

Add Method (Scenarios Collection)

Applies To

Scenarios.

Description

Creates a new scenario and adds it to the list of scenarios available for the current worksheet. Returns a Scenario object.

Syntax

object.**Add**(*name, changingCells, values, comment, locked, hidden*)

Elements

The **Add** method has the following object qualifier and named arguments:

object

Required. The Scenarios object.

name

Required. A string specifying the name for the new scenario.

changingCells

Required. A range giving the changing cells for the scenario.

values

Optional. An array containing the scenario values for the cells in *changingCells*. If omitted, the scenario values are assumed to be the current values in the cells of *changingCells*.

comment

Optional. A string specifying comment text for the scenario. When a new scenario is added, author name and date are automatically added at the beginning of the comment text.

locked
>   Optional. **True** if the scenario is locked to prevent changes. If this argument is omitted, the scenario is locked.

hidden
>   Optional. **True** if the scenario is hidden. If this argument is omitted, the scenario is not hidden.

Remarks   A scenario name must be unique; Microsoft Excel generates an error if you try to create a scenario with a name already in use.

Example   This example defines a scenario.

```
ActiveSheet.Scenarios.Add name:="Best Case", _
    changingCells:=ActiveSheet.Range("A1:A4"), _
    values:=Array(23, 5, 6, 21), comment:="Most favorable outcome."
```

Add Method (SeriesCollection)

Applies To   SeriesCollection.

Description   Adds one or more new series to the SeriesCollection.

Syntax   *object*.**Add**(*source, rowcol, seriesLabels, categoryLabels, replace*)

Elements   The **Add** method has the following object qualifier and named arguments:

object
>   Required. The SeriesCollection object.

source
>   Required. Specifies the new data, either as a Range or an array of data points.

rowcol
>   Optional. Specifies whether the new values are in the rows (**xlRows**) or columns (**xlColumns**) of the specified range. The default value is **xlColumns**.

seriesLabels
>   Optional. Ignored if *source* is an array. **True** if the first row or column contains the name of the data series. **False** if the first row or column contains the first data point of the series. If this argument is omitted, Microsoft Excel attempts to determine the series name location from the contents of the first row or column.

categoryLabels
>   Optional. Ignored if *source* is an array. **True** if the first row or column contains the name of the category labels. **False** if the first row or column contains the first data point of the series. If this argument is omitted, Microsoft Excel attempts to determine the category label location from the contents of the first row or column.

replace
Optional. If *categoryLabels* is **True** and *replace* is **True**, the specified categories replace the categories that currently exist for the series. If this argument is **False** or omitted, the existing categories will not be replaced.

See Also   **Extend** Method.

Example   This example adds column one to the series collection for chart one.

```
Charts(1).SeriesCollection.Add Columns(1), xlColumns
```

Add Method (Sheets Collection)

Applies To   Sheets.

Description   Creates a new worksheet, chart, module, dialog sheet or macro sheet.

Syntax   *object*.**Add**(*before, after, count, type*)

Elements   The **Add** method has the following object qualifier and named arguments:

object
Required. The Sheets object.

before
Optional. Specifies the sheet before which the new sheet is added. Must be an object, for example **ActiveWorkbook.Worksheets("Sheet1")**.

after
Optional. Specifies the sheet after which the new sheet is added. Must be an object, for example **ActiveWorkbook.ActiveSheet**.

count
Optional. The number of sheets to add. If omitted, the default is one.

type
Optional. The type of sheet to add. Must be one of **xlWorksheet**, **xlChart**, **xlModule**, **xlDialogSheet**, **xlExcel4MacroSheet**, or **xlExcel4IntlMacroSheet**. If omitted, the default is **xlWorksheet**.

Remarks   If *before* and *after* are omitted, the new sheet is inserted before the active sheet.

Examples   This example inserts a new worksheet before the active sheet.

```
ActiveWorkbook.Sheets.Add before:=ActiveWorkbook.ActiveSheet
```

This example adds two new dialog sheets after the first module.

```
ActiveWorkbook.Sheets.Add after:=ActiveWorkbook.Sheets("Module1"), _
    type:=xlDialogSheet, count:=2
```

Add Method (Styles Collection)

Applies To   Styles.

Description   Creates a new style and adds it to the list of styles available for the current workbook. Returns a Style object.

Syntax   *object*.**Add**(*name, basedOn*)

Elements   The **Add** method has the following object qualifier and named arguments:

object
Required. The Styles object.

name
Required. A string specifying the name for the new style.

basedOn
Optional. A reference to a cell that will be used as the basis for the new style. If specified, the newly created style will be given a style based on that cell. If omitted, the newly created style will be based on the **Normal** style.

Remarks   If a style with the specified name already exists, this method redefines the style based on the cell specified in *basedOn*. The following example redefines the Normal style based on the active cell:

```
ActiveWorkbook.Styles.Add name:="Normal", _
    basedOn:=ActiveCell
```

Examples   This example defines a style based on the active cell.

```
ActiveWorkbook.Styles.Add name:="myNewStyle", _
    basedOn:=ActiveCell
```

This example defines a new style that has only the Font property.

```
With ActiveWorkbook.Styles.Add(name:="theNewStyle")
    .IncludeNumber = False
    .IncludeFont = True
    .IncludeAlignment = False
    .IncludeBorder = False
    .IncludePatterns = False
    .IncludeProtection = False
    .Font.Name = "Arial"
    .Font.Size = 18
End With
```

Add Method (ToolbarButtons Collection)

Applies To	ToolbarButtons.
Description	Adds a new button to an existing toolbar.
Syntax	*object*.**Add(***button, before, onAction, pushed, enabled***)**
Elements	The **Add** method has the following object qualifier and named arguments:

object
> Required. The ToolbarButtons object.

button
> Optional. The button ID number, as an integer. If this argument is omitted, a gap is inserted in the toolbar. For a complete list of button IDs available to Visual Basic, see Appendix D in the *Visual Basic User's Guide*.

before
> Optional. Specifies the new button position. The new button will be inserted before the button that has this button ID number. If this argument is omitted, the button is inserted at the end of the toolbar.

onAction
> Optional. Specifies an initial value for the **OnAction** property, which is the name of the macro that runs when the button is clicked. If omitted with a built-in button, the button will have its built-in behavior. If omitted with a custom button, the Assign Macro dialog is displayed when the button is first clicked.

pushed
> Optional. Specifies an initial value for the **Pushed** property (**True** if the button appears pressed).

enabled
> Optional. Specifies an initial value for the **Enabled** property (**True** if the button is enabled).

See Also	**Enabled** Property, **OnAction** Property, **Pushed** Property.
Example	This example adds a new button to toolbar one.

```
Toolbars(1).ToolbarButtons.Add(101)
```

Add Method (Toolbars Collection)

Applies To   Toolbars.

Description   Creates a new toolbar. Returns a Toolbar object.

Syntax   *object*.**Add**(*name*)

Elements   The **Add** method has the following object qualifier and named arguments:

object
> Required. The Toolbars object.

name
> Optional. A string that specifies a name for the new toolbar. If omitted, Microsoft Excel uses a default name (such as "**Toolbar 1**").

Example   This example creates a new toolbar.

```
Toolbars.Add name:="myNewToolbar"
```

Add Method (Trendlines Collection)

Applies To   Trendlines.

Description   Creates a new Trendline.

Syntax   *object*.**Add**(*type, order, period, forward, backward, intercept, displayEquation, displayRSquared, name*)

Elements   The **Add** method has the following object qualifier and named arguments:

object
> Required. The Trendlines object.

type
> Optional. Specifies the trendline type (one of **xlLinear**, **xlLogarithmic**, **xlExponential**, **xlPolynomial**, **xlMovingAvg**, or **xlPower**). If omitted, the default is **xlLinear**.

order
> Required if *type* is **xlPolynomial**. Specifies the trendline order. Must be an integer from two to six, inclusive.

period

Required if *type* is **xlMovingAvg**. Specifies the trendline period. Must be an integer greater than one and less than the number of data points in the series you are adding a trendline to.

forward

Optional. Sets the number of periods (or units on a scatter chart) that the trendline extends forward.

backward

Optional. Sets the number of periods (or units on a scatter chart) that the trendline extends backward.

intercept

Optional. Sets the trendline intercept. If omitted, the intercept is automatically set by the regression.

displayEquation

Optional. **True** if the equation of the trendline is displayed on the chart (in the same data label as the R-squared value).

displayRSquared

Optional. **True** if the R-squared value of the trendline is displayed on the chart (in the same data label as the equation).

name

Optional. Specifies the name of the trendline as text. If this argument is omitted, an automatically generated name is used.

See Also   **Backward** Property, **DisplayEquation** Property, **DisplayRSquared** Property, **Forward** Property, **Intercept** Property, **Order** Property, **Period** Property.

Example   This example creates a new linear trendline.

```
Set newTrendline = _
    ActiveWorkbook.Charts(1).SeriesCollection(1).Trendlines.Add
```

Add Method (Workbooks Collection)

Applies To   Workbooks.

Description   Creates a new Workbook. The new workbook becomes the active workbook.

Syntax   *object*.**Add**(*template*)

Elements   The **Add** method has the following object qualifier and named arguments:

object
Required. The Workbooks object.

template
Optional. Determines how the new workbook is created. Can be a string specifying a template for the new workbook (the string can include a file path), or a constant to create a new workbook containing a single sheet (one of **xlWorksheet**, **xlChart**, **xlExcel4MacroSheet**, or **xlExcel4IntlMacroSheet**). If this argument is omitted, Microsoft Excel creates a new workbook with a number of blank sheets (the number of sheets is set by the **SheetsInNewWorkbook** property).

See Also   **ActiveWorkbook** Property, **SheetsInNewWorkbook** Property.

Example   This example creates a new default workbook.

```
Workbooks.Add
```

Add Method (Worksheets Collection)

Applies To   Worksheets.

Description   Creates a new Worksheet. The new worksheet becomes the active sheet.

Syntax   *object*.**Add**(*before, after, count, type*)

Elements   The **Add** method has the following object qualifier and named arguments:

object
Required. The Worksheets object.

before
Optional. Specifies the sheet before which the new sheet is added.

after
Optional. Specifies the sheet after which the new sheet is added.

count
Optional. The number of sheets to add. One if omitted.

type
Optional. Specifies the worksheet type (one of **xlWorksheet**, **xlExcel4MacroSheet**, or **xlExcel4IntlMacroSheet**). If omitted, the default is **xlWorksheet**.

Remarks   If *before* and *after* are omitted, the new sheet is inserted before the active sheet.

Example	This example inserts a new worksheet before the active sheet.

```
ActiveWorkbook.Worksheets.Add
```

AddChartAutoFormat Method

Applies To	Application.
Description	Adds a custom chart autoformat to the list of available chart autoformats.
Syntax	*object*.**AddChartAutoFormat**(*chart, name, description*)
Elements	The **AddChartAutoFormat** method has the following object qualifier and named arguments:

object
Required. The Application object.

chart
Required. A chart object that contains the format that will be applied when the new chart autoformat is applied.

name
Required. A string that represents the name of the autoformat.

description
Optional. A string that describes the custom autoformat.

See Also	**DeleteChartAutoFormat** Method, **SetDefaultChart** Method.
Example	This example adds a new autoformat based on chart one.

```
Application.AddChartAutoFormat _
    chart:=Charts("Chart1"), name:="Presentation Chart"
```

AddCustomList Method

Applies To	Application.
Description	Adds a custom list for custom autofill and/or custom sort.
Syntax	*object*.**AddCustomList**(*listArray, byRow*)

Elements   The **AddCustomList** method has the following object qualifier and named arguments:

object
> Required. The Application object.

listArray
> Required. An array of strings, or a Range.

byRow
> Optional. Only used if *listArray* is a Range. If **True**, Microsoft Excel creates a custom list from each row in the range. If **False**, Microsoft Excel creates a custom list from each column in the range. If this argument is omitted and there are more rows than columns (or an equal number of rows and columns) in the range, then Microsoft Excel creates a custom list from each column in the range. If this argument is omitted and there are more columns than rows in the range, then Microsoft Excel creates a custom list from each row in the range.

Remarks   If the list you are trying to add already exists, this method does nothing.

See Also   **CustomListCount** Property, **DeleteCustomList** Method, **GetCustomListNum** Method, **GetCustomListContents** Method.

Example   This example adds an array of strings as a custom list.

```
Application.AddCustomList Array("cogs", "sprockets", _
    "widgets", "gizmos")
```

AddFields Method

Applies To   PivotTable.

Description   Adds row, column and page fields to the pivot table.

Syntax   *object*.**AddFields(***rowField s* , *columnFields, pageFields, addToTable***)**

Elements   The **AddFields** method has the following object qualifier and named arguments:

object
> Required. The PivotTable object.

rowFields
> Optional. A PivotField (or an array of PivotFields) to be added as rows.

columnFields
> Optional. A PivotField (or an array of PivotFields) to be added as columns.

pageFields
> Optional. A PivotField (or an array of PivotFields) to be added as pages.

addToTable
> Optional. If **True**, the fields are added to the pivot table (none of the existing fields are replaced). If **False**, the new fields replace existing fields. The default is **False** if this argument is not specified.

Remarks   You must specify one of the field arguments.

See Also   **ColumnFields** Method, **DataFields** Method, **HiddenFields** Method, **PageFields** Method, **RowFields** Method, **VisibleFields** Method.

Example   This example replaces the existing column fields in the first pivot table with the Status and Closed_By fields.

```
ActiveSheet.PivotTables(1).AddFields _
    ColumnFields:=Array("Status", "Closed_By")
```

AddIn Object

Description   An add-in, either installed or not installed.

Remarks   While in a Visual Basic module, you create an add-in by choosing the Make Add-In command from the Tools menu. The AddIn object provides a programming interface to the Add-In Manager; it doesn't actually create an add-in.

AddIndent Property

Applies To   Button, Buttons, DrawingObjects, GroupObject, GroupObjects, Range, Style, TextBox, TextBoxes.

Description   **True** if text with the distributed text alignment style has extra space added at the beginning and end of each line. Read-write.

Syntax   *object*.**AddIndent**

Elements   *object*
> Required. The object to which this property applies.

Remarks   This property is available only in Far East versions of Microsoft Excel, and only
works for text with the **xlDistributed** alignment style in the direction of the text
(indent is added if the text **Orientation** is **xlVertical** and the **VerticalAlignment**
is **xlDistributed**, or if the text **Orientation** is **xlHorizontal** and the
HorizontalAlignment is **xlDistributed**).

See Also   **HorizontalAlignment** Property, **Orientation** Property, **VerticalAlignment**
Property.

Example   This example sets the active cell to use distributed horizontal alignment with extra
space at the beginning and end.

```
With ActiveCell
    .HorizontalAlignment = xlDistributed
    .AddIndent = True
End With
```

AddIns Method

Applies To   Application.

Description   Returns a single add-in (an AddIn object, Syntax 1) or the collection of add-ins (an
AddIns object, Syntax 2) that appears in the Add-Ins dialog box. Read-only.

Syntax 1   *object*.**AddIns**(*index*)

Syntax 2   *object*.**AddIns**

Elements   The **AddIns** method has the following object qualifier and named arguments:

object
Optional. The Application object.

index
Required for Syntax 1. The number of the add-in, or the title of the add-in, as a
string.

Example   This example displays the status of the Solver add-in.

```
Set currentAddIn = Application.AddIns("Solver")
If currentAddIn.Installed = True Then
    MsgBox "Solver add-in is installed"
Else
    MsgBox "Solver add-in is not installed"
End If
```

AddIns Object

Description	A collection of AddIn objects.

AddItem Method

Applies To	DrawingObjects, DropDown, DropDowns, ListBox, ListBoxes.
Description	Adds an item to a list box or dropdown list box.
Syntax	*object*.**AddItem**(*text, index*)
Elements	The **AddItem** method has the following object qualifier and named arguments:

object
Required. The object to which this method applies.

text
Required. Specifies the text string to add.

index
Optional. Specifies the position at which to add the new entry. If the list has fewer entries than the specified index, blank items are added from the end of the list to the specified position. If this argument is omitted, the item is appended to the existing list.

Remarks	Using this method clears any **ListFillRange**.
See Also	**List** Property, **RemoveItem** Method.
Example	This example adds a new item at the beginning of list box four.

```
DialogSheets(1).ListBoxes(4).AddItem text:="New Item", index:=1
```

AddMenu Method

Applies To	MenuItems.
Description	Adds a new submenu to the menu. This method can also be used to restore a built-in submenu that was previously deleted, by setting the *restore* argument to **True**.

Syntax	*object*.**AddMenu**(*caption, before, restore*)
Elements	The **AddMenu** method has the following object qualifier and named arguments:

object
Required. The MenuItems object.

caption
Required. The caption to use for the new submenu. To create an access key, put an ampersand (&) before the access-key letter.

before
Optional. If this argument is present, specifies the menu item before which this submenu should be inserted. May be a string containing the caption of the menu item (without the ampersand), a number indicating the position of the menu item, or a reference to the menu item.

restore
Optional. If this argument is **True**, Microsoft Excel will restore the previously deleted built-in submenu named by the *caption* argument. If **False** or omitted, Microsoft Excel will add a new submenu.

Example	This example adds a new submenu to the Help menu.

```
Application.MenuBars(1).Menus("Help").MenuItems.AddMenu("More")
```

Address Method

Applies To	Range.
Description	Returns the range reference, as a string in the language of the macro.
Syntax	*object*.**Address**(*rowAbsolute, columnAbsolute, referenceStyle, external, relativeTo*)
Elements	The **Address** method has the following object qualifier and named arguments:

object
Required. Returns a reference to this range.

rowAbsolute
Optional. If **True** or omitted, the row part of the reference is returned as an absolute reference.

columnAbsolute
Optional. If **True** or omitted, the column part of the reference is returned as an absolute reference.

referenceStyle
> Optional. If **xlA1** or omitted, the method returns an A1-style reference. If **xlR1C1**, the method returns an R1C1-style reference.

external
> Optional. If **True**, the method returns an external reference. If **False**, the method returns a local reference. The default is **False**.

relativeTo
> Optional. If *rowAbsolute* and *columnAbsolute* are **False**, and *referenceStyle* is **xlR1C1**, you must include a starting point for the relative reference. This argument is a Range object type that defines the starting point.

Remarks   If the reference contains more than one cell, *rowAbsolute* and *columnAbsolute* apply to all rows and columns.

See Also   **AddressLocal** Method, **Offset** Method.

Examples   The following example displays the text shown in the comments.

```
Set mc = Worksheets("Sheet1").Cells(1, 1)
MsgBox mc.Address()                              ' $A$1
MsgBox mc.Address(rowAbsolute:=False)            ' $A1
MsgBox mc.Address(referenceStyle:=xlR1C1)        ' R1C1
MsgBox mc.Address(referenceStyle:=xlR1C1, _
    rowAbsolute:=False,      _
    columnAbsolute:=False,   _
    relativeTo:=Worksheets(1).Cells(3, 3))       ' R[-2]C[-2]
```

AddressLocal Method

Applies To   Range.

Description   Returns the range reference, as a string in the language of the user.

Syntax   *object*.**AddressLocal**(*rowAbsolute, columnAbsolute, referenceStyle, external, relativeTo*)

Elements   The **AddressLocal** method has the following object qualifier and named arguments:

object
> Required. Returns a reference to this range.

rowAbsolute
> Optional. If **True** or omitted, the row part of the reference is returned as an absolute reference.

columnAbsolute
> Optional. If **True** or omitted, the column part of the reference is returned as an absolute reference.

referenceStyle
> Optional. If **xlA1** or omitted, the method returns an A1-style reference. If **xlR1C1**, the method returns an R1C1-style reference.

external
> Optional. If **True**, the method returns an external reference. If **False**, the method returns a local reference.

relativeTo
> Optional. If *rowAbsolute* and *columnAbsolute* are **False**, and **referenceStyle** is **xlR1C1**, then you must include a starting point for the relative reference. This argument is a Range object type that defines the starting point.

Remarks

If the reference contains more than one cell, *rowAbsolute* and *columnAbsolute* apply to all rows and columns.

See Also

Address Method, **Offset** Method.

Examples

Assume that the following example was created in the American English version of Microsoft Excel and then run in the German version. The example displays the text shown in the comments.

```
Set mc = Worksheets("Sheet1").Cells(1, 1)
MsgBox mc.AddressLocal()                            ' $A$1
MsgBox mc.AddressLocal(rowAbsolute:=False)          ' $A1
MsgBox mc.AddressLocal(referenceStyle:=xlR1C1)      ' Z1S1
MsgBox mc.AddressLocal(referenceStyle:=xlR1C1, _
    rowAbsolute:=False,       _
    columnAbsolute:=False,    _
    relativeTo:=Worksheets(1).Cells(3, 3))          ' Z(-2)S(-2)
```

AddVertex Method

Applies To

Drawing.

Description

Adds a vertex to the end of the drawing.

Syntax

object.**AddVertex**(*left, top*)

Elements

The **AddVertex** method has the following object qualifier and named arguments:

object
> Required. The Drawing object.

left
> Required. The left position of the new vertex in points (1/72 inch), relative to the upper left corner of the sheet.

top
> Required. The top position of the new vertex in points, relative to the upper left corner of the sheet.

See Also   **Add** Method (Drawings Collection), **Reshape** Method.

Example   This example creates a new open trapezoid.

```
With ActiveSheet.Drawings.Add(100, 100, 200, 100, False)
    .AddVertex 180, 200
    .AddVertex 80, 200
    .Border.Weight = xlMedium
End With
```

AdvancedFilter Method

Applies To   Range.

Description   Filters or copies from a list based on a criteria range. If the initial selection is a single cell, its current region is used.

Syntax   *object*.**AdvancedFilter**(*action, criteriaRange, copyToRange, unique*)

Elements   The **AdvancedFilter** method has the following object qualifier and named arguments:

object
> Required. The Range object.

action
> Required. Specifies the operation (either **xlFilterInPlace** or **xlFilterCopy**).

criteriaRange
> Optional. The criteria range. If omitted, there are no criteria.

copyToRange
> Required if *action* is **xlFilterCopy**, ignored otherwise. The destination range for the copied rows.

unique
> Optional. **True** means unique records only, **False** means all records that meet the criteria. If omitted, assumed **False**.

See Also   **AutoFilter** Method, **FilterMode** Property, **ShowAllData** Method.

Example   This example filters a database (named Database) based on a criteria range named Criteria.

```
Range("Database").AdvancedFilter _
    action:=xlFilterInPlace, _
    criteriaRange:=Range("Criteria")
```

AlertBeforeOverwriting Property

Applies To   Application.

Description   **True** if Microsoft Excel displays a message before overwriting non-blank cells during a drag and drop editing operation. Read-write.

Syntax   *object*.**AlertBeforeOverwriting**

Elements   *object*
                   Required. The Application object.

Example   This example causes Microsoft Excel to display an alert before overwriting non-blank cells during a drag and drop editing operation.

```
Application.AlertBeforeOverwriting = True
```

AltStartupPath Property

Applies To   Application.

Description   Returns or sets the name of the alternate startup directory or folder. Read-write. The name is a string.

Syntax   *object*.**AltStartupPath**

Elements   *object*
                   Required. The Application object.

Example   This example sets the alternate startup directory.

```
Application.AltStartupPath = "C:\EXCEL\MACROS"
```

And Operator

Description   Used to perform a logical conjunction on two expressions.

Syntax	*result = expression1* **And** *expression2*

Elements   The **And** operator syntax has these parts:

Part	Description
result	Any numeric variable.
expression1	Any expression.
expression2	Any expression.

Remarks   If, and only if, both expressions evaluate **True**, *result* is **True**. If either expression evaluates **False**, *result* is **False.** The following table illustrates how *result* is determined:

If expression1 is	And expression2 is	The result is
True	True	True
True	False	False
True	Null	Null
False	True	False
False	False	False
False	Null	False
Null	True	Null
Null	False	False
Null	Null	Null

The **And** operator also performs a bit-wise comparison of identically positioned bits in two numeric expressions and sets the corresponding bit in *result* according to the following truth table:

If bit in expression1 is	And bit in expression2 is	The result is
0	0	0
0	1	0
1	0	0
1	1	1

See Also   Operator Precedence.

Example   This example uses the **And** operator to perform a logical conjunction on two expressions.

```
A = 10: B = 8: C = 6 : D = Null          ' Initialize variables.
MyCheck = A > B And B > C                 ' Returns True.
MyCheck = B > A And B > C                 ' Returns False.
MyCheck = A > B And B > D                 ' Returns Null.
MyCheck = A And B                         ' Returns 8 (bit-wise comparison).
```

AppActivate Statement

Description   Activates an application window.

Syntax   **AppActivate** *title* [*,wait*]

Elements   The **AppActivate** statement syntax has these named-argument parts:

Part	Description
title	In Microsoft Windows, the *title* argument is the string in the title bar of the application window you want to activate.
	On the Macintosh (System 7.0 or later), the *title* argument is the application name. You can use the **MacID** function to specify an application's signature instead of the application name. For example,
	`AppActivate MacID("MSWD")`
	In addition, the task ID returned by the **Shell** function can be used, in place of *title*, to activate an application.
wait	Boolean value specifying whether the calling application has the focus before activating another. If **False** (default), the specified application is immediately activated, even if the calling application does not have the focus. If **True**, the calling application waits until it has the focus, then activates the specified application.

Remarks   The **AppActivate** statement changes the focus to the named application or window but does not affect whether it is maximized or minimized. Focus moves from the activated application window when the user takes some action to change the focus or close the window. Use the **Shell** function to start an application and set the window style.

In trying to find the application to activate, a comparison is made to try to find an application whose title string is an exact match with *title*. If unsuccessful, any application's title string that begins with *title* is activated. In Microsoft Windows, if there is more than one instance of the application named by *title*, one is arbitrarily activated.

If you use the **MacID** function with **AppActivate** in Microsoft Windows, an error occurs.

See Also   **MacID** Function, **Shell** Function, **SendKeys** Statement.

Example

This example illustrates various uses of the **AppActivate** statement to activate an application window. On the Macintosh, you can use the **MacID** function to specify the application's signature instead of the application's name. The **AppActivate** statement is available with Macintosh System 7.0 or later.

```
' In Microsoft Windows.
AppActivate "Microsoft Word"          ' Activate Microsoft Word.
' AppActivate can also use the return value of the Shell function.
MyAppID = Shell("C:\WORD\WINWORD.EXE", 1)    ' Run Microsoft Word.
AppActivate MyAppID                   ' Activate Microsoft Word.

' On the Macintosh.
AppActivate "Microsoft Word"          ' Activate Microsoft Word.

' MacID("MSWD") returns signature for Microsoft Word.
AppActivate MacID("MSWD")             ' Activate Microsoft Word.

' You can also use the return value of the Shell function.
ReturnValue = Shell("Microsoft Excel")   ' Run Microsoft Excel.
AppActivate ReturnValue               ' Activate Microsoft  Excel.
```

Application Object

Description

The Application object contains:

- Application-wide settings and options (options in the Tools Options dialog box, for example)
- Built-in worksheet functions such as SUM, AVERAGE, and COUNTA
- Methods that return top-level objects such as ActiveCell, ActiveSheet, and so on

Remarks

Many of the properties and methods that return the most common user-interface objects, such as the active cell (**ActiveCell** property) can be used without the Application object qualifier. For example, instead of writing `Application.ActiveCell.Font.Bold = True`, you can write `ActiveCell.Font.Bold = True`.

These properties and methods appear in the Object Browser under both the Application object and the Global object. To paste the form that does not require the Application qualifier, paste the property or method from the Global object.

Application Property

Applies To	All objects.
Description	Returns the Application that created this object. Read-only.
Syntax	*object*.**Application**
Elements	*object* Required. The object to which this property applies.
Remarks	The value of this property is "Microsoft Excel" if the object was created by Microsoft Excel.
See Also	**Creator** Property.
Example	This example runs a conditional block if an object was created by Microsoft Excel.

```
Set myObject = ActiveWorkbook
If myObject.Application.Value = "Microsoft Excel" Then
    MsgBox "This is a Microsoft Excel object"
Else
    MsgBox "This is not a Microsoft Excel object"
End If
```

ApplyDataLabels Method

Applies To	Chart, Point, Series.
Description	Applies data labels to the point, the series, or to all series on the chart.
Syntax	*object*.**ApplyDataLabels**(*type, legendKey*)
Elements	The **ApplyDataLabels** method has the following object qualifier and named arguments: *object* Required. The Chart, Point, or Series object.

type
   Optional. The type of data label, as shown in the following list.

Value	Meaning
xlNone	No data labels.
xlShowValue	Value for the point (assumed if this argument is not specified).
xlShowPercent	Percentage of the total. Only available for pie and doughnut charts.
xlShowLabel	Category for the point.
xlShowLabelAndPercent	Percentage of the total and category for the point. Only available for pie and doughnut charts.

legendKey
   Optional. If **True**, Microsoft Excel shows the legend key next to the point.

See Also   **DataLabel** Property, **HasDataLabel** Property, **HasDataLabels** Property.

Example   This example applies category labels to the first series.

```
ActiveChart.SeriesCollection(1).ApplyDataLabels type:=xlShowLabel
```

ApplyNames Method

Applies To   Range.

Description   Applies names to the cells in the range.

Syntax   *object*.**ApplyNames**(*names, ignoreRelativeAbsolute, useRowColumnNames, omitColumn, omitRow, order, appendLast*)

Elements   The **ApplyNames** method has the following object qualifier and named arguments:

object
   Required. The range where names will be applied.

names
   Optional. Contains an array of the names to apply. If omitted, all names on the sheet are applied to the range.

ignoreRelativeAbsolute
   Optional. If **True** or omitted, replaces references with names regardless of the reference types of either the names or references. If **False**, replaces absolute references only with absolute names, relative references only with relative names, and mixed references only with mixed names.

useRowColumnNames
> Optional. If **True** or omitted, Microsoft Excel uses the names of row and column ranges containing the specified range if names for the range cannot be found. If **False**, the *omitColumn* and *omitRow* arguments are ignored.

omitColumn
> Optional. If **True** or omitted, Microsoft Excel replaces the reference with the row-oriented name without including a column-oriented name if the referenced cell is in the same column as the formula and within a row-oriented named range.

omitRow
> Optional. If **True** or omitted, Microsoft Excel replaces the reference with the column-oriented name without including a row-oriented name if the referenced cell is in the same row as the formula within a column-oriented named range.

order
> Optional. Determines which range name is listed first when a cell reference is replaced by a row-oriented and column-oriented range name (either **xlRowThenColumn** or **xlColumnThenRow**).

appendLast
> Optional. If **True**, Microsoft Excel replaces the definitions of the names in *names* and also replaces the definitions of the last names defined. If *appendLast* is **False** or omitted, Microsoft Excel replaces the definitions of the names in *names* only.

Remarks   You can use the **Array** function to create the list of names for the *names* argument.

If you want to apply names to the entire sheet, use **Cells.ApplyNames**.

You cannot "unapply" names; to delete names, use the **Delete** method.

See Also   **Array** Function, **Delete** Method.

Example   This example applies names to the entire sheet.

```
Cells.ApplyNames names:=Array("Sales", "Profits")
```

ApplyOutlineStyles Method

Applies To   Range.

Description   Applies outlining styles to the range.

Syntax   *object*.**ApplyOutlineStyles**

Elements   *object*
> Required. The range where outlining styles will be applied.

Example

The following example applies automatic outlining styles to the selection. The selection must include the entire outline range.

```
Selection.ApplyOutlineStyles
```

Arc Object

Description

An arc graphic object drawn on a chart or worksheet.

Arcs Method

Applies To

Chart, DialogSheet, Worksheet.

Description

Returns a single arc (an Arc object, Syntax 1) or a collection of arcs (an Arcs object, Syntax 2) on the chart or sheet. Read-only.

Syntax 1

object.**Arcs(*index*)**

Syntax 2

object.**Arcs**

Elements

The **Arcs** method has the following object qualifier and named arguments.

object
Required. The object to which this method applies.

index
Required for Syntax 1. The name or number of the arc.

Example

This example selects the seventh and ninth arcs on the active sheet.

```
ActiveSheet.Arcs(Array(7, 9)).Select
```

Arcs Object

Description

A collection of Arc objects.

Area3DGroup Property

Applies To	Chart.
Description	Returns the area ChartGroup on a 3-D chart.
Syntax	*object*.**Area3DGroup**
Elements	*object*
	Required. The Chart object.
See Also	**AreaGroups** Method.
Example	This example sets the subtype for the 3-D area chart group.

```
Charts(1).Area3DGroup.SubType = 3
```

AreaGroups Method

Applies To	Chart.
Description	On a 2-D chart, returns a single area chart group (a ChartGroup object, Syntax 1), or a collection of the area chart groups (a ChartGroups collection, Syntax 2).
Syntax 1	*object*.**AreaGroups(*index*)**
Syntax 2	*object*.**AreaGroups**
Elements	The **AreaGroups** method has the following object qualifier and named arguments:
	object
	Required. The Chart object.
	index
	Required for Syntax 1. Specifies the chart group.
See Also	**Area3DGroup** Property.
Example	This example sets the subtype for the first area chart group.

```
Charts(1).AreaGroups(1).SubType = 3
```

Areas Method

Applies To	Range.
Description	Returns a single range (a Range object, Syntax 1), or a collection of all ranges (an Areas object, Syntax 2) in a multiple selection.
Syntax 1	*object*.**Areas**(*index*)
Syntax 2	*object*.**Areas**
Elements	*object* 　　Required. The multiple-selection range. *index* 　　Required for Syntax 1. The number of the range within the multiple selection.
Remarks	For a single selection, the **Areas** method returns a collection of one object, the original Range object itself. For a multiple selection, the **Areas** method returns a collection that contains one object for each selection.
See Also	**Union** Method.
Example	This example displays a message if the user tries to carry out a command on a multiple selection.

```
If Selection.Areas.Count > 1 Then
    MsgBox "Cannot do this to a multiple selection."
End If
```

Areas Object

Description	A collection of the areas in a Range. Each area is a Range. Areas objects are returned by the Areas method. Each area corresponds to the sections of a discontiguous (multiple) selection.

Arrange Method

Applies To	Windows.

Description   Arranges the windows on the screen.

Syntax   *object*.**Arrange**(*arrangeStyle, activeWorkbook, syncHorizontal, syncVertical*)

Elements   The **Arrange** method has the following object qualifier and named arguments:

object
   Required. The Windows object.

arrangeStyle
   Optional. Arrange windows in this style. Can have one of the following values:

Value	Meaning
xlTiled	Windows are tiled (the default value, used if *arrangeStyle* is omitted).
xlCascade	Windows are cascaded.
xlHorizontal	Windows are arranged horizontally.
xlVertical	Windows are arranged vertically.
xlIcons	Arranges the icons (not available on the Apple Macintosh).

activeWorkbook
   Optional. If **True**, arranges only the visible windows of the active workbook, instead of all the windows in Microsoft Excel. If **False** or omitted, arranges all of the windows.

syncHorizontal
   Optional. Ignored if *activeWorkbook* is **False** or omitted. If **True**, the windows of the active workbook are synchronized when scrolling horizontally. If **False** or omitted, the windows are not synchronized.

syncVertical
   Optional. Ignored if *activeWorkbook* is **False** or omitted. If **True**, the windows of the active workbook are synchronized when scrolling vertically. If **False** or omitted, the windows are not synchronized.

Example   This example tiles all the windows on the screen.

```
Application.Windows.Arrange
```

Array Function

Description   Returns a **Variant** containing an array.

Syntax	**Array**(*arglist*)
Elements	The *arglist* consists of a comma-delimited list of an arbitrary number of values that are assigned to the elements of the array contained within the **Variant**. If no arguments are specified, an array of zero-length is created.
Remarks	Although a **Variant** containing an array is conceptually different from an array whose elements are of type **Variant**, the way the array elements are accessed is the same. The notation used to refer to any element of an array consists of the variable name followed by parentheses containing an index number to the desired element. In the following example, the first statement creates a variable A as a **Variant**. The second statement assigns an array to the variable A. The final statement illustrates how to assign the value contained in the second array element to another variable.

```
Dim A As Variant
A = Array(10,20,30)
B = A(2)
```

The lower bound of an array created using the **Array** function is determined by the lower bound specified with the **Option Base** statement.

See Also	**Det***type* statements, **Dim** Statement, **Let** Statement, **Option Base** Statement.
Example	This example uses the **Array** function to return a **Variant** containing an array.

```
MyWeek = Array("Mon", "Tue", "Wed", "Thu", "Fri", "Sat", "Sun")
' Return values assume lower bound equals 1 (using Option Base).
MyDay = MyWeek(2)    ' Returns "Tue".
MyDay = MyWeek(4)    ' Returns "Thu".
```

ArrowHeadLength Property

Applies To	DrawingObjects, GroupObject, GroupObjects, Line, Lines.
Description	Returns or sets the length of the arrow head (one of **xlShort**, **xlMedium**, or **xlLong**). Read-write.
Syntax	*object*.**ArrowHeadLength**
Elements	*object*
	Required. The object to which this property applies.
See Also	**ArrowHeadWidth** Property, **ArrowHeadStyle** Property.

Example   This example sets the arrowhead length, width and style on line one.

```
With Charts(1).Lines(1)
    .ArrowHeadLength = xlShort
    .ArrowHeadWidth = xlNarrow
    .ArrowHeadStyle = xlOpen
End With
```

ArrowHeadStyle Property

Applies To   DrawingObjects, GroupObject, GroupObjects, Line, Lines.

Description   Returns or sets the arrow head type (one of **xlNone**, **xlOpen**, **xlClosed**, **xlDoubleOpen**, or **xlDoubleClosed**). Read-write.

Syntax   *object*.**ArrowHeadStyle**

Elements   *object*
           Required. The object to which this property applies.

See Also   **ArrowHeadLength** Property, **ArrowHeadWidth** Property.

Example   This example sets the arrowhead length, width and style on line one.

```
With Charts(1).Lines(1)
    .ArrowHeadLength = xlShort
    .ArrowHeadWidth = xlNarrow
    .ArrowHeadStyle = xlOpen
End With
```

ArrowHeadWidth Property

Applies To   DrawingObjects, GroupObject, GroupObjects, Line, Lines.

Description   Returns or sets the arrow head width (one of **xlNarrow**, **xlMedium**, **xlWide**). Read-write.

Syntax   *object*.**ArrowHeadWidth**

Elements   *object*
           Required. The object to which this property applies.

See Also   **ArrowHeadLength** Property, **ArrowHeadStyle** Property.

Example   This example sets the arrowhead length, width and style on line one.

```
With Charts(1).Lines(1)
    .ArrowHeadLength = xlShort
    .ArrowHeadWidth = xlNarrow
    .ArrowHeadStyle = xlOpen
End With
```

Asc Function

Description   Returns the character code corresponding to the first letter in a string.

Syntax   **Asc(*string*)**

Elements   The *string* named argument is any valid string expression. If the *string* contains no characters, a run-time error occurs.

See Also   Character Set, **Chr** Function.

Example   This example uses the **Asc** function to return a character code corresponding to the first letter in the string.

```
MyNumber = Asc("A")          ' Returns 65.
MyNumber = Asc("a")          ' Returns 97.
MyNumber = Asc("Apple")      ' Returns 65.
```

AskToUpdateLinks Property

Applies To   Application.

Description   **True** if Microsoft Excel asks the user to update links when opening files with links, or **False** if links are automatically updated with no dialog. Read-write.

Syntax   *object*.**AskToUpdateLinks**

Elements   *object*
                    Required. The Application object.

Example   This example causes Microsoft Excel to ask the user to update links when it opens a file with links.

```
Application.AskToUpdateLinks = True
```

Atn Function

Description	Returns the arctangent of a number.
Syntax	**Atn(***number***)**
Elements	The ***number*** named argument can be any valid numeric expression.
Remarks	The **Atn** function takes the ratio of two sides of a right triangle (***number***) and returns the corresponding angle in radians. The ratio is the length of the side opposite the angle divided by the length of the side adjacent to the angle.

The range of the result is -pi/2 to pi/2 radians.

To convert degrees to radians, multiply degrees by pi/180. To convert radians to degrees, multiply radians by 180/pi.

Note **Atn** is the inverse trigonometric function of **Tan**, which takes an angle as its argument and returns the ratio of two sides of a right triangle. Do not confuse **Atn** with the cotangent, which is the simple inverse of a tangent (1/tangent).

See Also	**Cos** Function, **Sin** Function, **Tan** Function.
Example	This example uses the **Atn** function to return the arctangent of a number.

```
Pi = 4 * Atn(1)      ' Calculate the value of pi.
```

Author Property

Applies To	AddIn, Workbook.
Description	Returns or sets the author of an object, as a string. Read-only for AddIn, read-write for Workbook.
Syntax	*object*.**Author**
Elements	*object* Required. The AddIn or Workbook object.
See Also	**Comments** Property, **Keyword** Property, **Subject** Property, **Title** Property.

Example

This example opens a new worksheet and creates a table of all the add-ins currently installed, showing their titles and authors.

```
Workbooks.Add
i = 1
Cells(1,1).Formula = "Title"
Cells(1,2).Formula = "Author"
Rows(1).Font.Bold = True
Rows(1).Font.Underline = True
For Each thisAddIn in AddIns
    If thisAddIn.Installed Then
        i = i + 1
        Cells(i,1).Formula = thisAddIn.Title
        Cells(i,2).Formula = thisAddIn.Author
    End If
Next
```

AutoFill Method

Applies To

Range.

Description

Performs an autofill on the cells in the range.

Syntax

object.**AutoFill**(*destination, type*)

Elements

The **AutoFill** method has the following object qualifier and named arguments:

object
    Required. The source range.

destination
    Required. A Range object that represents the cells to fill. The object must include the source range.

type
    Optional. Can be one of **xlFillDefault, xlFillSeries, xlFillCopy, xlFillFormats, xlFillValues, xlFillDays, xlFillWeekdays, xlFillMonths, xlFillYears, xlLinearTrend, xlGrowthTrend**. If **xlFillDefault** or omitted, the method selects the most appropriate type based on the source range.

Example

This example performs an autofill on cells A1:A20, based on the source range of A1:A2.

```
Set currentSourceRange = ActiveSheet.Range(Cells(1, 1),Cells(2, 1))
Set currentFillRange = ActiveSheet.Range(Cells(1, 1), Cells(20, 1))
currentSourceRange.AutoFill destination:=currentFillRange
```

AutoFilter Method

Applies To	Range.
Description	Syntax 1: Displays or hides the AutoFilter drop-down arrows.
	Syntax 2: Filters a list using the AutoFilter.
Syntax 1	*object*.**AutoFilter**
Syntax 2	*object*.**AutoFilter**(*field, criteria1, operator, criteria2*)
Elements	The **AutoFilter** method has the following object qualifier and named arguments:

object
Required. The Range object.

field
Required. The integer offset of the field on which to base the filter (from the left of the list — the leftmost field is field one).

criteria1
Optional. The criteria (a string; for example "101"). Use "=" to find blank fields, "<>" to find non-blank fields. If this argument is omitted, the criteria is **All**.

operator
Optional. Used with *criteria1* and *criteria2* to construct compound criteria. Can be either **xlAnd** or **xlOr**. If omitted, **xlAnd** is used.

criteria2
Optional. The second criteria (a string). Used with *criteria1* and *operator* to construct compound criteria.

See Also	**AdvancedFilter** Method, **AutoFilterMode** Property, **FilterMode** Property, **ShowAllData** Method.
Example	This example filters a list to show only the entries where field one is "Otis."

```
Range(Cells(1, 1), Cells(10, 10)).AutoFilter field:=1, _
    criteria1:="Otis"
```

AutoFilterMode Property

Applies To   Worksheet.

Description   **True** if the drop-down arrows for AutoFilter are currently displayed on the sheet. This property is independent of the **FilterMode** property. Read-write.

Syntax   *object*.**AutoFilterMode**

Elements   *object*
                     Required. The Worksheet object.

Remarks   This property will be **True** if the drop-down arrows are currently displayed. You can set this property to **False** to remove the arrows, but you cannot set it to **True**. Use the **AutoFilter** method to filter a list and display the drop-down arrows.

See Also   **AutoFilter** Method, **FilterMode** Property.

Example   This example displays the current state of the **AutoFilterMode** property.

```
If ActiveSheet.AutoFilterMode Then
    isOn = "On"
Else
    isOn = "Off"
End If
MsgBox "AutoFilterMode is " & isOn
```

AutoFit Method

Applies To   Range.

Description   Changes the width of the columns in the range or the height of the rows in the range for the best fit.

Syntax   *object*.**AutoFit**

Elements   *object*
                     Required. The range to apply the best fit to. Must be a row or a range of rows, or a column or a range of columns. Otherwise, this method generates an error.

Remark   One unit of column width is equal to the width of one character of the Normal style.

See Also   **ColumnWidth** Property, **RowHeight** Property.

Example   This example changes the width of columns A through I for best fit.

```
ActiveSheet.Range(Columns("A"), Columns("I")).AutoFit
```

AutoFormat Method (Chart object)

Applies To   Chart.

Description   Applies a built-in or custom autoformat to the specified chart.

Syntax   *object*.**AutoFormat**(*gallery, format*)

Elements   The **AutoFormat** method has the following object qualifier and named arguments:

object
Required. The Chart object.

gallery
Required. Specifies the built-in gallery. Can be one of **xl3DArea**, **xl3DBar**, **xl3DColumn**, **xl3DLine**, **xl3DPie**, **xl3DSurface**, **xlArea**, **xlBar**, **xlColumn**, **xlCombination**, **xlCustom**, **xlDefaultAutoFormat**, **xlDoughnut**, **xlLine**, **xlPie**, **xlRadar**, or **xlXYScatter**.

format
Optional. Specifies the option number for the built-in autoformats or a string containing the name of the custom autoformat if *gallery* is **xlCustom**.

See Also   **AutoFormat** Method (Range object).

Examples   This example applies the third radar autoformat.

```
Charts(1).AutoFormat xlRadar, 3
```

This example applies the "Monthly Sales" custom autoformat.

```
Charts(1).AutoFormat xlCustom, "Monthly Sales"
```

AutoFormat Method (Range object)

Applies To   Range.

Description   Automatically formats a range of cells using a predefined format.

Syntax   *object*.**AutoFormat**(*format, number, font, alignment, border, pattern, width*)

Elements

The **AutoFormat** method has the following object qualifier and named arguments:

object
Required. The range to format.

format
Optional. The name or number of the format to apply (one of **xlClassic1**, **xlClassic2**, **xlClassic3**, **xlAccounting1**, **xlAccounting2**, **xlAccounting3**, **xlAccounting4**, **xlColor1**, **xlColor2**, **xlColor3**, **xlList1**, **xlList2**, **xlList3**, **xl3DEffects1**, **xl3DEffects2**, **xlSimple**, or **xlNone**). If this argument is omitted, the default value is **xlClassic1**.

number
Optional. Corresponds to the Number check box in the AutoFormat dialog box. Can be **True** or **False** (**True** if omitted).

font
Optional. Corresponds to the Font check box in the AutoFormat dialog box. Can be **True** or **False** (**True** if omitted).

alignment
Optional. Corresponds to the Alignment check box in the AutoFormat dialog box. Can be **True** or **False** (**True** if omitted).

border
Optional. Corresponds to the Border check box in the AutoFormat dialog box. Can be **True** or **False** (**True** if omitted).

pattern
Optional. Corresponds to the Pattern check box in the AutoFormat dialog box. Can be **True** or **False** (**True** if omitted).

width
Optional. Corresponds to the Column Width/Row Height check box in the AutoFormat dialog box. Can be **True** or **False** (**True** if omitted).

Remarks

If the range is a single cell, this method also formats the current region around the cell. In other words, the **AutoFormat** method performs **CurrentRegion.AutoFormat** on the single cell.

In Japanese Microsoft Excel, the following additional formats are available: **xlLocalFormat1** and **xlLocalFormat2**.

See Also

AutoFormat Method (Chart object), **CurrentRegion** Property, **Style** Property.

Example

This example formats a range of cells using a predefined format.

```
Set currentSourceRange = ActiveSheet.Range(Cells(1, 1), Cells(8, 8))
currentSourceRange.AutoFormat format:=xlClassic1
```

AutomaticStyles Property

Applies To   Outline.

Description   **True** if the outline uses automatic styles. Read-write.

Syntax   *object*.**AutomaticStyles**

Elements   *object*
                    Required. The Outline object (**ActiveSheet.Outline**, for example).

Example   This example sets the outline on the active sheet to use automatic styles.

```
ActiveSheet.Outline.AutomaticStyles = True
```

AutoOutline Method

Applies To   Range.

Description   Automatically creates an outline for the specified range. If the range is a single cell, Microsoft Excel creates an outline for the entire sheet. The new outline replaces any existing outline.

Syntax   *object*.**AutoOutline**

Elements   *object*
                    Required. The Range object.

See Also   **ApplyOutlineStyles** Method, **ClearOutline** Method.

Example   This example creates an outline for the range A1:G37. The range must contain either a summary row or a summary column.

```
Range("A1:G37").AutoOutline
```

AutoScaling Property

Applies To   Chart.

Description   If **True**, Microsoft Excel scales a 3-D chart so that it is closer in size to the equivalent 2-D chart. The **RightAngleAxes** property must be **True**. Read-write.

Syntax	*object*.**AutoScaling**
Elements	*object*
	Required. The Chart object.
Example	This example scales the 3-D chart.

```
With Charts(1)
    .RightAngleAxes = True
    .AutoScaling = True
End With
```

AutoSize Property

Applies To	Button, Buttons, DrawingObjects, GroupObject, GroupObjects, TextBox, TextBoxes.
Description	**True** if the object will be automatically resized to fit the text it contains. Read-write.
Syntax	*object*.**AutoSize**
Elements	*object*
	Required. The object to which this property applies.
Remarks	This property is set to **False** if the object is resized manually (by the user or by the **Height** or **Width** properties).
Example	This example sets button one to automatically size to fit the text it contains.

```
ActiveSheet.Buttons(1).AutoSize = True
```

AutoText Property

Applies To	DataLabel, DataLabels.
Description	**True** if the object automatically generates appropriate text based on context. Read-write.
Syntax	*object*.**AutoText**
Elements	*object*
	Required. The DataLabel or DataLabels object.

Example   This example sets the data labels on series one to automatically generate appropriate text.

```
Charts(1).SeriesCollection(1).DataLabels.AutoText = True
```

AutoUpdate Property

Applies To   OLEObject.

Description   **True** if the OLE object updates automatically when the source changes. Valid only if the object is linked (its **OLEType** property must be **xlOLELink**). Read-only.

Syntax   *object*.**AutoUpdate**

Elements   *object*
    Required. The OLEObject.

Example   This example displays the auto update status for all OLE objects on the active worksheet.

```
Worksheets(1).Activate
Cells(1, 1) = "Name"
Cells(1, 2) = "Link Status"
Cells(1, 3) = "AutoUpdate Status"
i = 2
For Each obj In ActiveSheet.OLEObjects
    Cells(i, 1) = obj.Name
    If obj.OLEType = xlOLELink Then
        Cells(i, 2) = "Linked"
        Cells(i, 3) = obj.AutoUpdate
    Else
        Cells(i, 2) = "Embedded"
    End If
    i = i + 1
Next
```

Axes Method

Applies To   Chart.

Description   Returns a single axis (an Axis object, Syntax 1) or a collection of the axes on the chart (an Axes object, Syntax 2). Read-only.

Syntax 1	*object*.**Axes**(*type, axisGroup*)
Syntax 2	*object*.**Axes**
Elements	The **Axes** method has the following object qualifier and named arguments:

object
Required. The Chart object.

type
Required for Syntax 1. Specifies the axis to return. Can be one of **xlValue**, **xlCategory**, or **xlSeries** (**xlSeries** is only valid for 3-D charts).

axisGroup
Optional. Specifies the axis group (either **xlPrimary** or **xlSecondary**). If this argument is omitted, the primary group is used. 3-D charts have only one axis group.

Example	This example turns on major gridlines for the category (x) axis.

```
Charts(1).Axes(xlCategory).HasMajorGridlines = True
```

Axes Object

Description	A collection of Axis objects.

Axis Object

Description	An axis on a chart.

AxisBetweenCategories Property

Applies To	Axis.
Description	**True** if the value axis crosses the category (x) axis between categories.
Syntax	*object*.**AxisBetweenCategories**
Elements	*object* Required. The Axis object.
Remarks	This property only applies to category axes, and does not apply to 3-D charts.

Example   This example causes the value axis to cross the category (x) axis between categories.

```
ActiveChart.Axes(xlCategory).AxisBetweenCategories = True
```

AxisGroup Property

Applies To   Axis, ChartGroup, Series.

Description   Returns the group (either **xlPrimary** or **xlSecondary**) for the specified axis, chart group, or series. Read-write for Series; read-only for Axis and ChartGroup.

Syntax   *object*.**AxisGroup**

Elements   *object*
    Required. The Axis, ChartGroup, or Series object.

Remarks   For 3-D charts, only **xlPrimary** is valid.

Example   This example deletes the value axis if it is in the secondary group.

```
With ActiveChart.Axes(xlValue)
    If .AxisGroup = xlSecondary Then .Delete
End With
```

AxisTitle Object

Description   An axis title (a graphic object) on a chart.

AxisTitle Property

Applies To   Axis.

Description   Returns the AxisTitle for the specified axis. Read-only.

Syntax   *object*.**AxisTitle**

Elements   *object*
    Required. The Axis object.

Remarks   Setting **AxisTitle.Caption** to any string, even a blank string, forces the **HasTitle** property for that axis to **True**.

See Also　　　　ChartTitle Property, HasTitle Property, Title Property.

Example　　　　This example sets the category axis title text.

```
With ActiveChart.Axes(xlCategory).AxisTitle
    .Caption = "Category Axis"
    .Font.Italic = True
    .Font.Size = 17
End With
```

Background Property

Applies To　　　　Font.

Description　　　　Returns or sets the text background type (can be one of **xlAutomatic**, **xlOpaque**, or **xlTransparent**). This property is only used for text on charts. Read-write.

Syntax　　　　*object*.**Background**

Elements　　　　*object*
　　　　　　Required. The Font object.

Example　　　　This example sets the font size and background type of the title on chart one.

```
With ActiveSheet.ChartObjects(1).Chart.ChartTitle.Font
    .Size = 10
    .Background = xlTransparent
End With
```

Backward Property

Applies To　　　　Trendline.

Description　　　　Returns or sets the number of periods (or units on a scatter chart) that the trendline extends backward. Read-write.

Syntax　　　　*object*.**Backward**

Elements　　　　*object*
　　　　　　Required. The Trendline object.

See Also　　　　**Forward** Property.

Example   This example sets the number of units the trendline extends forward and backward.

```
With ActiveChart.SeriesCollection(1).Trendlines(1)
    .Forward = 5
    .Backward = 5
End With
```

Bar3DGroup Property

Applies To   Chart.

Description   Returns the bar ChartGroup on a 3-D chart.

Syntax   *object*.**Bar3DGroup**

Elements   *object*
                    Required. The Chart object.

See Also   **BarGroups** Method.

Example   This example sets the subtype for the 3-D bar chart group.

```
Charts(1).Bar3DGroup.SubType = 3
```

BarGroups Method

Applies To   Chart.

Description   On a 2-D chart, returns a single bar chart group (a ChartGroup object, Syntax 1), or a collection of the bar chart groups (a ChartGroups collection, Syntax 2).

Syntax 1   *object*.**BarGroups(*index*)**

Syntax 2   *object*.**BarGroups**

Elements   The **BarGroups** method has the following object qualifier and named arguments:

                    object
                    Required. The Chart object.

                    index
                    Required for Syntax 1. Specifies the chart group.

See Also	**Bar3DGroup** Property.
Example	This example sets the subtype for the first bar chart group.

```
Charts(1).BarGroups(1).SubType = 3
```

BaseField Property

Applies To	PivotField.
Description	Returns or sets the base field for the custom calculation. Valid only for data fields. Read-write.
Syntax	*object*.**BaseField**
Elements	*object* Required. The PivotField object.
Example	This example sets the base field to the "Year" field.

```
ActiveCell.PivotField.Calculation = xlDifferenceFrom
ActiveCell.PivotField.BaseField = "Year"
ActiveCell.PivotField.BaseItem = "1991"
```

BaseItem Property

Applies To	PivotField.
Description	Returns or sets the item in the base field for the custom calculation. Valid only for data fields. Read-write.
Syntax	*object*.**BaseItem**
Elements	*object* Required. The PivotField object.
Example	This example sets the base item to the "1991" item.

```
ActiveCell.PivotField.Calculation = xlDifferenceFrom
ActiveCell.PivotField.BaseField = "Year"
ActiveCell.PivotField.BaseItem = "1991"
```

BCCRecipients Property

Applies To   Mailer.

Description   Returns or sets the blind carbon copy recipients of the mailer. Read-write.

Syntax   *object*.**BCCRecipients**

Elements   *object*
Required. The Mailer object.

See Also   **CCRecipients** Property, **Enclosures** Property, **Mailer** Property, **Received** Property,**SendDateTime** Property, **Sender** Property, **SendMailer** Property, **Subject** Property, **ToRecipients** Property.

Remarks   This property is an array of strings specifying the address, in one of the following formats:

- A record in the Preferred Personal Catalog. These names are one level deep ("Fred" or "June").

- A full path specifying either a record in a personal catalog ("HD:Excel Folder:My Catalog:Barney") or a plain record ("HD:Folder:Martin").

- A relative path from the current working directory specifying either a personal catalog record ("My Catalog:Barney") or a plain record ("Martin").

- A path in a PowerShare catalog tree of the form "CATALOG_NAME:<node>:RECORD_NAME" where <node> is a path to a PowerShare catalog. An example of a complete path is "AppleTalk:North Building Zone:George's Mac".

See Also   **CCRecipients** Property, **Enclosures** Property, **Mailer** Property, **Received** Property,**SendDateTime** Property, **Sender** Property, **SendMailer** Property, **Subject** Property, **ToRecipients** Property.

Example   This example sets up the Mailer object for workbook one, and then sends the workbook.

```
With Workbooks(1)
    .HasMailer = True
    With .Mailer
        .Subject = "Here is the workbook"
        .ToRecipients = Array("Jean")
        .CCRecipients = Array("Adam", "Bernard")
        .BCCRecipients = Array("Chris")
        .Enclosures = Array("TestFile")
    End With
    .SendMailer
End With
```

Beep Statement

Description   Sounds a tone through the computer's speaker.

Syntax   **Beep**

Remarks   The frequency and duration of the beep depends on hardware, which may vary among computers.

Example   This example uses the **Beep** statement to sound three consecutive tones through the computer's speaker.

```
For I = 1 to 3   ' Loop 3 times.
    Beep         ' Sound a tone.
Next I
```

BlackAndWhite Property

Applies To   PageSetup.

Description   **True** if elements of the document will be printed in black and white. Read-write.

Syntax   *object*.**BlackAndWhite**

Elements   *object*
                      Required. The PageSetup object.

Remarks   This property applies only to worksheet pages.

Example   This example causes the active sheet to print in black and white.

```
ActiveSheet.PageSetup.BlackAndWhite = True
```

Bold Property

Applies To   Font.

Description   **True** if the font is bold. Read-write.

Syntax   *object*.**Bold**

Elements   *object*
    Required. The Font object (**ActiveCell.Font**, for example).

Example   This example sets the font to bold for the range A1:A5.

```
Range("A1", "A5").Font.Bold = True
```

Boolean Data Type

Boolean variables are stored as 16-bit (2-byte) numbers, but they can only be **True** or **False**. **Boolean** variables display as either True or False (when **Print** is used) or #TRUE# or #FALSE# (when **Write #** is used). Use the keywords **True** and **False** to assign one of the two states to **Boolean** variables.

When other numeric data types are converted to **Boolean** values, 0 becomes **False** while all other values become **True**. When **Boolean** values are converted to other data types, **False** becomes 0 while **True** becomes -1.

See Also   **CBool** Function, **DataType** Summary, **Def***type* Statements, **Integer** Data Type.

Border Object

Description   The border of a cell or graphic object.

Border Property

Applies To   Arc, Arcs, Axis, AxisTitle, ChartArea, ChartObject, ChartObjects, ChartTitle, CheckBox, CheckBoxes, DataLabel, DataLabels, DownBars, Drawing, DrawingObjects, Drawings, DropLines, ErrorBars, Floor, Gridlines, GroupObject, GroupObjects, HiLoLines, Legend, LegendKey, Line, Lines, OLEObject, OLEObjects, OptionButton, OptionButtons, Oval, Ovals, Picture, Pictures, PlotArea, Point, Rectangle, Rectangles, Series, SeriesLines, TextBox, TextBoxes, Trendline, UpBars, Walls.

Description   Returns or sets the Border of the object. Read-write.

Syntax   *object*.**Border**

Elements   *object*
                Required. The object to which this property applies.

Example   This example sets the color of the chart area border.

```
Charts(1).ChartArea.Border.Color = RGB(255, 0, 0)
```

BorderAround Method

Applies To   Range.

Description   Adds a border to a Range and sets the **Color**, **LineStyle**, and **Weight** properties for the new border.

Syntax   *object*.**BorderAround(***lineStyle, weight, colorIndex, color***)**

Elements

The **BorderAround** method has the following object qualifier and named arguments:

object
Required. The Range object.

lineStyle
Optional. Specifies the border line style. Can be one of **xlContinuous, xlDash, xlDot**, or **xlDouble.**

weight
Optional. Specifies the border weight. Can be one of **xlHairline, xlThin, xlMedium**, or **xlThick**. If omitted, **xlThin** is assumed.

colorIndex
Optional. Specifies the border color as a color index into the current color palette. Can be a number from one to 56, or the special constant **xlAutomatic** to use the window text color.

color
Optional. Specifies the border color as an RGB value.

Remarks

You can specify either *colorIndex* or *color*, but not both. If you do not specify either argument, Microsoft Excel uses the **xlAutomatic** color index.

Similarly, you can specify either *lineStyle* or *weight*, but not both. If you do not specify either argument, Microsoft Excel creates a default border.

This method outlines the entire range without filling it in. To set the borders of all the cells, you must set the **Color, LineStyle**, and **Weight** properties for the Borders collection. To clear the border, you must set the **LineStyle** property to **xlNone** for all the cells in the range.

Example

This example adds a thick red border to the range A1:G37.

```
Range("A1:G37").BorderAround color:=RGB(255, 0, 0), weight:=xlThick
```

Borders Method

Applies To   Range, Style.

Description   Returns a single border (a Border object, Syntax 1) or a collection of borders (a Borders object, Syntax 2). Read-write.

Syntax 1   *object*.**Borders(*index*)**

Syntax 2   *object*.**Borders**

Elements	The **Borders** method has the following object qualifier and named arguments:

object
> Required. The Range or Style object.

index
> Required for Syntax 1. Specifies the border (one of **xlTop**, **xlBottom**, **xlLeft**, or **xlRight**).

Examples	This example sets the color of the bottom border.

```
Application.Range("A1:A10").Borders(xlBottom).Color = RGB(255, 0, 0)
```

This example sets the color of all four borders at once.

```
Application.Range("A1:A10").Borders.Color = RGB(0,0,255)
```

Borders Object

Description	A collection of Border objects.

BottomMargin Property

Applies To	PageSetup.
Description	Returns or sets the size of the bottom margin, in points (1/72 inch). Read-write.
Syntax	*object*.**BottomMargin**
See Also	**LeftMargin** Property, **RightMargin** Property, **TopMargin** Property.
Elements	*object*
	Required. The PageSetup object (**ActiveSheet.PageSetup**, for example).
Remarks	Margins are set or returned in points. Use the **Application.InchesToPoints** or **Application.CentimetersToPoints** function to convert.
See Also	**LeftMargin** Property, **RightMargin** Property, **TopMargin** Property.

Examples   These examples set the bottom margin to 0.5 inch (36 points).

```
ActiveSheet.PageSetup.BottomMargin = Application.InchesToPoints(0.5)
ActiveSheet.PageSetup.BottomMargin = 36
```

This example displays the current bottom margin setting.

```
marginInches = ActiveSheet.PageSetup.BottomMargin / _
    Application.InchesToPoints(1)
MsgBox "The current bottom margin is " & marginInches & " inches"
```

BottomRightCell Property

Applies To   Arc, Button, ChartObject, CheckBox, Drawing, DropDown, EditBox, GroupBox, GroupObject, Label, Line, ListBox, OLEObject, OptionButton, Oval, Picture, Rectangle, ScrollBar, Spinner, TextBox.

Description   Returns the cell that lies under the bottom right corner of the object. For drawing objects, this property applies only when the drawing object is on a worksheet. Read-only.

Syntax   *object*.**BottomRightCell**

Elements   *object*
    Required. The object to which this property applies.

See Also   **TopLeftCell** Property.

Example   This example displays the reference for the cell under the bottom right corner of line one.

```
MsgBox "The bottom right corner is " & _
    Worksheets(1).Lines(1).BottomRightCell.Address
```

BringToFront Method

Applies To   Arc, Arcs, Button, Buttons, ChartObject, ChartObjects, CheckBox, CheckBoxes, Drawing, DrawingObjects, Drawings, DropDown, DropDowns, EditBox, EditBoxes, GroupBox, GroupBoxes, GroupObject, GroupObjects, Label, Labels, Line, Lines, ListBox, ListBoxes, OLEObject, OLEObjects, OptionButton, OptionButtons, Oval, Ovals, Picture, Pictures, Rectangle, Rectangles, ScrollBar, ScrollBars, Spinner, Spinners, TextBox, TextBoxes.

Description   Brings the object to the front of the z-order.

Syntax	*object*.**BringToFront**
Elements	*object*
	Required. The object to which this method applies.
See Also	**SendToBack** Method, **ZOrder** Property.
Example	This example brings line one to the front of the z-order.

```
ActiveSheet.DrawingObjects("Line 1").BringToFront
```

BuiltIn Property

Applies To	MenuBar, Toolbar, ToolbarButton.
Description	**True** if the object is built-in (part of Microsoft Excel, as opposed to a custom object). Read-only.
Syntax	*object*.**BuiltIn**
Elements	*object*
	Required. The MenuBar, Toolbar, or ToolbarButton object.
See Also	**BuiltInFace** Property.
Example	This example resets the face of each button that has a custom face.

```
For Each btn in Application.Toolbars(1).ToolbarButtons
    If btn.BuiltIn And Not btn.BuiltInFace Then
        btn.BuiltInFace = True
    End If
Next btn
```

BuiltInFace Property

Applies To	ToolbarButton.
Description	**True** if the button is using its built-in face. **False** if the button has a custom face. Read-write.
Syntax	*object*.**BuiltInFace**
Elements	*object*
	Required. The ToolbarButton object.

Remarks   This property can only be set to **True**, which forces the button to use its built-in face. You cannot set this property to **False**; to use a custom face, use the **CopyFace** and **PasteFace** methods (this sets the **BuiltInFace** property to **False**).

See Also   **BuiltIn** Property, **CopyFace** Method, **PasteFace** Method.

Example   This example resets the face of each built-in button that has a custom face.

```
For Each btn In Application.Toolbars(1).ToolbarButtons
    If btn.BuiltIn And Not btn.BuiltInFace Then
        btn.BuiltInFace = True
    End If
Next btn
```

Button Object

Description   A custom button graphic object on a chart or worksheet. Do not confuse the Button object with the ToolbarButton object, which is a button on a toolbar.

Buttons Method

Applies To   Chart, DialogSheet, Worksheet.

Description   Returns a single button (a Button object, Syntax 1) or a collection of buttons (a Buttons object, Syntax 2) on the chart or sheet. Read-only.

Syntax 1   *object*.**Buttons(*index*)**

Syntax 2   *object*.**Buttons**

Elements   The **Buttons** method has the following object qualifier and named arguments:

object
    Required. The object to which this method applies.

index
    Required for Syntax 1. The name or number of the button.

Example   This example deletes button one from the active worksheet.

```
ActiveSheet.Buttons(1).Delete
```

Buttons Object

Description   A collection of Button objects.

Calculate Method

Applies To   Application, Range, Worksheet.

Description   Calculates all open workbooks, a specific worksheet in a workbook, or a specified range of cells in a sheet, as shown in the following list:

To calculate	Example
All open workbooks	**Application.Calculate** or just **Calculate**
A specific worksheet	**Worksheets**(1)**.Calculate**
A specified range	**Worksheets**(1)**.Rows**(2)**.Calculate**

Syntax   *object*.**Calculate**

Elements   *object*
                Optional for Application, required for Worksheet and Range. Specifies where the calculation will occur.

Example   This example calculates the formulas in columns A, B, and C of worksheet Sheet1 in the active workbook.

```
Worksheets("Sheet1").Columns("A:C").Calculate
```

CalculateBeforeSave Property

Applies To   Application.

Description   **True** if workbooks are calculated before they are saved to disk (if the **Calculation** property is set to **xlManual**). This property is preserved even if you change the **Calculation** property. Read-write.

Syntax   *object*.**CalculateBeforeSave**

Elements	*object* Required. The Application object.
Example	This example causes Microsoft Excel to calculate workbooks before they are saved to disk.

```
Application.Calculation = xlManual
Application.CalculateBeforeSave = True
```

Calculation Property

Applies To   Application, PivotField.

Description   For the Application object, returns or sets the calculation mode, as shown in the following list. Read-write.

Value	Meaning
xlAutomatic	Recalculate automatically.
xlManual	Recalculate only at user's request.
xlSemiautomatic	Recalculate automatically, except for data tables.

For the PivotField object, returns or sets the type of calculation done by the specified pivot field (one of **xlDifferenceFrom**, **xlIndex**, **xlNormal**, **xlPercentDifferenceFrom**, **xlPercentOf**, **xlPercentOfColumn**, **xlPercentOfRow**, **xlPercentOfTotal**, or **xlRunningTotal**). Valid only for data fields. Read-write.

Syntax   *object*.**Calculation**

Elements   *object*
Required. The Application or PivotField object.

Examples   This example causes Microsoft Excel to calculate workbooks before they are saved to disk.

```
Application.Calculation = xlManual
Application.CalculateBeforeSave = True
```

This example sets the active field in a pivot table to calculate the difference from the base field.

```
ActiveCell.PivotField.Calculation = xlDifferenceFrom
ActiveCell.PivotField.BaseField = "Year"
ActiveCell.PivotField.BaseItem = "1991"
```

Call Statement

Description   Transfers control to a **Sub** procedure, **Function** procedure, dynamic-link library (DLL) procedure, or a Macintosh code resource procedure.

Syntax   [**Call**] *name* [*argumentlist*]

Elements   The **Call** statement syntax has these parts:

Part	Description
Call	Optional keyword; if specified, you must enclose *argumentlist* in parentheses. For example:
	`Call MyProc(0)`
name	Name of the procedure to call.
argumentlist	Comma-delimited list of variables, arrays, or expressions to pass to the procedure. Components of *argumentlist* may include the keywords **ByVal** or **ByRef** to describe how the arguments are to be treated by the called procedure. However, **ByVal** and **ByRef** can be used with **Call** only when making a call to a DLL procedure or a Macintosh code resource.

Remarks   You are never required to use the **Call** keyword when calling a procedure. However, if you use the **Call** keyword to call a procedure that requires arguments, *argumentlist* must be enclosed in parentheses. If you omit the **Call** keyword, you also must omit the parentheses around *argumentlist*. If you use either **Call** syntax to call any intrinsic or user-defined function, the function's return value is discarded.

To pass a whole array to a procedure, use the array name followed by empty parentheses.

See Also   **Declare** Statement.

Example   This example illustrates how the **Call** statement is used to transfer control to a **Sub** procedure, an intrinsic function, a dynamic-link library (DLL) procedure and a procedure in a Macintosh code resource.

```
' Call a Sub procedure.
Call PrintToDebugWindow("Hello World")
' The above statement causes control to be passed to the following
' Sub procedure.
Sub PrintToDebugWindow(AnyString)
    Debug.Print AnyString    ' Print to Debug window.
End Sub

' Call an intrinsic function. The return value of the function is
' discarded.
Call Shell(AppName, 1)   ' AppName contains the path of the
        ' executable.

' Call a Microsoft Windows DLL procedure.
Declare Sub MessageBeep Lib "User" (ByVal N As Integer)
Sub CallMyDll()
    Call MessageBeep(0) ' Call Windows DLL procedure.
    MessageBeep 0    ' Call again without Call keyword.
End Sub

' Call a Macintosh Code Resource.
Declare Sub MessageAlert Lib "MyHd:MyAlert" Alias "MyAlert" (ByVal N _
As Integer)
Sub CallMyCodeResource()
    Call MessageAlert(0)' Call Macintosh code resource.
    MessageAlert 0   ' Call again without Call keyword.
End Sub
```

Caller Property

Applies To   Application.

Description   Returns information about how Visual Basic was called (see the Remarks section for details). Read-only.

Syntax   *object*.**Caller**

Elements   *object*
        Required. The Application object.

Remarks

This property returns information about how Visual Basic was called, as shown in the following table.

Caller	Return
A custom function entered in a single cell	A **Range** specifying that cell
A custom function, part of an array formula in a range of cells	A **Range** specifying that range of cells
An Auto_Open, Auto_Close, Auto_Activate, or Auto_Deactivate macro	The name of the document as text
A command on a menu	An array of three elements specifying the command's position number, the menu number, and the menu bar number
The user clicked on a drawing object	The specifier of that object as a string
A tool on a toolbar	An array of two elements specifying the tool position number and the toolbar name as text
A macro set by the **OnDoubleClick** or **OnEntry** properties.	The name of the chart object identifier or cell reference, if applicable, to which the macro applies
Run manually from the Tools Macro dialog box, or for any reason not described above	The #REF! error value

This property returns information about how Visual Basic was called, not how the current procedure was called. For example, if the user presses button 4, which calls Macro1, and Macro1 calls Macro2, and Macro2 uses the **Caller** property, the property will return "Button 4".

If you need to write a macro which behaves differently based on whether it is called from a button or a menu item, you should specify an argument for the macro in the Assign Macro To Object... dialog box.

CancelButton Property

Applies To   Button, Buttons, DrawingObjects.

Description	Applies only to buttons in a user-defined dialog. **True** if the button is automatically selected when the ESCAPE key is pressed or when the system menu close box or menu item is selected. When the user presses the ESCAPE key, the Cancel button is selected, and Microsoft Excel runs the macro identified by the button's **OnAction** property.
Syntax	*object*.**CancelButton**
Elements	*object* Required. The object to which this property applies.
Remarks	Set this property for a button if you want some code to always run when the dialog is canceled, even if it is cancelled by the ESCAPE key or the system menu. Only one button in the dialog can have the Cancel property set to **True** at any given time. Setting one will reset this property for all other buttons on the sheet.
See Also	**DismissButton** Property.
Example	This example sets the **CancelButton** property for button four.

```
ActiveWorkbook.DialogSheets(1).Buttons(4).CancelButton = True
```

CanPlaySounds Property

Applies To	Application.
Description	**True** if the computer can play sound notes. Read-only.
Syntax	*object*.**CanPlaySounds**
Elements	*object* Required. The Application object.
See Also	**CanRecordSounds** Property.
Example	This example uses the **CanPlaySounds** property to determine if the computer can play sound notes. If it can, then it plays the sound note in cell A1.

```
soundPlayCapable = Application.CanPlaySounds
If soundPlayCapable Then
    Cells(1, 1).SoundNote.Play
End If
```

CanRecordSounds Property

Applies To	Application.
Description	**True** if the computer can record sound notes. Read-only.
Syntax	*object*.**CanRecordSounds**
Elements	*object* Required. The Application object.
See Also	**CanPlaySounds** Property.
Example	This example uses the **CanRecordSounds** property to determine if the computer can record sound notes. If it can, then it records a sound note into cell A1.

```
soundRecordCapable = Application.CanRecordSounds
If soundRecordCapable Then
    Cells(1, 1).SoundNote.Record
End If
```

Caption Property

Applies To	Application, AxisTitle, Button, Buttons, Characters, ChartTitle, CheckBox, CheckBoxes, DataLabel, DataLabels, DialogFrame, DrawingObjects, DropDown, DropDowns, EditBox, EditBoxes, GroupBox, GroupBoxes, Label, Labels, Menu, MenuBar, MenuItem, OptionButton, OptionButtons, TextBox, TextBoxes, Window.
Description	The **Caption** property has several different meanings, depending on the object type to which it is applied. The **Caption** property is read-write, except as noted in the following list.

Object type	Meaning
Application	The name that appears in the title bar of the main Microsoft Excel window. If you don't set a name, or if you set the name to **Empty**, then this property returns "Microsoft Excel". Read-only on the Apple Macintosh.
AxisTitle	The axis title text.
Button	The button text.
Characters	The text of this range of characters.

Object type	Meaning
ChartTitle	The chart title text.
Controls	The control text (check box, dialog frame, drop down, edit box, group box, label, and option button).
DataLabel	The data label text.
Menu	The name of the menu. Use an ampersand (&) before the letter that you want to be the command underline (for example, "&File").
MenuBar	The menu bar text.
MenuItem	The name of the menu item (command). Use an ampersand (&) before the letter that you want to be the command underline (for example, "E&xit").
TextBox	The text in the text box.
Window	The name that appears in the title bar of the document window. When you set the name, you can use that name as the index to the **Windows** property; see Example 2. You can restore the default document name by setting the **Caption** property to **Empty**.

Syntax

object.**Caption**

Elements

object
   Required. The object to which this property applies.

See Also

Text Property.

Examples

This example sets the name that appears in the title bar of the main Microsoft Excel window to be a custom name.

```
Application.Caption = "Blue Sky Airlines Reservation System"
```

This example sets the name of the first window in the workbook to be Consolidated Balance Sheet. This name is then used as the index argument to the Windows property.

```
ActiveWorkbook.Windows(1).Caption = "Consolidated Balance Sheet"
ActiveWorkbook.Windows("Consolidated Balance Sheet") _
    .ActiveSheet.Calculate
```

Category Property

Applies To   Name.

Description   If the name refers to a custom function or command, this property returns or sets the category for this name as a string translated to the language of the macro. Read-write.

Syntax   *object*.**Category**

Elements   *object*
        Required. The Name object.

See Also   **MacroType** Property.

Example   This example displays the name category in the language of the macro.

```
With ActiveWorkbook.Names(1)
    If .MacroType <> xlNone Then
        MsgBox "The category for this name is " & .Category
    Else
        MsgBox "This name does not refer to" & _
            " a custom function or command."
    End If
End With
```

CategoryLocal Property

Applies To   Name.

Description   If the name refers to a custom function or command, this property returns or sets the category for this name as a string in the language of the user. Read-write.

Syntax   *object*.**CategoryLocal**

Elements   *object*
        Required. The Name object.

See Also   **Category** Property, **MacroType** Property.

Example   This example displays the name category in the language of the user.

```
With ActiveWorkbook.Names(1)
    If .MacroType <> xlNone Then
        MsgBox "The category for this name is " & .CategoryLocal
    Else
        MsgBox "This name does not refer to" _ &
            " a custom function or command."
    End If
End With
```

CategoryNames Property

Applies To   Axis.

Description   Returns or sets all the category names for the specified axis, as a text array. When you set this property, you can set it to an array or a Range containing the category names. Read-write.

Syntax   *object*.**CategoryNames**

Elements   *object*
          Required. The Axis object.

Remarks   Category names are really a property of the "special" series in an axis grouping. Deleting or modifying that special series will change the category names for all series using the axis.

See Also   **Formula** Property, **Values** Property, **XValues** Property,

Examples   This example sets the category names to the values in cells B1:B5.

```
Set ActiveChart.Axes(xlCategory).CategoryNames = _
    Worksheets(1).Range("B1:B5")
```

This example uses an array to set individual category names.

```
ActiveChart.Axes(xlCategory).CategoryNames = _
    Array ("1985", "1986", "1987", "1988", "1989")
```

CBool Function

Description   Converts an expression to a **Boolean**.

Syntax	**CBool**(*expression*)
Elements	The *expression* argument is any valid numeric expression.
Remarks	If *expression* is zero, **False** is returned; otherwise, **True** is returned. If *expression* can't be interpreted as a numeric value, a run-time error occurs.
See Also	Data Type Summary.
Example	This example uses the **CBool** function to convert an expression to a **Boolean**. If the expression evaluates to a nonzero value, **CBool** returns **True**; otherwise, it returns **False**.

```
A = 5 : B = 5              ' Define variables.
Check = CBool(A = B)         ' Check contains True.
A = 0                      ' Define variable.
Check = CBool(A)           ' Check contains False.
```

CCRecipients Property

Applies To	Mailer
Description	Returns or sets the carbon copy (indirect) recipients of the mailer. Read-write.
Syntax	*object*.**CCRecipients**
Elements	*object* Required. The Mailer object.
Remarks	This property is an array of strings specifying the address, in one of the following formats:

- A record in the Preferred Personal Catalog. These names are one level deep ("Fred" or "June").

- A full path specifying either a record in a personal catalog ("HD:Excel Folder:My Catalog:Barney") or a plain record ("HD:Folder:Martin").

- A relative path from the current working directory specifying either a personal catalog record ("My Catalog:Barney") or a plain record ("Martin").

- A path in a PowerShare catalog tree of the form "CATALOG_NAME:<node>:RECORD_NAME" where <node> is a path to a PowerShare catalog. An example of a complete path is "AppleTalk:North Building Zone:George's Mac".

See Also	**BCCRecipients** Property, **Enclosures** Property, **Mailer** Property, **Received** Property, **SendDateTime** Property, **Sender** Property, **SendMailer** Method, **Subject** Property, **ToRecipients** Property.
Example	This example sets up the Mailer object for workbook one, and then sends the workbook.

```
With Workbooks(1)
    .HasMailer = True
    With .Mailer
        .Subject = "Here is the workbook"
        .ToRecipients = Array("Jean")
        .CCRecipients = Array("Adam", "Bernard")
        .BCCRecipients = Array("Chris")
        .Enclosures = Array("TestFile")
    End With
    .SendMailer
End With
```

CCur Function

Description	Converts an expression to a **Currency**.
Syntax	**CCur**(*expression*)
Elements	The *expression* argument is any valid numeric or string expression.
Remarks	In general, you can document your code using the data type conversion functions to show that the result of some operation should be expressed as a particular data type rather than the default data type. For example, use **CCur** to force currency arithmetic in cases where single-precision, double-precision, or integer arithmetic normally would occur.
	You should use the **CCur** function instead of **Val** to provide internationally-aware conversions from any other data type to a **Currency**. For example, different decimal separators are properly recognized depending on the locale setting of your computer, as are different thousand separators and various currency options.
	If *expression* lies outside the acceptable range for the **Currency** data type, an error occurs.
See Also	Data Type Summary.

Example

This example uses the **CCur** function to convert an expression to a **Currency**.

```
MyDouble = 543.214588            ' MyDouble is a Double.
MyCurr = CCur(MyDouble * 2)       ' Convert result (1086.4292) to
                               ' Currency.
```

CDate Function

Description

Converts an expression to a **Date**.

Syntax

CDate(*date*)

Elements

The *date* argument is any valid date expression.

Remarks

Use the **IsDate** function to determine if *date* can be converted to a date or time. **CDate** recognizes date and time literals as well as some numbers that fall within the range of acceptable dates. When converting a number to a date, the whole number portion is converted to a date. Any fractional part of the number is converted to a time of day, starting at midnight.

CDate recognizes date formats according to the international settings of your system. The correct order of day, month, and year may not be determined if it is provided in a format other than one of the recognized date settings. In addition, a long date format is not recognized if it also contains the day-of-the-week string.

Note A **CVDate** function is also provided for compatibility with previous versions of Visual Basic. However, since there is now an intrinsic **Date** type, there is no further need for **CVDate**. The syntax of the **CVDate** function is identical to the **CDate** function. The difference is that it returns a **Variant** whose subtype is Date instead of an actual **Date** type. The same effect can be achieved by converting an expression to a **Date** and then assigning it to a **Variant**. This technique is consistent with the conversion of all other intrinsic types to their equivalent **Variant** subtypes.

See Also

Data Type Summary, **IsDate** Function.

Example   This example uses the **CDate** function to convert a string to a **Date**. In general, it is bad programming practice to hard code dates/times as strings as shown in this example. Use date literals instead.

```
MyDate = "February 12, 1969"      ' Define date.
MyShortDate = CDate(MyDate)       ' Convert to Date data type.
MyTime = "4:35:47 PM"             ' Define time.
MyShortTime = CDate(MyTime)       ' Convert to Date data type.
```

CDbl Function

Description   Converts an expression to a **Double**.

Syntax   **CDbl**(*expression*)

Elements   The *expression* argument is any valid numeric or string expression.

Remarks   In general, you can document your code using the data type conversion functions to show that the result of some operation should be expressed as a particular data type rather than the default data type. For example, use **CDbl** or **CSng** to force double- or single-precision arithmetic in cases where currency or integer arithmetic normally would occur.

You should use the **CDbl** function instead of **Val** to provide internationally-aware conversions from any other data type to a **Double**. For example, different decimal separators and thousands separators are properly recognized depending on the locale setting of your system.

See Also   Data Type Summary.

Example   This example uses the **CDbl** function to convert an expression to a **Double**.

```
MyCurr = CCur(234.456784)          ' MyCurr is a Currency.
MyDouble = CDbl(MyCurr * 8.2 * 0.01)   ' Convert result to Double.
```

Cell Error Values

You can insert a cell error value into a cell or you can test the value of a cell for an error value using the **CVErr** function. The cell error values have constants assigned to them as shown in the following table.

Constant	Error number	Cell error value
xlErrDiv0	2007	#DIV/0!
xlErrNA	2042	#N/A
xlErrName	2029	#NAME?
xlErrNull	2000	#NULL!
xlErrNum	2036	#NUM!
xlErrRef	2023	#REF!
xlErrValue	2015	#VALUE!

See Also   **CVErr** Function.

Examples   This example inserts the seven cell error values into cells A1:A7 on the first worksheet.

```
myErrorArray = Array(xlErrDiv0, xlErrNA, xlErrName, xlErrNull, _
        xlErrNum, xlErrRef, xlErrValue)
For i = 1 To 7
    Worksheets(1).Cells(i, 1).Value = CVErr(myErrorArray(i - 1))
Next i
```

This example displays a message if the active cell contains a cell error value. You can use this example as a framework for handling cell error values.

```
If IsError(ActiveCell Value) Then
    errval = ActiveCell Value
    Select Case errval
        Case CVErr(xlErrDiv0)
            MsgBox "#DIV/0! error"
        Case CVErr(xlErrNA)
            MsgBox "#N/A error"
        Case CVErr(xlErrName)
            MsgBox "#NAME? error"
        Case CVErr(xlErrNull)
            MsgBox "#NULL! error"
        Case CVErr(xlErrNum)
            MsgBox "#NUM! error"
        Case CVErr(xlErrRef)
            MsgBox "#REF! error"
        Case CVErr(xlErrValue)
            MsgBox "#VALUE! error"
        Case Else
            MsgBox "This should never happen!!"
    End Select
End If
```

CellDragAndDrop Property

Applies To	Application.
Description	**True** if Cell Drag and Drop editing is on. Read-write.
Syntax	*object*.**CellDragAndDrop**
Elements	*object* Required. The Application object.
Example	This example switches to Cell Drag and Drop editing if it is not already on.

```
dragAndDropEnabled = Application.CellDragAndDrop
If Not dragAndDropEnabled Then
    Application.CellDragAndDrop = True
End If
```

Cells Method

Applies To	Application, Range, Worksheet.
Description	Returns a single cell (Syntax 1 and 2) or a collection of cells (Syntax 3) as a Range. The action of the **Cells** method depends on the object to which it is applied, as shown in the following table:

Object type	Action
Application	If the active document is a worksheet, **Application.Cells** is equivalent to **ActiveSheet.Cells**, which returns a collection of cells on the active worksheet. Otherwise, the **Cells** method returns an error.
Range	Returns a collection of cells from the range.
Worksheet	Returns a collection of cells from the worksheet.

Syntax 1	*object*.**Cells(*rowIndex, columnIndex*)**
Syntax 2	*object*.**Cells(*rowindex*)**
Syntax 3	*object*.**Cells**

Elements

The **Cells** method has the following object qualifier and named arguments:

object
> Optional for Application, required for Worksheet and Range. The object that contains the cells.If you omit the object qualifier, the **Cells** method applies to the active worksheet of the active workbook.

rowIndex
> Required for Syntax 1. The row number of the cell you want to access, starting with 1 for row 1 (for Application and Worksheet) or the first row in the Range.

> Required for Syntax 2. A long integer specifying the index number of the cell you want to access, in row-major order. A1 is Cells(1), A2 is Cells(257) for Application and Worksheet; Range.Cells(1) is the top left cell in the Range.

columnIndex
> Required for Syntax 1. A number or string indicating the column number of the cell you want to access, starting with 1 or "A" for column A (for Application or Worksheet) or the first column in the Range.

Remarks

Syntax 1 uses a row number and a column number or letter as index arguments. For more information about this syntax, see the Range object.

Syntax 2 uses a single number as an index argument. The index is 1 for cell A1, 2 for cell B1, 3 for cell C1, 257 for cell A2, and so on.

The *rowIndex* and *columnIndex* arguments are relative offsets when you apply the **Cells** method to a Range object. In other words, specifying a *rowIndex* of 1 returns cells in the first row of the range, not the first row of the worksheet. For example, if the selection is cell C3, then **Selection.Cells(2, 2)** returns cell D4 (you can use the method to index outside the original range).

If you apply Syntax 3 to a Range, it returns the same Range object (in other words, it does nothing).

If you apply Syntax 3 to a Worksheet, it returns a collection of all the cells in the worksheet (all the cells, not just the cells that are currently in use).

See Also

Range Method.

Examples

This example sets the font size of cell C5 on the active worksheet to 14-point.

```
Application.Cells(5, 3).Font.Size = 14
```

This example clears the formula in the first cell on the active sheet.

```
ActiveSheet.Cells(1).ClearContents
```

This example sets the font for every cell in the active worksheet to 8-point Arial.

```
With Cells.Font
    .Name = "Arial"
    .Size = 8
End With
```

CenterFooter Property

Applies To   PageSetup.

Description   Returns or sets the center part of the footer. Read-write.

Syntax   *object*.**CenterFooter**

Elements   *object*
     Required. The PageSetup object (**ActiveSheet.PageSetup**, for example).

Remarks   Special format codes can be used in the footer text. For more information, search the online Visual Basic Reference for Formatting Codes for Headers and Footers.

See Also   **CenterHeader** Property, **LeftFooter** Property, **LeftHeader** Property, **RightFooter** Property, **RightHeader** Property.

Example   This example prints the name of the document and the page number at the bottom of each page.

```
ActiveSheet.PageSetup.CenterFooter = "&F page &P"
```

CenterHeader Property

Applies To   PageSetup.

Description   Returns or sets the center part of the header. Read-write.

Syntax	*object*.**CenterHeader**
Elements	*object*
	Required. The PageSetup object (**ActiveSheet.PageSetup**, for example).
Remarks	Special format codes can be used in the header text. For more information, search the online Visual Basic Reference for Formatting Codes for Headers and Footers.
See Also	**CenterFooter** Property, **LeftFooter** Property, **LeftHeader** Property, **RightFooter** Property, **RightHeader** Property.
Example	This example prints the date and page number at the top of each page.

```
ActiveSheet.PageSetup.CenterHeader = "&D page &P of &N"
```

CenterHorizontally Property

Applies To	PageSetup.
Description	**True** if the sheet is centered horizontally on the page. Read-write.
Syntax	*object*.**CenterHorizontally**
Elements	*object*
	Required. The PageSetup object (**ActiveSheet.PageSetup**, for example).
See Also	**CenterVertically** Property.
Example	This example centers the worksheet horizontally.

```
ActiveSheet.PageSetup.CenterHorizontally = True
```

CenterVertically Property

Applies To	PageSetup.
Description	**True** if the sheet is centered vertically on the page. Read-write.
Syntax	*object*.**CenterVertically**
Elements	*object*
	Required. The PageSetup object (**ActiveSheet.PageSetup**, for example).
See Also	**CenterHorizontally** Property.

Example	This example centers the worksheet vertically.

```
ActiveSheet.PageSetup.CenterVertically = True
```

CentimetersToPoints Method

Applies To	Application.
Description	Converts a measurement in centimeters into points (0.035 centimeters).
Syntax	*object*.**CentimetersToPoints**(*centimeters*)
Elements	The **CentimetersToPoints** method has the following object qualifier and named arguments:

object
> Required. The Application object.

centimeters
> Required. Specifies the centimeter value to convert to points.

See Also	**InchesToPoints** Method.
Example	This example sets the left margin to five centimeters.

```
ActiveSheet.PageSetup.LeftMargin = Application.CentimetersToPoints(5)
```

ChangeFileAccess Method

Applies To	Workbook.
Description	Changes the access permissions for the workbook. This may require loading an updated version from the disk.
Syntax	*object*.**ChangeFileAccess**(*mode, writePassword, notify*)
Elements	The **ChangeFileAccess** method has the following object qualifier and named arguments:

object
> Required. The Workbook object.

mode
> Required. Specifies the new access mode (one of **xlReadWrite** or **xlReadOnly**).

writePassword

Optional. If the file is write reserved and *mode* is **xlReadWrite**, specifies the write-reserved password. Ignored if there is no password for the file or *mode* is **xlReadOnly**.

notify

Optional. **True** if you wish to be notified if the file cannot be immediately accessed. Assumed to be **True** if omitted.

Remarks   If you have a file open in read-only mode, you do not have exclusive access to the file. If you change a file from read-only to read-write, Microsoft Excel must load a new copy of the file to ensure that no changes were made while you had the file open as read-only.

Example   This example sets the active workbook to read-only.

```
ActiveWorkbook.ChangeFileAccess(xlReadOnly)
```

ChangeLink Method

Applies To   Workbook.

Description   Changes a link from one document to another.

Syntax   *object*.**ChangeLink**(*name, newName, type*)

Elements   The **ChangeLink** method has the following object qualifier and named arguments:

object

Required. The Workbook object.

name

Required. Specifies the name of the Microsoft Excel or DDE/OLE link to change, as returned from the **LinkSources** method.

newName

Required. The new name of the link.

type

Optional. Specifies the link type (either **xlExcelLinks** or **xlOLELinks**). If omitted, the default is **xlExcelLinks**. Use **xlOLELinks** for both DDE and OLE links.

Examples   This example changes a Microsoft Word for Windows link.

```
ActiveWorkbook.ChangeLink "WinWord|'C:\DOC1.DOC'!DDE_LINK1", _
    "WinWord|'C:\DOC2.DOC'!DDE_LINK2", xlOLELinks
```

This example changes a Microsoft Excel link.

```
ActiveWorkbook.ChangeLink "c:\excel\book1.xls", _
    "c:\excel\book2.xls", xlExcelLinks
```

ChangeScenario Method

Applies To   Scenario.

Description   Changes the scenario to have a new set of changing cells and (optionally) scenario values.

Syntax   *object*.**ChangeScenario**(*changingCells, values*)

Elements   The **ChangeScenario** method has the following object qualifier and named arguments:

object
   Required. The Scenario object.

changingCells
   Required. A Range that specifies the new set of changing cells for the scenario. The changing cells must be on the same sheet as the scenario.

values
   Optional. An array containing the new scenario values for the changing cells. If omitted, the scenario values are assumed to be the current values in the changing cells.

Remarks   If you specifiy *values*, the array must contain an element for each cell in the *changingCells* range, or Microsoft Excel generates an error.

See Also   **ChangingCells** Property, **Comment** Property.

Example   This example sets the changing cells for the scenario to the range A1:A10.

```
ActiveSheet.Scenarios(1).ChangeScenario ActiveSheet.Range("A1:A10")
```

ChangingCells Property

Applies To   Scenario.

Description   Returns a Range containing the changing cells for a scenario. Read only.

Syntax   *object*.**ChangingCells**

Elements   *object*
          Required. The Scenario object.

See Also   **ChangeScenario** Method, **Comment** Property.

Example   This example selects the changing cells for the first scenario.

```
ActiveSheet.Scenarios(1).ChangingCells.Select
```

Character Sets

Ansi Character Set

American National Standards Institute (ANSI) 8-bit character set used by Microsoft Windows that allows you to represent up to 256 characters (0-255) using your keyboard. The first 128 characters (0-127) correspond to the letters and symbols on a standard U.S. keyboard. The second 128 characters (128-255) represent special characters, such as letters in international alphabets, accents, currency symbols, and fractions.

Ascii Character Set

American Standard Code for Information Interchange (ASCII) 7-bit character set widely used to represent letters and symbols found on a standard U.S. keyboard. The ASCII character set is the same as the first 128 characters (0-127) in the ANSI character set.

0 - 127

0	■	32	[space]	64	@	96	`
1	■	33	!	65	A	97	a
2	■	34	"	66	B	98	b
3	■	35	#	67	C	99	c
4	■	36	$	68	D	100	d
5	■	37	%	69	E	101	e
6	■	38	&	70	F	102	f
7	■	39	'	71	G	103	g
8	* *	40	(	72	H	104	h
9	* *	41	)	73	I	105	i
10	* *	42	*	74	J	106	j
11	■	43	+	75	K	107	k
12	■	44	,	76	L	108	l
13	* *	45	-	77	M	109	m
14	■	46	.	78	N	110	n
15	■	47	/	79	O	111	o
16	■	48	0	80	P	112	p
17	■	49	1	81	Q	113	q
18	■	50	2	82	R	114	r
19	■	51	3	83	S	115	s
20	■	52	4	84	T	116	t
21	■	53	5	85	U	117	u
22	■	54	6	86	V	118	v
23	■	55	7	87	W	119	w
24	■	56	8	88	X	120	x
25	■	57	9	89	Y	121	y

26	■	58	:	90	Z	122	z
27	■	59	;	91	[	123	{
28	■	60	<	92	\	124	|
29	■	61	=	93	]	125	}
30	■	62	>	94	^	126	~
31	■	63	?	95	_	127	■

* * Values 8, 9, 10, and 13 convert to backspace, tab, linefeed, and carriage return characters, respectively. They have no graphical representation but, depending on the application, may affect the visual display of text.

■ These characters aren't supported by Microsoft Windows.

128 - 255

128	■	160	[space]	192	À	224	à
129	■	161	¡	193	Á	225	á
130	■	162	¢	194	Â	226	â
131	■	163	£	195	Ã	227	ã
132	■	164	¤	196	Ä	228	ä
133	■	165	¥	197	Å	229	å
134	■	166	¦	198	Æ	230	æ
135	■	167	§	199	Ç	231	ç
136	■	168	¨	200	È	232	è
137	■	169	©	201	É	233	é
138	■	170	ª	202	Ê	234	ê
139	■	171	«	203	Ë	235	ë
140	■	172	¬	204	Ì	236	ì
141	■	173	-	205	Í	237	í
142	■	174	®	206	Î	238	î
143	■	175	¯	207	Ï	239	ï
144	■	176	°	208	Ð	240	ð
145	'	177	±	209	Ñ	241	ñ

146	’	178	²	210	Ò	242	ò
147	■	179	³	211	Ó	243	ó
148	■	180	´	212	Ô	244	ô
149	■	181	μ	213	Õ	245	õ
150	■	182	¶	214	Ö	246	ö
151	■	183	·	215	×	247	÷
152	■	184	¸	216	Ø	248	ø
153	■	185	¹	217	Ù	249	ù
154	■	186	º	218	Ú	250	ú
155	■	187	»	219	Û	251	û
156	■	188	¼	220	Ü	252	ü
157	■	189	½	221	Ý	253	ý
158	■	190	¾	222	Þ	254	þ
159	■	191	¿	223	ß	255	ÿ

■   These characters aren't supported by Microsoft Windows.

Characters Method

Applies To   AxisTitle, Button, Buttons, ChartTitle, CheckBox, CheckBoxes, DataLabel, DialogFrame, DrawingObjects, DropDown, DropDowns, EditBox, EditBoxes, GroupBox, GroupBoxes, Label, Labels, OptionButton, OptionButtons, Range, TextBox, TextBoxes.

Description   Returns a range of Characters within the object text. This allows you to format characters within a text string.

Syntax   *object*.**Characters**(*start, length*)

Elements   The **Characters** method has the following object qualifier and named arguments:

object
   Required. The object to which this method applies.

start
> Optional. The first character to return. If this argument is one or omitted, this method returns a range of characters starting with the first character.

length
> Optional. The number of characters to return. If this argument is omitted, this method returns the remainder of the string after the *start* character.

Remarks
For a Range object, this method will fail if it is used with arguments and the cell does not contain a text value. You can use this method without arguments to obtain a set of characters for the entire range, but you cannot use the method with arguments.

Example
This example makes the third character in the active cell a subscript.

```
ActiveCell.Characters(3, 1).Font.Subscript = True
```

Characters Object

Description
A collection of characters (in other words, the text or a subset of the text) in a cell, text box, or custom button graphic object.

Chart Object

Description
A chart in a workbook.

Chart Property

Applies To
ChartObject.

Description
Returns the Chart contained in the object. Read-only.

Syntax
object.**Chart**

Elements
object
> Required. The object to which this property applies.

Example   This example sets the chart in ChartObject one to use auto scaling.

```
ActiveSheet.ChartObjects(1).Chart.AutoScaling = True
```

ChartArea Object

Description   The chart area of a chart.

ChartArea Property

Applies To   Chart.

Description   Returns the complete ChartArea for the chart. Read-only.

Syntax   *object*.**ChartArea**

Elements   *object*
         Required. The Chart object.

Example   This example sets the chart area color to red.

```
Charts(1).ChartArea.Interior.Color = RGB(255,0,0)
```

ChartGroup Object

Description   A chart group on a chart.

ChartGroups Method

Applies To   Chart.

Description	Returns a single chart group (a ChartGroup object, Syntax 1) or a collection of all the chart groups in the chart (a ChartGroups object, Syntax 2). Every type of group is included in the returned collection.
Syntax 1	*object*.**ChartGroups**(*index*)
Syntax 2	*object*.**ChartGroups**
Elements	The **ChartGroups** method has the following object qualifier and named arguments:

object
    Required. The Chart object.

index
    Required for Syntax 1. The number of the chart group.

Example	This example makes chart group one an area chart.

```
ActiveChart.ChartGroups(1).Type = xlArea
```

ChartGroups Object

Description	A collection of ChartGroup objects.

ChartObject Object

Description	An embedded chart on a sheet. The ChartObject acts as a container for a chart. The ChartObject provides the size.

ChartObjects Method

Applies To	Chart, DialogSheet, Worksheet.
Description	Returns a single chart (a ChartObject object, Syntax 1) or a collection of all the embedded charts (a ChartObjects object, Syntax 2) on the chart or sheet.

Syntax 1	*object*.**ChartObjects(*index*)**
Syntax 2	*object*.**ChartObjects**
Elements	The **ChartObjects** method has the following object qualifier and named arguments:

object
> Required. The object to which this method applies. If you specify a Chart object, it must be a chart sheet (it cannot be an embedded chart).

index
> Required for Syntax 1. The name or number of the chart (can be an array to specify more than one).

Remarks	This method is not equivalent to the **Charts** method. This method returns embedded charts; the **Charts** method returns chart sheets. Use the **Chart** property to return the chart sheet for an embedded chart object.
See Also	**Charts** Method.
Example	This example brings chart one on the active sheet to the front of the z-order.

```
ActiveSheet.ChartObjects(1).BringToFront
```

ChartObjects Object

Description	A collection of ChartObject objects.

Charts Method

Applies To	Application, Workbook.
Description	Returns a single chart (a Chart object, Syntax 1) or a collection of the charts (a Charts object, Syntax 2) in the workbook.
Syntax 1	*object*.**Charts(*index*)**
Syntax 2	*object*.**Charts**
Elements	The **Charts** method has the following object qualifier and named arguments:

object
> Optional for Application, required for Workbook. The object to which this method applies.

index
> Required for Syntax 1. The name or number of the chart (can be an array to specify more than one).

Remarks   Using this method with no object qualifier is equivalent to **ActiveWorkbook.Charts**.

See Also   **ChartObjects** Method.

Example   This example turns on major gridlines for the category (x) axis on the first chart on the active workbook.

```
Charts(1).Axes(xlCategory).HasMajorGridlines = True
```

Charts Object

Description   A collection of charts in a workbook.

ChartSize Property

Applies To   PageSetup.

Description   Returns or sets the method used when scaling a chart to fit on a page, as shown in the following table. Read-write.

Value	Meaning
xlScreenSize	Print the chart the same size as it appears on the screen.
xlFitToPage	Print the chart as large as possible, while retaining the chart's height-to-width ratio as shown on the screen.
xlFullPage	Print the chart to fit the page, adjusting the height-to-width ratio as necessary.

Syntax   *object*.**ChartSize**

Elements   *object*
> Required. The PageSetup object (**ActiveSheet.PageSetup**, for example).

Remarks   This property applies only to chart sheets (it cannot be used with embedded charts).

Example   This example scales the first chart in the workbook so that it fits a full page.

```
ActiveWorkbook.Charts(1).PageSetup.ChartSize = xlFullPage
```

ChartTitle Object

Description   The title of a chart.

ChartTitle Property

Applies To   Chart.

Description   Returns the ChartTitle for the specified chart. Read-only.

Syntax   *object*.**ChartTitle**

Elements   *object*
                   Required. The Chart object.

See Also   **AxisTitle** Property, **HasTitle** Property, **Title** Property.

Example   This example sets the active chart title text.

```
With ActiveChart
    .HasTitle = True
    .ChartTitle.Text = "February Sales"
    .ChartTitle.Font.Bold = True
    .ChartTitle.Font.Size = 18
End With
```

ChartWizard Method

Applies To   Chart.

Description   Modifies the properties of the given chart. Allows a chart to be quickly formatted
                   without setting all the individual properties. This method is non-interactive, and
                   changes only the specified properties.

Syntax

*object.*ChartWizard(*source, gallery, format, plotBy, categoryLabels, seriesLabels, hasLegend, title, categoryTitle, valueTitle, extraTitle*)

Elements

The **ChartWizard** method has the following object qualifier and named arguments:

object
  Required. The Chart object.

source
  Optional. Specifies a range that contains the source data for the chart. If this argument is omitted, Microsoft Excel uses the current selection.

gallery
  Optional. Specifies the chart type (one of **xlArea**, **xlBar**, **xlColumn**, **xlLine**, **xlPie**, **xlRadar**, **xlXYScatter**, **xlCombination**, **xl3DArea**, **xl3DBar**, **xl3DColumn**, **xl3DLine**, **xl3DPie**, **xl3DSurface**, or **xlDoughnut**).

format
  Optional. Specifies the option number for the built-in autoformats. Can be a number from 1 to 10, depending on the gallery type. If this argument is omitted, Microsoft Excel chooses a default value based on the gallery type and data source.

plotBy
  Optional. Specifies whether the data for each series is in rows or columns (either **xlRows** or **xlColumns**).

categoryLabels
  Optional. An integer specifying the number of rows or columns within the source range containing category labels. Legal values are from zero to one less than the maximum number of the corresponding categories or series.

seriesLabels
  Optional. An integer specifying the number of rows or columns within the source range containing series labels. Legal values are from zero to one less than the maximum number of the corresponding categories or series.

hasLegend
  Optional. **True** to include a legend.

title
  Optional. Chart title text.

categoryTitle
  Optional. Category (x) axis title text.

valueTitle
  Optional. Value axis title text.

extraTitle
  Optional. Series axis title for 3-D charts, second value axis title for 2-D charts.

Example

This example reformats chart one into a line chart and adds a legend and x- and y-axis titles.

```
ActiveWorkbook.Charts(1).ChartWizard _
    gallery:=xlLine, _
    hasLegend:=True, categoryTitle:="Year", valueTitle:="Sales"
```

ChDir Statement

Description

Changes the current directory or folder.

Syntax

ChDir *path*

Elements

The *path* named argument is a string expression that identifies which directory or folder becomes the new default directory or folder{bmc emdash.bmp}may include drive. If no drive is specified, **ChDir** changes the default directory or folder on the current drive.

Remarks

In Microsoft Windows, the **ChDir** statement changes the default directory but not the default drive. For example, if the default drive is C, the following statement changes the default directory on drive D, but C remains the default drive:

```
ChDir "D:\TMP"
```

On the Macintosh, the default drive always changes to whatever drive is specified in *path*.

See Also

ChDrive Statement, **CurDir** Function, **Dir** Function, **MkDir** Statement, **RmDir** Statement.

Example

This example uses the **ChDir** statement to change the current directory or folder.

```
' Change current directory or folder to "MYDIR".
ChDir "MYDIR"

' In Microsoft Windows.
' Assume "C:" is the current drive.  The following statement changes
' the default directory on drive "D:". "C:" remains the current drive.
ChDir "D:\WINDOWS\SYSTEM"

' On the Macintosh.
' Changes default folder and default drive.
ChDir "HD:MY FOLDER"
```

ChDrive Statement

Description   Changes the current drive.

Syntax   **ChDrive** *drive*

Elements   The *drive* named argument is a string expression that specifies an existing drive. If you supply a zero-length argument (""), the current drive doesn't change. In Microsoft Windows, if the argument *drive* is a multiple-character string, **ChDrive** uses only the first letter. On the Macintosh, **ChDrive** changes the current folder to the root folder of the specifed drive.

See Also   **ChDir** Statement, **CurDir** Function, **MkDir** Statement, **RmDir** Statement.

Example   This example uses the **ChDrive** statement to change the current drive.

```
' In Microsoft Windows.
ChDrive "D"      ' Make "D" the current drive.

' On the Macintosh.
' Make "MY DRIVE" the current drive
ChDrive "MY DRIVE:"

' Make "MY DRIVE" the current drive and
'    current folder since it's the root.
ChDrive "MY DRIVE:MY FOLDER"
```

CheckBox Object

Description   A check box control on a worksheet or dialog sheet.

Remarks   Check boxes have position and dimension but no formatting properties. The background and font of the check box is fixed.

CheckBoxes Method

Applies To   Chart, DialogSheet, Worksheet.

Description   Returns a single check box (a CheckBox object, Syntax 1) or a collection of check boxes on the chart or sheet (a CheckBoxes object, Syntax 2).

Syntax 1	*object*.**CheckBoxes(*index*)**
Syntax 1	*object*.**CheckBoxes**
Elements	The **CheckBoxes** method has the following object qualifier and named arguments:

object
 Required. The Chart, DialogSheet, or Worksheet object.

index
 Required for Syntax 1. Specifies the name or number of the check box (can be an array to specify more than one).

Example This example displays the number of check boxes on dialog sheet one.

```
cCheckBox = ActiveWorkbook.DialogSheets(1).CheckBoxes.Count
MsgBox "There are " & cCheckBox & " check boxes on dialog sheet one."
```

CheckBoxes Object

Description   A collection of CheckBox objects.

Checked Property

Applies To	MenuItem.
Description	**True** if the menu item is checked. Read-write.
Syntax	*object*.**Checked**
Elements	*object*
	Required. The MenuItem object.
Example	This example checks menu item four on menu one.

```
ActiveMenuBar.Menus(1).MenuItems(4).Checked = True
```

CheckSpelling Method

Applies To   Application, Button, Buttons, Chart, CheckBox, CheckBoxes, DialogFrame, DialogSheet, DrawingObjects, GroupBox, GroupBoxes, GroupObject,

GroupObjects, Label, Labels, OptionButton, OptionButtons, Range, TextBox, TextBoxes, Worksheet.

Description

Syntax 1: Checks the spelling of an object. This form has no return value; Microsoft Excel displays the Spelling dialog box.

Syntax 2: Checks the spelling of a single word. Returns **True** if the word is found in one of the dictionaries, **False** if it is not.

Syntax 1

object.**CheckSpelling(***customDictionary, ignoreUppercase, alwaysSuggest***)**

Syntax 2

object.**CheckSpelling(***word, customDictionary, ignoreUppercase***)**

Elements

The **CheckSpelling** method has the following object qualifier and named arguments:

object
Required. The object to which this method applies. Use the Application object to check a single word (Syntax 2).

customDictionary
Optional. A string indicating the filename of the custom dictionary to examine if the word is not found in the main dictionary. If omitted, the currently specified dictionary is used.

ignoreUppercase
Optional. If **True**, Microsoft Excel will ignore words that are in all uppercase. If **False**, Microsoft Excel will check words that are in all uppercase. If omitted, the current setting will be used.

alwaysSuggest
Optional. If **True**, Microsoft Excel will display a list of suggested alternate spellings when an incorrect spelling is found. If **False**, Microsoft Excel will wait for you to input the correct spelling. If omitted, the current setting will be used.

word
Required (used with Application object only). The word you want to check.

Remarks

To check headers, footers, and objects, use **Worksheet.CheckSpelling**.

To check only cells and notes, use **Worksheet.Cells.CheckSpelling**.

Example

This example checks the spelling of the active sheet.

```
ActiveSheet.CheckSpelling
```

ChildField Property

Applies To   PivotField.

Description	Returns the child pivot field for the specified field (if the field is grouped and has a child field). Read-only.
Syntax	*object*.**ChildField**
Elements	*object* Required. The PivotField object.
Remarks	If the specified field has no child field, this property causes an error.
Example	This example displays the name of the child pivot field for the active field.

```
MsgBox "The name of the child field is " & _
     ActiveCell.PivotField.ChildField.Name
```

ChildItems Method

Applies To	PivotField, PivotItem.
Description	Returns one pivot item (a PivotItem object, Syntax 1) or a collection of all the pivot items (a PivotItems object, Syntax 2) that are group children in the specified field, or children of the specified item. Read-only.
Syntax 1	*object*.**ChildItems**(*index*)
Syntax 2	*object*.**ChildItems**
Elements	The **ChildItems** method has the following object qualifier and named arguments:

object
    Required. The PivotField or PivotItem object.

index
    Required for Syntax 1. The number or name of the pivot item to return (can be an array to specify more than one).

Example	This example adds the names of all the group children of the active field to a list box.

```
For Each pvtItem in ActiveCell.PivotField.ChildItems
     childItemListBox.AddItem(pvtItem.Name)
Next pvtItem
```

Chr Function

Description	Returns the character associated with the specified character code.

Syntax	**Chr**(*charcode*)
Elements	The *charcode* named argument is a number in the range 0 to 255, inclusive, that identifies a character.
Remarks	Numbers from 0 to 31 are the same as standard, nonprintable ASCII codes. For example, **Chr**(10) returns a linefeed character.
See Also	**Asc** Function, Character Set, **Str** Function.
Example	This example uses the **Chr** function to return the character associated with the specified character code.

```
MyChar = Chr(65)' Returns A.
MyChar = Chr(97)' Returns a.
MyChar = Chr(62)' Returns >.
MyChar = Chr(37)' Returns %.
```

CInt Function

Description	Converts an expression to an **Integer**.
Syntax	**CInt**(*expression*)
Elements	The *expression* argument is any valid numeric or string expression.
Remarks	In general, you can document your code using the data type conversion functions to show that the result of some operation should be expressed as a particular data type rather than the default data type. For example, use **CInt** or **CLng** to force integer arithmetic in cases where currency, single-precision, or double-precision arithmetic normally would occur.

You should use the **CInt** function instead of **Val** to provide internationally-aware conversions from any other data type to an **Integer**. For example, different decimal separators are properly recognized depending on the locale setting of your system, as are different thousand separators.

If *expression* lies outside the acceptable range for the **Integer** data type, an error occurs.

Note **CInt** differs from the **Fix** and **Int** functions that truncate, rather than round, the fractional part of a number. When the fractional part is exactly 0.5, the **CInt** function always rounds it to the nearest even number. For example, 0.5 rounds to 0, and 1.5 rounds to 2.

See Also	Data Type Summary, **Fix** Function, **Int** Function.

Example   This example uses the **CInt** function to convert a value to an **Integer**.

```
MyDouble = 2345.5678          ' MyDouble is a Double.
MyInt = CInt(MyDouble)        ' MyInt contains 2346.
```

CircularReference Property

Applies To   Worksheet.

Description   Returns the Range containing the first circular reference on the sheet, or **Nothing** if there is no circular reference present. The circular reference must be removed before calculation can proceed. Read-only.

Syntax   *object*.**CircularReference**

Elements   *object*
                Required. The Worksheet object.

Example   This example selects the range containing the first circular reference.

```
ActiveSheet.CircularReference.Select
```

Clear Method

Applies To   ChartArea, Range.

Description   Clears the entire range or chart area.

Syntax   *object*.**Clear**

Elements   *object*
                Required. The ChartArea or Range object.

See Also   **ClearFormats** Method, **ClearContents** Method.

Example   This example clears cells A1 through G37.

```
Range("A1:G37").Clear
```

ClearArrows Method

Applies To   Worksheet.

Description	Clears the tracer arrows on the worksheet. Tracer arrows are added by the auditing feature.
Syntax	*object*.**ClearArrows**
Elements	*object* Required. The Worksheet object.
See Also	**ShowDependents** Method, **ShowErrors** Method, **ShowPrecedents** Method.
Example	This example clears tracer arrows on the active sheet.

```
ActiveSheet.ClearArrows
```

ClearContents Method

Applies To	ChartArea, Range.
Description	Clears the formulas from the range. Clears the data from a chart but leaves the formatting.
Syntax	*object*.**ClearContents**
Elements	*object* Required. The Chart or Range object.
Example	This example clears the formulas from cells A1 through G37.

```
Range("A1:G37").ClearContents
```

ClearFormats Method

Applies To	ChartArea, Floor, LegendKey, PlotArea, Point, Range, Series, Trendline, Walls.
Description	Clears the formatting of the object.
Syntax	*object*.**ClearFormats**
Elements	*object* Required. The object to which this method applies.
See Also	**Clear** Method, **ClearContents** Method.
Example	This example clears all formatting from the range A1:G37.

```
Range("A1", "G37").ClearFormats
```

ClearNotes Method

Applies To	Range.
Description	Clears the note and the sound notes from all the cells in the range.
Syntax	*object*.**ClearNotes**
Elements	*object*
	Required. Clear notes and sound notes from this range.
See Also	**NoteText** Method, **SoundNote** Property,
Example	This example clears all notes and sound notes in columns A through C.

```
ActiveSheet.Range(Columns("A"), Columns("C")).ClearNotes
```

ClearOutline Method

Applies To	Range.
Description	Clears the outline for the specified range.
Syntax	*object*.**ClearOutline**
Elements	*object*
	Required. The Range object.
See Also	**AutoOutline** Method.
Example	This example clears the outline for the range A1:G37.

```
Range("A1:G37").ClearOutline
```

ClipboardFormats Property

Applies To	Application.
Description	Returns the formats currently on the Clipboard, as an array of numeric values. To determine if a particular format is present, compare each element in the array with the appropriate constant shown in the table below. Read-only.

Syntax

object.**ClipboardFormats**

Elements

object

Required. The Application object.

Remarks

This property is available in Microsoft Windows and on the Apple Macintosh. Some formats may be available only on the Apple Macintosh, or only in Microsoft Windows.

This property returns an array of numeric values. To determine if a particular clipboard format is present, compare each element of the array to one of the constants below.

xlClipboardFormatBIFF	**xlClipboardFormatBIFF2**
xlClipboardFormatBIFF3	**xlClipboardFormatBIFF4**
xlClipboardFormatBinary	**xlClipboardFormatBitmap**
xlClipboardFormatCGM	**xlClipboardFormatCSV**
xlClipboardFormatDIF	**xlClipboardFormatDspText**
xlClipboardFormatEmbeddedObject	**xlClipboardFormatEmbedSource**
xlClipboardFormatLink	**xlClipboardFormatLinkSource**
xlClipboardFormatLinkSourceDesc	**xlClipboardFormatMovie**
xlClipboardFormatNative	**xlClipboardFormatObjectDesc**
xlClipboardFormatObjectLink	**xlClipboardFormatOwnerLink**
xlClipboardFormatPICT	**xlClipboardFormatPrintPICT**
xlClipboardFormatRTF	**xlClipboardFormatScreenPICT**
xlClipboardFormatStandardFont	**xlClipboardFormatStandardScale**
xlClipboardFormatSYLK	**xlClipboardFormatTable**
xlClipboardFormatText	**xlClipboardFormatToolFace**
xlClipboardFormatToolFacePICT	**xlClipboardFormatVALU**
xlClipboardFormatWK1	

Example

This example displays a message box if the clipboard contains a rich-text format object.

```
aFmts = Application.ClipboardFormats
For Each fmt in aFmts
    If fmt = xlClipboardFormatRTF Then
        MsgBox "Clipboard contains rich text"
    End If
Next
```

CLng Function

Description   Converts an expression to a **Long**.

Syntax   **CLng**(*expression*)

Elements   The *expression* argument is any valid numeric or string expression.

Remarks   In general, you can document your code using the data type conversion functions to show that the result of some operation should be expressed as a particular data type rather than the default data type. For example, use **CInt** or **CLng** to force integer arithmetic in cases where currency, single-precision, or double-precision arithmetic normally would occur.

You should use the **CLng** function instead of **Val** to provide internationally-aware conversions from any other data type to a **Long**. For example, different decimal separators are properly recognized depending on the locale setting of your system, as are different thousand separators.

If *expression* lies outside the acceptable range for the **Long** data type, an error occurs.

Note **CLng** differs from the **Fix** and **Int** functions that truncate, rather than round, the fractional part of a number. When the fractional part is exactly 0.5, the **CLng** function always rounds it to the nearest even number. For example, 0.5 rounds to 0, and 1.5 rounds to 2.

See Also   Data Type Summary, **Fix** Function, **Int** Function.

Example   This example uses the **CLng** function to convert a value to a **Long**.

```
MyVal1 = 25427.45 : MyVal2 = 25427.55    ' MyVal1, MyVal2 are Doubles.
MyLong1 = CLng(MyVal1)                        ' MyLong1 contains 25427.
MyLong2 = CLng(MyVal2)                        ' MyLong2 contains 25428.
```

Close Method

Applies To   Window, Workbook, Workbooks.

Description	Closes the object. The Workbooks collection uses Syntax 1. Window and Workbook objects use Syntax 2.
Syntax 1	*object*.**Close**
Syntax 2	*object*.**Close**(*saveChanges, fileName, routeWorkbook*)
Elements	The **Close** method has the following object qualifier and named arguments:

object
Required. The object to close.

saveChanges
Optional. If there are no changes to the workbook in the window, this argument is ignored. If there are changes to the workbook, and there are other windows open on the workbook, this argument is ignored. If there are changes to the workbook, and there are no other windows open on the workbook, this argument takes the following action:

Value	Action
True	Saves the changes to the workbook. If there is not yet a filename associated with the workbook, then *fileName* is used. If *fileName* is omitted, the user is asked to supply a filename.
False	Does not save the changes to this file.
Omitted	Displays a dialog box asking the user whether or not to save changes.

fileName
Optional. Save changes under this filename,

routeWorkbook
Optional. If the workbook does not need to be routed to the next recipient (has no routing slip, or is already routed), this argument is ignored. Otherwise, Microsoft Excel routes the workbook as shown in the following table.

Value	Meaning
True	Sends the workbook to the next recipient.
False	Does not send the workbook.
Omitted	Displays a dialog box asking the user if the workbook should be sent.

Remarks	Closing a workbook from Visual Basic does not run any Auto_Close macros in the workbook. Use the **RunAutoMacros** method to run the auto close macros.
Example	This example closes the active window and discards any changes.

```
ActiveWindow.Close saveChanges := False
```

Close Statement

Description   Concludes input/output (I/O) to a file opened using the **Open** statement.

Syntax   **Close** [*filenumberlist*]

Elements   The *filenumberlist* argument can be one or more file numbers using the following syntax, where *filenumber* is any valid file number:

[#]*filenumber*][,[#]*filenumber*] ...

Remarks   If you omit *filenumberlist*, all active files opened by the **Open** statement are closed.

When you close files that were opened for **Output** or **Append**, the final buffer of output is written to the operating system buffer for that file. All buffer space associated with the closed file is released.

When the **Close** statement executes, the association of a file with its file number ends.

See Also   **End** Statement, **Open** Statement, **Reset** Statement, **Stop** Statement.

Example   This example uses the **Close** statement to close all three files opened for **Output**.

```
For I = 1 To 3                      ' Loop 3 times.
    FileName = "TEST" & I             ' Create file name.
    Open FileName For Output As #I     ' Open file.
    Print #I, "This is a test."        ' Write string to file.
Next I
Close                               ' Close all 3 open files.
```

Color Property

Applies To   Border, Borders, Font, Interior.

Description   Returns or sets the primary color of the object, as shown in the following table. The color is a long integer, created with the **RGB** function. Read-write.

Object	Color
Border	The color of the border.
Borders	The color of all four borders of a range. If they are not the same, returns **Null**.
Font	The color of the font.
Interior	The cell shading color or drawing object fill color.

Syntax   *object*.**Color**

Elements   *object*
　　　　　　Required. The object to which this property applies.

Remark   If the color is Automatic, the **Color** property returns the automatic color as an RGB value (a long integer). Use the **ColorIndex** property to determine if the color is Automatic.

Example   This example sets the color of the tick labels on the value axis.

```
Charts(1).Axes(xlValue).TickLabels.Font.Color = RGB(0, 255, 0)
```

ColorButtons Property

Applies To   Application.

Description   **True** if toolbars are displayed using colored faces. Read-write.

Syntax   *object*.**ColorButtons**

Elements   *object*
　　　　　　　Required. The Application object.

See Also   **LargeButtons** Property.

Example   This example turns off colored toolbar faces.

```
Application.ColorButtons = False
```

ColorIndex Property

Applies To   Border, Borders, Font, Interior.

Description	Returns or sets the color of the border, font, or interior, as shown in the following table. The color is specified as an index value into the current color palette, or the special constant **xlAutomatic** to use the automatic fill style. Read-write.

Object	ColorIndex
Border	Color of the border.
Borders	Color of all four borders. Returns **Null** if all four colors are not the same.
Font	Color of the font. Specify **xlAutomatic** to use the automatic color.
Interior	Color of the interior fill. Set this property to **xlNone** to specify no fill. Set this property to **xlAutomatic** to specify the automatic fill (for drawing objects).

Syntax	*object*.**ColorIndex**
Elements	*object* Required. The object to which this property applies.
Remarks	This property specifies a color as an index into the workbook color palette. You can use the **Colors** property to return the current color palette.
See Also	**Color** Property, **Colors** Property, **PatternColor** Property.
Example	This example sets the color of rectangle one to the tenth color in the palette.

```
ActiveSheet.Rectangles(1).Border.ColorIndex = 10
```

Colors Property

Applies To	Workbook.
Description	Returns or sets an array of colors (from one to 56) in the palette for the workbook. Read-write.
Syntax	*object*.**Colors**
Elements	*object* Required. The Workbook object.
See Also	**ColorIndex** Property.
Example	This example sets the color palette for the active workbook to be the same as the palette for BOOK2.XLS.

```
ActiveWorkbook.Colors = Workbooks("BOOK2.XLS").Colors
```

Column Property

Applies To	Range.
Description	Returns the first column of the first area in the range, as a number. Read-only.
Syntax	*object*.**Column**
Elements	*object*
	Required. The range containing the column to return.
Remarks	Column A returns 1, column B returns 2, and so on.
	To return the number of the last column in the range, use

```
myRange.Columns(myRange.Columns.Count).Column
```

See Also	**Columns** Method, **Row** Property, **Rows** Method.
Example	This example returns the number of the first column in the multiple selection that contains B3:C5 and D7:E9.

```
Set r1 = Range(Cells(3, 2), Cells(5, 3))
Set r2 = Range(Cells(7, 4), Cells(9, 5))
Set multipleSelection = Union(r1, r2)
MsgBox "First column in the multiple selection is " & _
    multipleSelection.Column      'Displays the number 2
```

Column3DGroup Property

Applies To	Chart.
Description	Returns the column ChartGroup on a 3-D chart.
Syntax	*object*.**Column3DGroup**
Elements	*object*
	Required. The Chart object.
See Also	**ColumnGroups** Method.
Example	This example sets the subtype for the 3-D column chart group.

```
Charts(1).Column3DGroup.SubType = 4
```

ColumnDifferences Method

Applies To   Range.

Description   Returns a Range that contains all the cells whose contents are different than the comparison cell in each column. The comparison cell is the one in the same row as *comparison*.

Syntax   *object*.**ColumnDifferences(***comparison***)**

Elements   The **ColumnDifferences** method has the following object qualifier and named arguments:

object
     Required. The range containing the cells to compare.

comparison
     Required. A cell in the comparison row.

See Also   **RowDifferences** Method.

Example   This example selects the cells in column one whose contents are different from the active cell.

```
Columns(1).ColumnDifferences(ActiveCell).Select
```

ColumnFields Method

Applies To   PivotTable.

Description   Returns a single pivot field (a PivotField object, Syntax 1) or a collection of the pivot fields (a PivotFields object, Syntax 2) that are currently showing as column fields. Read-only.

Syntax 1   *object*.**ColumnFields(***index***)**

Syntax 2   *object*.**ColumnFields**

Elements   The **ColumnFields** method has the following object qualifier and named arguments:

object
     Required. The PivotTable object.

index
> Required for Syntax 1. The name or number of the pivot field to return (can be an array to specify more than one).

See Also **DataFields** Method, **HiddenFields** Method, **PageFields** Method, **PivotFields** Method, **RowFields** Method, **VisibleFields** Method.

Example This example adds the active pivot table column field names to a list box.

```
For Each clmField In ActiveCell.PivotTable.ColumnFields
    columnFieldListBox.AddItem(clmField.Name)
Next clmField
```

ColumnGrand Property

Applies To PivotTable.

Description **True** if the pivot table shows column grand totals. Read-write.

Syntax *object*.**ColumnGrand**

See Also **RowGrand** Property.

Elements *object*
> Required. The PivotTable object.

Example This example sets the active pivot table to show column grand totals.

```
ActiveCell.PivotTable.ColumnGrand = True
```

ColumnGroups Method

Applies To Chart.

Description On a 2-D chart, returns a single column chart group (a ChartGroup object, Syntax 1), or a collection of the column chart groups (a ChartGroups collection, Syntax 2).

Syntax 1 *object*.**ColumnGroups**(*index*)

Syntax 2 `object.ColumnGroups`

Elements	The **ColumnGroups** method has the following object qualifier and named arguments:

object
Required. The Chart object.

index
Required for Syntax 1. Specifies the chart group.

See Also   **Column3DGroup** Property.

Example   This example sets the subtype for the first column chart group.

```
Charts(1).ColumnGroups(1).SubType = 3
```

ColumnRange Property

Applies To   PivotTable.

Description   Returns the Range that contains the pivot table column area. Read-only.

Syntax   *object*.**ColumnRange**

Elements   *object*
Required. The PivotTable object.

See Also   **DataBodyRange** Property, **DataLabelRange** Property, **PageRange** Property, **RowRange** Property.

Example   This example selects the column headers for the active pivot table.

```
ActiveCell.PivotTable.ColumnRange.Select
```

Columns Method

Applies To   Application, Range, Worksheet.

Description   Returns a single column (Syntax 1) or a collection of columns (Syntax 2). A column is a Range object.

Syntax 1   *object*.**Columns**(*index*)

Syntax 2   *object*.**Columns**

Elements	The **Columns** method has the following object qualifier and named arguments.

object
> Optional for Application, required for Range and Worksheet. The object that contains the columns.

index
> Required for Syntax 1. The name or number of the column.

Remarks	When applied to a Range object that is a multiple selection, this method returns columns from the first area of the range only. For example, if the Range object is a multiple selection with two areas, A1:B2 and C3:D4, **Selection.Columns.Count**, returns 2, not 4. To use this method on a range that may contain a multiple selection, test **Areas.Count** to determine if the range is a multiple selection, and if it is, then loop over each area in the range; see the second example.
See Also	**Range** Method, **Rows** Method.
Examples	This example formats the font of the first column (column A) of the active worksheet as bold.

```
ActiveSheet.Columns(1).Font.Bold = True
```

This example displays the number of columns in the selection. The code tests for a multiple selection and if one exists, loops on the areas of the multiple selection.

```
areaCount = Selection.Areas.Count
If areaCount <= 1 Then
    MsgBox "The selection contains " & _
        Selection.Columns.Count & " columns."
Else
    For i = 1 To areaCount
        MsgBox "Area " & i & " of the selection contains " & _
            Selection.Areas(i).Columns.Count & " columns."
    Next i
End If
```

ColumnWidth Property

Applies To	Range.
Description	Returns or sets the width of all columns in the range. Read-write.
Syntax	*object*.**ColumnWidth**
Elements	*object*

> Required. Return or set column widths for this range.

Remarks	One unit of column width is equal to the width of a character of the Normal style. For proportional fonts, the width of the character 0 (zero) is used.
	Use the **Width** property to return the width of a column in points.
	If all columns in the range have the same width, the **ColumnWidth** property returns the width. If columns in the range have different widths, the property returns **Null**.
See Also	**RowHeight** Property.
Example	This example doubles the width of columns A and B on the active worksheet.

```
With ActiveSheet.Range(Columns("A"), Columns("B"))
    .ColumnWidth = .ColumnWidth * 2
End With
```

CommandUnderlines Property

Applies To	Application.
Description	Returns or sets the state of the command underlines, as shown in the following list.

Value	Meaning
xlOn	Command underlines are on.
xlOff	Command underlines are off.
xlAutomatic	Command underlines appear when you activate the menus.

Syntax	*object*.**CommandUnderlines**
Elements	*object*
	Required. The Application object.
Remarks	In Microsoft Excel for Windows, reading this property always returns **xlOn**, and setting this property to anything but **xlOn** is an error.
Example	This example turns off command underlines in Microsoft Excel for the Macintosh.

```
Application.CommandUnderlines = xlOff
```

Comment Property

Applies To	Scenario.

Description	Returns or sets the comment associated with the scenario. The comment text cannot exceed 255 characters. Read-write.
Syntax	*object*.**Comment**
Elements	*object* Required. The Scenario object.
See Also	**ChangeScenario** Method, **ChangingCells** Property.
Example	This example sets the comment for the first scenario.

```
ActiveSheet.Scenarios(1).Comment = "Worst case July 1993 sales"
```

Comments Property

Applies To	AddIn, Workbook.
Description	Returns or sets the comments for an object, as a string. Read-only for AddIn, read-write for Workbook.
Syntax	*object*.**Comments**
Elements	*object* Required. The AddIn or Workbook object.
See Also	**Author** Property, **Keywords** Property, **Subject** Property, **Title** Property.
Example	This example sets the comments for the active workbook.

```
ActiveWorkbook.Comments = "This workbook has been reviewed."
```

Comparison Operators

Description	Used to compare expressions.
Syntax	*result = expression1 comparisonoperator expression2* *result = object1* **Is** *object2* *result = string* **Like** *pattern*

Elements

Comparison operators have these parts:

Part	Description
result	Any numeric variable.
expression	Any expression.
comparisonoperator	Any comparison operator.
object	Any object name.
string	Any string expression.
pattern	Any string expression or range of characters.

Remarks

The **Is** and **Like** operators have specific comparison functionality that differs from the operators in the following table. The following table contains a list of the comparison operators and the conditions that determine whether *result* is **True**, **False**, or **Null**:

Operator	Description	True if	False if	Null if
<	Less than	*expression1* < *expression2*	*expression1* >= *expression2*	*expression1* or *expression2* = **Null**
<=	Less than or equal to	*expression1* <= *expression2*	*expression1* > *expression2*	*expression1* or *expression2* = **Null**
>	Greater than	*expression1* > *expression2*	*expression1* <= *expression2*	*expression1* or *expression2* = **Null**
>=	Greater than or equal to	*expression1* >= *expression2*	*expression1* < *expression2*	*expression1* or *expression2* = **Null**
=	Equal to	*expression1* = *expression2*	*expression1* <> *expression2*	*expression1* or *expression2* = **Null**
<>	Not equal to	*expression1* <> *expression2*	*expression1* = *expression2*	*expression1* or *expression2* = **Null**

When comparing two expressions, you may not be able to easily determine whether the expressions are being compared as numbers or as strings. The following table shows how the expressions are compared or what results when either expression is not a **Variant**:

If	Then
Both expressions are numeric data types (**Integer**, **Long**, **Single**, **Double**, or **Currency**)	Perform a numeric comparison.
Both expressions are **String**	Perform a string comparison.

If	Then
One expression is a numeric data type and the other is a **Variant** that is, or can be, a number	Perform a numeric comparison.
One expression is a numeric data type and the other is a string **Variant** that can't be converted to a number	A `Type Mismatch` error occurs.
One expression is a **String** and the other is any **Variant** (except a **Null**)	Perform a string comparison.
One expression is **Empty** and the other is a numeric data type	Perform a numeric comparison, using 0 as the **Empty** expression.
One expression is **Empty** and the other is a **String**	Perform a string comparison, using a zero-length string as the **Empty** expression.

If *expression1* and *expression2* are both **Variant** expressions, their underlying type determines how they are compared. The following table shows how the expressions are compared or what results from the comparison, depending on the underlying type of the **Variant**:

If	Then
Both **Variant** expressions are numeric	Perform a numeric comparison.
Both **Variant** expressions are strings	Perform a string comparison.
One **Variant** expression is numeric and the other is a string	The numeric expression is less than the string expression.
One **Variant** expression is **Empty** and the other is numeric	Perform a numeric comparison, using 0 as the **Empty** expression.
One **Variant** expression is **Empty** and the other is a string	Perform a string comparison, using a zero-length string as the **Empty** expression.
Both **Variant** expressions are **Empty**	The expressions are equal.

Note   If a **Currency** is compared with a **Single** or **Double**, the **Single** or **Double** is converted to a **Currency**. This causes any fractional part of the **Single** or **Double** value less than 0.0001 to be lost and may cause two values to compare as equal when they are not. When a **Single** is compared to a **Double**, the **Double** is rounded to the precision of the **Single**.

See Also   **Is** Operator, **Like** Operator, Operator Precedence, **Option Compare** Statement.

Example

This example shows various uses of comparison operators, which you use to compare expressions.

```
MyResult = (45 < 35)      ' Returns False.
MyResult = (45 = 45)      ' Returns True.
MyResult = (4 <> 3)       ' Returns True.
MyResult = ("5" > "4")    ' Returns True.
Var1 = "5" : Var2 = 4     ' Initialize variables.
MyResult = (Var1 > Var2)  ' Returns True.
Var1 = 5 : Var2 = Empty
MyResult = (Var1 > Var2)  ' Returns True.
Var1 = 0 : Var2 = Empty
MyResult = (Var1 = Var2)  ' Returns True.
```

Consolidate Method

Applies To

Range.

Description

Consolidates data from multiple ranges on multiple worksheets into a single range on a single worksheet.

Syntax

object.**Consolidate**(*sources, function, topRow, leftColumn, createLinks*)

Elements

object
　　Required. The destination range.

sources
　　Optional. Specifies the sources of the consolidation as an array of text reference strings in R1C1-style notation. The references must include the full path of sheets to consolidate.

function
　　Optional. The consolidation function (one of **xlAverage**, **xlCount**, **xlCountNums**, **xlMax**, **xlMin**, **xlProduct**, **xlStDev**, **xlStDevP**, **xlSum**, **xlVar**, or **xlVarP**).

topRow
　　Optional. If **True**, data is consolidated based on column header titles in the top row of the consolidation ranges. If **False** or omitted, data is consolidated by position.

leftColumn
　　Optional. If **True**, data is consolidated based on row titles in the left column of the consolidation ranges. If **False** or omitted, data is consolidated by position.

createLinks
　　Optional. If **True**, the consolidation uses worksheet links. If **False**, the consolidation copies the data.

See Also	**ConsolidationFunction** Property, **ConsolidationOptions** Property, **ConsolidationSources** Property, **Style** Property.
Example	This example consolidates data on Sheet1 and Sheet2, using the MAX function.

```
Worksheets(1).Cells(1, 1).Consolidate _
    sources:=Array("Sheet1!R2C2:R37C6", "Sheet2!R2C2:R37C6"), _
    function:=xlMax
```

ConsolidationFunction Property

Applies To	Worksheet.
Description	Returns the function code used for the current consolidation (one of **xlAverage**, **xlCount**, **xlCountNums**, **xlMax**, **xlMin**, **xlProduct**, **xlStDev**, **xlStDevP**, **xlSum**, **xlVar**, or **xlVarP**). Read-only.
Syntax	*object*.**ConsolidationFunction**
Elements	*object* Required. The Worksheet object.
See Also	**Consolidate** Method, **ConsolidationOptions** Property, **ConsolidationSources** Property.
Example	This example displays a message box if the current consolidation is using the SUM function.

```
If ActiveSheet.ConsolidationFunction = xlSum Then
    MsgBox "This worksheet uses the SUM function for consolidation."
End If
```

ConsolidationOptions Property

Applies To	Worksheet.
Description	Returns a three-element array of consolidation options, as shown in the following table. If the element is **True**, that option is set. Read-only.

Element	Meaning
1	Labels in top row.
2	Labels in left column.
3	Create links for data.

Syntax	*object*.**ConsolidationOptions**
Elements	*object* Required. The Worksheet object.
See Also	**Consolidate** Method, **ConsolidationFunction** Property, **ConsolidationSources** Property.
Example	This example displays the consolidation options for the active worksheet.

```
aOptions = ActiveSheet.ConsolidationOptions
Cells(1, 1) = "Labels in top row"
Cells(2, 1) = "Labels in left column"
Cells(3, 1) = "Create links for data"
For i = 1 To 3
    If aOptions(i) Then
        Cells(i, 2) = "True"
    Else
        Cells(i, 2) = "False"
    End If
Next i
```

ConsolidationSources Property

Applies To	Worksheet.
Description	Returns an array of string values that name the source sheets for the worksheet's current consolidation. Returns **Empty** if there is no consolidation on the sheet. Read-only.
Syntax	*object*.**ConsolidationSources**
Elements	*object* Required. The Worksheet object.
See Also	**Consolidate** Method, **ConsolidationFunction** Property, **ConsolidationOptions** Property.

Example	This example displays the names of the source sheets for the consolidation for the active worksheet.

```
Cells(1, 1) = "Consolidation Sources"
aSources = ActiveSheet.ConsolidationSources
If IsEmpty(aSources) Then
    Cells(2, 1) = "none"
Else
    For i = 1 To UBound(aSources)
        Cells(i + 1, 1) = aSources(i)
    Next i
End If
```

Const Statement

Description

Declares constants for use in place of literal values.

Syntax

[**Public** | **Private**] **Const** *constname* [**As** *type*] = *expression*

Elements

The **Const** statement syntax has these parts:

Part	Description
Public	Used at module level to declare constants that are available to all procedures in all modules. Not allowed in procedures.
Private	Used at module level to declare constants that are available only within the module where the declaration is made. Not allowed in procedures.
constname	Name of the constant; follows standard variable naming conventions.
type	Data type of the constant; may be **Boolean**, **Integer**, **Long**, **Currency**, **Single**, **Double**, **Date**, **String**, or **Variant**. Use a separate **As** *type* clause for each constant being declared.
expression	Literal, other constant, or any combination including arithmetic or logical operators except **Is**.

Remarks

If not explicitly specified using either **Public** or **Private**, constants are **Private** by default.

Several constant declarations can be combined on the same line by separating each constant assignment with a comma. If constant declarations are combined in this way, the **Public** or **Private** keywords, if used, apply to all of them.

You can't use string concatenation, variables, user-defined or intrinsic functions (such as **Chr**) in expressions assigned to constants.

Tip The special characters left bracket ([), question mark (**?**), number sign (**#**), and asterisk (*****) can be used to match themselves directly only by enclosing them in brackets. The right bracket (]) can't be used within a group to match itself, but it can be used outside a group as an individual character. Constants can make your programs self-documenting and easier to modify. Unlike variables, constants can't be inadvertently changed while your program is running.

If you don't explicitly declare the constant type (using **As** *type*), the constant is given a data type that is most appropriate for the expression provided.

Constants declared in **Sub**, **Function**, or **Property** procedures are local to that procedure. A constant declared outside a procedure is defined throughout the module in which it is declared. You can use constants anywhere you would use an expression.

See Also   **Def***type* Statement, **Let** Statement.

Example   This example uses the **Const** statement to declare constants for use in place of literal values.

```
' Constants are Private by default.
Const MyVar = 459

' Declare Public constant.
Public Const MyString = "HELP"

' Declare Private Integer constant.
Private Const MyInt As Integer = 5

' Declare multiple constants on same line.
Const MyStr = "Hello", MyDouble As Double = 3.4567
```

ConstrainNumeric Property

Applies To   Application.

Description   **True** if handwriting recognition is limited to numbers and punctuation only. Read-write. This property is available only if you are using Microsoft Windows for Pen Computing. If you try to return or set this property under any other operating system, an error occurs.

Syntax   *object*.**ConstrainNumeric**

Elements   *object*
            Required. The Application object.

Example

This example limits handwriting recognition to numbers and punctuation only if the computer is running under Microsoft Windows for Pen Computing.

```
If Application.WindowsForPens Then
    Application.ConstrainNumeric = True
End If
```

ConvertFormula Method

Applies To

Application.

Description

Converts cell references in a formula between the A1 and R1C1 reference styles, between relative and absolute references, or both.

Syntax

object.**ConvertFormula**(*formula, fromReferenceStyle, toReferenceStyle, toAbsolute, relativeTo*)

Elements

The **ConvertFormula** method has the following object qualifier and named arguments:

object
　　Required. The Application object.

formula
　　Required. A string containing the formula that you want to convert. This must be a valid formula and it must begin with an equal sign.

fromReferenceStyle
　　Required. The reference style of the formula. May be either **xlA1** or **xlR1C1**.

toReferenceStyle
　　Optional. The reference style you want returned. May be either **xlA1** or **xlR1C1**. If omitted, the reference style is not changed (the formula stays in the style specified by *fromReferenceStyle*).

toAbsolute
　　Optional. Specifies the converted reference type (one of **xlAbsolute**, **xlAbsRowRelColumn**, **xlRelRowAbsColumn**, or **xlRelative).** If this argument is omitted, the reference type is not changed.

relativeTo
　　Optional. A Range object that contains one cell. This object determines the cell to which relative references relate.

Example   This example converts a SUM formula that contains R1C1-style references to an equivalent formula that contains A1-style references, and then displays the result.

```
inputFormula = "=SUM(R10C2:R15C2)"
MsgBox Application.ConvertFormula( _
    formula:=inputFormula, _
    fromReferenceStyle:=xlR1C1, _
    toReferenceStyle:=xlA1)
```

Copy Method

Applies To   Arc, Arcs, Button, Buttons, Chart, ChartArea, ChartObject, ChartObjects, Charts, CheckBox, CheckBoxes, DialogSheet, DialogSheets, Drawing, DrawingObjects, Drawings, DropDown, DropDowns, EditBox, EditBoxes, GroupBox, GroupBoxes, GroupObject, GroupObjects, Label, Labels, Line, Lines, ListBox, ListBoxes, Module, Modules, OLEObject, OLEObjects, OptionButton, OptionButtons, Oval, Ovals, Picture, Pictures, Point, Range, Rectangle, Rectangles, ScrollBar, ScrollBars, Series, Sheets, Spinner, Spinners, TextBox, TextBoxes, ToolbarButton, Worksheet, Worksheets.

Description   Syntax 1: Copies the control or drawing object to the Clipboard. Copies a picture of the point or series to the Clipboard.

Syntax 2: Copies the Range to the specified range, or to the Clipboard.

Syntax 3: Copies the sheet to another location in the workbook.

Syntax 4: Copies a toolbar button to another position, either on the same toolbar or to another toolbar.

Syntax 1   *object*.**Copy**

Syntax 2   *object*.**Copy**(*destination*)

Syntax 3   *object*.**Copy**(*before, after*)

Syntax 4   *object*.**Copy**(*toolbar, before*)

Elements   The **Copy** method has the following object qualifier and named arguments:

object
Required. The object to which this method applies. Copying a Chart object uses Syntax 3, and copies the entire chart sheet. To copy only the chart area, use Syntax 1 with the ChartArea object.

destination
> Optional. Specifies the new range where the specified range will be copied. If this argument is omitted, Microsoft Excel copies the range to the clipboard.

before
> Syntax 3: Optional. The sheet before which this sheet will be copied. You cannot specify *before* if you specify *after*.

> Syntax 4: Required. Specifies the new button position as a number from one to the number of exisiting buttons + one. Gaps count as one position. Buttons to the right of this position are moved right (or down) to make room for the copied button.

after
> Optional. The sheet after which this sheet will be copied. You cannot specify *after* if you specify *before*.

toolbar
> Required for Syntax 4. Specifies the toolbar object to copy the button to.

Remarks

If you do not specify either *before* or *after*, Microsoft Excel creates a new workbook containing the copied sheet.

To copy a button and insert a gap before the copied button, first insert a gap on the destination toolbar using the ToolbarButtons **Add** method, then copy the button to the position after the new gap.

See Also

Move Method, **Paste** Method.

Examples

This example copies button one to the Clipboard.

```
ActiveSheet.Buttons(1).Copy
```

This example copies sheet one after sheet three.

```
Sheets("Sheet1").Copy after := Sheets("Sheet3")
```

This example copies worksheet one before worksheet nine on Book2.

```
Application.Worksheets("Sheet1").Copy _
    before := Workbooks("Book2").Worksheets("Sheet9")
```

CopyFace Method

Applies To   ToolbarButton.

Description   Copies the specified button face to the Clipboard. This method copies only the bitmap button face, not the button itself.

Syntax	*object*.**CopyFace**
Elements	*object* Required. The ToolbarButton object.
See Also	**BuiltIn** Property, **BuiltInFace** Property, **PasteFace** Method.
Example	This example copies the bitmap face of button one on toolbar one and pastes it onto the face of button three.

```
With Toolbars(1)
    .ToolbarButtons(1).CopyFace
    .ToolbarButtons(3).PasteFace
End With
```

CopyObjectsWithCells Property

Applies To	Application.
Description	**True** if drawing objects are cut, copied, extracted, and sorted with cells. Read-write.
Syntax	*object*.**CopyObjectsWithCells**
Elements	*object* Required. The Application object.
Example	This example causes Microsoft Excel to cut, copy, extract and sort drawing objects with cells.

```
Application.CopyObjectsWithCells = True
```

CopyPicture Method

Applies To	Arc, Arcs, Button, Buttons, Chart, ChartObject, ChartObjects, CheckBox, CheckBoxes, DialogFrame, Drawing, DrawingObjects, Drawings, DropDown, DropDowns, EditBox, EditBoxes, GroupBox, GroupBoxes, GroupObject, GroupObjects, Label, Labels, Line, Lines, ListBox, ListBoxes, OLEObject, OLEObjects, OptionButton, OptionButtons, Oval, Ovals, Picture, Pictures, Range, Rectangle, Rectangles, ScrollBar, ScrollBars, Spinner, Spinners, TextBox, TextBoxes.
Description	Copies the object to the Clipboard as a Picture. Syntax 2 is used for the Chart object. Syntax 1 is used for all other objects.

Syntax 1	*object*.**CopyPicture**(*appearance, format*)
Syntax 2	*object*.**CopyPicture**(*appearance, format, size*)
Elements	The **CopyPicture** method has the following object qualifier and named arguments:

object
Required. The object to copy.

appearance
Optional. Specifies how the picture should be copied. If **xlScreen** or omitted, the picture is copied as closely as possible to the picture displayed on the screen. If **xlPrinter**, the picture is copied as it would be printed.

format
Optional. Specifies the format of the picture (one of **xlPicture** or **xlBitmap**). If omitted, picture format is used.

size
Optional. Specifies the size of the copied picture when the object is a chart that is on a chart sheet (not embedded on a worksheet). If **xlPrinter** or omitted, the picture is copied as closely as possible to the printed size. If **xlScreen**, the picture is copied as closely as possible to the size as displayed on the screen.

Remarks	This method creates a Picture object on the Clipboard, regardless of the copied object.
	If you copy a range, it must be made up of adjacent cells.
See Also	**Copy** Method, **Paste** Method.
Example	This example copies a screen image of the range to the Clipboard, as a bitmap.

```
Application.Range("C5:G37").CopyPicture xlScreen, xlBitmap
```

Corners Object

Description	The corners of a 3-D chart. The only thing you can do to the chart corners is to select them; when the corners are selected, you can rotate and resize the 3-D chart.

Corners Property

Applies To	Chart.

Description	Returns the Corners of a 3-D chart. The corners cannot be formatted; this property can be used only to select the corners of the chart. Read-only.
Syntax	*object*.**Corners**
Elements	*object*
	Required. The Chart object.
Example	This example selects the corners of the chart.

```
Charts(1).Corners.Select
```

Cos Function

Description	Returns the cosine of an angle.
Syntax	**Cos(*number*)**
Elements	The ***number*** named argument can be any valid numeric expression that expresses an angle in radians.
Remarks	The **Cos** function takes an angle and returns the ratio of two sides of a right triangle. The ratio is the length of the side adjacent to the angle divided by the length of the hypotenuse.
	The result lies in the range -1 to 1.
	To convert degrees to radians, multiply degrees by pi/180. To convert radians to degrees, multiply radians by 180/pi.
See Also	**Atn** Function, **Sin** Function, **Tan** Function.
Example	This example uses the **Cos** function to return the cosine of an angle.

```
MyAngle = 1.3              ' Define angle in radians.
MySecant = 1 / Cos(MyAngle)    ' Calculate secant.
```

Count Property

Applies To	All collections.
Description	Returns the number of items in the collection. Read-only.

Syntax	*object*.**Count**
Elements	*object*
	Required. The object to which this property applies.
Example	This example displays the number of menus on the active menu bar.

```
MsgBox "The active menu bar contains " & _
    ActiveMenuBar.Menus.Count & " menus."
```

CreateBackup Property

Applies To	Workbook.
Description	**True** if a backup will be created when this file is saved. Read-only.
Syntax	*object*.**CreateBackup**
Elements	*object*
	Required. The Workbook object.
Example	This example saves the workbook BOOK1.XLS as NEWBOOK.XLS if a backup is created when saving.

```
With Workbooks("BOOK1.XLS")
    If .CreateBackup Then .SaveAs "NEWBOOK.XLS"
End With
```

CreateNames Method

Applies To	Range.
Description	Creates names in the given range based on text labels in the sheet.
Syntax	*object*.**CreateNames(***top, left, bottom, right***)**
Elements	The **CreateNames** method has the following object qualifier and named arguments:
	object
	Required. Create names in this range.
	top
	Optional. Corresponds to the Top Row checkbox in the Create dialog box. Can be **True** or **False**.

left
>Optional. Corresponds to the Left Column checkbox in the Create dialog box. Can be **True** or **False**.

bottom
>Optional. Corresponds to the Bottom Row checkbox in the Create dialog box. Can be **True** or **False**.

right
>Optional. Corresponds to the Right Column checkbox in the Create dialog box. Can be **True** or **False**.

See Also   **Delete** Method.

Example   This example creates names for cells B1:B3 based on the text in cells A1:A3. Notice that you have to include the cells that contain the names in the range, even though the names are created only for cells B1:B3.

```
Set rangeToName = ActiveSheet.Range(Cells(1, 1), Cells(3, 2))
rangeToName.CreateNames
```

CreateObject Function

Description   Creates an OLE Automation object.

Syntax   **CreateObject(*class*)**

Elements   The *class* named argument uses the syntax: "*appname.objecttype*" and has these parts:

Part	Description
appname	The name of the application providing the object.
objecttype	The type or class of object to create.

Remarks

> **Note** If an application that supports OLE Automation exposes an object library, it is preferable to use the functions defined within the library for object creation rather than use **CreateObject**.

Each application that supports OLE Automation provides at least one type of object. For example, a word processing application may provide an application object, a document object, and a toolbar object.

Use this function to create an OLE Automation object and assign the object to an object variable. To do this, use the **Set** statement to assign the object returned by **CreateObject** to the object variable. For example:

```
Set WordBasicObject = CreateObject("Word.Basic")
```

When this code is executed, the application creating the object is started, if it is not already running (Microsoft Word in this example), and an object of the specified type is created. Once an object is created, you reference it in code using the object variable you defined. In the above example, you access properties and methods of the new object using the object variable, WordBasicObject. For example:

```
WordBasicObject.Insert "Hello, world."
WordBasicObject.FilePrint
WordBasicObject.FileSaveAs "C:\DOCS\TEST.DOC"
```

See Also   **GetObject** Function, **Set** Statement.

CreatePublisher Method

Applies To   Chart, Range.

Description   Creates a publisher based on a Chart or a Range. Available only on the Apple Macintosh with System 7 or later.

Syntax   *object*.**CreatePublisher**(*edition, appearance, size, containsPICT, containsBIFF, containsRTF, containsVALU*)

Elements   The **CreatePublisher** method has the following object qualifier and named arguments:

object
　　Required. The Chart or Range object.

edition
　　Optional. The file name of the edition to be created. If omitted, a default of <Document Name> Edition #*n* is used.

appearance
　　Optional. One of **xlPrinter** or **xlScreen**.

size
　　Optional (used only with Chart objects). One of **xlPrinter** or **xlScreen**.

containsPICT
　　Optional. **True** if the publisher should include PICT format. Assumed **True** if not specified.

containsBIFF
Optional. **True** if the publisher should include BIFF format. Assumed **True** if not specified for a Range, **False** for a Chart.

containsRTF
Optional. **True** if the publisher should include RTF format. Assumed **True** if not specified for a Range, **False** for a Chart..

containsVALU
Optional. **True** if the publisher should include VALU format. Assumed **True** if not specified for a Range, **False** for a Chart.

Example   This example creates a publisher based on the first chart in the active workbook.

```
ActiveWorkbook.Charts(1).CreatePublisher
```

CreateSummary Method

Applies To   Scenarios.

Description   Creates a new worksheet containing a summary report for the scenarios on the specified worksheet.

Syntax   *object*.**CreateSummary**(*reportType*, *resultCells*)

Elements   The **CreateSummary** method has the following object qualifier and named arguments:

object
Required. The Scenarios collection object.

reportType
Optional. Specifies the report type (either **xlStandardSummary** or **xlPivotTable**). If this argument is omitted, a standard report is created.

resultCells
Optional. A range containing the result cells on the specified worksheet. Normally, this range refers to one or more cells containing the formulas that depend on the changing cell values for your model -- that is, the cells that show the results of a particular scenario. If this argument is omitted, no result cells are included in the report.

Example   This example creates a summary of the scenarios on the active worksheet, with result cells in the range C4:C9.

```
ActiveSheet.Scenarios.CreateSummary _
    resultCells := ActiveSheet.Range("C4:C9")
```

Creator Property

Applies To	All objects.
Description	Returns the application that created this object, as a 32-bit integer. If the object was created by Microsoft Excel, this property returns the string XCEL, which is the hexadecimal number 5843454C. Read-only.
Syntax	*object*.**Creator**
Elements	*object* Required. The object to which this property applies.
Remark	The **Creator** property is designed to be used in Microsoft Excel for the Apple Macintosh, where each application has a four-character creator code. For example, Microsoft Excel has the creator code XCEL.
See Also	**Application** Property.
Example	This example displays a message about the creator of myObject.

```
Set myObject = ActiveWorkbook
If myObject.Creator = &h5843454c Then
    MsgBox "This is a Microsoft Excel object"
Else
    MsgBox "This is not a Microsoft Excel object"
End If
```

Crosses Property

Applies To	Axis.
Description	Returns or sets the point on the specified axis where the other axis crosses, as shown in the following list. Read-write.

Value	Meaning
xlAutomatic	Microsoft Excel sets the axis crossing.
xlMinimum	The axis crosses at the minimum value.
xlMaximum	The axis crosses at the maximum value.
xlCustom	The **CrossesAt** property specifies the crossing point.

Syntax	*object*.**Crosses**
Elements	*object*
	Required. The Axis object.

Remarks   This property is not available for 3-D charts or radar charts.

This property can be used for both category and value axes. On the category axis, **xlMinimum** sets the value axis to cross at the first category, and **xlMaximum** sets the value axis to cross at the last category.

xlMinimum and **xlMaximum** can have different meanings, depending on the axis.

See Also   **CrossesAt** Property

Example   This example sets the value axis to cross the category (x) axis at the maximum x value.

```
ActiveChart.Axes(xlCategory).Crosses = xlMaximum
```

CrossesAt Property

Applies To   Axis.

Description   Returns or sets the point on the value axis where the category (x) axis crosses. Applies only to the value axis. Read-write.

Syntax   *object*.**CrossesAt**

Elements   *object*
        Required. The Axis object.

Remarks   Setting this property causes the **Crosses** property to change to **xlCustom**.

This property is not available for 3-D charts or radar charts.

See Also   **Crosses** Property.

Example   This example sets the category (x) axis to cross the value axis at value 3.

```
With ActiveChart.Axes(xlValue)
    .Crosses = xlCustom
    .CrossesAt = 3
End With
```

CSng Function

Description   Converts an expression to a **Single**.

Syntax   **CSng**(*expression*)

Elements   The *expression* argument is any valid numeric or string expression.

Remarks   In general, you can document your code using the data type conversion functions to show that the result of some operation should be expressed as a particular data type rather than the default data type. For example, use **CDbl** or **CSng** to force double- or single-precision arithmetic in cases where currency or integer arithmetic normally would occur.

You should use the **CSng** function instead of **Val** to provide internationally-aware conversions from any other data type to a **Single**. For example, different decimal separators are properly recognized depending on the locale setting of your system, as are different thousand separators.

If *expression* lies outside the acceptable range for the **Single** data type, an error occurs.

See Also   Data Type Summary.

Example   This example uses the **CSng** function to convert a value to a **Single**.

```
                                    ' MyDouble1, MyDouble2 are Doubles.
MyDouble1 = 75.3421115 : MyDouble2 = 75.3421555
MySingle1 = CSng(MyDouble1)     ' MySingle1 contains 75.34211.
MySingle2 = CSng(MyDouble2)     ' MySingle2 contains 75.34216.
```

CStr Function

Description   Converts an expression to a **String**.

Syntax   **CStr**(*expression*)

Elements   The *expression* argument is any valid numeric or string expression.

Remarks   In general, you can document your code using the data type conversion functions to show that the result of some operation should be expressed as a particular data type rather than the default data type. For example, use **CStr** to force the result to be expressed as a **String**.

You should use the **CStr** function instead of **Str** to provide internationally-aware conversions from any other data type to a **String**. For example, different decimal separators are properly recognized depending on the locale setting of your system.

The data in *expression* determines what is returned according to the following table:

If expression is	CStr returns
Boolean	**String** containing **True** or **False** (translated as appropriate for locale).
Date	**String** containing a date in the short-date format of your system.
Null	A run-time error.
Empty	A zero-length **String** ("").
Error	A **String** containing the word **Error** (translated as appropriate for locale) followed by the error number.
Other Numeric	A **String** containing the number.

See Also Data Type Summary, **Str** Function.

Example This example uses the **CStr** function to convert a numeric value to a **String**.

```
MyDouble = 437.324        ' MyDouble is a Double.
MyString = CStr(MyDouble)        ' MyString contains "437.324".
```

CurDir Function

Description Returns the current path.

Syntax **CurDir**[(*drive*)]

Elements The *drive* argument is a string expression that specifies an existing drive. In Microsoft Windows, if no drive is specified or if *drive* is zero-length (""), **CurDir** returns the path for the current drive. On the Macintosh, **CurDir** ignores any *drive* specified and simply returns the path for the current drive.

See Also **ChDir** Statement, **ChDrive** Statement, **MkDir** Statement, **RmDir** Statement.

Example   This example uses the **CurDir** function to return the current path.

```
' In Microsoft Windows.
' Assume current path on C Drive is  "C:\WINDOWS\SYSTEM".
' Assume current path on D Drive is "D:\EXCEL".
' Assume C is the current drive.
MyPath = CurDir           ' Returns "C:\WINDOWS\SYSTEM".
MyPath = CurDir("C")         ' Returns "C:\WINDOWS\SYSTEM".
MyPath = CurDir("D")         ' Returns "D:\EXCEL".

' On the Macintosh.
' Drive letters are ignored. Path for current drive is returned.
' Assume current path on HD Drive is  "HD:MY FOLDER".
' Assume HD is the current drive.
' Drive MD also exists on the machine.
MyPath = CurDir           ' Returns "HD:MY FOLDER".
MyPath = CurDir("HD")        ' Returns "HD:MY FOLDER".
MyPath = CurDir("MD")        ' Returns "HD:MY FOLDER".
```

Currency Data Type

Currency variables are stored as 64-bit (8-byte) numbers in an integer format, scaled by 10,000 to give a fixed-point number with 15 digits to the left of the decimal point and 4 digits to the right. This representation provides a range of -922,337,203,685,477.5808 to 922,337,203,685,477.5807. The type-declaration character for **Currency** is @ (character code 64).

The **Currency** data type is useful for calculations involving money and for fixed-point calculations in which accuracy is particularly important.

See Also   **CCur** Function, **Def***type* Statements, **Long** Data Type.

CurrentArray Property

Applies To   Range.

Description   If this cell is part of an array, returns a Range that is the entire array. Read-only.

Syntax   *object*.**CurrentArray**

Elements   *object*
　　　　　　　　Required. A single cell to test.

See Also	**CurrentRegion** Property, **HasArray** Property.
Example	Assume that the active cell is A1 and that the active cell is part of an array that includes cells A1:A10. This example sets the object variable arrayRange to the range that represents the entire array that contains the active cell.

```
Set arrayRange = ActiveCell.CurrentArray
```

CurrentPage Property

Applies To	PivotField.
Description	Returns or sets the current page showing for the page field (only valid for page fields). Read-write.
Syntax	*object*.**CurrentPage**
Elements	*object* Required. The PivotField object.
Remarks	To set this property, set it to the name of the page. Set it to "All" to set all pages showing.
Example	This example sets the current page to the "1990" page.

```
ActiveCell.PivotTable.PivotFields("Year").CurrentPage = "1990"
```

CurrentRegion Property

Applies To	Range.
Description	Returns a Range that is the current region. The current region is a range bounded by any combination of blank rows and blank columns. Read-only.
Syntax	*object*.**CurrentRegion**
Elements	*object* Required. The range inside the region.
Remarks	This property is useful for many operations that automatically expand the selection to include the entire current region, such as the **AutoFormat** method.
See Also	**CurrentArray** Property.

Example   This example selects the current region.

```
Selection.CurrentRegion.Select
```

CustomListCount Property

Applies To   Application.

Description   Returns the number of defined custom lists (including built-in lists). Read-only.

Syntax   *object*.**CustomListCount**

Elements   *object*
                     Required. The Application object.

See Also   **AddCustomList** Method, **DeleteCustomList** Method, **GetCustomListNum**
                     Method, **GetCustomListContents** Method.

Example   This example displays the number of custom lists currently defined.

```
MsgBox "There are currently " & Application.CustomListCount & _
    " defined custom lists."
```

Cut Method

Applies To   Arc, Arcs, Button, Buttons, ChartObject, ChartObjects, CheckBox, CheckBoxes,
                     Drawing, DrawingObjects, Drawings, DropDown, DropDowns, EditBox,
                     EditBoxes, GroupBox, GroupBoxes, GroupObject, GroupObjects, Label, Labels,
                     Line, Lines, ListBox, ListBoxes, OLEObject, OLEObjects, OptionButton,
                     OptionButtons, Oval, Ovals, Picture, Pictures, Range, Rectangle, Rectangles,
                     ScrollBar, ScrollBars, Spinner, Spinners, TextBox, TextBoxes.

Description   Cuts the object to the Clipboard or to a specified destination.

Syntax   *object*.**Cut**(*destination*)

Elements   The **Cut** method has the following object qualifier and named arguments:

                     object
                     Required. The object to cut.

                     destination
                     Optional (used only with Range objects). Specifies the range where the object
                     should be pasted. If omitted, the object is cut to the Clipboard. The destination
                     range must be a single cell or an enlarged multiple of the range to be cut.

Remarks	The cut range must be made up of adjacent cells.
	Only embedded charts can be cut.
See Also	**Copy** Method, **Paste** Method.
Example	This example cuts a range and places it on the Clipboard.

```
Application.Range("A1:G37").Cut
```

CutCopyMode Property

Applies To	Application.
Description	Returns or sets the Cut or Copy mode status, as shown in the following lists. Read-write.

Return value	Description
False	Not in Cut or Copy mode
xlCopy	In Copy mode
xlCut	In Cut mode

Set value	Description
False	Cancels Cut or Copy mode and removes the moving border.
True	Cancels Cut or Copy mode and removes the moving border. In Microsoft Excel for the Macintosh, this also places the contents of the selection in the Macintosh clipboard.

Syntax	*object*.**CutCopyMode**
Elements	*object* Required. The Application object.
Example	This example places the contents of your selection (if there is one) in the clipboard in Microsoft Excel for the Macintosh.

```
cutCopyModeState = Application.CutCopyMode
If cutCopyModeState Then
    Application.CutCopyMode = True
End If
```

CVar Function

Description	Converts an expression to a **Variant**.
Syntax	**CVar**(*expression*)
Elements	The *expression* argument is any valid numeric or string expression.
Remarks	In general, you can document your code using the data type conversion functions to show that the result of some operation should be expressed as a particular data type rather than the default data type. For example, use **CVar** to force the result to be expressed as a **Variant**.
See Also	Data Type Summary.
Example	This example uses the **CVar** function to convert an expression to a **Variant**.

```
MyInt = 4534                     ' MyInt is an Integer.
MyVar = CVar(MyInt & "000")          ' MyVar contains 4534000.
```

CVErr Function

Description	Returns a **Variant** of subtype **Error** containing an error number specified by the user.
Syntax	**CVErr**(*errornumber*)
Elements	The *errornumber* argument is any valid error number.
Remarks	Use the **CVErr** function to create user-defined errors in user-created procedures. For example, if you create a function that accepts several arguments and normally returns a string, you can have your function evaluate the input arguments to ensure they are within acceptable range. If they are not, it is likely that your function will not return what you expect. In this event, **CVErr** allows you to return an error number that tells you what action to take.
	Note that implicit conversion of an **Error** is not allowed. For example, you can't directly assign the return value of **CVErr** to a non-**Variant** variable. However, you can perform an explicit conversion (using **CInt**, **CDbl**, and so on) of the value returned by **CVErr** and assign that to a variable of the appropriate data type.
See Also	Data Type Summary, **IsError** Function.

Example   This example uses the **CVErr** function to return an Error **Variant**. The user-defined function `CalculateDouble` returns an error if the argument passed to it isn't a number. **CVErr** is useful for returning user-defined errors from user-defined procedures. Use the **IsError** function to test if the value is an error.

```
                              ' Define CalculateDouble Function procedure.
Function CalculateDouble(Number)
    If IsNumeric(Number) Then
        CalculateDouble = Number * 2     ' Return result.
    Else
        CalculateDouble = CVErr(2001)    ' Return a user-defined error
    End If                               ' number.
End Function
```

Data Type Summary

The following table shows the supported data types, including their storage sizes and ranges.

Data type	Storage size	Range
Boolean	2 bytes	**True** or **False**.
Integer	2 bytes	-32,768 to 32,767.
Long (long integer)	4 bytes	-2,147,483,648 to 2,147,483,647.
Single (single-precision floating-point)	4 bytes	-3.402823E38 to -1.401298E-45 for negative values; 1.401298E-45 to 3.402823E38 for positive values.
Double (double-precision floating-point)	8 bytes	-1.79769313486232E308 to -4.94065645841247E-324 for negative values; 4.94065645841247E-324 to 1.79769313486232E308 for positive values.
Currency (scaled integer)	8 bytes	-922,337,203,685,477.5808 to 922,337,203,685,477.5807.
Date	8 bytes	January 1, 100 to December 31, 9999.
Object	4 bytes	Any **Object** reference.
String	1 byte per character	0 to approximately 2 billion (approximately 65,535 for Microsoft Windows version 3.1 and earlier).

Data type	Storage size	Range
Variant	16 bytes + 1 byte for each character	Any numeric value up to the range of a **Double** or any character text.
User-defined (using Type)	Number required by elements	The range of each element is the same as the range of its data type.

See Also

Boolean Data Type, **Currency** Data Type, **Date** Data Type, **Def***type* Statements, **Double** Data Type, **Integer** Data Type, **Long** Data Type, **Object** Data Type, **Single** Data Type, **String** Data Type, **Type** Statement, **Variant** Data Type.

DataBodyRange Property

Applies To   PivotTable.

Description   Returns the Range that contains the pivot table data area. Read-only.

Syntax   *object*.**DataBodyRange**

Elements   *object*
        Required. The PivotTable object.

See Also   **ColumnRange** Property, **DataLabelRange** Property, **PageRange** Property, **RowRange** Property.

Example   This example selects the active pivot table data.

```
ActiveCell.PivotTable.DataBodyRange.Select
```

DataEntryMode Property

Applies To   Application.

Description   Returns or sets Data Entry mode, as shown in the following list. When in Data Entry mode, you can enter data only in the unlocked cells of the currently selected range. Read-write.

Value	Meaning
xlOn	Data Entry mode on.
xlOff	Data Entry mode off.
xlStrict	Data Entry mode on, and ESC will not exit the Data Entry mode.

Syntax   *object*.**DataEntryMode**

Elements   *object*
                Required. The Application object.

Example   This example turns Data Entry mode off if it is on.

```
If (Application.DataEntryMode = xlOn) Or _
    (Application.DataEntryMode = xlStrict) Then
        Application.DataEntryMode = xlOff
End If
```

DataFields Method

Applies To   PivotTable.

Description   Returns a single pivot field (a PivotField object, Syntax 1) or a collection of the pivot fields (a PivotFields object, Syntax 2) which are currently showing as data fields. Read-only.

Syntax 1   *object*.**DataFields**(*index*)

Syntax 2   *object*.**DataFields**

Elements   The **DataFields** method has the following object qualifier and named arguments:

object
        Required. The PivotTable object.

index
        Required for Syntax 1. The name or number of the pivot field to return (can be an array to specify more than one).

See Also   **ColumnFields** Method, **HiddenFields** Method, **PageFields** Method, **PivotFields** Method, **RowFields** Method, **VisibleFields** Method.

Example

This example adds the active pivot table data field names to a list box.

```
For Each dtaField In ActiveCell.PivotTable.DataFields
    dataFieldListBox.AddItem(dtaField.Name)
Next
```

DataLabel Object

Description

A data label on a chart series, or a data label on a single point of a chart series.

DataLabel Property

Applies To

Point, Trendline.

Description

Returns the DataLabel associated with the point or trendline. Read-only.

Syntax

object.**DataLabel**

Elements

object
    Required. The Point or Trendline object.

See Also

ApplyDataLabels Method, **HasDataLabel** Property.

Example

This example turns on the data label for point seven on series three, and then sets the datalabel color.

```
With ActiveChart.SeriesCollection(3).Points(7)
    .HasDataLabel = True
    .ApplyDataLabels type:=xlValue
    .DataLabel.Font.Color = RBG(0, 0 ,255)
End With
```

DataLabelRange Property

Applies To

PivotTable.

Description

Returns the Range that contains the pivot table data field labels. Read-only.

Syntax

object.**DataLabelRange**

Elements	*object* Required. The PivotTable object.
See Also	**ColumnRange** Property, **DataBodyRange** Property, **PageRange** Property, **RowRange** Property.
Example	This example selects the data field labels in the active pivot table.

```
ActiveCell.PivotTable.DataLabelRange.Select
```

DataLabels Method

Applies To	Series.
Description	Returns a single data label (a DataLabel object, Syntax 1) or a collection of all data labels for the series (a DataLabels collection, Syntax 2).
Syntax 1	*object*.**DataLabels**(*index*)
Syntax 2	*object*.**DataLabels**
Elements	The **DataLabels** method has the following object qualifier and named arguments:

object
    Required. The Series object.

index
    Required for Syntax 1. The number of the data label.

Remarks	If the series has the Show Value option on for the data labels, the returned collection can contain up to one label for each point. Data labels can be turned on or off for individual points in the series.
	If the series is on an area chart and has the Show Label option on for the data labels, the returned collection contains only a single label, which is the label for the area series.
See Also	**DataLabel** Property.
Example	This example sets the data labels for series one to show their value and key.

```
With Charts(1).SeriesCollection(1).DataLabels
    .ShowLegendKey = True
    .Type = xlValue
End With
```

DataLabels Object

Description   A collection of all the DataLabel objects for the points on a series.

DataRange Property

Applies To   PivotField, PivotItem.

Description   Returns a Range as shown in the following table. Read-only.

Object	DataRange
Data field	Data contained in the field
Row, Column, or Page field	Items in the field
Item	Data qualified by the item

Syntax   *object*.**DataRange**

Elements   *object*
                       Required. The PivotField or PivotItem object.

Examples   This example selects the data in the field (if the field is a data field), or the items in the field (if the field is a row, column, or page field).

```
ActiveCell.PivotField.DataRange.Select
```

This example selects the data qualified by the active pivot item.

```
ActiveCell.PivotItem.DataRange.Select
```

DataSeries Method

Applies To   Range.

Description   Creates a data series in the range.

Syntax   *object*.**DataSeries**(*rowcol, type, date, step, stop, trend*)

Elements   The **DataSeries** method has the following object qualifier and named arguments:

object
Required. Where the data series will be created.

rowcol
Optional. Can be **xlRows** or **xlColumns** to enter the data series in rows or columns, respectively. If omitted, the size and shape of the range is used.

type
Optional. Can be **xlLinear**, **xlGrowth**, **xlChronological**, or **xlAutoFill**. If omitted, it is **xlLinear**.

date
Optional. If the *type* argument is **xlChronological**, this indicates the date unit by which to step, either **xlDay**, **xlWeekday**, **xlMonth**, or **xlYear**. If omitted, it is **xlDay**.

step
Optional. The step value for the series. If omitted, it is assumed to be 1.

stop
Optional. The stop value for the series. If omitted, the method fills to the end of the range.

trend
Optional. If **True**, the method creates a linear or growth type of trend. If **False** or omitted, the method creates a standard data series.

Example   This example creates a series of twelve dates. The series contains the first day of every month in 1994 and is created in the range A1:A12.

```
Set dateRange = ActiveSheet.Range(Cells(1, 1), Cells(12, 1))
ActiveSheet.Cells(1, 1).Formula = "1-JAN-1994"
dateRange.DataSeries type:=xlChronological, date:=xlMonth
```

DataType Property

Applies To   PivotField.

Description   Returns a constant describing the type of data in the pivot field. Can be **xlText**, **xlNumber**, or **xlDate**. Read-only.

Syntax   *object*.**DataType**

Elements   *object*
Required. The PivotField object.

Example   This example displays a message box if the active field contains text.

```
If ActiveCell.PivotField.DataType = xlText Then
    MsgBox "This field contains text."
End If
```

Date Data Type

Date variables are stored as 64-bit (8-byte) numbers that represent dates ranging from 1 January 100 to 31 December 9999 and times from 0:00:00 to 23:59:59. Any recognizable literal date values can be assigned to **Date** variables. Literal dates must be enclosed within number sign characters (#). For example, #January 1, 1993# or #1 Jan 93#.

Date variables display dates according to the short date format recognized by your computer. Times display according to the time format (either 12- or 24-hour) recognized by your computer.

When other numeric data types are converted to **Date**, values to the left of the decimal represent date information while values to the right of the decimal represent time. Midnight is 0 and midday is .5. Negative whole numbers represent dates before 30 December 1899. When **Date** variables are converted to other numeric data types, they appear only as numbers.

See Also   **CDate** Function, Data Type Summary, **Def***type* Statements, **Double** Data Type, **Variant** Data Type.

Date Function

Description   Returns the current system date.

Syntax   **Date**

Remarks   To set the system date, use the **Date** statement.

See Also   **CDate** Function, **Date** Statement, **Format** Function, **Now** Function, **Time** Function, **Time** Statement.

Example   This example uses the **Date** function to return the current system date.

```
MyDate = Date    ' MyDate contains current system date.
```

Date Statement

Description   Sets the current system date.

Syntax   **Date** = *date*

Elements   For MS-DOS® computers, the *date* argument must be a date from January 1, 1980 through December 31, 2099, or an error occurs. For the Macintosh, *date* must be a date from January 1, 1904 through December 31, 2040. For all other systems, *date* is limited to dates from January 1, 100 through December 31, 9999.

Remarks

Note If you use the **Date** statement to set the date on computers using versions of MS-DOS earlier than version 3.3, the change remains in effect only until you change it again or turn off your computer. Many computers have a battery-powered CMOS RAM that retains date and time information when the computer is turned off. However, to permanently change the date on computers running earlier versions of MS-DOS, you may have to use your Setup disk or perform some equivalent action. Refer to the documentation for your particular system.

See Also   **Date** Function, **Time** Function, **Time** Statement.

Example   This example uses the **Date** statement to set the computer system date.

```
' In the development environment, the date literal will display in short
' format using the locale settings of your code.

MyDate = #February 12, 1985#        ' Assign a date.
Date = MyDate                       ' Change system date.
```

Date1904 Property

Applies To   Workbook.

Description   **True** if this workbook uses the 1904 date system. Read-write.

Syntax   *object*.**Date1904**

Elements   *object*
                Required. The Workbook object.

Example   This example causes Microsoft Excel to use the 1904 date system for the active workbook.

```
ActiveWorkbook.Date1904 = True
```

DateSerial Function

Description   Returns a date for a specified year, month, and day.

Syntax   **DateSerial(***year,month,day***)**

Elements   The **DateSerial** function syntax has these named-argument parts:

Part	Description
year	Number between 100 and 9999, inclusive, or a numeric expression.
month	Number between 1 and 12, inclusive, or a numeric expression.
day	Number between 1 and 31, inclusive, or a numeric expression.

Remarks   To specify a date, such as December 31, 1991, the range of numbers for each **DateSerial** argument should be in the normally accepted range for the unit; that is; 1-31 for days and 1-12 for months. However, you can also specify relative dates for each argument using any numeric expression that represents some number of days, months, or years before or after a certain date.

The following example uses numeric expressions instead of absolute date numbers. Here the **DateSerial** function returns a date that is the day before the first day (1 - 1) of two months before August (8 - 2) of 10 years before 1990 (1990 - 10); in other words, May, 31, 1980.

```
DateSerial(1990 - 10, 8 - 2, 1 - 1)
```

For the *year* argument, values between 0 and 99, inclusive, are interpreted as the years 1900-1999. For all other *year* arguments, use a complete four-digit year (for example, 1800).

If the date specified by the three arguments, either directly or by expression, falls outside the acceptable range of dates, an error occurs.

See Also   **Date** Function, **Date** Statement, **DateValue** Function, **Day** Function, **Month** Function, **Now** Function, **TimeSerial** Function, **TimeValue** Function, **Weekday** Function, **Year** Function.

Example   This example uses the **DateSerial** function to return the date for the specified year, month and day.

```
' MyDate contains the date for February 12, 1969.
MyDate = DateSerial(1969, 2, 12)        ' Return a date.
```

DateValue Function

Description   Returns a date.

Syntax   **DateValue(*date*)**

Elements   The *date* named argument is normally a string expression representing a date from January 1, 100 through December 31, 9999. However, *date* can also be any expression that can represent a date, a time, or both a date and time, in that range.

Remarks   If the *date* argument includes time information, **DateValue** doesn't return it. However, if *date* includes invalid time information (such as "89:98"), an error occurs.

If *date* is a string that includes only numbers separated by valid date separators, **DateValue** recognizes the order for month, day, and year according to the Short Date format you specified for your system. **DateValue** also recognizes unambiguous dates that contain month names, either in long or abbreviated form. For example, in addition to recognizing 12/30/1991 and 12/30/91, **DateValue** also recognizes December 30, 1991 and Dec 30, 1991.

If the year part of *date* is omitted, **DateValue** uses the current year from your computer's system date.

See Also   **CDate** Function, **Date** Function, **Date** Statement, **DateSerial** Function, **Day** Function, **Month** Function, **Now** Function, **TimeSerial** Function, **TimeValue** Function, **Weekday** Function, **Year** Function.

Example   This example uses the **DateValue** function to convert a string to a date. In general, it is bad programming practice to hard code dates/times as strings as shown in this example. Use date literals instead.

```
MyDate = DateValue("February 12, 1969")        ' Return a date.
```

Day Function

Description   Returns a whole number between 1 and 31, inclusive, representing the day of the month.

Syntax	**Day**(*date*)
Elements	The *date* named argument is limited to a date or numbers and strings, in any combination, that can represent a date. If *date* contains no valid data, **Null** is returned.
See Also	**Date** Function, **Date** Statement, **Hour** Function, **Minute** Function, **Month** Function, **Now** Function, **Second** Function, **Weekday** Function, **Year** Function.
Example	This example uses the **Day** function to obtain the day of the month from a specified date.

```
' In the development environment, the date literal will display in short
' format using the locale settings of your code.
MyDate = #February 12, 1969#          ' Assign a date.
MyDay = Day(MyDate)                    ' MyDay contains 12.
```

DDEAppReturnCode Property

Applies To	Application.
Description	Returns the application-specific DDE return code that was contained in the last DDE acknowledge message received by Microsoft Excel. Read-only.
Syntax	*object*.**DDEAppReturnCode**
Elements	*object* Optional. The Application object.
Example	This example sets the variable appErrorCode to the DDE return code.

```
appErrorCode = Application.DDEAppReturnCode
```

DDEExecute Method

Applies To	Application.
Description	Runs a command or takes other actions in another application via the specified DDE channel.
Syntax	*object*.**DDEExecute**(*channel, string*)

Elements   The **DDEExecute** method has the following object qualifier and named arguments:

object
  Optional. The Application object.

channel
  Required. The channel number returned by the **DDEInitiate** method.

string
  Required. The message defined in the receiving application.

Remarks   An error occurs if the method call is not successful.

The **DDEExecute** method is designed to send commands to another application. You can also use it to send keystrokes to an application, although the **SendKeys** method is the preferred way to send keystrokes. The *string* argument can specify any single key, or any key combined with ALT, CTRL, or SHIFT, or any combination of those keys (in Microsoft Excel for Windows) or COMMAND, CTRL, OPTION, or SHIFT or any combination of those keys (in Microsoft Excel for the Macintosh). Each key is represented by one or more characters, such as "a" for the character a, or "{ENTER}" for the ENTER key.

To specify characters that aren't displayed when you press the key, such as ENTER or TAB, use the codes shown in the following table. Each code in the table represents one key on the keyboard.

Key	Code
BACKSPACE	"{BACKSPACE}" or "{BS}"
BREAK	"{BREAK}"
CAPS LOCK	"{CAPSLOCK}"
CLEAR	"{CLEAR}"
DELETE OR DEL	"{DELETE}" or "{DEL}"
DOWN ARROW	"{DOWN}"
END	"{END}"
ENTER (NUMERIC KEYPAD)	"{ENTER}"
ENTER	"~" (tilde)
ESC	"{ESCAPE} or {ESC}"
HELP	"{HELP}"
HOME	"{HOME}"
INS	"{INSERT}"
LEFT ARROW	"{LEFT}"
NUM LOCK	"{NUMLOCK}"

Key	Code
PAGE DOWN	"{PGDN}"
PAGE UP	"{PGUP}"
RETURN	"{RETURN}"
RIGHT ARROW	"{RIGHT}"
SCROLL LOCK	"{SCROLLLOCK}"
TAB	"{TAB}"
UP ARROW	"{UP}"
F1 THROUGH F15	"{F1}" through "{F15}"

In Microsoft Excel for Windows, you can also specify keys combined with SHIFT and/or CTRL and/or ALT. In Microsoft Excel for the Macintosh, you can also specify keys combined with SHIFT and/or CTRL and/or OPTION and/or COMMAND. To specify a key combined with another key or keys, use the following table.

To combine with	Precede the key code by
SHIFT	"+" (plus sign)
CTRL	"^" (caret)
ALT OR OPTION	"%" (percent sign)
COMMAND	"*" (asterisk)

Example

This example shows how to open a channel to Word for Windows, open the Word document FORMLETR.DOC, and then send the Print command from the File menu to Word.

```
channelNumber = Application.DDEInitiate("WinWord", "FORMLETR.DOC")
Application.DDEExecute channelNumber, "[FILEPRINT]"
Application.DDETerminate channelNumber
```

DDEInitiate Method

Applies To   Application.

Description   Opens a DDE channel to an application.

Syntax   *object*.**DDEInitiate**(*app, topic*)

Elements   The **DDEInitiate** method has the following object qualifier and named arguments.

object
   Optional. The Application object.

app
> Required. A string containing the application name.

topic
> Required. A string that describes something in the application to which you are opening a channel, usually a document of that application.

Remarks   If successful, the **DDEInitiate** method returns the number of the open channel. All subsequent DDE functions use this number to specify the channel.

Example   This example shows how to open a channel to Word for Windows, open the Word document FORMLETR.DOC, and then send the Print command from the File menu to Word.

```
channelNumber = Application.DDEInitiate("WinWord", "FORMLETR.DOC")
Application.DDEExecute channelNumber, "[FILEPRINT]"
Application.DDETerminate channelNumber
```

DDEPoke Method

Applies To   Application.

Description   Sends data to an application.

Syntax   *object*.**DDEPoke(*channel, item, data*)**

Elements   The **DDEPoke** method has the following object qualifier and named arguments.

object
> Optional. The Application object.

channel
> Required. The channel number returned by the **DDEInitiate** method.

item
> Required. The item to which the data is to be sent.

data
> Required. The data to send to the application.

Remarks   An error occurs if the method call is not successful.

Example   This example shows how to open a channel to Word for Windows, open the Word document SALES.DOC, and then insert the contents of cell A1 at the beginning of the document.

```
channelNumber = Application.DDEInitiate("WinWord", "SALES.DOC")
Set rangeToPoke = Cells(1, 1)
Application.DDEPoke channelNumber, "\StartOfDoc", rangeToPoke
Application.DDETerminate channelNumber
```

DDERequest Method

Applies To   Application.

Description   Requests information from the specified application. This method always returns an array; for more information, see the example.

Syntax   *object*.**DDERequest**(*channel, item*)

Elements   The **DDERequest** method has the following object qualifier and named arguments.

object
    Optional. The Application object.

channel
    Required. The channel number returned by the **DDEInitiate** method.

item
    Required. The item to request.

Example   This example shows how to open a channel to the System topic in Word for Windows, and then use the Topics item to return a list of all open documents. The list is returned in column A.

```
channelNumber = Application.DDEInitiate("WinWord", "System")
returnList = Application.DDERequest(channelNumber, "Topics")
For i = LBound(returnList) To UBound(returnList)
    Cells(i, 1).Formula = returnList(i)
Next i
Application.DDETerminate channelNumber
```

DDETerminate Method

Applies To   Application.

Description   Closes a channel to another application.

Syntax   *object*.**DDETerminate**(*channel*)

Elements   The **DDETerminate** method has the following object qualifier and named arguments.

object
    Optional. The Application object.

channel
Required. The channel number returned by the **DDEInitiate** method.

Example
This example shows how to open a channel to Word for Windows, open the Word document FORMLETR.DOC, send the Print command from the File menu to Word, and then close the channel to Word..

```
channelNumber = Application.DDEInitiate("WinWord", "FORMLETR.DOC")
Application.DDEExecute channelNumber, "[FILEPRINT]"
Application.DDETerminate channelNumber
```

Debug Object

Description
The **Debug** object is accessed with the keyword **Debug**, and is used to send output to the Debug window at run time.

See Also
Debug Window.

Declare Statement

Description
Used at module level to declare references to external procedures in a dynamic-link library (DLL) or Macintosh code resource.

Syntax 1
[**Public** | **Private**] **Declare Sub** *name* [**CDecl**] **Lib** "*libname*" [**Alias** "*aliasname*"][([*arglist*])]

Syntax 2
[**Public** | **Private**] **Declare Function** *name* [**CDecl**] **Lib** "*libname*" [**Alias** "*aliasname*"] [([*arglist*])][**As** *type*]

Elements
The **Declare** statement syntax has these parts:

Part	Description
Public	Used to declare procedures that are available to all other procedures in all modules.
Private	Used to declare procedures that are available only within the module where the declaration is made.
Sub	Indicates that the procedure doesn't return a value.
Function	Indicates that the procedure returns a value that can be used in an expression.
name	Any valid procedure name.

Part	Description
CDecl	For the Macintosh only. Indicates that the procedure uses C language argument order, naming conventions, and calling conventions.
Lib	Indicates that a DLL or code resource contains the procedure being declared. The **Lib** clause is required for all declarations.
libname	Name of the DLL or code resource that contains the declared procedure.
Alias	Indicates that the procedure being called has another name in the DLL or is in a Macintosh code resource. This is useful when the external procedure name is the same as a keyword. You can also use **Alias** when a DLL procedure has the same name as a **Public** variable or constant or any other procedure in the same scope. **Alias** is also useful if any characters in the DLL procedure name aren't allowed in names.
aliasname	Name of the procedure in the DLL or code resource.
	In Microsoft Windows, if the first character is not a #, *aliasname* is the name of the procedure's entry point in the DLL. If # is the first character, all characters that follow must indicate the ordinal number of the procedure's entry point.
	On the Macintosh, the syntax to specify the code resource type is as follows:
	"[*resourcetype*]$[*resourcename*]"
	The *resourcetype* is any valid 4-character constant. If omitted, the default *resourcetype* is CODE. The *resourcename* is the procedure name in the code resource. If *resourcename* is omitted, it is assumed to be the same as *name*.
arglist	List of variables representing arguments that are passed to the procedure when it is called.
type	Data type of the value returned by a **Function** procedure; may be **Boolean**, **Integer**, **Long**, **Currency**, **Single**, **Double**, **Date**, **String** (variable length only), **Object**, **Variant**, a user-defined type, or an object type.

The *arglist* argument has the following syntax and parts:

[**Optional**][**ByVal** | **ByRef**][**ParamArray**] *varname*[( )][**As** *type*]

Part	Description
Optional	Indicates that an argument is not required. If used, all subsequent arguments in *arglist* must also be optional and declared using the **Optional** keyword. All **Optional** arguments must be **Variant**. **Optional** can't be used for any argument if **ParamArray** is used.
ByVal	Indicates that the argument is passed by value.
ByRef	Indicates that the argument is passed by reference.
ParamArray	Used only as the last argument in *arglist* to indicate that the final argument is an **Optional** array of **Variant** elements. The **ParamArray** keyword allows you to provide an arbitrary number of arguments. May not be used with **ByVal**, **ByRef**, or **Optional**.
varname	Name of the variable representing the argument being passed to the procedure; follows standard variable naming conventions.
type	Data type of the argument passed to the procedure; may be **Boolean**, **Integer**, **Long**, **Currency**, **Single**, **Double**, **Date**, **String** (variable length only), **Object**, **Variant**, a user-defined type, or an object type.

Remarks

For **Function** procedures, the data type of the procedure determines the data type it returns. You can use an **As** clause following the *arglist* to specify the return type of the function. Within *arglist* you can use an **As** clause to specify the data type of any of the arguments passed to the procedure. In addition to specifying any of the standard data types, you can specify **As Any** in the *arglist* to inhibit type checking and allow any data type to be passed to the procedure.

Empty parentheses indicate that the **Sub** or **Function** procedure has no arguments and that arguments should be checked to ensure that none are passed. In the following example, First takes no arguments. If you use arguments in a call to First, an error occurs:

```
Declare Sub First Lib "MyLib" ()
```

If you include an argument list, the number and type of arguments are checked each time the procedure is called. In the following example, First takes one **Long** argument:

```
Declare Sub First Lib "MyLib" (X As Long)
```

Note You can't have fixed-length strings in the argument list of a **Declare** statement because only variable-length strings can be passed to procedures. Fixed-length strings can appear as procedure arguments, but they are converted to variable-length strings before being passed.

See Also   **Call** Statement.

Example   This example shows how the **Declare** statement is used at the module level to declare a reference to an external procedure in a dynamic-link library (DLL) or Macintosh code resource.

```
' In Microsoft Windows.
Declare Sub MessageBeep Lib "User" (ByVal N As Integer)

' On the Macintosh.
Declare Sub MessageAlert Lib "MyHd:MyAlert" Alias "MyAlert" (ByVal N _
As Integer)
```

DefaultButton Property

Applies To   Button, Buttons, DialogSheet, DrawingObjects.

Description   Applies only to buttons in a user-defined dialog.

For Button objects, this property is **True** if the button is the default button for a user-defined dialog. The default button is indicated by a thick border. When the user presses the ENTER key, the default button is selected, and Microsoft Excel runs the macro identified by the button's **OnAction** property. Read-write.

For DialogSheet objects, this property is the name of the button that is the default while a dialog is running. Read-write.

Syntax   *object*.**DefaultButton**

Elements   *object*
    Required. The object to which this property applies.

Remarks   When the dialog is not displayed, this property can be used with the Button object to return or set the initial default button (the default button when the dialog is first displayed). Only one button on the dialog can be the default button. Setting this property resets the property for all other buttons on the dialog sheet.

When the dialog is displayed, use this property in an event procedure to return or set the current default button. In this case, the property is the button ID as a string, and the property is applied to the DialogSheet object. You cannot apply this property to a Button object when the dialog is displayed.

See Also   **CancelButton** Property.

Examples   This example sets button four to be the initial default button. You can only set the initial default button when the dialog is not running.

```
ActiveWorkbook.DialogSheets(1).Buttons(4).DefaultButton = True
```

This example sets button five to be the current default button on dialog sheet one. You can only set the current default button while the dialog is running.

```
With ActiveWorkbook.DialogSheets(1)
    .DefaultButton = .Buttons(5).Name
End With
```

DefaultFilePath Property

Applies To   Application.

Description   Returns or sets the default path Microsoft Excel uses when it opens files. Read-write.

Syntax   *object*.**DefaultFilePath**

Elements   *object*
    Required. The Application object.

Example   This example displays the current default file path.

```
MsgBox "The current default file path is " & _
    Application.DefaultFilePath
```

Def*type* Statements

Description   Used at module level to set the default data type for variables and **Function** procedures whose names start with the specified characters.

Syntax   **DefBool** *letterrange*[*,letterrange*] . . .

DefInt *letterrange*[*,letterrange*] . . .

DefLng *letterrange*[*,letterrange*] . . .

DefCur *letterrange*[*,letterrange*] . . .

DefSng *letterrange*[*,letterrange*] . . .

DefDbl *letterrange*[*,letterrange*] . . .

DefDate *letterrange*[,*letterrange*] . . .

DefStr *letterrange*[,*letterrange*] . . .

DefObj *letterrange*[,*letterrange*] . . .

DefVar *letterrange*[,*letterrange*] . . .

Elements

The argument *letterrange* has the following syntax:

letter1[-*letter2*]

The arguments *letter1* and *letter2* specify the name range for which you can set a default data type. Each argument represents the first letter of the variable or **Function** procedure name and can be any letter of the alphabet. The case of letters in *letterrange* isn't significant.

Remarks

The statement name determines the data type:

Statement	Data Type
DefBool	**Boolean**
DefInt	**Integer**
DefLng	**Long**
DefCur	**Currency**
DefSng	**Single**
DefDbl	**Double**
DefDate	**Date**
DefStr	**String**
DefObj	**Object**
DefVar	**Variant**

For example, in the following program fragment, `Message` is a string variable:

```
DefStr A-Q
. . .
Message = "Out of stack space."
```

A **Def***type* statement affects only the module where it is used. For example, a **DefInt** statement in one module affects only the default data type of variables and **Function** procedures declared in that module; the default data type of variables in other modules is unaffected. If not explicitly declared with a **Def***type* statement, the default data type for all variables and all **Function** procedures is **Variant**.

When you specify a letter range, it usually defines the data type for variables that begin with letters in the lower 128 characters of the character set. However, when you specify the letter range A-Z, you set the default to the specified data type for all variables, including any that begin with international characters from the extended part of the character set (128-255).

Once the range A-Z has been specified, you can't further redefine any subranges of variables using **Def**_type_ statements. In fact, once a range has been specified, if you include a previously defined letter in another **Def**_type_ statement, an error occurs. However, you can explicitly specify the data type of any variable, defined or not, using a **Dim** statement with an **As** _type_ clause. For example, you can use the following code at module level to define a variable as a **Double** even though the default data type is **Integer**:

```
DefInt A-Z
Dim TaxRate As Double
```

Def_type_ statements don't affect elements of user-defined types since they must be explicitly declared.

See Also   Character Set, **Let** Statement.

Example   This example shows various uses of the **Def**_type_ statements to set default data types of variables and function procedures whose names start with specified characters. The default data type can be overridden only by explicit assignment using the **Dim** statement. **Def**_type_ statements can only be used at the module-level.

```
' Variable names beginning with A through K default to Integer.
DefInt A-K

' Variable names beginning with L through Z default to String.
DefStr L-Z

CalcVar = 4                  ' Initialize Integer.
StringVar = "Hello there"      ' Initialize String.
AnyVar = "Hello"               ' Causes "Type mismatch" error.
Dim Calc As Double             ' Explicitly set the type to Double.
Calc = 2.3455             ' Assign a Double.

' Deftype statements also apply to function procedures.
CalcNum = ATestFunction(4)       ' Call user-defined function.

' ATestFunction function procedure definition.
Function ATestFunction(INumber)
    ATestFunction = INumber * 2 ' Return value is an integer.
End Function
```

Delete Method

Applies To Arc, Arcs, Axis, AxisTitle, Button, Buttons, Characters, Chart, ChartObject, ChartObjects, Charts, ChartTitle, CheckBox, CheckBoxes, DataLabel, DataLabels, DialogSheet, DialogSheets, DownBars, Drawing, DrawingObjects, Drawings, DropDown, DropDowns, DropLines, EditBox, EditBoxes, ErrorBars, Gridlines, GroupBox, GroupBoxes, GroupObject, GroupObjects, HiLoLines, Label, Labels, Legend, LegendEntry, LegendKey, Line, Lines, ListBox, ListBoxes, Menu, MenuBar, MenuItem, Module, Modules, Name, OLEObject, OLEObjects, OptionButton, OptionButtons, Oval, Ovals, Picture, Pictures, Point, Range, Rectangle, Rectangles, Scenario, ScrollBar, ScrollBars, Series, SeriesLines, Sheets, SoundNote, Spinner, Spinners, Style, TextBox, TextBoxes, TickLabels, Toolbar, ToolbarButton, Trendline, UpBars, Worksheet, Worksheets.

Description Deletes the object. Syntax 2 applies only to Range objects.

Syntax 1 *object*.**Delete**

Syntax 2 *object*.**Delete**(*shift*)

Elements *object*
Required. The object to which this method applies. Syntax 2 applies only to Range objects.

shift
Optional. Specifies how to shift cells to replace the deleted cells (either **xlToLeft**, or **xlUp**). If this argument is omitted, Microsoft Excel selects a default based on the shape of the range.

Remarks Attempts to delete a built-in Toolbar or MenuBar object will fail, but will not cause an error. This allows you to use a **For Each** loop to delete all custom tool bars or menu bars.

Deleting a Point or LegendKey deletes the entire series.

Example This example deletes oval one on the active sheet.

```
ActiveSheet.Ovals(1).Delete
```

DeleteChartAutoFormat Method

Applies To Application.

Description Removes a custom chart autoformat from the list of available chart autoformats.

Syntax	*object*.**DeleteChartAutoFormat(***name***)**
Elements	The **DeleteChartAutoFormat** method has the following object qualifier and named arguments:

object
　　Required. The Application object.

name
　　Required. Specifies the name of the custom autoformat to remove.

See Also	**AddChartAutoFormat** Method, **SetDefaultChart** Method.
Example	This example deletes the "Presentation Chart" custom autoformat.

```
Application.DeleteChartAutoFormat name:="Presentation Chart"
```

DeleteCustomList Method

Applies To	Application.
Description	Deletes a custom list.
Syntax	*object*.**DeleteCustomList(***listNum***)**
Elements	The **DeleteCustomList** method has the following object qualifier and named arguments:

object
　　Required. The Application object.

listNum
　　Required. The custom list number. This number must be greater than or equal to five (Microsoft Excel has four built-in custom lists that cannot be deleted).

Remarks	This method generates an error if the list number is less than five or a matching custom list does not exist.
See Also	**AddCustomList** Method, **CustomListCount** Property, **GetCustomListNum** Method, **GetCustomListContents** Method.
Example	This example deletes a custom list.

```
n = Application.GetCustomListNum(Array("cogs", "sprockets", _
    "widgets", "gizmos"))
Application.DeleteCustomList n
```

DeleteNumberFormat Method

Applies To   Workbook.

Description   Deletes a custom number format from the workbook.

Syntax   *object*.**DeleteNumberFormat**(*numberFormat*)

Elements   The **DeleteNumberFormat** method has the following object qualifier and named arguments:

object
　　Required. The Workbook object.

numberFormat
　　Required. A string that names the number format to delete.

Example   This example deletes the number format "000-00-0000" from the active workbook.

```
ActiveWorkbook.DeleteNumberFormat("000-00-0000")
```

Delivery Property

Applies To   RoutingSlip.

Description   Returns or sets the delivery method used when routing (one of **xlOneAfterAnother** or **xlAllAtOnce**). Read-write before routing starts, read-only once routing is in progress.

Syntax   *object*.**Delivery**

Elements   *object*
　　Required. The RoutingSlip object.

Example   This example sends BOOK1.XLS to three recipients, one after the other.

```
Workbooks("BOOK1.XLS").HasRoutingSlip = True
With Workbooks("BOOK1.XLS").RoutingSlip
    .Delivery = xlOneAfterAnother
    .Recipients = Array("Adam Bendel", "Jean Selva", "Bernard Gabor")
    .Subject = "Here is BOOK1.XLS"
    .Message = "Here is the workbook. What do you think?"
End With
Workbooks("BOOK1.XLS").Route
```

Dependents Property

Applies To   Range.

Description   Returns a Range that contains all of the dependents of a cell. This may be a multiple selection (a union of Range objects) if there is more than one dependent. Read-only.

Syntax   *object*.**Dependents**

Elements   *object*
         Required. Returns dependents for this cell.

See Also   **DirectDependents** Property, **DirectPrecedents** Property, **Precedents** Property, **ShowDependents** Method.

Example   This example selects the dependents of the active cell.

```
ActiveCell.Dependents.Select
```

DepthPercent Property

Applies To   Chart.

Description   Returns or sets the depth of a 3-D chart as a percentage of the chart width (between 20 and 2000 percent). Read-write.

Syntax   *object*.**DepthPercent**

Elements   *object*
         Required. The Chart object.

See Also   **HeightPercent** Property.

Example   This example sets the chart depth to 50 percent of its width.

```
Charts(1).DepthPercent = 50
```

Deselect Method

Applies To   Chart.

Description   Cancels the selection for the specified chart.

Syntax	*object*.**Deselect**
Elements	*object* Required. The Chart object.
See Also	**Select** Method, **Selection** Property.
Example	This example cancels the selection for chart one.

```
Charts(1).Deselect
```

Dialog Object

Description   A built-in Microsoft Excel dialog box.

DialogBox Method

Applies To   Range.

Description   Displays a dialog box defined by a dialog-box definition table on a Microsoft Excel version 4.0 macro sheet. Returns the number of the chosen control, or **False** if the user chooses the Cancel button.

Syntax   *object*.**DialogBox**

Elements   *object*
Required. A dialog-box definition table.

Remark   This method is included for backward compatibility with the Microsoft Excel version 4.0 macro language.

Example   This example runs a Microsoft Excel version 4.0 dialog box and then displays the return value in a message box. The dialogRange variable refers to the dialog-box definition table on the Microsoft Excel version 4.0 macro sheet.

```
result = dialogRange.DialogBox
If Not result Then
    ' user cancelled the dialog box
Else
    ' result is position number of chosen control
End If
```

DialogFrame Object

Description   The dialog frame provides the backdrop for user-defined dialogs. It has no
                    formatting properties, only a position, a size, and a caption. Only one dialog frame
                    exists per dialog sheet, and it cannot be deleted or moved in front of any other
                    graphic object. Dialog frames do not exist on the worksheet.

DialogFrame Property

Applies To   DialogSheet.

Description   Returns the DialogFrame associated with this dialog sheet. Read only.

Syntax   *object*.**DialogFrame**

Elements   *object*
                       Required. The DialogSheet object.

Example   This example sets the height and width of the dialog frame.

```
With ActiveWorkbook.DialogSheets(1).DialogFrame
    .Height = 144
    .Width = 196
End With
```

Dialogs Method

Applies To   Application.

Description   Returns a single built-in dialog (a Dialog object, Syntax 1) or a collection of all
                    built-in dialogs (a Dialogs object, Syntax 2). Read-only.

Syntax 1   *object*.**Dialogs(*index*)**

Syntax 2   *object*.**Dialogs**

Elements   The **Dialogs** method has the following object qualifier and named arguments:

                    object
                       Required. The Application object.

index

Required for Syntax 1. A built-in constant. See the following Remarks section for more information.

Remarks

Using the **Dialogs** and **Show** methods, you can display approximately 200 built-in dialog boxes. Each dialog box has a constant assigned to it; these constants all begin with xlDialog. You can use the Object Browser to browse the list of dialog box constants. From the View menu, choose Object Browser, select the Microsoft Excel library, and then select the Constants object. Scroll the list in the Methods/Properties box until you find the constants that begin with xlDialog. The constants correspond to dialog box names; for example, the constant for the Find File dialog box is **xlDialogFindFile**.

The **Dialogs** method may fail if you try to show a dialog box in an incorrect context. For example, to display the Format Data Labels dialog box (using the Visual Basic expression **Application.Dialogs(xlDialogDataLabel).Show**), the active sheet must be a chart, otherwise the method fails.

See Also

Show Method.

Example

This example displays the dialog box for the Open command on the File menu.

```
Application.Dialogs(xlDialogOpen).Show
```

Dialogs Object

Description   A collection of Dialog objects.

DialogSheet Object

Description   A dialog sheet in a workbook.

DialogSheets Method

Applies To   Application, Workbook.

Description   Returns a single dialog sheet (a DialogSheet object, Syntax 1) or a collection of all dialog sheets (a DialogSheets object, Syntax 2) in the workbook. Read-only.

Syntax 1	*object*.**DialogSheets(***index***)**
Syntax 2	*object*.**DialogSheets**
Elements	The **DialogSheets** method has the following object qualifier and named arguments:

object
> Optional for Application, required for Workbook. The object that contains dialog sheets.

index
> Required for Syntax 1. The name or number of the dialog sheet to return.

Remarks	Using this method with no object qualifier is a shortcut for **ActiveWorkbook.DialogSheets**.
Example	This example displays the number of dialog sheets in the active workbook.

```
MsgBox "There are " & ActiveWorkbook.DialogSheets.Count & _
    " dialog sheets in this workbook."
```

DialogSheets Object

Description   A collection of DialogSheet objects.

Dim Statement

Description   Declares variables and allocates storage space.

Syntax   **Dim** *varname*[([*subscripts*])][**As** *type*][,*varname*[([*subscripts*])][**As** *type*]] . . .

Elements

The **Dim** statement syntax has these parts:

Part	Description
varname	Name of the variable; follows standard variable naming conventions.
subscripts	Dimensions of an array variable; up to 60 multiple dimensions may be declared. The *subscripts* argument uses the following syntax:
	[*lower* **To**] *upper* [,[*lower* **To**] *upper*] **. . .**
type	Data type of the variable; may be **Boolean**, **Integer**, **Long**, **Currency**, **Single**, **Double**, **Date**, **String** (for variable-length strings), **String** * *length* (for fixed-length strings), **Object**, **Variant**, a user-defined type, or an object type. Use a separate **As** *type* clause for each variable you declare.

Remarks

Variables declared with **Dim** at the module level are available to all procedures within the module. At the procedure level, variables are available only within the procedure.

Use the **Dim** statement at module or procedure level to declare the data type or object type of a variable. For example, the following statement declares a variable as an **Integer**.

```
Dim NumberOfEmployees As Integer
```

If you do not specify a data type or object type, and there is no **Def***type* statement in the module, the variable is **Variant** by default.

When variables are initialized, a numeric variable is initialized to 0, a variable-length string is initialized to a zero-length string, and a fixed-length string is filled with zeros. **Variant** variables are initialized to **Empty**. Each element of a user-defined type variable is initialized as if it was a separate variable. A variable that refers to an object must be assigned an existing object using the **Set** statement before it can be used. Until it is assigned an object, the declared object variable has the special value **Nothing**, which indicates that it does not refer to any particular instance of an object.

You can also use the **Dim** statement with empty parentheses to declare dynamic arrays. After declaring a dynamic array, use the **ReDim** statement within a procedure to define the number of dimensions and elements in the array. If you try to redeclare a dimension for an array variable whose size was explicitly specified in a **Private**, **Public** or **Dim** statement, an error occurs.

Tip When you use the **Dim** statement in a procedure, it is a generally accepted programming practice to put the **Dim** statement at the beginning of the procedure.

See Also

Array Function, **Option Base** Statement, **Private** Statement, **Public** Statement, **ReDim** Statement, **Set** Statement, **Static** Statement, **Type** Statement.

Example

This example shows various uses of the **Dim** statement to declare variables. The **Dim** statement is also used to declare arrays. The default lower bound for array subscripts is 0 and can be overridden at the module level using the **Option Base** statement.

```
' AnyValue and MyValue are declared as Variant by default with values
' set to Empty.
Dim AnyValue, MyValue

'  Explicitly declare a variable of type Integer.
Dim Number As Integer

' Multiple declarations on a single line. AnotherVar is of type Variant
' since its type is omitted.
Dim AnotherVar, Choice As Boolean, BirthDate As Date

' DayArray is an array of Variants with 51 elements indexed,
' starting at 0 thru 50, assuming Option Base is set to 0 (default) for
' the current module.
Dim DayArray(50)

' Matrix is a two-dimensional array of integers.
Dim Matrix(3,4) As Integer

' MyMatrix is a three-dimensional array of doubles with explicit
' bounds.
Dim MyMatrix(1 To 5,  4 To 9,  3 To 5) As Double

' BirthDay is an array of dates with indexes from 1 to 10.
Dim BirthDay(1 To 10) As Date

' MyArray is a dynamic array.
Dim MyArray()
```

Dir Function

Description

Returns the name of a file, directory, or folder that matches a specified pattern or file attribute, or the volume label of a drive.

Syntax

Dir[(*pathname*[,*attributes*])]

Elements

The **Dir** function syntax has these parts:

Part	Description
pathname	String expression that specifies a file name—may include directory or folder, and drive. **Null** is returned if *pathname* is not found.
attributes	Constant or numeric expression, the sum of which specifies file attributes. If omitted, all normal files are returned that match *pathname*.

The *attributes* argument has these constants and values:

Constant	Value	File Attribute
vbNormal	0	Normal.
vbHidden	2	Hidden.
vbSystem	4	System—not available on the Macintosh.
vbVolume	8	Volume label; if specified, all attributes are ignored—not available on the Macintosh.
vbDirectory	16	Directory or folder.

Note These constants are specified by Visual Basic. As a result, the names can be used anywhere in your code in place of the actual values.

Remarks

Dir supports the use of '*' (multiple character) and '?' (single character) wildcards to specify multiple files. However, on the Macintosh, these characters are treated as valid file name characters and can't be used as wildcards to specify multiple files.

Since the Macintosh does not support wildcards, use the file type to identify groups of files. You can use the **MacID** function to specify file type instead of using the file names. For example, the following statement returns the name of the first "TEXT" file in the current folder:

```
Dir("", MacID("TEXT"))
```

If you use the **MacID** function with **Dir** in Microsoft Windows, an error occurs.

Any *attribute* value greater than 256 is considered a **MacID** value.

You must specify *pathname* the first time you call the **Dir** function, or an error occurs. If you also specify file attributes, *pathname* must be included.

Dir returns the first file name that matches *pathname*. To get any additional file names that match *pathname*, call **Dir** again with no arguments. When no more file names match, **Dir** returns a zero-length string. Once a zero-length string is returned, you must specify *pathname* in subsequent calls or an error occurs. You can change to a new *pathname* without retrieving all of the file names that match the current *pathname*. However, you can't recursively call the **Dir** function.

Tip Because file names are retrieved in no particular order, you may want to store returned file names in an array and then sort the array.

See Also   **ChDir** Statement, **CurDir** Function, **MacID** Function.

DirectDependents Property

Applies To   Range.

Description   Returns a Range that contains all of the direct dependents of a cell. This may be a multiple selection (a union of Range objects) if there is more than one dependent. Read-only.

Syntax   *object*.**DirectDependents**

Elements   *object*
    Required. Return direct dependents for this cell.

See Also   **Dependents** Property, **DirectPrecedents** Property, **Precedents** Property, **ShowDependents** Method.

Example   This example selects the direct dependents of the active cell.

```
ActiveCell.DirectDependents.Select
```

DirectPrecedents Property

Applies To   Range.

Description   Returns a Range that contains all of the direct precedents of a cell. This may be a multiple selection (a union of Range objects) if there is more than one precedent. Read-only.

Syntax	*object*.**DirectPrecedents**
Elements	*object* Required. Return direct precedents for this cell.
See Also	**Dependents** Property, **DirectDependents** Property, **Precedents** Property, **ShowPrecedents** Method.
Example	This example selects the direct precedents of the active cell.

```
ActiveCell.DirectPrecedents.Select
```

DismissButton Property

Applies To	Button, Buttons, DrawingObjects.
Description	**True** if the button will automatically close a user-defined dialog when the button is clicked. Any number of buttons on the dialog can have the **DismissButton** property set to **True**. Read-write.
Syntax	*object*.**DismissButton**
Elements	*object* Required. The object to which this property applies.

When you click a button that has the **DismissButton** property set to **True**, three steps are taken:

1. The button's **OnAction** procedure runs. If you want to do any custom data validation, then do it in this procedure. If validation fails, you can set the **DismissButton** property to False, in which case the dialog remains visible. Remember to reset the **DismissButton** property to **True** when validation passes.

2. When the **OnAction** procedure ends and the **DismissButton** property is **True**, edit fields on the dialog are automatically validated to ensure that they contain data of the type specified by their **InputType** properties. If automatic validation fails, Microsoft Excel displays an alert, the offending edit box gets the focus, and the dialog remains visible.

3. If automatic validation passes, then the dialog closes and the **Show** method that called the dialog returns **True**.

If no button in the dialog has the **DismissButton** property set to **True**, then you must explicitly call the **Hide** method or cancel the dialog to close it.

See Also	**CancelButton** Property, **Hide** Method, **InputType** Property, **OnAction** Property, **Show** Method.

Example

This example sets the **DismissButton** property for each button on the dialog sheet.

```
For Each bt in ActiveWorkbook.DialogSheets(1).Buttons
    bt.DismissButton = True
Next bt
```

Display3DShading Property

Applies To

CheckBox, CheckBoxes, DrawingObjects, DropDown, DropDowns, GroupBox, GroupBoxes, ListBox, ListBoxes, OptionButton, OptionButtons, ScrollBar, ScrollBars, Spinner, Spinners.

Description

True if the control uses 3-D visual effects. This property applies only to controls on worksheets and charts. Read-write.

Syntax

object.**Display3DShading**

Elements

object
    Required. The object to which this property applies.

Example

This example sets check box one to use 3-D shading.

```
ActiveSheet.CheckBoxes(1).Display3DShading = True
```

DisplayAlerts Property

Applies To

Application.

Description

True if Microsoft Excel displays certain alerts and messages while a macro is running. Read-write.

Syntax

object.**DisplayAlerts**

Elements

object
    Required. The Application object.

Remarks

Defaults to **True**. Set this to **False** if you do not want to be disturbed by prompts and alert messages while a macro is running, and want Microsoft Excel to choose the default response.

If you set this property to **False**, Microsoft Excel sets it back to **True** when your macro stops running.

Example   This example closes the active workbook. The user is not prompted to save changes
                     (if any), and those changes are not saved.

```
Application.DisplayAlerts = False
ActiveWorkbook.Close
```

DisplayAutomaticPageBreaks Property

Applies To   DialogSheet, Worksheet.

Description   **True** if automatic page breaks should be displayed for this sheet. Read-write.

Syntax   *object*.**DisplayAutomaticPageBreaks**

Elements   *object*
                     Required. The object to which this property applies.

Example   This example causes the active worksheet to display automatic page breaks.

```
ActiveSheet.DisplayAutomaticPageBreaks = True
```

DisplayBlanksAs Property

Applies To   Chart.

Description   Returns or sets how blank cells are plotted on a chart (one of **xlNotPlotted**,
                     xlInterpolated, or **xlZero**). Read-write.

Syntax   *object*.**DisplayBlanksAs**

Elements   *object*
                     Required. The Chart object.

Example   This example causes Microsoft Excel not to plot blank cells.

```
ActiveWorkbook.Charts(1).DisplayBlanksAs = xlNotPlotted
```

DisplayClipboardWindow Property

Applies To   Application.

Description	Apple Macintosh only. **True** if the clipboard window is displayed. Set this property to **True** to display the clipboard window. Read-write.
Syntax	*object*.**DisplayClipboardWindow**
Elements	*object* Required. The Application object.
Remarks	In Microsoft Windows, this property retains its value, but does nothing.
Example	This example displays the clipboard window.

```
Application.DisplayClipboardWindow = True
```

DisplayDrawingObjects Property

Applies To	Workbook.
Description	Returns or sets how drawing objects are displayed, as shown in the following table. Read-write.

Value	Meaning
xlAll	Show all drawing objects.
xlPlaceholders	Show only placeholders.
xlHide	Hide all drawing objects.

Syntax	*object*.**DisplayDrawingObjects**
Elements	*object* Required. The Workbook object.
Example	This example hides all the drawing objects in the active workbook.

```
ActiveWorkbook.DisplayDrawingObjects = xlHide
```

DisplayEquation Property

Applies To	Trendline.
Description	**True** if the equation for the trendline is displayed on the chart (in the same data label as the R-squared value). Setting this property to **True** automatically turns on data labels. Read-write.

Syntax	*object*.**DisplayEquation**
Elements	*object* Required. The Trendline object.
See Also	**Add** Method (Trendlines Collection), **DisplayRSquared** Property.
Example	This example displays the R-squared value and equation for trendline one.

```
With ActiveWorkbook.Charts(1).SeriesCollection(1).Trendlines(1)
    .DisplayRSquared = True
    .DisplayEquation = True
End With
```

DisplayExcel4Menus Property

Applies To	Application.
Description	**True** if Microsoft Excel displays Excel 4 menu bars; **False** if Microsoft Excel displays the Excel 5 menu bars. Read-write.
Syntax	*object*.**DisplayExcel4Menus**
Elements	*object* Required. The Application object.
Example	This example switches to Microsoft Excel version 5 menus if version 4 menus are currently in use.

```
If Application.DisplayExcel4Menus Then
    Application.DisplayExcel4Menus = False
End If
```

DisplayFormulaBar Property

Applies To	Application.
Description	**True** if the formula bar is displayed. Read-write.
Syntax	*object*.**DisplayFormulaBar**
Elements	*object* Required. The Application object.

Example   This example saves the current state of the **DisplayFormulaBar** property, and then sets the property to **False** so the formula bar is not displayed.

```
saveFormulaBar = Application.DisplayFormulaBar
Application.DisplayFormulaBar = False
```

DisplayFormulas Property

Applies To   Window.

Description   **True** if the window is displaying formulas, or **False** if the window is displaying values. Read-write.

Syntax   *object*.**DisplayFormulas**

Elements   *object*
              Required. The Window object.

Remarks   This property applies only to worksheets and macro sheets.

Example   This example changes the active window to display formulas.

```
ActiveWindow.DisplayFormulas = True
```

DisplayFullScreen Property

Applies To   Application.

Description   **True** if Microsoft Excel is in full-screen mode. Read-write.

Syntax   *object*.**DisplayFullScreen**

Elements   *object*
              Required. The Application object.

Remarks   Full-screen mode maximizes the application window to cover the entire screen and hides the application title bar (in Microsoft Windows). Toolbars, the status bar, and the formula bar maintain separate display settings for full-screen and normal mode.

Example   This example causes Microsoft Excel to display in full-screen mode.

```
Application.DisplayFullScreen = True
```

DisplayGridlines Property

Applies To   Window.

Description   **True** if gridlines are displayed. Read-write.

Syntax   *object*.**DisplayGridlines**

Elements   *object*
    Required. The Window object.

Remarks   This property applies only to worksheets and macro sheets.

    This property affects only displayed gridlines. Use the **PrintGridlines** property to control gridline printing.

Example   This example displays gridlines in the active window.

```
ActiveWindow.DisplayGridlines = True
```

DisplayHeadings Property

Applies To   Window.

Description   **True** if both row and column headings are displayed, **False** if no headings are displayed. Read-write.

Syntax   *object*.**DisplayHeadings**

Elements   *object*
    Required. The Window object.

Remarks   This property applies only to worksheets and macro sheets.

    This property affects only displayed headings. Use the **PrintHeadings** property to control heading printing.

Example   This example turns off row and column headings in the active window.

```
ActiveWindow.DisplayHeadings = False
```

DisplayHorizontalScrollBar Property

Applies To	Window.
Description	**True** if the horizontal scrollbar is displayed. Read-write.
Syntax	*object*.**DisplayHorizontalScrollBar**
Elements	*object* 　　Required. The Window object.
See Also	**DisplayVerticalScrollBar** Property, **DisplayScrollBars** Property, **TabRatio** Property.
Example	This example turns on the horizontal scroll bar.

```
ActiveWindow.DisplayHorizontalScrollBar = True
```

DisplayInfoWindow Property

Applies To	Application.
Description	**True** if the Info window is displayed. Set this property to **True** to display the Info window. Read-write.
Syntax	*object*.**DisplayInfoWindow**
Elements	*object* 　　Required. The Application object.
Example	This example displays the Info window.

```
Application.DisplayInfoWindow = True
```

DisplayNoteIndicator Property

Applies To	Application.
Description	**True** if cells containing notes contain note indicators (small dots in their upper-right corners). Read-write.

Syntax	*object*.**DisplayNoteIndicator**
Elements	*object*
	Required. The Application object.
Example	This example saves the current state of the **DisplayNoteIndicator** property and then sets the property to **True** so cells with notes will have note indicators.

```
saveNoteIndicator = Application.DisplayNoteIndicator
Application.DisplayNoteIndicator = True
```

DisplayOutline Property

Applies To	Window.
Description	**True** if outline symbols are displayed. Read-write.
Syntax	*object*.**DisplayOutline**
Elements	*object*
	Required. The Window object.
Remarks	This property applies only to worksheets and macro sheets.
Example	This example displays outline symbols for the active window.

```
ActiveWindow.DisplayOutline = True
```

DisplayRecentFiles Property

Applies To	Application.
Description	**True** if the most recently used (MRU) file list is displayed in the File menu. Read-write.
Syntax	*object*.**DisplayRecentFiles**
Elements	*object*
	Required. The Application object.
Example	This example turns off the most recently used file list.

```
Application.DisplayRecentFiles = False
```

DisplayRightToLeft Property

Applies To	Window.
Description	**True** if the window displays right-to-left instead of left-to-right. Read-write.
Syntax	*object*.**DisplayRightToLeft**
Elements	*object* Required. The Window object.
Remarks	This property is only available in Arabic and Hebrew Microsoft Excel.
Example	This example sets window one to display right-to-left.

```
ActiveWorkbook.Windows(1).DisplayRightToLeft = True
```

DisplayRSquared Property

Applies To	Trendline.
Description	**True** if the R-squared value of the trendline is displayed on the chart (in the same data label as the equation). Setting this property to **True** automatically turns on data labels. Read-write.
Syntax	*object*.**DisplayRSquared**
Elements	*object* Required. The Trendline object.
See Also	**Add** Method (Trendlines Collection), **DisplayEquation** Property.
Example	This example displays the R-squared value and equation for trendline one.

```
With ActiveWorkbook.Charts(1).SeriesCollection(1).Trendlines(1)
    .DisplayRSquared = True
    .DisplayEquation = True
End With
```

DisplayScrollBars Property

Applies To	Application.

Description	**True** if scroll bars are visible for all workbooks. Read-write.
Syntax	*object*.**DisplayScrollBars**
Elements	*object* Required. The Application object.
See Also	**DisplayHorizontalScrollBar** Property, **DisplayVerticalScrollBar** Property.
Example	This example turns off scroll bars for all workbooks.

```
Application.DisplayScrollBars = False
```

DisplayStatusBar Property

Applies To	Application.
Description	**True** if the status bar is displayed. Read-write.
Syntax	*object*.**DisplayStatusBar**
Elements	*object* Required. The Application object.
See Also	**StatusBar** Property.
Example	This example saves the current state of the **DisplayStatusBar** property, and then sets the property to **True** so the status bar is visible.

```
saveStatusBar = Application.DisplayStatusBar
Application.DisplayStatusBar = True
```

DisplayVerticalScrollBar Property

Applies To	DrawingObjects, EditBox, EditBoxes, Window.
Description	**True** if the vertical scrollbar is displayed. Read-write.
Syntax	*object*.**DisplayVerticalScrollBar**
Elements	*object* Required. The object to which this property applies.
See Also	**DisplayHorizontalScrollBar** Property, **DisplayScrollBars** Property.

| **Example** | This example turns on the vertical scroll bar. |

```
ActiveWindow.DisplayVerticalScrollBar = True
```

DisplayWorkbookTabs Property

Applies To	Window.
Description	**True** if the workbook tabs are displayed. Read-write.
Syntax	*object*.**DisplayWorkbookTabs**
Elements	*object* Required. The Window object.
See Also	**TabRatio** Property.
Example	This example turns on the workbook tabs.

```
ActiveWindow.DisplayWorkbookTabs = True
```

DisplayZeros Property

Applies To	Window.
Description	**True** if zero values are displayed. Read-write.
Syntax	*object*.**DisplayZeros**
Elements	*object* Required. The Window object.
Remarks	This property applies only to worksheets and macro sheets.
Example	This example sets the active window to display zero values.

```
ActiveWindow.DisplayZeros = True
```

Do...Loop Statement

| **Description** | Repeats a block of statements while a condition is **True** or until a condition becomes **True**. |

Syntax 1   **Do** [{**While** | **Until**} *condition*]
                  [*statements*]
                  [**Exit Do**]
                  [*statements*]
                  Loop

Syntax 2   **Do**
                  [*statements*]
                  [**Exit Do**]
                  [*statements*]
                  Loop [{**While** | **Until**}*condition*]

Elements   The **Do...Loop** statement syntax has these parts:

Part	Description
condition	Expression that is **True** or **False**.
statements	One or more statements that are repeated while or until *condition* is **True**.

Remarks   The **Exit Do** can only be used within a **Do...Loop** control structure to provide an
                  alternate way to exit a **Do...Loop**. Any number of **Exit Do** statements may be
                  placed anywhere in the **Do...Loop**. Often used with the evaluation of some
                  condition (for example, **If...Then**), **Exit Do** transfers control to the statement
                  immediately following the **Loop**.

                  When used within nested **Do...Loop** statements, **Exit Do** transfers control to the
                  loop that is one nested level above the loop where it occurs.

See Also   **Exit** Statement, **For...Next** Statement, **While...Wend** Statement.

Example   This example shows how **Do...Loop** statements can be used. The inner **Do...Loop**
                  statement loops 10 times, sets the value of the flag to **False**, and exits prematurely
                  using the **Exit Do** statement. The outer loop exits immediately upon checking the
                  value of the flag.

```
Check = True : Counter = 0        ' Initialize variables.
Do   ' Outer Loop.
    Do While Counter < 20         ' Inner Loop.
        Counter = Counter + 1     ' Increment Counter.
        If Counter = 10 Then      ' If condition is true.
            Check = False         ' Set value of flag to False.
            Exit Do               ' Exit inner loop.
        End If
    Loop
Loop Until Check = False          ' Exit outer loop immediately.
```

DoEvents Statement

Description   Yields execution so that the operating system can process other events.

Syntax   **DoEvents**

Remarks   **DoEvents** passes control to the operating system. Control is not returned until the operating system has finished processing the events in its queue and, for Microsoft Windows only, all keys in the **SendKeys** queue have been sent.

If parts of your code take up too much processor time, use **DoEvents** periodically to relinquish control to the operating system so that events, such as keyboard input and mouse clicks, can be processed without significant delay.

Caution   Make sure the procedure that has given up control with **DoEvents** is not executed again from a different part of your code before the first **DoEvents** call returns; this could cause unpredictable results. In addition, do not use **DoEvents** if other applications could possibly interact with your procedure in unforeseen ways during the time you have yielded control.

Example   This example uses the **DoEvents** Statement to cause execution to yield to the operating system once every 1000 iterations of the loop.

```
For I = 1 To 150000 ' Start loop.
    If I Mod 1000 = 0 Then   ' If loop has repeated 1000 times.
        DoEvents             ' Yield to operating system.
    End If
Next I                       ' Increment loop counter.
```

Double Data Type

Double (double-precision floating-point) variables are stored as 64-bit (8-byte) numbers ranging in value from -1.79769313486232E308 to -4.94065645841247E-324 for negative values and from 4.94065645841247E-324 to 1.79769313486232E308 for positive values. The type-declaration character for **Double** is # (character code 35).

See Also   **CDbl** Function, Data Type Summary, **Def***type* Statements, **Single** Data Type.

DoubleClick Method

Applies To   Application.

Description   Equivalent to double-clicking the active cell or currently selected object.

Syntax   *object*.**DoubleClick**

Elements   *object*
                    Required. The Application object.

See Also   **OnDoubleClick** Property.

Example   This example double-clicks the active cell or selected object.

```
Application.DoubleClick
```

DoughnutGroups Method

Applies To   Chart.

Description   On a 2-D chart, returns a single doughnut chart group (a ChartGroup object, Syntax 1), or a collection of the doughnut chart groups (a ChartGroups collection, Syntax 2).

Syntax 1   *object*.**DoughnutGroups**(*index*)

Syntax 2   *object*.**DoughnutGroups**

Elements   The **DoughnutGroups** method has the following object qualifier and named arguments:

                    object
                    Required. The Chart object.

                    index
                    Required for Syntax 1. Specifies the chart group.

Example   This example sets the starting angle for the first doughnut group.

```
Charts(1).DoughnutGroups(1).FirstSliceAngle = 45
```

DoughnutHoleSize Property

Applies To   ChartGroup.

Description   Returns or sets the size of the hole in a doughnut chart group. The hole size is expressed as a percentage of the chart size from 10 to 90 percent. Read-write.

Syntax   *object*.**DoughnutHoleSize**

Elements   *object*
                    Required. The ChartGroup object.

Example   This example sets the hole size for doughnut chart group one.

```
ActiveChart.DoughnutGroups(1).DoughnutHoleSize = 10
```

DownBars Object

Description   A down bar on a chart.

DownBars Property

Applies To   ChartGroup.

Description   Returns the DownBars on a line chart. Applies only to line charts. Read-only.

Syntax   *object*.**DownBar**

Elements   *object*
                    Required. The ChartGroup object.

See Also   **HasUpDownBars** Property, **UpBars** Property.

Example   This example turns on up and down bars for the first chart group, and then sets their colors.

```
With ActiveChart.ChartGroups(1)
    .HasUpDownBars = True
    .DownBars.Interior.Color = RGB(255, 0, 0)
    .UpBars.Interior.Color = RGB(0, 0, 255)
End With
```

Draft Property

Applies To   PageSetup.

Description   **True** if the sheet will be printed without graphics. Read-write.

Syntax   *object*.**Draft**

Elements   *object*
        Required. The PageSetup object.

Remarks   Setting this property to **True** makes printing faster (at the expense of not printing graphics).

See Also   **PrintObject** Property.

Example   This example turns off graphics printing.

```
ActiveSheet.PageSetup.Draft = True
```

Drawing Object

Description   A graphic object created by the Freehand, Freeform, or Filled Freeform buttons.

DrawingObjects Method

Applies To   Chart, DialogSheet, Worksheet.

Description   Returns a single drawing object (Syntax 1) or a collection of all the drawing objects (Syntax 2) on the chart, worksheet, or dialog sheet. Returns all drawing objects, including graphic objects, pictures, embedded objects, and embedded charts.

Syntax 1   *object*.**DrawingObjects(***index***)**

Syntax 2   *object*.**DrawingObjects**

Elements   The **DrawingObjects** method has the following object qualifier and named arguments:

        object
        Required. The Chart, DialogSheet, or Worksheet object.

index
> Required for Syntax 1. The name or number of the drawing object. Can be an array to return several drawing objects.

Example   This example deletes drawing object three on the active worksheet.

```
ActiveSheet.DrawingObjects(3).Delete
```

DrawingObjects Object

Description   A collection of all graphic objects on a sheet.

Drawings Method

Applies To   Chart, DialogSheet, Worksheet.

Description   Returns a single drawing (a Drawing object, Syntax 1) or a collection of drawings (a Drawings object, Syntax 2) on the chart, dialog sheet, or worksheet. Drawings are created by the Freeform, Freehand, and Filled Freeform buttons on the Drawing toolbar.

Syntax 1   *object*.**Drawings(*index*)**

Syntax 2   *object*.**Drawings**

Elements   The **Drawings** method has the following object qualifier and named arguments:

object
> Required. The Chart, DialogSheet, or Worksheet object.

index
> Required for Syntax 1. The name or number of the drawing to return. More than one index can be specified.

Example   This example brings drawing one to the front of worksheet one.

```
Worksheets(1).Drawings(1).BringToFront
```

Drawings Object

Description   A collection of Drawing objects.

DropDown Object

Description   A drop-down list box, either editable or non-editable. One item in the list may be chosen, and in editable versions you can type in arbitrary text in an edit field.

DropDownLines Property

Applies To   DrawingObjects, DropDown, DropDowns.

Description   Returns or sets the number of list lines displayed in the drop-down portion of a drop-down list box. Read-write.

Syntax   *object*.**DropDownLines**

Elements   *object*
                   Required. The object to which this property applies.

Remarks   This property is ignored on the Apple Macintosh.

Example   This example sets the number of list lines in drop-down list box four.

```
Application.DialogSheets(1).DropDowns(4).DropDownLines = 10
```

DropDowns Method

Applies To   Chart, DialogSheet, Worksheet.

Description   Returns a single drop-down list box control (a DropDown object, Syntax 1) or a collection of drop-down list box controls on the chart or sheet (a DropDowns object, Syntax 2).

Syntax 1	*object*.**DropDowns**(*index*)
Syntax 2	*object*.**DropDowns**
Elements	The **DropDowns** method has the following object qualifier and named arguments:

object
  Required. The Chart, DialogSheet, or Worksheet object.

index
  Required for Syntax 1. Specifies the name or number of the drop-down list box control (can be an array to specify more than one).

Example	This example sets the number of list lines in drop-down list box one.

```
Application.DialogSheets(1).DropDowns(1).DropDownLines = 10\
```

DropDowns Object

Description	A collection of DropDown objects.

DropLines Object

Description	Drop lines on a chart.

DropLines Property

Applies To	ChartGroup.
Description	Returns or sets the DropLines for a series on a line or area chart. Applies only to line or area charts. Read-write.
Syntax	*object*.**DropLines**
Elements	*object* Required. The ChartGroup object.
See Also	**HasDropLines** Property.

Example   This example turns on drop lines for the first chart group, and then sets their line style, weight, and color.

```
With ActiveChart.ChartGroups(1)
    .HasDropLines = True
    With .DropLines.Border
        .LineStyle = xlThin
        .Weight = xlMedium
        .Color = RGB(255, 0, 0)
    End With
End With
```

Duplicate Method

Applies To   Arc, Arcs, Button, Buttons, ChartObject, ChartObjects, CheckBox, CheckBoxes, Drawing, DrawingObjects, Drawings, DropDown, DropDowns, EditBox, EditBoxes, GroupBox, GroupBoxes, GroupObject, GroupObjects, Label, Labels, Line, Lines, ListBox, ListBoxes, OLEObject, OLEObjects, OptionButton, OptionButtons, Oval, Ovals, Picture, Pictures, Rectangle, Rectangles, ScrollBar, ScrollBars, Spinner, Spinners, TextBox, TextBoxes.

Description   Duplicates the object and returns a reference to the new copy.

Syntax   *object*.**Duplicate**

Elements   *object*
        Required. The object to which this method applies.

Example   This example duplicates oval one, and then selects the copy.

```
Set dOval = ActiveSheet.Ovals(1).Duplicate
dOval.Select
```

Edit Method

Applies To   ToolbarButton.

Description   Starts the button editor for the specified toolbar button.

Syntax   *object*.**Edit**

Elements   *object*
        Required. The ToolbarButton object.

Example   This example starts the button editor for button five on toolbar one.

```
Application.Toolbars(1).ToolbarButtons(5).Edit
```

EditBox Object

Description   Edit boxes allow text input on dialogs.

Remarks   Unlike other controls, edit boxes do not have a numeric value and cannot be linked to cells.

EditBoxes Method

Applies To   DialogSheet.

Description   Returns a single edit box control (an EditBox object, Syntax 1) or a collection of edit box controls on the sheet (an EditBoxes object, Syntax 2).

Syntax 1   *object*.**EditBoxes(*index*)**

Syntax 2   *object*.**EditBoxes**

Elements   The **EditBoxes** method has the following object qualifier and named arguments:

object
　　Required. The DialogSheet object.

index
　　Required for Syntax 1. Specifies the name or number of the edit box (can be an array to specify more than one).

Example   This example displays the number of edit boxes on dialog sheet one.

```
cEditBoxes = Application.DialogSheets(1).EditBoxes.Count
MsgBox "There are " & cEditBoxes & "edit boxes on dialog sheet one."
```

EditBoxes Object

Description   A collection of EditBox objects.

EditDirectlyInCell Property

Applies To   Application.

Description   **True** if Microsoft Excel allows editing in cells. Read-write.

Syntax   *object*.**EditDirectlyInCell**

Elements   *object*
                    Required. The Application object.

Example   This example enables editing in cells.

```
Application.EditDirectlyInCell = True
```

EditionOptions Method

Applies To   Workbook.

Description   Sets options for publishers and subscribers in the workbook. Available only on the Apple Macintosh running System 7.

Syntax   *object*.**EditionOptions**(*type, option, name, reference, appearance, chartSize, formats*)

Elements   The **EditionOptions** method has the following object qualifier and named arguments:

                    object
                    Required. The Workbook object.

                    type
                    Required. Specifies the edition type to change (either **xlPublisher** or **xlSubscriber**).

                    option
                    Required. Specifies the type of information to set for the edition. If *type* is **xlPublisher**, then *option* can be one of **xlCancel**, **xlSendPublisher**, **xlSelect**, **xlAutomaticUpdate**, **xlManualUpdate**, or **xlChangeAttributes**. If *type* is **xlSubscriber**, then *option* can be one of **xlCancel**, **xlUpdateSubscriber**, **xlOpenSource**, **xlAutomaticUpdate**, or **xlManualUpdate**.

                    name
                    Optional. Specifies the name of the edition, as returned from the **LinkSources** method. If *name* is omitted, *reference* must be specified.

reference
Optional (required if *name* is not specified). Specifies the edition reference as text in R1C1-style form. This argument is required if there is more than one publisher or subscriber with the same edition name in the workbook, or if the *name* argument is omitted.

appearance
Optional. If *option* is **xlChangeAttributes**, specifies whether the edition is published as shown on screen (**xlScreen**) or as shown when printed (**xlPrinter**).

chartSize
Optional. If *option* is **xlChangeAttributes** and the published object is a chart, specifies the size of the edition (either **xlScreen** or **xlPrinter**). If the edition is not a chart, omit this argument.

formats
Optional. If *option* is **xlChangeAttributes**, specifies the format of the published edition. Can be any combination of **xlPICT**, **xlBIFF**, **xlRTF**, or **xlVALU**.

Elevation Property

Applies To	Chart.
Description	Returns or sets the elevation of the 3-D chart view, in degrees. Read-write.
Syntax	*object*.**Elevation**
Elements	*object* Required. The Chart object.
Remarks	The chart elevation is the height at which you view the chart, in degrees. The default is 15 for most chart types. The value of this property must be between -90 and 90, except for 3-D bar charts, where it must be between 0 and 44.
See Also	**Perspective** Property, **Rotation** Property.
Example	This example sets the chart elevation to 34 degrees.

```
Charts(1).Elevation = 34
```

EnableCancelKey Property

Applies To	Application.

Description   Controls how Microsoft Excel handles CTRL+BREAK (or ESC or COMMAND+PERIOD) user interruptions of the running procedure, as shown in the following table. Read-write.

Value	Meaning
xlDisabled	Cancel key trapping is completely disabled.
xlInterrupt	Interrupt the current procedure and allow the user to debug or end the procedure.
xlErrorHandler	The interrupt is sent to the running procedure as an error, trappable by an error handler setup with an **On Error GoTo** statement. The trappable error code is 18.

Syntax   *object*.**EnableCancelKey**

Elements   *object*
Required. The Application object.

Remarks   Use this property very carefully. If you use **xlDisabled**, there is no way to interrupt a runaway loop or other non-self-terminating code. If you use **xlErrorHandler** but your error handler always returns using the **Resume** statement, there is also no way to stop runaway code.

The **EnableCancelKey** property is always reset to **xlInterrupt** whenever Microsoft Excel returns to the idle state and no code is running. To trap or disable cancellation in your procedure you must explicitly change the **EnableCancelKey** property every time the procedure is called.

See Also   Trappable Errors.

Example   This example shows how the **EnableCancelKey** property can be used to set up a custom cancellation handler.

```
On Error GoTo handleCancel
Application.EnableCancelKey = xlErrorHandler
MsgBox "This may take a long time: press ESC to cancel"
For x = 1 To 1000000     ' Do something 1,000,000 times (long!)
    ' do something here
Next x

handleCancel:
If Err = 18 Then
    MsgBox "You cancelled"
End If
```

Enabled Property

Applies To   Arc, Arcs, Button, Buttons, ChartObject, ChartObjects, CheckBox, CheckBoxes, Drawing, DrawingObjects, Drawings, DropDown, DropDowns, EditBox, EditBoxes, GroupBox, GroupBoxes, GroupObject, GroupObjects, Label, Labels, Line, Lines, ListBox, ListBoxes, Menu, MenuItem, OLEObject, OLEObjects, OptionButton, OptionButtons, Oval, Ovals, Picture, Pictures, Rectangle, Rectangles, ScrollBar, ScrollBars, Spinner, Spinners, TextBox, TextBoxes, ToolbarButton.

Description   **True** if the control, drawing object, or menu item is enabled. Read-write, except for Menu, which is write-only.

Syntax   *object*.**Enabled**

Elements   *object*
                     Required. The object to which this property applies.

Remarks   A disabled menu item is gray. A disabled toolbar button is gray and it beeps when it is pressed.

See Also   **Pushed** Property.

Example   This example disables all the buttons with custom faces on toolbar one.

```
For Each btn In Application.Toolbars(1).ToolbarButtons
    If Not btn.BuiltInFace Then
        btn.Enabled = False
    End If
Next btn
```

EnableTipWizard Property

Applies To   Application.

Description   **True** if the TipWizard is enabled. Read-write.

Syntax   *object*.**EnableTipWizard**

Elements   *object*
                     Required. The Application object.

Example   This example enables the TipWizard.

```
Application.EnableTipWizard = True
```

Enclosures Property

Applies To   Mailer.

Description   Returns or sets the enclosed files attached to the workbook mailer, as an array of strings, with each string indicating the pathname of a file to attach as an enclosure. Relative paths are allowed, and are assumed to be based on the current directory. Read-write.

Syntax   *object*.**Enclosures**

Elements   *object*
    Required. The Mailer object.

See Also   **BCCRecipients** Property, **CCRecipients** Property, **Mailer** Property, **Received** Property, **SendDateTime** Property, **Sender** Property, **SendMailer** Property, **Subject** Property, **ToRecipients** Property.

Example   This example sets up the Mailer object for workbook one, and then sends the workbook.

```
With Workbooks(1)
    .HasMailer = True
    With .Mailer
        .Subject = "Here is the workbook"
        .ToRecipients = Array("Jean")
        .CCRecipients = Array("Adam", "Bernard")
        .BCCRecipients = Array("Chris")
        .Enclosures = Array("TestFile")
    End With
    .SendMailer
End With
```

End Method

Applies To   Range.

Description   Returns a cell (a Range object) at the end of the region that contains the source range. Equivalent to pressing END+UP ARROW, END+DOWN ARROW, END+LEFT ARROW, OR END+RIGHT ARROW.

Syntax   *object*.**End(***direction***)**

Elements   The **End** method has the following object qualifier and named arguments:

object
    Required. A cell in the range.

direction
Required. Specifies the direction to move. One of **xlToLeft**, **xlToRight**, **xlUp**, or **xlDown**.

Examples   This example selects cell B1.

```
Range("B4").End(xlUp).Select
```

This example selects cell IV4.

```
Range("B4").End(xlToRight).Select
```

End Statement

Description   Ends a procedure or block.

Syntax   **End**

End Function

End If

End Property

End Select

End Sub

End Type   ·

End With

Elements   The **End** statement syntax has these forms:

Statement	Description
End	Terminates procedure execution. Never required by itself but may be placed anywhere in a procedure to close files opened with the **Open** statement and to clear variables.
End Function	Required to end a **Function** statement.
End If	Required to end a block **If...Then...Else** statement.
End Property	Required to end a **Property Let**, **Property Get**, or **Property Set** procedure.
End Select	Required to end a **Select Case** statement.

Statement	Description
End Sub	Required to end a **Sub** statement.
End Type	Required to end a user-defined type definition (**Type** statement).
End With	Required to end a **With** statement.

Remarks

Note When executed, the **End** statement resets all module-level variables and all static local variables in all modules. If you need to preserve the value of these variables, use **Stop** instead. You can then resume execution while preserving the value of those variables.

See Also

Exit Statement, **Function** Statement, **If...Then...Else** Statement, **Property Get** Statement, **Property Let** Statement, **Property Set** Statement, **Select Case** Statement, **Stop** Statement, **Sub** Statement, **Type** Statement, **With** Statement.

Example

This example uses the **End** Statement to end code execution, a **Select Case** block, and a **Sub** procedure.

```
Sub EndStatementDemo()
    For Number = 1 To 2      ' Loop 2 times.
        Select Case Number   ' Evaluate Number.
            Case 1  ' If Number equals 1.
                Debug.Print Number  ' Print value to Debug window.
            Case Else        ' If Number does not equal 1.
                End          ' Terminate procedure execution.
        End Select           ' End of Select Case Statement.
    Next Number
End Sub ' End of Sub procedure.
```

EndStyle Property

Applies To   ErrorBars.

Description   Returns or sets the end style for the error bars (either **xlCap** or **xlNoCap**). Read-write.

Syntax   *object*.**EndStyle**

Elements   *object*
        Required. The ErrorBars object.

Example   This example sets the end style for the error bars on series one.

```
ActiveChart.SeriesCollection(1).ErrorBars.EndStyle = xlCap
```

EntireColumn Property

Applies To   Range.

Description   Returns the entire column or columns that contain the range. A column is a Range object. Read-only.

Syntax   *object*.**EntireColumn**

Elements   *object*
                   Required. The range containing the column or columns to return.

See Also   **EntireRow** Property.

Example   This example selects the entire column that contains the active cell.

```
ActiveCell.EntireColumn.Select
```

EntireRow Property

Applies To   Range.

Description   Returns the entire row or rows that contain the range. A row is a Range object. Read-only.

Syntax   *object*.**EntireRow**

Elements   *object*
                   Required. The range containing the row or rows to return.

See Also   **EntireColumn** Property.

Example   This example selects the entire row that contains the active cell.

```
ActiveCell.EntireRow.Select
```

EOF Function

Description   Returns a value that indicates whether the end of a file has been reached.

Syntax   **EOF**(*filenumber*)

Elements   The *filenumber* named argument is any valid file number.

Remarks   Use **EOF** to avoid an error when attempting to get input past the end of a file.

False is returned unless the end of the file has been reached; then **True** is returned. When used with files opened for **Random** or **Binary** access, **EOF** returns **False** unless the last executed **Get** statement is unable to read an entire record; then **True** is returned.

See Also   **Loc** Function, **LOF** Function, **Open** Statement.

Example   This example uses the **EOF** function to detect the end of a file. For purposes of this example, assume that MyFile is a text file with a few lines of text.

```
Open "MyFile" For Input As #1        ' Open file for input.
Do While Not EOF(1)                  ' Check for end of file.
    Line Input #1, InputData         ' Read line of data.
    Debug.Print InputData            ' Print to Debug window.
Loop
Close #1                             ' Close file.
```

Eqv Operator

Description   Used to perform a logical equivalence on two expressions.

Syntax   *result* = *expression1* **Eqv** *expression2*

Elements   The **Eqv** operator syntax has these parts:

Part	Description
result	Any numeric variable.
expression1	Any expression.
expression2	Any expression.

Remarks   If either expression is a **Null**, *result* is also a **Null**. When neither expression is a **Null**, *result* is determined according to the following table:

If expression1 is	And expression2 is	The result is
True	True	True
True	False	False
False	True	False
False	False	True

The **Eqv** operator performs a bit-wise comparison of identically positioned bits in two numeric expressions and sets the corresponding bit in *result* according to the following truth table:

If bit in *expression1* is	And bit in *expression2* is	The *result* is
0	0	1
0	1	0
1	0	0
1	1	1

See Also   Operator Precedence.

Example   This example uses the **Eqv** operator to perform logical equivalence on two expressions.

```
A = 10: B = 8: C = 6 : D = Null      ' Initialize variables.
MyCheck = A > B Eqv B > C            ' Returns True.
MyCheck = B > A Eqv B > C            ' Returns False.
MyCheck = A > B Eqv B > D            ' Returns Null.
MyCheck = A Eqv B                    ' Returns -3
                                     (bit-wise comparison).
```

Erase Statement

Description   Reinitializes the elements of fixed-size arrays and deallocates dynamic-array storage space.

Syntax   **Erase** *arraylist*

Elements   The *arraylist* argument is one or more comma-delimited array variables to be erased.

Remarks   It is important to know whether an array is fixed-size (ordinary) or dynamic because **Erase** behaves differently depending on the type of array. No memory is recovered for fixed-size arrays. **Erase** sets the elements of a fixed array as follows:

Type of array	Effect of Erase on fixed-array elements
Fixed numeric array	Sets each element to zero.
Fixed string array (variable length)	Sets each element to zero-length ("").
Fixed string array (fixed length)	Sets each element to zero.

Type of array	Effect of Erase on fixed-array elements
Fixed **Variant** array	Sets each element to **Empty**.
Array of user-defined types	Sets each element as if it were a separate variable.
Array of objects	Sets each element to the special value **Nothing**.

Erase frees the memory used by dynamic arrays. Before your program can refer to the dynamic array again, it must redeclare the array variable's dimensions using a **ReDim** statement.

See Also   **Array** Function, **Dim** Statement, **Private** Statement, **Public** Statement, **ReDim** Statement, **Static** Statement.

Example   This example uses the **Erase** statement to reinitialize the elements of fixed-size arrays and deallocate dynamic-array storage space.

```
' Declare array variables.
Dim NumArray(10) As Integer          ' Integer array.
Dim StrVarArray(10) As String        ' Variable-string array.
Dim StrFixArray(10) As String * 10   ' Fixed-string array.
Dim VarArray(10) As Variant          ' Variant array.
Dim DynamicArray() As Integer        ' Dynamic array.
ReDim DynamicArray(10)               ' Allocate storage space.
Erase NumArray                   ' Each element set to 0.
Erase StrVarArray                  ' Each element set to "".
Erase StrFixArray                  ' Each element set to 0.
Erase VarArray                 ' Each element set to Empty.
Erase DynamicArray                ' Free memory used by array.
```

Err Statement

Description   Sets **Err** to a specific value.

Syntax   **Err** = *errornumber*

Elements   The *errornumber* argument can be any valid error number or 0, which means no run-time error occurred.

Remarks   **Err** is used to record whether a run-time error has occurred and identifies the error. Use the **Err** statement to set **Err** to a nonzero, whole number to communicate error information between procedures. For example, you might use one of the unassigned run-time error numbers as an application-specific error number. To determine which error numbers are being used, use the **Error** function, the **Error** statement, or both. To avoid conflict with existing error numbers, create user-defined errors by defining your first error at 65,535 and work down from there.

You can also set **Err** to 0 using any form of the **Resume** or **On Error** statement or by executing an **Exit Sub**, **Exit Function** or **Exit Property** statement within an error handler. In addition, the **Error** statement can set **Err** to any value to simulate any run-time error.

See Also   **Erl** Function, **Err** Function, **Error** Function, **Error** Statement.

Example   This example shows how the **Err** statement is used to clear an error by setting **Err** to 0. Error number 55 is generated to illustrate its usage.

```
On Error Resume Next              ' Enable error handling.
Open "TESTFILE" For Output as #1   ' Open file for output.
Kill "TESTFILE"                  ' Attempt to delete open file.
Select Case Err                  ' Evaluate Error Number.
    Case 55                      ' "File already open" error.
        Close #1                 ' Close open file.
        Kill "TESTFILE"           ' Delete file.
        Err = 0                  ' Reset Err to 0.
    Case Else
        ' Handle other situations here...
End Select
```

Err, Erl Functions

Description   Returns error status.

Syntax   **Err**

Erl

Remarks   After an error occurs, the **Err** function returns a number that is the run-time error number, identifying the error. The **Erl** function returns a number that is the line number of the line in which the error occurred, or the numbered line most closely preceding it.

Because **Err** and **Erl** return meaningful values only after an error has occurred, they are usually used in error-handling routines to determine the error and corrective action. Both **Err** and **Erl** are reset to 0 after any form of the **Resume** or **On Error** statement and after an **Exit Sub** or **Exit Function** statement within an error-handling routine.

Caution If you set up an error handler using **On Error GoTo** and that error handler calls another procedure, the value of **Err** and **Erl** may be reset to 0. To make sure that the value doesn't change, assign the values of **Err** or **Erl** to variables before calling another procedure or before executing **Resume**, **On Error**, **Exit Sub**, **Exit Function**, or **Exit Property**.

You can directly set the value returned by the **Err** function using the **Err** statement. You can set values for both **Err** and **Erl** indirectly using the **Error** statement.

The **Erl** function returns only a line number, not a line label, located at or before the line producing the error. Line numbers greater than 65,529 are treated as line labels and can't be returned by **Erl**. If your procedure has no line numbers, or if there is no line number before the point at which an error occurs, **Erl** returns 0.

See Also   **Err** Statement, **Error** Function, **Error** Statement, **On Error** Statement, **Resume** Statement., Trappable Errors.

Example   ·   This example shows an error-handling routine which uses the **Err** and **Erl** functions. If there are no additional errors, **Err** returns error number 11 and **Erl** returns line 1030.

```
Sub ErrDemo()
1010  On Error GoTo ErrorHandler        ' Set up an error handler.
1020  B = 1: C = 0                       ' Initialize variables.
1030  A = B \ C              ' Cause a "Division by zero" error.
1040  Exit Sub
ErrorHandler:                  ' Error handler.
    ErrorNumber = Err            ' Get run-time error number.
    ErrorLine = Erl              ' Get line number.
    Resume Next              ' Resume execution at next line.
End Sub
```

Error Function

Description   Returns the error message that corresponds to a given error number.

Syntax	**Error**[(*errornumber*)]
Elements	The *errornumber* argument can be any valid error number. If *errornumber* is not defined, an error occurs. If omitted, the message corresponding to the most recent run-time error is returned. If no run-time error has occurred, **Error** returns a zero-length string (**""**).
Remarks	Use the **Err** function to return the error number for the most recent run-time error.
See Also	**Erl** Function, **Err** Function, **Error** Statement, Trappable Errors.
Example	This example uses the **Error** function to print error messages that correspond to the specified error numbers.

```
For ErrorNumber = 61 To 64          ' Loop through values 61 - 64.
    Debug.Print Error(ErrorNumber)  ' Print error to Debug window.
Next ErrorNumber
```

Error Statement

Description	Simulates the occurrence of an error.
Syntax	**Error** *errornumber*
Elements	The *errornumber* can be any valid error number.
Remarks	If *errornumber* is defined, the **Error** statement simulates the occurrence of that error; that is, it sets the value of **Err** to *errornumber*.
	To define your own error numbers, use a number greater than any of the standard error numbers. To avoid conflict with existing error numbers, create user-defined errors by defining your first error at 65,535 and work down from there.
	If an **Error** statement is executed when no error-handling routine is enabled, an error message is displayed and execution stops. If the **Error** statement specifies an error number that is not used, an error message is displayed.
See Also	**Erl** Function, **Err** Function, **Error** Function, **On Error** Statement, **Resume** Statement, Trappable Errors.
Example	This example uses the **Error** statement to simulate error 11.

```
On Error Resume Next    ' Enable error handling.
Error 11                ' Simulate the "Division by zero" error.
```

ErrorBar Method

Applies To	Series.
Description	Applies error bars to the series.
Syntax	*object*.**ErrorBar**(*direction, include, type, amount, minusValues*)
Elements	The **ErrorBar** method has the following object qualifier and named arguments:

object
Required. The Series object.

direction
Optional. Specifies the error bar direction (can be **xlX** or **xlY**; X is only available for scatter charts). If omitted, error bars are applied in the Y direction.

include
Optional. Specifies the error bar parts to include (one of **xlPlusValues**, **xlMinusValues**, **xlNone**, or **xlBoth**). If omitted, both error bars are included.

type
Optional. Specifies the error bar type (one of **xlFixedValue**, **xlPercent**, **xlStDev**, **xlStError**, or **xlCustom**).

amount
Optional. The error amount. Used for only the positive error amount when *type* = **xlCustom**.

minusValues
Optional. The negative error amount when *type* = **xlCustom**.

See Also	**ErrorBars** Property, **HasErrorBars** Property.
Example	This example applies standard error bars in the Y direction, including both positive and negative.

```
ActiveChart.SeriesCollection(1).ErrorBar _
    direction:=xlY, include:=xlBoth, type:=xlStError
```

ErrorBars Object

Description	Error bars on a chart.

ErrorBars Property

Applies To   Series.

Description   Returns the ErrorBars for the series. Read-only.

Syntax   *object*.**ErrorBars**

Elements   *object*
        Required. The Series object.

See Also   **ErrorBar** Method, **HasErrorBars** Property.

Example   This example sets the error bar color.

```
With ActiveChart.SeriesCollection(1)
    .HasErrorBars = True
    .ErrorBars.Border.Color = RGB(0, 255, 0)
End With
```

Evaluate Method

Applies To   Application, Chart, DialogSheet, Worksheet.

Description   Converts a Microsoft Excel name to an object or to a value.

Syntax   *object*.**Evaluate(*name*)**

Elements   The **Evaluate** method has the following object qualifier and named arguments:

object
    Optional for Application, required for Chart, DialogSheet, and Worksheet.
    Contains the named object.

name
    Required. The name of the object, using Microsoft Excel's naming convention.

Remarks   The following names in Microsoft Excel may be used with this method:

A1-style references. Any reference to a single cell using A1 notation. All references are considered to be absolute references.

Ranges. You may use the range, intersect, and union operators (colon, space, and comma) with references.

Defined names in the language of the macro.

External references using the ! operator. These references could be to a cell or a name defined in another workbook, for example, **Evaluate("[BOOK1.XLS]Sheet1!A1")**.

Graphic objects using their Microsoft Excel name (**"Oval 3"**, for example). You cannot use the number alone.

Note Using square brackets (for example, **[A1:C5]**) is identical to calling the **Evaluate** method with a string argument. For example, the following expression pairs are equivalent:

```
[a1].Value = 25
Evaluate("A1").Value = 25
trigVariable = [SIN(45)]
trigVariable = Evaluate("SIN(45)")
Set firstCellInSheet = Workbooks("BOOK1.XLS").Sheets(4).[A1]
Set firstCellInSheet = Workbooks("BOOK1.XLS").Sheets(4).Evaluate("A1")
```

The advantage of using square brackets is that it is shorter. The advantage of using **Evaluate** is that the argument is a string, so you can construct the string in your code or use a Visual Basic variable.

Example

This example turns on bold formatting in cell A1.

```
boldCell = "A1"
Application.Evaluate(boldCell).Font.Bold = True
```

Excel4IntlMacroSheets Method

Applies To

Application, Workbook.

Description

Returns a Microsoft Excel 4.0 international macro sheet (a Worksheet object, Syntax 1) or a collection of all Microsoft Excel 4.0 international macro sheets (a Worksheets object, Syntax 2) in the workbook. Read-only.

Syntax 1

object.**Excel4IntlMacroSheets**(*index*)

Syntax 2

object.**Excel4IntlMacroSheets**

Elements

The **Excel4IntlMacroSheets** method has the following object qualifier and named arguments:

object
> Optional for Application, required for Workbook. The object that contains Microsoft Excel 4.0 international macro sheets.

index
>Required for Syntax 1. The name or number of the Microsoft Excel 4.0 international macro sheet to return.

Remarks   Using this method with no object qualifier is a shortcut for **ActiveWorkbook.Excel4IntlMacroSheets**.

See Also   **Excel4MacroSheets** Method, **Worksheets** Method.

Example   This example displays the number of Microsoft Excel 4.0 international macro sheets in the active workbook.

```
MsgBox "There are " & ActiveWorkbook.Excel4IntlMacroSheets.Count & _
    " Microsoft Excel 4.0 international macro sheets in this workbook"
```

Excel4MacroSheets Method

Applies To   Application, Workbook.

Description   Returns a Microsoft Excel 4.0 macro sheet (a Worksheet object, Syntax 1) or a collection of all Microsoft Excel 4.0 macro sheets (a Worksheets object, Syntax 2) in the workbook. Read-only.

Syntax 1   *object*.**Excel4MacroSheets(*index*)**

Syntax 2   *object*.**Excel4MacroSheets**

Elements   The **Excel4MacroSheets** method has the following object qualifier and named arguments:

object
>Optional for Application, required for Workbook. The object that contains Microsoft Excel 4.0 macro sheets.

index
>Required for Syntax 1. The name or number of the Microsoft Excel 4.0 macro sheet to return.

Remarks   Using this method with no object qualifier is a shortcut for **ActiveWorkbook.Excel4MacroSheets**.

See Also   **Excel4IntlMacroSheets** Method, **Worksheets** Method.

Example   This example displays the number of Microsoft Excel 4.0 macro sheets in the active workbook.

```
MsgBox "There are " & ActiveWorkbook.Excel4MacroSheets.Count & _
    " Microsoft Excel 4.0 macro sheets in this workbook"
```

ExecuteExcel4Macro Method

Applies To   Application.

Description   Runs a Microsoft Excel 4.0 macro function and returns the results of the function. Returned type depends on the function. Read-write.

Syntax   *object*.**ExecuteExcel4Macro**(*string*)

Elements   The **ExecuteExcel4Macro** method has the following object qualifier and named arguments:

object
Optional. The Application object.

string
Required. A Microsoft Excel 4.0 macro language function without the equal sign. All references must be given as R1C1 strings. If *string* contains embedded double quotation marks, then you must double them. For example, to run the macro function =MID("sometext",1,4), *string* would have to be "MID(""sometext"",1,4)".

Remarks   The Microsoft Excel 4.0 macro is not evaluated in the context of the current workbook or sheet. This means that any references should be external and should specify an explicit workbook name. For example, to run a Microsoft Excel 4.0 macro "My_Macro" in Book1 you must use "Book1!My_Macro()". If you do not specify the workbook name, this method fails.

See Also   **Run** Method.

Example   This example runs the ZOOM macro function on a worksheet.

```
Worksheets(1).Activate
Application.ExecuteExcel4Macro "ZOOM(50)"
```

Exit Statement

Description   Exits a block of **Do...Loop**, **For...Next**, **Function**, **Sub**, or **Property** code.

Syntax	**Exit Do**
	Exit For
	Exit Function
	Exit Property
	Exit Sub
Elements	The **Exit** statement syntax has these forms:

Statement	Description
Exit Do	Provides a way to exit a **Do...Loop** statement. It can be used only inside a **Do...Loop** statement. **Exit Do** transfers control to the statement following the **Loop** statement. When used within nested **Do...Loop** statements, **Exit Do** transfers control to the loop that is one nested level above the loop where it occurs.
Exit For	Provides a way to exit a **For** loop. It can be used only in a **For...Next** or **For Each...Next** loop. **Exit For** transfers control to the statement following the **Next** statement. When used within nested **For** loops, **Exit For** transfers control to the loop that is one nested level above the loop where it occurs.
Exit Function	Immediately exits the **Function** procedure in which it appears. Execution continues with the statement following the statement that called the **Function**.
Exit Property	Immediately exits the **Property** procedure in which it appears. Execution continues with the statement following the statement that called the **Property** procedure.
Exit Sub	Immediately exits the **Sub** procedure in which it appears. Execution continues with the statement following the statement that called the **Sub**.

Remarks   Do not confuse **Exit** statements with **End** statements. **Exit** does not define the end of a structure.

See Also   **Do...Loop** Statement, **End** Statement, **For...Next** Statement, **Function** Statement, **Property Get** Statement, **Property Let** Statement, **Property Set** Statement, **Stop** Statement, **Sub** Statement.

Example   This example uses the **Exit** statement to exit a **For...Next** loop, a **Do...Loop**, and a **Sub** procedure.

```
Sub ExitStatementDemo()
    Do                    ' Set up infinite loop.
    For I = 1 To 1000     ' Loop 1000 times.
    MyNum = Int(Rnd * 1000) ' Generate random numbers.
    Select Case MyNum     ' Evaluate random number.
    Case 7: Exit For      ' If 7, exit For...Next.
    Case 29: Exit Do      ' If 29, exit Do...Loop.
    Case 54: Exit Sub     ' If 54, exit Sub procedure.
    End Select
    Next I
    Loop
End Sub
```

Exp Function

Description   Returns *e* (the base of natural logarithms) raised to a power.

Syntax   **Exp(*number*)**

Elements   The ***number*** named argument can be any valid numeric expression.

Remarks   If the value of ***number*** exceeds 709.782712893, an error occurs. The constant *e* is approximately 2.718282.

Note The **Exp** function complements the action of the **Log** function and is sometimes referred to as the antilogarithm.

See Also   **Log** Function.

Example   This example uses the **Exp** function to return *e* raised to a power.

```
' Define angle in radians.
MyAngle = 1.3
' Calculate hyperbolic sine.
MyHSin = (Exp(MyAngle) - Exp(- 1 * MyAngle)) / 2
```

Explosion Property

Applies To   Point, Series.

Description	Returns or sets the percentage of pie-chart or doughnut-chart slice explosion. Zero is no explosion (the tip of the slice is in the center of the pie). Read-write.
Syntax	*object*.Explosion
Elements	*object* Required. The Point or Series object.
Example	This example sets the explosion value for point five on the active chart.

```
ActiveChart.SeriesCollection(1).Points(5).Explosion = 50
```

Extend Method

Applies To	SeriesCollection.
Description	Adds new data points to an existing series collection.
Syntax	*object*.**Extend**(*source, rowcol, categoryLabels*)
Elements	The **Extend** method has the following object qualifier and named arguments:

object
Required. The SeriesCollection object.

source
Required. Specifies the new data to be added to the SeriesCollection, either as a Range or an array of data points.

rowcol
Optional. Specifies whether the new values are in the rows (**xlRows**) or columns (**xlColumns**) of the given range source. If this argument is omitted, Microsoft Excel attempts to determine where the values are by the size and orientation of the selected range or dimensions of the array. This argument is ignored if the source data is in an array.

categoryLabels
Optional. Ignored if *source* is an array. **True** if the first row or column contains the name of the category labels. **False** if the first row or column contains the first data point of the series. If this argument is omitted, Microsoft Excel attempts to determine the category label location from the contents of the first row or column.

See Also	**Add** Method (SeriesCollection).
Example	This example adds the data in column one to series collection one.

```
Application.Charts(1).SeriesCollection.Extend _
    Worksheets(1).Columns(1), xlColumns, False
```

FileAttr Function

Description	Returns file mode or operating system file handle information for files opened using the **Open** statement.
Syntax	**FileAttr(*filenumber,returnType*)**
Elements	The **FileAttr** function syntax has these named-argument parts:

Part	Description
filenumber	Any valid file number.
returnType	Number indicating the type of information to return: specify **1** to return a value indicating the file mode; specify **2** to return the operating system file handle.

Return Values   When the *returnType* argument is 1, the following return values indicate the file mode:

Value	File Mode
1	Input
2	Output
4	Random
8	Append
32	Binary

See Also   **GetAttr** Function, **Open** Statement, **SetAttr** Statement.

Example   This example uses the **FileAttr** function to return the file mode and file handle of an open file.

```
FileNum = 1                      ' Assign file number.
Open "TESTFILE" For Append As FileNum    ' Open file.
Handle = FileAttr(FileNum, 1)        ' Returns 8 (Append file mode).
Mode = FileAttr(FileNum, 2)      ' Returns file handle.
Close FileNum                    ' Close file.
```

FileConverters Property

Applies To	Application.
Description	Returns a list of installed file converters as a text array. Each row in the array contains information about a single file converter, as shown in the following table. Returns **Null** if there are no converters installed. Read-only.

Column	Contents
1	The long name of the converter, including the filetype search string in Microsoft Windows (for example "Lotus 1-2-3 Files (*.wk*)").
2	The path name of the converter DLL or code resource.
3	The file extension search string in Microsoft Windows or the four-character file type on the Apple Macintosh.

Syntax

object.**FileConverters**

Elements

object
    Required. The Application object.

Example

This example sets the `foundMultiplan` variable to **True** if the Multiplan file converter is installed.

```
installedCvts = Application.FileConverters
foundMultiplan = False
If Not IsNull(installedCvts) Then
    For row = 1 To UBound(installedCvts, 1)
        If installedCvts(row, 1) Like "*Multiplan*" Then
            foundMultiplan = True
            Exit For
        End If
    Next row
End If
```

FileCopy Statement

Description

Copies a file.

Syntax

FileCopy *source*, *destination*

Elements

The **FileCopy** statement syntax has these named argument parts:

Part	Description
source	String expression that specifies the name of the file to be copied{bmc emdash.bmp}may include directory or folder, and drive.
destination	String expression that specifies the target file name{bmc emdash.bmp}may include directory or folder, and drive.

Remarks

Open files can only be copied for read-only access.

See Also

Kill Statement, **Name** Statement.

Example

This example uses the **FileCopy** statement to copy one file to another. For purposes of this example, assume that SRCFILE is a file containing some data.

```
SourceFile = "SRCFILE"              ' Define source file name.
DestinationFile = "DESTFILE"        ' Define target file name.
FileCopy SourceFile, DestinationFile      ' Copy source to target.
```

FileDateTime Function

Description

Returns a date that indicates the date and time when a file was created or last modified .

Syntax

FileDateTime(*pathname*)

Elements

The *pathname* named argument is a string expression that specifies a file name{bmc emdash.bmp}may include directory or folder, and drive.

See Also

FileLen Function, **GetAttr** Function.

Example

This example uses the **FileDateTime** function to get the date and time when a file was created or last modified. The format of the date and time displayed is based on the locale settings of your system.

```
' Assume TESTFILE was last modified on February 12 1993 at 4:35:47 PM.
' Assume United States/English locale settings.
MyStamp = FileDateTime("TESTFILE")        ' Returns "2/12/93 4:35:47 PM".
```

FileFormat Property

Applies To

Workbook.

Description

Returns the file format and/or type of the workbook, as shown in the following list. Read-only.

xlAddIn	xlExcel3	xlTextMSDOS
xlCSV	xlExcel4	xlTextWindows
xlCSVMac	xlExcel4Workbook	xlTextPrinter
xlCSVMSDOS	xlIntlAddIn	xlWK1
xlCSVWindows	xlIntlMacro	xlWK3
xlDBF2	xlNormal	xlWKS
xlDBF3	xlSYLK	xlWQ1
xlDBF4	xlTemplate	xlWK3FM3
xlDIF	xlText	xlWK1FMT
xlExcel2	xlTextMac	xlWK1ALL

Syntax   *object*.**FileFormat**

Elements   *object*
      Required. The Workbook object.

Remarks   The following additional formats are available in Far East Microsoft Excel:
xlWJ2WD1, **xlExcel2FarEast**, and **xlWorks2FarEast.**

Example   This example saves the active workbook in Normal file format if its current file
format is WK3.

```
If ActiveWorkbook.FileFormat = xlWK3 Then
    ActiveWorkbook.SaveAs fileFormat:=xlNormal
End If
```

FileLen Function

Description   Returns the length of a file in bytes.

Syntax   **FileLen(*pathname*)**

Elements   The ***pathname*** named argument is a string expression that specifies a file
name{bmc emdash.bmp}may include directory or folder, and drive.

Remarks   If the specified file is open when the **FileLen** function is called, the value returned
represents the last saved disk size of the file.

To obtain the length of an open file, use the **LOF** function.

See Also   **FileDateTime** Function, **GetAttr** Function, **LOF** Function.

Example	This example uses the **FileLen** function to return the length of a file in bytes. For purposes of this example, assume that TESTFILE is a file containing some data.

```
MySize = FileLen("TESTFILE")    ' Returns file length (bytes).
```

FillAcrossSheets Method

Applies To	Sheets, Worksheets.
Description	Copies a range to the same area on all other worksheets in a collection.
Syntax	*object*.**FillAcrossSheets**(*range, type*)
Elements	The **FillAcrossSheets** method has the following object qualifier and named arguments:

object
Required. The Sheets or Worksheets object.

range
Required. Specifies the range to fill across the worksheets in the collection. The range must be from a worksheet within the collection.

type
Optional. Specifies how to copy the range (one of **xlAll**, **xlContents**, or **xlFormulas**). The default is **xlAll** if this argument is omitted.

Example	This example fills the range A1:C5 on sheets one, five and seven.

```
x = Array("Sheet1", "Sheet5", "Sheet7")
Sheets(x).FillAcrossSheets _
    Worksheets("Sheet1").Range("A1:C5")
```

FillDown Method

Applies To	Range.
Description	Fills down from the top cell or cells of the range to the bottom. Copies the contents and formats of the cell or cells in the top row of a range into the rest of the rows in the range.
Syntax	*object*.**FillDown**
Elements	*object* Required. The range to fill.
See Also	**AutoFill** Method, **FillLeft** Method, **FillRight** Method, **FillUp** Method.

Example   This example copies the contents and formats from cell A1 to A10.

```
Range("A1", "A10").FillDown
```

FillLeft Method

Applies To   Range.

Description   Fills left from the rightmost cell or cells of the range to the left. Copies the contents and formats of the cell or cells in the right column of a range into the rest of the columns in the range.

Syntax   *object*.**FillLeft**

Elements   *object*
                 Required. The range to fill.

See Also   **AutoFill** Method, **FillDown** Method, **FillRight** Method, **FillUp** Method.

Example   This example copies the contents and formats from cell H1 into the range A1:H1.

```
Range("A1", "H1").FillLeft
```

FillRight Method

Applies To   Range.

Description   Fills right from the leftmost cell or cells of the range to the right. Copies the contents and formats of the cell or cells in the left column of a range into the rest of the columns in the range.

Syntax   *object*.**FillRight**

Elements   *object*
                 Required. The range to fill.

See Also   **AutoFill** Method, **FillDown** Method, **FillLeft** Method, **FillUp** Method.

Example   This example copies the contents and formats from cell A1 into the range A1:H1.

```
Range("A1", "H1").FillRight
```

FillUp Method

Applies To   Range.

Description   Fills up from the bottommost cell or cells of the range to the top. Copies the contents and formats of the cell or cells in the bottom row of a range into the rest of the rows in the range.

Syntax   *object*.**FillUp**

Elements   *object*
                        Required. The range to fill.

See Also   **AutoFill** Method, **FillDown** Method, **FillLeft** Method, **FillRight** Method.

Example   This example copies the contents and formats from cell A10 into the range A1:A10.

```
Range("A1:A10").FillUp
```

FilterMode Property

Applies To   Worksheet.

Description   **True** if the worksheet is in filter mode. Read-only.

Syntax   *object*.**FilterMode**

Elements   *object*
                        Required. The Worksheet object.

Remarks   This property will be **True** if the worksheet contains a filtered list in which there are hidden rows.

See Also   **AdvancedFilter** Method, **AutoFilter** Method, **AutoFilterMode** Property, **ShowAllData** Method.

Example   This example displays a message box that shows the current status of the **FilterMode** property.

```
If ActiveSheet.FilterMode Then
    isItOn = "On"
Else
    isItOn = "Off"
End If
MsgBox "Filter mode is " & isItOn
```

Find Method

Applies To   Range.

Description   Finds a cell containing specific information in a range, and returns the first cell (a Range object) where it is found. Does not affect the selection or active cell.

For help about using the **Find** worksheet function in Visual Basic, see Using Worksheet Functions in Visual Basic.

Syntax   *object*.**Find**(*what, after, lookIn, lookAt, searchOrder, searchDirection, matchCase*)

Elements   The **Find** method has the following object qualifier and named arguments:

object
   Required. The range to search.

what
   Required. The contents for which you want to search. May be a string, or any Microsoft Excel data type.

after
   Optional. The first cell after which you want to search. This corresponds to the position of the active cell when a search is done from the user interface. If omitted, the top left cell of the range is used as the starting point for the search. *After* must be one cell in the range. (See the examples for an explanation.)

lookIn
   Optional. One of **xlFormulas**, **xlValues**, or **xlNotes**. If omitted, **xlFormulas** is assumed.

lookAt
   Optional. May be **xlWhole** or **xlPart**; if omitted it is **xlPart**.

searchOrder
   Optional. One of **xlByRows** (to search row-major) or **xlByColumns** (to search column-major). If omitted, **xlByRows** is assumed.

searchDirection
   Optional. **xlNext** or **xlPrevious**; if omitted it is **xlNext**.

matchCase
   Optional. If **True**, case-sensitive search is performed. If **False** or omitted, case-insensitive search is performed.

Remarks   The **FindNext** and **FindPrevious** methods can be used to repeat the search.

To find cells matching more complicated patterns, use **For Each** with the **Like** operator. For example, the following code searches for all cells in the range A1:C5 that use a font starting with the letters "Cour". When it finds a match, it changes the font to Times New Roman:

```
For Each c In [A1:C5]
    If c.Font.Name Like "Cour*" Then
        c.Font.Name = "Times New Roman"
    End If
Next
```

See Also   **FindNext** Method, **FindPrevious** Method, **InStr** Function, **Len** Function, **Mid** Function, **Replace** Method.

Examples   These examples show typical uses for the **Find** method:

```
' Find "Phoenix" in Column H and activate it:
Columns("H").Find("Phoenix").Activate

' Search in column A for the first occurrence of the
' string "oscar", which appears below (but not in) A3, and select it:
Columns("A").Find("oscar", after := [A3]).Select

' User selects A1:C5 and makes B3 active.
' Then they search for "word". This is the equivalent in Basic:
Selection.Find("word", after := ActiveCell).Activate
' To find the next occurrence:
Selection.FindNext(after := ActiveCell).Activate
```

FindFile Method

Applies To   Application.

Description   Displays the dialog box for the Find File command. This dialog can only be displayed interactively (it cannot be preset).

Syntax   *object*.**FindFile**

Elements   *object*
     Required. The Application object.

Example   This example displays the dialog box for the Find File command.

```
Application.FindFile
```

FindNext Method

Applies To   Range.

Description   Continues a search started with the **Find** method. Finds the next cell matching the same conditions and returns that cell (a Range object). Does not affect the selection or active cell.

Syntax   *object*.**FindNext(*after*)**

Elements   The **FindNext** method has the following object qualifier and named arguments:

object
Required. The range to search.

after
Optional. The first cell after which you want to search. This corresponds to the position of the active cell when a search is done from the user interface. If omitted, the top left cell of the range is used as the starting point for the search.

See Also   **Find** Method, **FindPrevious** Method, **Replace** Method.

Example   This example finds the next two occurrences of the word "Phoenix":

```
' Find "Phoenix" in Column H and select it:
Columns("H").Find("Phoenix").Activate
' Now find the next occurrence:
Columns("H").FindNext(ActiveCell).Activate
' Now find the first occurrence in column A:
Columns("A").FindNext().Activate
```

FindPrevious Method

Applies To   Range.

Description   Continues a search started with the **Find** method. Finds the previous cell matching the same conditions and returns that cell (a Range object). Does not affect the selection or active cell.

Syntax   *object*.**FindPrevious(*after*)**

Elements   The **FindPrevious** method has the following object qualifier and named arguments:

object
Required. The range to search.

after
> Optional. The first cell before which you want to search. This corresponds to the position of the active cell when a search is done from the user interface. If omitted, the top left cell of the range is used as the starting point for the search (because the search proceeds backwards from this cell, it immediately wraps around to the bottom right cell in the range).

See Also   **Find** Method, **FindNext** Method, **Replace** Method.

Example   This example finds the previous occurrence of the word "Phoenix".

```
' Find "Phoenix" in Column H and select it:
Columns("H").Find("Phoenix").Activate
' Now find the previous occurrence:
Columns("H").FindPrevious(ActiveCell).Activate
```

FirstPageNumber Property

Applies To   PageSetup.

Description   Returns or sets the first page number that will be used for printing this sheet (the default value is **xlAutomatic**). Read-write.

Syntax   *object*.**FirstPageNumber**

Elements   *object*
> Required. The PageSetup object (**ActiveSheet.PageSetup**, for example).

Example   This example sets the first page number for this sheet to 100.

```
ActiveSheet.PageSetup.FirstPageNumber = 100
```

FirstSliceAngle Property

Applies To   ChartGroup.

Description   Returns or sets the angle of the first pie or doughnut slice for a pie, 3-D pie, or doughnut chart, in degrees clockwise from vertical. Applies only to pie, 3-D pie, and doughnut charts. Read-write.

Syntax   *object*.**FirstSliceAngle**

Elements   *object*
> Required. The ChartGroup object.

Example   This example sets the angle for the first slice in the first chart group.

```
ActiveChart.ChartGroups(1).FirstSliceAngle = 15
```

FitToPagesTall Property

Applies To   PageSetup.

Description   Returns or sets how many pages tall the worksheet will be scaled to when it is printed. The **Zoom** property must be **False**, or this property is ignored. Read-write.

Syntax   *object*.**FitToPagesTall**

Elements   *object*
                     Required. The PageSetup object (**ActiveSheet.PageSetup**, for example).

Remarks   If this property is **False**, Microsoft Excel scales the worksheet according to the **FitToPagesWide** property.

                     This property applies only to worksheets.

Example   This example causes the active sheet to print exactly one page wide and tall.

```
With ActiveSheet.PageSetup
    .Zoom = False
    .FitToPagesTall = 1
    .FitToPagesWide = 1
End With
```

FitToPagesWide Property

Applies To   PageSetup.

Description   Returns or sets how many pages wide the worksheet will be scaled when it is printed. The **Zoom** property must be **False,** or this property is ignored. Read-write.

Syntax   *object*.**FitToPagesWide**

Elements   *object*
                     Required. The PageSetup object (**ActiveSheet.PageSetup**, for example).

Remarks   If this property is **False**, Microsoft Excel scales the worksheet according to the **FitToPagesTall** property.

                     This property applies only to worksheets.

Example

This example causes the active sheet to print exactly one page wide and tall.

```
With ActiveSheet.PageSetup
    .Zoom = False
    .FitToPagesTall = 1
    .FitToPagesWide = 1
End With
```

FixedDecimal Property

Applies To

Application.

Description

All data entered after this property is set to **True** will be formatted with the number of fixed decimal places set by the **FixedDecimalPlaces** property.

Syntax

object.**FixedDecimal**

Elements

object
    Required. The Application object.

Example

This example sets the **FixedDecimal** property to **True**, and then sets the **FixedDecimalPlaces** property to 4. Entering "30000" after this code runs produces "3" on the worksheet, and entering "12500" produces "1.25."

```
Application.FixedDecimal = True
Application.FixedDecimalPlaces = 4
```

FixedDecimalPlaces Property

Applies To

Application.

Description

Returns or sets the number of fixed decimal places used when the **FixedDecimal** property is set to **True**. Read-write.

Syntax

object.**FixedDecimalPlaces**

Elements

object
    Required. The Application object.

Example

This example sets the **FixedDecimal** property to **True**, and then sets the **FixedDecimalPlaces** property to 4. Entering "30000" after this code runs produces "3" on the worksheet, and entering "12500" produces "1.25."

```
Application.FixedDecimal = True
Application.FixedDecimalPlaces = 4
```

Floor Object

Description   The floor of a 3-D chart.

Floor Property

Applies To   Chart.

Description   Returns the Floor of the 3-D chart. Read-only.

For help about using the **Floor** worksheet function in Visual Basic, see Using Worksheet Functions in Visual Basic.

Syntax   *object*.**Floor**

Elements   *object*
                    Required. The Chart object.

Example   This example sets the chart floor color.

```
Charts(1).Floor.Interior.Color = RGB(255, 0, 0)
```

Focus Property

Applies To   DialogSheet.

Description   Returns or sets the dynamic focus of the running dialog box, as a string containing the ID for the control with the focus. The control with the focus is where user keyboard input is directed, and the focus is visually indicated by a dashed rectangle around the control or around selections within the control. Read-write.

Syntax   *object*.**Focus**

Elements   *object*
                    Required. The DialogSheet object.

Remarks   Reading and setting this property while the dialog is not running will cause an error. While the dialog is running, setting this property will attempt to change the focus to the specified control. Not all controls will accept the focus, and the dialog manager may refuse to move the focus under certain conditions. Reading this property always returns the ID of the control with the focus.

Example

This example sets the focus to edit box one if it does not contain a number.

```
If Not IsNumeric(myDialog.EditBoxes(1).Text) Then
    myDialog.Focus = myDialog.EditBoxes(1).Name
End If
```

Font Object

Description

A font description. The Font object contains all font attributes (font name, font size, color, and so on) as properties.

Font Property

Applies To

AxisTitle, Button, Buttons, Characters, ChartArea, ChartTitle, DataLabel, DataLabels, DrawingObjects, GroupObject, GroupObjects, Legend, LegendEntry, PlotArea, Range, Style, TextBox, TextBoxes, TickLabels.

Description

Returns or sets the Font of the object. Read-write.

Syntax

object.**Font**

Elements

object
     Required. The object to which this property applies.

See Also

Font Object.

Example

This example sets the font in the active cell to 14-point bold italic.

```
With ActiveCell.Font
    .Size = 14
    .Bold = True
    .Italic = True
End With
```

FontStyle Property

Applies To

Font.

Description

Returns or sets the font style (as a string). Read-write.

Syntax	*object*.**FontStyle**
Elements	*object* Required. The Font object.
Remarks	Changing this property may affect other Font properties (such as **Bold** and **Italic**). Unlike most properties, this property is always in the language of the system because the system determines which fonts are available. So instead of being able to use "Bold" from an English macro running on Spanish Windows, you must use "Negrita." Use the separate Font object properties to work around this restriction.
See Also	**Font** Object, **Background** Property, **Bold** Property, **Color** Property, **ColorIndex** Property, **Italic** Property, **Name** Property, **OutlineFont** Property, **Shadow** Property, **Size** Property, **Strikethrough** Property, **Subscript** Property, **Superscript** Property, **Underline** Property.
Example	This example sets the font style for cell A1.

```
Cells(1, 1).Font.FontStyle = "Bold Italic"
```

FooterMargin Property

Applies To	PageSetup.
Description	Returns or sets the distance from the bottom of the page to the footer, in points (1/72 inch). Read-write.
Syntax	*object*.**FooterMargin**
Elements	*object* Required. The PageSetup object.
See Also	**BottomMargin** Property, **HeaderMargin** Property, **LeftMargin** Property, **RightMargin** Property, **TopMargin** Property.
Example	This example sets the footer margin to one-half inch.

```
ActiveSheet.PageSetup.FooterMargin = Application.InchesToPoints(0.5)
```

For Each...Next Statement

Description	Repeats a group of statements for each element in an array or collection.

Syntax	**For Each** *element* **In** *group* 　　[*statements*] 　　[**Exit For**] 　　[*statements*] **Next** [*element*]
Elements	The **For Each...Next** statement syntax has these parts:

Part	Description
element	Variable used to iterate through the elements of the collection or array. For collections, *element* can only be a **Variant** variable, a generic **Object** variable, or any specific OLE Automation object variable. For arrays, *element* can only be a **Variant** variable.
group	Name of an object collection or array (except an array of user-defined types).
statements	One or more statements that are executed on each item in *collection*.

Important When using **For Each... Next** with arrays, you can only read the value contained in the array elements indicated by the control variable *element*. You cannot set the value by assigning a value to *element*.

Remarks

The **For Each** block is entered if there is at least one element in *group*. Once the loop has been entered, all the statements in the loop are executed for the first element in *group*. Then, as long as there are more elements in *group*, the statements in the loop continue to execute for each element. When there are no more elements in *group*, the loop is exited and execution continues with the statement following the **Next** statement.

The **Exit For** can only be used within a **For Each...Next** or **For...Next** control structure to provide an alternate way to exit. Any number of **Exit For** statements may be placed anywhere in the loop. The **Exit For** is often used with the evaluation of some condition (for example, **If...Then**), and transfers control to the statement immediately following **Next**.

You can nest **For Each...Next** loops by placing one **For Each...Next** loop within another. However, each loop *element* must be unique.

Note If you omit *element* in a **Next** statement, execution continues as if you had included it. If a **Next** statement is encountered before its corresponding **For** statement, an error occurs.

You can't use the **For Each...Next** statement with an array of user-defined types because a **Variant** can't contain a user-defined type.

See Also

Do...Loop Statement, **Exit** Statement, **For...Next** Statement, **While...Wend** Statement.

Example

This example uses the **For Each...Next** statement to search the `Text` property of all elements in a collection for the existence of the string "Hello". In the example, `MyObject` is a text-related object and is an element of the collection `MyCollection`. Both are generic names used for illustration purposes only.

```
Found = False   ' Initialize variable.
For Each MyObject In MyCollection   ' Iterate through each element.
    If MyObject.Text = "Hello" Then ' If Text equals "Hello".
        Found = True' Set Found to True.
        Exit For' Exit loop.
    End If
Next
```

For...Next Statement

Description

Repeats a group of statements a specified number of times.

Syntax

For *counter* = *start* **To** *end* [**Step** *step*]
    [*statements*]
    [**Exit For**]
    [*statements*]
Next [*counter*]

Elements

The **For...Next** statement syntax has these parts:

Part	Description
counter	Numeric variable used as a loop counter. The variable can't be any array element or any element of a user-defined type.
start	Initial value of *counter*.
end	Final value of *counter*.
step	Amount *counter* is changed each time through the loop. If not specified, *step* defaults to one.
statements	One or more statements between **For** and **Next** that are executed the specified number of times.

Remarks

The *step* argument can be either positive or negative. The value of the *step* argument determines loop processing as follows:

Value	Loop executes if
Positive or 0	*counter* <= *end*
Negative	*counter* >= *end*

Once the loop starts and all statements in the loop have executed, *step* is added to *counter*. At this point, either the statements in the loop execute again (based on the same test that caused the loop to execute initially), or the loop is exited and execution continues with the statement following the **Next** statement.

Tip Changing the value of *counter* while inside a loop can make it more difficult to read and debug.

The **Exit For** can only be used within a **For Each...Next** or **For...Next** control structure to provide an alternate way to exit. Any number of **Exit For** statements may be placed anywhere in the loop. The **Exit For** is often used with the evaluation of some condition (for example, **If...Then**), and transfers control to the statement immediately following **Next**.

You can nest **For...Next** loops by placing one **For...Next** loop within another. Give each loop a unique variable name as its *counter*. The following construction is correct:

```
For I = 1 To 10
    For J = 1 To 10
        For K = 1 To 10
            . . .
        Next K
    Next J
Next I
```

Note If you omit *counter* in a **Next** statement, execution continues as if you had included it. If a **Next** statement is encountered before its corresponding **For** statement, an error occurs.

See Also

Do...Loop Statement, **Exit** Statement, **For Each...Next** Statement, **While...Wend** Statement.

Example

This example uses the **For...Next** statement to create a string that contains 10 instances of the numbers 0 through 9, each string separated from the other by a single space. The outer loop uses a loop counter variable that is decremented each time through the loop.

```
For Words = 10 To 1 Step -1 ' Set up 10 repetitions.
    For Chars = 0 To 9  ' Set up 10 repetitions.
        MyString = MyString & Chars ' Append number to string.
    Next Chars
    MyString = MyString & " "    ' Append a space.
Next Words
```

Format Function

Description   Formats an expression according to instructions contained in a format expression.

Syntax   **Format**(*expression*[,*format*])

Elements   The **Format** function syntax has these parts:

Part	Description
expression	Any valid *expression*.
format	A valid named or user-defined format expression.

Remarks

To Format These	Do This
Numbers	Use predefined named numeric formats or create user-defined numeric formats.
Dates and times	Use predefined named date/time formats or create user-defined date/time formats.
Date and time serial numbers	Use date and time formats or numeric formats.
Strings	Create your own user-defined string formats.

If you try to format a number without specifying *format*, **Format** provides the same functionality as the **Str** function. However, positive numbers formatted as strings using **Format** lack the leading space reserved for displaying the sign of the value; whereas, those converted using **Str** retain the leading space.

Example   This example shows various uses of the **Format** function to format values using both named and user-defined formats. For the date separator (/), time separator (:) and AM/ PM literal, the actual formatted output displayed by your system depends on the settings at the time. When times and dates are listed back in the development environment, the short time and short date formats of the code locale are used. When displayed by running code, the short time and short date formats of the system locale are used, which may be different from the code locale. For this example, English - US is assumed.

```
' MyTime and MyDate will be displayed in the development environment
' using current system short time and short date settings.
MyTime = #17:04:23#
MyDate = #January 27, 1993#

' Returns current system time in the system-defined long time format.
MyStr = Format(Time, "Long Time")

' Returns current system date in the system-defined long date format.
MyStr = Format(Date, "Long Date")
```

```
MyStr = Format(MyTime, "h:m:s")              ' Returns "17:4:23".
MyStr = Format(MyTime, "hh:mm:ss AMPM")      ' Returns "05:04:23 PM".
MyStr = Format(MyDate, "dddd, mmm d yyyy")
    ' Returns "Wednesday, Jan 27 1993".

' If format is not supplied, a string is returned.
MyStr = Format(23)                           ' Returns "23".

' User-defined formats.
MyStr = Format(5459.4, "##,##0.00")          ' Returns "5,459.40".
MyStr = Format(334.9, "###0.00")             ' Returns "334.90".
MyStr = Format(5, "0.00%")                   ' Returns "500.00%".
MyStr = Format("HELLO", "<")                 ' Returns "hello".
MyStr = Format("This is it", ">")            ' Returns "THIS IS IT".
```

Different Formats for Different Numeric Values

A format expression for numbers can have from one to four sections separated by semicolons. (If the *format* argument contains one of the predefined formats, only one section is allowed.)

If you use	The result is
One section only	The format expression applies to all values.
Two sections	The first section applies to positive values and zeros, the second to negative values.
Three sections	The first section applies to positive values, the second to negative values, and the third to zeros.
Four sections	The first section applies to positive values, the second to negative values, the third to zeros, and the fourth to **Null** values.

The following example has two sections: the first defines the format for positive values and zeros; the second section defines the format for negative values.

`"$#,##0;($#,##0)"`

If you include semicolons with nothing between them, the missing section is printed using the format of the positive value. For example, the following format displays positive and negative values using the format in the first section and displays "Zero" if the value is zero.

`"$#,##0;;\Z\e\r\o"`

Different Formats for Different String Values

A format expression for strings can have one section, or two sections separated by a semicolon.

If you use	The result is
One section only	The format applies to all string data.
Two sections	The first section applies to string data, the second to **Null** values and zero-length strings.

Named Date/Time Formats

The following table identifies the predefined date and time format names:

Format Name	Description
General Date	Display a date and/or time. For real numbers, display a date and time (for example, 4/3/93 05:34 PM); if there is no fractional part, display only a date (for example, 4/3/93); if there is no integer part, display time only (for example, 05:34 PM). Date display is determined by your system settings.
Long Date	Display a date according to your system's long date format.
Medium Date	Display a date using the medium date format appropriate for the language version of the host application.
Short Date	Display a date using your system's short date format.
Long Time	Display a time using your system's long time format: includes hours, minutes, seconds.
Medium Time	Display time in 12-hour format using hours and minutes and the AM/PM designator.
Short Time	Display a time using the 24-hour format (for example, 17:45).

Named Numeric Formats

The following table identifies the predefined numeric format names:

Format name	Description
General Number	Display number as is, with no thousand separators.
Currency	Display number with thousand separator, if appropriate; display negative numbers enclosed in parentheses; display two digits to the right of the decimal separator. Note that output is based on system settings.
Fixed	Display at least one digit to the left and two digits to the right of the decimal separator.
Standard	Display number with thousands separator, at least one digit to the left and two digits to the right of the decimal separator.

Format name	Description
Percent	Display number multiplied by 100 with a percent sign (%) appended to the right; always displays two digits to the right of the decimal separator.
Scientific	Use standard scientific notation.
Yes/No	Display No if number is 0; otherwise, display Yes.
True/False	Display **False** if number is 0; otherwise, display **True**.
On/Off	Display Off if number is 0; otherwise, display On.

See Also   **Named Date/Time** Formats.

User-Defined Date/Time Formats

The following table identifies characters you can use to create user-defined date/time formats:

Character	Description
:	Time separator. In some locales, other characters may be used to represent the time separator. The time separator separates hours, minutes, and seconds when time values are formatted. The actual character used as the time separator in formatted output is determined by your system settings.
/	Date separator. In some locales, other characters may be used to represent the date separator. The date separator separates the day, month, and year when date values are formatted. The actual character used as the date separator in formatted output is determined by your system settings.
c	Display the date as ddddd and display the time as t t t t t, in that order. Display only date information if there is no fractional part to the date serial number; display only time information if there is no integer portion.
d	Display the day as a number without a leading zero (1-31).
dd	Display the day as a number with a leading zero (01-31).
ddd	Display the day as an abbreviation (Sun-Sat).

Character	Description
dddd	Display the day as a full name (Sunday-Saturday).
ddddd	Display a date as a complete date (including day, month, and year), formatted according to your system's short date format setting. For Microsoft Windows, the default short date format is m/d/yy.
dddddd	Display a date serial number as a complete date (including day, month, and year) formatted according to the long date setting recognized by your system. For Microsoft Windows, the default long date format is mmmm dd, yyyy.
w	Display the day of the week as a number (1 for Sunday through 7 for Saturday).
ww	Display the week of the year as a number (1-53).
m	Display the month as a number without a leading zero (1-12). If m immediately follows h or hh, the minute rather than the month is displayed.
mm	Display the month as a number with a leading zero (01-12). If m immediately follows h or hh, the minute rather than the month is displayed.
mmm	Display the month as an abbreviation (Jan-Dec).
mmmm	Display the month as a full month name (January-December).
q	Display the quarter of the year as a number (1-4).
y	Display the day of the year as a number (1-366).
yy	Display the year as a 2-digit number (00-99).
yyyy	Display the year as a 4-digit number (100-9999).
h	Display the hour as a number without leading zeros (0-23).

Character	Description
hh	Display the hour as a number with leading zeros (00-23).
n	Display the minute as a number without leading zeros (0-59).
nn	Display the minute as a number with leading zeros (00-59).
s	Display the second as a number without leading zeros (0-59).
ss	Display the second as a number with leading zeros (00-59).
t t t t t	Display a time as a complete time (including hour, minute, and second), formatted using the time separator defined by the time format recognized by your system. A leading zero is displayed if the leading zero option is selected and the time is before 10:00 A.M. or P.M. The default time format is h:mm:ss.
AM/PM	Use the 12-hour clock and display an uppercase AM with any hour before noon; display an uppercase PM with any hour between noon and 11:59 P.M.
am/pm	Use the 12-hour clock and display a lowercase AM with any hour before noon; display a lowercase PM with any hour between noon and 11:59 P.M.
A/P	Use the 12-hour clock and display an uppercase A with any hour before noon; display an uppercase P with any hour between noon and 11:59 P.M.
a/p	Use the 12-hour clock and display a lowercase A with any hour before noon; display a lowercase P with any hour between noon and 11:59 P.M.
AMPM	Use the 12-hour clock and display the AM string literal as defined by your system with any hour before noon; display the PM string literal as defined by your system with any hour between noon and 11:59 P.M. AMPM can be either uppercase or lowercase, but the case of the string displayed matches the string as defined by your system settings. For Microsoft Windows, the default format is AM/PM.

Examples   The following are examples of user-defined date and time formats for December 7, 1958:

Format	Display
m/d/yy	12/7/58
d-mm	7-Dec
d-mmmm-yy	7-December-58
d-mmmm	7 December
mmmm-yy	December 58
hh:mm AM/PM	08:50 PM
h:mm:ss a/p	8:50:35 p
h:mm	20:50
h:mm:ss	20:50:35
m/d/yy h:mm	12/7/58 20:50

User-Defined Numeric Formats

The following table identifies characters you can use to create user-defined number formats:

Character	Description
None	**No formatting**
	Display the number with no formatting.
0	**Digit placeholder**
	Display a digit or a zero. If the expression has a digit in the position where the 0 appears in the format string, display it; otherwise, display a zero in that position.
	If the number has fewer digits than there are zeros (on either side of the decimal) in the format expression, display leading or trailing zeros. If the number has more digits to the right of the decimal separator than there are zeros to the right of the decimal separator in the format expression, round the number to as many decimal places as there are zeros. If the number has more digits to the left of the decimal separator than there are zeros to the left of the decimal separator in the format expression, display the extra digits without modification.
#	**Digit placeholder**
	Display a digit or nothing. If the expression has a digit in the position where the # appears in the format string, display it; otherwise, display nothing in that position.

Character	Description
	This symbol works like the 0 digit placeholder, except that leading and trailing zeros aren't displayed if the number has the same or fewer digits than there are # characters on either side of the decimal separator in the format expression.
.	**Decimal placeholder**
	In some locales, a comma is used as the decimal separator. The decimal placeholder determines how many digits are displayed to the left and right of the decimal separator. If the format expression contains only number signs to the left of this symbol, numbers smaller than 1 begin with a decimal separator. If you always want a leading zero displayed with fractional numbers, use 0 as the first digit placeholder to the left of the decimal separator instead. The actual character used as a decimal placeholder in the formatted output depends on the Number Format recognized by your system.
%	**Percentage placeholder**
	The expression is multiplied by 100. The percent character (%) is inserted in the position where it appears in the format string.
,	**Thousand separator**
	In some locales, a period is used as a thousand separator. The thousand separator separates thousands from hundreds within a number that has four or more places to the left of the decimal separator. Standard use of the thousand separator is specified if the format contains a thousand separator surrounded by digit placeholders (0 or #). Two adjacent thousand separators or a thousand separator immediately to the left of the decimal separator (whether or not a decimal is specified) means "scale the number by dividing it by 1000, rounding as needed."" You can scale large numbers using this technique. For example, you can use the format string "##0,," to represent 100 million as 100. Numbers smaller than 1 million are displayed as 0. Two adjacent thousand separators in any position other than immediately to the left of the decimal separator are treated simply as specifying the use of a thousand separator. The actual character used as the thousand separator in the formatted output depends on the Number Format recognized by your system.
:	**Time separator**
	In some locales, other characters may be used to represent the time separator. The time separator separates hours, minutes, and seconds when time values are formatted. The actual character used as the time separator in formatted output is determined by your system settings.
/	**Date separator**

Character	Description
	In some locales, other characters may be used to represent the date separator. The date separator separates the day, month, and year when date values are formatted. The actual character used as the date separator in formatted output is determined by your system settings.
E- E+ e- e+	**Scientific format**
	If the format expression contains at least one digit placeholder (0 or #) to the right of E-, E+, e-, or e+, the number is displayed in scientific format and E or e is inserted between the number and its exponent. The number of digit placeholders to the right determines the number of digits in the exponent. Use E- or e- to place a minus sign next to negative exponents. Use E+ or e+ to place a minus sign next to negative exponents and a plus sign next to positive exponents.
- + $ ( ) space	**Display a literal character**
	To display a character other than one of those listed, precede it with a backslash (\) or enclose it in double quotation marks (" ").
****	**Display the next character in the format string**
	Many characters in the format expression have a special meaning and can't be displayed as literal characters unless they are preceded by a backslash. The backslash itself isn't displayed. Using a backslash is the same as enclosing the next character in double quotation marks. To display a backslash, use two backslashes (\\).
	Examples of characters that can't be displayed as literal characters are the date- and time-formatting characters (a, c, d, h, m, n, p, q, s, t, w, y, and /:), the numeric-formatting characters (#, 0, %, E, e, comma, and period), and the string-formatting characters (@, &, <, >, and !).
"ABC"	**Display the string inside the double quotation marks**
	To include a string in *format* from within code, you must use **Chr**(34) to enclose the text (34 is the character code for a double quotation mark).

Examples   Some sample format expressions for numbers are shown below. (These examples all assume that your system's locale setting is English-US.) The first column contains the format strings. The other columns contain the output that results if the formatted data has the value given in the column headings.

Format (*format*)	Positive 5	Negative 5	Decimal .5	Null
Zero-length string	5	-5	0.5	
0	5	-5	1	
0.00	5.00	-5.00	0.50	
#,##0	5	-5	1	
#,##0.00;;;Nil	5.00	-5.00	0.50	Nil
$#,##0;($#,##0)	$5	($5)	$1	
$#,##0.00;($#,##0.00)	$5.00	($5.00)	$0.50	
0%	500%	-500%	50%	
0.00%	500.00%	-500.00%	50.00%	
0.00E+00	5.00E+00	-5.00E+00	5.00E-01	
0.00E-00	5.00E00	-5.00E00	5.00E-01	

User-Defined String Formats

You can use any of the following characters to create a format expression for strings:

Character	Description
@	**Character placeholder**

Display a character or a space. If the string has a character in the position where the @ appears in the format string, display it; otherwise, display a space in that position. Placeholders are filled from right to left unless there is an ! character in the format string. See below.

&	**Character placeholder**

Display a character or nothing. If the string has a character in the position where the & appears, display it; otherwise, display nothing. Placeholders are filled from right to left unless there is an ! character in the format string. See below.

<	**Force lowercase**

Display all characters in lowercase format.

Character	Description
>	**Force uppercase**
	Display all characters in uppercase format.
!	**Force left to right fill of placeholders**
	The default is to fill from right to left.

Formula Property

Applies To   Button, Buttons, Picture, Pictures, Range, Series, TextBox, TextBoxes.

Description   Returns or sets the object's formula, in A1-style notation and the language of the macro. Read-write.

Syntax   *object*.**Formula**

Elements   *object*
　　Required. The object to which this property applies.

Remarks   If the cell contains a constant, this property returns the constant. If the cell is empty, it returns an empty string. If the cell contains a formula, it returns the formula as a string, in the same format as it would be displayed in the formula bar (including the equal sign).

If you set the value or formula of a cell to a date, Microsoft Excel checks to see if that cell is already formatted with one of the date or time number formats. If not, it changes the number format to the default short date number format.

If the range is a one- or two-dimensional range, you can set the formula to a Visual Basic array of the same dimensions. Similarly, you can put the formula into a Visual Basic array.

Setting the formula of a multi-cell range fills all cells in the range with the formula.

When used with a Picture object, the formula must use absolute A1-style notation.

See Also   **FormulaArray** Property, **FormulaLocal** Property, **FormulaR1C1** Property, **FormulaR1C1Local** Property.

Example   This example sets the formula in cell A1.

```
Application.Cells(1, 1).Formula = "=$A$4+$A$10"
```

FormulaArray Property

Applies To   Range.

Description   Returns or sets the formula of a range, entered as an array. Returns (or can be set to) a single formula or a Visual Basic array. If the specified range is not array entered, this property returns **Null**. Read-write.

Syntax   *object*.**FormulaArray**

Elements   *object*
    Required. Return the array formula for this range.

See Also   **Formula** Property.

Example   This example enters the number 3 as an array constant in A1:C5.

```
Range(Cells(1, 1), Cells(5, 3)).FormulaArray = "=3"
```

FormulaHidden Property

Applies To   Range, Style.

Description   **True** if the formula will be hidden when the workbook or worksheet is protected. Read-write.

Syntax   *object*.**FormulaHidden**

Elements   *object*
    Required. The range this property applies to.

Remarks   Do not confuse this property with the **Hidden** property.

See Also   **Locked** Property, **Protect** Method, **Unprotect** Method.

Example   This example hides the formulas in column one when the workbook or worksheet is protected.

```
Columns(1).FormulaHidden = True
```

FormulaLocal Property

Applies To   Range, Series.

Description   Returns or sets the formula for the object, using A1-style references in the user's language. Read-write.

Syntax	*object*.**FormulaLocal**
Elements	*object* Required. The Range or Series object.
Remarks	If the cell contains a constant, this property returns the constant. If the cell is empty, it returns an empty string. If the cell contains a formula, it returns the formula as a string, in the same format as it would be displayed in the formula bar (including the equal sign).
	If you set the value or formula of a cell to a date, Microsoft Excel checks to see if that cell is already formatted with one of the date or time number formats. If not, it changes the number format to the default short date number format.
	If the range is a one- or two-dimensional range, you can set the formula to a Visual Basic array of the same dimensions. Similarly, you can put the formula into a Visual Basic array.
	Setting the formula of a multi-cell range fills all cells in the range with the formula.
See Also	**Formula** Property, **FormulaArray** Property, **FormulaR1C1** Property, **FormulaR1C1Local** Property.
Example	This example sets the formula in the active cell from cell A10.

```
ActiveCell.FormulaLocal = Range("A10").FormulaLocal
```

FormulaR1C1 Property

Applies To	Range, Series.
Description	Returns or sets the formula for the object, using R1C1-style notation in the language of the macro.
Syntax	*object*.**FormulaR1C1**
Elements	*object* Required. The Range or Series object.
Remarks	If the cell contains a constant, this property returns the constant. If the cell is empty, it returns an empty string. If the cell contains a formula, it returns the formula as a string, in the same format as it would be displayed in the formula bar (including the equal sign).
	If you set the value or formula of a cell to a date, Microsoft Excel checks to see if that cell is already formatted with one of the date or time number formats. If not, it changes the number format to the default short date number format.

If the range is a one- or two-dimensional range, you can set the formula to a Visual Basic array of the same dimensions. Similarly, you can put the formula into a Visual Basic array.

Setting the formula of a multi-cell range fills all cells in the range with the formula.

See Also   **Formula** Property, **FormulaArray** Property, **FormulaLocal** Property, **FormulaR1C1Local** Property.

Example   This example sets the formula in the active cell from cell A10.

```
ActiveCell.FormulaR1C1 = Cells(10, 1).FormulaR1C1
```

FormulaR1C1Local Property

Applies To   Range, Series.

Description   Returns or sets the the formula for the object, using R1C1-style notation in the user's language.

Syntax   *object*.**FormulaR1C1Local**

Elements   *object*
Required. The Range or Series object.

Remarks   If the cell contains a constant, this property returns the constant. If the cell is empty, it returns an empty string. If the cell contains a formula, it returns the formula as a string, in the same format as it would be displayed in the formula bar (including the equal sign).

If you set the value or formula of a cell to a date, Microsoft Excel checks to see if that cell is already formatted with one of the date or time number formats. If not, it changes the number format to the default short date number format.

If the range is a one- or two-dimensional range, you can set the formula to a Visual Basic array of the same dimensions. Similarly, you can put the formula into a Visual Basic array.

Setting the formula of a multi-cell range fills all cells in the range with the formula.

See Also   **Formula** Property, **FormulaArray** Property, **FormulaLocal** Property, **FormulaR1C1** Property.

Example   This example sets the formula in the active cell from cell A10.

```
ActiveCell.FormulaR1C1Local = Range("A10").FormulaR1C1Local
```

Forward Property

Applies To   Trendline.

Description Returns or sets the number of periods (or units on a scatter chart) that the trendline extends forward. Read-write.

Syntax   *object*.**Forward**

Elements   *object*
                Required. The Trendline object.

See Also   **Backward** Property, **ForwardMailer** Method.

Example   This example sets the number of units the trendline extends forward and backward.

```
With ActiveWorkbook.Charts(1).SeriesCollection(1).Trendlines(1)
    .Forward = 5
    .Backward = 5
End With
```

ForwardMailer Method

Applies To   Workbook.

Description Sets up the workbook mailer for forwarding by creating a new mailer that is pre-set with the subject and enclosures of the existing mailer. Valid only when the workbook has a received mailer attached (you can only forward a workbook you have received). Available only in Microsoft Excel for the Apple Macintosh with the PowerTalk mail system extension installed.

Syntax   *object*.**ForwardMailer**

Elements   *object*
                Required. The Workbook object.

Remarks   After you use this method to set up a workbook mailer for forwarding, you can change the mailer settings (if necessary) with the **Mailer** property and then use the **SendMailer** method to forward the workbook.

                This method generates an error if it is used in Microsoft Windows.

See Also   **Mailer** Property, **MailSystem** Property, **SendMailer** Method.

Example   This example forwards the active workbook.

```
ActiveWorkbook.ForwardMailer
```

FreeFile Function

Description	Returns the next file number available for use by the **Open** statement.
Syntax	**FreeFile**[(*rangenumber*)]
Elements	The *rangenumber* argument specifies the range from which the next free file number is to be returned. Specify a **0** (default) to return a file number in the range 1 to 255, inclusive. Specify a **1** to return a file number in the range 256 to 511.
Remarks	Use **FreeFile** when you need to supply a file number and you want to make sure the file number is not already in use.
See Also	**Open** Statement.
Example	This example uses the **FreeFile** function to return the next available file number. Five files are opened for output within the loop and some sample data is written to each.

```
For MyIndex = 1 to 5                          ' Loop 5 times.
    FileNumber = FreeFile                     ' Get unused file number.
    Open "TEST" & MyIndex _
        For Output As #FileNumber             ' Create file name.
    Write #FileNumber, "This is a sample"     ' Output text.
    Close #FileNumber                         ' Close file.
Next MyIndex
```

FreezePanes Property

Applies To	Window.
Description	**True** if split panes are frozen. Read-write.
Syntax	*object*.**FreezePanes**
Elements	*object* Required. The Window object.
Remarks	It is possible for **FreezePanes** to be **True** and **Split** to be **False**, or vice versa. This property applies only to worksheets and macro sheets.
Example	This example freezes split panes in the active window.

```
ActiveWindow.FreezePanes = True
```

Function Statement

Description

Declares the name, arguments, and code that form the body of a **Function** procedure.

Syntax

[**Public** | **Private**][**Static**] **Function** *name* [(*arglist*)][**As** *type*]
   [*statements*]
   [*name = expression*]
   [**Exit Function**]
   [*statements*]
   [*name = expression*]
End Function

Elements

The **Function** statement syntax has these parts:

Part	Description
Public	Indicates that the **Function** procedure is accessible to all other procedures in all modules. If used in a private module (one that contains an **Option Private** statement) the procedure is not available outside the project.
Private	Indicates that the **Function** procedure is accessible only to other procedures in the module where it is declared.
Static	Indicates that the **Function** procedure's local variables are preserved between calls. The **Static** attribute doesn't affect variables that are declared outside the **Function**, even if they are used in the procedure.
name	Name of the **Function**; follows standard variable naming conventions.
arglist	List of variables representing arguments that are passed to the **Function** procedure when it is called. Multiple variables are separated by commas.
type	Data type of the value returned by the **Function** procedure; may be **Boolean**, **Integer**, **Long**, **Currency**, **Single**, **Double**, **Date**, **String** (except fixed length), **Object**, **Variant** or any user-defined type. Arrays of any type can't be returned, but a **Variant** containing an array can.
statements	Any group of statements to be executed within the body of the **Function** procedure.
expression	Return value of the **Function**.

The *arglist* argument has the following syntax and parts:

[**Optional**][**ByVal** | **ByRef**][**ParamArray**] *varname*[( )][**As** *type*]

Part	Description
Optional	Indicates that an argument is not required. If used, all subsequent arguments in *arglist* must also be optional and declared using the **Optional** keyword. All **Optional** arguments must be **Variant**. **Optional** can't be used for any argument if **ParamArray** is used.
ByVal	Indicates that the argument is passed by value.
ByRef	Indicates that the argument is passed by reference.
ParamArray	Used only as the last argument in *arglist* to indicate that the final argument is an **Optional** array of **Variant** elements. The **ParamArray** keyword allows you to provide an arbitrary number of arguments. May not be used with **ByVal**, **ByRef**, or **Optional**.
varname	Name of the variable representing the argument; follows standard variable naming conventions.
type	Data type of the argument passed to the procedure; may be **Boolean**, **Integer**, **Long**, **Currency**, **Single**, **Double**, **Date**, **String** (variable length only), **Object**, **Variant**, a user-defined type, or an object type.

Remarks

If not explicitly specified using either **Public** or **Private**, **Function** procedures are **Public** by default. If **Static** is not used, the value of local variables is not preserved between calls.

All executable code must be in procedures. You can't define a **Function** procedure inside another **Function**, **Sub**, or **Property** procedure.

The **Exit Function** keywords cause an immediate exit from a **Function** procedure. Program execution continues with the statement following the statement that called the **Function** procedure. Any number of **Exit Function** statements can appear anywhere in a **Function** procedure.

Like a **Sub** procedure, a **Function** procedure is a separate procedure that can take arguments, perform a series of statements, and change the values of its arguments. However, unlike a **Sub** procedure, a **Function** procedure can be used on the right hand side of an expression in the same way you use any intrinsic function, such as **Sqr**, **Cos**, or **Chr**, when you want to use the value returned by the function.

You call a **Function** procedure using the function name, followed by the argument list in parentheses, in an expression. If the function has no arguments, you still must include the parentheses. See the **Call** statement for specific information on how to call **Function** procedures.

Caution

Function procedures can be recursive; that is, they can call themselves to perform a given task. However, recursion can lead to stack overflow. The **Static** keyword is usually not used with recursive **Function** procedures.

To return a value from a function, assign the value to the function name. Any number of such assignments can appear anywhere within the procedure. If no value is assigned to *name*, the procedure returns a default value: a numeric function returns 0, a string function returns a zero-length string (""), and a **Variant** function returns **Empty**. A function that returns an object reference returns **Nothing** if no object reference is assigned to *name* (using **Set**) within the **Function**.

The following example shows how to assign a return value to a function named BinarySearch. In this case, **False** is assigned to the name to indicate that some value was not found.

```
Function BinarySearch(. . .) As Boolean
. . .
    ' Value not found. Return a value of False.
    If lower > upper Then
        BinarySearch = False
        Exit Function
    End If
. . .
End Function
```

Variables used in **Function** procedures fall into two categories: those that are explicitly declared within the procedure and those that are not. Variables that are explicitly declared in a procedure (using **Dim** or the equivalent) are always local to the procedure. Other variables used but not explicitly declared in a procedure are also local unless they are explicitly declared at some higher level outside the procedure.

Caution A procedure can use a variable that is not explicitly declared in the procedure, but a name conflict can occur if anything you have defined at the module level has the same name. If your procedure refers to an undeclared variable that has the same name as another procedure, constant or variable, it is assumed that your procedure is referring to that module-level name. Explicitly declare variables to avoid this kind of conflict. You can use an **Option Explicit** statement to force explicit declaration of variables.

Caution

Arithmetic expressions may be rearranged to increase internal efficiency. Avoid using a **Function** procedure in an arithmetic expression when the function changes the value of variables in the same expression.

See Also

Call Statement, **Dim** Statement, **Option Explicit** Statement, **Property Get** Statement, **Property Let** Statement, **Property Set** Statement, **Set** Statement, **Static** Statement, **Sub** Statement.

Example

This example uses the **Function** statement to declare the name, arguments and code that form the body of a **Function** procedure.

```
' The following user-defined function returns the square root of the
' argument passed to it.
Function CalculateSquareRoot(NumberArg As Double) As Double
    If NumberArg < 0 Then               ' Evaluate argument.
        Exit Function                   ' Exit to calling procedure.
    Else
        CalculateSquareRoot = Sqr(NumberArg)    ' Return square root.
    EndIf
End Function

' Using the ParamArray keyword enables a function to accept a variable
' number of arguments. In the following definition, FirstArg is passed
' by value.
Function CalcSum(ByVal FirstArg As Integer, ParamArray OtherArgs())

' If the function is invoked as...
ReturnValue = CalcSum(4,3,2,1)

' Local variables get the following values: FirstArg=4, OtherArgs(1)=3,
' OtherArgs(2) = 2 and so on, assuming default lower bound for
' arrays = 1.

' If a function's arguments are defined as...
Function MyFunc(MyStr As String, Optional MyArg1, Optional MyArg2)

' It can be invoked in the following ways.
RetVal = MyFunc("Hello", 2, "World")    ' All 3 arguments supplied.
RetVal = MyFunc("Test", , 5)            ' Second argument omitted.
RetVal = MyFunc("Test")                 ' First argument only.
```

FunctionWizard Method

Applies To

Range.

Description

Starts the Function Wizard for the upper left cell of the range.

Elements

object
    Required. The Range object.

Example

This example starts the Function Wizard for the active cell.

```
ActiveCell.FunctionWizard
```

GapDepth Property

Applies To   Chart.

Description   Returns or sets the distance between the data series in a 3-D chart, as a percentage of the marker width (between 0 and 500). Read-write.

Syntax   *object*.**GapDepth**

Elements   *object*
     Required. The Chart object.

Example   This example sets the distance between the data series on a 3-D chart to 200 percent of the marker width.

```
Charts(1).GapDepth = 200
```

GapWidth Property

Applies To   ChartGroup.

Description   Returns or sets the space between bar or column clusters as a percentage of the width of a bar or column. This property must be between 0 and 500. Read-write.

Syntax   *object*.**GapWidth**

Elements   *object*
     Required. The ChartGroup object.

See Also   **Overlap** Property.

Example   This example sets the space between column clusters to 50 percent of the width of a column.

```
Charts(1).ChartGroups(1).GapWidth = 50
```

Get Statement

Description   Reads from an open disk file into a variable.

Syntax   **Get** [#]*filenumber*,[*recnumber*],*varname*

Elements

The **Get** statement syntax has these parts:

Part	Description
filenumber	Any valid file number.
recnumber	Record number (**Random** mode files) or byte number (**Binary** mode files) at which reading begins.
varname	Valid variable name into which data is read.

Remarks

The first record/byte in a file is at position 1, the second record/byte is at position 2, and so on. If you omit *recnumber*, the next record or byte (the one after the last **Get** or **Put** statement or the one pointed to by the last **Seek** function) is read. Delimiting commas must be included, for example:

```
Get #4,,FileBuffer
```

For files opened in **Random** mode, the following rules apply:

- If the length of the data being read is less than the length specified in the **Len** clause of the **Open** statement, **Get** still reads subsequent records on record-length boundaries. The space between the end of one record and the beginning of the next record is padded with the existing contents of the file buffer. Because the amount of padding data can't be determined with any certainty, it is generally a good idea to have the record length match the length of the data being read.

- If the variable being read into is a variable-length string, **Get** reads a 2-byte descriptor containing the string length and then the data that goes into the variable. Therefore, the record length specified by the **Len** clause in the **Open** statement must be at least 2 bytes greater than the actual length of the string.

- If the variable being read into is a **Variant** of numeric type, **Get** reads 2 bytes identifying the **VarType** of the **Variant** and then the data that goes into the variable. For example, when reading a **Variant** of **VarType** 3, **Get** reads 6 bytes: 2 bytes identifying the **Variant** as **VarType** 3 (**Long**) and 4 bytes containing the **Long** data. The record length specified by the **Len** clause in the **Open** statement must be at least 2 bytes greater than the actual number of bytes required to store the variable.

- If the variable being read into is a **String Variant** (**VarType** 8), **Get** reads 2 bytes identifying the **VarType**, 2 bytes indicating the length of the string, and then the string data. The record length specified by the **Len** clause in the **Open** statement must be at least 4 bytes greater than the actual length of the string.

- If the variable being read into is any other type of variable (not a variable-length string or a **Variant**), **Get** reads only the variable data. The record length specified by the **Len** clause in the **Open** statement must be greater than or equal to the length of the data being read.

- **Get** reads elements of user-defined types as if each were being read individually except that there is no padding between elements. The record length specified by the **Len** clause in the **Open** statement must be greater than or equal to the sum of all the bytes required to read the individual elements.

For files opened in **Binary** mode, all of the **Random** rules apply except that:

- In **Binary** mode, the **Len** clause in the **Open** statement has no effect. **Get** reads all variables from disk contiguously; that is, with no padding between records.

- **Get** reads variable-length strings that aren't elements of user-defined types without expecting the 2-byte length descriptor. The number of bytes read equals the number of characters already in the string. For example, the following statements read 10 bytes from file number 1:

```
VarString = String(10," ")
Get #1,,VarString
```

See Also

Open Statement, **Put** Statement, **Type** Statement, **VarType** Function.

Example

This example uses the **Get** statement to read data from a disk file into a variable. For purposes of this example, assume that TESTFILE is a file containing five records of the user-defined type Record.

```
Type Record                 ' Define user-defined type.
    ID As Integer
    Name As String * 20
End Type
Dim MyRecord As Record      ' Declare variable.

' Open sample file for random access.
Open "TESTFILE" For Random As #1 Len = Len(MyRecord)

' Read the sample file using the Get statement.
Position = 3                ' Define record number.
Get #1, Position, MyRecord  ' Read third record.
Close #1                    ' Close file.
```

GetAttr Function

Description

Returns a number representing the attributes of a file, directory or folder, or volume label.

Syntax	**GetAttr(*pathname*)**
Elements	The ***pathname*** named argument is a string expression that specifies a file name—may include directory or folder, and drive.
Return Values	The value returned by **GetAttr** is the sum of the following attribute values:

Value	Constant	File Attribute
0	vbNormal	Normal.
1	vbReadonly	Read-only.
2	vbHidden	Hidden.
4	vbSystem	System file{bmc emdash.bmp}not available on the Macintosh.
8	vbVolume	Volume label{bmc emdash.bmp}not available on the Macintosh.
16	vbDirectory	Directory or folder.
32	vbArchive	File has changed since last backup{bmc emdash.bmp}not available on the Macintosh.

Note These constants are specified by Visual Basic. As a result, the names can be used anywhere in your code in place of the actual values.

Remarks	To determine which attributes are set, use the **And** operator to perform a bit-wise comparison of the value returned by the **GetAttr** function and the value of the individual file attribute you want. If the result is not zero, that attribute is set for the named file. For example, the return value of the following **And** expression is zero if the Archive attribute is not set:

```
Result = GetAttr(FName) And vbArchive
```

A nonzero value is returned if the Archive attribute is set.

See Also	**FileAttr** Function, **SetAttr** Statement.
Example	This example uses the **GetAttr** statement to determine the attributes of a file and directory or folder.

```
' Assume file TESTFILE has hidden attribute set.
MyAttr = GetAttr("TESTFILE")          ' Returns 2.

' Assume file TESTFILE has hidden and read-only attributes set.
MyAttr = GetAttr("TESTFILE")          ' Returns 3.

' Assume MYDIR is a directory or folder.
MyAttr = GetAttr("MYDIR")             ' Returns 16.
```

GetCustomListContents Method

Applies To   Application.

Description   Returns a custom list (an array of strings) for a specified list number.

Syntax   *object*.**GetCustomListContents**(*listNum*)

Elements   The **GetCustomListContents** method has the following object qualifier and named arguments:

object
    Required. The Application object.

listNum
    Required. The list number.

Remarks   This method generates an error if a corresponding list does not exist.

See Also   **AddCustomList** Method, **CustomListCount** Property, **DeleteCustomList** Method, **GetCustomListNum** Method.

Example   This example sets the listArray variable to the number six custom list.

```
On Error Goto err_handler
listArray = Application.GetCustomListContents(6)
Exit Sub
err_handler:
    MsgBox("GetCustomListContents error occurred")
    Resume Next
```

GetCustomListNum Method

Applies To   Application.

Description   Returns the custom list number for an array of strings. Both built-in and custom defined lists can be matched using this method.

Syntax   *object*.**GetCustomListNum**(*listArray*)

Elements   The **GetCustomListNum** method has the following object qualifier and named arguments:

object
  Required. The Application object.

listArray
  Required. An array of strings.

Remarks   This method generates an error if a corresponding list does not exist.

See Also   **AddCustomList** Method, **CustomListCount** Property, **DeleteCustomList** Method, **GetCustomListContents** Method.

Example   This example deletes a custom list.

```
n = Application.GetCustomListNum(Array("cogs", "sprockets", _
    "widgets", "gizmos"))
Application.DeleteCustomList n
```

GetObject Function

Description   Retrieves an OLE Automation object from a file.

Syntax   **GetObject([*pathname*][,*class*])**

Elements   The **GetObject** function syntax has these named-argument parts:

Part	Description
pathname	The full path and name of the file containing the object to retrieve. If *pathname* is omitted, *class* is required.
class	A string representing the class of the object.

The *class* argument uses the syntax: "*appname.objecttype*" and has these parts:

Part	Description
appname	The name of the application providing the object.
objecttype	The type or class of object to create.

Remarks

Note If an application which supports OLE Automation exposes an object library, it is preferable to use the functions defined within the library for object access rather than use **GetObject**.

Use the **GetObject** function to access an OLE Automation object from a file and assign the object to an object variable. To do this, use the **Set** statement to assign the object returned by **GetObject** to the object variable. For example:

```
Set CADObject = GetObject("C:\CAD\SCHEMA.CAD")
```

When this code is executed, the application associated with the specified file name is started and the object in the specified file is activated.

If *pathname* is a zero-length string (""), **GetObject** returns a new object instance of the specified type. If the *pathname* argument is omitted entirely, **GetObject** returns the currently active object of the specified type. If no object of the specified type exists, an error occurs.

The above example shows how to activate an entire file. However, some applications allow you to activate part of a file. To do this, add an exclamation point (!) to the end of the file name followed by a string that identifies the part of the file you want to activate. For information on how to create this string, see the documentation for the application that created the object.

For example, in a drawing application you might have multiple layers to a drawing stored in a file. You could use the following code to activate a layer within a drawing called SCHEMA.CAD:

```
Set LayerObject = GetObject("C:\CAD\SCHEMA.CAD!Layer3")
```

If you do not specify the object's *class*, the OLE.DLLs determine the application to invoke and the object to activate based on the file name you provide. Some files, however, may support more than one class of object. For example, a drawing might support three different types of objects: an application object, a drawing object, and a toolbar object, all of which are part of the same file. To specify which object in a file you want to activate, use the optional *class* argument. For example:

```
Set MyObject = GetObject("C:\DRAWINGS\SAMPLE.DRW", "FIGMENT.DRAWING")
```

In the above example, FIGMENT is the name of a drawing application and DRAWING is one of the object types it supports.

Once an object is activated, you reference it in code using the object variable you defined. In the above example, you access properties and methods of the new object using the object variable MyObject. For example:

```
MyObject.Line 9, 90
MyObject.InsertText 9, 100, "Hello, world."
MyObject.SaveAs "C:\DRAWINGS\SAMPLE.DRW"
```

See Also   **CreateObject** Function, **Set** Statement.

GetOpenFilename Method

Applies To   Application.

Description   Displays the standard Open dialog box and gets a filename from the user without actually opening any files.

Syntax   *object*.**GetOpenFilename**(*fileFilter, filterIndex, title, buttonText*)

Elements   The **GetOpenFilename** method has the following object qualifier and named arguments:

object
    Required. The Application object.

fileFilter
    Optional. A string specifying file filtering criteria.

    In Microsoft Windows, this string consists of pairs of file filter strings followed by the MS-DOS wildcard file filter specification, with each part and each pair separated by commas. Each separate pair is listed in the File Type drop-down list box. For example, the following string specifies two file filters -- text and addin:

```
"Text Files (*.txt),*.txt,Add-In Files (*.xla),*.xla"
```

    To use multiple MS-DOS wildcard expressions for a single file filter type, separate the wildcard expressions with semicolons. For example:

```
"Visual Basic Files (*.bas; *.txt),*.bas;*.txt".
```

    If omitted on Windows, this argument defaults to "All Files (*.*),*.*".

    On the Apple Macintosh, this string is a list of comma-separated file type codes, ("TEXT,XLA,XLS4"). Spaces are significant and should not be inserted before or after the comma separators unless they are part of the file type code. If omitted, this argument defaults to all file types.

filterIndex
    Optional. Microsoft Windows only (ignored on the Apple Macintosh). Specifies the index number of the default file filtering criteria from one to the number of filters specified in *fileFilter*. If this argument is omitted or greater than the number of filters present, the first file filter is used.

title
    Optional. Microsoft Windows only (ignored on the Apple Macintosh). Specifies the dialog title. If this argument is omitted, the dialog title is "Open".

buttonText

Optional. Apple Macintosh only (ignored in Microsoft Windows). Specifies the text used for the Open button in the dialog box. If this argument is omitted, the button text is "Open".

Remarks

This method returns the selected filename or the name entered by the user. The returned name may include a path specification. Returns **False** if the user cancels the dialog box.

This method may change the current drive or directory.

See Also

GetSaveAsFileName Method, **Open** Method.

Example

This example displays the Open dialog box for text files, and then displays the filename that the user chose in a message box.

```
fileToOpen = Application.GetOpenFilename("Text Files (*.txt), *.txt")
MsgBox "Open " & fileToOpen
```

GetSaveAsFilename Method

Applies To

Application.

Description

Displays the standard Save As dialog box and gets a filename from the user without actually saving any files.

Syntax

object.**GetSaveAsFilename**(*initialFilename, fileFilter, filterIndex, title, buttonText*)

Elements

The **GetSaveAsFilename** method has the following object qualifier and named arguments:

object

Required. The Application object.

initialFilename

Optional. Specifies the suggested filename. If this argument is omitted, Microsoft Excel uses the active workbook's name.

fileFilter

Optional. A string specifying file filtering criteria.

In Microsoft Windows, this string consists of pairs of file filter strings followed by the MS-DOS wildcard file filter specification, with each part and each pair separated by commas. Each separate pair is listed in the File Type drop-down list box. For example, the following string specifies two file filters -- text and addin:

```
"Text Files (*.txt), *.txt, Add-In Files (*.xla), *.xla"
```

To use multiple MS-DOS wildcard expressions for a single file filter type, separate the wildcard expressions with semicolons. For example:

```
"Visual Basic Files (*.bas; *.txt),*.bas;*.txt"
```

If omitted on Windows, this argument defaults to "All Files (*.*),*.*".

On the Apple Macintosh, this string is a list of comma-separated file type codes, ("TEXT,XLA,XLS4"). Spaces are significant and should not be inserted before or after the comma separators unless they are part of the file type code. If omitted, this argument defaults to all file types.

filterIndex

Optional. Microsoft Windows only (ignored on the Apple Macintosh). Specifies the index number of the default file filtering criteria from one to the number of filters specified in *fileFilter*. If this argument is omitted or greater than the number of filters present, the first file filter is used.

title

Optional. Microsoft Windows only (ignored on the Apple Macintosh). Specifies the dialog title. If this argument is omitted, the dialog title is "Save As".

buttonText

Optional. Apple Macintosh only (ignored in Microsoft Windows). Specifies the text used for the Save button in the dialog box. If this argument is omitted, the button text is "Save".

Remarks

This method returns the selected filename or the name entered by the user. The returned name may include a path specification. Returns **False** if the user cancels the dialog box.

This method may change the current drive or directory.

See Also

GetOpenFileName Method, **Save** Method, **SaveAs** Method.

Example

This example displays the Save As dialog box with the file filter set to text files.

```
fileSaveName = Application.GetSaveAsFilename( _
    fileFilter:="Text Files (*.txt), *.txt")
MsgBox "Save as " & fileSaveName
```

GoalSeek Method

Applies To   Range.

Description   Calculates the values necessary to achieve a specific goal. If the goal is an amount returned by a formula, this calculates a value that, when supplied to your formula, causes the formula to return the number you want. Returns **True** if the goal seek is successful.

Syntax   *object*.**GoalSeek**(*goal, changingCell*)

Elements   The **GoalSeek** method has the following object qualifier and named arguments:

object
   Required. The specified range must be a single cell.

goal
   Required. The value you want returned in this cell.

changingCell
   Required. A Range object indicating which cell should be changed to achieve the target value.

Example   Suppose a worksheet has a cell named Polynomial containing the formula =(X^3)+(3*X^2)+6 and another cell named X that is empty. This example finds a value for the cell X so that Polynomial contains the value 15.

```
Range("Polynomial").GoalSeek goal:=15, changingCell:=Range("X")
```

GoSub...Return Statement

Description   Branch to and return from a subroutine within a procedure.

Syntax   **GoSub** *line*
   . . .
   line
   . . .
   Return

Elements   The *line* argument can be any line label or line number.

Remarks	You can use **GoSub** and **Return** anywhere in a procedure, but **GoSub** and the corresponding **Return** must be in the same procedure. A subroutine can contain more than one **Return** statement, but the first **Return** statement encountered causes the flow of execution to branch back to the statement immediately following the most recently executed **GoSub** statement.

> **Note** You can't enter or exit **Sub** procedures with **GoSub...Return**.

> **Tip** Creating separate procedures which you can call may provide a more structured alternative to using **GoSub...Return**.

See Also	**End** Statement, **GoTo** Statement, **On...GoSub** Statement, **On...GoTo** Statement, **Sub** Statement.
Example	This example uses **GoSub** to call a subroutine within a **Sub** procedure. The **Return** statement causes the execution to resume at the statement immediately following the **Gosub** statement. The **Exit Sub** statement is used to prevent control from accidentally flowing into the subroutine.

```
Sub GosubDemo()
    Num = 10                ' Initialize variable.
    GoSub MyRoutine           ' Branch to subroutine.
    Debug.Print Num           ' Print value upon return.
    Exit Sub                ' Exit Sub procedure.
MyRoutine:                  ' Start of subroutine.
    Num = Num \ 2             ' Halve the value.
    Return                  ' Return from subroutine.
End Sub
```

Goto Method

Applies To	Application.
Description	Selects any range or Visual Basic procedure in any workbook, and activates that workbook if it is not already active.
Syntax	*object*.**Goto**(*reference, scroll*)

Elements	The **Goto** method has the following object qualifier and named arguments:

object
Required. The Application object.

reference
Required. Specifies the destination. Can be a range or a string containing a Visual Basic procedure name.

scroll
Optional. If this argument is **True**, Microsoft Excel scrolls the window so that the top left corner of the range appears in the top left corner of the window. If **False** or omitted, Microsoft Excel does not scroll the window.

Remarks   This method differs from the **Select** method in the following ways.

- If you specify a range on a sheet that is not on top, Microsoft Excel will switch to that sheet before selecting. (If you use **Select** with a range on a sheet that is not on top, the range will be selected but the sheet will not be activated).

- This method has a *scroll* argument that lets you scroll the destination window.

- When you use the **Goto** method, the previous selection (before the **Goto** method runs) is added to the array of previous selections (for more information, see the **PreviousSelections** property). You can use this feature to quickly jump between up to four selections.

- The **Select** method has a *replace* argument; the **Goto** method does not.

See Also   **Select** Method.

Example   This example selects cell A154 and scrolls the window to display the range.

```
Application.Goto reference:=Worksheets(1).Range("A154"), _
    scroll:=True
```

GoTo Statement

Description   Branches unconditionally to a specified line within a procedure.

Syntax   **GoTo** *line*

Elements   The *line* argument can be any line label or line number.

Remarks   **GoTo** can branch only to lines within the procedure where it appears.

Note

Too many **GoTo** statements can be difficult to read and debug. Use structured control statements (**Do...Loop**, **For...Next**, **If...Then...Else**, **Select Case**) whenever possible.

See Also

Do...Loop Statement, **For...Next** Statement, **GoSub...Return** Statement, **If...Then...Else** Statement, **Select Case** Statement.

Example

This example uses the **GoTo** statement to branch to line labels within a procedure.

```
Sub GotoStatementDemo()
    Number = 1            ' Initialize variable.
    ' Evaluate Number and branch to appropriate label.
    If Number = 1 Then GoTo Line1 Else GoTo Line2

Line1:
    MyString = "Number equals 1"
    GoTo LastLine            ' Go to LastLine.
Line2:
    ' The following statement never gets executed.
    MyString = "Number equals 2"
LastLine:
    Debug.Print MyString     ' Print 1 in Debug window.
End Sub
```

GridlineColor Property

Applies To   Window.

Description   Returns or sets the gridline color as an RGB value. Read-write.

Syntax   *object*.**GridlineColor**

Elements   *object*
                   Required. The Window object.

See Also   **DisplayGridlines** Property, **GridlineColorIndex** Property.

Example   This example sets the active window gridline color to red.

```
ActiveWindow.GridlineColor = RGB(255,0,0)
```

GridlineColorIndex Property

Applies To   Window.

Description   Returns or sets the gridline color as an index into the current color palette. Read-write.

Syntax   *object*.**GridlineColorIndex**

Elements   *object*
                    Required. The Window object.

Remarks   Set this property to **xlAutomatic** to specify the automatic color.

See Also   **DisplayGridlines** Property, **GridlineColor** Property.

Example   This example sets the active window gridline color.

```
ActiveWindow.GridlineColorIndex = 10        ' use palette color 10
```

Gridlines Object

Description   Major gridlines or minor gridlines on a chart.

Group Method

Applies To   Arcs, Buttons, ChartObjects, CheckBoxes, DrawingObjects, Drawings, DropDowns, EditBoxes, GroupBoxes, GroupObjects, Labels, Lines, ListBoxes, OLEObjects, OptionButtons, Ovals, Pictures, Range, Rectangles, ScrollBars, Spinners, TextBoxes.

Description   Syntax 1: Demotes a range in an outline (in other words, increases its outline level). The range should be an entire row or column, or a range of rows or columns.

Groups a discontiguous range in a pivot table.

Groups multiple controls or drawing objects together; returns a new GroupObject.

Syntax 2: Performs numeric or date grouping in a pivot table field.

Syntax 1	*object*.**Group**
Syntax 2	*object*.**Group**(*start, end, by, periods*)
Elements	The **Group** method has the following object qualifier and named arguments:

object
Required. The object to which this method applies.

start
Optional. The first value to be grouped. If omitted or **True**, the first value in the field is used.

end
Optional. The last value to be grouped. If omitted or **True**, the last value in the field is used.

by
Optional. If the field is numeric, specifies the size of each group.

If the field is a date, specifies the number of days in each group if *periods* is set to **days**. Otherwise *by* is ignored.

If this argument is omitted, a default group size is automatically chosen.

periods
Optional. An array of boolean values specifying the period for the group, as shown in the following table.

1   Seconds

2   Minutes

3   Hours

4   Days

5   Months

6   Quarters

7   Years

If an element of the array is **True**, a group is created for the corresponding time. If the element is **False,** no group is created. This argument is ignored if the field is not a date field.

See Also   **OutlineLevel** Property, **Ungroup** Method.

Examples

This example creates a group from the first, third, and fifth drawing objects.

```
Set myGroup = ActiveSheet.DrawingObjects(Array(1, 3, 5)).Group
myGroup.Select
```

This example groups a date field in a pivot table. The field is grouped from January 1, 1993 to December 31, 1993, by ten-day periods. The field contains the active cell.

```
ActiveCell.Group start:="1/1/1993", end:="12/31/1993", by:=10, _
    periods:=Array(False, False, False, True, False, False, False)
```

GroupBox Object

Description

Static frame used to label and group sets of option buttons (OptionButton objects) and other controls.

Remarks

Group boxes have no font or background formatting but do have an accelerator key. Group boxes can be positioned and sized.

Group boxes control how option buttons select and clear. All option buttons with an upper-left corner contained within the group box boundaries are considered to be part of a group, and at most one option button within that group can be selected any time.

GroupBoxes Method

Applies To

Chart, DialogSheet, Worksheet.

Description

Returns a single group box control (a GroupBox object, Syntax 1) or a collection of group box controls on the chart or sheet (a GroupBoxes object, Syntax 2).

Syntax 1

object.**GroupBoxes(***index***)**

Syntax 2

object.**GroupBoxes**

Elements

The **GroupBoxes** method has the following object qualifier and named arguments:

object
    Required. The Chart, DialogSheet, or Worksheet object.

index
    Required for Syntax 1. Specifies the name or number of the group box (can be an array to specify more than one).

Example   This example displays the number of group boxes on dialog sheet one.

```
cGroupBoxes = Application.DialogSheets(1).GroupBoxes.Count
MsgBox "There are " & cGroupBoxes & _
    " group boxes on dialog sheet one."
```

GroupBoxes Object

Description   A collection of GroupBox objects.

GroupLevel Property

Applies To   PivotField.

Description   Returns the placement of the specified field within a group of fields (if the field is a member of a grouped set of fields). Read-only.

Syntax   *object*.**GroupLevel**

Elements   *object*
                     Required. The PivotField object.

Remarks   The highest-level parent field (leftmost parent field) is **GroupLevel** one, its child is **GroupLevel** two, and so on.

Example   This example displays a message box if the active field has **GroupLevel** one.

```
If (ActiveCell.PivotField.GroupLevel = 1) Then
    MsgBox "This is the highest-level parent field."
End If
```

GroupObject Object

Description   A group of graphic objects.

GroupObjects Method

Applies To   Chart, DialogSheet, Worksheet.

Description   Returns a single group (a GroupObject object, Syntax 1) or a collection of all the groups (a GroupObjects object, Syntax 2) on the chart, worksheet, or dialog sheet.

Syntax 1   *object*.**GroupObjects(*index*)**

Syntax   *object*.**GroupObjects**

Elements   The **GroupObjects** method has the following object qualifier and named arguments:

object
Required. The Chart, DialogSheet or Worksheet object.

index
Required for Syntax 1. The name or number of the group (can be an array to specify more than one).

Example   This example ungroups group one on worksheet one.

```
Worksheets(1).GroupObjects(1).Ungroup
```

GroupObjects Object

Description   A collection of GroupObject objects.

HasArray Property

Applies To   Range.

Description   **True** if the specified cell is a part of an array. Read-only.

Syntax   *object*.**HasArray**

Elements   *object*
Required. The cell to test.

See Also   **CurrentArray** Property.

Example	This example deletes the active cell if it is not part of an array.

```
If Not ActiveCell.HasArray Then
    ActiveCell.Delete
Else
    MsgBox "You can't delete a cell that is part of an array."
End If
```

HasAutoFormat Property

Applies To	PivotTable.
Description	**True** if the pivot table is automatically formatted when it is refreshed or when fields are moved. Read-write.
Syntax	*object*.**AutoFormat**
Elements	*object* Required. The PivotTable object.
Example	This example causes the active pivot table to be automatically reformatted when it is refreshed or when fields are moved.

```
ActiveCell.PivotTable.HasAutoFormat = True
```

HasAxis Property

Applies To	Chart.
Description	Indicates which Axes exist on the current chart, as a two-dimensional array of Boolean values. Read-write.
	The first array dimension indicates the axis (one of **xlCategory**, **xlValue**, or **xlSeries**). Series axes apply only to 3-D charts.
	The second array dimension indicates the axis group (**xlPrimary** or **xlSecondary**). Read-write. 3-D charts have only one set of axes.
Syntax	*object*.**HasAxis**
Elements	*object* Required. The Chart object.
Remarks	Microsoft Excel may create or delete axes if you change the chart type or change the **AxisGroup** property.

See Also	**Axes** object.
Example	This example turns on the primary value axis for the chart.

```
Charts(1).HasAxis(xlValue, xlPrimary) = True
```

HasDataLabel Property

Applies To	Point.
Description	**True** if the point has a data label. Read-write.
Syntax	*object*.**HasDataLabel**
Elements	*object* Required. The Point object.
See Also	**ApplyDataLabels** Method, **DataLabel** Property, **HasDataLabels** Property.
Example	This example turns on the data label for point seven on series three, and then sets the datalabel color.

```
With ActiveChart.SeriesCollection(3).Points(7)
    .HasDataLabel = True
    .ApplyDataLabels type:=xlValue
    .DataLabel.Font.Color = RGB(0, 0, 255)
End With
```

HasDataLabels Property

Applies To	Series.
Description	**True** if the series has data labels. Read-write.
Syntax	*object*.**HasDataLabels**
Elements	*object* Required. The Series object.
See Also	**ApplyDataLabels** Method, **DataLabel** Property, **HasDataLabels** Property.
Example	This example turns on data labels for series three.

```
With ActiveChart.SeriesCollection(3)
    .HasDataLabels = True
    .ApplyDataLabels type:=xlValue
End With
```

HasDropLines Property

Applies To   ChartGroup.

Description   **True** if the line or area chart has drop lines. Applies only to line and area charts. Read-write.

Syntax   *object*.**HasDropLines**

Elements   *object*
                    Required. The ChartGroup object.

See Also   **DropLines** Property.

Example   This example turns on drop lines for the first chart group, and then sets their line style, weight, and color.

```
With ActiveChart.ChartGroups(1)
    .HasDropLines = True
    With .DropLines.Border
        .LineStyle = xlThin
        .Weight = xlMedium
        .Color = RGB(255, 0, 0)
    End With
End With
```

HasErrorBars Property

Applies To   Series.

Description   **True** if the series has error bars. This property is not available on 3-D charts. Read-write.

Syntax   *object*.**HasErrorBars**

Elements   *object*
                    Required. The Series object.

See Also   **ErrorBar** Method, **ErrorBars** Property.

Example   This example sets the error bar color.

```
With ActiveChart.SeriesCollection(1)
    .HasErrorBars = True
    .ErrorBars.Border.Color = RGB(0, 255, 0)
End With
```

HasFormula Property

Applies To   Range.

Description   **True** if all cells in the range contain formulas; **False** if no cell in the range contains a formula; **Null** otherwise. Read-only.

Syntax   *object*.**HasFormula**

Elements   *object*
                      Required. The range to test.

Example   This example uses the **HasFormula** property to run a portion of the macro if the specified range contains formulas.

```
If Range("A1:A10").HasFormula Then
    'all the cells in the range contain formulas
Else
    'at least one cell in the range does not contain a formula
End If
```

HasHiLoLines Property

Applies To   ChartGroup.

Description   **True** if the line chart has high-low lines. Applies only to line charts. Read-write.

Syntax   *object*.**HasHiLoLines**

Elements   *object*
                      Required. The ChartGroup object.

See Also   **HiLoLines** Property.

Example   This example turns on high-low lines for the first chart group, and then sets their line style, weight, and color.

```
With ActiveChart.ChartGroups(1)
    .HasHiLoLines = True
    With .HiLoLines.Border
        .LineStyle = xlThin
        .Weight = xlMedium
        .Color = RGB(255, 0, 0)
    End With
End With
```

HasLegend Property

Applies To   Chart.

Description   **True** if the chart has a legend. Read-write.

Syntax   *object*.**HasLegend**

Elements   *object*
　　　　　　Required. The Chart object.

See Also   **Legend** Property.

Example   This example turns on the chart legend and then sets its color.

```
Charts(1).HasLegend = True
Charts(1).Legend.Font.Color = RGB(0,255,0)
```

HasMailer Property

Applies To   Workbook.

Description   **True** if the workbook has a mailer. Available only in Microsoft Excel for the Apple Macintosh with the PowerTalk mail system extension installed. Read-write.

Syntax   *object*.**HasMailer**

Elements   *object*
　　　　　　Required. The Workbook object.

See Also   **Mailer** Property, **MailSystem** Property, **SendMailer** Method.

Example   This example replies to the active workbook.

```
With ActiveWorkbook
    If .HasMailer Then
        .Reply
        .Mailer.Subject = "Here's my reply"
        .SendMailer
    End If
End With
```

HasMajorGridlines Property

Applies To   Axis.

Description	**True** if the axis has major gridlines. Only axes in the primary axis group can have gridlines. Read-write.
Syntax	*object*.**HasMajorGridlines**
Elements	*object* Required. The Axis object.
See Also	**AxisGroup** Property, **HasMinorGridlines** Property, **MajorGridlines** Property, **MinorGridlines** Property.
Example	This example sets the color of the major gridlines for the value axis.

```
With ActiveChart.Axes(xlValue)
    If .HasMajorGridlines Then
        .MajorGridlines.Border.Color = RGB(0, 0, 255)
    End If
End With
```

HasMinorGridlines Property

Applies To	Axis.
Description	**True** if the axis has minor gridlines. Only axes in the primary axis group can have gridlines. Read-write.
Syntax	*object*.**HasMinorGridlines**
Elements	*object* Required. The Axis object.
See Also	**AxisGroup** Property, **HasMajorGridlines** Property, **MajorGridlines** Property, **MinorGridlines** Property.
Example	This example sets the color of the minor gridlines for the value axis.

```
With ActiveChart.Axes(xlValue)
    If .HasMinorGridlines Then
        .MinorGridlines.Border.Color = RGB(0, 255, 0)
    End If
End With
```

HasPassword Property

Applies To	Workbook.

Description	**True** if the workbook has a protection password. Read-only.
Syntax	*object*.**HasPassword**
Elements	*object* Required. The Workbook object.
Remarks	You can assign a protection password to a workbook with the **SaveAs** method.
Example	This example displays a message that reminds you that the workbook PROFIT92.XLS has a protection password and quits Microsoft Excel if the **HasPassword** property is **True**.

```
If Workbooks("PROFIT92.XLS").HasPassword Then
    MsgBox "PROFIT92.XLS is protected." & _
        " To read, please obtain the password" & _
        " from the Network Administrator."
    Application.Quit
End If
```

HasRadarAxisLabels Property

Applies To	ChartGroup.
Description	**True** if a radar chart has axis labels. Applies only to radar charts. Read-write.
Syntax	*object*.**HasRadarAxisLabels**
Elements	*object* Required. The ChartGroup object.
See Also	**RadarAxisLabels** Property.
Example	This example turns on radar axis labels for the first chart group, and sets their color.

```
With ActiveChart.ChartGroups(1)
    .HasRadarAxisLabels = True
    .RadarAxisLabels.Font.Color = RGB(255, 0, 0)
End With
```

HasRoutingSlip Property

Applies To	Workbook.
Description	**True** if the workbook has a RoutingSlip. Read-write.

Syntax	*object*.**HasRoutingSlip**
Elements	*object* Required. The Workbook object.
Remarks	Setting this property to **True** creates a routing slip with default values. Setting the property to **False** deletes the routing slip.
See Also	**RoutingSlip** Property.
Example	This example creates a routing slip for BOOK1.XLS, and then sends the workbook to three recipients, one after the other.

```
Workbooks("BOOK1.XLS").HasRoutingSlip = True
With Workbooks("BOOK1.XLS").RoutingSlip
    .Delivery = xlOneAfterAnother
    .Recipients = Array("Adam Bendel", "Jean Selva", "Bernard Gabor")
    .Subject = "Here is BOOK1.XLS"
    .Message = "Here is the workbook. What do you think?"
End With
Workbooks("BOOK1.XLS").Route
```

HasSeriesLines Property

Applies To	ChartGroup.
Description	True if a stacked column or bar chart has series lines. Applies only to stacked column and bar charts. Read-write.
Syntax	*object*.**HasSeriesLines**
Elements	*object* Required. The ChartGroup object.
See Also	**SeriesLines** Property.
Example	This example turns on series lines for the first chart group, and then sets their line style, weight, and color.

```
With ActiveChart.ChartGroups(1)
    .HasSeriesLines = True
    With .SeriesLines.Border
        .LineStyle = xlThin
        .Weight = xlMedium
        .Color = RGB(255, 0, 0)
    End With
End With
```

HasTitle Property

Applies To	Axis, Chart.
Description	True if the axis or chart has a visible title. Read-write.
Syntax	*object*.**HasTitle**
Elements	*object*
	Required. The Axis or Chart object.
Remarks	An axis title is an AxisTitle object.
	A chart title is a ChartTitle object.
Example	This example sets the value axis title to read "Population Growth" in 17-point italic.

```
With ActiveWorkbook.Charts(1).Axes(xlValue)
    .HasTitle = True
    With .AxisTitle
        .Caption = "Population Growth"
        .Font.Italic = True
        .Font.Size = 17
    End With
End With
```

HasUpDownBars Property

Applies To	ChartGroup.
Description	**True** if a line chart has up and down bars. Applies only to line charts. Read-write.
Syntax	*object*.**HasUpDownBars**
Elements	*object*
	Required. The ChartGroup object.
See Also	**DownBars** Property, **UpBars** Property.
Example	This example turns on up and down bars for the first chart group, and then sets their colors.

```
With ActiveChart.ChartGroups(1)
    .HasUpDownBars = True
    .DownBars.Interior.Color = RGB(255, 0, 0)
    .UpBars.Interior.Color = RGB(0, 0, 255)
End With
```

HeaderMargin Property

Applies To   PageSetup.

Description   Returns or sets the distance from the top of the page to the header, in points (1/72 inch). Read-write.

Syntax   *object*.**HeaderMargin**

Elements   *object*
                      Required. The PageSetup object.

See Also   **BottomMargin** Property, **FooterMargin** Property, **LeftMargin** Property, **RightMargin** Property, **TopMargin** Property.

Example   This example sets the header margin to one-half inch.

```
ActiveSheet.PageSetup.HeaderMargin = Application.InchesToPoints(0.5)
```

Height Property

Applies To   Application, Arc, Arcs, Button, Buttons, ChartArea, ChartObject, ChartObjects, CheckBox, CheckBoxes, DialogFrame, Drawing, DrawingObjects, Drawings, DropDown, DropDowns, EditBox, EditBoxes, GroupBox, GroupBoxes, GroupObject, GroupObjects, Label, Labels, Legend, Line, Lines, ListBox, ListBoxes, OLEObject, OLEObjects, OptionButton, OptionButtons, Oval, Ovals, Picture, Pictures, PlotArea, Range, Rectangle, Rectangles, ScrollBar, ScrollBars, Spinner, Spinners, TextBox, TextBoxes, Toolbar, Window.

Description   Returns or sets the height of an object, in points (1/72 inch).

Syntax   *object*.**Height**

Elements   *object*
                      Required. The object to which this property applies. Read-write for all objects, except as shown in the following table.

Remarks   The height set or returned depends on the specified object.

Object type	Height
Application	Height of the main Application window. On the Apple Macintosh this is always equal to the total height of the screen, in points. Setting this value to something else on the Macintosh will have no effect. Under Microsoft Windows, if the window is minimized, this property is read-only and refers to the height of the icon. If the window is maximized, this property cannot be set. Use the **WindowState** property to determine the window state.
Range	Height of the range. Read-only.
Toolbar	Height of the toolbar. Returns the exact height of the toolbar in points. Use the **Width** property to change the size of the toolbar. Read-only.
Window	Height of the window. Use the **UsableHeight** property to determine the maximum size for the window.
	You cannot set this property if the window is maximized or minimized. Use the **WindowState** property to determine the window state.
Arc, Button, ChartArea, ChartObject, CheckBox, DialogFrame, Drawing, DrawingObjects, DropDown, EditBox, GroupBox, GroupObject, Label, Legend, Line, ListBox, OLEObject, OptionButton, Oval, Picture, PlotArea, Rectangle, ScrollBar, Spinner, TextBox	Height of the object.

You can use negative numbers to set the **Height** and **Width** properties of the following drawing objects: Arc, Button, CheckBox, Drawing, DropDown, EditBox, GroupBox, GroupObject, Label, Line, ListBox, OLEObject, OptionButton, Oval, Picture, Rectangle, ScrollBar, Spinner, and TextBox. This causes the object to reflect or translate (the behavior depends on the object), after which the **Top** and **Left** properties change to describe the new position. The **Height** and **Width** properties always return positive numbers.

See Also   **Left** Property, **Top** Property, **Width** Property.

Example   This example sets the height of oval one to one inch (72 points).

```
ActiveSheet.Ovals(1).Height = 72
```

HeightPercent Property

Applies To   Chart.

Description   Returns or sets the height of a 3-D chart as a percentage of the chart width (between 5 and 500 percent). Read-write.

Syntax   *object*.**HeightPercent**

Elements   *object*
        Required. The Chart object.

See Also   **DepthPercent** Property.

Example   This example sets the chart height to 80 percent of its width.

```
Charts(1).HeightPercent = 80
```

Help Method

Applies To   Application.

Description   Displays a Help topic.

Syntax   *object*.**Help**(*helpFile, helpContextID*)

Elements   The **Help** method has the following object qualifier and named arguments:

object
        Required. The Application object.

helpFile
        Optional. The name of the online Help file you wish to display. If this argument is not specified, Microsoft Excel's Help file is used.

helpContextID
        Optional. Specifies the context ID for the Help topic. If this argument is not specified, the contents topic is displayed.

Example   This example displays the contents screen for the Help file OTISAPP.HLP.

```
Application.Help "OTISAPP.HLP"
```

HelpButton Property

Applies To   Button, Buttons, DrawingObjects.

Description	Applies only to buttons in a user-defined dialog box. If **True**, then pressing the Help key runs the macro identified by the button's **OnAction** property. If **False**, pressing the Help key does nothing. The Help key is F1 in Microsoft Excel for Windows and COMMAND+? in Microsoft Excel for the Macintosh. Read-write.
Syntax	*object*.**HelpButton**
Elements	*object* Required. The object to which this property applies.
Remarks	Only one button in the dialog box can have the **HelpButton** property set to **True** at any given time; setting the property resets it for all other buttons in the dialog box. If the user presses the Help key in a dialog box that has no Help button, nothing happens.
See Also	**Help** Method.
Example	This example sets the **HelpButton** property for button five.

```
Application.DialogSheets(1).Buttons(5).HelpButton = True
```

Hex Function

Description	Returns a string representing the hexadecimal value of a number.
Syntax	**Hex(*number*)**
Elements	The ***number*** named argument is any valid numeric expression.
Remarks	If ***number*** is not already a whole number, it is rounded to the nearest whole number before being evaluated.

If *number* is	Hex returns
Null	An error.
Empty	Zero (0).
Any other number	Up to eight hexadecimal characters.

You can represent hexadecimal numbers directly by preceding numbers in the proper range with &H. For example, &H10 represents decimal 16 in hexadecimal notation.

See Also	**Oct** Function.

Example   This example uses the **Hex** function to return the hexadecimal value of a number.

```
MyHex = Hex(5)      ' Returns 5.
MyHex = Hex(10)     ' Returns A.
MyHex = Hex(459)    ' Returns 1CB.
```

Hidden Property

Applies To   Range, Scenario.

Description   Range object: **True** if the rows or columns are hidden. The specified range must span an entire column or row. Read-write.

Scenario object: **True** if the scenario is hidden. The default value is **False**. Read-write.

Syntax   *object*.**Hidden**

Elements   *object*
                    Required. The object to which this property applies.

Remark   Do not confuse this property with the **FormulaHidden** property.

Examples   These examples show some typical uses for the **Hidden** property.

```
Columns(1).Hidden = True        ' Hide column A
Rows.Hidden = False             ' Unhide all rows

' Hide columns A through F
Range(Columns("A"), Columns("F")).Hidden = True

' Hide every other column starting with A
j = 0
For Each i in Columns
    If j = 0 Then
        i.Hidden = True
        j = 1
    Else
        i.Hidden = False
        j = 0
    End If
Next
```

HiddenFields Method

Applies To   PivotTable.

Description   Returns a single pivot field (a PivotField object, Syntax 1) or a collection of the pivot fields (a PivotFields object, Syntax 2) that are currently not showing as row, column, page or data fields. Read-only.

Syntax 1   *object*.**HiddenFields**(*index*)

Syntax 2   *object*.**HiddenFields**

Elements   The **HiddenFields** method has the following object qualifier and named arguments:

object
    Required. The PivotTable object.

index
    Required for Syntax 1. The name or number of the pivot field to return (can be an array to specify more than one).

See Also   **ColumnFields** Method, **DataFields** Method, **PageFields** Method, **PivotFields** Method, **RowFields** Method, **VisibleFields** Method.

Example   This example adds the active pivot table hidden field names to a list box.

```
For Each hdnField In ActiveCell.PivotTable.HiddenFields
    hiddenFieldListBox.AddItem(hdnField.Name)
Next
```

HiddenItems Method

Applies To   PivotField.

Description   Returns one hidden pivot item (a PivotItem object, Syntax 1) or a collection of all the hidden pivot items (a PivotItems object, Syntax 2) in the specified field. Read-only.

Syntax 1   *object*.**HiddenItems**(*index*)

Syntax 2   *object*.**HiddenItems**

Elements   The **HiddenItems** method has the following object qualifier and named arguments:

object
    Required. The PivotField object.

index
    Required for Syntax 1. The number or name of the pivot item to return (can be an array to specify more than one).

See Also   **ChildItems** Method, **ParentItems** Method, **PivotItems** Method, **VisibleItems** Method.

Example   This example adds the names of all the hidden items in the active field to a list box.

```
For Each pvtItem in ActiveCell.PivotField.HiddenItems
    hiddenItemListBox.AddItem(pvtItem.Name)
Next pvtItem
```

Hide Method

Applies To   DialogSheet.

Description   Hides a dialog. If the dialog is not currently displayed, an error occurs.

Syntax   *object*.**Hide(*cancel*)**

Elements   The **Hide** method has the following object qualifier and named arguments:

object
Required. The DialogSheet object.

cancel
Optional. If **True**, the dialog is cancelled without validating edit-box contents. If **False** or omitted, edit box contents are validated before returning. No macros assigned to Cancel or OK buttons are run in either case.

Remarks   If *cancel* is **False** and edit fields in the dialog could not be validated then this method returns **False**, and the dialog does not exit. Otherwise, this method returns **True**.

Example   This example hides the active dialog.

```
ActiveDialog.Hide
```

HiLoLines Object

Description   High-low lines on a chart.

HiLoLines Property

Applies To   ChartGroup.

Description   Returns or sets the HiLoLines for a series on a line chart. Applies only to line charts. Read-write.

Syntax   *object*.**HiLoLines**

Elements   *object*
                    Required. The ChartGroup object.

See Also   **HasHiLoLines** Property.

Example   This example turns on high-low lines for the first chart group, and then sets their
                    line style, weight, and color.

```
With ActiveChart.ChartGroups(1)
    .HasHiLoLines = True
    With .HiLoLines.Border
        .LineStyle = xlThin
        .Weight = xlMedium
        .Color = RGB(255, 0, 0)
    End With
End With
```

HorizontalAlignment Property

Applies To   AxisTitle, Button, Buttons, ChartTitle, DataLabel, DataLabels, DrawingObjects,
                    GroupObject, GroupObjects, Range, Style, TextBox, TextBoxes.

Description   Returns or sets the horizontal alignment for the object. Can be one of **xlCenter**,
                    xlDistributed, **xlJustify**, **xlLeft**, or **xlRight** for all objects. In addition, the Range
                    or Style object can be set to **xlCenterAcrossSelection**, **xlFill**, or **xlGeneral**. Read-
                    write.

Syntax   *object*.**HorizontalAlignment**

Elements   *object*
                    Required. The object to which this property applies.

Remarks   The **xlDistributed** alignment style works only in Far East versions of Microsoft
                    Excel.

See Also   **AddIndent** Property, **VerticalAlignment** Property.

Example   This example centers the chart title.

```
ActiveChart.ChartTitle.HorizontalAlignment = xlCenter
```

Hour Function

Description   Returns a whole number between 0 and 23, inclusive, representing the hour of the day.

Syntax   **Hour(*time*)**

Elements   The *time* named argument is limited to a time or numbers and strings, in any combination, that can represent a time. If *time* contains no valid data, **Null** is returned.

See Also   **Day** Function, **Minute** Function, **Now** Function, **Second** Function, **Time** Function, **Time** Statement.

Example   This example uses the **Hour** function to obtain the hour from a specified time.

```
' In the development environment, the time (date literal) will display
' in short format using the locale settings of your code.
MyTime = #4:35:17 PM#        ' Assign a time.
MyHour = Hour(MyTime)        ' MyHour contains 16.
```

Id Property

Applies To   ToolbarButton.

Description   The button identification number of the button (built-in buttons only). Read-only.

Syntax   *object*.**Id**

Elements   *object*
                 Required. The ToolbarButton object.

Example   This example sets the buttonId variable to the identification number for button one on toolbar two.

```
buttonId = Toolbars(2).ToolbarButtons(1).Id
```

If...Then...Else Statement

Description   Conditionally executes a group of statements, depending on the value of an expression.

Syntax 1	**If** *condition* **Then** *statements* [**Else** *elsestatements*]

Syntax 2	**If** *condition* **Then**
	  [*statements*]
	[**ElseIf** *condition-n* **Then**
	  [*elseifstatements*]] . . .
	[**Else**
	  [*elsestatements*]]
	End If

Elements

Syntax 1 has these parts:

Part	Description
condition	Numeric or string expression that evaluates **True** or **False**.
statements	One or more statements separated by colons; executed if *condition* is **True**.
elsestatements	One or more statements separated by colons; executed if *condition* is **False**.

Syntax 2 has these parts:

Part	Description
condition	Expression that is **True** or **False**.
statements	One or more statements executed if *condition* is **True**.
condition-n	Numeric or string expression that evaluates **True** or **False**.
elseifstatements	One or more statements executed if associated *condition-n* is **True**.
elsestatements	One or more statements executed if no previous *condition-n* expressions are **True**.

Remarks

You can use the single-line form (Syntax 1) for short, simple tests. However, the block form (Syntax 2) provides more structure and flexibility than the single-line form and is usually easier to read, maintain, and debug.

Note With Syntax 1 it is possible to have multiple statements executed as the result of an **If...Then** decision, but they must all be on the same line and separated by colons, as in the following statement:

```
If A > 10 Then A = A + 1 : B = B + A : C = C + B
```

When executing a block **If** (Syntax 2), *condition* is tested. If *condition* is **True**, the statements following **Then** are executed. If *condition* is **False**, each **ElseIf** condition (if any) is evaluated in turn. When a **True** condition is found, the statements immediately following the associated **Then** are executed. If none of the

ElseIf conditions are **True** (or if there are no **ElseIf** clauses), the statements following **Else** are executed. After executing the statements following **Then** or **Else**, execution continues with the statement following **End If**.

The **Else** and **ElseIf** clauses are both optional. You can have as many **ElseIf** clauses as you want in a block **If**, but none can appear after an **Else** clause. Block **If** statements can be nested; that is, contained within one another.

What follows the **Then** keyword is examined to determine whether or not a statement is a block **If**. If anything other than a comment appears after **Then** on the same line, the statement is treated as a single-line **If** statement.

A block **If** statement must be the first statement on a line. The **Else**, **ElseIf**, and **End If** parts of the statement can have only a line number or line label preceding them. The block **If** must end with an **End If** statement.

Tip **Select Case** may be more useful when evaluating a single expression that has several possible actions.

See Also   **Select Case** Statement.

Example   This example shows uses of the **If...Then...Else** statement.

```
Number = 53          ' Initialize variable.
If Number < 10 Then
    Digits = 1
ElseIf Number < 100 Then
' Condition evaluates to True so the next statement is executed.
    Digits = 2
Else
    Digits = 3
End If
' Assign a value using the single line form of syntax.
If Digits = 1 Then MyString = "One" Else MyString = "More than one"
```

IgnoreRemoteRequests Property

Applies To   Application.

Description   **True** if remote DDE requests are ignored. Read-write.

Syntax   *object*.**IgnoreRemoteRequests**

Elements   *object*
                    Required. The Application object.

Example   This example saves the current state of the **IgnoreRemoteRequests** property, and
                    then sets the property to **True** so remote DDE requests are ignored.

```
saveIgnoreRequests = Application.IgnoreRemoteRequests
Application.IgnoreRemoteRequests = True
```

IMEStatus Function

Description   Returns the current Input Method Editor (IME) mode of Microsoft Windows;
                     available in Far East versions only.

Syntax   **IMEStatus**

Return Values   Japanese locale:

Value	Description
0	No operation.
1	IME on.
2	IME off.
3	IME disabled.
4	Hiragana double-byte characters (DBC).
5	Katakana DBC.
6	Katakana single-byte characters (SBC).
7	Alphanumeric DBC.
8	Alphanumeric SBC.

Korean locale:

Value	Description
0	No operation.
1	IME on.
2	IME off.
3	IME disabled.
4	Hangeul DBC.
5	Hanja conversion.
6	Reserved for consistency of **IMEStatus** information and future Hanja word conversion requirements.
7	Alphanumeric DBC.
8	Alphanumeric SBC.

Imp Operator

Description   Used to perform a logical implication on two expressions.

Syntax   *result* = *expression1* **Imp** *expression2*

Elements   The **Imp** operator syntax has these parts:

Part	Description
result	Any numeric variable.
expression1	Any expression.
expression2	Any expression.

Remarks   The following table illustrates how *result* is determined:

If expression1 is	And expression2 is	The result is
True	True	True
True	False	False
True	Null	Null
False	True	True
False	False	True
False	Null	True
Null	True	True
Null	False	Null
Null	Null	Null

The **Imp** operator performs a bit-wise comparison of identically positioned bits in two numeric expressions and sets the corresponding bit in *result* according to the following truth table:

If bit in *expression1* is	And bit in *expression2* is	The *result* is
0	0	1
0	1	1
1	0	0
1	1	1

See Also   Operator Precedence.

Example   This example uses the **Imp** Operator to perform logical implication on two expressions.

```
A = 10: B = 8: C = 6 : D = Null      ' Initialize variables.
MyCheck = A > B Imp B > C            ' Returns True.
MyCheck = A > B Imp C > B            ' Returns False.
MyCheck = B > A Imp C > B            ' Returns True.
MyCheck = B > A Imp C > D            ' Returns True.
MyCheck = C > D Imp B > A            ' Returns Null.
MyCheck = B Imp A                    ' Returns -1 (bit-wise comparison).
```

Import Method

Applies To   SoundNote.

Description   Imports a sound note from a file.

Syntax	*object*.**Import**(*file, resource*)
Elements	The **Import** method has the following object qualifier and named arguments:

object
    Required. The SoundNote object.

file
    Required. The name of the file containing sounds.

resource
    Required for the Apple Macintosh (not used with Microsoft Windows). The name or number of the sound resource in the file to import.

See Also	**Play** Method, **Record** Method.
Example	This example adds a sound note to the active cell.

```
ActiveCell.SoundNote.Import "C:\SOUNDS\CHIMES.WAV"
```

InchesToPoints Method

Applies To	Application.
Description	Converts a measurement in inches into points (1/72 inch).
Syntax	*object*.**InchesToPoints**(*inches*)
Elements	The **InchesToPoints** method has the following object qualifier and named arguments:

object
    Required. The Application object.

inches
    Required. Specifies the inch value to convert to points.

See Also	**CentimetersToPoints** Method.
Example	This example sets the left margin to 2.5 inches

```
ActiveSheet.PageSetup.LeftMargin = Application.InchesToPoints(2.5)
```

IncludeAlignment Property

Applies To	Style.

Description	**True** if the style includes the **AddIndent**, **HorizontalAlignment**, **VerticalAlignment**, **WrapText**, and **Orientation** properties. Read-write.
Syntax	*object*.**IncludeAlignment**
Elements	*object* Required. The Style object.
See Also	**IncludeBorder** Property, **IncludeFont** Property, **IncludeNumber** Property, **IncludePatterns** Property, **IncludeProtection** Property.
Example	This example sets the style in the active cell to include the alignment properties.

```
ActiveCell.Style.IncludeAlignment = True
```

IncludeBorder Property

Applies To	Style.
Description	**True** if the style includes the **Borders** properties. Read-write.
Syntax	*object*.**IncludeBorder**
Elements	*object* Required. The Style object.
See Also	**IncludeAlignment** Property, **IncludeFont** Property, **IncludeNumber** Property, **IncludePatterns** Property, **IncludeProtection** Property.
Example	This example sets the style in the active cell to include borders.

```
ActiveCell.Style.IncludeBorder = True
```

IncludeFont Property

Applies To	Style.
Description	**True** if the style includes the **Font** property. Read-write.
Syntax	*object*.**IncludeFont**
Elements	*object* Required. The Style object.
See Also	**IncludeAlignment** Property, **IncludeBorder** Property, **IncludeNumber** Property, **IncludePatterns** Property, **IncludeProtection** Property.

| Example | This example sets the style in the active cell to include the font property. |

```
ActiveCell.Style.IncludeFont = True
```

IncludeNumber Property

Applies To	Style.
Description	**True** if the style includes the **NumberFormat** property. Read-write.
Syntax	*object*.**IncludeNumber**
Elements	*object* Required. The Style object.
See Also	**IncludeAlignment** Property, **IncludeBorder** Property, **IncludeFont** Property, **IncludePatterns** Property, **IncludeProtection** Property.
Example	This example sets the style in the active cell to include the number format property.

```
ActiveCell.Style.IncludeNumber = True
```

IncludePatterns Property

Applies To	Style.
Description	**True** if the style includes the **Interior** properties. Read-write.
Syntax	*object*.**IncludePatterns**
Elements	*object* Required. The Style object.
See Also	**IncludeAlignment** Property, **IncludeBorder** Property, **IncludeFont** Property, **IncludeNumber** Property, **IncludeProtection** Property.
Example	This example sets the style in the active cell to include interior patterns.

```
ActiveCell.Style.IncludePatterns = True
```

IncludeProtection Property

Applies To	Style.

Description	**True** if the style includes the **FormulaHidden** and **Locked** protection properties. Read-write.
Syntax	*object*.**IncludeProtection**
Elements	*object* Required. The Style object.
See Also	**IncludeAlignment** Property, **IncludeBorder** Property, **IncludeFont** Property, **IncludeNumber** Property, **IncludePatterns** Property.
Example	This example sets the style in the active cell to include the protection properties.

```
ActiveCell.Style.IncludeProtection = True
```

Index Property

Applies To	Arc, Button, Chart, ChartObject, CheckBox, DialogSheet, Drawing, DropDown, EditBox, GroupBox, GroupObject, Label, LegendEntry, Line, ListBox, Menu, MenuBar, MenuItem, Module, Name, OLEObject, OptionButton, Oval, Pane, Picture, Rectangle, Scenario, ScrollBar, Spinner, TextBox, Trendline, Window, Worksheet.
Description	Returns the index number of the object within the collection of similar objects. Read-only. For help about using the **Index** worksheet function in Visual Basic, see Using Worksheet Functions in Visual Basic.
Syntax	*object*.**Index**
Elements	*object* Required. The object to which this property applies.
Example	This example displays the index number of an object passed to this procedure.

```
MsgBox "The index number of this object is " & obj.Index
```

InnerDetail Property

Applies To	PivotTable.
Description	Returns or sets the name of the field which will be shown as detail when the **ShowDetail** property is **True** for the innermost row or column field. Read-write.

Syntax	*object*.**InnerDetail**
Elements	*object*
	Required. The PivotTable object.
See Also	**ShowDetail** Property.
Example	This example sets the **InnerDetail** property to the "Region" field.

```
ActiveCell.PivotTable.InnerDetail = "Region"
```

Input # Statement

Description	Reads data from an open sequential file and assigns the data to variables.
Syntax	**Input #***filenumber*,*varlist*
Elements	The **Input #** statement syntax has these parts:

Part	Description
filenumber	Any valid file number.
varlist	Comma-delimited list of variables that are assigned values read from the file: can't be an array or object variable. However, variables that describe an element of an array or user-defined type may be used.

Remarks   When read, standard string or numeric data is assigned to variables as is. The following table illustrates how other input data is treated:

Data	Value assigned to variable
Delimiting comma or blank line	**Empty**.
#NULL#	**Null**.
#TRUE# or #FALSE#	**True** or **False.**
#yyyy-mm-dd hh:mm:ss#	The date and/or time represented by the expression.
#ERROR *errornumber*#	*errornumber* (variable is a **Variant** tagged as an error).

Double quotation marks (**"**) within input data are ignored.

Data items in a file must appear in the same order as the variables in *varlist* and be matched with variables of the same data type. If a variable is numeric and the data is not, zero is assigned to the variable.

If the end of the file is reached while a data item is being input, the input is terminated and an error occurs.

Note In order to correctly read data from a file into variables, you should always use the **Write #** statement instead of the **Print #** statement to write the data to the files. Using **Write #** ensures that each separate data field is properly delimited.

See Also   **Input** Function, **Write #** Statement.

Example   This example uses the **Input #** statement to read data from a file into two variables. For purposes of this example, assume that TESTFILE is a file with a few lines of data written to it using the **Write #** statement; that is, each line contains a string in quotations and a number separated by a comma, for example, ("Hello", 234).

```
Open "TESTFILE" For Input As #1        ' Open file for input.
Do While Not EOF(1)                    ' Loop until end of file.
    Input #1, MyString, MyNumber       ' Read data into variables.
    Debug.Print MyString, MyNumber     ' Print data to Debug window.
Loop
Close #1                               ' Close file.
```

Input Function

Description   Returns characters (bytes) from an open sequential file.

Syntax   **Input**(*number*,[#]*filenumber*)

Elements   The **Input** function syntax has these parts:

Part	Description
number	Any valid numeric expression specifying the number of characters to return.
filenumber	Any valid file number.

Remarks   Use this function only with files opened in **Input** or **Binary** mode.

Unlike the **Input #** statement, the **Input** function returns all of the characters it reads including commas, carriage returns, linefeeds, quotation marks, and leading spaces.

Note Another function (**InputB**) is provided for use with the double-byte character sets (DBCS) used in some Asian locales. Instead of specifying the number of characters to return, *number* specifies the number of bytes. In areas where DBCS is not used, **InputB** behaves the same as **Input**.

See Also   **Input #** Statement.

Example   This example uses the **Input** function to read one character at a time from a file and print it to the Debug window. For purposes of this example, assume that TESTFILE is a text file with a few lines of sample data.

```
Open "TESTFILE" For Input As #1         ' Open file.
Do While Not EOF(1)                     ' Loop until end of file.
    MyChar = Input(1, #1)               ' Get one character.
    Debug.Print MyChar                  ' Print to Debug window.
Loop
Close #1                                ' Close file.
```

InputBox Function

Description   Displays a prompt in a dialog box, waits for the user to input text or choose a button, and returns the contents of the text box.

Syntax   **InputBox(***prompt*[*,title*][*,default*][*,xpos*][*,ypos*][*,helpfile,context*]**)**

Elements   The **InputBox** function syntax has these named-argument parts:

Part	Description
prompt	String expression displayed as the message in the dialog box. The maximum length of *prompt* is approximately 1024 characters, depending on the width of the characters used. If *prompt* consists of more than one line, be sure to include a carriage return (character code 13), or carriage return linefeed (character code 10) between each line.
title	String expression displayed in the title bar of the dialog box. If you omit *title*, nothing is placed in the title bar.
default	String expression displayed in the text box as the default response if no other input is provided. If you omit *default*, the text box is displayed empty.

Part	Description
xpos	Numeric expression that specifies, in twips, the horizontal distance of the left edge of the dialog box from the left edge of the screen. If *xpos* is omitted, the dialog box is horizontally centered.
ypos	Numeric expression that specifies, in twips, the vertical distance of the upper edge of the dialog box from the top of the screen. If *ypos* is omitted, the dialog box is vertically positioned approximately one-third of the way down the screen.
helpfile	String expression that identifies the Help file to use to provide context-sensitive Help for the dialog box. If *helpfile* is provided, *context* must also be provided.
context	Numeric expression that is the Help context number the Help author assigned to the appropriate Help topic. If *context* is provided, *helpfile* must also be provided.

Remarks

When both *helpfile* and *context* are supplied, a Help button is automatically added to the dialog box.

If the user chooses OK or presses Enter, the **InputBox** function returns whatever is in the text box. If the user chooses Cancel, the function returns a zero-length string ("").

See Also

MsgBox Function.

Example

This example shows various ways to use the **InputBox** function to prompt the user to enter a value. If the x and y positions are omitted, the dialog is automatically centered for the respective axes. The variable MyValue contains the value entered by the user if the user chooses OK or presses ENTER. If the user chooses Cancel, a zero-length string is returned.

```
Message = "Enter a value between 1 and 3"    ' Set prompt.
Title = "InputBox Demo"                       ' Set title.
Default = "1"                                 ' Set default.
' Display message, title, and default value.
MyValue = InputBox(Message, Title, Default)

' Use helpfile and context. The help button is added automatically.
MyValue = InputBox(Message, Title, , , , "DEMO.HLP", 10)

' Display dialog at position 100,100
MyValue = InputBox(Message, Title, Default, 100, 100)
```

InputBox Method

Applies To   Application.

Description   Displays a dialog box for user input. Returns the information entered in the dialog box.

Syntax   *object*.**InputBox**(*prompt, title, default, left, top, helpFile, helpContextID, type*)

Elements   The **InputBox** method has the following object qualifier and named arguments:

object
Required. The Application object.

prompt
Required. The message to be displayed in the dialog box. This may be a string, a number, a date, or a Boolean value.

title
Optional. The title for the input box. If this argument is omitted, the title bar is empty.

default
Optional. Specifies a value to be put in the edit box when the dialog box is initially displayed. If this argument is omitted, the edit box is left empty. This value may be a Range.

left
Optional. Specifies an x position for the dialog box, in points, from the top left of the screen. One point is 1/72 inch.

top
Optional. Specifies a y position for the dialog box, in points, from the top left of the screen.

helpFile
Optional. The name of the online Help file for this input box. If the *helpFile* and *helpContextID* arguments are present, a Help button will appear in the dialog.

helpContextID
Optional. The context ID of the Help topic in *helpFile*.

type
> Optional. Specifies the return data type. If this argument is omitted, the dialog box returns text. May have one of the following values:

Value	Meaning
0	A formula
1	A number
2	Text (a string)
4	A logical value (**True** or **False**)
8	A cell reference, as a Range object
16	An error value, such as #N/A
64	An array of values

> You can use the sum of the allowable values for *type*. For example, for an input box that can accept text or numbers, set *type* equal to **1 + 2**.

Remarks

Use **InputBox** to display a simple dialog box so you can enter information to be used in a macro. The dialog box has an OK and a Cancel button. If you choose the OK button, **InputBox** returns the value entered in the dialog box. If you choose the Cancel button, **InputBox** returns **False**.

If *type* = 0, **InputBox** returns the formula in the form of text, for example, "=2*PI()/360". If there are any references in the formula, they are returned as A1-style references. (Use **ConvertFormula** to convert between reference styles.)

If *type* = 8, **InputBox** returns a Range. You must use the **Set** statement to assign the result to a Range, as shown in the following example.

```
Set myRange = InputBox(prompt := "Sample", type := 8)
```

If you do not use the **Set** statement, the variable is set to the value in the Range, rather than the Range itself.

If you use the **InputBox** method to ask the user for a formula, you must use the **FormulaLocal** property to assign the formula to a Range. The input formula will be in the user's language. The **InputBox** method differs from the **InputBox** function because it allows selective validation of the user's input, and it can be used with Microsoft Excel objects, error values and formulas. **Application.InputBox** calls the **InputBox** method; **InputBox** with no object qualifier calls the **InputBox** function.

Example

This example asks for the name of a context string.

```
stringToFind = Application.InputBox("Context string to find?", _
    "Search String")
```

InputType Property

Applies To	DrawingObjects, EditBox, EditBoxes.
Description	Returns or sets what type of input validation is applied to the contents of an edit box (one of **xlFormula, xlInteger**, **xlNumber**, **xlReference**, or **xlText**). Read-write.
Syntax	*object*.**InputType**
Elements	*object* Required. The object to which this property applies.
Example	This example sets edit box one to require an integer.

```
Application.DialogSheets(1).Editboxes(1).InputType = xlInteger
```

Insert Method

Applies To	Characters, Pictures, Range.
Description	Syntax 1 (Range object): Inserts a cell or a range of cells into the worksheet or macro sheet and shifts other cells away to make space.
	Syntax 2 (Characters object): Inserts a string before the selected characters.
	Syntax 3 (Pictures object): Inserts the specified file as a picture.
Syntax 1	*object*.**Insert**(*shift*)
Syntax 2	*object*.**Insert**(*string*)
Syntax 3	*object*.**Insert**(*filename, converter*)
Elements	The **Insert** method has the following object qualifier and named arguments: *object* Required. Insert cells at this range (Syntax 1) or insert string before this character (Syntax 2).
	shift Optional. Specifies which way to shift the cells, either **xlToRight** or **xlDown**. If omitted, a default is used based on the shape of the range.
	string Required. The string to insert.

filename
> Required. Specifies the file to insert.

converter
> Required. Specifies the picture converter to use when loading the file. Can be one of **xlBMP, xlWMF, xlPLT, xlCGM, xlHGL, xlPIC, xlEPS, xlDRW, xlTIF, xlWPG, xlDXF, xlPCX,** or **xlPCT.**

Examples   This example inserts a new row before row four.

```
Rows(4).Insert
```

This example inserts a cell at A1:C5 and shifts cells down.

```
Range("A1:C5").Insert(xlDown)
```

This example inserts an entire row at the current selection.

```
Selection.EntireRow.Insert
```

This example replaces the first 3 characters of the first text box in the sheet with the string "New" formatted bold.

```
With ActiveSheet.TextBoxes(1).Characters(1,3)
    .Insert "New"
    .Font.Bold = True
End With
```

This example adds the string "Done" to the end of a text box by inserting the new string after the last character in the text box.

```
With ActiveSheet.TextBoxes(1)
    .Characters(.Characters.Count + 1).Insert ("Done")
End With
```

InsertFile Method

Applies To   Module.

Description   Adds text from a file to the end of the module.

Syntax   *object*.**InsertFile**(*fileName, merge*)

Elements   The **InsertFile** method has the following object qualifier and named arguments:

object
> Required. The Module object.

fileName
> Required. The name of the file containing the text that you wish to insert.

merge
> Optional. If **True,** the new file is merged, so that all declarations are at the top of the module and all procedures are below the declarations. If **False** or omitted, the new file is inserted at the insertion point.

Remarks   You cannot insert text into a running code module. This applies both to running procedures as well as modules containing code that is stacked waiting to run after the current procedure returns.

Example   This example adds text from a file to module one.

```
ActiveWorkbook.Modules(1).InsertFile fileName:="MYMACRO.TXT"
```

Installed Property

Applies To   AddIn.

Description   **True** if the add-in is installed. Read-write.

Syntax   *object*.**Installed**

Elements   *object*
> Required. The AddIn object.

Remarks   Setting this property to **True** installs the add-in and calls its Auto_Add functions. Setting this property to **False** removes the add-in and calls its Auto_Remove functions.

Example   This example installs the Analysis Tools add-in.

```
AddIns("Analysis Tools").Installed = True
```

InStr Function

Description   Returns the position of the first occurrence of one string within another.

Syntax   **InStr(**[*start,*]*string1,string2*[*,compare*]**)**

Elements

The **InStr** function syntax has these parts:

Part	Description
start	Numeric expression that sets the starting position for each search. If omitted, search begins at the first character position. If *start* contains no valid data, an error occurs. *Start* is required if *compare* is specified.
string1	String expression being searched. If *string1* contains no valid data, **Null** is returned.
string2	String expression sought. If *string2* contains no valid data, **Null** is returned.
compare	Number specifying the type of string comparison. Specify **1** to perform a textual case-insensitive comparison. Specify **0** (default) to perform a binary comparison. If *compare* is **Null**, an error occurs. *Start* is required if *compare* is specified. If *compare* is omitted, the setting of **Option Compare** is used to determine the type of comparison.

Return Values

Value	Description
0	*string1* is zero-length.
start	*string2* is zero-length.
0	*string2* not found.
Position at which match is found	*string2* is found within *string1*.
0	*start* > *string2*.

Remarks

Note When **Option Compare Text** is specified, comparisons are textual and case-insensitive. When **Option Compare Binary** is specified, comparisons are strictly binary.

Note Another function (**InStrB**) is provided for use with the double-byte character sets (DBCS) used in some Asian locales. Instead of returning the character position of the first occurence of one string within another, **InStrB** returns the byte position. In areas where DBCS is not used, **InStrB** behaves the same as **InStr**.

See Also

Option Compare Statement.

Example

This example uses the **InStr** function to return the position of the first occurrence of one string within another.

```
SearchString ="XXpXXpXXPXXP"      ' String to search in.
SearchChar = "P"                  ' Search for "P".

' A textual comparison starting at position 4. Returns 6.
MyPos = InStr(4, SearchString, SearchChar, 1)

' A binary comparison starting at position 1. Returns 9.
MyPos = InStr(1, SearchString, SearchChar, 0)

' Comparison is binary by default (if last argument is omitted).
MyPos = InStr(SearchString, SearchChar)       ' Returns 9.

MyPos = InStr(1, SearchString, "W") ' Returns 0.
```

Int Function, Fix Function

Description

Returns the integer portion of a number.

Syntax

Int(*number*)
Fix(*number*)

Elements

The *number* argument can be any valid numeric expression. If *number* contains no valid data, **Null** is returned.

Remarks

Both **Int** and **Fix** remove the fractional part of *number* and return the resulting integer value.

The difference between **Int** and **Fix** is that if *number* is negative, **Int** returns the first negative integer less than or equal to *number,* whereas **Fix** returns the first negative integer greater than or equal to *number.* For example, **Int** converts -8.4 to -9, and **Fix** converts -8.4 to -8.

Fix(*number*) is equivalent to:

```
Sgn(number) * Int(Abs(number))
```

See Also

CInt Function.

Example

This example illustrates how the **Int** and **Fix** functions return integer portions of numbers. In the case of a negative number argument, the **Int** function returns the the first negative integer less than or equal to the number; whereas, the **Fix** function returns the first negative integer greater than or equal to the number.

```
MyNumber = Int(99.8)      ' Returns 99.
MyNumber = Fix(99.2)      ' Returns 99.
MyNumber = Int(-99.8)     ' Returns -100.
MyNumber = Fix(-99.8)     ' Returns -99.
MyNumber = Int(-99.2)     ' Returns -100.
MyNumber = Fix(-99.2)     ' Returns -99.
```

Integer Data Type

Integer variables are stored as 16-bit (2-byte) numbers ranging in value from -32,768 to 32,767. The type-declaration character for **Integer** is % (character code 37).

You can also use **Integer** variables to represent enumerated values. An enumerated value can contain a finite set of unique whole numbers, each of which has special meaning in the context in which it is used. Enumerated values provide a convenient way to select among a known number of choices. For example, when asking the user to select a color from a list, you could have 0 = black, 1 = white, and so on. It is good programming practice to define constants using the **Const** statement for each enumerated value.

See Also

CInt Function, **Long** Data Type, **Variant** Data Type.

Interactive Property

Applies To

Application.

Description

True if Microsoft Excel is in interactive mode; this property is usually **True**. If you set it to **False**, Microsoft Excel will block all input from the keyboard and mouse (except input to dialog boxes that are displayed by your code). Blocking user input will prevent the user from interfering with the macro as it moves or activates Microsoft Excel objects. Read-write.

Syntax

object.**Interactive**

Elements

object
    Required. The Application object.

Intercept Property

Applies To   Trendline.

Description   Returns or sets the point where the trendline crosses the value axis. Read-write.

For help about using the **Intercept** worksheet function in Visual Basic, see Using Worksheet Functions in Visual Basic.

Syntax   *object*.**Intercept**

Elements   *object*
                     Required. The Trendline object.

Remarks   Setting this property causes the **InterceptIsAuto** property to be set to **False**.

See Also   **InterceptIsAuto** Property.

Example   This example causes trendline one to cross the value axis at five.

```
ActiveWorkbook.Charts(1).SeriesCollection(1) _
    .Trendlines(1).Intercept = 5
```

InterceptIsAuto Property

Applies To   Trendline.

Description   **True** if the point where the trendline crosses the value axis is automatically determined by the regression. Read-write.

Syntax   *object*.**InterceptIsAuto**

Elements   *object*
                     Required. The Trendline object.

Remarks   Setting the **Intercept** property causes this property to be set to **False**.

See Also   **Intercept** Property.

Example   This example causes the trendline intercept point to be automatically determined.

```
ActiveWorkbook.Charts(1).SeriesCollection(1) _
    .Trendlines(1).InterceptIsAuto = True
```

Interior Object

Description   The interior of a cell or graphic object.

Interior Property

Applies To   Arc, Arcs, AxisTitle, ChartArea, ChartObject, ChartObjects, ChartTitle, CheckBox, CheckBoxes, DataLabel, DataLabels, DownBars, Drawing, DrawingObjects, Drawings, Floor, GroupObject, GroupObjects, Legend, LegendKey, OLEObject, OLEObjects, OptionButton, OptionButtons, Oval, Ovals, Picture, Pictures, PlotArea, Point, Range, Rectangle, Rectangles, Series, Style, TextBox, TextBoxes, UpBars, Walls.

Description   Returns or sets the Interior of the object. Read-write.

Syntax   *object*.**Interior**

Elements   *object*
                          Required. The object to which this property applies.

Example   This example sets the interior color for cell A1.

```
Range("A1").Interior.Color = RGB(255,0,0)
```

International Property

Applies To   Application.

Description   Returns a 45-element array containing information about the current country and international settings. Read-only.

Syntax	*object*.**International(***index***)**
Elements	*object*

    Required. The Application object.

index

Optional. Specifies a single setting to return, as shown in the following table:

Index	Built-In Constant	Type	Meaning
1	xlCountryCode	number	Country version of Microsoft Excel.
2	xlCountrySetting	number	Current country setting in the Microsoft Windows Control Panel or the country number as determined by your Apple system software.
3	xlDecimalSeparator	text	Decimal separator.
4	xlThousandsSeparator	text	Zero or thousands separator.
5	xlListSeparator	text	List separator.
6	xlUpperCaseRowLetter	text	Uppercase Row letter (for R1C1 references).
7	xlUpperCaseColumnLetter	text	Uppercase Column letter.
8	xlLowerCaseRowLetter	text	Lowercase Row letter.
9	xlLowerCaseColumnLetter	text	Lowercase Column letter.
10	xlLeftBracket	text	Character used instead of the left bracket ([) in R1C1 relative references.
11	xlRightBracket	text	Character used instead of the right bracket (]).
12	xlLeftBrace	text	Character used instead of the left brace ({) in array literals.
13	xlRightBrace	text	Character used instead of the right brace (}).
14	xlColumnSeparator	text	Character used to separate columns in array literals.
15	xlRowSeparator	text	Character used to separate rows.
16	xlAlternateArraySeparator	text	Alternate array item separator to use if the current array separator is the same as the decimal separator.
17	xlDateSeparator	text	Date separator (*/* in US).
18	xlTimeSeparator	text	Time separator (**:** in US).
19	xlYearCode	text	Year symbol in number formats (**y** in US).
20	xlMonthCode	text	Month symbol (**m**).

Index	Built-In Constant	Type	Meaning
21	xlDayCode	text	Day symbol (**d**).
22	xlHourCode	text	Hour symbol (**h**).
23	xlMinuteCode	text	Minute symbol (**m**).
24	xlSecondCode	text	Second symbol (**s**).
25	xlCurrencyCode	text	Currency symbol (**$**).
26	xlGeneralFormatName	text	Name of the **General** number format.
27	xlCurrencyDigits	number	Number of decimal digits to use in currency formats.
28	xlCurrencyNegative	number	Indicates the currency format for negative currencies: 0 = ($x) or (x$) 1 = -$x or -x$ 2 = $-x or x-$ 3 = $x- or x$- Note: The position of the currency symbol is determined by 37.
29	xlNoncurrencyDigits	number	Number of decimal digits to use in non-currency formats.
30	xlMonthNameChars	number	Number of characters to use in month names.
31	xlWeekdayNameChars	number	Number of characters to use in weekday names.
32	xlDateOrder	number	Indicates the date order: 0 = month-day-year 1 = day-month-year 2 = year-month-day
33	xl24HourClock	Boolean	**True** if using 24-hour time; **False** if using 12-hour time.
34	xlNonEnglishFunctions	Boolean	**True** if not displaying functions in English.
35	xlMetric	Boolean	**True** if using the metric system; **False** if using the English measurement system.
36	xlCurrencySpaceBefore	Boolean	**True** if adding a space before the currency symbol.
37	xlCurrencyBefore	Boolean	**True** if the currency symbol precedes the currency values; **False** if it goes after.
38	xlCurrencyMinusSign	Boolean	**True** if using a minus sign for negative numbers; **False** if using parentheses.

Index	Built-In Constant	Type	Meaning
39	xlCurrencyTrailingZeros	Boolean	**True** if trailing zeros are displayed for zero currency values.
40	xlCurrencyLeadingZeros	Boolean	**True** if leading zeros are displayed for zero currency values.
41	xlMonthLeadingZero	Boolean	**True** if a leading zero is displayed in months when months are displayed as numbers.
42	xlDayLeadingZero	Boolean	**True** if a leading zero is displayed in days.
43	xl4DigitYears	Boolean	**True** if using 4-digit years; **False** if using 2-digit years.
44	xlMDY	Boolean	**True** if the date order is Month-Day-Year when dates are displayed in the long form; **False** if the date order is Day-Month-Year.
45	xlTimeLeadingZero	Boolean	**True** if the leading zero is shown in the time.

Example

This example uses the **International** property to display the international decimal separator.

```
MsgBox "The decimal separator is " & _
    Application.International(xlDecimalSeparator)
```

Intersect Method

Applies to

Application.

Description

Returns the rectangular intersection of two or more ranges.

Syntax

object.**Intersect**(*arg1, arg2, ...*)

Elements

The **Intersect** method has the following object qualifier and named arguments:

object
Optional. The Application object.

arg1, arg2, ...
Required. The intersecting ranges. At least two Range objects must be specified.

See Also

Union Method.

Example   This example selects the intersection of named ranges range1 and range2.

```
Application.Intersect(Range("range1"), Range("range2")).Select
```

InvertIfNegative Property

Applies To   LegendKey, Point, Series.

Description   **True** if Microsoft Excel inverts the pattern in the item when it corresponds to a negative number. Read-write.

Syntax   *object*.**InvertIfNegative**

Elements   *object*
Required. The LegendKey, Point, or Series object.

Example   This example inverts the pattern for negative values on series one.

```
ActiveChart.SeriesCollection(1).InvertIfNegative = True
```

Is Operator

Description   Used to compare two object reference variables.

Syntax   *result* = *object1* **Is** *object2*

Elements   The **Is** operator syntax has these parts:

Part	Description
result	Any numeric variable.
object1	Any object name.
object2	Any object name.

Remarks   If *object1* and *object2* both refer to the same object, *result* is **True**; if they do not, *result* is **False**. Two variables can be made to refer to the same object in several ways.

In the following example, A has been set to refer to the same object as B:

```
Set A = B
```

The following example makes A and B refer to the same object as C:

```
Set A = C
Set B = C
```

See Also	Operator Precedence, **Set** Statement.
Example	This example uses the **Is** operator to compare two object references. All the object variables used here are generic names and for illustration purposes only.

```
Set YourObject = MyObject              ' Assign object references.
Set ThisObject = MyObject
Set ThatObject = OtherObject
MyCheck = YourObject Is ThisObject     ' Returns True.
MyCheck = ThatObject Is ThisObject     ' Returns False.
' Assume MyObject <> OtherObject
MyCheck = MyObject Is ThatObject       ' Returns False.
```

IsArray Function

Description	Returns a value indicating whether a variable is an array.
Syntax	**IsArray(*varname*)**
Elements	The *varname* named argument can be any variable.
Remarks	**IsArray** returns **True** if the variable is an array; otherwise, it returns **False**.
See Also	**Array** Function, **IsDate** Function, **IsEmpty** Function, **IsError** Function, **IsMissing** Function, **IsNull** Function, **IsNumeric** Function, **IsObject** Function, **TypeName** Function, **Variant** Data Type, **VarType** Function.
Example	This example uses the **IsArray** function to check if a variable is an array.

```
Dim MyArray(1 To 5) As Integer     ' Declare array variable.
YourArray = Array(1, 2, 3)         ' Use Array function.
MyCheck = IsArray(MyArray)         ' Returns True.
MyCheck = IsArray(YourArray)       ' Returns True.
```

IsDate Function

Description	Returns a value indicating whether an expression can be converted to a date.
Syntax	**IsDate(*expression*)**
Elements	The *expression* named argument can be any date or string expression recognizable as a date or time.
Remarks	**IsDate** returns **True** if the expression is a date or can legally be converted to a date; otherwise, it returns **False**. The range of valid dates is January 1, 100 A.D. through December 31, 9999 A.D.

See Also   **CDate** Function, **Date** Data Type, **IsArray** Function, **IsEmpty** Function, **IsError** Function, **IsMissing** Function, **IsNull** Function, **IsNumeric** Function, **IsObject** Function, **TypeName** Function, **Variant** Data Type, **VarType** Function.

Example   This example uses the **IsDate** function to determine if an expression can be converted to a date.

```
MyDate = "February 12, 1969"
YourDate = #2/12/69#
NoDate = "Hello"
MyCheck = IsDate(MyDate)        ' Returns True.
MyCheck = IsDate(YourDate)      ' Returns True.
MyCheck = IsDate(NoDate)        ' Returns False.
```

IsEmpty Function

Description   Returns a value indicating whether a variable has been initialized.

Syntax   **IsEmpty(*expression*)**

Elements   The *expression* named argument can be any numeric or string expression. However, because **IsEmpty** is used to determine if individual variables are initialized, the *expression* argument is most often a single variable name.

Remarks   **IsEmpty** returns **True** if the variable is **Empty**; otherwise, it returns **False**. **False** is always returned if *expression* contains more than one variable.

See Also   **IsArray** Function, **IsDate** Function, **IsError** Function, **IsMissing** Function, **IsNull** Function, **IsNumeric** Function, **IsObject** Function, **TypeName** Function, **Variant** Data Type, **VarType** Function.

Example   This example uses the **IsEmpty** function to determine whether or not a variable has been initialized.

```
MyCheck = IsEmpty(MyVar)        ' Returns True.
MyVar = Null                    ' Assign Null.
MyCheck = IsEmpty(MyVar)        ' Returns False.
MyVar = Empty                   ' Assign Empty.
MyCheck = IsEmpty(MyVar)        ' Returns True.
```

IsError Function

Description   Returns a value indicating whether an expression is an error value.

Syntax   **IsError(*expression*)**

Elements	The *expression* named argument can be any numeric expression used to indicate an error value.
Remarks	Error values are created by converting real numbers to error values using the **CVErr** function. The **IsError** function is used to determine if a numeric expression represents an error. **IsError** returns **True** if the *expression* argument indicates an error; otherwise, it returns **False**.
See Also	**IsArray** Function, **IsDate** Function, **IsEmpty** Function, **IsMissing** Function, **IsNull** Function, **IsNumeric** Function, **IsObject** Function, **CVErr** Function, **TypeName** Function, **Variant** Data Type, **VarType** Function.
Example	This example uses the **IsError** function to check if a numeric expression is an error value. The **CVErr** function is used to return an **Error Variant** from a user-defined function.

```
' Assume UserFunction is a user-defined function procedure that returns
' an error value; e.g., return value assigned with the statement
' UserFunction = CVErr(32767) where 32767 is a user-defined number.
ReturnVal = UserFunction()
MyCheck = IsError(ReturnVal)          ' Returns True.
```

IsGap Property

Applies To	ToolbarButton.
Description	**True** if the button is really a gap (an extended space between buttons). Read-only.
Syntax	*object*.**IsGap**
Elements	*object* Required. The ToolbarButton object.
Example	This example sets the buttonIsGap variable to **True** if the third button on toolbar one is a gap.

```
buttonIsGap = Application.ToolBars(1).ToolbarButtons(3).IsGap
```

IsMissing Function

Description	Returns a value indicating whether an optional argument has been passed to a procedure.

Syntax	**IsMissing(*argname*)**
Elements	The ***argname*** named argument is the name of an optional procedure argument.
Remarks	The **IsMissing** function is used in a procedure that has optional arguments, including **ParamArray** arguments, to determine whether an argument has been passed to the procedure. **IsMissing** returns **True** if no value has been passed for the specified argument; otherwise, it returns **False**.
See Also	**IsArray** Function, **IsDate** Function, **IsEmpty** Function, **IsError** Function, **IsNull** Function, **IsNumeric** Function, **IsObject** Function, **Function** Statement, **Property Get** Statement, **Property Let** Statement, **Property Set** Statement, **Sub** Statement, **TypeName** Function, **Variant** Data Type, **VarType** Function.
Example	This example uses the **IsMissing** function to check if an optional argument has been passed to a user-defined procedure.

```
' The following statements call the user-defined function procedure.
ReturnValue = ReturnTwice()          ' Returns Null.
ReturnValue = ReturnTwice(2)         ' Returns 4.

' Function procedure definition.
Function ReturnTwice(Optional A)
    If IsMissing(A) Then
        ' If argument is missing, return a Null.
        ReturnTwice = Null
    Else
        ' If argument is present, return twice the value.
        ReturnTwice = A * 2
    End If
End Function
```

IsNull Function

Description	Returns a value that indicates whether an expression contains no valid data (**Null**).
Syntax	**IsNull(*expression*)**
Elements	The ***expression*** named argument can be any numeric or string expression.
Remarks	**IsNull** returns **True** if *expression* is **Null**, that is, it contains no valid data; otherwise, **IsNull** returns **False**. If *expression* consists of more than one variable, **Null** in any variable causes **True** to be returned for the entire expression.

The **Null** value indicates that the **Variant** contains no valid data. **Null** is not the same as **Empty**, which indicates that a variable has not yet been initialized. It is also not the same as a zero-length string, which is sometimes referred to as a null string.

Important Use the **IsNull** function to determine whether an expression contains a **Null** value. Expressions that you might expect to evaluate **True** under some circumstances, such as If Var = Null and If Var <> Null, are always **False**. This is because any expression containing a **Null** is itself **Null** and therefore **False**.

See Also

IsArray Function, **IsDate** Function, **IsEmpty** Function, **IsError** Function, **IsMissing** Function, **IsNumeric** Function, **IsObject** Function, **TypeName** Function, **Variant** Data Type, **VarType** Function.

Example

This example uses the **IsNull** function to determine if a variable contains a **Null**.

```
MyCheck = IsNull(MyVar)      ' Returns False.
MyVar = ""
MyCheck = IsNull(MyVar)      ' Returns False.
MyVar = Null
MyCheck = IsNull(MyVar)      ' Returns True.
```

IsNumeric Function

Description

Returns a value indicating whether an expression can be evaluated as a number.

Syntax

IsNumeric(*expression*)

Elements

The *expression* named argument can be any numeric or string expression.

Remarks

IsNumeric returns **True** if the entire *expression* is recognized as a number; otherwise, it returns **False**.

IsNumeric returns **False** if *expression* is a date expression.

See Also

IsArray Function, **IsDate** Function, **IsEmpty** Function, **IsError** Function, **IsMissing** Function, **IsNull** Function, **IsObject** Function, **TypeName** Function, **Variant** Data Type, **VarType** Function.

Example   This example uses the **IsNumeric** function to determine if a variable can be evaluated as a number.

```
MyVar = "53"                    ' Assign value.
MyCheck = IsNumeric(MyVar)      ' Returns True.
MyVar = "459.95"                ' Assign value.
MyCheck = IsNumeric(MyVar)      ' Returns True.
MyVar = "45 Help"               ' Assign value.
MyCheck = IsNumeric(MyVar)      ' Returns False.
```

IsObject Function

Description   Returns a value indicating whether an expression references a valid OLE Automation object.

Syntax   **IsObject(*expression*)**

Elements   The *expression* named argument can be any expression.

Remarks   **IsObject** returns **True** if *expression* is a valid reference to an actual object; otherwise, it returns **False**.

See Also   **IsArray** Function, **IsDate** Function, **IsEmpty** Function, **IsError** Function, **IsMissing** Function, **IsNull** Function, **IsNumeric** Function, **Object** Data Type, **Set** Statement, **TypeName** Function, **Variant** Data Type, **VarType** Function.

Example   This example uses the **IsObject** function to determine if a variable references a valid object. `MyObject` and `YourObject` are object variables of the same type. They are generic names used here for illustration purposes only.

```
Dim MyInt As Integer            ' Declare variable.
Set YourObject = MyObject       ' Assign an object reference.
MyCheck = IsObject(YourObject)  ' Returns True.
MyCheck = IsObject(MyInt)       ' Returns False.
```

Italic Property

Applies To   Font.

Description   **True** if the font is italic. Read-write.

Syntax   *object*.**Italic**

Elements   *object*
           Required. The Font object (**ActiveCell.Font**, for example).

Example   This example sets the font to italic for the range A1:A5.

```
Range("A1", "A5").Font.Italic = True
```

Item Method

Applies To   All collections.

Description   Returns part of a collection. The **Item** method works like the accessor method for a collection. For example, the following code:

```
ActiveWorkbook.Worksheets.Item(1)
```

Is equivalent to:

```
ActiveWorkbook.Worksheets(1)
```

The **Item** method is not generally required; you can usually use the collection-accessor form. However, you may need to use the **Item** method to return part of a collection if you assign a variable to the collection and pass it to a function or sub procedure, as shown in the following example.

```
Sub UseItem(wk as Worksheets)
    wk.Item(1).PageSetup.BottomMargin = 120      'must use Item here
End Sub
```

For more information about acccessing an individual member of a collection, see the method named for the collection (the **Worksheets** Method, for example).

Iteration Property

Applies To   Application.

Description   **True** if Microsoft Excel will use iteration to resolve circular references. Read-write.

Syntax   *object*.**Iteration**

Elements   *object*
        Required. The Application object.

See Also   **MaxIterations** Property, **MaxChange** Property.

Example   This example saves the current state of the **Iteration** property, and then sets the property to **True**, so Microsoft Excel will use iteration to resolve circular references.

```
saveIteration = Application.Iteration
Application.Iteration = True
```

Justify Method

Applies To   Range.

Description   Rearranges the text in a range so that it fills the range evenly.

Syntax   *object*.**Justify**

Elements   *object*
         Required. The range to justify.

Remarks   If the range is not large enough, Microsoft Excel displays a message that text will extend below the range. If you choose the OK button, justified text will replace the contents in cells extending beyond the selected range. To prevent this message from appearing, set the **DisplayAlerts** property to **False**, in which case the text will always replace the contents in cells below the range.

Example   This example justifies text in the active cell.

```
ActiveCell.Justify
```

Keywords

A keyword is a word or symbol recognized as part of the programming language; for example, a statement, function name, or operator.

In Visual Basic, there are two types of keywords:

Type	Description
Restricted	Keywords that should not be used to name procedures.
Unrestricted	Keywords that may be used without restriction. Many of the unrestricted keywords are system or application-provided functions, methods, properties, and statement names that are unknown to the compiler. This allows you to define your own procedures with the same name. For example, if you create a FileCopy procedure and call it from within your application, your version of FileCopy is used, rather than the system-provided **FileCopy** statement.

Restricted Keywords

The following keywords are restricted:

Abs	**And**	**Any**	**As**
B *	**BF***	**Boolean**	**ByRef**
ByVal	**Call**	**Case**	**CBool**
CCur	**CDate**	**CDbl**	**CDecl**
CInt	**Circle** *	**CLng**	**Close**
Const	**Command** *	**CSng**	**CStr**
CurDir	**Currency**	**CVar**	**CVDate**
CVErr	**Date**	**Debug**	**Declare**
DefBool	**DefCur**	**DefDate**	**DefDbl**
DefInt	**DefLng**	**DefObj**	**DefSng**
DefStr	**DefVar**	**Dim**	**Dir**
Do	**Double**	**Each**	**Else**
ElseIf	**Empty**	**End**	**EndIf**
Environ *	**Eqv**	**Erase**	**Error**
Exit	**F** *	**False**	**Fix**
For	**Format**	**FreeFile**	**Function**
Get	**Global** *	**Go**	**GoSub**
GoTo	**If**	**Imp**	**In**
Input	**InputB**	**Instr**	**InstrB**
Int	**Integer**	**Is**	**LBound**
Len	**LenB**	**Let**	**Like**
Line *	**Load** *	**LoadPicture** *	**Local** *
Lock	**Long**	**Loop**	**LSet**

Me *	Mid	MidB	Mod
Name	New *	Next	Not
Nothing	Null	Object	On
Open	Option	Optional	Or
ParamArray	Point *	Preserve	Print
Private	Property	PSet *	Public
Put	QBColor *	ReDim	Rem
Resume	Return	RSet	Scale *
SavePicture *	Seek	Select	Set
Sgn	Shared	Single	Spc
Static	Stop	StrComp	String
Sub	Tab	Then	To
True	Type	TypeOf *	UBound
Unload *	Unlock	Until	Variant
Wend	While	Width	With
Write	Xor		

* Keyword restricted for future expansion of the language or to maintain compatibility with existing editions of Visual Basic.

Keywords Property

Applies To   AddIn, Workbook.

Description   Returns or sets the keywords for an object, as a string. Read-only for AddIn, read-write for Workbook.

Syntax   *object*.**Keywords**

Elements   *object*
    Required. The AddIn or Workbook object.

See Also   **Author** Property, **Comments** Property, **Subject** Property, **Title** Property.

Example   This example sets the keywords for the active workbook.

```
ActiveWorkbook.Keywords = "yellow, orange, blue, green"
```

Kill Statement

Description   Deletes files from a disk.

Syntax   **Kill** *pathname*

Elements   The *pathname* named argument is a string expression that specifies one or more file names to be deleted{bmc emdash.bmp}may include directory or folder, and drive.

Remarks   **Kill** supports the use of '*****' (multiple character) and '**?**' (single character) wildcards to specify multiple files. However, on the Macintosh, these characters are treated as valid file name characters and can't be used as wildcards to specify multiple files.

Since the Macintosh does not support wildcards, use the file type to identify groups of files to delete. You can use the **MacID** function to specify file type instead of repeating the command with separate file names. For example, the following statement deletes all 'TEXT' files in the current folder.

```
Kill MacID("TEXT")
```

If you use the **MacID** function with **Kill** in Microsoft Windows, an error occurs.

An error occurs if you try to use **Kill** to delete an open file.

To delete directories, use the **RmDir** statement.

See Also   **RmDir** Statement, **MacID** Function.

Example   This example uses the **Kill** statement to delete a file from a disk. Since the Macintosh does not support wildcards, you can use the **MacID** function to specify the file type instead of the file name.

```
' Assume TESTFILE is a file containing some data.
Kill "TestFile"      ' Delete file.

' In Microsoft Windows.
' Delete all *.txt files in current directory.
Kill "*.txt"

' On the Macintosh.
' Use the MacID function to delete all PICT files in current folder
Kill MacID("PICT")
```

Label Object

Description   Static text objects on dialog sheets.

Remarks	Labels have no font or background formatting but do have an accelerator key. Labels can be positioned and sized. Labels do not exist on worksheets.

LabelRange Property

Applies To	PivotField, PivotItem.
Description	PivotField: Returns the cell containing the field label. If there are multiple cells containing this label, they are all returned. Read-only.
	PivotItem: Returns a Range containing all the cells in the pivot table that contain the item.
Syntax	*object*.**LabelRange**
Elements	*object* Required. The PivotField or PivotItem object.
Example	This example selects the active field header cell.

```
ActiveCell.PivotField.LabelRange.Select
```

Labels Method

Applies To	Chart, DialogSheet, Worksheet.
Description	Returns a single label (a Label object, Syntax 1) or a collection of labels on the sheet (a Labels object, Syntax 2).
Syntax 1	*object*.**Labels**(*index*)
Syntax 2	*object*.**Labels**
Elements	The **Labels** method has the following object qualifier and named arguments:
	object Required. The Chart, DialogSheet or Worksheet object.
	index Required for Syntax 1. Specifies the name or number of the label (can be an array to specify more than one).
Example	This example displays the number of labels on dialog sheet one.

```
cLabels = Application.DialogSheets(1).Labels.Count
MsgBox "There are " & cLabels & " labels on dialog sheet one."
```

Labels Object

Description   A collection of Label objects.

LargeButtons Property

Applies To   Application.

Description   **True** if Microsoft Excel is using large toolbar buttons. **False** if Microsoft Excel is using standard toolbar buttons. Read-write.

Syntax   *object*.**LargeButtons**

Elements   *object*
    Required. The Application object.

See Also   **ColorButtons** Property.

Example   This example displays the large toolbar buttons.

```
Application.LargeButtons = True
```

LargeChange Property

Applies To   DrawingObjects, ScrollBar, ScrollBars.

Description   Returns or sets the amount that the scroll box increments or decrements for a page scroll (when the user clicks in the scroll bar body region). Read-write.

Syntax   *object*.**LargeChange**

Elements   *object*
    Required. The object to which this property applies.

See Also   **SmallChange** Property.

Example   This example sets the scroll bar to move two units for each line scroll and 10 units for each page scroll.

```
With ActiveSheet.ScrollBars(1)
    .SmallChange = 2
    .LargeChange = 10
End With
```

LargeScroll Method

Applies To   Pane, Window.

Description   Scrolls the window by pages.

Syntax   *object*.**LargeScroll**(*down, up, toRight, toLeft*)

Elements   The **LargeScroll** method has the following object qualifier and named arguments:

object
> Required. The window to scroll.

down
> Optional. The number of pages to scroll the window down.

up
> Optional. The number of pages to scroll the window up.

toRight
> Optional. The number of pages to scroll the window right.

toLeft
> Optional. The number of pages to scroll the window left.

Remarks   If *down* and *up* are both specified, the window is scrolled by the difference of the arguments. For example, if *down* is three and *up* is six, the window is scrolled up three pages.

If *toLeft* and *toRight* are both specified, the window is scrolled by the difference of the arguments. For example, if *toLeft* is three and *toRight* is six, the window is scrolled right three pages.

Any of the arguments can be a negative number.

See Also   **SmallScroll** Method.

Example   This example scrolls the active window down three pages.

```
ActiveWindow.LargeScroll down:=3
```

LBound Function

Description   Returns the smallest available subscript for the indicated dimension of an array.

Syntax

LBound(*arrayname*[,*dimension*])

Elements

The **LBound** statement syntax has these parts:

Part	Description
arrayname	Name of the array variable; follows standard variable naming conventions.
dimension	Whole number indicating which dimension's lower bound is returned. Use 1 for the first dimension, 2 for the second, and so on. If *dimension* is omitted, 1 is assumed.

Remarks

The **LBound** function is used with the **UBound** function to determine the size of an array. Use the **UBound** function to find the upper limit of an array dimension.

LBound returns the values listed in the table below for an array with the following dimensions:

```
Dim A(1 To 100, 0 To 3, -3 To 4)
```

Statement	Return Value
LBound(A, 1)	1
LBound(A, 2)	0
LBound(A, 3)	-3

The default lower bound for any dimension is either 0 or 1, depending on the setting of the **Option Base** statement.

Arrays for which dimensions are set using the **To** clause in a **Dim**, **Private**, **Public**, **ReDim**, or **Static** statement can have any integer value as a lower bound.

See Also

Dim Statement, **Private** Statement, **Public** Statement, **Option Base** Statement, **ReDim** Statement, **Static** Statement, **UBound** Function.

Example

This example uses the **LBound** function to determine the smallest available subscript for the indicated dimension of an array. Use the **Option Base** statement to override the default base array subscript value of 0.

```
Dim MyArray(1 To 10, 5 To 15, 10 To 20)  ' Declare array variables.
Dim AnyArray(10)
Lower = LBound(MyArray, 1)      ' Returns 1.
Lower = LBound(MyArray, 3)      ' Returns 10.
Lower = LBound(AnyArray)        ' Returns 0 or 1,
                                ' depending on setting of Option Base.
```

LCase Function

Description   Returns a string that has been converted to lowercase.

Syntax   **LCase(*string*)**

Elements   The *string* named argument is any valid string expression. If *string* contains no valid data, **Null** is returned.

Remarks   Only uppercase letters are converted to lowercase; all lowercase letters and nonletter characters remain unchanged.

See Also   **UCase** Function.

Example   This example uses the **LCase** function to return a lowercase version of a string.

```
Uppercase = "Hello World 1234"    ' String to convert.
Lowercase = LCase(UpperCase)      ' Returns "hello world 1234".
```

Left Function

Description   Returns a specified number of characters from the left side of a string.

Syntax   **Left(*string*,*length*)**

Elements   The **Left** function syntax has these named-argument parts:

Part	Description
string	String expression from which the leftmost characters are returned. If *string* contains no valid data, **Null** is returned.
length	Numeric expression indicating how many characters to return. If 0, a zero-length string is returned. If greater than or equal to the number of characters in *string*, the entire string is returned.

Remarks   To determine the number of characters in *string*, use the **Len** function.

Note Another function (**LeftB**) is provided for use with the double-byte character sets (DBCS) used in some Asian locales. Instead of specifying the number of characters to return, *length* specifies the number of bytes. In areas where DBCS is not used, **LeftB** behaves the same as **Left**.

See Also   **Len** Function, **Mid** Function, **Right** Function.

Example

This example uses the **Left** function to return a specified number of characters from the left side of a string.

```
AnyString = "Hello World"      ' Define string.
MyStr = Left(AnyString, 1)     ' Returns "H".
MyStr = Left(AnyString, 7)     ' Returns "Hello W".
MyStr = Left(AnyString, 20)    ' Returns "Hello World".
```

Left Property

Applies To

Application, Arc, Arcs, AxisTitle, Button, Buttons, ChartArea, ChartObject, ChartObjects, ChartTitle, CheckBox, CheckBoxes, DataLabel, DataLabels, DialogFrame, Drawing, DrawingObjects, Drawings, DropDown, DropDowns, EditBox, EditBoxes, GroupBox, GroupBoxes, GroupObject, GroupObjects, Label, Labels, Legend, Line, Lines, ListBox, ListBoxes, OLEObject, OLEObjects, OptionButton, OptionButtons, Oval, Ovals, Picture, Pictures, PlotArea, Range, Rectangle, Rectangles, ScrollBar, ScrollBars, Spinner, Spinners, TextBox, TextBoxes, Toolbar, Window.

Description

Returns or sets the position of the specified object, in points (1/72 inch). Read-write, except for the Range object.

Syntax

object.**Left**

Elements

object
    Required. The object to which this property applies.

Remarks

The **Left** property has several different meanings, depending on the object it is applied to.

Object	Meaning
Application	The distance from the left edge of the physical screen to the left edge of the main Microsoft Excel window, in points.
ClipboardWindow	Macintosh only. The left position of the window, in points, measured from the left edge of the usable area (below the menus, left-docked toolbars, and/or the formula bar).
Range	The distance from the left edge of column A to the left edge of the range, in points. If the range is discontinuous, the first area is used. If the range is more than one column wide, the leftmost column in the range is used. Read-only.

Object	Meaning
Toolbar	If the toolbar is docked (its **Position** property is not **xlFloating**), the number of points from the left edge of the toolbar to the left edge of the toolbar's docking area.
	If the toolbar is floating, the number of points from the left edge of the toolbar to the left edge of the Microsoft Excel workspace.
Window	The left position of the window, in points, measured from the left edge of the usable area.
Arc, AxisTitle, Button, ChartArea, ChartTitle, CheckBox, DataLabel, DialogFrame, Drawing, DrawingObjects, DropDown, EditBox, GroupObject, GroupBox, Label, Legend, Line, ListBox, OLEObject, OptionButton, Oval, Picture, PlotArea, Rectangle, ScrollBar, Spinner, TextBox	The left position of the object, in points, measured from the left edge of column A (on a worksheet) or the upper left of the chart area (on a chart).

If the window is maximized, the **Application.Left** property returns a negative number that varies based on the width of the window border. Setting **Application.Left** to zero will make the window a tiny bit smaller than it would if the application window were maximized. In other words, if **Application.Left** is zero, the left border of the main Microsoft Excel window will just be visible on screen.

On the Apple Macintosh, **Application.Left** is always zero. Setting this value to something else on the Macintosh will have no effect.

With Microsoft Windows, if the Microsoft Excel window is minimized, **Application.Left** controls the position of the icon.

See Also   **Height** Property, **Top** Property, **Width** Property.

Example   This example moves oval one so that it just touches the left edge of the first column.

```
ActiveSheet.Ovals(1).Left = 0
```

LeftFooter Property

Applies To   PageSetup.

Description   Returns or sets the left part of the footer. Read-write.

Syntax	*object*.**LeftFooter**
Elements	*object* Required. The PageSetup object (**ActiveSheet.PageSetup**, for example).
Remarks	Special format codes can be used in the footer text. For more information, search the online Visual Basic Reference for Formatting Codes for Headers and Footers.
See Also	**CenterFooter** Property, **CenterHeader** Property, **LeftHeader** Property, **RightFooter** Property, **RightHeader** Property.
Example	This example prints the page number on the lower-left corner of every page.

```
ActiveSheet.PageSetup.LeftFooter = "&P"
```

LeftHeader Property

Applies To	PageSetup.
Description	Returns or sets the left part of the header. Read-write.
Syntax	*object*.**LeftHeader**
Elements	*object* Required. The PageSetup object (**ActiveSheet.PageSetup**, for example).
Remarks	Special format codes can be used in the footer text. For more information, search the online Visual Basic Reference for Formatting Codes for Headers and Footers.
See Also	**CenterFooter** Property, **CenterHeader** Property, **LeftFooter**Property, **RightFooter** Property, **RightHeader** Property.
Example	This example prints the date in the upper-left corner of every page.

```
ActiveSheet.PageSetup.LeftHeader = "&D"
```

LeftMargin Property

Applies To	PageSetup.
Description	Returns or sets the size of the left margin, in points (1/72 inch). Read-write.
Syntax	*object*.**LeftMargin**
Elements	*object* Required. The PageSetup object (**ActiveSheet.PageSetup**, for example).

Remarks   Margins are set or returned in points. Use the **Application.InchesToPoints** or **Application.CentimetersToPoints** function to convert.

See Also   **BottomMargin** Property, **RightMargin** Property, **TopMargin** Property.

Examples   This example sets the left margin to 1.5 inches.

```
ActiveSheet.PageSetup.LeftMargin = _
    Application.InchesToPoints(1.5)
```

This example sets the left margin to 2 centimeters.

```
ActiveSheet.PageSetup.LeftMargin = _
    Application.CentimetersToPoints(2)
```

This example sets the variable leftMarginInches to the current left margin setting, in inches.

```
leftMarginInches = ActiveSheet.PageSetup.LeftMargin / _
    Application.InchesToPoints(1)
```

Legend Object

Description   The legend of a chart.

Legend Property

Applies To   Chart

Description   Returns the Legend for the chart. Read-only.

Syntax   *object*.**Legend**

Elements   *object*
           Required. The Chart object.

See Also   HasLegend Property

Example   This example turns on the chart legend and then sets its color.

```
Charts(1).HasLegend = True
Charts(1).Legend.Font.Color = RGB(0,255,0)
```

LegendEntries Method

Applies To	Legend.
Description	Returns a single legend entry (a LegendEntry object, Syntax 1) or a collection of legend entries for the legend (a LegendEntries object, Syntax 2).
Syntax 1	*object*.**LegendEntries**(*index*)
Syntax 2	*object*.**LegendEntries**
Elements	The **LegendEntries** method has the following object qualifier and named arguments:

object
> Required. The Legend object.

index
> Required for Syntax 1. Specifies the name or number of the legend entry.

Example   This example selects legend entry three.

```
Application.Charts(1).Legend.LegendEntries(3).Select
```

LegendEntries Object

Description   A collection of LegendEntry objects.

LegendEntry Object

Description   Text and data marker labels contained within a charting legend.

Each legend entry has two parts. The LegendEntry object contains the text of the entry and a way to access the marker portion of the entry. The LegendKey object is associated with each entry. It encapsulates the formatting properties for the entry.

The text of a legend entry comes from the series name, and it cannot be changed. LegendEntry objects support font formatting, and they can be deleted. No pattern formatting is supported for legend entries. The position and size of entries cannot be changed.

LegendKey Object

Description   Text and data marker labels contained within a charting legend.

Each legend entry has two parts. The LegendEntry object contains the text of the entry and a way to access the marker portion of the entry. The LegendKey object is associated with each entry. It encapsulates the formatting properties for the entry. Formatting the LegendKey causes the entire series associated with the entry to be formatted.

The LegendKey object associated with an entry is accessed via a property of the LegendEntry object. The marker encapsulates pattern formatting for the legend marker and its associated series or trendline. Legend markers cannot be deleted or cleared.

LegendKey Property

Applies To   LegendEntry.

Description   Returns the LegendKey object associated with the entry.

Syntax   *object*.**LegendKey**

Elements   *object*
         Required. The LegendEntry object.

Example   This example selects the legend key for legend entry five.

```
Application.Charts(1).Legend.LegendEntries(5).LegendKey.Select
```

Len Function

Description   Returns the number of characters in a string or the number of bytes required to store a variable.

Syntax	**Len**(*string* | *varname*)
Elements	The **Len** function syntax has these parts:

Part	Description
string	Any valid string expression. If *string* contains no valid data, **Null** is returned.
varname	Any valid variable name. If *varname* contains no valid data, **Null** is returned.

Remarks

Caution **Len** may not be able to determine the actual number of storage bytes required when used with user-defined data types.

Note Another function (**LenB**) is provided for use with the double-byte character sets (DBCS) used in some Asian locales. Instead of returning the number of characters in a string, **LenB** returns the number of bytes used to represent that string. In areas where DBCS is not used, **LenB** behaves the same as **Len**.

See Also **InStr** Function.

Example This example uses the **Len** function to return the number of characters in a string or the number of bytes required to store a variable.

```
Type CustomerRecord                 ' Define user-defined type.
    ID As Integer
    Name As String * 10
    Address As String * 30
End Type
Dim Customer As CustomerRecord      ' Declare variables.
Dim MyInt As Integer, MyCur As Currency
MyString = "Hello World"            ' Initialize.
MyLen = Len(MyInt)                  ' Returns 2.
MyLen = Len(Customer)               ' Returns 42.
MyLen = Len(MyString)               ' Returns 11.
MyLen = Len(MyCur)                  ' Returns 8.
```

Let Statement

Description Assigns the value of an expression to a variable or property.

Syntax	[**Let**] *varname* = *expression*
Elements	The **Let** statement syntax has these parts:

Part	Description
varname	Name of the variable or property; follows standard variable naming conventions.
expression	Value assigned to the variable.

Remarks

In order to simplify Basic code, the optional **Let** keyword is most often omitted.

A value expression can be assigned to a variable only if it is of a data type that is compatible with the variable. You can't assign string expressions to numeric variables, and you can't assign numeric expressions to string variables. If you do, an error occurs at compile time.

Variant variables can be assigned either string or numeric expressions. However, the reverse is not always true. Any **Variant** except a **Null** can be assigned to a string variable, but only a **Variant** whose value can be interpreted as a number can be assigned to a numeric variable. Use the **IsNumeric** function to determine if the **Variant** can be converted to a number.

Caution   Assigning an expression of one numeric data type to a variable of a different numeric data type coerces the value of the expression into the data type of the resulting variable.

Let statements can be used to assign one record variable to another only when both variables are of the same user-defined type. Use the **LSet** statement to assign record variables of different user-defined types. Use the **Set** statement to assign object references to variables.

See Also

Const Statement, Data Type Summary, **IsNumeric** Function, **LSet** Statement, **Set** Statement, **Variant** Data Type.

Example

This example uses statements with and without the **Let** statement to assign the value of an expression to a variable.

```
' The following variable assignments use the Let statement.
Let MyStr = "Hello World"
Let MyInt = 5

' The following are the same assignments without the Let statement.
MyStr = "Hello World"
MyInt = 5
```

LibraryPath Property

Applies To   Application.

Description   Returns the path to the LIBRARY directory, not including the final separator. Read-only.

Syntax   *object*.**LibraryPath**

Elements   *object*
        Required. The Application object.

Example   This example opens the file OSCAR.XLA in the LIBRARY directory.

```
f = Application.LibraryPath & "\OSCAR.XLA"
Workbooks.Open filename:=f
```

Like Operator

Description   Used to compare two strings.

Syntax   *result* = *string* **Like** *pattern*

Elements   The **Like** operator syntax has these parts:

Part	Description
result	Any numeric variable.
string	Any string expression.
pattern	Any string expression conforming to the pattern-matching conventions described in the following section.

Remarks   If *string* matches *pattern*, *result* is **True**; if there is no match, *result* is **False**; and if either *string* or *pattern* is a **Null**, *result* is also a **Null**.

        The behavior of the **Like** operator depends on the **Option Compare** statement. Unless otherwise specified, the default string-comparison method for each module is **Option Compare Binary**.

Option Compare Binary results in string comparisons based on a sort order derived from the internal binary representations of the characters. In Microsoft Windows, sort order is determined by the code page. On the Macintosh, sort order is determined by the character set. In the following example, a typical binary sort order is shown:

$$A < B < E < Z < a < b < e\ < z < À < Ê < Ø < à < ê < ø$$

Option Compare Text results in string comparisons based on a case-insensitive textual sort order determined by your system's locale. The same characters shown above, when sorted using **Option Compare Text**, produce the following text sort order:

$$(A{=}a)\ < (\ À{=}à) < (B{=}b) < (E{=}e) < (Ê{=}ê) < (Z{=}z) < (Ø{=}ø)$$

Built-in pattern matching provides a versatile tool for string comparisons. The pattern-matching features allow you to use wildcard characters, character lists, or character ranges, in any combination, to match strings. The following table shows the characters allowed in *pattern* and what they match:

Character(s) in *pattern*	Matches in *string*
?	Any single character.
*	Zero or more characters.
#	Any single digit (0-9).
[*charlist*]	Any single character in *charlist*.
[!*charlist*]	Any single character not in *charlist*.

A group of one or more characters (*charlist*) enclosed in brackets ([ ]) can be used to match any single character in *string* and can include almost any character code, including digits.

Note The special characters left bracket ([), question mark (?), number sign (#), and asterisk (*) can be used to match themselves directly only by enclosing them in brackets. The right bracket (]) can't be used within a group to match itself, but it can be used outside a group as an individual character.

In addition to a simple list of characters enclosed in brackets, *charlist* can specify a range of characters by using a hyphen (-) to separate the upper and lower bounds of the range. For example, [A-Z] in *pattern* results in a match if the corresponding character position in *string* contains any of the uppercase letters in the range A through Z. Multiple ranges are included within the brackets without any delimiters.

The meaning of a specified range depends on the character ordering valid at run time (as determined by **Option Compare** and the locale setting of the system the code is running on). Using the same example shown above with **Option Compare**

Binary, the range [A-E] matches A, B and E. With **Option Compare Text**, [A-E] matches A, a, À, à, B, b, E, e. Note that it does not match Ê or ê because accented characters fall after unaccented characters in the sort order.

Other important rules for pattern matching include the following:

- An exclamation point (!) at the beginning of *charlist* means that a match is made if any character except the ones in *charlist* are found in *string*. When used outside brackets, the exclamation point matches itself.

- The hyphen (-) can appear either at the beginning (after an exclamation mark if one is used) or at the end of *charlist* to match itself. In any other location, the hyphen is used to identify a range of characters.

- When a range of characters is specified, they must appear in ascending sort order (from lowest to highest). [A-Z] is a valid pattern, but [Z-A] is not.

- The character sequence [ ] is ignored; it is considered a zero-length string.

See Also   **Instr** Function, Operator Precedence, **Option Compare** Statement, **StrComp** Function.

Example   This example uses the **Like** operator to compare a string to a pattern.

```
MyCheck = "aBBBa" Like "a*a"            ' Returns True.
MyCheck = "F" Like "[A-Z]"             ' Returns True.
MyCheck = "F" Like "[!A-Z]"           ' Returns False.
MyCheck = "a2a" Like "a#a"            ' Returns True.
MyCheck = "aM5b" Like "a[L-P]#[!c-e]"  ' Returns True.
MyCheck = "BAT123khg" Like "B?T*"     ' Returns True.
MyCheck = "CAT123khg" Like "B?T*"     ' Returns False.
```

Line Input # Statement

Description   Reads a line from an open sequential file and assigns it to a string variable.

Syntax   **Line Input #***filenumber,varname*

Elements   The **Line Input #** statement syntax has these parts:

Part	Description
filenumber	Any valid file number.
varname	Valid string variable name.

Remarks   The **Line Input #** statement reads from a file one character at a time until it encounters a carriage return (**Chr**(13)) or carriage return-linefeed sequence. Carriage return-linefeed sequences are skipped rather than appended to the character string.

See Also   **Input #** Statement.

Example   This example uses the **Line Input #** statement to read a line from a sequential file and assign it to a variable. For purposes of this example, assume that TESTFILE is a text file with a few lines of sample data.

```
Open "TESTFILE" For Input As #1        ' Open file.
Do While Not EOF(1)                    ' Loop until end of file.
    Line Input #1, TextLine            ' Read line into variable.
    Debug.Print TextLine               ' Print to Debug window.
Loop
Close #1                               ' Close file.
```

Line Object

Description   A line graphic object drawn on a chart or worksheet.

Line3DGroup Property

Applies To   Chart.

Description   Returns the line ChartGroup on a 3-D chart.

Elements   *object*
                Required. The Chart object.

See Also   **LineGroups** Method.

Example   This example makes the 3-D line group an area group.

```
Charts(1).Line3DGroup.Type = xl3DArea
```

LineGroups Method

Applies To   Chart.

Description	On a 2-D chart, returns a single line chart group (a ChartGroup object, Syntax 1), or a collection of the line chart groups (a ChartGroups collection, Syntax 2).
Syntax 1	*object*.**LineGroups**(*index*)
Syntax 2	*object*.**LineGroups**
Elements	The **LineGroups** method has the following object qualifier and named arguments:

object
   Required. The Chart object.

index
   Required for Syntax 1. Specifies the chart group.

See Also	**Line3DGroup** Property.
Example	This example sets the subtype for the first line group.

```
Charts(1).LineGroups(1).SubType = 2
```

Lines Method

Applies To	Chart, DialogSheet, Worksheet.
Description	Returns a single line (a Line object, Syntax 1) or a collection of lines (a Lines object, Syntax 2) on the chart, dialog sheet, or worksheet. Read-only.
Syntax 1	*object*.**Lines**(*index*)
Syntax 2	*object*.**Lines**
Elements	The **Lines** method has the following object qualifier and named arguments:

object
   Required. The object to which this method applies.

index
   Required for Syntax 1. The name or number of the line.

Remarks	This property returns both lines and arrows. The only difference between a line and an arrow is the **ArrowHeadStyle** property.
Example	This example deletes line three on the active sheet.

```
ActiveSheet.Lines(3).Delete
```

Lines Object

Description   A collection of Line objects.

LineStyle Property

Applies To   Border, Borders.

Description   Returns or sets the line style of the border. Can be one of **xlContinuous, xlDash, xlDot, xlDashDot, xlDashDotDot, xlGray50, xlGray75, xlGray25, xlDouble, xlNone,** or **xlAutomatic.** Read-write.

Syntax   *object*.**LineStyle**

Elements   *object*
                       Required. The Border or Borders object.

Example   This example sets major gridlines on the value axis to 50 percent gray.

```
Charts(1).Axes(xlValue).MajorGridlines.Border.LineStyle = xlGray50
```

LinkCombo Method

Applies To   DrawingObjects.

Description   Creates a combination list-edit box from a list box and an edit box. The edit box and list box to be linked must be the only two objects in the DrawingObjects collection.

Syntax   *object*.**LinkCombo(*link*)**

Elements   The **LinkCombo** method has the following object qualifier and named arguments:

                       object
                       Required. The DrawingObjects collection.

                       link
                       Optional. If omitted or **True**, the objects are linked so that the edit box text is always updated to the current selection in the list box whenever the user selects a new list box item. If **False**, the link between the objects is broken.

Remarks	This function is only useful on a dialog sheet, because edit boxes are not allowed on a worksheet or chart. To see how to use the **LinkCombo** method, use the macro recorder to record creating a Combination List-Edit control on a dialog sheet.
See Also	**DrawingObjects** Method, **EditBox** object, **LinkedObject** Property, **ListBox** object.
Example	This example links edit box one and list box two on the active dialog sheet.

```
ActiveDialog.DrawingObjects( _
    Array("List Box 1", "Edit Box 2")).LinkCombo
```

LinkedCell Property

Applies To	CheckBox, CheckBoxes, DrawingObjects, DropDown, DropDowns, ListBox, ListBoxes, OptionButton, OptionButtons, ScrollBar, ScrollBars, Spinner, Spinners.
Description	Returns or sets the cell or cells (as a string reference) linked to the control's value. When a value is placed in the cell, the control takes this value. Likewise, if the value of the control changes, that value is also placed in the cell.
Syntax	*object*.**LinkedCell**
Elements	*object* Required. The object to which this property applies.
Remarks	This property cannot be used with multi-select list boxes.
Example	This example links list box one to cells A1:A5.

```
ActiveDialog.Listboxes(1).LinkedCell = "Sheet1!A1:A5"
```

LinkedObject Property

Applies To	DropDown, EditBox, ListBox.
Description	Returns the name of the object linked to an edit box, list box, or drop-down control. For a DropDown object, returns the name of the drop-down control if it can be edited, or **False** if it is not editable. Read-only.
Syntax	*object*.**LinkedObject**
Elements	*object* Required. The object to which this property applies.
See Also	**LinkCombo** Method.

Example

This example sets the focus to the object linked to edit box four.

```
With Application.DialogSheets(1)
    .Focus = .EditBoxes(4).LinkedObject
End With
```

LinkInfo Method

Applies To   Workbook.

Description   Returns information on link date and update state.

Syntax   *object*.**LinkInfo**(*name, linkInfo, type, editionRef*)

Elements   The **LinkInfo** method has the following object qualifier and named arguments:

object
Required. The Workbook object.

name
Required. Specifies the name of the link, as returned from the **LinkSources** method.

linkInfo
Required. Specifies the type of information to be returned about the link (either **xlUpdateState** or **xlEditionDate**). **xlEditionDate** applies only to editions. For **xlUpdateState**, this method returns 1 if the link updates automatically, or 2 if the link must be updated manually.

type
Optional. Specifies the type of link to return. Can be one of **xlOLELinks** (also handles DDE links), **xlPublishers**, or **xlSubscribers.**

editionRef
Optional. If the link is an edition, this argument specifies the edition reference as a string in R1C1-style form. This argument is required if there are more than one publisher or subscriber with the same name in the workbook.

Example   This example displays a message box if the link updates automatically.

```
If ActiveWorkbook.LinkInfo( _
        "WinWord|'C:\MSGFILE.DOC'!DDE_LINK1", xlUpdateState, _
        xlOLELink) = 1 Then
    MsgBox "Automatic update"
End If
```

LinkSources Method

Applies To	Workbook.
Description	Returns an array of links in the workbook. The names in the array are the names of the linked documents, editions, or DDE or OLE servers. Returns **Empty** if there are no links.
Syntax	*object*.**LinkSources**(*type*)
Elements	The **LinkSources** method has the following object qualifier and named arguments:

object
    Required. The Workbook object.

type
    Optional. Specifies the type of link to return. Can be one of **xlExcelLinks**, **xlOLELinks** (also handles DDE links), **xlPublishers**, or **xlSubscribers.**

Remarks	The format of the array is a single-dimensional array for all types but publisher and subscriber. The returned strings contain the name of the link source in the notation appropriate for the link type. For example, DDE links use the "Server|Document!Item" syntax.
	For publisher and subscriber links, the returned array is two-dimensional. The first column of the array contains the names of the edition, and the second column contains the references of the editions as text.
Example	This example displays a list of Microsoft Excel links in the active workbook.

```
aLinks = ActiveWorkbook.LinkSources(xlExcelLinks)
If Not IsEmpty(aLinks) Then
    For i = 1 to UBound(aLinks)
        Cells(i, 1) = aLinks(i)
    Next i
End If
```

List Property

Applies To	DrawingObjects, DropDown, DropDowns, ListBox, ListBoxes.
Description	Returns or sets the text entries in a list box or drop-down list box, as an array of strings (Syntax 1), or returns or sets a single text entry (Syntax 2). Returns an error if there are no entries in the list. Read-write.

Syntax 1	*object*.**List**
Syntax 2	*object*.**List**(*index*)
Elements	*object*
	Required. The object to which this property applies.
	index
	Required for syntax 2. The text entry number.
Remarks	Setting this property clears any **ListFillRange**.
See Also	**AddItem** Method, **ListCount** Property, **RemoveItem** Method.
Examples	This example sets the entries in list box one.

```
Application.DialogSheets(1).ListBoxes(1).List = _
    Array("cogs", "widgets", "sprockets", "gizmos")
```

This example sets entry four in list box one.

```
Application.DialogSheets(1).ListBoxes(1).List(4) = "gadgets"
```

ListBox Object

Description   A scrollable list of items. One item in the list may be selected by the user. Microsoft Excel does not support multi-select list boxes on user-defined dialogs or worksheets.

You can fill the list either from a range of cells (by specifying the **ListFillRange** property) or by specifying each item (using the **AddItem** or **RemoveItem** methods or the **List** property).

ListBoxes Method

Applies To   Chart, DialogSheet, Worksheet.

Description   Returns a single list-box control (a ListBox object, Syntax 1) or a collection of list-box controls on the chart or sheet (a ListBoxes object, Syntax 2).

Syntax 1	*object*.**ListBoxes**(*index*)
Syntax 2	*object*.**ListBoxes**
Elements	The **ListBoxes** method has the following object qualifier and named arguments:

object
   Required. The Chart, DialogSheet, or Worksheet object.

index
   Required for Syntax 1. Specifies the name or number of the list box (can be an array to specify more than one).

Example   This example sets the entries in list box one.

```
Application.DialogSheets(1).Listboxes(1).List = _
    Array("cogs", "widgets", "sprockets", "gizmos")
```

ListBoxes Object

Description   A collection of ListBox objects.

ListCount Property

Applies To   DropDown, ListBox.

Description   Returns the number of entries in a list box or drop-down list box. Returns zero if there are no entries in the list. Read-only.

Syntax   *object*.**ListCount**

Elements   *object*
   Required. The object to which this property applies.

See Also   **List** Property.

Example   This example displays the number of entries in list box one.

```
cEntries = Application.DialogSheets(1).ListBoxes(1).ListCount
MsgBox "There are " & cEntries & " entries in list box one."
```

ListFillRange Property

Applies To   DrawingObjects, DropDown, DropDowns, ListBox, ListBoxes.

Description   Returns or sets the worksheet range used to fill the list box, as a string. Setting this property destroys any existing list in the list box. Read-write.

Syntax   *object*.**ListFillRange**

Elements   *object*
                    Required. The object to which this property applies.

Remarks   Microsoft Excel reads the contents of every cell in the range and puts it into the list box. The list will track changes in the range cells.

                    If the list in the list box was created with the **AddItem** method, this property returns an empty string ("").

See Also   **AddItem** Method, **List** Property, **RemoveItem** Method.

Example   This example fills list box four with the range A1:A10 on sheet one.

```
Application.DialogSheets(1).Listboxes(4).ListFillRange = _
    "Sheet1!A1:A10"
```

ListIndex Property

Applies To   DrawingObjects, DropDown, DropDowns, ListBox, ListBoxes.

Description   Returns or sets the index of the currently selected item in a list box or drop-down list box. Read-write.

Syntax   *object*.**ListIndex**

Elements   *object*
                    Required. The object to which this property applies.

Remarks   This property cannot be used with multi-select list boxes. Use the **Selected** property instead.

See Also   **MultiSelect** Property, **Selected** Property, **Value** Property.

Example   This example selects item four in list box four.

```
Application.DialogSheets(1).ListBoxes(4).ListIndex = 4
```

ListNames Method

Applies To	Range.
Description	Pastes a list of all non-hidden names on the worksheet, beginning at the first cell of the range.
Syntax	*object*.**ListNames**
Elements	*object* Required. Identifies the worksheet for which to list names, and the start of the range where the names will be listed.
Remarks	Use the **Names** method to return a collection of all the names on a worksheet.
Example	This example pastes a list of all non-hidden names defined on the worksheet, beginning at the active cell.

```
ActiveCell.ListNames
```

Loc Function

Description	Returns the current read/write position within an open file.
Syntax	**Loc(*filenumber*)**
Elements	The *filenumber* named argument is any valid file number.
Remarks	The following describes the return value for each file access mode:

File Access	Return Value
Random	Number of the last record read from or written to the file.
Sequential	Current byte position in the file divided by 128.
Binary	Position of the last byte read or written.

See Also	**EOF** Function, **LOF** Function, **Open** Statement.
Example	This example uses the **Loc** function to return the current read/write position within an open file. For purposes of this example, assume that TESTFILE is a text file with a few lines of sample data.

```
Open "TESTFILE" For Input As #1      ' Open file just created.
Do While Not EOF(1)                  ' Loop until end of file.
    Line Input #1, MyLine            ' Read line into variable.
    MyLocation = Loc(1)          ' Get current position within file.
    Debug.Print MyLine; Tab; MyLocation      ' Print to Debug window.
Loop
```

LocationInTable Property

Applies To   Range.

Description   Returns a constant that describes the part of the PivotTable which contains the top left corner of the specified range. Can be one of **xlRowHeader**, **xlColumnHeader**, **xlPageHeader**, **xlDataHeader**, **xlRowItem**, **xlColumnItem**, **xlPageItem**, **xlDataItem**, or **xlTableBody**. Read-only.

Syntax   *object*.**LocationInTable**

Elements   *object*
          Required. The Range object.

Example   This example displays a message box if the active cell is in the body of the pivot table.

```
If ActiveCell.LocationInTable = xlTableBody Then
    MsgBox "The active cell is in the body of the table."
End If
```

Lock...Unlock Statements

Description   Controls access by other processes to all or part of a file opened using the **Open** statement.

Syntax   **Lock** [#]*filenumber*[,*recordrange*]

          ...

          Unlock [#]*filenumber*[,*recordrange*]

Elements   The **Lock** and **Unlock** statement syntax has these parts:

Part	Description
filenumber	Any valid file number.
recordrange	The range of records to lock or unlock.

The *recordrange* argument has the following syntax and parts:

recnumber | [*start*] **To** *end*

Part	Description
recnumber	Record number (**Random** mode files) or byte number (**Binary** mode files) at which locking or unlocking begins.
start	Number of the first record or byte to lock or unlock.
end	Number of the last record or byte to lock or unlock.

Remarks   The **Lock** and **Unlock** statements are used in environments where several processes might need access to the same file.

Lock and **Unlock** statements are always used in pairs. The arguments to **Lock** and **Unlock** must match exactly.

The first record/byte in a file is at position 1, the second record/byte is at position 2, and so on. If you specify just one record, then only that record is locked or unlocked. If you specify a range of records and omit a starting record (*start*), all records from the first record to the end of the range (*end*) are locked or unlocked. Using **Lock** without *recnumber* locks the entire file; using **Unlock** without *recnumber* unlocks the entire file.

If the file has been opened for sequential input or output, **Lock** and **Unlock** affect the entire file, regardless of the range specified by *start* and *end*.

Caution Be sure to remove all locks with an **Unlock** statement before closing a file or terminating your program. Failure to remove locks produces unpredictable results.

See Also   **Open** Statement.

Example   This example illustrates the use of the **Lock** and **Unlock** statements. While a record is being modified, access by other processes to the record is denied. For purposes of this example, assume that TESTFILE is a file containing five records of the user-defined type Record.

```
Type Record                              ' Define user-defined type.
    ID As Integer
    Name As String * 20
End Type
Dim MyRecord As Record                   ' Declare variable.

' Open sample file for random access.
Open "TESTFILE" For Random Shared As #1 Len = Len(MyRecord)
RecordNumber = 4                         ' Define record number.
Lock #1, RecordNumber                    ' Lock record.
Get #1, RecordNumber, MyRecord           ' Read record.
MyRecord.ID = 234                        ' Modify record.
MyRecord.Name = "John Smith"
Put #1, RecordNumber, MyRecord           ' Write modified record.
Unlock #1, RecordNumber                  ' Unlock current record.
Close #1                                 ' Close file.
```

Locked Property

Applies To   Arc, Arcs, Button, Buttons, ChartObject, ChartObjects, CheckBox, CheckBoxes, DialogFrame, Drawing, DrawingObjects, Drawings, DropDown, DropDowns, EditBox, EditBoxes, GroupBox, GroupBoxes, GroupObject, GroupObjects, Label, Labels, Line, Lines, ListBox, ListBoxes, OLEObject, OLEObjects, OptionButton, OptionButtons, Oval, Ovals, Picture, Pictures, Range, Rectangle, Rectangles, Scenario, ScrollBar, ScrollBars, Spinner, Spinners, Style, TextBox, TextBoxes.

Description   **False** if the object can be modified when the sheet is protected. Read-write.

Syntax   *object*.**Locked**

Elements   *object*
        Required. The Range object.

See Also   **FormulaHidden** Property, **Protect** Method, **Unprotect** Method.

Example   This example unlocks cells A1:G37 so they can be modified when the sheet is protected.

```
Range("A1:G37").Locked = False
ActiveSheet.Protect
```

LockedText Property

Applies To   Button, Buttons, CheckBox, CheckBoxes, DialogFrame, DrawingObjects, GroupBox, GroupBoxes, Label, Labels, OptionButton, OptionButtons, TextBox, TextBoxes.

Description   **True** if the text in the object will be locked to prevent changes when the document is protected. Read-write.

Syntax   *object*.**LockedText**

Elements   *object*
        Required. The object to which this property applies.

See Also   **Protect** Method, **ProtectContents** Property.

Example   This example locks the text in button one.

```
ActiveSheet.Buttons(1).LockedText = True
```

LOF Function

Description   Returns the size, in bytes, of a file opened using the **Open** statement.

Syntax   **LOF(*filenumber*)**

Elements   The *filenumber* named argument is any valid file number.

Remarks   To obtain the length of a file that is not open, use the **FileLen** function.

See Also   **EOF** Function, **FileLen** Function, **Loc** Function, **Open** Statement.

Example   This example uses the **LOF** function to determine the size of an open disk file. For purposes of this example, assume that TESTFILE is a text file containing sample data.

```
Open "TESTFILE" For Input As #1      ' Open file.
FileLength = LOF(1)                  ' Get length of file.
Close #1                             ' Close file.
```

Log Function

Description   Returns the natural logarithm of a number.

Syntax   **Log(*number*)**

Elements   The *number* named argument can be any valid numeric expression greater than 0.

Remarks   The natural logarithm is the logarithm to the base e. The constant e is approximately 2.718282.

You can calculate base-n logarithms for any number x by dividing the natural logarithm of x by the natural logarithm of n as follows:

$$\text{Log}n(x) = \textbf{Log}(x) / \textbf{Log}(n)$$

The following example illustrates a custom **Function** that calculates base-10 logarithms:

```
Static Function Log10(X)
    Log10 = Log(X) / Log(10#)
End Function
```

See Also   **Exp** Function.

Example

This example uses the **Log** function to return the natural logarithm of a number.

```
' Define angle in radians.
MyAngle = 1.3
' Calculate inverse hyperbolic sine.
MyLog = Log(MyAngle + Sqr(MyAngle * MyAngle + 1))
```

Long Data Type

Long (long integer) variables are stored as signed 32-bit (4-byte) numbers ranging in value from -2,147,483,648 to 2,147,483,647. The type-declaration character for **Long** is **&** (character code 38).

See Also

CLng Function, Data Type Summary, **Def**type Statements, **Integer** Data Type.

LSet Statement

Description

Left aligns a string within a string variable, or copies a variable of one user-defined type to another variable of a different user-defined type.

Syntax

LSet stringvar = string

LSet varname1 = varname2

Elements

The **LSet** statement syntax has these parts:

Part	Description
stringvar	Name of string variable.
string	String expression to be left aligned within stringvar.
varname1	Variable name of the user-defined type being copied to.
varname2	Variable name of the user-defined type being copied from.

Remarks

LSet replaces any leftover characters in stringvar with spaces.

If string is longer than stringvar, **LSet** places only the leftmost characters, up to the length of the stringvar, in stringvar.

Only user-defined types containing **Integer**, **Long**, **Double**, **Single**, **String** (fixed-length), or **Currency** types may be copied. The following example copies the contents of RecTwo (a user-defined type variable) to RecOne (a variable of another user-defined type):

```
Type TwoString
    StrFld As String * 2
End Type

Type ThreeString
    StrFld As String * 3
End Type

Dim RecOne As TwoString, RecTwo As ThreeString
LSet RecOne = RecTwo
```

Because RecOne is 2 bytes long, only 2 bytes are copied from RecTwo. **LSet** copies only the number of bytes in the shorter of the two user-defined type variables.

See Also   **RSet** Statement.

Example   This example uses the **LSet** statement to left align a string within a string variable and to copy a variable of one user-defined type to another variable of a different user-defined type.

```
MyString = "0123456789"            ' Initialize string.
LSet MyString = "<-Left"           ' MyString contains "<-Left   ".

' LSet is also used to copy a variable of one user-defined type to
' another variable of a different user-defined type.
' Module level.

Type AType                         ' Define types.
    AName As String * 10
    AAdd As String * 10
End Type
Type BType
    BName As String * 5
    BAdd As String * 5
End Type

' Procedure level.
Dim AVar As AType, BVar As BType   ' Declare variables.
AVar.AName = "John Smith"          ' Define fields.
AVar.AAdd = "Rodeo Drv."
LSet BVar = AVar                   ' Copy variables.

' After copying, values are truncated.
Debug.Print BVar.BName             ' Prints "John ".
Debug.Print BVar.BAdd              ' Prints "Smith".
```

LTrim, RTrim, and Trim Functions

Description   Returns a copy of a string without leading spaces (**LTrim**), trailing spaces (**RTrim**), or both leading and trailing spaces (**Trim**).

Syntax   **LTrim**(*string*)

RTrim(*string*)

Trim(*string*)

Elements   The *string* named argument is any valid string expression. If *string* contains no valid data, **Null** is returned.

See Also   **Left** Function, **Right** Function.

Example   This example uses the **LTrim** and **RTrim** functions to strip leading and trailing spaces from a string variable. Using the **Trim** function alone achieves the same result.

```
MyString = "  <-Trim->  "              ' Initialize.
TrimString = LTrim(MyString)           ' TrimString = "<-Trim->  ".
TrimString = RTrim(MyString)           ' TrimString = "  <-Trim->".
TrimString = LTrim(RTrim(MyString))    ' TrimString = "<-Trim->".
' Using the Trim function alone achieves the same result.
TrimString = Trim(MyString)            ' TrimString = "<-Trim->".
```

MacID Function

Description   Used only on the Macintosh to convert a four-character constant to a value that may be used by **Dir**, **Kill**, **Shell**, and **AppActivate**.

Syntax   **MacID**(*constant*)

Elements   The *constant* named argument consists of four-characters used to specify a resource type, file type, application signature, or Apple Event. For example, TEXT, OBIN, MSWD (Microsoft Word), XCEL (Microsoft Excel), and so on.

Remarks   **MacID** is used with **Dir** and **Kill** to specify a Macintosh file type. Since the Macintosh does not support '*' and '?' as wildcards, you can use a four-character constant instead to identify groups of files. For example, the following statement returns 'TEXT' type files from the current folder:

```
Dir("", MacID("TEXT"))
```

MacID is used with **Shell** and **AppActivate** to specify an application using the application's unique signature.

See Also   **AppActivate** Statement, **Dir** Function, **Kill** Statement, **Shell** Function.

Example   This example shows various uses of the **MacID** function. The **MacID** function is not available in Microsoft Windows.

```
' Return the first text file in folder HD:My Folder.
FileName = Dir("HD:My Folder:", MacID("TEXT"))

' Deletes all "TEXT" files in the current folder.
Kill MacID("TEXT")

' Run Microsoft Excel.
ReturnValue = Shell(MacID("XCEL"))

' Activate Microsoft Word.
 AppActivate MacID("MSWD")
```

MacroType Property

Applies To   Name.

Description   Returns or sets what the name refers to, as shown in the following table. Read-write.

Value	Meaning
xlCommand	Name is a user-defined macro.
xlFunction	Name is a user-defined function.
xlNone	Name is not a function or macro.

Syntax   *object*.**MacroType**

Elements   *object*
                    Required. The Name object.

See Also   **Category** Property.

Example   This example displays the name category in the language of the macro.

```
With ActiveWorkbook.Names(1)
    If .MacroType <> xlNone Then
        MsgBox "The category for this name is " & .Category
    Else
        MsgBox "This name does not refer " & _
            "to a custom function or command."
    End If
End With
```

MacScript Statement

Description   Executes an AppleScript script; available on the Macintosh using System 7.0 or later.

Syntax   **MacScript** *script*

Elements   The *script* named argument is a string expression specifying the name of an AppleScript script.

Remarks   Multiline scripts may be created by embedding carriage return characters (**Chr**(13)).

See Also   **MacID** Function.

Mailer Object

Description   The PowerTalk Mailer for a workbook. This object is available only on the Apple Macintosh with the PowerTalk system extension installed.

Mailer Property

Applies To   Workbook.

Description   Returns the PowerTalk Mailer attached to the workbook. Read-only .

Syntax   *object*.**Mailer**

Elements   *object*
　　　　　　Required. The Workbook object.

Remarks   The Mailer object contains the properties needed to mail workbooks with PowerTalk. To mail a workbook, turn on the mailer with the **HasMailer** property, set the mailer properties, and then send the workbook and mailer with the **SendMailer** method.

See Also   **SendMailer** Method, **BCC Recipients** Property, **CCRecipients** Property, **Enclosures** Property, **Received** Property,**SendDateTime** Property, **Sender** Property, **SendMailer** Property, **Subject** Property, **ToRecipients** Property.

Example   This example sets up the Mailer object for workbook one, and then sends the workbook.

```
With Workbooks(1)
    .HasMailer = True
    With .Mailer
        .Subject = "Here is the workbook"
        .ToRecipients = Array("Jean")
        .CCRecipients = Array("Adam", "Bernard")
        .BCCRecipients = Array("Chris")
        .Enclosures = Array("TestFile")
    End With
    .SendMailer
End With
```

MailLogoff Method

Applies To   Application.

Description   Closes an established MAPI mail session.

Syntax   *object*.**MailLogoff**

Elements   *object*
        Required. The Application object.

See Also   **MailLogon** Method, **MailSession** Property, **SendMail** Method.

Example   This example closes the established mail session if there is one.

```
If Not IsNull(Application.MailSession) Then Application.MailLogoff
```

MailLogon Method

Applies To   Application.

Description   Logs into MAPI Mail and establishes a mail session. A mail session must be established before mail or document routing functions can be used.

Syntax   *object*.**MailLogon(***name, password, downloadNewMail***)**

Elements   The **MailLogon** method has the following object qualifier and named arguments:

    object
        Required. The Application object.

name
> Optional. The mail account name. If omitted, the default mail account name is used.

password
> Optional. The mail account password.

downloadNewMail
> Optional. If True, new mail is downloaded immediately.

Remarks   Previously established mail sessions are logged off before an attempt is made to establish the new session.

Omit both the name and password parameters to piggyback on the system default mail session.

See Also   **MailLogoff** Method, **MailSession** Property, **SendMail** Method.

Example   This example logs into MAPI mail and forces an immediate download of any new mail.

```
If IsNull(Application.MailSession) Then
    Application.MailLogon "oscarx", "mypassword", True
End If
```

MailSession Property

Applies To   Application.

Description   Returns the MAPI mail session number as a hexadecimal string (if there is an active session), or **Null** if there is no session. Read-only.

Syntax   *object*.**MailSession**

Elements   *object*
> Required. The Application object.

Remarks   This property is not used on PowerTalk mail systems.

See Also   **MailLogon** Method, **MailLogoff** Method, **MailSystem** Property, **SendMail** Method.

Example   This example closes the established mail session if there is one.

```
If Not IsNull(Application.MailSession) Then Application.MailLogoff
```

MailSystem Property

Applies To	Application.
Description	Returns the mail system installed on the host machine (one of **xlNoMailSystem**, **xlMAPI**, or **xlPowerTalk**). Read-only.
Syntax	*object*.**MailSystem**
Elements	*object* Required. The Application object.
See Also	**MailLogoff** Method, **MailLogon** Method, **MailSession** Property, **SendMail** Method.
Example	This example sends the current document if the host machine is using MAPI.

```
If Application.MailSystem = xlMAPI Then
    ActiveWorkbook.SendMail "Jean Selva", "Sampl e Subject"

End If
```

MajorGridlines Property

Applies To	Axis.
Description	Returns the major Gridlines for the specified axis. Only axes in the primary axis group can have gridlines. Read-only.
Syntax	*object*.**MajorGridlines**
Elements	*object* Required. The Axis object.
See Also	**AxisGroup** Property, **HasMajorGridlines** Property, **HasMinorGridlines** Property, **MinorGridlines** Property.
Example	This example sets the color of the major gridlines for the value axis.

```
With ActiveChart.Axes(xlValue)
    If .HasMajorGridlines Then
        .MajorGridlines.Border.Color = RGB(0, 0, 255)    'set color to
blue
    End If
End With
```

MajorTickMark Property

Applies To	Axis.
Description	Returns or sets the type of major tick mark for the specified axis (one of **xlNone**, **xlInside**, **xlOutside**, or **xlCross**). Read-write.
Syntax	*object*.**MajorTickMark**
Elements	*object* Required. The Axis object.
See Also	**MinorTickMark** Property.
Example	This example sets the value axis to use outside major tick marks.

```
ActiveChart.Axes(xlValue).MajorTickMark = xlOutside
```

MajorUnit Property

Applies To	Axis.
Description	Returns or sets the major units for the value axis. Applies only to the value axis. Read-write.
Syntax	*object*.**MajorUnit**
Elements	*object* Required. The Axis object.
Remarks	Setting this property sets the **MajorUnitIsAuto** property to **False.** Use the **TickMarkSpacing** property to set tick mark spacing on the category axis.
See Also	**MajorUnitIsAuto** Property, **MinorUnit** Property, **MinorUnitIsAuto** Property, **TickMarkSpacing** Property.
Example	This example sets the major and minor units for the value axis.

```
With ActiveChart.Axes(xlValue)
    .MajorUnit = 100
    .MinorUnit = 20
End With
```

MajorUnitIsAuto Property

Applies To	Axis.
Description	**True** if Microsoft Excel calculates major units for the value axis. Applies only to the value axis. Read-write.
Syntax	*object*.**MajorUnitIsAuto**
Elements	*object* Required. The Axis object.
Remarks	Setting the **MajorUnit** property sets this property to **False**.
See Also	**MajorUnit** Property, **MinorUnit** Property, **MinorUnitIsAuto** Property, **TickMarkSpacing** Property.
Example	This example sets Microsoft Excel to calculate major and minor units for the value axis.

```
With ActiveChart.Axes(xlValue)
    .MajorUnitIsAuto = True
    .MinorUnitIsAuto = True
End With
```

MarkerBackgroundColor Property

Applies To	LegendKey, Point, Series.
Description	Returns or sets the marker background color as an RGB value. Line, scatter and radar charts only. Read-write.
Syntax	*object*.**MarkerBackgroundColor**
Elements	*object* Required. The LegendKey, Point, or Series object.
See Also	**MarkerBackgroundColorIndex** Property, **MarkerForegroundColor** Property, **MarkerStyle** Property.
Example	This example sets the marker background and foreground color for the second point on a series.

```
With ActiveChart.SeriesCollection(1).Points(2)
    .MarkerBackgroundColor = RGB(0,255,0)
    .MarkerForegroundColor = RGB(255,0,0)
End With
```

MarkerBackgroundColorIndex Property

Applies To   LegendKey, Point, Series.

Description   Returns or sets the marker background color as an index into the current color palette (a value from one to 56, or **xlNone** if there is no background color). Line, scatter and radar charts only. Read-write.

Syntax   *object*.**MarkerBackgroundColorIndex**

Elements   *object*
                      Required. The LegendKey, Point, or Series object.

See Also   **MarkerBackgroundColor** Property, **MarkerForegroundColor** Property, **MarkerStyle** Property.

Example   This example sets the marker background and foreground color (as an index) for the second point on a series.

```
With ActiveChart.SeriesCollection(1).Points(2)
    .MarkerBackgroundColorIndex = 1
    .MarkerForegroundColorIndex = 2
End With
```

MarkerForegroundColor Property

Applies To   LegendKey, Point, Series.

Description   Returns or sets the foreground color of the marker, specified as an RGB value. Line, scatter and radar charts only. Read-write.

Syntax   *object*.**MarkerForegroundColor**

Elements   *object*
                      Required. The LegendKey, Point, or Series object.

See Also   **MarkerBackgroundColor** Property, **MarkerBackgroundColorIndex** Property, **MarkerForegroundColorIndex** Property, **MarkerStyle** Property.

Example   This example sets the marker background and foreground color for the second point on a series.

```
With ActiveChart.SeriesCollection(1).Points(2)
    .MarkerBackgroundColor = RGB(0,255,0)
    .MarkerForegroundColor = RGB(255,0,0)
End With
```

MarkerForegroundColorIndex Property

Applies To   LegendKey, Point, Series.

Description   Returns or sets the marker foreground color as an index into the current color palette (a value from one to 56, or **xlNone** if there is no foreground color). Line, scatter and radar charts only. Read-write.

Syntax   *object*.**MarkerForegroundColorIndex**

Elements   *object*
                      Required. The LegendKey, Point, or Series object.

See Also   **MarkerBackgroundColorIndex** Property, **MarkerForegroundColor** Property, **MarkerStyle** Property.

Example   This example sets the marker background and foreground color (as an index) for the second point on a series.

```
With ActiveChart.SeriesCollection(1).Points(2)
    .MarkerBackgroundColorIndex = 1
    .MarkerForegroundColorIndex = 2
End With
```

MarkerStyle Property

Applies To   LegendKey, Point, Series.

Description   Returns or sets the marker style for a point or series on a line chart, a scatter chart, or a radar chart. Read-write.

Syntax   *object*.**MarkerStyle**

Elements   *object*
                      Required. The LegendKey, Point or Series object.

Remarks   This property can have one of the following values.

Value	Meaning
xlNone	No markers.
xlAutomatic	Automatic markers.
xlSquare	Square markers.
xlDiamond	Diamond-shaped markers.
xlTriangle	Triangular markers.
xlX	Square markers with an X.

Value	Meaning
xlStar	Square markers with an asterisk.
xlDot	Short bar markers.
xlDash	Long bar markers.
xlCircle	Circular markers.
xlPlus	Square markers with a plus sign.
xlPicture	Picture markers.

See Also   **MarkerBackgroundColor** Property, **MarkerBackgroundColorIndex** Property, **MarkerForegroundColorIndex** Property, **MarkerStyle** Property.

Example   This example sets the marker style for the first series.

```
ActiveChart.SeriesCollection(1).MarkerStyle = xlCircle
```

MathCoprocessorAvailable Property

Applies To   Application.

Description   **True** if a math coprocessor is available. Read-only.

Syntax   *object*.**MathCoprocessorAvailable**

Elements   *object*
        Required. The Application object.

Example   This example displays a message box if a math coprocessor is not available.

```
If Not Application.MathCoprocessorAvailable Then
    MsgBox "This macro requires a math coprocessor"
End If
```

Max Property

Applies To   DrawingObjects, ScrollBar, ScrollBars, Spinner, Spinners.

Description   Returns or sets the maximum value of a scroll bar or spinner range. The scroll bar or spinner will not take on values above this maximum value. Read-write.

For help about using the **Max** worksheet function in Visual Basic, see Using Worksheet Functions in Visual Basic.

Syntax	*object*.**Max**
Elements	*object*
	Required. The object to which this property applies.
Remarks	The value of the **Max** property must be greater than the value of the **Min** property.
See Also	**Min** Property.
Example	This example sets the minimum and maximum values for scroll bar one.

```
With Application.DialogSheets(1).ScrollBars(1)
    .Min = 20
    .Max = 50
End With
```

MaxChange Property

Applies To	Application.
Description	Returns or sets the maximum amount of change that is used in each iteration as Microsoft Excel tries to resolve circular references. Read-write.
Syntax	*object*.**MaxChange**
Elements	*object*
	Required. The Application object.
Remarks	The **MaxIterations** property sets the maximum number of iterations used when resolving circular references.
See Also	**Iteration** Property, **MaxIteration** Property.
Example	This example saves the current setting of the **MaxChange** property and then sets the maximum change for each iteration to 0.1.

```
saveMaxChange = Application.MaxChange
Application.MaxChange = 0.1
```

MaximumScale Property

Applies To	Axis.
Description	Returns or sets the maximum value on the value axis. Applies only to the value axis. Read-write.

Syntax	*object*.**MaximumScale**
Elements	*object* Required. The Axis object.
Remarks	Setting this property sets the **MaximumScaleIsAuto** property to **False**.
See Also	**MaximumScalesAuto** Property, **MinimumScale** Property, **MinimumScaleIsAuto** Property.
Example	This example sets the maximum and minimum values for the value axis.

```
With ActiveChart.Axes(xlValue)
    .MinimumScale = 10
    .MaximumScale = 120
End With
```

MaximumScaleIsAuto Property

Applies To	Axis.
Description	**True** if Microsoft Excel calculates the maximum value for the value axis. Applies only to the value axis. Read-write.
Syntax	*object*.**MaximumScaleIsAuto**
Elements	*object* Required. The Axis object.
Remarks	Setting the **MaximumScale** property sets this property to **False**.
See Also	**MaximumScale** Property, **MinimumScale** Property, **MinimumScaleIsAuto** Property.
Example	This example sets Microsoft Excel to calculate the minimum and maximum values for the value axis.

```
With ActiveChart.Axes(xlValue)
    .MinimumScaleIsAuto = True
    .MaximumScaleIsAuto = True
End With
```

MaxIterations Property

Applies To	Application.

Description	Returns or sets the maximum number of iterations that will be allowed to resolve a circular reference. Read-write.
Syntax	*object*.**MaxIterations**
Elements	*object* Required. The Application object.
Remarks	The **MaxChange** property sets the maximum amount of change used in each iteration when resolving circular references.
See Also	**Iteration** Property, **MaxChange** Property.
Example	This example saves the current value of the **MaxIterations** property and then sets the maximum number of iterations to 1000.

```
saveMaxIterations = Application.MaxIterations
Application.MaxIterations = 1000
```

MemoryFree Property

Applies To	Application.
Description	Returns the amount of memory that is still available for Microsoft Excel to use, in bytes. Read-only.
Syntax	*object*.**MemoryFree**
Elements	*object* Required. The Application object.
See Also	**MemoryTotal** Property, **Memory Used** Property.
Example	This example displays a message box showing the number of free bytes.

```
MsgBox "Microsoft Excel has " & _
    Application.MemoryFree & " bytes free"
```

MemoryTotal Property

Applies To	Application.
Description	Returns the total amount of memory that is available to Microsoft Excel, including memory already in use, in bytes. Read-only.

Syntax	*object*.**MemoryTotal**
Elements	*object* Required. The Application object.
Remarks	**MemoryTotal** is equal to **MemoryUsed** + **MemoryFree**.
See Also	**MemoryFree** Property, **Memory Used** Property.
Example	This example displays a message box showing the total number of available bytes.

```
MsgBox "Microsoft Excel has " & Application.MemoryTotal & _
    " total bytes available"
```

MemoryUsed Property

Applies To	Application.
Description	Returns the amount of memory that is currently in use by Microsoft Excel, in bytes. Read-only.
Syntax	*object*.**MemoryUsed**
Elements	*object* Required. The Application object.
See Also	**MemoryFree** Property, **Memory Total** Property.
Example	This example displays a message box showing the number of bytes currently used.

```
MsgBox "Microsoft Excel is currently using " & _
    Application.MemoryUsed & " bytes"
```

Menu Object

Description	A drop-down menu, shortcut menu, or cascading menu.

MenuBar Object

Description	A built-in or custom menu bar.

MenuBars Method

Applies To   Application.

Description   Returns a single menu bar (a MenuBar object, Syntax 1) or a collection of the top-level menu bars (the MenuBars object, Syntax 2). Read-only.

Syntax 1   *object*.**MenuBars(*index*)**

Syntax 2   *object*.**MenuBars**

Elements   The **MenuBars** method has the following object qualifier and named arguments:

object
Optional. The Application object.

index
Required for Syntax 1. The name or number of the menu bar. Several predefined constants are available, as shown in the following list.

Constant	Description
xlWorksheet	Worksheet, macro sheet and dialog sheet.
xlChart	Chart
xlModule	Visual Basic module
xlNoDocuments	No documents open
xlInfo	Info Window
xlWorksheetShort	Short Worksheet menu (for Microsoft Excel version 3 compatibility)
xlChartShort	Short Chart menu (for Microsoft Excel version 3 compatibility)
xlWorksheet4	Old worksheet menu bar (for Microsoft Excel version 4 compatibility)
xlChart4	Old chart menu bar (for Microsoft Excel version 4 compatibility)

Example

This example displays the number of menus in the main worksheet menu bar, adds a menu called "Extra", and then displays the new number of menus in the menu bar.

```
Set worksheetMenuBars = Application.MenuBars(xlWorksheet)
With worksheetMenuBars
    numberOfMenus = .Menus.Count
    MsgBox "There are " & numberOfMenus & _
        " menus in the menubar"
    .Menus.Add "Extra"
    numberOfMenus = .Menus.Count
    MsgBox "There are now " & numberOfMenus & _
        " menus in the menubar"
End With
```

MenuBars Object

Description

A collection of MenuBar objects.

MenuItem Object

Description

A menu item. A menu item can be a command or a separator bar.

MenuItems Method

Applies To

Menu.

Description

Returns a single menu item (a MenuItem object, Syntax 1), or a collection of the menu items (a MenuItems object, Syntax 2) on the menu. Read-only.

Syntax 1

object.**MenuItems(*index*)**

Syntax 2

object.**MenuItems**

Elements

The **MenuItems** method has the following object qualifier and named arguments:

object
　　Required. The Menu object.

index
　　Required for Syntax 1. The name or number of the menu item.

Example   This example adds a menu item to the Help menu on the active menu bar.

```
With ActiveMenuBar.Menus("Help")
    Set mi = .MenuItems.Add("&More Help", "my_Help_Macro")
End With
```

MenuItems Object

Description   A collection of MenuItem objects.

Menus Method

Applies To   MenuBar.

Description   Returns a single menu (a Menu object, Syntax 1), or a collection of the menus (a Menus object, Syntax 2) on the menu bar. Read-only.

Syntax 1   *object*.**Menus(*index*)**

Syntax 2   *object*.**Menus**

Elements   The **Menus** method has the following object qualifier and named arguments:

object
     Required. The MenuBar object.

index
     Required for Syntax 1. The name or number of the menu. Can be one of the following constants:

Constant	Description
xlWorksheet	Worksheet and macro sheet and dialog sheet.
xlChart	Chart
xlModule	Visual Basic module
xlNoDocuments	No documents open
xlInfo	Info Window
xlWorksheetShort	Short Worksheet menu (Microsoft Excel 3 compatibility)
xlChartShort	Short Chart menu (Microsoft Excel 3 compatibility)

Constant	Description
xlWorksheet4	Old worksheet menu bar (Microsoft Excel 4 compatibility)
xlChart4	Old chart menu bar (Microsoft Excel 4 compatibility)

Example   This example adds a menu item to the Help menu on the active menu bar.

```
With ActiveMenuBar.Menus("Help")
    Set mi = .MenuItems.Add("&More Help", "my_Help_Macro")
End With
```

Menus Object

Description   A collection of Menu objects.

Merge Method

Applies To   Scenarios, Styles.

Description   Syntax 1: Merges the scenarios from another sheet into the collection of scenarios.

Syntax 2: Merges the styles from another workbook into the collection of styles.

Syntax 1   *object*.**Merge**(*source*)

Syntax 2   *object*.**Merge**(*workbook*)

Elements   The **Merge** method has the following object qualifier and named arguments:

object
    Required. The Scenarios or Styles object.

source
    Required for Syntax 1. The Worksheet object, or name of the sheet containing scenarios to merge.

workbook
    Required for Syntax 2. The Workbook object containing styles to merge.

Example   This example merges the styles from workbook two into the active workbook.

```
ActiveWorkbook.Styles.Merge Workbooks(2)
```

Message Property

Applies To   RoutingSlip.

Description   Returns or sets the message text of the routing slip. This text is used as the body text of mail messages used to route the workbook. Read-write.

Syntax   *object*.**Message**

Elements   *object*
        Required. The RoutingSlip object.

See Also   **Subject** Property.

Example   This example sends BOOK1.XLS to three recipients, one after the other.

```
Workbooks("BOOK1.XLS").HasRoutingSlip = True
With Workbooks("BOOK1.XLS").RoutingSlip
    .Delivery = xlOneAfterAnother
    .Recipients = Array("Adam Bendel", "Jean Selva", "Bernard Gabor")
    .Subject = "Here is BOOK1.XLS"
    .Message = "Here is the workbook. What do you think?"
End With
Workbooks("BOOK1.XLS").Route
```

Mid Function

Description   Returns a specified number of characters from a string.

Syntax   **Mid**(*string*,*start*[,*length*])

Elements   The **Mid** function syntax has these parts:

Part	Description
string	String expression from which characters are returned. If *string* contains no valid data, **Null** is returned.
start	Character position in *string* at which the part to be taken begins. If *start* is greater than the number of characters in *string*, **Mid** returns a zero-length string.
length	Number of characters to return. If omitted or if there are fewer than *length* characters in the text (including the character at *start*), all characters from the *start* position to the end of the string are returned.

Remarks   To determine the number of characters in *string*, use the **Len** function.

> **Note**   Another function (**MidB**) is provided for use with the double-byte character sets (DBCS) used in some Asian locales. Instead of specifying the number of characters to return, *length* specifies the number of bytes. In areas where DBCS is not used, **MidB** behaves the same as **Mid**.

See Also   **Left** Function, **Len** Function, **LTrim** Function, **Mid** Statement, **Right** Function, **RTrim** Function, **Trim** Function.

Example   This example uses the **Mid** function to return a specified number of characters from a string.

```
MyString = "Mid Function Demo"      ' Create text string.
FirstWord = Mid(MyString, 1, 3)     ' Returns "Mid".
LastWord = Mid(MyString, 14, 4)     ' Returns "Demo".
MidWords = Mid(MyString, 5)         ' Returns "Function Demo".
```

Mid Statement

Description   Replaces a specified number of characters in a string variable with characters from another string.

Syntax   **Mid**(*stringvar*,*start*[,*length*])=*string*

Elements   The **Mid** statement syntax has these parts:

Part	Description
stringvar	Name of string variable to modify.
start	Character position in *stringvar* where the replacement of text begins.
length	Number of characters to replace. If omitted, all of *string* is used.
string	String expression that replaces part of *stringvar*.

Remarks   The number of characters replaced is always less than or equal to the number of characters in *stringvar*.

See Also   **Mid** Function.

| Example | This example uses the **Mid** statement to replace a specified number of characters in a string variable with characters from another string. |

```
MyString = "The dog jumps"        ' Initialize string.
Mid(MyString, 5, 3) = "fox"       ' MyString = "The fox jumps".
Mid(MyString, 5) = "cow"          ' MyString = "The cow jumps".
Mid(MyString, 5) = "cow jumped over"
                                  ' MyString = "The cow jumpe".
Mid(MyString, 5, 3) = "duck"      ' MyString = "The duc jumps".
```

Min Property

Applies To	DrawingObjects, ScrollBar, ScrollBars, Spinner, Spinners.
Description	Returns or sets the minimum value of a scroll bar or spinner range. The scroll bar or spinner will not take on values below this minimum value. Read-write.
	For help about using the **Min** worksheet function in Visual Basic, see Using Worksheet Functions in Visual Basic.
Syntax	*object*.**Min**
Elements	*object* Required. The object to which this property applies.
Remarks	The value of the **Min** property must be less than the value of the **Max** property.
See Also	**Max** Property.
Example	This example sets the minimum and maximum values for scroll bar one.

```
With Application.DialogSheets(1).ScrollBars(1)
    .Min = 20
    .Max = 50
End With
```

MinimumScale Property

Applies To	Axis.
Description	Returns or sets the minimum value on the value axis. Applies only to the value axis. Read-write.

Syntax	*object*.**MinimumScale**
Elements	*object* Required. The Axis object.
Remarks	Setting this property sets the **MinimumScaleIsAuto** property to **False**.
See Also	**MaximumScale** Property, **MaximumScalesAuto** Property, **MinimumScalesAuto** Property.
Example	This example sets the maximum and minimum values on the value axis.

```
With ActiveChart.Axes(xlValue)
    .MinimumScale = 10
    .MaximumScale = 120
End With
```

MinimumScaleIsAuto Property

Applies To	Axis.
Description	**True** if Microsoft Excel calculates the minimum value for the value axis. Applies only to the value axis. Read-write.
Syntax	*object*.**MinimumScaleIsAuto**
Elements	*object* Required. The Axis object.
Remarks	Setting the **MinimumScale** property sets this property to **False**.
See Also	**MaximumScale** Property, **MaximumScalesAuto** Property, **MinimumScales** Property.
Example	This example sets Microsoft Excel to calculate the minimum and maximum values for the value axis.

```
With ActiveChart.Axes(xlValue)
    .MinimumScaleIsAuto = True
    .MaximumScaleIsAuto = True
End With
```

MinorGridlines Property

Applies To	Axis.

Description	Returns the minor Gridlines for the specified axis. Only axes in the primary axis group can have gridlines. Read-only.
Syntax	*object*.**MinorGridlines**
Elements	*object* Required. The Axis object.
See Also	**AxisGroup** Property, **HasMajorGridlines** Property, **HasMinorGridlines** Property, **MajorGridlines** Property.
Example	This example sets the color of the minor gridlines for the value axis.

```
With ActiveChart.Axes(xlValue)
    If .HasMinorGridlines Then
        .MinorGridlines.Border.Color = RGB(0, 0, 255)    'set color to
blue
    End If
End With
```

MinorTickMark Property

Applies To	Axis.
Description	Returns or sets the type of minor tick mark for the specified axis (one of **xlNone**, **xlInside**, **xlOutside**, or **xlCross**). Read-write.
Syntax	*object*.**MinorTickMark**
Elements	*object* Required. The Axis object.
See Also	**MajorTickMark** Property.
Example	This example sets the category (x) axis to use inside minor tick marks.

```
ActiveChart.Axes(xlCategory).MinorTickMark = xlInside
```

MinorUnit Property

Applies To	Axis.
Description	Returns or sets the minor units on the value axis. Applies only to the value axis. Read-write.

Syntax	*object*.**MinorUnit**
Elements	*object* Required. The Axis object.
Remarks	Setting this property sets the **MinorUnitIsAuto** property to **False.** Use the **TickMarkSpacing** property to set tick mark spacing on the category axis.
See Also	**MajorUnit** Property, **MajorUnitIsAuto** Property, **MinorUnitIsAuto** Property, **TickMarkSpacing** Property.
Example	This example sets the major and minor units for the value axis.

```
With ActiveChart.Axes(xlValue)
    .MajorUnit = 100
    .MinorUnit = 20
End With
```

MinorUnitIsAuto Property

Applies To	Axis.
Description	**True** if Microsoft Excel calculates minor units for the value axis. Applies only to the value axis. Read-write.
Syntax	*object*.**MinorUnitIsAuto**
Elements	*object* Required. The Axis object.
Remarks	Setting the **MinorUnit** property sets this property to **False.**
See Also	**MajorUnit** Property, **MajorUnitIsAuto** Property, **MinorUnit** Property, **TickMarkSpacing** Property.
Example	This example sets Microsoft Excel to calculate major and minor units for the value axis.

```
With ActiveChart.Axes(xlValue)
    .MajorUnitIsAuto = True
    .MinorUnitIsAuto = True
End With
```

Minute Function

Description   Returns a whole number between 0 and 59, inclusive, representing the minute of the hour.

Syntax   **Minute(*time*)**

Elements   The *time* named argument is limited to a time or numbers and strings, in any combination, that can represent a time. If *time* contains no valid data, **Null** is returned.

See Also   **Day** Function, **Hour** Function, **Now** Function, **Second** Function, **Time** Function, **Time** Statement.

Example   This example uses the **Minute** function to obtain the minute of the hour from a specified time.

```
' In the development environment, the time (date literal) will display
' in short format using the locale settings of your code.
MyTime = #4:35:17 PM#           ' Assign a time.
MyMinute = Minute(MyTime)       ' MyMinute contains 35.
```

MkDir Statement

Description   Creates a new directory or folder.

Syntax   **MkDir *path***

Elements   The ***path*** named argument is a string expression that identifies the directory or folder to be created{bmc emdash.bmp}may include drive. If no drive is specified, **MkDir** creates the new directory or folder on the current drive.

Remarks   In Microsoft Windows, if you use **MkDir** to create a directory whose name contains an embedded space, you may be able to access it with some applications, but you can't remove it using standard operating system commands. To remove such a directory, use the **RmDir** statement.

See Also   **ChDir** Statement, **CurDir** Function, **RmDir** Statement.

Example   This example uses the **MkDir** statement to create a directory or folder. If the drive is not specified, the new directory or folder is created on the current drive.

```
MkDir "MYDIR"    ' Make new directory or folder.
```

Mod Operator

Description   Divides two numbers and returns only the remainder.

Syntax   *result = number1* **Mod** *number2*

Elements   The **Mod** operator syntax has these parts:

Part	Description
result	Any numeric variable.
number1	Any numeric expression.
number2	Any numeric expression.

Remarks   The modulus, or remainder, operator divides *number1* by *number2* (rounding floating-point numbers to integers) and returns only the remainder as *result*. For example, in the following expression, A (which is *result*) equals 5.

```
A = 19 Mod 6.7
```

Usually, the data type of *result* is an **Integer**, **Integer** variant, **Long**, or **Variant** containing a **Long**, regardless of whether or not *result* is a whole number. Any fractional portion is truncated. However, if any expression is a **Null**, *result* is also a **Null**. Any expression that is **Empty** is treated as 0.

See Also   Operator Precedence.

Example   This example uses the **Mod** operator to divide two numbers and return only the remainder. If either number is a floating-point number, it is first rounded to an integer.

```
MyResult = 10 Mod 5        ' Returns 0.
MyResult = 10 Mod 3        ' Returns 1.
MyResult = 12 Mod 4.3      ' Returns 0.
MyResult = 12.6 Mod 5      ' Returns 3.
```

Module Object

Description   A Visual Basic module in a workbook.

Modules Method

Applies To   Application, Workbook.

Description	Returns a module (a Module object, Syntax 1) or a collection of all modules (a Modules object, Syntax 2) in the workbook. Read-only.
Syntax 1	*object*.**Modules**(*index*)
Syntax 2	*object*.**Modules**
Elements	The **Modules** method has the following object qualifier and named arguments:

object
> Required. The Workbook object.

index
> Required for Syntax 1. The name or number of the module to return.

Example	This example displays the number of modules available in the active workbook.

```
MsgBox "There are " & ActiveWorkbook.Modules.Count & _
    " modules in this workbook."
```

Modules Object

Description	A collection of Module objects.

Month Function

Description	Returns a whole number between 1 and 12, inclusive, representing the month of the year.
Syntax	**Month(*date*)**
Elements	The *date* named argument is limited to a date or numbers and strings, in any combination, that can represent a date. If *date* contains no valid data, **Null** is returned.
See Also	**Date** Function, **Date** Statement, **Day** Function, **Now** Function, **Weekday** Function, **Year** Function.
Example	This example uses the **Month** function to obtain the month from a specified date.

```
' In the development environment, the date literal will display in short
' format using the locale settings of your code.
MyDate = #February 12, 1969#       ' Assign a date.
MyMonth = Month(MyDate)            ' MyMonth contains 2.
```

MouseAvailable Property

Applies To	Application.
Description	**True** if a mouse is available (always **True** on the Macintosh). Read-only.
Syntax	*object*.**MouseAvailable**
Elements	*object*
	Required. The Application object.
Example	This example sets the variable `systemMouseAvailable` to **True** if a mouse is available.

```
systemMouseAvailable = Application.MouseAvailable
```

Move Method

Applies To   Chart, Charts, DialogSheet, DialogSheets, Module, Modules, Sheets, ToolbarButton, Worksheet, Worksheets.

Description   Syntax 1: Moves the sheet to another location in the workbook.

Syntax 2: Moves a toolbar button to another position, either on the same toolbar or to another toolbar.

Syntax 1   *object*.**Move**(*before, after*)

Syntax 2   *object*.**Move**(*toolbar, before*)

Elements   The **Move** method has the following object qualifier and named arguments:

object
　　Required. The object to which this method applies.

before
　　Syntax 1: Optional. The sheet before which this sheet will be moved. You cannot specify *before* if you specify *after*.

　　Syntax 2: Required. Specifies the new button position as a number from 1 to the number of existing buttons + 1. Gaps count as one position. Buttons to the right of this position are moved right (or down) to make room for the moved button.

after
　　Optional. The sheet after which this sheet will be moved. You cannot specify *after* if you specify *before*.

toolbar
　　Required for Syntax 2. Specifies the toolbar object to move the button to.

Remarks   If you do not specify either *before* or *after*, Microsoft Excel creates a new workbook containing the moved sheet.

See Also   **Copy** Method.

Example   This example moves Sheet1 after Sheet9 in Book2.

```
Application.Worksheets("Sheet1").Move _
    after:= Workbooks("Book2").Worksheets("Sheet9")
```

MoveAfterReturn Property

Applies To   Application.

Description   **True** if the selection will be moved as soon as the ENTER (RETURN) key is pressed. Read-write.

Syntax   *object*.**MoveAfterReturn**

Elements   *object*
          Required. The Application object.

Example   This example saves the current state of the **MoveAfterReturn** property and then sets the property to **True**, so selections will be moved as soon as the ENTER key is pressed.

```
saveMoveAfter = Application.MoveAfterReturn
Application.MoveAfterReturn = True
```

MsgBox Function

Description   Displays a message in a dialog box, waits for the user to choose a button, and returns a value indicating which button the user has chosen.

Syntax

MsgBox(*prompt*[*,buttons*][*,title*][*,helpfile,context*])

Elements

The **MsgBox** function syntax has these named-argument parts:

Part	Description
prompt	String expression displayed as the message in the dialog box. The maximum length of *prompt* is approximately 1024 characters, depending on the width of the characters used. If *prompt* consists of more than one line, be sure to include a carriage return (character code 13) or carriage return linefeed (character code 10) between each line.
buttons	Numeric expression that is the sum of values specifying the number and type of buttons to display, the icon style to use, the identity of the default button, and the modality. If omitted, the default value for *buttons* is 0.
title	String expression displayed in the title bar of the dialog box. If you omit *title*, nothing is placed in the title bar.
helpfile	String expression that identifies the Help file to use to provide context-sensitive Help for the dialog box. If *helpfile* is provided, *context* must also be provided.
context	Numeric expression that is the Help context number the Help author assigned to the appropriate Help topic. If *context* is provided, *helpfile* must also be provided.

The *buttons* named argument has these values:

Constant	Value	Description
vbOKOnly	0	Display OK button only.
vbOKCancel	1	Display OK and Cancel buttons.
vbAbortRetryIgnore	2	Display Abort, Retry, and Ignore buttons.
vbYesNoCancel	3	Display Yes, No, and Cancel buttons.
vbYesNo	4	Display Yes and No buttons.
vbRetryCancel	5	Display Retry and Cancel buttons.
vbCritical	16	Display Critical Message icon.
vbQuestion	32	Display Warning Query icon.
vbExclamation	48	Display Warning Message icon.
vbInformation	64	Display Information Message icon.
vbDefaultButton1	0	First button is default.
vbDefaultButton2	256	Second button is default.
vbDefaultButton3	512	Third button is default.

Constant	Value	Description
vbApplicationModal	0	Application modal; the user must respond to the message box before continuing work in the current application.
vbSystemModal	4096	System modal; all applications are suspended until the user responds to the message box.

The first group of values (0-5) describes the number and type of buttons displayed in the dialog box; the second group (16, 32, 48, 64) describes the icon style; the third group (0, 256, 512) determines which button is the default, and the fourth group (0, 4096) determines the modality of the message box. When adding numbers to create a final value for the argument *buttons*, use only one number from each group.

Note These constants are specified by Visual Basic. As a result, the names can be used anywhere in your code in place of the actual values.

Return Values

Constant	Value	Button Selected
vbOK	1	OK
vbCancel	2	Cancel
vbAbort	3	Abort
vbRetry	4	Retry
vbIgnore	5	Ignore
vbYes	6	Yes
vbNo	7	No

Remarks

When both *helpfile* and *context* are provided, a Help button is automatically added to the dialog box.

If the dialog box displays a Cancel button, pressing the ESC key has the same effect as choosing Cancel. If the dialog box contains a Help button, context-sensitive Help is provided for the dialog box. However, no value is returned until one of the other buttons is chosen.

See Also

InputBox Function.

Example   The example uses the **MsgBox** function to display a critical-error message in a dialog box with Yes and No buttons. The No button is specified as the default response. The value returned by the **MsgBox** function depends on the button chosen by the user. For purposes of this example, assume that DEMO.HLP is a Help file that contains a topic with context number equal to 1000.

```
Msg = "Do you want to continue ?"        ' Define message.
Style = vbYesNo + vbCritical + vbDefaultButton2
                                         ' Define buttons.
Title = "MsgBox Demonstration"           ' Define title.
Help = "DEMO.HLP"                        ' Define help file.
Ctxt = 1000                              ' Define topic context.

' Display message.
Response = MsgBox(Msg, Style, Title, Help, Ctxt)
If Response = vbYES Then                  ' User chose Yes button.
    MyString = "Yes"                      ' Perform some action.
Else                                      ' User chose No button.
    MyString = "No"                       ' Perform some action.
End If
```

MultiLine Property

Applies To   DrawingObjects, EditBox, EditBoxes.

Description   **True** if the edit box is multi-line enabled. Read-write.

Syntax   *object*.**MultiLine**

Elements   *object*
          Required. The object to which this property applies.

Example   This example enables edit box one for multi-line input.

```
Application.DialogSheets(1).EditBoxes(1).MultiLine = True
```

MultiSelect Property

Applies To   DrawingObjects, ListBox, ListBoxes.

Description   Returns or sets the selection mode of the list box (or collection of list boxes). Can be one of **xlNone**, **xlSimple**, or **xlExtended**. Read-write.

Syntax	*object*.**MultiSelect**
Elements	*object* Required. The object to which this property applies.
Remarks	**Single select** (**xlNone**) allows only one item at a time to be selected. Any click or spacebar press deselects the currently selected item and selects the clicked-upon item.

Simple multi-select (**xlSimple**) toggles the selection on an item in the list when it is selected with the mouse or the spacebar is pressed when the focus is on the item. This mode is appropriate for pick lists where multiple items are often selected.

Extended multi-select (**xlExtended**) normally acts like a single-selection list box, so that mouse clicks on an item cancel all other selected items. When you hold down SHIFT while clicking the mouse or pressing an ARROW key, items are sequentially selected from the current item as the user navigates. When you hold down CTRL while clicking the mouse, single items are added to the list selection. This mode is appropriate when multiple items are allowed but not often used.

You can use the **Value** or **ListIndex** properties to get and set the selected item in a single-select list box. You must use the **Selected** property to get and set the selected items in a multi-select list box.

Multi-select list boxes cannot be linked to cells with the **LinkedCell** property.

See Also	**ListIndex** Property, **Selected** Property, **Value** Property.
Example	This example sets list box one to allow extended multiple selections.

```
ActiveSheet.ListBoxes(1).MultiSelect = True
```

Name Object

Description	A defined name. Names can be built-in, such as Database, Print_Area, and Auto_Open, or they can be custom names.

Name Property

Applies To	AddIn, Application, Arc, AxisTitle, Button, Chart, ChartArea, ChartObject, ChartTitle, CheckBox, Corners, DataLabel, DataLabels, DialogFrame, DialogSheet, DownBars, Drawing, DropDown, DropLines, EditBox, ErrorBars, Floor, Font, Gridlines, GroupBox, GroupObject, HiLoLines, Label, Legend, Line, ListBox, Module, Name, OLEObject, OptionButton, Oval, Picture, PivotField,

PivotItem, PivotTable, PlotArea, Range, Rectangle, Scenario, ScrollBar, Series, SeriesLines, Spinner, Style, TextBox, TickLabels, Toolbar, ToolbarButton, Trendline, UpBars, Walls, Workbook, Worksheet.

Description   Returns or sets the name of the object. See the Remarks section for details.

Syntax   *object*.**Name**

Elements   *object*
    Required. The object to which this property applies.

Remarks   The meaning of this property depends on the object, as shown in the following table. The name of a Range object is a Name object. For every other object, the name is a string.

Object	Name
AddIn	The filename of the add-in, not including its path on disk. Read-only.
Application	The name of the application. Read-only.
Chart	If the chart is a page in the workbook, this is the name of that page as shown on the tab. If the chart is an embedded object, it is the name of the object. Read-write.
Control or drawing object	The name of the control or drawing object, in the language of the macro. Read-write.
DialogSheet, Module, Worksheet	The name of the sheet, as shown on the tab. Read-write.
Font	The name of the font.
Name	The name itself. If it is one of the built-in names it will be translated to the language of the macro. Read-write.
OLEObject	The name of the object. Read-write.
PivotField	The name of the field in the pivot table. Read-write.
PivotItem	The name of the item in the pivot table field. Read-write.
PivotTable	The name of the pivot table. Read-write.
Range	The name of the range (this is a Name object). Assign to this property to define a name. If the range has multiple names, returns the first one. Read-write.
Scenario	The name of the scenario. Read-write.
Series	The name of the series. Read-write.
Style	The name of the style. If the style is a built-in style, this will return the name of the style in the language of the macro. Read only.

Object	Name
Toolbar	The name of the toolbar. If the toolbar is built-in, returns the name in the language of the user. Read-write for custom toolbars, read-only for built-in toolbars.
ToolbarButton	The name of the button, as a string. Read-write.
Trendline	The name of the trendline as it will appear in the legend. Read-write.
Workbook	The name of the workbook, not including its path on disk. Read-only .

See Also   **NameLocal** Property.

Example   This example displays the name and localized name of a style.

```
With ActiveWorkbook.Styles(1)
    MsgBox "The name of the style is " & .Name
    MsgBox "The localized name of the style is " & .NameLocal
End With
```

Name Statement

Description   Renames a disk file, directory, or folder.

Syntax   **Name** *oldpathname* **As** *newpathname*

Elements   The **Name** statement syntax has these parts:

Part	Description
oldpathname	String expression that specifies the existing file name and location{bmc emdash.bmp}may include directory or folder, and drive.
newpathname	String expression that specifies the new file name and location{bmc emdash.bmp}may include directory or folder, and drive. The file specified by *newpathname* can't already exist.

Remarks   Both *newpathname* and *oldpathname* must be on the same drive. If the path in *newpathname* exists and is different from the path in *oldpathname*, the **Name** statement moves the file to the new directory or folder and renames the file, if necessary. If *newpathname* and *oldpathname* have different paths and the same file name, **Name** moves the file to the new location and leaves the file name unchanged. Using **Name**, you can move a file from one directory or folder to another, but you can't move a directory or folder.

Name supports the use of '*' (multiple character) and '?' (single character) wildcards. However, on the Macintosh, these characters are treated as valid file name characters and can't be used as wildcards to specify multiple files.

Using **Name** on an open file produces an error. You must close an open file before renaming it.

See Also   **Kill** Statement.

Example   This example uses the **Name** statement to rename a file. For purposes of this example, assume that the directories or folders that are specified already exist.

```
OldName = "OLDFILE" : NewName = "NEWFILE"      ' Define file names.
Name OldName As NewName                        ' Rename file.

' In Microsoft Windows.
OldName = "C:\MYDIR\OLDFILE" : NewName = "C:\YOURDIR\NEWFILE"
Name OldName As NewName                        ' Move and rename file.

' On the Macintosh.
OldName = "HD:MY FOLDER:OLDFILE" : NewName = "HD:YOUR FOLDER:NEWFILE"
Name OldName As NewName                        ' Move and rename
file.
```

NameIsAuto Property

Applies To   Trendline.

Description   **True** if Microsoft Excel automatically determines the name of the trendline. Read-write.

Syntax   *object*.**NameIsAuto**

Elements   *object*
    Required. The Trendline object.

Example   This example causes Microsoft Excel to automatically determine the name for trendline one.

```
ActiveWorkbook.Charts(1).SeriesCollection(1) _
    .Trendlines(1).NameIsAuto = True
```

NameLocal Property

Applies To   Name, Style.

Description	Returns or sets the name of the object, in the language of the user. Read-write for Name, read-only for Style.
Syntax	*object*.**NameLocal**
Elements	*object* Required. The Name or Style object.
Remarks	If the style is a built-in style, this property returns the name of the style in the language of the current locale.
See Also	**Name** Property.
Example	This example displays the name and localized name of a style.

```
With ActiveWorkbook.Styles(1)
    MsgBox "The name of the style is " & .Name
    MsgBox "The localized name of the style is " & .NameLocal
End With
```

Names Method

Applies To	Application, Workbook.
Description	Returns a single name (a Name object, Syntax 1) or a collection of names (the Names object, Syntax 2). Read-only.
Syntax 1	*object*.**Names(***index, indexLocal, refersTo***)**
Syntax 2	*object*.**Names**
Elements	The **Names** method has the following object qualifier and named arguments:

object
Optional for Application, required for Workbook. Specifies the object containing names to return.

index
Optional (Syntax 1 requires one of the three arguments). The name or number of the defined name to return.

indexLocal
Optional (Syntax 1 requires one of the three arguments). The name of the defined name, in the language of the user. No names will be translated if you use this argument.

refersTo
Optional (Syntax 1 requires one of the three arguments). What the name refers to. This allows you to get a name by what it refers to.

Remark	For Syntax 1, you must specify one (and only one) of the three arguments.
	This method returns names in the active workbook for the Application object.
Example	This example displays the number of defined names in the active workbook.

```
MsgBox "This workbook has " & ActiveWorkbook.Names.Count & _
    " defined names"
```

Names Object

Description   A collection of Name objects.

Naming-Conflict Errors

A naming-conflict bug can occur even if you use **Option Explicit**, which normally protects you from such situations. For example, if you use an undeclared identifier in a **For...Next** loop in a procedure, and that variable has the same name as one with wider scope, you can inadvertently change the variable with wider scope:

```
Option Explicit ' Forces declaration before use of variables.
Dim X    ' Module-level declaration of X.

Sub AnyProc()
    ' A Dim X statement here would prevent a bug.
    For X = 0 to 25 ' Loop counter not declared in its procedure.
        Print X ' This X is the same as the module-level X.
    Next X
    Call AnotherProc
End Sub
Sub AnotherProc()
    X = X + 1
    Print X ' This X has value of loop counter in AnyProc.
End Sub
```

See Also   **For...Next** Statement, **Option Explicit** Statement.

NavigateArrow Method

Applies To   Range.

Description	Navigates a tracer arrow for the specified range to the precedent, dependent, or error-causing cell or cells. Selects the precedent, dependent, or error cell and returns the new selection Range object. This method causes an error if applied to a cell without visible tracer arrows.
Syntax	*object*.**NavigateArrow**(*towardPrecedent, arrowNumber, linkNumber*)
Elements	The **NavigateArrow** method has the following object qualifier and named arguments:

object
Required. The Range object.

towardPrecedent
Required. Specifies the direction to navigate (**True** to navigate toward precedents or **False** to navigate toward dependents).

arrowNumber
Optional. Specifies the arrow number to navigate, corresponding to the numbered reference in the cell's formula. If this argument is omitted, this first arrow is navigated.

linkNumber
Optional. If the arrow is an external reference arrow, this argument indicates which external reference to follow. If this argument is omitted, the first external reference is followed.

Example	This example navigates a tracer arrow toward precedent cells.

```
Range("A1:A153").NavigateArrow True, 1
```

NewWindow Method

Applies To	Window, Workbook.
Description	Creates a new window for the workbook, or a copy of the specified window.
Syntax	*object*.**NewWindow**
Elements	*object* Required. The Window or Workbook object.
Example	This example creates a new window for the workbook BOOK1.XLS.

```
Workbooks("BOOK1.XLS").NewWindow
```

Next Property

Applies To	Chart, DialogSheet, Module, Range, Worksheet.
Description	Returns the next sheet or cell (a Range object). Read-only.
Syntax	*object*.**Next**
Elements	*object*
	Required. The object to which this property applies.
Remarks	If the object is a range, this property emulates the TAB key, although the property returns the next cell without selecting it.
	On a protected sheet, this property returns the next unlocked cell. On an unprotected sheet, this always returns the cell to the right of the specified cell.
See Also	**ActivateNext** Method, **Previous** Property.
Example	This example activates the next unlocked cell (if the sheet is unprotected, this is the cell immediately to the right of the active cell).

```
ActiveCell.Next.Activate
```

NextLetter Method

Applies To	Application.
Description	Opens the oldest unread Microsoft Excel letter from the In Tray. Available only in Microsoft Excel for the Apple Macintosh with the PowerTalk mail system extension installed.
Syntax	*object*.**NextLetter**
Elements	*object*
	Required. The Application object.
Remarks	This method returns a Workbook object for the newly opened workbook, or **Null** if there are no more workbooks to open.
	This method generates an error if it is used in Microsoft Windows.
See Also	**MailSystem** Property, **SendMail** Method.
Example	This example opens the oldest unread Microsoft Excel letter from the In Tray.

```
If Application.MailSystem = xlPowerTalk Then _
    Application.NextLetter
```

Not Operator

Description   Used to perform logical negation on an expression.

Syntax   *result* = **Not** *expression*

Elements   The **Not** operator syntax has these parts:

Part	Description
result	Any numeric variable.
expression	Any expression.

Remarks   The following table illustrates how *result* is determined:

If expression is	Then result is
True	False
False	True
Null	Null

In addition, the **Not** operator inverts the bit values of any variable and sets the corresponding bit in *result* according to the following truth table:

Bit in expression	Bit in result
0	1
1	0

See Also   Operator Precedence.

Example   This example uses the **Not** operator to perform logical negation on an expression.

```
A = 10: B = 8: C = 6 : D = Null ' Initialize variables.
MyCheck = Not(A > B)    ' Returns False.
MyCheck = Not(B > A)    ' Returns True.
MyCheck = Not(C > D)    ' Returns Null.
MyCheck = Not A ' Returns -11 (bit-wise comparison).
```

NoteText Method

Applies To   Range.

Description   Returns or sets the cell note associated with the upper-left cell in this range. Read-write.

Syntax	*object*.**NoteText**(*text, start, length*)
Elements	*object*

> *object*
> Required. The range to which this property applies.

> *text*
> Optional. If specified, contains the text to add to the note (up to 255 characters). The text is inserted starting at position *start*, replacing *length* characters of the existing note. If this argument is omitted, this method returns the current text of the note starting at position *start*, for *length* characters.

> *start*
> Optional. Specifies the starting position for the set or returned text. If omitted, this method starts at the first character. This argument is omitted if there is no existing note. Specify a number larger than the number of characters in the existing note to append text to the note.

> *length*
> Optional. Specifies the number of characters to set or return. If this argument is omitted, Microsoft Excel sets or returns characters from the start position to the end of the note (up to 255 characters) If there are more than 255 characters from *start* to the end of the note, this method returns only 255 characters.

Remarks   To add a note containing more than 255 characters, use this method once to specify the first 255 characters, then append the remainder of the note 255 characters at a time.

See Also   **ClearNotes** Method.

Example   This example sets the cell note for the active cell.

```
ActiveCell.NoteText "This may change!"
```

Now Function

Description   Returns the current date and time according to the setting of your computer's system date and time.

Syntax   **Now**

Remarks

Note   When displayed directly, the **Now** function's return value is displayed as a string using the short date and time formats you specified for your system.

See Also   **Date** Function, **Date** Statement, **Day** Function, **Hour** Function, **Minute** Function, **Month** Function, **Second** Function, **Time** Function, **Time** Statement, **Weekday** Function, **Year** Function.

Example   This example uses the **Now** function to return the current system date and time.

```
Today = Now    ' Get current system date and time.
```

NumberFormat Property

Applies To   DataLabel, DataLabels, PivotField, Range, Style, TickLabels.

Description   Returns or sets the format code for the object (as a string). Read-write.

Syntax   *object*.**NumberFormat**

Elements   *object*
                  Required. The object to which this property applies.

Remark   For the PivotField object, the **NumberFormat** property can be set only for a data field.

                  The format code is the same string as the Format Codes option in the Format Cells dialog box.. The **Format** function uses different format code strings than the **NumberFormat** and **NumberFormatLocal** properties.

See Also   **Format** Function, **NumberFormatLinked** Property, **NumberFormatLocal** Property.

Example   These examples set the number format for cell A17, row one and column C.

```
Range("A17").NumberFormat = "General"
Rows(1).NumberFormat = "hh:mm:ss"
Columns("C").NumberFormat = "$#,##0.00_);[Red]($#,##0.00)"
```

NumberFormatLinked Property

Applies To   DataLabel, DataLabels, TickLabels.

Description   **True** if the number format is linked to the cells (so that the number format changes in the labels when it changes in the cells). Read-write.

Syntax   *object*.**NumberFormatLinked**

Elements   *object*
                  Required. The DataLabel, DataLabels, or TickLabels object.

Example   This example links the tick label number format to its cells for the value axis.

```
Charts(1).Axes(xlValue).TickLabels.NumberFormatLinked = True
```

NumberFormatLocal Property

Applies To   Range, Style.

Description   Returns or sets the format code for the object as a string, in the language of the user (not the language of the macro writer). Read-write.

Syntax   *object*.**NumberFormatLocal**

Elements   *object*
                         Required. The Range or Style object.

Remark   The **Format** function uses different format code strings than the **NumberFormat** and **NumberFormatLocal** properties.

See Also   **Format** Function, **NumberFormat** Property.

Example   This example displays the number format for cell A17.

```
MsgBox "The number format for cell A17 is " & _
    Range("A17").NumberFormatLocal
```

Object Data Type

Object variables are stored as 32-bit (4-byte) addresses that refer to objects within an application. A variable declared as an **Object** is one that can subsequently be assigned (using the **Set** statement) to refer to any object produced by the application.

See Also   Data Type Summary, **Def***type* Statements, **IsObject** Function, **Variant** Data Type.

Object Property

Applies To   OLEObject.

Description   Returns the OLE Automation object associated with this OLE object. Read-only.

Syntax   *object*.**Object**

Elements   *object*
                         Required. The OLEObject.

Example   This example inserts text into an embedded Microsoft Word document.

```
Set wordObj = ActiveSheet.OLEObjects(1)
wordObj.Activate
With wordObj.Object.Application.WordBasic
    .Insert "Start here"
End With
```

Oct Function

Description   Returns a string representing the octal value of a number.

Syntax   **Oct(*number*)**

Elements   The *number* named argument is any valid numeric expression.

Remarks   If *number* is not already a whole number, it is rounded to the nearest whole number before being evaluated.

If *number* is	Oct returns
Null	An error.
Empty	Zero (0).
Any other number	Up to 11 octal characters.

You can represent octal numbers directly by preceding numbers in the proper range with &O. For example, &O10 is the octal notation for decimal 8.

See Also   **Hex** Function.

Example   This example uses the **Oct** function to return the octal value of a number.

```
MyOct = Oct(4)   ' Returns 4.
MyOct = Oct(8)   ' Returns 10.
MyOct = Oct(459)    ' Returns 713.
```

Offset Method

Applies To   Range.

Description   Returns a range at an offset to the specified range.

Syntax	*object*.**Offset(***rowOffset, columnOffset***)**
Elements	The **Offset** method has the following object qualifier and named arguments:

object
Required. Return a range offset to this one.

rowOffset
Optional. Number of rows (positive, negative, or zero) by which to offset the range. If omitted, zero is assumed.

columnOffset
Optional. Number of columns (positive, negative, or zero) by which to offset the range. If omitted, zero is assumed.

See Also	**Address** Method.
Example	This example activates the cell three columns to the right and three rows down from the active cell.

```
ActiveCell.Offset(3, 3).Activate
```

OLEObject Object

Description	A chart embedded on a worksheet, or a linked or embedded OLE object.

OLEObjects Method

Applies To	Chart, DialogSheet, Worksheet.
Description	Returns a single OLE Object (an OLEObject, Syntax 1) or a collection of all OLE objects (an OLEObjects collection, Syntax 2) on the chart or sheet. Read-only.
Syntax 1	*object*.**OLEObjects(***index***)**
Syntax 2	*object*.**OLEObjects**
Elements	The **OLEObjects** method has the following object qualifier and named arguments:

object
Required. The Chart, DialogSheet, or Worksheet object.

index
Required for Syntax 1. The name or number of the OLE object.

See Also	**Charts** Method, **OLEType** Property.

Example   This example creates a list of link types for OLE objects in the active sheet.

```
i = 2
Cells(1, 1).Value = "Link Type"
For Each ob In ActiveSheet.OLEObjects
    If ob.OLEType = xlOLELink Then
        Cells(i, 1) = "Linked"
    Else
        Cells(i, 1) = "Embedded"
    End If
    i = i + 1
Next
```

OLEObjects Object

Description   A collection of OLEObject objects.

OLEType Property

Applies To   OLEObject.

Description   Returns **xlOLELink** if the object is linked (exists outside of the file), or **xlOLEEmbed** if the object is embedded (is entirely contained within the file). Read-only.

Syntax   *object*.**OLEType**

Elements   *object*
                 Required. The OLEObject.

See Also   **OLEObjects** Method.

Example   This example creates a list of link types for OLE objects in the active sheet.

```
i = 2
Cells(1, 1).Value = "Link Type"
For Each ob In ActiveSheet.OLEObjects
    If ob.OLEType = xlOLELink Then
        Cells(i, 1) = "Linked"
    Else
        Cells(i, 1) = "Embedded"
    End If
    i = i + 1
Next
```

On Error Statement

Description   Enables an error-handling routine and specifies the location of the routine within a procedure; can also be used to disable an error-handling routine.

Syntax   **On Error GoTo** *line*

On Error Resume Next

On Error GoTo 0

Elements   The **On Error** statement syntax can have any of the following forms:

Statement	Description
On Error GoTo *line*	Enables the error-handling routine that starts at *line*, which is any line label or line number. Thereafter, if a run-time error occurs, control branches to *line*. The specified *line* must be in the same procedure as the **On Error** statement. If it isn't, a compile-time error occurs.
On Error Resume Next	Specifies that when a run-time error occurs, control goes to the statement immediately following the statement where the error occurred. In other words, execution continues.
On Error GoTo 0	Disables any enabled error handler in the current procedure.

Remarks   If you don't use an **On Error** statement, any run-time error that occurs is fatal; that is, an error message is generated and execution stops.

If an error occurs while an error handler is active (between the occurrence of the error and a **Resume**, **Exit Sub**, **Exit Function**, or **Exit Property** statement), the current procedure's error handler can't handle the error. If the calling procedure has an enabled error handler, control is returned to the calling procedure and its error handler is activated to handle the error. If the calling procedure's error handler is also active, control is passed back through any previous calling procedures until an inactive error handler is found. If no inactive error handler is found, the error is fatal at the point at which it actually occurred. Each time the error handler passes control back to the calling procedure, that procedure becomes the current procedure. Once an error is handled by an error handler in any procedure, execution resumes in the current procedure at the point designated by the **Resume** statement.

Notice that an error-handling routine is not a **Sub** or **Function** procedure. It is a block of code marked by a line label or line number.

Error-handling routines rely on the value in **Err** to determine the cause of the error. The error-handling routine should test or save this value before any other error can occur or before a procedure that could cause an error is called. The value in **Err** reflects only the most recent error. You can use the **Error** function to return the error message associated with any given run-time error number returned by **Err**.

On Error Resume Next causes execution to continue with the statement immediately following the statement that caused the run-time error, or with the statement immediately following the most recent call out of the procedure containing the error-handling routine. This allows execution to continue despite a run-time error. You can then build the error-handling routine in line with the procedure rather than transferring control to another location within the procedure.

On Error GoTo 0 disables error handling in the current procedure. It doesn't specify line 0 as the start of the error-handling code, even if the procedure contains a line numbered 0. Without an **On Error GoTo 0** statement, an error handler is automatically disabled when a procedure is exited.

To prevent error-handling code from running when no error has occurred, place an **Exit Sub, Exit Function**, or **Exit Property** statement, as appropriate, immediately ahead of the error-handling routine, as in the following example:

```
Sub InitializeMatrix(Var1, Var2, Var3, Var4)
    On Error GoTo ErrorHandler
    . . .
    Exit Sub
ErrorHandler:
    . . .
    Resume Next
End Sub
```

Here, the error-handling code follows the **Exit Sub** statement and precedes the **End Sub** statement to separate it from the normal procedure flow. This is only one possible solution; error-handling code can be placed anywhere in a procedure.

See Also   **Erl** Function, **Err** Function, **Error** Function, **Resume** Statement, Trappable Errors.

Example

This example uses the **On Error GoTo** statement to specify the location of an error-handling routine within a procedure. Attempting to delete an open file generates error number 55. The error is handled in the error-handling routine and control is then returned to the statement that caused it.

```
Sub OnErrorStatementDemo()
    On Error GoTo ErrorHandler      ' Enable error-handling routine.
    Open "TESTFILE" For Output as #1 ' Open file for output.
    Kill "TESTFILE"                  ' Attempt to delete open file.
    Exit Sub' Exit Sub before error handler.
ErrorHandler:                        ' Error-handling routine.
    Select Case Err                    ' Evaluate Error Number.
        Case 55                      ' "File already open" error.
            Close #1                   ' Close open file.
        Case Else

                                     ' Handle other situations here...

    End Select
    Resume                           ' Resume execution at same line
                                     ' that caused the error.
End Sub
```

On...GoSub, On...GoTo Statements

Description

Branch to one of several specified lines, depending on the value of an expression.

Syntax

On *expression* **GoSub** *destinationlist*

On *expression* **GoTo** *destinationlist*

Elements

The **On**...**GoSub** and **On**...**GoTo** statement syntax has these parts:

Part	Description
expression	Any numeric expression that evaluates to a whole number between 0 and 255, inclusive. If *expression* is any number other than a whole number, it is rounded before it is evaluated.
destinationlist	List of line numbers or line labels separated by commas.

Remarks

The value of *expression* determines which line in *destinationlist* is branched to. If the value of *expression* is less than 1 or greater than the number of items in the list, one of the following results occurs:

If expression is:	Then
Equal to 0	Control drops to the statement following **On...GoSub** or **On...GoTo**.
Greater than number of items in list	Control drops to the statement following **On...GoSub** or **On...GoTo**.
Negative	An error occurs.
Greater than 255	An error occurs.

You can mix line numbers and line labels in the same list. There is no practical limit to the number of line labels and line numbers you can use with **On...GoSub** and **On...GoTo**. However, if you use more labels or numbers than will fit on a single line, you must use the line-continuation character to continue the logical line onto the next physical line.

Tip **Select Case** provides a more structured and flexible way to perform multiple branching.

See Also

GoSub...Return Statement, **GoTo** Statement, **Select Case** Statement.

Example

This example uses the **On...GoSub** and **On...GoTo** statements to branch to subroutines and line labels respectively.

```
Sub OnGosubGotoDemo()
    Number = 2                   ' Initialize variable.
                                 ' Branch to Sub2.
    On Number GoSub Sub1, Sub2   ' Execution resumes here after
                                 ' On...GoSub.
    On Number GoTo Line1, Line2  ' Branch to Line2.
                 ' Execution does not resume here after On...GoTo.
    Exit Sub
Sub1:
    MyString = "In Sub1" : Return
Sub2:
    MyString = "In Sub2" : Return
Line1:
    MyString = "In Line1"
Line2:
    MyString = "In Line2"
End Sub
```

OnAction Property

Applies To	Arc, Arcs, Button, Buttons, ChartObject, ChartObjects, CheckBox, CheckBoxes, DialogFrame, Drawing, DrawingObjects, Drawings, DropDown, DropDowns, EditBox, EditBoxes, GroupBox, GroupBoxes, GroupObject, GroupObjects, Label, Labels, Line, Lines, ListBox, ListBoxes, OLEObject, OLEObjects, OptionButton, OptionButtons, Oval, Ovals, Picture, Pictures, Rectangle, Rectangles, ScrollBar, ScrollBars, Spinner, Spinners, TextBox, TextBoxes, ToolbarButton.
Description	Returns or sets the name of a macro that runs when the object is clicked. Read-write.
Syntax	*object*.**OnAction**
Elements	*object* Required. The object to which this property applies.
Example	This example causes the "my_Debug_Macro" macro to run when the third button on toolbar one is clicked.

```
Application.ToolBars(1).ToolbarButtons(3).OnAction = "my_Debug_Macro"
```

OnCalculate Property

Applies To	Application, Worksheet.
Description	Returns or sets the name of the macro that runs whenever you recalculate the worksheet. Read-write.
Syntax	*object*.**OnCalculate**
Elements	*object* Required. The object to which this property applies.
Remarks	Setting this property for a worksheet overrides any macro that may be set for the application. Set this property to empty text ("") to remove the macro. A macro set to run by the **OnCalculate** property is not run by actions taken by other macros. For example, a macro set by **OnCalculate** will not run if a macro calls the **Calculate** method, but will be run if you change data in a sheet set to calculate automatically or choose the Calc Now button.

Example	This example causes Microsoft Excel to run "my_Recalc_Macro" when you recalculate any worksheet in the application (unless that worksheet sets the **OnCalculate** property for itself).

```
Application.OnCalculate = "my_Recalc_Macro"
```

OnData Property

Applies To	Application, Worksheet.
Description	Returns or sets the name of the procedure that runs when DDE- or OLE-linked data arrives in Microsoft Excel. The specified procedure runs only when data arrives from another application. Read-write.
Syntax	*object*.**OnData**
Elements	*object* Required. The object to which this property applies.
Remarks	Set this property to " " (empty text) to remove the procedure.
Example	This example runs my_Worksheet_Data_Handler if data arrives in the active worksheet, and runs my_Global_Data_Handler if data arrives anywhere else.

```
ActiveSheet.OnData = "my_Worksheet_Data_Handler"
Application.OnData = "my_Global_Data_Handler"
```

OnDoubleClick Property

Applies To	Application, Chart, DialogSheet, Module, Worksheet.
Description	Returns or sets the name of the macro that runs whenever you double-click anywhere on the chart or sheet. Read-write.
Syntax	*object*.**OnDoubleClick**
Elements	*object* Required. The Application, Chart, DialogSheet, Module, or Worksheet object.
Remarks	Setting this property for a worksheet overrides any macro that may be set for the application.
	This property overrides Microsoft Excel's normal double-click behavior, such as editing data in a cell or displaying a formatting dialog box.
	Set this property to empty text ("") to remove the macro.

See Also	**DoubleClick** Method.
Example	This example causes Microsoft Excel to run the macro "my_DblClick_Macro" when you double-click anywhere on the active sheet.

```
ActiveSheet.OnDoubleClick = "my_DblClick_Macro"
```

OnEntry Property

Applies To	Application, Worksheet.
Description	Returns or sets the name of the procedure that runs whenever you enter data using the formula bar or when you edit data in a cell. Read-write.
Syntax	*object*.**OnEntry**
Elements	*object* Required. The object to which this property applies.
Remarks	The procedure does not run when you use edit commands or macro functions.
	Set this property to " " (empty text) to remove the procedure.
	To determine which cell had data entered in it, use the **Caller** property.
Example	This example runs my_Worksheet_Entry_Procedure when data is entered on the active worksheet, and my_Global_Entry_Procedure when data is entered anywhere else.

```
ActiveSheet.OnEntry = "my_Worksheet_Entry_Procedure"
Application.OnEntry = "my_Global_Entry_Procedure"
```

OnKey Method

Applies To	Application.
Description	Runs a specified procedure when a particular key or key combination is pressed.
Syntax	*object*.**OnKey**(*key, procedure*)
Elements	The **OnKey** method has the following object qualifier and named arguments:
	object Required. The Application object.
	key Required. A string indicating the keystroke.

procedure

Optional. A string indicating the name of the procedure. If *procedure* is " " (empty text), nothing happens when *key* is pressed. This form of **OnKey** disables the normal meaning of keystrokes in Microsoft Excel. If *procedure* is omitted, *key* reverts to its normal meaning in Microsoft Excel, and any special key assignments made with previous **OnKey** methods are cleared.

Remarks

The *key* argument can specify any single key, or any key combined with ALT, CTRL, or SHIFT, or any combination of those keys (in Microsoft Excel for Windows) or COMMAND, CTRL, OPTION, or SHIFT or any combination of those keys (in Microsoft Excel for the Macintosh). Each key is represented by one or more characters, such as "a" for the character a, or "{ENTER}" for the ENTER key.

To specify characters that aren't displayed when you press the key, such as ENTER or TAB, use the codes shown in the following table. Each code in the table represents one key on the keyboard.

Key	Code
BACKSPACE	"{BACKSPACE}" or "{BS}"
BREAK	"{BREAK}"
CAPS LOCK	"{CAPSLOCK}"
CLEAR	"{CLEAR}"
DELETE or DEL	"{DELETE}" or "{DEL}"
DOWN ARROW	"{DOWN}"
END	"{END}"
ENTER (numeric keypad)	"{ENTER}"
ENTER	"~" (tilde)
ESC	"{ESCAPE} or {ESC}"
HELP	"{HELP}"
HOME	"{HOME}"
INS	"{INSERT}"
LEFT ARROW	"{LEFT}"
NUM LOCK	"{NUMLOCK}"
PAGE DOWN	"{PGDN}"
PAGE UP	"{PGUP}"
RETURN	"{RETURN}"
RIGHT ARROW	"{RIGHT}"
SCROLL LOCK	"{SCROLLLOCK}"
TAB	"{TAB}"
UP ARROW	"{UP}"
F1 through F15	"{F1}" through "{F15}"

In Microsoft Excel for Windows, you can also specify keys combined with SHIFT and/or CTRL and/or ALT. In Microsoft Excel for the Macintosh, you can also specify keys combined with SHIFT and/or CTRL and/or OPTION and/or COMMAND. To specify a key combined with another key or keys, use the following table:

To combine with	Precede the key code by
SHIFT	"+" (plus sign)
CTRL	"^" (caret)
ALT or OPTION	"%" (percent sign)
COMMAND	"*" (asterisk)

To assign a procedure to one of the special characters (+, ^, %, and so on), enclose the character in braces. See the example for details.

Examples

This example assigns my_InsertItem_Procedure to the key sequence CTRL+PLUS SIGN and my_SpecialPrint_Procedure to the key sequence SHIFT+CTRL+RIGHT.

```
Application.OnKey "^{+}", "my_InsertItem_Procedure"
Application.OnKey "+^{RIGHT}", "my_SpecialPrint_Procedure"
```

This example returns SHIFT+CTRL+RIGHT to its normal meaning.

```
Application.OnKey "+^{RIGHT}"
```

This example disables the SHIFT+CTRL+RIGHT key sequence.

```
Application.OnKey "+^{RIGHT}", ""
```

OnRepeat Method

Applies To

Application.

Description

Sets the Repeat menu item and the name of the procedure that will run if you choose Repeat from the Edit menu after running the procedure that sets this property.

Syntax

object.**OnRepeat**(*text, procedure*)

Elements

The **OnRepeat** method has the following object qualifier and named arguments:

object
Required. The Application object.

text
Required. Specifies the text that appears with the Repeat command on the Edit menu.

procedure
> Required. Specifies the name of the procedure that will run when you choose Repeat from the Edit menu.

Remarks
If a procedure does not use the OnRepeat method, the Repeat command repeats the most recently run procedure.

The procedure must use the **OnRepeat** and **OnUndo** methods last, to prevent the repeat or undo procedures from being overwritten by subsequent actions in the procedure.

See Also
OnUndo Method, **Repeat** Method.

Example
This example sets the repeat and undo procedures.

```
Application.OnRepeat "Repeat VB Procedure", _
    "Book1.xls!My_Repeat_Sub"
Application.OnUndo "Undo VB Procedure", _
    "Book1.xls!My_Undo_Sub"
```

OnSheetActivate Property

Applies To
Application, Chart, DialogSheet, Module, Workbook, Worksheet.

Description
Returns or sets the name of the macro that runs when the user activates the specified sheet (Chart, DialogSheet, Module, or Worksheet object), any sheet in the specified workbook (Workbook object), or any sheet in any open workbook (Application object). Read-write.

Syntax
object.**OnSheetActivate**

Elements
object
> Required. The object to which this property applies.

Remark
To disable an **OnSheetActivate** macro, set the property to an empty string, as shown in the examples.

See Also
OnSheetDeactivate Property, **OnWindow** Property, **RunAutoMacros** Method.

Examples
This example sets the **OnSheetActivate** property to the macro "my_Activate_Sub" in Module1 in the active workbook. This macro will run whenever the user activates a sheet in any workbook.

```
Application.OnSheetActivate = ActiveWorkbook.Name & _
    "!Module1.my_Activate_Sub"
```

This example disables the **OnSheetActivate** macro.

```
Application.OnSheetActivate = ""
```

OnSheetDeactivate Property

Applies To   Application, Chart, DialogSheet, Module, Workbook, Worksheet.

Description   Returns or sets the name of the macro that runs when the user deactivates the specified sheet (Chart, DialogSheet, Module, or Worksheet object), any sheet in the specified workbook (Workbook object), or any sheet in any open workbook (Application object). Read-write.

Syntax   *object*.**OnSheetDeactivate**

Elements   *object*
     Required. The object to which this property applies.

See Also   **OnSheetActivate** Property, **OnWindow** Property, **RunAutoMacros** Method.

Example   This example sets the **OnSheetDeactivate** property to the macro "my_Deactivate_Sub" in Module1 in the active workbook. This macro will run whenever the user deactivates a sheet in any workbook.

```
Application.OnSheetDeactivate = ActiveWorkbook.Name & _
    "!Module1.my_Deactivate_Sub"
```

OnTime Method

Applies To   Application.

Description   Schedules a procedure to run at a specified time in the future (either at a specific time of day or after a specific period has passed).

Syntax   *object*.**OnTime**(*earliestTime, procedure, latestTime, schedule*)

Elements   The **OnTime** method has the following object qualifier and named arguments:

object
     Required. The Application object.

earliestTime
     Required. The time when you want this procedure to run.

procedure
     Required. The name of the procedure to run.

latestTime
     Optional. The latest time the procedure can be run. For example, if *latestTime* is set to *earliestTime* + 30 and Microsoft Excel is not in Ready, Copy, Cut, or Find mode at *earliestTime* because another procedure is running, Microsoft

Excel will wait 30 seconds for the first procedure to complete. If Microsoft Excel is not in Ready mode within 30 seconds, the procedure will not run. If this argument is omitted, Microsoft Excel will wait until the procedure can be run.

schedule
Optional. **False** to clear a previously set **OnTime** procedure. **True** (or omitted) to schedule a new procedure.

Remarks   Use `Now + TimeValue(time)` to schedule something at a time after the current time. Use `TimeValue(time)` to schedule something at a specific time.

Examples   This example runs my_Procedure 15 seconds from now:

```
Application.OnTime Now + TimeValue("00:00:15"), "my_Procedure"
```

This example runs my_Procedure at 5 P.M.:

```
Application.OnTime TimeValue("17:00:00"), "my_Procedure"
```

This example cancels the **OnTime** setting from the previous example:

```
Application.OnTime TimeValue("17:00:00"), "my_Procedure",,False
```

OnUndo Method

Applies To   Application.

Description   Sets the Undo menu item and the name of the procedure that will run if you choose Undo from the Edit menu after running the procedure that sets this property.

Syntax   *object*.**OnUndo**(*text, procedure*)

Elements   The **OnUndo** method has the following object qualifier and named arguments:

object
Required. The Application object.

text
Required. Specifies the text that appears with the Undo command on the Edit menu.

procedure
Required. Specifies the name of the procedure that runs when you choose Undo from the Edit menu.

Remarks   If a procedure does not use the OnUndo method, the Undo command is disabled.

The procedure must use the **OnRepeat** and **OnUndo** methods last, to prevent the repeat or undo procedures from being overwritten by subsequent actions in the procedure.

See Also	**OnRepeat** Method, **Repeat** Method.
Example	This example sets the repeat and undo procedures.

```
Application.OnRepeat "Repeat VB Procedure", _
    "Book1.xls!My_Repeat_Sub"
Application.OnUndo "Undo VB Procedure", _
    "Book1.xls!My_Undo_Sub"
```

OnWindow Property

Applies To	Application, Window.
Description	Returns or sets the name of the procedure that runs whenever you switch to a window. Read-write.
Syntax	*object*.**OnWindow**
Elements	*object*
	Required. The object to which this property applies.
Remarks	The procedure specified by this property does not run when other procedures switch to the window or when a command to switch to a window is received through a DDE channel. Instead, the procedure responds to a user's actions, such as clicking a window with the mouse, choosing the Go To command from the Edit menu, and so on.
	If a worksheet or macro sheet has an Auto_Activate or Auto_Deactivate macro defined for it, those macros will be run after the procedure specified by **OnWindow**.
Example	This example runs my_Stock_Procedure when you switch to the STOCKS.XLS window.

```
Application.Windows("STOCKS.XLS").OnWindow = "my_Stock_Procedure"
```

Open Method

Applies To	Workbooks.
Description	Opens a workbook.

Syntax

object.**Open**(*fileName, updateLinks, readOnly, format, password, writeResPassword, ignoreReadOnlyRecommended, origin, delimiter, editable, notify, converter*)

Elements

object
Required. The Workbooks object.

fileName
Specifies the filename of the workbook to open.

updateLinks
Optional. Specifies how links in the file are updated. If this argument is omitted, the user is prompted to determine how to update links. Otherwise, this argument is one of the following:

0	No updates
1	Updates external but not remote references
2	Updates remote but not external references
3	Updates both remote and external references

If Microsoft Excel is opening a file in the WKS, WK1, or WK3 format and the *updateLinks* argument is 2, Microsoft Excel generates charts from the graphs attached to the file. If the argument is 0, no charts are created.

readOnly
Optional. If **True**, the workbook is opened in read-only mode.

format
Optional. If Microsoft Excel is opening a text file, this argument specifies the delimiter character, as shown in the following list. If this argument is omitted, the current delimiter is used.

Value	Delimiter
1	Tabs
2	Commas
3	Spaces
4	Semicolons
5	Nothing
6	Custom character, see the *delimiter* argument.

password
Optional. A string containing the password required to open a protected workbook. If omitted and the workbook requires a password, the user is prompted for the password.

writeResPassword
> Optional. A string containing the password required to write to a write-reserved workbook. If omitted and the workbook requires a password, the user will be prompted for the password.

ignoreReadOnlyRecommended
> Optional. If **True** and the workbook was saved with the Read-Only Recommended option, Microsoft Excel does not display the read-only recommended message.

origin
> Optional. If the file is a text file, this indicates where it originated (so that code pages and CR/LF can be mapped correctly). May be one of **xlMacintosh**, **xlWindows**, or **xlMSDOS**. If this argument is omitted, the current operating system is used.

delimiter
> Optional. If the file is a text file and the *format* argument is 6, this is a string that specifies the character to use as the delimiter. For example, Chr(9) for tabs, "","" for commas, ";" for semicolons, or a custom character. Only the first character of the string is used.

editable
> Optional. If the file is a Microsoft Excel 4.0 add-in, using **True** opens the addin so that it is a visible window. If **False** or omitted, the add-in is opened hidden and it cannot be unhidden. This option does not apply for Microsoft Excel 5.0 Addins. If the file is not an addin, specifying **True** prevents the running of any Auto_Open macros.

notify
> Optional. If the file cannot be opened in the mode requested by *readOnly*, specifying **True** adds the file to the file notification list. Microsoft Excel will open the file read-only, poll the file notification list, and then notify the user when the file becomes available. If this argument is **False** or omitted, no notification is requested, and attempts to open an unavailable file will fail.

converter
> Optional. Specifies the index of the first file converter to try when opening the file. The specified file converter is tried first, then all other converters are tried if the specified converter does not recognize the file. The converter index is the row number of the converters returned by the **FileConverters** property.

Remarks   If the workbook being opened has any Auto_Open macros in it, they will not be run when you open the file from Visual Basic. If you want to run the Auto_Open macro, you must use the **RunAutoMacros** method.

See Also   **Activate** Method, **Close** Method, **FileConverters** Property, **OpenText** Method.

Example   This example opens the workbook OSCAR.XLS with the password "drowssap.""

```
Workbooks.Open fileName:="OSCAR.XLS", password:="drowssap"
```

Open Statement

Description   Enables input/output (I/O) to a file.

Syntax   **Open** *pathname* [**For** *mode*] [**Access** *access*] [*lock*] **As** [#]*filenumber* [**Len**=*reclength*]

Elements   The **Open** statement syntax has these parts:

Part	Description
pathname	String expression that specifies a file name{bmc emdash.bmp}may include directory or folder, and drive.
mode	Keyword specifying the file mode: **Append**, **Binary**, **Input**, **Output**, or **Random**.
access	Keyword specifying the operations permitted on the open file: **Read**, **Write**, or **Read Write**.
lock	Keyword specifying the operations permitted on the open file by other processes: **Shared**, **Lock Read**, **Lock Write**, **Lock Read Write**.
filenumber	A valid file number in the range 1 to 511, inclusive. Use the **FreeFile** function to obtain the next available file number.
reclength	Number less than or equal to 32,767 (bytes). For files opened for random access, this value is the record length. For sequential files, this value is the number of characters buffered.

Remarks   You must open a file before any I/O operation can be performed on it. **Open** allocates a buffer for I/O to the file and determines the mode of access to use with the buffer.

If the file specified by *pathname* doesn't exist, it is created when a file is opened for **Append**, **Binary**, **Output**, or **Random** modes.

If the file is already opened by another process and the specified type of access is not allowed, the **Open** operation fails and an error occurs.

The **Len** clause is ignored if *mode* is **Binary**.

Important In **Binary**, **Input**, and **Random** modes, you can open a file using a different file number without first closing the file. In **Append** and **Output** modes, you must close a file before opening it with a different file number.

On the Macintosh, the file mode specified in the **Open** statement determines the initial **Creator** and **Type** property settings:

File mode	Creator	Type
Output	????	TEXT
Append	????	TEXT
Random	????	OBIN
Binary	????	OBIN
Unspecified	????	OBIN

See Also

Close Statement, **FreeFile** Function.

Example

This example illustrates various uses of the **Open** statement to enable input/output to a file.

```
' Open in sequential-input mode.
Open "TESTFILE" For Input As #1

' Open in binary-file mode for writing operations only.
Open "TESTFILE" For Binary Access Write As #1

' Open file in random-access mode. The file contains records of the
' user-defined type Record.
Type Record           ' Define user-defined type.
    ID As Integer
    Name As String * 20
End Type
Dim MyRecord As Record   ' Declare variable.
Open "TESTFILE" For Random As #1 Len = Len(MyRecord)

' Open for sequential output; any process can read/write to file.
Open "TESTFILE" For Output Shared As #1

' Open in binary-file mode for reading; other processes can't read
' file.
Open "TESTFILE" For Binary Access Read Lock Read As #1
```

OpenLinks Method

Applies To

Workbook.

Description

Opens the supporting documents for a link or links.

Syntax	*object*.**OpenLinks**(*name, readOnly, type*)
Elements	The **OpenLinks** method has the following object qualifier and named arguments:

object
Required. The Workbook object.

name
Required. Specifies the name of the Microsoft Excel or DDE/OLE link, as returned from the **LinkSources** method (can be an array of names to specify more than one link).

readOnly
Optional. **True** if the documents are opened read-only. **False** if omitted.

type
Optional. Specifies the link type. Can be one of **xlExcelLinks**, **xlOLELinks** (also handles DDE links), **xlPublishers**, or **xlSubscribers**. **xlExcelLinks** if omitted.

Examples	This example opens the link supporting documents.

```
ActiveWorkbook.OpenLinks "WinWord|'C:\MSGFILE.DOC'!DDE_LINK1", _
    xlOLELinks
```

This example opens all supporting Microsoft Excel documents for the active workbook.

```
ActiveWorkbook.OpenLinks _
    name:=ActiveWorkbook.LinkSources(xlExcelLinks)
```

OpenText Method

Applies To	Workbooks.
Description	Loads and parses a text file as a new workbook with a single sheet containing the parsed text-file data.
Syntax	*object*.**OpenText**(*filename, origin, startRow, dataType, textQualifier, consecutiveDelimiter, tab, semicolon, comma, space, other, otherChar, fieldInfo*)
Elements	The **OpenText** method has the following object qualifier and named arguments:

object
Required. The Workbooks object.

filename
Required. Specifies the filename of the text file to open and parse.

origin

Optional. Specifies the origin of the text file (one of **xlMacintosh**, **xlWindows**, or **xlMSDOS**). If this argument is omitted, the method uses the current setting in the File Origin option of the Text Import Wizard.

startRow

Optional. The row number at which to start parsing text. The first row is 1. If omitted, 1 is assumed.

dataType

Optional. Specifies the column format of the data within the file (either **xlDelimited** or **xlFixedWidth**). The default is **xlDelimited**.

textQualifier

Optional. Specifies the text qualifier. Can be one of **xlDoubleQuote**, **xlSingleQuote**, or **xlNone**. The default is **xlDoubleQuote**.

consecutiveDelimiter

Optional. **True** if consecutive delimiters should be considered as one delimiter. The default is **False**.

tab

Optional. **True** if *dataType* is **xlDelimited** and the tab character is a delimiter. The default is **False**.

semicolon

Optional. **True** if *dataType* is **xlDelimited** and the semicolon character is a delimiter. The default is **False**.

comma

Optional. **True** if *dataType* is **xlDelimited** and the comma character is a delimiter. The default is **False**.

space

Optional. **True** if *dataType* is **xlDelimited** and the space character is a delimiter. The default is **False**.

other

Optional. **True** if *dataType* is **xlDelimited** and the character specified by the *otherChar* argument is a delimiter. The default is **False**.

otherChar

Optional (required if *other* is **True**). Specifies the delimiter character when *other* is True. If more than one character is specified, only the first character of the string is used, remaining characters are ignored.

fieldInfo

Optional. An array containing parse information for the individual columns of data. The interpretation depends on the value of *dataType*.

When the data is delimited, this argument is an array of two-element arrays, with each two-element array specifying the conversion options for a particular column. The first element is the column number (one based), and the second element is one of the following numbers specifying how the column in parsed:

1   General

2   Text

3   MDY date

4   DMY date

5   YMD date

6   MYD date

7   DYM date

8   YDM date

9   Skip the column

The column specifiers may be in any order. If a column specifier is not present for a particular column in the input data, the column is parsed using the General setting. This example causes the third column to be skipped, the first column to be parsed as text, and the remaining columns in the source data to be parsed with the General setting:

```
Array(Array(3, 9), Array(1, 2))
```

If the source data has fixed-width columns, the first element of each two-element array specifies the starting character position in the column (as an integer; character zero is the first character). The second element of the two-element array specifies the parse option for the column as a number from one through nine, as listed above.

The following example parses two columns from a fixed-width file, with the first column starting at the beginning of the line and extending for 10 characters. The second column starts at position 15 and goes to the end of the line. To avoid including the characters between position 10 and position 15, a skipped column entry is added.

```
Array(Array(0, 1), Array(10, 9), Array(15, 1))
```

See Also   **Close** Method, **Open** Method, **TextToColumns** Method.

Example   This example opens the file DATA.TXT using tab delimiters.

```
Workbooks.OpenText filename:="DATA.TXT", _
    dataType:=xlDelimited, tab:=True
```

OperatingSystem Property

Applies To	Application.
Description	Returns the name and version number of the current operating system. For example, "Windows 3.10" or "Macintosh 7.00". Read-only.
Syntax	*object*.**OperatingSystem**
Elements	*object* Required. The Application object.
Example	This example displays the name of the operating system.

```
MsgBox "Microsoft Excel is using " & Application.OperatingSystem
```

Operator Precedence

When several operations occur in an expression, each part is evaluated and resolved in a predetermined order. That order is known as operator precedence. Parentheses can be used to override the order of precedence and force some parts of an expression to be evaluated before others. Operations within parentheses are always performed before those outside. Within parentheses, however, normal operator precedence is maintained.

When expressions contain operators from more than one category, arithmetic operators are evaluated first, comparison operators are evaluated next, and logical operators are evaluated last. Comparison operators all have equal precedence; that is, they are evaluated in the left to right order in which they appear. Arithmetic and logical operators are evaluated in the following order of precedence:

Arithmetic	Comparison	Logical
Exponentiation (^)	Equality (=)	Not
Negation (-)	Inequality (<>)	And
Multiplication and division (*,/)	Less than (<)	Or
Integer division (\)	Greater than (>)	Xor
Modulo arithmetic (**Mod**)	Less than or Equal to (<=)	Eqv
Addition and subtraction (+,-)	Greater than or Equal to (>=)	Imp
String concatenation (**&**)	**Like**	**Is**

When multiplication and division occur together in an expression, each operation is evaluated as it occurs from left to right. Likewise, when addition and subtraction occur together in an expression, each operation is evaluated in order of appearance from left to right.

The string concatenation operator (**&**) is not really an arithmetic operator, but in precedence it does fall after all arithmetic operators and before all comparison operators. Similarly, the **Like** operator, while equal in precedence to all comparison operators, is actually a pattern-matching operator. The **Is** operator is an object reference comparison operator. It does not compare objects or their values; it checks only to determine if two object references refer to the same object.

Arithmetic Operators	^ Operator
	* Operator
	/ Operator
	\ Operator
	Mod Operator
	+ Operator
	- Operator
Concatenation Operators	**&** Operator
	+ Operator
Logical Operators	**And** Operator
	Eqv Operator
	Imp Operator
	Not Operator
	Or Operator
	Xor Operator

Option Base Statement

Description   Used at module level to declare the default lower bound for array subscripts.

Syntax

Option Base {0 | 1}

Remarks

If used, the **Option Base** statement must appear in a module before any statements that declare variables or define constants.

Since the default base is **0**, the **Option Base** statement is never required. However, if used, it can appear only once in a module and must precede array declarations that include dimensions.

The **Option Base** statement has no effect on arrays within user-defined types for which the lower bound is always 0.

Tip The **To** clause in the **Dim**, **Private**, **Public**, **ReDim**, and **Static** statements provides a more flexible way to control the range of an array's subscripts. However, if you don't explicitly set the lower bound with a **To** clause, you can use **Option Base** to change the default lower bound to 1.

The **Option Base** statement only affects the lower bound of arrays in the module where the statement is located.

See Also

Dim Statement, **LBound** Function, **Option Compare** Statement, **Option Explicit** Statement, **Option Private** Statement, **Private** Statement, **Public** Statement, **ReDim** Statement, **Static** Statement.

Example

This example uses the **Option Base** statement to override the default base array subscript value of 0. The **LBound** function returns the smallest available subscript for the indicated dimension of an array. The **Option Base** statement is used at the module-level only.

```
' Set default array subscripts to 1.
Option Base 1

Dim MyArray(20), TwoDArray(3,4)     ' Declare array variables.
Dim ZeroArray(0 To 5)               ' Override default base subscript.
' Use LBound function to test lower bounds of arrays.
Lower = LBound(MyArray)             ' Returns 1.
Lower = LBound(TwoDArray, 2)        ' Returns 1.
Lower = LBound(ZeroArray)           ' Returns 0.
```

Option Compare Statement

Description

Used at module level to declare the default comparison mode to use when string data is compared.

Syntax	**Option Compare** {**Binary**	**Text**}
Remarks	If used, the **Option Compare** statement must appear in a module before any statements that declare variables or define constants.

The **Option Compare** statement specifies the string comparison method (**Binary** or **Text**) for a module. If a module doesn't include an **Option Compare** statement, the default text comparison method is **Binary**.

Option Compare Binary results in string comparisons based on a sort order derived from the internal binary representations of the characters. In Microsoft Windows, sort order is determined by the code page. On the Macintosh, sort order is determined by the character set. In the following example, a typical binary sort order is shown:

```
A < B < E < Z < a < b < e  < z < À < Ê < Ø < à < ê < ø
```

Option Compare Text results in string comparisons based on a case-insensitive textual sort order determined by your system's locale. The same characters shown above, when sorted using **Option Compare Text**, produce the following text sort order:

```
(A=a) < ( À=à) < (B=b) < (E=e) < (Ê=ê) < (Z=z) < (Ø=ø)
```

See Also	Character Set, **InStr** Function, **Option Base** Statement, **Option Explicit** Statement, **Option Private** Statement, **StrComp** Function.
Example	This example uses the **Option Compare** statement to set the default string comparison mode. The **Option Compare** statement is used at the module-level only.

```
' Set the string comparison method to Binary.
Option Compare Binary      ' i.e. "AAA" less than "aaa"
' Set the string comparison method to Text.
Option Compare Text        ' i.e. "AAA" equal to "aaa".
```

Option Explicit Statement

Description	Used at module level to force explicit declaration of all variables in that module.
Syntax	**Option Explicit**
Remarks	If used, the **Option Explicit** statement must appear in a module before any statements that declare variables or define constants.

If you don't use the **Option Explicit** statement, all undeclared variables are **Variant** unless the default type is otherwise specified with a **Def***type* statement.

When you use the **Option Explicit** statement, you must explicitly declare all variables using the **Dim**, **Private**, **Public**, **ReDim**, or **Static** statements. If you attempt to use an undeclared variable name, an error occurs at compile time.

Tip Use **Option Explicit** to avoid incorrectly typing the name of an existing variable or to avoid risking confusion in code where the scope of the variable is not clear.

See Also **Const** Statement, **Dim** Statement, **Function** Statement, **Option Base** Statement, **Option Compare** Statement, **Option Private** Statement, **Private** Statement, **Public** Statement, **ReDim** Statement, **Static** Statement, **Sub** Statement.

Example This example uses the **Option Explicit** statement to force you to explicitly declare all variables. Attempting to use an undeclared variable gives you an error at compile time. The **Option Explicit** statement is used at the module-level only.

```
Option Explicit  ' Force explicit variable declaration.
Dim MyVar        ' Declare variable.
MyInt = 10       ' Undeclared variable generates error.
MyVar = 10       ' Will not generate error.
```

Option Private Statement

Description Used at module level to indicate that an entire module is **Private**.

Syntax **Option Private Module**

Remarks If used, the **Option Private** statement must appear in a module before any statements that declare variables or define constants.

The public parts (variables, objects, and user-defined types declared at module level) of modules declared **Private** using the **Option Private** statement are still available within the project containing the module, but they are not available to other applications or projects.

See Also **Option Base** Statement, **Option Compare** Statement, **Option Explicit** Statement, **Private** Statement.

Example This **Option Private** statement is used at the module-level to indicate that the entire module is private.

```
Option Private Module   ' Indicate that module is private.
```

OptionButton Object

Description   Option buttons (also known as radio buttons) allow the user to select one of a list of options.

Remarks   Option buttons are usually placed within a group box control (GroupBox object). Option buttons have no font, border, or pattern formatting, but they can be positioned and sized.

OptionButtons Method

Applies To   Chart, DialogSheet, Worksheet.

Description   Returns a single option button control (an OptionButton object, Syntax 1) or a collection of option button controls on the chart or sheet (an OptionButtons object, Syntax 2).

Syntax 1   *object*.**OptionButtons(***index***)**

Syntax 2   *object*.**OptionButtons**

Elements   The **OptionButtons** method has the following object qualifier and named arguments:

object
     Required. The Chart, DialogSheet, or Worksheet object.

index
     Required for Syntax 1. Specifies the name or number of the option button (can be an array to specify more than one).

Example   This example displays the number of option buttons on dialog sheet one.

```
cOptionButtons = Application.Dialogsheets(1).OptionButtons.Count
MsgBox "There are " & cOptionButtons & _
    " option buttons on dialog sheet one."
```

OptionButtons Object

Description   A collection of OptionButton objects.

Or Operator

Description   Used to perform a logical disjunction on two expressions.

Syntax   *result = expression1* **Or** *expression2*

Elements   The **Or** operator syntax has these parts:

Part	Description
result	Any numeric variable.
expression1	Any expression.
expression2	Any expression.

Remarks   If either or both expressions evaluate **True**, *result* is **True**. The following table illustrates how *result* is determined:

If expression1 is	And expression2 is	The result is
True	**True**	**True**
True	**False**	**True**
True	**Null**	**True**
False	**True**	**True**
False	**False**	**False**
False	**Null**	**Null**
Null	**True**	**True**
Null	**False**	**Null**
Null	**Null**	**Null**

The **Or** operator also performs a bit-wise comparison of identically positioned bits in two numeric expressions and sets the corresponding bit in *result* according to the following truth table:

If bit in *expression1* is	And bit in *expression2* is	The *result* is
0	0	0
0	1	1
1	0	1
1	1	1

See Also   Operator Precedence.

Example

This example uses the **Or** operator to perform logical disjunction on two expressions.

```
A = 10: B = 8: C = 6 : D = Null     ' Initialize variables.
MyCheck = A > B Or B > C              ' Returns True.
MyCheck = B > A Or B > C              ' Returns True.
MyCheck = A > B Or B > D              ' Returns True.
MyCheck = B > D Or B > A              ' Returns Null.
MyCheck = A Or B    ' Returns 10 (bit-wise comparison).
```

Order Property

Applies To

PageSetup, Trendline.

Description

PageSetup object: Returns or sets the order that Microsoft Excel uses to number pages when printing a large worksheet (either **xlDownThenOver** or **xlOverThenDown**). Read-write.

Trendline object: Returns or sets the trendline order (an integer greater than one) when the trendline **Type** is **xlPolynomial**. Read-write.

Syntax

object.**Order**

Elements

object
   Required. The PageSetup or Trendline object.

Remarks

For the PageSetup object, this property applies only to worksheets.

Example

This example makes Microsoft Excel break the active worksheet into pages by moving over first, then down.

```
ActiveSheet.PageSetup.Order = xlOverThenDown
```

OrganizationName Property

Applies To

Application.

Description

Returns the registered organization name (as a string). Read-only.

Syntax

object.**OrganizationName**

Elements

object
   Required. The Application object.

Example

This example sets the string variable usersWorkplace to the registered organization name.

```
usersWorkplace = Application.OrganizationName
```

Orientation Property

Applies To

AxisTitle, Button, Buttons, ChartTitle, DataLabel, DataLabels, DrawingObjects, GroupObject, GroupObjects, PageSetup, PivotField, Range, Style, TextBox, TextBoxes, TickLabels.

Description

Returns or sets the object's orientation, as shown in the following table.

Object	Orientation
PageSetup	Portrait or landscape printing mode. One of **xlPortrait** or **xlLandscape**.
PivotField	Location of the field in the pivot table. One of **xlHidden**, **xlRowField**, **xlColumnField**, **xlPageField**, or **xlDataField**.
AxisTitle, Button, ChartTitle, DataLabel, DrawingObjects, GroupObject, RadarAxisLabels, Range, Style, TextBox, TickLabels	The text orientation. One of **xlHorizontal**, **xlVertical**, **xlUpward**, or **xlDownward**. Can also be **xlAutomatic** for TickLabels only.

Syntax

object.**Orientation**

Elements

object
Required. The object to which this property applies.

Examples

This example displays the orientation for the active field.

```
Select Case ActiveCell.PivotField.Orientation
    Case xlHidden
        MsgBox "Hidden field"
    Case xlRowField
        MsgBox "Row field"
    Case xlColumnField
        MsgBox "Column field"
    Case xlPageField
        MsgBox "Page field"
    Case xlDataField
        MsgBox "Data field"
End Select
```

This example sets the first worksheet to print in landscape mode.

```
Worksheets(1).PageSetup.Orientation = xlLandscape
```

Outline Object

Description   An outline on a document.

The Outline object contains outline settings for a worksheet. The following properties and methods control outlining for worksheet ranges:

ApplyOutlineStyles Method

AutoOutline Method

ClearOutline Method

DisplayOutline Property

Group Method

OutlineLevel Property

ShowDetail Property

Ungroup Method

Outline Property

Applies To   Worksheet.

Description   Returns an Outline object for the specified worksheet.

Syntax   *object*.**Outline**

Elements   *object*
        Required. The Worksheet object.

Example   This example sets the outline for the active sheet to use automatic styles

```
ActiveSheet.Outline.AutomaticStyles = True
```

OutlineFont Property

Applies To	Font.
Description	**True** if the font is an outline font. Read-write.
Syntax	*object*.**OutlineFont**
Elements	*object*
	Required. The Font object (**ActiveCell.Font**, for example).
Remarks	This property has no effect in Microsoft Windows, but its value is retained (it can be set and returned).
Example	This example sets the font for the active cell to an outline font.

```
ActiveCell.Font.OutlineFont = True
```

OutlineLevel Property

Applies To	Range.
Description	Returns or sets the current row or column outline level of the specified row or column. Read-write.
Syntax	*object*.**OutlineLevel**
Elements	*object*
	Required. The row or column for which to set outline level. The range should be a row or a column, or a range of rows or columns.
Remarks	Level one is the outermost summary level.
See Also	**EntireColumn** Property, **EntireRow** Property.
Example	This example sets the outline level for row two to one.

```
Rows(2).OutlineLevel = 1
```

Oval Object

Description	An oval graphic object drawn on a chart or worksheet.

Ovals Method

Applies To   Chart, DialogSheet, Worksheet.

Description   Returns a single oval (an Oval object, Syntax 1) or a collection of ovals (an Ovals object, Syntax 2). Read-only.

Syntax 1   *object*.**Ovals(*index*)**

Syntax 2   *object*.**Ovals**

Elements   The **Ovals** method has the following object qualifier and named arguments:

object
    Required. The object containing the ovals.

index
    Required for Syntax 1. The name or number of the oval.

Example   This example deletes oval three on the active sheet.

```
ActiveSheet.Ovals(3).Delete
```

Ovals Object

Description   A collection of Oval objects.

Overlap Property

Applies To   ChartGroup.

Description   Specifies how bars and columns are positioned. Can be a value from -100 to 100. Applies only to bar and column charts. Read-write.

Syntax   *object*.**Overlap**

Elements   *object*
    Required. The ChartGroup object.

Remarks   If this property is set to -100, bars are positioned so that there is one bar width between them. With zero overlap, there is no space between bars (one bar starts immediately after the preceding bar). At 100 overlap, bars are positioned on top of each other.

See Also   **GadWidth** Property.

Example

This example sets the overlap for the first chart group to -50.

```
ActiveWorkbook.Charts(3).ChartGroups(1).Overlap = -50
```

PageBreak Property

Applies To

Range.

Description

Returns or sets the location of a page break (one of **xlNone**, **xlManual**, or **xlAutomatic**). Read-write.

Syntax

object.**PageBreak**

Elements

object
    Required. Controls page break location, as shown in the following table.

Specified Range	Page break location
Entire column	Left of the column
Entire row	Above the row
Neither	Above and to the left of the range. In this case, you can set the page break, but not return it.

Remarks

This property can return the location of either automatic or manual page breaks, but it can only set the location of manual breaks (it can only be set to **xlManual** or **xlNone).**

To remove all manual page breaks on a worksheet, set **Cells.PageBreak** to **xlNone**.

Examples

The following examples show some typical uses for the **PageBreak** property.

```
' Set a manual page break above row 25:
Rows(25).PageBreak = xlManual

' Set a manual page break to the left of column J
Columns("J").PageBreak = xlManual

' Get rid of both of those page breaks
Rows(25).PageBreak = xlNone
Columns("J").PageBreak = xlNone

' Another way to get rid of both page breaks
Range("J25").PageBreak = xlNone
```

PageFields Method

Applies To	PivotTable.
Description	Returns a single pivot field (a PivotField object, Syntax 1) or a collection of the pivot fields (a PivotFields object, Syntax 2) that are currently showing as page fields. Read-only.
Syntax 1	*object*.**PageFields**(*index*)
Syntax 2	*object*.**PageFields**
Elements	The **PageFields** method has the following object qualifier and named arguments:

object
> Required. The PivotTable object.

index
> Required for Syntax 1. The name or number of the pivot field to return (can be an array to specify more than one).

See Also	**ColumnFields** Method, **DataFields** Method, **HiddenFields** Method, **PivotFields** Method, **RowFields** Method, **VisibleFields** Method.
Example	This example adds the active pivot table page field names to a list box.

```
For Each pgField In ActiveCell.PivotTable.PageFields
    pageFieldListBox.AddItem(pgField.Name)
Next pgField
```

PageRange Property

Applies To	PivotTable.
Description	Returns the Range that contains the pivot table page area. Read-only.
Syntax	*object*.**PageRange**
Elements	*object* Required. The PivotTable object.
See Also	**ColumnRange** Property, **DataBodyRange** Property, **DataLabelRange** Property, **RowRange** Property.
Example	This example selects the active pivot table page headers.

```
ActiveCell.PivotTable.PageRange.Select
```

PageSetup Object

Description   A page setup description. The PageSetup object contains all page setup attributes (left margin, bottom margin, paper size, and so on) as properties.

PageSetup Property

Applies To   Chart, DialogSheet, Module, Window, Worksheet.

Description   Returns a PageSetup object that contains all of the page setup settings for this object. Read-only.

Syntax   *object*.**PageSetup**

Elements   *object*
                       Required. The object to which this property applies.

Example   This example sets the center header text for chart one.

```
Charts(1).PageSetup.CenterHeader = "December Sales"
```

Pane Object

Description   A pane of a window.

Panes Method

Applies To   Window.

Description   Returns one pane (a Pane object, Syntax 1) or a collection of all the panes (a Panes object, Syntax 2) in a window. Read-only.

Syntax 1   *object*.**Panes**(*index*)

Syntax 2   *object*.**Panes**

Elements   The **Panes** method has the following object qualifier and named arguments:

                       object
                       Required. The Window object.

index
Required for Syntax 1. The name or number of the pane.

Remarks   This property is only available on windows that can be split (worksheets and Microsoft Excel 4.0 macro sheets).

Examples   This example displays the number of panes on the active window.

```
MsgBox "There are " & ActiveWindow.Panes.Count & _
    " panes in the active window"
```

This example activates the top left pane on the active window.

```
ActiveWindow.Panes(1).Activate
```

Panes Object

Description   A collection of Pane objects.

PaperSize Property

Applies To   PageSetup.

Description   Windows only. Returns or sets the size of the paper. Read-write.

Syntax   *object*.**PaperSize**

Elements   *object*
Required. The PageSetup object (**ActiveSheet.PageSetup**, for example).

Remarks   This property may have one of the following values.

Value	Meaning
xlPaperLetter	Letter (8 1/2 x 11 in.)
xlPaperLetterSmall	Letter Small (8 1/2 x 11 in.)
xlPaperTabloid	Tabloid (11 x 17 in.)
xlPaperLedger	Ledger (17 x 11 in.)
xlPaperLegal	Legal (8 1/2 x 14 in.)
xlPaperStatement	Statement (5 1/2 x 8 1/2 in.)
xlPaperExecutive	Executive (7 1/2 x 10 1/2 in.)
xlPaperA3	A3 (297 x 420 mm)
xlPaperA4	A4 (210 x 297 mm)

Value	Meaning
xlPaperA4Small	A4 Small (210 x 297 mm)
xlPaperA5	A5 (148 x 210 mm)
xlPaperB4	B4 (250 x 354 mm)
xlPaperB5	B5 (182 x 257 mm)
xlPaperFolio	Folio (8 1/2 x 13 in.)
xlPaperQuarto	Quarto (215 x 275 mm)
xlPaper10x14	10 x 14 in.
xlPaper11x17	11 x 17 in.
xlPaperNote	Note (8 1/2 x 11 in.)
xlPaperEnvelope9	Envelope #9 (3 7/8 x 8 7/8 in.)
xlPaperEnvelope10	Envelope #10 (4 1/8 x 9 1/2 in.)
xlPaperEnvelope11	Envelope #11 (4 1/2 x 10 3/8 in.)
xlPaperEnvelope12	Envelope #12 (4 1/2 x 11 in.)
xlPaperEnvelope14	Envelope #14 (5 x 11 1/2 in.)
xlPaperCsheet	C size sheet
xlPaperDsheet	D size sheet
xlPaperEsheet	E size sheet
xlPaperEnvelopeDL	Envelope DL (110 x 220 mm)
xlPaperEnvelopeC3	Envelope C3 (324 x 458 mm)
xlPaperEnvelopeC4	Envelope C4 (229 x 324 mm)
xlPaperEnvelopeC5	Envelope C5 (162 x 229 mm)
xlPaperEnvelopeC6	Envelope C6 (114 x 162 mm)
xlPaperEnvelopeC65	Envelope C65 (114 x 229 mm)
xlPaperEnvelopeB4	Envelope B4 (250 x 353 mm)
xlPaperEnvelopeB5	Envelope B5 (176 x 250 mm)
xlPaperEnvelopeB6	Envelope B6 (176 x 125 mm)
xlPaperEnvelopeItaly	Envelope (110 x 230 mm)
xlPaperEnvelopeMonarch	Envelope Monarch (3 7/8 x 7 1/2 in.)
xlPaperEnvelopePersonal	Envelope (3 5/8 x 6 1/2 in.)
xlPaperFanfoldUS	U.S. Standard Fanfold (14 7/8 x 11 in.)
xlPaperFanfoldStdGerman	German Standard Fanfold (8 1/2 x 12 in.)
xlPaperFanfoldLegalGerman	German Legal Fanfold (8 1/2 x 13 in.)
xlPaperUser	User defined

Some printers may not support all paper sizes.

Example   This example sets the paper size to legal.

```
ActiveSheet.PageSetup.PaperSize = xlPaperLegal
```

Parent Property

Applies To   All objects.

Description   Returns the parent object for the specified object. Read-only.

Syntax   *object*.**Parent**

Elements   *object*
                     Required. The object to which this property applies.

Example   This example displays the name of the chart that contains myAxis.

```
Set myAxis = Charts(1).Axes(xlValue)
MsgBox myAxis.Parent.Name
```

ParentField Property

Applies To   PivotField.

Description   Returns the pivot field that is the group parent of the object. The field must be
                     grouped and have a parent field. Read-only.

Syntax   *object*.**ParentField**

Elements   *object*
                     Required. The PivotField object.

Example   This example displays the name of the pivot field that is the group parent of the
                     active field.

```
MsgBox "The active field is a child of the field " & _
    ActiveCell.PivotField.ParentField.Name
```

ParentItem Property

Applies To   PivotItem.

Description   Returns the parent pivot item in the parent PivotField (the field must be grouped so
                     that it has a parent). Read-only.

Syntax	*object*.**ParentItem**
Elements	*object* Required. The PivotItem object.
Example	This example displays the name of the parent pivot item for the active item.

```
MsgBox "This item is a subitem of " & _
    ActiveCell.PivotItem.ParentItem.Name
```

ParentItems Method

Applies To	PivotField.
Description	Returns one pivot item (a PivotItem object, Syntax 1) or a collection of all the pivot items (a PivotItems object, Syntax 2) that are group parents in the specified field. The specified field must be a group parent of another field. Read-only.
Syntax 1	*object*.**ParentItems**(*index*)
Syntax 2	*object*.**ParentItems**
Elements	The **ParentItems** method has the following object qualifier and named arguments:
	object Required. The PivotField object.
	index Required for Syntax 1. The number or name of the pivot item to return (can be an array to specify more than one).
See Also	**ChildItems** Method, **HiddenItems** Method, **PivotItems** Method, **VisibleItems** Method.
Example	This example adds the names of all the items that are group parents in the active field to a list box.

```
For Each pvtItem in ActiveCell.PivotField.ParentItems
    parentItemListBox.AddItem pvtItem.Name
Next pvtItem
```

ParentShowDetail Property

Applies To	PivotItem.

Description	**True** if the specified item is showing because one of its parents is showing detail; **False** if the specified item is not showing because one of its parents is hiding detail. This property is only available if the item is grouped. Read-only.
Syntax	*object*.**ParentShowDetail**
Elements	*object* Required. The PivotItem object.
Example	This example displays a dialog box if the specified item is not showing because the item's parent is hiding detail.

```
If Not targetItem.ParentShowDetail Then
    MsgBox "The target item is not showing."
End If
```

Parse Method

Applies To	Range.
Description	Parses a range of data and breaks it into multiple cells. Distributes the contents of the range to fill several adjacent columns; the range can be no more than one column wide.
Syntax	*object*.**Parse**(*parseLine, destination*)
Elements	The **Parse** method has the following object qualifier and named arguments:

object
Required. The range to parse.

parseLine
Optional. The parse line, as a string. This is a string containing left and right brackets to indicate where the cells should be split. For example, "[xxx][xxx]" would put the first three characters into the first column, and the next three characters into the second column of the destination range. If omitted, Microsoft Excel guesses where to split the columns based on the spacing of the top left cell in the range. If you want to use a different range to guess the parse line, use a Range as the *parseLine* argument. That range must be one of the cells that is being parsed. The *parseLine* argument cannot be longer than 255 characters, including the brackets and spaces.

destination
Optional. A range indicating the upper-left corner of the destination for the parsed data. If omitted, Microsoft Excel will parse in place.

Remarks	Use a range as the *parseLine* argument to recognize data that you've read from files created by another application, such as a database (see the example for details).

Examples   These examples show some typical uses for the **Parse** method. Use the second example if the top row of your data contains field names, and all the other rows contain the actual data, so you want Microsoft Excel to use the second row to guess how to parse the data.

```
' Parse column 1 into columns 2:3 using [xxx] [xxx]:
Columns(1).Parse "[xxx] [xxx]", Cells(1, 2)

' Parse column 1 into columns 2:x based on cell A2:
Columns(1).Parse Cells(2,1), Cells(1,2)
```

Paste Method (Chart Object)

Applies To   Chart.

Description   Pastes chart data from the Clipboard into the specified Chart.

Syntax   *object*.**Paste(*type*)**

Elements   *object*
      Required. The Chart object.

      type
      Optional. If another chart is in the clipboard, specifies the chart information to paste (one of **xlFormats**, **xlFormulas**, or **xlAll**). The default is **xlAll**. If there is data other than a chart in the clipboard, this parameter cannot be used.

Remarks   This method changes the current selection.

See Also   **Copy** Method, **Cut** Method, **Paste** Method (DialogSheet or Worksheet Objects).

Example   This example pastes data from the range B1:B5 into chart one.

```
Range("B1:B5").Copy
Charts(1).Paste
```

Paste Method (DialogSheet or Worksheet Object)

Applies To   DialogSheet, Worksheet.

Description   Pastes the contents of the Clipboard onto the sheet.

Syntax   *object*.**Paste(*destination, link*)**

Elements   *object*
      Required. The DialogSheet or Worksheet object.

destination
> Optional. A Range specifying where the Clipboard contents should be placed. If omitted, the current selection is used. This argument can only be specified if the contents of the Clipboard can be pasted into a range — it cannot be used with drawing objects. If this argument is specified, the *link* argument cannot be used.

link
> Optional. If **True**, a link is established to the source of the pasted data. If this argument is specified, the *destination* argument cannot be used.

Remarks   If you do not specify the *destination* argument, you must select the destination range before you use this method.

This method may modify the sheet selection depending on the contents of the Clipboard. For example, pasted drawing objects remain selected.

See Also   **Copy** Method, **Cut** Method, **Paste** Method (Chart object), **PasteSpecial** Method.

Example   This example copies data from cells C1:C5 to cells D1:D5.

```
Range("C1:C5").Copy
ActiveSheet.Paste destination:=Range("D1:D5")
```

Paste Method (Pictures Object)

Applies To   Pictures.

Description   Pastes a picture from the Clipboard to a sheet or chart. The position of the new picture is determined by the current selection.

Syntax   *object*.**Paste**(*link*)

Elements   *object*
> Required. The Pictures object.

link
> Optional. If **True**, a link is established between the pasted picture and the source data. The default is **False**.

See Also   **Copy** Method, **Cut** Method.

Example   This example pastes a picture from the Clipboard to cell A1 on the active worksheet.

```
Range("A1").Select
ActiveSheet.Pictures.Paste
```

Paste Method (Point or Series Object)

Applies To	Point, Series.
Description	Pastes a picture from the Clipboard as the marker on the selected point or series. This method can be used on column, bar, line, or radar charts, and it sets the **MarkerStyle** to **xlPicture**.
Syntax	*object*.**Paste**
Elements	*object*
	Required. The Point or Series object.
See Also	**Copy** Method, **Cut** Method, **MarkerStyle** Property.
Example	This example copies a picture to the Clipboard and then pastes it into the first series on chart one.

```
Worksheets(1).Activate
ActiveSheet.Pictures(1).Copy
Charts(1).Activate
ActiveChart.SeriesCollection(1).Paste
```

Paste Method (SeriesCollection Object)

Applies To	SeriesCollection.
Description	Pastes data from the Clipboard to the specified series collection.
Syntax	*object*.**Paste**(*rowcol, seriesLabels, categoryLabels, replace, newSeries*)
Elements	*object*
	Required. The SeriesCollection object.

rowcol

Optional. Specifies whether the values corresponding to a particular data series are in rows (**xlRows**) or columns (**xlColumns**). The default is **xlColumns**.

seriesLabels

Optional. If **True**, Microsoft Excel uses the contents of the cell in the first column of each row (or first row of each column) as the name of the data series in that row (or column). If **False** (or omitted), Microsoft Excel uses the contents of the cell in the first column of each row (or first row of each column) as the first data point of the data series.

categoryLabels
> Optional. If **True**, Microsoft Excel uses the contents of the first row (or column) of the selection as the categories for the chart. If **False** (or omitted), Microsoft Excel uses the contents of the first row (or column) as the first data series in the chart.

replace
> Optional. If **True**, Microsoft Excel applies categories while replacing existing categories with information from the copied cell range. If **False**, Microsoft Excel applies new categories without replacing any old ones.

newSeries
> Optional. Specifies whether the data is to be pasted as new series (**True**) or as new points on existing series (**False**). The default is **True**.

See Also   **Add** Method (Collection object), **ChartWizard** Method, **Copy** Method, **Cut** Method, **Extend** Method.

Example   This example copies data to the Clipboard from cells C1:C5 and pastes the data to chart three as a new series.

```
Range("C1:C5").Copy
Charts(3).SeriesCollection.Paste
```

PasteFace Method

Applies To   ToolbarButton.

Description   Pastes a bitmap button face from the Clipboard onto the specified button.

Syntax   *object*.**PasteFace**

Elements   *object*
> Required. The ToolbarButton object.

See Also   **BuiltInFace** Property, **CopyFace** Method.

Example   This example copies the bitmap face of button one on toolbar one and pastes it onto the face of button three.

```
With Toolbars(1)
    .ToolbarButtons(1).CopyFace
    .ToolbarButtons(3).PasteFace
End With
```

PasteSpecial Method (DialogSheet or Worksheet Object)

Applies To   DialogSheet, Worksheet.

Description   Pastes the contents of the Clipboard onto the sheet using a specified format. Use this method to paste data from other applications or paste in a specific format.

Syntax   *object*.**PasteSpecial**(*format, link, displayAsIcon, iconFileName, iconIndex, iconLabel*)

Elements   *object*
    Required. The DialogSheet or Worksheet object.

format
    Required. Specifies the clipboard format of the data to paste (as text).

link
    Optional. If **True**, a link is established to the source of the pasted data. If the source data is not suitable for linking or the source application doesn't support linking, this parameter is ignored. The default value is **False**.

displayAsIcon
    Optional. If **True**, the pasted data is displayed as an icon. The default value is **False**.

iconFileName
    Optional. The name of the file that contains the icon to use if *displayAsIcon* is **True**.

iconIndex
    Optional. The index number of the icon within the icon file.

iconLabel
    Optional. The text label of the icon.

Remarks   You must select the destination range before you use this method.

This method may modify the sheet selection depending on the contents of the Clipboard. For example, pasted drawing objects remain selected.

See Also   **Cut** Method, **Copy** Method, **Paste** Method, **PasteSpecial** Method (Range Object).

Examples　This example pastes a Microsoft Word document object from the Clipboard into cell D1.

```
Range("D1").Select
ActiveSheet.PasteSpecial format:="Word Document Object"
```

This example pastes the Microsoft Word document object and displays it as an icon.

```
Range("F5").Select
ActiveSheet.PasteSpecial format:="Word Document Object", _
    displayAsIcon:=True, iconFileName:="MOREICONS.DLL", _
    iconIndex:=9, iconLabel:="Form Letter"
```

PasteSpecial Method (Range Object)

Applies To　Range.

Description　Pastes a Range from the Clipboard to the specified range.

Syntax　*object*.**PasteSpecial**(*paste, operation, skipBlanks, transpose*)

Elements　The **PasteSpecial** method has the following object qualifier and named arguments:

object
　Required. The Range object.

paste
　Optional. Specifies the part of the range to be pasted (one of **xlAll**, **xlFormulas**, **xlValues**, **xlFormats**, or **xlNotes**). If omitted, the default is **xlAll**.

operation
　Optional. Specifies the paste operation (one of **xlNone**, **xlAdd**, **xlSubtract**, **xlMultiply**, or **xlDivide**). If omitted, the default is **xlNone**.

skipBlanks
　Optional. If **True**, blank cells in the Range on the Clipboard will not be pasted into the destination. If omitted, the default is **False**.

transpose
　Optional. If **True**, rows and columns are transposed when the Range is pasted. If omitted, the default is **False**.

See Also　**Cut** Method, **Copy** Method, **Paste** Method, **PasteSpecial** Method (Worksheet Object).

Example	This example copies replaces the data in cells D1:D5 with the sum of the existing contents and cells C1:C5.

```
Range("C1:C5").Copy
Range("D1:D5").PasteSpecial operation:=Add
```

Path Property

Applies To	AddIn, Application, Workbook.
Description	Returns the complete path of the object (as a string), without including the final separator and name of the object. Read-only.
Syntax	*object*.**Path**
Elements	*object*
	Optional for Application, required for AddIn and Workbook. The object to which this property applies.
Example	This example sets the variable `currentExcelPath` to the complete path of Microsoft Excel.

```
currentExcelPath = Application.Path
```

PathSeparator Property

Applies To	Application.
Description	Returns the character ":" in Microsoft Excel for the Macintosh; "\" in Microsoft Excel for Windows. Read-only.
Syntax	*object*.**PathSeparator**
Elements	*object*
	Required. The Application object.
Example	This example sets the variable `currentSystemPathSeparator` to the current path separator.

```
currentSystemPathSeparator = Application.PathSeparator
```

Pattern Property

Applies To   Interior.

Description   Returns or sets the pattern of the interior. Read-write.

Syntax   *object*.**Pattern**

Elements   *object*
                    Required. The Interior object.

Remarks   This property can have one of the following values.

xlAutomatic	**xlHorizontal**
xlChecker	**xlLightDown**
xlCrissCross	**xlLightHorizontal**
xlDown	**xlLightUp**
xlGray16	**xlLightVertical**
xlGray25	**xlNone**
xlGray50	**xlSemiGray75**
xlGray75	**xlSolid**
xlGray8	**xlUp**
xlGrid	**xlVertical**

See Also   **PatternColor** Property.

Example   This example adds a crisscross pattern to the interior of oval one.

```
ActiveSheet.Ovals(1).Interior.Pattern = xlCrissCross
```

PatternColor Property

Applies To   Interior.

Description   Returns or sets the interior pattern color as an RGB value. Read-write.

Syntax	*object*.**PatternColor**
Elements	*object* Required. The Interior object.
See Also	**Color** Property, **Pattern** Property, **PatternColorIndex** Property.
Example	This example sets the interior pattern color for rectangle one.

```
ActiveSheet.Rectangles(1).Interior.PatternColor = RGB(255,0,0)
```

PatternColorIndex Property

Applies To	Interior.
Description	Returns or sets the interior pattern color as an index into the current color palette. Read-write.
Syntax	*object*.**PatternColorIndex**
Elements	*object* Required. The Interior object.
Remarks	Set this property to **xlAutomatic** to specify the automatic pattern for cells or the automatic fill style for drawing objects. Set this property to **xlNone** to specify no pattern (this is the same as setting **Interior.Pattern** to **xlNone**).
See Also	**Color** Property, **Colors** Property, **Pattern** Property, **PatternColor** Property.
Example	This example sets the pattern color (as an index) for rectangle one.

```
ActiveSheet.Rectangles(1).Interior.PatternColorIndex = 5
```

Period Property

Applies To	Trendline.
Description	Returns or sets the period of the trendline (applies only if this is a moving average trendline; its **Type** property must be **xlMovingAvg**). Read-write.
Syntax	*object*.**Period**
Elements	*object* Required. The Trendline object.
See Also	**Type** Property.

Example   This example sets the period for trendline one if its type is **xlMovingAvg**.

```
With ActiveWorkbook.Charts(1).SeriesCollection(1).Trendlines(1)
    If .Type = xlMovingAvg Then .Period = 10
End With
```

Perspective Property

Applies To   Chart.

Description   Returns or sets the perspective for the 3-D chart view. Must be between 0 and 100. This property is ignored if the **RightAngleAxes** property is **True**. Read-write.

Syntax   *object*.**Perspective**

Elements   *object*
       Required. The Chart object.

See Also   **Elevation** Property, **RightAngleAxes** Property, **Rotation** Property.

Example   This example sets the chart perspective to 70.

```
Charts(1).Perspective = 70
```

PhoneticAccelerator Property

Applies To   Button, Buttons, CheckBox, CheckBoxes, DrawingObjects, GroupBox, GroupBoxes, Label, Labels, OptionButton, OptionButtons.

Description   Returns or sets the phonetic keyboard accelerator key character for the control (this property is available only in Far East Microsoft Excel). The phonetic accelerator is used when the system accelerator mode is switched to phonetic characters (as opposed to roman characters, which use the **Accelerator** property). Read-write.

Syntax   *object*.**PhoneticAccelerator**

Elements   *object*
       Required. The object to which this property applies.

See Also   **Accelerator** Property.

Example   This example sets the accelerator and phonetic accelerator for button four.

```
With DialogSheets(1).Buttons(4)
    .Accelerator = "E"
    .PhoneticAccelerator = "1"
End With
```

Picture Object

Description   A graphic object created by the Camera button, or a bitmap or metafile pasted on a sheet.

Pictures Method

Applies To   Chart, DialogSheet, Worksheet.

Description   Returns a single picture (a Picture object, Syntax 1) or a collection of pictures (a Pictures object, Syntax 2). Read-only.

Syntax 1   *object*.**Pictures**(*index*)

Syntax 2   *object*.**Pictures**

Elements   The **Pictures** method has the following object qualifier and named arguments:

object
     Required. The object containing the pictures.

index
     Required for Syntax 1. The name or number of the picture.

Example   This example deletes the picture three on the active sheet.

```
ActiveSheet.Pictures(3).Delete
```

Pictures Object

Description   A collection of Picture objects.

PictureType Property

Applies To   Point, Series.

Description   Returns or sets how pictures are displayed on a column or bar picture chart, as shown in the following table. Applies only to column and bar picture charts. Read-write.

Value	Meaning
xlStretch	Stretch the picture to reach the necessary value.
xlStack	Stack the pictures to reach the necessary value.
xlScale	Stack the pictures, but use the **PictureUnit** property to determine what unit each picture represents.

Syntax *object*.**PictureType**

Elements *object*
Required. The Point or Series object.

See Also **PictureUnit** Property.

Example This example sets the first series to stretch pictures.

```
ActiveChart.SeriesCollection(1).PictureType = xlStretch
```

PictureUnit Property

Applies To Point, Series.

Description Returns or sets the unit for each picture on a column or bar picture chart if the **PictureType** property is set to **xlScale** (if not, this property is ignored). Read-write.

Syntax *object*.**PictureUnit**

Elements *object*
Required. The Point or Series object.

See Also **PictureType** Property.

Example This example sets the first series to stack pictures and uses each picture to represent five units.

```
With ActiveChart.SeriesCollection(1)
    .PictureType = xlScale
    .PictureUnit = 5
End With
```

Pie3DGroup Property

Applies To Chart.

Description Returns the pie ChartGroup on a 3-D chart. Read-write.

Syntax	*object*.**Pie3DGroup**
Elements	*object* Required. The Chart object.
See Also	**PieGroups** Method.
Example	This example makes the 3-D pie group an area group.

```
Charts(1).Pie3DGroup.Type = xl3DArea
```

PieGroups Method

Applies To	Chart.
Description	On a 2-D chart, returns a single pie chart group (a ChartGroup object, Syntax 1), or a collection of the pie chart groups (a ChartGroups collection, Syntax 2).
Syntax 1	*object*.**PieGroups**(*index*)
Syntax 2	*object*.**PieGroups**
Elements	The **PieGroups** method has the following object qualifier and named arguments:
	object Required. The Chart object.
	index Required for Syntax 1. Specifies the chart group.
See Also	**Pie3DGroup** Property.
Example	This example makes the first pie group an area group.

```
Charts(1).PieGroups(1).Type = xlArea
```

PivotField Object

Description	A pivot field in a pivot table.

PivotField Property

Applies To	Range.

Description	Returns the PivotField containing the top left corner of the range. Read-only.
Syntax	*object*.**Field**
Elements	*object* Required. The Range object.
Example	This example displays the name of the pivot field containing the active cell.

```
MsgBox "The active cell is inside the field " & _
    ActiveCell.PivotField.Name
```

PivotFields Method

Applies To	PivotTable.
Description	Returns a single pivot field (a PivotField object, Syntax 1) or a collection of the visible and hidden pivot fields (a PivotFields object, Syntax 2) in the pivot table. Read-only.
Syntax 1	*object*.**PivotFields(*index*)**
Syntax 2	*object*.**PivotFields**
Elements	The **PivotFields** method has the following object qualifier and named arguments:
	object Required. The PivotTable object.
	index Required for Syntax 1. The name or number of the pivot field to return (can be an array to specify more than one).
See Also	**ColumnFields** Method, **DataFields** Method, **HiddenFields** Method, **PageFields** Method, **RowFields** Method, **VisibleFields** Method.
Example	This example adds the active pivot table field names to a list box.

```
For Each pvtField In ActiveCell.PivotTable.PivotFields
    pivotFieldListBox.AddItem(pvtField.Name)
Next pvtField
```

PivotFields Object

Description	A collection of PivotField objects.

PivotItem Object

Description   A pivot item in a pivot field.

PivotItem Property

Applies To   Range.

Description   Returns the PivotItem containing the top left corner of the range. Read-only.

Syntax   *object*.**PivotItem**

Elements   *object*
                    Required. The Range object.

Example   This example displays the name of the pivot item containing the active cell.

```
MsgBox "The active cell is inside the item " & _
    ActiveCell.PivotItem.Name
```

PivotItems Method

Applies To   PivotField.

Description   Returns a single pivot item (a PivotItem object, Syntax 1) or a collection of all the visible and hidden pivot items (a PivotItems object, Syntax 2) in the specified field. Read-only.

Syntax 1   *object*.**PivotItems(*index*)**

Syntax 2   *object*.**PivotItems**

Elements   The **PivotItems** method has the following object qualifier and named arguments:

                    object
                    Required. The PivotField object.

                    index
                    Required for Syntax 1. The number or name of the pivot item to return (can be an array to specify more than one).

See Also   **ChildItems** Method, **HiddenItems** Method, **ParentItems** Method, **VisibleItems** Method.

Example   This example adds the names of all items in the active field to a list box.

```
For Each pvtItem in ActiveCell.PivotField.PivotItems
    pvtItemListBox.AddItem(pvtItem.Name)
Next pvtItem
```

PivotItems Object

Description   A collection of PivotItem objects.

PivotTable Object

Description   A pivot table on a sheet.

The PivotTable object contains PivotField objects which in turn contain PivotItem objects.

Because pivot table programming can be complex, it is generally easier to record pivot table actions, using the Record Macro command from the Tools menu.

PivotTable Property

Applies To   Range.

Description   Returns the PivotTable containing the top left corner of the specified range. Read-only.

Syntax   *object*.**PivotTable**

Elements   *object*
            Required. The Range object.

Example   This example displays the name of the pivot table containing the active cell.

```
MsgBox "The active cell is in pivot table " & _
    ActiveCell.PivotTable.Name
```

PivotTables Method

Applies To	Worksheet.
Description	Returns a single pivot table (a PivotTable object, Syntax 1) or a collection of all the pivot tables (a PivotTables object, Syntax 2) in a worksheet. Read-only.
Syntax 1	*object*.**PivotTables**(*index*)
Syntax 2	*object*.**PivotTables**
Elements	The **PivotTables** method has the following object qualifier and named arguments:

object
　　Required. The Worksheet object.

index
　　Required for Syntax 1. The name or number of the pivot table (can be an array
　　to specify more than one).

See Also	**PivotFields** Method, **PivotItems** Method.
Example	This example adds the names of all the pivot tables on worksheet one to a list box.

```
For Each pvt in Worksheets(1).PivotTables
    pivotTableListBox.AddItem pvt.Name
Next pvt
```

PivotTables Object

Description	A collection of PivotTable objects.

PivotTableWizard Method

Applies To	Worksheet.
Description	Creates a PivotTable. This method does not display the Pivot Table Wizard.

Syntax

object.**PivotTableWizard**(*sourceType, sourceData, tableDestination, tableName, rowGrand, columnGrand, saveData, hasAutoFormat, autoPage*)

Elements

The **PivotTableWizard** method has the following object qualifier and named arguments:

object
Required. The Worksheet object.

sourceType
Optional. Describes the source of the pivot table data, as shown in the following list. If you specify this argument, you must also specify *sourceData*.

Value	Meaning
xlConsolidation	Multiple consolidation ranges
xlDatabase	Microsoft Excel list or database
xlExternal	Data from another application
xlPivotTable	Same source as another pivot table

If *sourceType* and *sourceData* are not specified, Microsoft Excel assumes that the source type is **xlDatabase**, and the source data comes from the named range Database. If the named range does not exist, Microsoft Excel uses the current region if the current selection is in a range of more than 10 cells containing data. If this is not true, this method will fail.

sourceData
Optional. The data for the new pivot table. A Range, an array of ranges, or a text constant representing the name of another pivot table. For an external database, this is a two-element array. The first element is the connection string specifying the ODBC source for the data. The second element is the SQL query string used to get the data. If you specify this argument, you must specify *sourceType*. If the active cell is inside the *sourceData* range, you must specify *tableDestination*.

tableDestination
Optional. A Range specifying where the pivot table should be placed on the worksheet. If this argument is not specified, the pivot table is placed at the active cell.

tableName
Optional. The name of the pivot table to be created, given as a string.

rowGrand
Optional. If **True**, the new pivot table shows row grand totals. If **False**, row grand totals are omitted.

columnGrand
Optional. If **True**, the new pivot table shows column grand totals. If **False**, column grand totals are omitted.

saveData
> Optional. If **True**, data is saved with the table. If **False**, only the table definition is saved.

hasAutoFormat
> Optional. If **True**, Microsoft Excel automatically formats the pivot table when it is refreshed or when fields are moved.

autoPage
> Optional. Valid only if *sourceType* is **xlConsolidation**. If **True**, Microsoft Excel creates a page field for the consolidation. If **False**, you must create the page field or fields.

Example   This example creates a new pivot table from a Microsoft Excel database (contained in the range A1:C100).

```
ActiveSheet.PivotTableWizard xlDatabase, Range("A1:C100")
```

Placement Property

Applies To   Arc, Arcs, Button, Buttons, ChartObject, ChartObjects, CheckBox, CheckBoxes, Drawing, DrawingObjects, Drawings, DropDown, DropDowns, EditBox, EditBoxes, GroupBox, GroupBoxes, GroupObject, GroupObjects, Label, Labels, Line, Lines, ListBox, ListBoxes, OLEObject, OLEObjects, OptionButton, OptionButtons, Oval, Ovals, Picture, Pictures, Rectangle, Rectangles, ScrollBar, ScrollBars, Spinner, Spinners, TextBox, TextBoxes.

Description   Returns or sets how the object is attached to the cells below it. Can be one of **xlMoveAndSize**, **xlMove**, or **xlFreeFloating**. Can be used only on objects in a worksheet. Read-write.

Syntax   *object*.**Placement**

Elements   *object*
> Required. The object to which this property applies.

Example   This example sets oval one to be a free-floating object.

```
ActiveSheet.Ovals(1).Placement = xlFreeFloating
```

Play Method

Applies To   SoundNote.

Description   Plays the sound note.

Syntax	*object*.**Play**
Elements	*object* Required. The SoundNote object.
Remarks	To play sounds, you must have sound hardware installed in your computer.
See Also	**Record** Method.
Example	This example plays the sound notes for all cells in the selection.

```
For Each c In Selection.Cells
    c.SoundNote.Play
Next
```

PlotArea Object

Description	The plot area of a chart.

PlotArea Property

Applies To	Chart.
Description	Returns the PlotArea of a chart. Read-only.
Syntax	*object*.**PlotArea**
Elements	*object* Required. The Chart object.
Example	This example sets the chart plot area color.

```
Charts(1).PlotArea.Border.Color = RGB(255,0,0)
```

PlotOrder Property

Applies To	Series.
Description	Returns or sets the plot order for this series within the chart group. Read-write.

Syntax	*object*.**PlotOrder**
Elements	*object* Required. The Series object.
Remarks	Plot order can only be set within a chart group (you cannot set the plot order for the entire chart if you have more than one chart type). A chart group is a collection of series with the same chart type and subtype.
	Changing the plot order of one series will cause the plot orders of the other series on the chart group to adjust as necessary.
Example	This example makes the third series plot fourth in the first chart group.

```
ActiveChart.ChartGroups(1).SeriesCollection(3).PlotOrder = 4
```

PlotVisibleOnly Property

Applies To	Chart.
Description	**True** if only visible cells are plotted (**False** if both visible and hidden cells are plotted). Read-write.
Syntax	*object*.**PlotVisibleOnly**
Elements	*object* Required. The Chart object.
Example	This example causes Microsoft Excel to plot only visible cells on chart one.

```
ActiveWorkbook.Charts(1).PlotVisibleOnly = True
```

Point Object

Description	A single point in a series.

Points Method

Applies To	Series.
Description	Returns a single point (a Point object, Syntax 1) or a collection of all of the points (a Points object, Syntax 2) in the series. Read-only.

Syntax 1	*object*.**Points(*index*)**
Syntax 2	*object*.**Points**
Elements	The **Points** method has the following object qualifier and named arguments:

object
    Required. The Series object.

index
    Required for Syntax 1. The name or number of the point.

Example	This example applies a data label to the first point in the series.

```
ActiveChart.SeriesCollection(1).Points(1).ApplyDataLabels
```

Points Object

Description	A collection of Point objects.

Position Property

Applies To	Legend, PivotField, PivotItem, Toolbar.
Description	Returns or sets the position of the specified object, as shown in the following table. Read-write.

Object	Position
Legend	Position of the legend on the chart. One of **xlBottom, xlCorner, xlTop, xlRight**, or **xlLeft**.
PivotField	Position of the field (first, second, third, and so on) among all the fields in its orientation (Rows, Columns, Pages, Data).
PivotItem	Position of the item in its field, if the item is currently showing.
Toolbar	Position of the toolbar. One of **xlTop**, **xlLeft**, **xlRight**, **xlBottom**, or **xlFloating**.

Syntax	*object*.**Position**
Elements	*object* Required. The object to which this property applies.

Examples   This example sets the active pivot field to position one.

```
ActiveCell.PivotField.Position = 1
```

This example displays the position number of the active pivot item.

```
MsgBox "The active item is in position number " & _
    ActiveCell.PivotItem.Position
```

Precedents Property

Applies To   Range.

Description   Returns a Range that contains all of the precedents of a cell. This may be a multiple selection (a union of Range objects) if there is more than one precedent. Read-only.

Syntax   *object*.**Precedents**

Elements   *object*
                   Required. Return precedents for this cell.

See Also   **Dependents** Property, **DirectDependents** Property, **DirectPrecedents** Property, **ShowPrecedents** Method.

Example   This example selects the precedents of the active cell.

```
ActiveCell.Precedents.Select
```

PrecisionAsDisplayed Property

Applies To   Workbook.

Description   **True** if calculations in this workbook will be done using only the precision of the numbers as they are displayed. Read-write.

Syntax   *object*.**PrecisionAsDisplayed**

Elements   *object*
                   Required. The Workbook object.

Example   This example causes calculations on the active workbook to use only the precision of the numbers as they are displayed.

```
ActiveWorkbook.PrecisionAsDisplayed = True
```

PrefixCharacter Property

Applies To	Range.
Description	Returns the prefix character for the cell. Read-only.
Syntax	*object*.**PrefixCharacter**
Elements	*object* Required. Return the prefix character for this cell.
Remarks	If the **TransitionNavigKeys** property is **False**, this character will be ' for a text label, or blank. If the **TransitionNavigKeys** property is **True**, this will be ' for a left-justified label, " for a right-justified label, ^ for a centered label, \ for a repeated label, or blank.
Example	This example displays the prefix character for the active cell.

```
MsgBox "The prefix character is " & ActiveCell.PrefixCharacter
```

Previous Property

Applies To	Chart, DialogSheet, Module, Range, Worksheet.
Description	Returns the previous sheet or cell (a Range object). Read-only.
Syntax	*object*.**Previous**
Elements	*object* Required. The object to which this property applies.
Remarks	If the object is a range, this property emulates SHIFT+TAB, although the property returns the previous cell without selecting it.
	On a protected sheet, this property returns the previous unlocked cell. On an unprotected sheet, this always returns the cell to the left of the specified cell.
See Also	**ActivatePrevious** Method, **Next** Property.
Example	This example activates the cell before the active cell.

```
ActiveCell.Previous.Activate
```

PreviousSelections Property

Applies To	Application.

Description   Returns an array of the four previous ranges or names selected. Read-only. Each time you go to a range or cell using the Name Box or GoTo command from the Edit Menu, or a macro calls the **Goto** method, whatever range was selected before is added to this array as element number one, and the other items in the array are moved down.

Syntax   *object*.**PreviousSelections**

Elements   *object*
        Required. The Application object.

Example   This example returns the first range or name in the list of previous selections.

```
Application.PreviousSelections(1).Select
```

Print # Statement

Description   Writes display-formatted data to a sequential file.

Syntax   **Print #***filenumber*,[*outputlist*]

Elements   The **Print #** statement syntax has these parts:

Part	Description
filenumber	Any valid file number.
outputlist	Expression or list of expressions to print.

The *outputlist* argument has the following syntax and parts:

[{**Spc(***n***)** | **Tab[(***n***)]**}][*expression*][*charpos*]

Part	Description
Spc(*n***)**	Used to insert space characters in the output, where *n* is the number of space characters to insert.
Tab(*n***)**	Used to position the insertion point to an absolute column number, where *n* is the column number. Use **Tab** with no argument to position the insertion point at the beginning of the next print zone.
expression	Numeric or string expressions to print.
charpos	Specifies the insertion point for the next character. Use a semicolon to specify the insertion point to be immediately after the last character displayed. Use **Tab(***n***)** to position the insertion point to an absolute column number. Use **Tab** with no argument to position the insertion point at the beginning of the next print zone. If *charpos* is omitted, the next character is printed on the next line.

Remarks   If you omit *outputlist* and include only a list separator after *filenumber*, a blank line prints to the file. Multiple expressions can be separated with either a space or a semicolon. A space has the same effect as a semicolon.

All data written to the file using **Print #** is internationally aware; that is, the data is properly formatted (using the appropriate decimal separator) and the keywords are output in the language appropriate for the international locale specified for your system.

For **Boolean** data, either True or False is printed. The **True** and **False** keywords are translated, as appropriate, according to the locale setting specified for your system.

Date data is written to the file using the standard short date format recognized by your system. When either the date or the time component is missing or zero, only the provided part gets written to the file.

Nothing is written to the file if *outputlist* data is **Empty**. However, if *outputlist* data is **Null**, Null is written to the file. Again, the **Null** keyword is translated, as appropriate.

For error data, the output appears as Error errorcode. The **Error** keyword is translated, as appropriate, when written to the file.

Because **Print #** writes an image of the data to the file, you must delimit the data so it prints correctly. If you use **Tab** with no arguments to move the print position to the next print zone, **Print #** also writes the spaces between print fields to the file.

Note If, at some future time, you want to read the data from a file using the **Input #** statement, use the **Write #** statement instead of the **Print #** statement to write the data to the file. Using **Write #** ensures the integrity of each separate data field by properly delimiting it, so that it can be read back in using **Input #**. Using **Write #** also ensures that it can be correctly read in any locale.

See Also   **Open** Statement, **Print** Method, **Spc** Function, **Tab** Function, **Write #** Statement.

Example

This example uses the **Print #** statement to write data to a file.

```
Open "TESTFILE" For Output As #1          ' Open file for output.
Print #1, "This is a test"          ' Print text to file.
Print #1,                      ' Print blank line to file.
Print #1, "Zone 1"; Tab ; "Zone 2" ' Print in two print zones.
Print #1, "Hello" ; " " ; "World"   ' Separate strings with space.
Print #1, Spc(5) ; "5 leading spaces " ' Print 5 leading spaces.
Print #1, Tab(10) ; "Hello"        ' Print word at col 10.

' Assign Boolean, Date, Null and Error values.
MyBool = False : MyDate = #February 12, 1969# : MyNull = Null
MyError = CVErr(32767)
' True, False, Null and Error are translated using locale settings of
' your system. Date literals are written using standard short date
' format.
Print #1, MyBool ; " is a Boolean value"
Print #1, MyDate ; " is a date"
Print #1, MyNull ; " is a null value"
Print #1, MyError ; " is an error value"
Close #1                                ' Close file.
```

Print Method

Applies To

Debug.

Description

Prints text in the Immediate pane of the Debug window.

Syntax

[*object.*]**Print** [*outputlist*]

Elements

The **Print** method syntax has these parts:

Part	Description
object	Object expression that evaluates to the **Debug** object.
outputlist	Expression or list of expressions to print. If omitted, a blank line is printed.

The *outputlist* argument has the following syntax and parts:

[{**Spc**(*n*) | **Tab**[(*n*)]}][*expression*][*charpos*]

Part	Description
Spc(*n*)	Used to insert space characters in the output, where *n* is the number of space characters to insert.
Tab(*n*)	Used to position the insertion point at an absolute column number where *n* is the column number. Use **Tab** with no argument to position the insertion point at the beginning of the next print zone.
expression	Numeric or string expressions to print.
charpos	Specifies the insertion point for the next character. Use a semicolon to specify the insertion point to immediately follow the last character displayed. Use **Tab**(*n*) to position the insertion point at an absolute column number. Use **Tab** with no argument to position the insertion point at the beginning of the next print zone. If *charpos* is omitted, the next character is printed on the next line.

Remarks

Multiple expressions can be separated with either a space or a semicolon. A space has the same effect as a semicolon.

All data printed to the Immediate pane is internationally aware; that is, the data is properly formatted (using the appropriate decimal separator) and the keywords are output in the language appropriate for the international locale specified for your system.

For **Boolean** data, either True or False is printed. The **True** and **False** keywords are translated, as appropriate, according to the locale setting specified for your system.

Date data is written using the standard short date format recognized by your system. When either the date or the time component is missing or zero, only the data provided gets written.

Nothing is written if *outputlist* data is **Empty**. However, if *outputlist* data is **Null**, Null is output. Again, the **Null** keyword is translated, as appropriate, when output.

For error data, the output appears as `Error errorcode`. The **Error** keyword is translated, as appropriate, when output.

Note Because the **Print** method normally prints with proportionally-spaced characters, it is important to remember that there is no correlation between the number of characters printed and the number of fixed-width columns those characters occupy. For example, a wide letter, such as a "W", occupies more than one fixed-width column, whereas a narrow letter, such as an "i", occupies less. To account for cases where wider than average characters are used, you must ensure that your tabular columns are positioned far enough apart. Alternatively, you can print using a fixed-pitch font (such as Courier) to ensure that each character uses only one column.

See Also   **Debug** Object, **Print #** Statement, **Spc** Function, **Tab** Function.

Example   This example uses the **Print** method to output text to the **Debug** object; that is, display text in the Debug window.

```
For I = 11 To 20    ' Loop 10 times.
    ' Print each value on a new line.
    Debug.Print I
Next I

For I = 11 To 20    ' Loop 10 times.
    ' Print values on the same line, next to each other.
    Debug.Print I;
Next I

Debug.Print Spc(10) ; "Hello there" ' Print 10 spaces before.
Debug.Print Tab(20) ; "This is a test" ' Print at column 20.
Debug.Print "Hello"; Tab; Tab; "There" ' Print 2 print zones apart.
```

PrintArea Property

Applies To   PageSetup.

Description   Returns or sets the range to print, as a string using A1-style references in the language of the macro. Read-write.

Syntax   *object*.**PrintArea**

Elements   *object*
                   Required. The PageSetup object.

Remarks   Set this property to **False** or to the empty string ("") to set the print area to the entire sheet.

This property applies only to worksheet pages.

See Also   **PrintOut** Method.

Examples   This example sets the print area to the range A1:C5.

```
ActiveSheet.PageSetup.PrintArea = "A1:C5"
```

This example sets the print area to the current selection.

```
ActiveSheet.PageSetup.PrintArea = Selection.Address
```

PrintGridlines Property

Applies To   PageSetup.

Description   **True** if cell gridlines are printed on the page. Read-write.

Syntax   *object*.**PrintGridlines**

Elements   *object*
        Required. The PageSetup object (**ActiveSheet.PageSetup**, for example).

Remarks   This property applies only to worksheets.

See Also   **DisplayGridlines** Property.

Example   This example prints cell gridlines when the active sheet is printed.

```
ActiveSheet.PageSetup.PrintGridlines = True
```

PrintHeadings Property

Applies To   PageSetup.

Description   **True** if row and column headings are printed with this page. Read-write.

Syntax   *object*.**PrintHeadings**

Elements   *object*
        Required. The PageSetup object (**ActiveSheet.PageSetup**, for example).

Remarks   This property applies only to worksheets.

The **DisplayHeadings** property controls on-screen heading display.

Example   This example turns off heading printing for the active worksheet.

```
ActiveSheet.PageSetup.PrintHeadings = False
```

PrintNotes Property

Applies To   PageSetup.

Description   **True** if cell notes will be printed along with the sheet. Read-write.

Syntax   *object*.**PrintNotes**

Elements   *object*
                      Required. The PageSetup object.

Remarks   This property applies only to worksheet pages.

Example   This example turns off notes printing.

```
ActiveSheet.PageSetup.PrintNotes = False
```

PrintObject Property

Applies To   Arc, Arcs, Button, Buttons, ChartObject, ChartObjects, CheckBox, CheckBoxes, Drawing, DrawingObjects, Drawings, DropDown, DropDowns, EditBox, EditBoxes, GroupBox, GroupBoxes, GroupObject, GroupObjects, Label, Labels, Line, Lines, ListBox, ListBoxes, OLEObject, OLEObjects, OptionButton, OptionButtons, Oval, Ovals, Picture, Pictures, Rectangle, Rectangles, ScrollBar, ScrollBars, Spinner, Spinners, TextBox, TextBoxes.

Description   **True** if the object will be printed when the document is printed. Read-write.

Syntax   *object*.**PrintObject**

Elements   *object*
                      Required. The object to which this property applies.

See Also   **PrintOut** Method.

Example   This example sets oval one to print with the worksheet.

```
ActiveSheet.Ovals(1).PrintObject = True
```

PrintOut Method

Applies To   Chart, Charts, DialogSheet, DialogSheets, Module, Modules, Range, Sheets, Window, Workbook, Worksheet, Worksheets.

Description   Prints the object.

Syntax   *object*.**PrintOut**(*from, to, copies, preview*)

Elements   The **PrintOut** method has the following object qualifier and named arguments:

object
   Required. The object to print.

from
   Optional. The number of the page with which to start printing. If omitted, printing starts at the beginning.

to
   Optional. The number of the last page to print. If omitted, printing goes to the last page.

copies
   Optional. The number of copies to print. If omitted, one copy is printed.

preview
   Optional. If **True**, Microsoft Excel invokes print preview before printing the object. If **False** (or omitted) the object is printed immediately.

Remarks   "Pages" in the descriptions of *from* and *to* refers to printed pages -- not overall pages in the sheet or workbook.

This method applies to the Window object only when it is the Info Window.

See Also   **PrintArea** Property, **PrintPreview** Method.

Example   This example prints the active sheet.

```
ActiveSheet.PrintOut
```

PrintPreview Method

Applies To   Chart, Charts, DialogSheet, DialogSheets, Range, Sheets, Window, Workbook, Worksheet, Worksheets.

Description   Shows a preview of the object as it would be printed.

Syntax	*object*.**PrintPreview**
Elements	*object* Required. The object to preview.
See Also	**PrintOut** Method.
Example	This example shows a print preview of the active sheet.

```
ActiveSheet.PrintPreview
```

PrintQuality Property

Applies To	PageSetup.
Description	Returns or sets the print quality, as a two-element array containing both horizontal and vertical print quality. Some printers may not support vertical print quality. Read-write.
Syntax	*object*.**PrintQuality**
Elements	*object* Required. The PageSetup object.
Remarks	This property always returns a two-element array, even if the printer does not support vertical print quality.
Examples	This example sets print quality on a printer with non-square pixels. The array specifies both horizontal and vertical print quality.

```
ActiveSheet.PageSetup.PrintQuality = Array(240, 140)
```

This example displays the current horizontal print quality setting.

```
MsgBox "Horizontal Print Quality is " & _
    ActiveSheet.PageSetup.PrintQuality(1)
```

PrintTitleColumns Property

Applies To	PageSetup.
Description	Returns or sets the columns containing the cells to be repeated on the left of each page, as a string in A1-style notation in the language of the macro. Read-write.

Syntax	*object*.**PrintTitleColumns**
Elements	*object* Required. The PageSetup object.
Remarks	If you specify only part of a column or columns, Microsoft Excel expands the range to full columns.
	Set this property to **False** or to the empty string ("") to turn off title columns.
	This property applies only to worksheet pages.
See Also	**PrintTitleRows** Property.
Example	This example sets row three to the print title row, and columns one through three as the title columns.

```
ActiveSheet.PageSetup.PrintTitleRows = ActiveSheet.Rows(3)
ActiveSheet.PageSetup.PrintTitleColumns = ActiveSheet.Columns("A:C")
```

PrintTitleRows Property

Applies To	PageSetup.
Description	Returns or sets the rows containing the cells to be repeated on the top of each page, as a string in A1-style notation in the language of the macro. Read-write.
Syntax	*object*.**PrintTitleRows**
Elements	*object* Required. The PageSetup object.
Remarks	If you specify only part of a row or rows, Microsoft Excel expands the range to full rows.
	Set this property to **False** or to the empty string ("") to turn off title rows.
	This property applies only to worksheet pages.
See Also	**PrintTitleColumns** Property.
Example	This example sets row three to the print title row, and columns one through three to the title columns.

```
ActiveSheet.PageSetup.PrintTitleRows = ActiveSheet.Rows(3)
ActiveSheet.PageSetup.PrintTitleColumns = ActiveSheet.Columns("A:C")
```

Private Statement

Description   Used at module level to declare private variables and allocate storage space.

Syntax   **Private** *varname*[([*subscripts*])][**As** *type*][,*varname*[([*subscripts*])][**As** *type*]] **. . .**

Elements   The **Private** statement syntax has these parts:

Part	Description
varname	Name of the variable; follows standard variable naming conventions.
subscripts	Dimensions of an array variable; up to 60 multiple dimensions may be declared. The *subscripts* argument uses the following syntax: [*lower* **To**] *upper* [,[*lower* **To**] *upper*] **. . .**
type	Data type of the variable; may be **Boolean**, **Integer**, **Long**, **Currency**, **Single**, **Double**, **Date**, **String** (for variable-length strings), **String** * *length* (for fixed-length strings), **Object**, **Variant**, a user-defined type, or an object type. Use a separate **As** *type* clause for each variable being defined.

Remarks   **Private** variables are available only to the module in which they are declared.

Use the **Private** statement to declare the data type or object type of a variable. For example, the following statement declares a variable as an **Integer**:

```
Private NumberOfEmployees As Integer
```

If you do not specify a data type or object type, and there is no **Def***type* statement in the module, the variable is **Variant** by default.

When variables are initialized, a numeric variable is initialized to 0, a variable-length string is initialized to a zero-length string, and a fixed-length string is filled with zeros. **Variant** variables are initialized to **Empty**. Each element of a user-defined type variable is initialized as if it was a separate variable. A variable that refers to an object must be assigned an existing object using the **Set** statement before it can be used. Until it is assigned an object, the declared object variable has the special value **Nothing**, which indicates that it does not refer to any particular instance of an object.

You can also use the **Private** statement with empty parentheses to declare dynamic arrays. After declaring a dynamic array, use the **ReDim** statement within a procedure to define the number of dimensions and elements in the array. If you try to redeclare a dimension for an array variable whose size was explicitly specified in a **Private**, **Public** or **Dim** statement, an error occurs.

See Also   **Array** Function, **Const** Statement, **Dim** Statement, **Function** Statement, **Option Base** Statement, **Option Private** Statement, **Property Get** Statement, **Property Let** Statement, **Property Set** Statement, **Public** Statement, **ReDim** Statement, **Static** Statement, **Sub** Statement, **Type** Statement.

Example   This **Private** statement is used at the module-level to declare variables as private; that is, they are available only to the module in which they are declared.

```
Private Number As Integer                ' Private integer variable.
Private NameArray (1 To 5) As String        ' Private array variable.
Private MyVar, YourVar, ThisVar As Integer'Multiple declarations.
```

PromptForSummaryInfo Property

Applies To   Application.

Description   **True** if Microsoft Excel asks for summary info when files are initially saved. Read-write.

Syntax   *object*.**PromptForSummaryInfo**

Elements   *object*
                  Required. The Application object.

Example   This example causes Microsoft Excel to ask for summary info when files are initially saved.

```
Application.PromptForSummaryInfo = True
```

Property Get Statement

Description   Declares the name, arguments, and code that form the body of a **Property** procedure, which gets the value of a property.

Syntax

[**Public** | **Private**][**Static**] **Property Get** *name* [(*arglist*)][**As** *type*]
    [*statements*]
    [*name = expression*]
    [**Exit Property**]
    [*statements*]
    [*name = expression*]
End Property

Elements

The **Property Get** statement syntax has these parts:

Part	Description
Public	Indicates that the **Property Get** procedure is accessible to all other procedures in all modules. If used in a private module (one that contains an **Option Private** statement) the procedure is not available outside the project.
Private	Indicates that the **Property Get** procedure is accessible only to other procedures in the module where it is declared.
Static	Indicates that the **Property Get** procedure's local variables are preserved between calls. The **Static** attribute doesn't affect variables that are declared outside the **Property Get** procedure, even if they are used in the procedure.
name	Name of the **Property Get** procedure; follows standard variable naming conventions, except that the name can be the same as a **Property Let** or **Property Set** procedure in the same module.
arglist	List of variables representing arguments that are passed to the **Property Get** procedure when it is called. Multiple variables are separated by commas.
type	Data type of the value returned by the **Property Get** procedure; may be **Boolean**, **Integer**, **Long**, **Currency**, **Single**, **Double**, **Date**, **String** (except fixed length), **Object**, or **Variant**. Arrays of any type can't be returned, but a **Variant** containing an array can.
statements	Any group of statements to be executed within the body of the **Property Get** procedure.
expression	Value of the property returned by the procedure defined by the **Property Get** statement.

The *arglist* argument has the following syntax and parts:

[**Optional**][**ByVal** | **ByRef**] *varname*[( )][**As** *type*]

Part	Description
Optional	Indicates that an argument is not required. If used, all subsequent arguments in *arglist* must also be optional and declared using the **Optional** keyword. All **Optional** arguments must be **Variant**.
ByVal	Indicates that the argument is passed by value.

Part	Description
ByRef	Indicates that the argument is passed by reference.
varname	Name of the variable representing the argument; follows standard variable naming conventions.
type	Data type of the argument passed to the **Property Get** procedure; may be **Boolean**, **Integer**, **Long**, **Currency**, **Single**, **Double**, **Date**, **String** (variable length only), **Object**, **Variant**, a user-defined type, or an object type.

Remarks

If not explicitly specified using either **Public** or **Private**, **Property** procedures are **Public** by default. If **Static** is not used, the value of local variables is not preserved between calls.

All executable code must be in procedures. You can't define a **Property Get** procedure inside another **Sub**, **Function**, or **Property** procedure.

The **Exit Property** keywords cause an immediate exit from a **Property Get** procedure. Program execution continues with the statement following the statement that called the **Property Get** procedure. Any number of **Exit Property** statements can appear anywhere in a **Property Get** procedure.

Like a **Sub** and **Property Let** procedure, a **Property Get** procedure is a separate procedure that can take arguments, perform a series of statements, and change the values of its arguments. However, unlike a **Sub** or **Property Let** procedure, a **Property Get** procedure can be used on the right-hand side of an expression in the same way you use a **Function** or a property name when you want to return the value of a property.

See Also

Function Statement, **Property Let** Statement, **Property Set** Statement, **Sub** Statement.

Example

This example uses the **Property Get** Statement to define a property procedure that gets the value of a property that identifies, as a string, the current color of a pen in a drawing package:

```
Dim CurrentColor As Integer
Const BLACK = 0, RED = 1, GREEN = 2, BLUE = 3

' Returns the current color of the pen as a string
Property Get PenColor() As String
    Select Case CurrentColor
        Case RED
            PenColor = "Red"
        Case GREEN
            PenColor = "Green"
        Case BLUE
            PenColor = "Blue"
    End Select
End Property

' The following line gets the color of the pen
' calling the Property Get procedure.
ColorName = PenColor()
```

Property Let Statement

Description

Declares the name, arguments, and code that form the body of a **Property Let** procedure, which assigns a value to a property.

Syntax

[**Public** | **Private**][**Static**] **Property Let** *name* [(*arglist*)]
    [*statements*]
    [**Exit Property**]
    [*statements*]
End Property

Elements

The **Property Let** statement syntax has these parts:

Part	Description
Public	Indicates that the **Property Let** procedure is accessible to all other procedures in all modules. If used in a private module (one that contains an **Option Private** statement), the procedure is not available outside the project.
Private	Indicates that the **Property Let** procedure is accessible only to other procedures in the module where it is declared.

Part	Description
Static	Indicates that the **Property Let** procedure's local variables are preserved between calls. The **Static** attribute doesn't affect variables that are declared outside the **Property Let** procedure, even if they are used in the procedure.
name	Name of the **Property Let** procedure; follows standard variable naming conventions, except that the name can be the same as a **Property Get** or **Property Set** procedure in the same module.
arglist	List of variables representing arguments that are passed to the **Property Let** procedure when it is called. Multiple variables are separated by commas. The last argument is the value assigned to the property on the right-hand side of an expression.
statements	Any group of statements to be executed within the body of the **Property Let** procedure.

The *arglist* argument has the following syntax and parts:

[**ByVal** | **ByRef**] *varname*[( )][**As** *type*]

Part	Description
ByVal	Indicates that the argument is passed by value.
ByRef	Indicates that the argument is passed by reference.
varname	Name of the variable representing the argument; follows standard variable naming conventions.
type	Data type of the argument passed to the **Property Let** procedure; may be **Boolean**, **Integer**, **Long**, **Currency**, **Single**, **Double**, **Date**, **String** (variable length only), **Object**, **Variant**, a user-defined type, or an object type.

Note Every **Property Let** statement must define at least one argument for the procedure it defines. That argument (or the last argument if there is more than one) will contain the actual value to be assigned to the property when the procedure defined by the **Property Let** statement is invoked.

Remarks

If not explicitly specified using either **Public** or **Private**, **Property** procedures are **Public** by default. If **Static** is not used, the value of local variables is not preserved between calls.

All executable code must be in procedures. You can't define a **Property Let** procedure inside another **Sub**, **Function**, or **Property** procedure.

The **Exit Property** keywords cause an immediate exit from a **Property Let** procedure. Program execution continues with the statement following the statement that called the **Property Let** procedure. Any number of **Exit Property** statements can appear anywhere in a **Property Let** procedure.

Like a **Function** and **Property Get** procedure, a **Property Let** procedure is a separate procedure that can take arguments, perform series of statements, and change the value of its arguments. However, unlike a **Function** and **Property Get** procedure, both of which return a value, a **Property Let** procedure can only be used on the left side of a property assignment expression or **Let** statement.

See Also

Function Statement, **Let** Statement, **Property Get** Statement, **Property Set** Statement, **Sub** Statement.

Example

This example uses the **Property Let** statement to define a procedure that assigns a value to a property that identifies the pen color for a drawing package.

```
Dim CurrentColor As Integer
Const BLACK = 0, RED = 1, GREEN = 2, BLUE = 3

' Sets the pen color property for a Drawing package.
' The module level variable 'CurrentColor' is set to
' a numeric value that identifies the color used for drawing.
Property Let PenColor(ColorName as String)
    Select Case ColorName          ' Check color name string.
        Case "Red"
            CurrentColor = RED      ' Assign value for Red.
        Case "Green"
            CurrentColor = GREEN     ' Assign value for Green.
        Case "Blue"
            CurrentColor = BLUE     ' Assign value for Blue.
        Case Else
            CurrentColor = BLACK     ' Assign default value.
    End Select
End Property

' The following line sets the PenColor property for a drawing package
' by calling the Property Let procedure.

PenColor() = "Red"
```

Property Set Statement

Description

Declares the name, arguments, and code that form the body of a **Property** procedure, which sets a reference to an object.

Syntax

[**Public** | **Private**][**Static**] **Property Set** *name* [(*arglist*)]

    [*statements*]
    [**Exit Property**]
    [*statements*]
End Property

Elements

The **Property Set** statement syntax has these parts:

Part	Description
Public	Indicates that the **Property Set** procedure is accessible to all other procedures in all modules. If used in a private module (one that contains an **Option Private** statement), the procedure is not available outside the project.
Private	Indicates that the **Property Set** procedure is accessible only to other procedures in the module where it is declared.
Static	Indicates that the **Property Set** procedure's local variables are preserved between calls. The **Static** attribute doesn't affect variables that are declared outside the **Property Set** procedure, even if they are used in the procedure.
name	Name of the **Property Set** procedure; follows standard variable naming conventions, except that the name can be the same as a **Property Get** or **Property Let** procedure in the same module.
arglist	List of variables representing arguments that are passed to the **Property Set** procedure when it is called. Multiple variables are separated by commas. The last argument is the object reference used on the right-hand side of an object reference assignment.
statements	Any group of statements to be executed within the body of the **Property** procedure.

The *arglist* argument has the following syntax and parts:

[**ByVal** | **ByRef**] *varname*[( )][**As** *type*]

Part	Description
ByVal	Indicates that the argument is passed by value.
ByRef	Indicates that the argument is passed by reference.
varname	Name of the variable representing the argument; follows standard variable naming conventions.

Part	Description
type	Data type of the argument passed to the **Property Set** procedure; may be **Boolean**, **Integer**, **Long**, **Currency**, **Single**, **Double**, **Date**, **String** (variable length only), **Object**, **Variant**, a user-defined type, or an object type.

Note Every **Property Set** statement must define at least one argument for the procedure it defines. That argument (or the last argument if there is more than one) will contain the actual object reference for the property when the procedure defined by the **Property Set** statement is invoked.

Remarks

If not explicitly specified using either **Public** or **Private**, **Property** procedures are **Public** by default. If **Static** is not used, the value of local variables is not preserved between calls.

All executable code must be in procedures. You can't define a **Property Set** procedure inside another **Sub**, **Function**, or **Property** procedure.

The **Exit Property** keywords cause an immediate exit from a **Property Set** procedure. Program execution continues with the statement following the statement that called the **Property Set** procedure. Any number of **Exit Property** statements can appear anywhere in a **Property Set** procedure.

Like a **Function** and **Property Get** procedure, a **Property Set** procedure is a separate procedure that can take arguments, perform a series of statements, and change the value of its arguments. However, unlike a **Function** and **Property Get** procedure, both of which return a value, a **Property Set** procedure can only be used on the left side of an object reference assignment (**Set** statement).

See Also

Function Statement, **Property Get** Statement, **Property Let** Statement, **Sub** Statement.

Example

This example uses the **Property Set** statement to declare a property procedure which sets a reference to an object.

```
' The Pen property may be set to different Pen implementations.
Property Set Pen(P As Object)
    Set CurrentPen = P      ' Assign Pen to object.
End Property
```

Protect Method

Applies To

Chart, DialogSheet, Module, Workbook, Worksheet.

Description	Protects a chart, dialog sheet, Visual Basic module or worksheet (Syntax 1), or a workbook (Syntax 2) so that it cannot be modified.
Syntax 1	*object*.**Protect**(*password, drawingObjects, contents, scenarios*)
Syntax 2	*object*.**Protect**(*password, structure, windows*)
Elements	The **Protect** method has the following object qualifier and named arguments:

object
> Required. The Chart, DialogSheet, Module, or Worksheet (Syntax 1) or Workbook object (Syntax 2).

password
> Optional. A string that specifies a case-sensitive password for the sheet or workbook. If omitted, you can unprotect the sheet or workbook without a password. If specified, you must specify the password to unprotect the sheet or workbook. If you forget the password, you cannot unprotect the sheet or workbook. It's a good idea to keep a list of your passwords and their corresponding document names in a safe place.

drawingObjects
> Optional. **True** to protect the drawing objects on the sheet. For a dialog sheet, this protects the layout of the controls. If this argument is omitted, the drawing objects are not protected. Ignored for Visual Basic modules.

contents
> Optional. **True** (or omitted) to protect the contents of the object. For a Visual Basic Module, this protects the source code. For a chart, this protects the entire chart. For a dialog sheet, this protects the dialog layout and text of the dialog controls. For a worksheet, this protects the cells.

scenarios
> Optional. **True** (or omitted) to protect scenarios. This argument is valid only for worksheets.

structure
> Optional. **True** to protect the structure of the workbook (the relative position of the sheets). If this argument is omitted, the structure is not protected.

windows
> Optional. **True** to protect the windows of the sheet or workbook. If omitted, the windows are not protected.

Remarks	Using the **Protect** method causes an error if the workbook is already protected.
See Also	**Locked** Property, **ProtectContents** Property, **ProtectDrawingObjects** Property, **ProtectScenerios** Property, **ProtectStructure** Property, **ProtectWindows** Property, **Unprotect** Method.
Example	This example protects the active workbook.

```
ActiveWorkbook.Protect password := "drowssap"
```

ProtectContents Property

Applies To   Chart, DialogSheet, Module, Worksheet.

Description   **True** if the contents of a sheet are protected. For a Visual Basic Module, this protects the source code. For a chart, this protects the entire chart. For a dialog sheet, this protects the dialog layout and text of the dialog controls. For a worksheet, this protects the cells. Read-only.

Syntax   *object*.**ProtectContents**

Elements   *object*
                        Required. The Chart, DialogSheet, Module, or Worksheet object.

See Also   **Locked** Property, **Protect** Method, **ProtectWindows** Property, **Unprotect** Method.

Example   This example displays a message box if the contents of the active sheet are protected.

```
If ActiveSheet.ProtectContents Then
    MsgBox "The contents of the active sheet are protected."
End If
```

ProtectDrawingObjects Property

Applies To   Chart, DialogSheet, Worksheet.

Description   **True** if the drawing objects of a sheet are protected. On a dialog sheet, this protects the layout of the controls. Read-only.

Syntax   *object*.**ProtectDrawingObjects**

Elements   *object*
                        Required. The Chart, DialogSheet, or Worksheet object.

See Also   **Locked** Property, **Protect** Method, **ProtectContents** Property, **Unprotect** Method.

Example   This example displays a message box if the drawing objects on the active sheet are protected.

```
If ActiveSheet.ProtectDrawingObjects Then
    MsgBox "The drawing objects on the active sheet are protected."
End If
```

ProtectScenarios Property

Applies To	Worksheet.
Description	**True** if the worksheet scenarios are protected. Read-only.
Syntax	*object*.**ProtectScenarios**
Elements	*object* Required. The Worksheet object.
See Also	**Protect** Method, **Unprotect** Method.
Example	This example displays a message box if scenarios are protected on the active worksheet.

```
If ActiveSheet.ProtectScenarios Then _
    MsgBox "Scenarios are protected on this worksheet."
```

ProtectStructure Property

Applies To	Workbook.
Description	**True** if the order of the sheets in the workbook is protected. Read-only.
Syntax	*object*.**ProtectStructure**
Elements	*object* Required. The Workbook object.
See Also	**Protect** Method, **ProtectWindows** Property, **Unprotect** Method.
Example	This example displays a message advising you of the results of protecting the structure of the workbook PROFIT92.XLS.

```
If Workbooks("PROFIT92.XLS").ProtectStructure Then
    MsgBox "Remember, you cannot delete, add, or change " & _
        "the location of any sheets in this workbook."
End If
```

ProtectWindows Property

Applies To	Workbook.
Description	**True** if the windows of the workbook are protected. Read-only.

Syntax	*object*.**ProtectWindows**
Elements	*object* Required. The Workbook object.
See Also	**Protect** Method, **ProtectStructure** Property, **Unprotect** Method.
Example	This example displays a message advising you of the results of protecting the windows of the workbook PROFIT92.XLS.

```
If Workbooks("PROFIT92.XLS").ProtectWindows Then
    MsgBox "Remember, you cannot rearrange any window in this workbook."
End If
```

Public Statement

Description	Used at module level to declare public variables and allocate storage space.
Syntax	**Public** *varname*[([*subscripts*])][**As** *type*][,*varname*[([*subscripts*])][**As** *type*]] ...
Elements	The **Public** statement syntax has these parts:

Part	Description
varname	Name of the variable; follows standard variable naming conventions.
subscripts	Dimensions of an array variable; up to 60 multiple dimensions may be declared. The argument *subscripts* uses the following syntax: [*lower* **To**] *upper* [,[*lower* **To**] *upper*] ...

type   Data type of the variable; may be **Boolean**, **Integer**, **Long**, **Currency**, **Single**, **Double**, **Date**, **String** (for variable-length strings), **String** * *length* (for fixed-length strings), **Object**, **Variant**, a user-defined type, or an object type. Use a separate **As** *type* clause for each variable being defined.

Remarks   Variables declared using the **Public** statement are available to all procedures in all modules in all applications unless **Option Private Module** is in effect; in which case, the variables are **Public** only within the project in which they reside.

Use the **Public** statement to declare the data type or object type of a variable. For example, the following statement declares a variable as an **Integer**:

```
Public NumberOfEmployees As Integer
```

If you do not specify a data type or object type and there is no **Def***type* statement in the module, the variable is **Variant** by default.

When variables are initialized, a numeric variable is initialized to 0, a variable-length string is initialized to a zero-length string, and a fixed-length string is filled with zeros. **Variant** variables are initialized to **Empty**. Each element of a user-defined type variable is initialized as if it was a separate variable. A variable that refers to an object must be assigned an existing object using the **Set** statement before it can be used. Until it is assigned an object, the declared object variable has the special value **Nothing**, which indicates that it does not refer to any particular instance of an object.

You can also use the **Public** statement with empty parentheses to declare dynamic arrays. After declaring a dynamic array, use the **ReDim** statement within a procedure to define the number of dimensions and elements in the array. If you try to redeclare a dimension for an array variable whose size was explicitly specified in a **Private**, **Public** or **Dim** statement, an error occurs.

See Also

Array Function, **Const** Statement, **Dim** Statement, **Option Base** Statement, **Option Private** Statement, **Private** Statement, **ReDim** Statement, **Static** Statement, **Type** Statement.

Example

The **Public** statement is used at the module-level to declare variables as public; that is, they are available to all procedures in all modules in all applications unless **Option Private Module** is in effect.

```
Public Number As Integer                    ' Public integer variable.
Public NameArray(1 To 5) As String    ' Public array variable.
Public MyVar, YourVar, ThisVar As Integer
                                      ' Multiple declarations.
```

Pushed Property

Applies To

ToolbarButton.

Description

True if the button appears pressed down. Read-write.

Syntax

object.**Pushed**

Elements

object
    Required. The ToolbarButton object.

Remark

You cannot set this property for a built-in button. You can only set it for a custom button, and then only if the button has a procedure attached to it.

See Also

Enabled Property.

Example

This example adds a custom button to toolbar one, attaches the my_Macro procedure to it, and then makes the button appear pressed.

```
Set btn = Toolbars(1).ToolbarButtons.Add(button:=220, before:=3)
btn.OnAction = "my_Macro"
btn.Pushed = True
```

Put Statement

Description   Writes from a variable to a disk file.

Syntax   **Put** [#]*filenumber*,[*recnumber*],*varname*

Elements   The **Put** statement syntax has these parts:

Part	Description
filenumber	Any valid file number.
recnumber	Record number (**Random** mode files) or byte number (**Binary** mode files) at which writing begins.
varname	Name of variable containing data to be written to disk.

Remarks   The first record/byte in a file is at position 1, the second record/byte is at position 2, and so on. If you omit *recnumber*, the next record or byte (the one after the last **Get** or **Put** statement or the one pointed to by the last **Seek** function) is written. You must include delimiting commas, for example:

```
Put #4,,FileBuffer
```

For files opened in **Random** mode, the following rules apply:

- If the length of the data being written is less than the length specified in the **Len** clause of the **Open** statement, **Put** still writes subsequent records on record-length boundaries. The space between the end of one record and the beginning of the next record is padded with the existing contents of the file buffer. Because the amount of padding data can't be determined with any certainty, it is generally a good idea to have the record length match the length of the data being written.

- If the variable being written is a variable-length string, **Put** writes a 2-byte descriptor containing the string length and then the variable. The record length specified by the **Len** clause in the **Open** statement must be at least 2 bytes greater than the actual length of the string.

- If the variable being written is a **Variant** of a numeric type, **Put** writes 2 bytes identifying the **VarType** of the **Variant** and then the variable. For example, when writing a **Variant** of **VarType** 3, **Put** writes 6 bytes: 2 bytes identifying the **Variant** as **VarType** 3 (**Long**) and 4 bytes containing the **Long** data. The record length specified by the **Len** clause in the **Open** statement must be at least 2 bytes greater than the actual number of bytes required to store the variable.

- If the variable being written is a **String Variant** (**VarType** 8), **Put** writes 2 bytes identifying the **VarType**, 2 bytes indicating the length of the string, and then the string data. The record length specified by the **Len** clause in the **Open** statement must be at least 4 bytes greater than the actual length of the string.

- If the variable being written is any other type of variable (not a variable-length string and not a **Variant**), **Put** writes only the variable data. The record length specified by the **Len** clause in the **Open** statement must be greater than or equal to the length of the data being written.

- **Put** writes elements of user-defined types as if each were written individually, except there is no padding between elements. The record length specified by the **Len** clause in the **Open** statement must be greater than or equal to the sum of all the bytes required to write the individual elements.

For files opened in **Binary** mode, all of the **Random** rules apply except that:

- The **Len** clause in the **Open** statement has no effect. **Put** writes all variables to disk contiguously; that is, with no padding between records.

- **Put** writes variable-length strings that are not elements of user-defined types without the 2-byte length descriptor. The number of bytes written equals the number of characters in the string. For example, the following statements write 10 bytes to file number 1:

```
VarString$ = String$(10," ")
Put #1,,VarString$
```

See Also   **Get** Statement, **Open** Statement, **VarType** Function.

Example

This example uses the **Put** statement to write data to a disk file. Five records of the user-defined type Record are written to the file.

```
' Define user-defined type.
Type Record
    ID As Integer
    Name As String * 20
End Type
Dim MyRecord As Record                    ' Declare variable.

' Open file for random access.
Open "TESTFILE" For Random As #1 Len = Len(MyRecord)
For RecordNumber = 1 To 5                 ' Loop 5 times.
    MyRecord.ID = RecordNumber            ' Define ID.
    MyRecord.Name = "My Name" & RecordNumber          ' Create a
string.
    Put #1, RecordNumber, MyRecord        ' Write record to file.
Next RecordNumber
Close #1                                  ' Close file.
```

QueryGetData Function

Description

Builds a new query.

This function is contained in the XLQuery add-in. Before you use the function, you must establish a reference to the XLQuery add-in using the References command from the Tools menu. For more information, see "Calling Procedures in Another Workbook," in the *Visual Basic User's Guide*.

Syntax

QueryGetData(*connectionString, queryText, keepQueryDef, fieldNames, rowNumbers, destination, execute*)

Elements

The **QueryGetData** function has the following named arguments:

connectionString

Required. A string that contains database connection information, such as the data source name, user ID, and passwords, necessary to make a SQL connection to an external data source. For example, "DSN=Myserver; Server=server1; UID=dbayer; PWD=buyer1; Database=nwind".

queryText

Required. A string that contains the SQL language query to be run on the data source.

keepQueryDef

Optional. If **True** or omitted, preserves the query definition. If **False**, the query definition is lost and the data from the query is no longer a data range.

fieldNames
> Optional. If **True** or omitted, places field names from Microsoft Query into the first row of the data range. If **False**, the field names are discarded.

rowNumbers
> Optional. If True, places row numbers from Microsoft Query into the first column in the data range. If **False** or omitted, the row numbers are discarded.

destination
> Optional. The destination for the returned data, as a Range object. If destination is in a data range then that data range is changed to reflect the new SQL query. The default destination is the active cell or the selection.

execute
> Optional. If **True** or omitted, the query is run immediately. If **False**, the query text is added to a buffer and the query is not run until a subsequent **QueryGetData** function call with the execute argument set to **True**. When this occurs, Microsoft Query runs all query text in the buffer.

See Also   **QueryGetDataDialog** Function, **QueryRefresh** Function.

QueryGetDataDialog Function

Description   Builds a new query. Equivalent to choosing the Get External Data command from the Data menu.

This function is contained in the XLQuery add-in. Before you use the function, you must establish a reference to the XLQuery add-in using the References command from the Tools menu. For more information, see "Calling Procedures in Another Workbook," in the *Visual Basic User's Guide*.

Syntax   **QueryGetDataDialog(***connectionString, queryText, keepQueryDef, fieldNames, rowNumbers, destination, execute***)**

Elements   The **QueryGetData** function has the following named arguments:

connectionString
> Required. A string that contains database connection information, such as the data source name, user ID, and passwords, necessary to make a SQL connection to an external data source. For example, "DSN=Myserver; Server=server1; UID=dbayer; PWD=buyer1; Database=nwind".

queryText
> Required. A string that contains the SQL language query to be run on the data source.

keepQueryDef

Optional. If **True** or omitted, preserves the query definition. If **False**, the query definition is lost and the data from the query is no longer a data range.

fieldNames

Optional. If **True** or omitted, places field names from Microsoft Query into the first row of the data range. If **False**, the field names are discarded.

rowNumbers

Optional. If True, places row numbers from Microsoft Query into the first column in the data range. If **False** or omitted, the row numbers are discarded.

destination

Optional. The destination for the returned data, as a Range object. If destination is in a data range then that data range is changed to reflect the new SQL query. The default destination is the active cell or the selection.

execute

Optional. If **True** or omitted, the query is run immediately. If **False**, the query text is added to a buffer and the query is not run until a subsequent **QueryGetData** function call with the execute argument set to **True**. When this occurs, Microsoft Query runs all query text in the buffer.

See Also   **QueryGetData** Function, **QueryRefresh** Function.

QueryRefresh Function

Description   Refreshes the data in a data range returned by the Microsoft Query tool.

This function is contained in the XLQuery add-in. Before you use the function, you must establish a reference to the XLQuery add-in using the References command from the Tools menu. For more information, see "Calling Procedures in Another Workbook,"" in the *Visual Basic User's Guide*.

Syntax   **QueryRefresh(*ref*)**

Elements   The **QueryRefresh** function has the following named argument:

ref

Optional. A single cell, as a Range object, that is inside a data range. If *ref* is not in a data range then the function returns the #REF! error value.

See Also   **QueryGetData** Function, **QueryGetDataDialog** Function.

Quit Method

Applies To   Application.

Description   Quits Microsoft Excel. Does not run any Auto_Close macros before quitting.

Syntax   *object*.**Quit**

Elements   *object*
    Required. The Application object.

Remarks   If unsaved workbooks are open when you use this method, Microsoft Excel displays a dialog box asking if you want to save the changes. You can prevent this by saving all workbooks before using the **Quit** method or by setting the **DisplayAlerts** property to **False.** When this property is **False**, Microsoft Excel does not display the dialog box when you quit with unsaved workbooks, and it quits without saving them.

If you set the **Saved** property for a workbook to **True** without saving it to the disk, Microsoft Excel will quit without asking you to save the workbook.

Example   This example saves any open documents and closes the application.

```
For Each w In Application.Workbooks
    w.Save
Next w
Application.Quit
```

RadarAxisLabels Property

Applies To   ChartGroup

Description   Returns or sets the radar axis labels (a TickLabels collection) for this chart group. Read-write.

Syntax   *object*.**RadarAxisLabels**

Elements   *object*
    Required. The ChartGroup object.

See Also   **HasRadarAxisLabels** Property.

Example   This example turns on radar axis labels for the first chart group, and sets their color.

```
With ActiveChart.ChartGroups(1)
    .HasRadarAxisLabels = True
    .RadarAxisLabels.Font.Color = RGB(255, 0, 0)
End With
```

RadarGroups Method

Applies To   Chart.

Description   On a 2-D chart, returns a single radar chart group (a ChartGroup object, Syntax 1), or a collection of the radar chart groups (a ChartGroups collection, Syntax 2).

Syntax 1   *object*.**RadarGroups(*index*)**

Syntax 2   *object*.**RadarGroups**

Elements   The **RadarGroups** method has the following object qualifier and named arguments:

object
    Required. The Chart object.

index
    Required for Syntax 1. Specifies the chart group.

Example   This example makes the first radar group a filled radar group.

```
Charts(1).RadarGroups(1).SubType = 2
```

Randomize Statement

Description   Initializes the random-number generator.

Syntax   **Randomize [*number*]**

Elements   The *number* named argument can be any valid numeric expression.

Remarks   **Randomize** uses *number* to initialize a random-number generator, giving it a new seed value. If you omit *number,* the value returned by the **Timer** function is used as the new seed value.

If **Randomize** is not used, the same initial seed is always used to start the sequence.

Use the **Randomize** statement without an argument to provide a random seed based on the system timer to initialize the random-number generator before **Rnd** is called.

See Also   **Rnd** Function, **Timer** Function.

Example   This example uses the **Randomize** statement to initialize the random-number generator. Because the number argument has been omitted, **Randomize** uses the return value from the **Timer** function as the new seed value.

```
' Initialize random-number generator.
Randomize
' Generate random value between 1 and 6.
MyAngle = Int((6 * Rnd) + 1)
```

Range Method

Applies To   Application, Range, Worksheet.

Description   Returns a cell or range of cells.

Syntax 1   *object*.**Range**(*cell1*)

Syntax 2   *object*.**Range**(*cell1, cell2*)

Elements   The **Range** method has the following object qualifier and named arguments:

object
   Optional for Application, required for Range and Worksheet. The object to which this method applies.

cell1
   Required for Syntax 1. The name of the range. This must be an A1-style reference in the language of the macro. It may include the range operator ':' (colon), the intersection operator ' ' (space), or the union operator ',' (comma). It may include dollar signs, but they are ignored. Any part of the range may use a local defined name. If you use a name, the name is assumed to be in the language of the macro.

cell1, cell2
   Required for Syntax 2. The cells at the top left and bottom right of the range. Each one may be a Range containing exactly a single cell (or an entire column or entire row), or a string naming a single cell in the language of the macro.

Remarks   When used with no object qualifier, this method is a shortcut for **ActiveSheet.Range**.

When applied to a Range object, the method is relative to the range object. For example, if the selection is cell C3, then **Selection.Range("B1")** returns cell D3 because it is relative to the Range object returned by the **Selection** property. On the other hand, the code **ActiveSheet.Range("B1")** always returns cell B1.

See Also   **Cells** Method.

Examples   This example copies cells A1:J10 to the Clipboard. The example uses Syntax 1.

```
Application.Range("A1:J10").Copy
```

This example sets the font of cells A1:C5 to italic. The example uses Syntax 2.

```
Range(Cells(1, 1), Cells(5, 3)).Font.Italic = True
```

Range Object

Description   A cell, row, column, selection of cells, multiple selection, or 3-D range.

Working with the Range Object

Here are several examples of how to use the most important properties and methods of the Range object.

Cells Method

Use the **Cells** method to return a single cell, as shown in the following examples:

```
Cells(1, 1).Value = 24                'Set the value of cell A1 to 24
Cells(2, 1).Formula = "=SUM(B1:B5)"   'Enter a formula in cell A2
```

Although you can also use Range("A1") or just [a1] to return cell A1, these forms are not as useful as the Cells(rowIndex, columnIndex) notation. The following example shows why the Cells(rowIndex, columnIndex) is so useful (copy the code into a module and then run it from a worksheet):

```
Sub SetUpTable()
    For theYear = 1 To 5
        Cells(1, theYear + 1).Value = 1990 + theYear
    Next theYear
    For theQuarter = 1 To 4
        Cells(theQuarter + 1, 1).Value = "Q" & theQuarter
    Next theQuarter
End Sub
```

Although you could use Visual Basic's string functions to manipulate A1-style references, it's much easier (and much better programming practice) to use the Cells(1, 1) notation.

Range Method

Use the **Range** method to return a rectangular range of cells. The following example fills the range A1:H8 with the string "Test":

```
Sub FillTheRange()
    Range(Cells(1, 1), Cells(8, 8)).Value = "Test"
End Sub
```

You can also use the **Range** method to return a named range, as shown in the following example:

```
Sub ClearDatabaseCriteria()
    Range("Criteria").ClearContents
End Sub
```

Multiple Selections

Use the **Union** method and **Range** method to return multiple selections. The following example creates an object called myMultipleSelection, defines it as the multiple selection of A1:B2 and C3:D4, and then selects it:

```
Sub ShowMultipleSelection()
    Dim r1, r2, myMultipleSelection As Range
    Set r1 = Range(Cells(1, 1), Cells(2, 2))
    Set r2 = Range(Cells(3, 3), Cells(4, 4))
    Set myMultipleSelection = Union(r1, r2)
    myMultipleSelection.Select
End Sub
```

If you work with multiple selections, the **Areas** method is very useful. It divides a multiple selection into individual Range objects and then returns them as a collection. You can use the **Count** property on the returned collection to check for a multiple selection, as shown in the following example:

```
Sub NoMultipleSelections()
    numberOfSelectedAreas = Selection.Areas.Count
    If numberOfSelectedAreas > 1 Then
        MsgBox "You cannot carry out this command on multiple
selections"
    End If
End Sub
```

Offset Method

When you record macros using relative references, the macro recorder uses the **Offset** method to specify the selections you make on a worksheet. For example, this is what is recorded in a Visual Basic module when you move the active cell from A1 to B2:

```
Sub Macro(1)
    Selection.Offset(1, 1).Range("A1").Select
End Sub
```

ReadOnly Property

Applies To	Workbook.
Description	**True** if the workbook has been opened as read-only. Read-only.
Syntax	*object*.**ReadOnly**
Elements	*object* Required. The Workbook object.
See Also	**Open** Method, **SaveAs** Method.
Example	This example saves the active workbook as NEWFILE.XLS if it is read-only.

```
If ActiveWorkbook.ReadOnly Then
    ActiveWorkbook.SaveAs fileName:="NEWFILE.XLS"
End If
```

ReadOnlyRecommended Property

Applies To	Workbook.
Description	**True** if the workbook was saved as read-only recommended. Read-only.
Syntax	*object*.**ReadOnlyRecommended**
Elements	*object* Required. The Workbook object.
Remarks	When you open a document that was saved as read-only recommended, Microsoft Excel displays a message recommending that you open the document as read-only.
	Use the **SaveAs** method to change this property.
See Also	**Open** Method, **SaveAs** Method.

Example

In this example, if the workbook BUDGET93.XLS is saved as read-only recommended, the code saves it as TESTFILE.XLS.

```
With Workbooks("BUDGET93.XLS")
    If .ReadOnlyRecommended Then
        .SaveAs fileName:="TESTFILE.XLS"
    End If
End With
```

Received Property

Applies To

Mailer.

Description

True if the workbook mailer has been received (it is has been sent by another user to the current user) and the current user has not modified the mailer by using the **Reply**, **ReplyAll**, or **ForwardMailer** methods. PowerTalk requires that mailers be received before they can be forwarded or replied to. Read-only.

Syntax

object.**Received**

Elements

object
        Required. The Mailer object.

See Also

BCCRecipient Property, **CCRecipients** Property, **Enclosures** Property, **ForwardMailer** Method, **Mailer** Property, **Reply** Method, **ReplyAll** Method, **SendDateTime** Property, **Sender** Property, **SendMailer** Property, **Subject** Property, **ToRecipients** Property.

Example

This example displays the current state of the Received property.

```
With ActiveWorkbook
    If .HasMailer Then
        If .Mailer.Received Then
            state = "True"
        Else
            state = "False"
        End If
        MsgBox "Received property is " & state
    Else
        MsgBox "The workbook has no mailer"
    End If
End With
```

Recipients Property

Applies To   RoutingSlip.

Description   Returns or sets the recipients on the routing slip (as an array of strings). Read-write.

Syntax   *object*.**Recipients**

Elements   *object*
                  Required. The RoutingSlip object.

Remarks   The order of the recipient list defines the delivery order if the routing delivery option is **xlOneAfterAnother**. If a routing slip is in progress, only those recipients who have not already received and routed the document are returned or set.

Example   This example sends BOOK1.XLS to three recipients, one after the other.

```
Workbooks("BOOK1.XLS").HasRoutingSlip = True
With Workbooks("BOOK1.XLS").RoutingSlip
    .Delivery = xlOneAfterAnother
    .Recipients = Array("Adam Bendel", "Jean Selva", "Bernard Gabor")
    .Subject = "Here is BOOK1.XLS"
    .Message = "Here is the workbook. What do you think?"
    .ReturnWhenDone = True
End With
Workbooks("BOOK1.XLS").Route
```

Record Method

Applies To   SoundNote.

Description   Displays the Record dialog box so you can record a sound note.

Syntax   *object*.**Record**

Elements   *object*
                  Required. The SoundNote object.

Remarks   To record sounds, you must have sound hardware installed in your computer.

See Also   **Play** Method.

Example   This example displays the Record dialog box so you can record a sound note into the active cell.

```
ActiveCell.SoundNote.Record
```

RecordMacro Method

Applies To Application.

Description Records code if the macro recorder is on.

Syntax *object*.**RecordMacro**(*basicCode, xlmCode*)

Elements The **RecordMacro** method has the following object qualifier and named arguments:

object
  Required. The Application object.

basicCode
  Optional. A string that specifies the Visual Basic code that will be recorded if the macro recorder is recording into a Visual Basic module. The string will be recorded on one line. If the string contains a carriage return (ASCII character 10, or **Chr$(10)** in code), it will be recorded on more than one line.

xlmCode
  Optional. A string that specifies the formula that will be recorded if the macro recorder is recording into a Microsoft Excel version 4.0 macro sheet. The string will be recorded into one cell. If the string does not begin with an equal sign, a comment is recorded.

Remarks The **RecordMacro** method cannot record into the active module (the module in which the **RecordMacro** method exists).

If *basicCode* is omitted, and the application is recording into Visual Basic, Microsoft Excel will record a suitable **Application.Run** statement.

If *xlmCode* is omitted, and the application is recording into Microsoft Excel version 4.0, Microsoft Excel will record a suitable **RUN** macro function.

To prevent recording (for example, if the user cancels your dialog box), call this function with two empty strings.

Example This example records Visual Basic code or an XLM formula.

```
Application.RecordMacro basicCode:="Application.Run ""MySub"" ", _
    xlmCode:="=MySub()"
```

RecordRelative Property

Applies To Application.

Description	**True** if macros are recorded using relative references; **False** if recording is absolute. Read-only.
Syntax	*object*.**RecordRelative**
Elements	*object* Required. The Application object.
Example	This example sets the string variable `theRightAddress` to return the address of A1 as the string "$A$1" if **RecordRelative** is **False**; otherwise, it returns it as the string "R1C1".

```
If Application.RecordRelative = False Then
    theRightAddress = Cells(1,1).Address()
Else
    theRightAddress = Cells(1,1).Address(referenceStyle := xlR1C1)
End If
```

Rectangle Object

Description	A rectangle graphic object drawn on a chart or worksheet.

Rectangles Method

Applies To	Chart, DialogSheet, Worksheet.
Description	Returns a single rectangle (a Rectangle object, Syntax 1) or a collection of rectangles (a Rectangles object, Syntax 2). Read-only.
Syntax 1	*object*.**Rectangles**(*index*)
Syntax 2	*object*.**Rectangles**
Elements	The **Rectangles** method has the following object qualifier and named arguments:
	object Required. The object containing the rectangles.
	index Required for Syntax 1. The name or number of the rectangle.
Example	This example deletes rectangle three on the active sheet.

```
ActiveSheet.Rectangles(3).Delete
```

Rectangles Object

Description   A collection of Rectangle objects.

ReDim Statement

Description   Used at the procedure level to declare dynamic-array variables and allocate or reallocate storage space.

Syntax   **ReDim** [**Preserve**] *varname*(*subscripts*) [**As** *type*][,*varname*(*subscripts*) [**As** *type*]] **. . .**

Elements   The **ReDim** statement syntax has these parts:

Part	Description
Preserve	Preserves the data in an existing array when you change the size of the last dimension.
varname	Name of the variable; follows standard variable naming conventions.
subscripts	Dimensions of an array variable; up to 60 multiple dimensions may be declared. The *subscripts* argument uses the following syntax: [*lower* **To**] *upper* [,[*lower* **To**] *upper*] **. . .**
type	Data type of the variable; may be **Boolean**, **Integer**, **Long**, **Currency**, **Single**, **Double**, **Date**, **String** (for variable-length strings), **String** * *length* (for fixed-length strings), **Object**, **Variant**, a user-defined type, or an object type. Use a separate **As** *type* clause for each variable being defined. For a **Variant** containing an array, *type* describes the type of each element of the array, but does not change the **Variant** to some other type.

Remarks   The **ReDim** statement is usually used to size or resize a dynamic array that has already been formally declared using a **Private**, **Public** or **Dim** statement with empty parentheses (without dimension subscripts).

You can use the **ReDim** statement repeatedly to change the number of elements and dimensions in an array. However, you can't declare an array of one data type and later use **ReDim** to change the array to another data type, unless the array is contained in a **Variant**. If the array is contained in a **Variant**, the type of the elements can be changed using an **As** *type* clause.

If you use the **Preserve** keyword, you can resize only the last array dimension and you can't change the number of dimensions at all. For example, if your array has only one dimension, you can resize that dimension because it is the last and only dimension. However, if your array has two or more dimensions you can only change the size of the last dimension and still preserve the contents of the array. The following example shows how you can increase the size of the last dimension of a dynamic array without erasing any existing data contained in the array.

```
ReDim X(10, 10, 10)
. . .
ReDim Preserve X(10, 10, 15)
```

Caution If you make an array smaller than it was, data in the eliminated elements will be lost.

When variables are initialized, a numeric variable is initialized to 0, a variable-length string is initialized to a zero-length string, and a fixed-length string is filled with zeros. **Variant** variables are initialized to **Empty**. Each element of a user-defined type variable is initialized as if it was a separate variable. A variable that refers to an object must be assigned an existing object using the **Set** statement before it can be used. Until it is assigned an object, the declared object variable has the special value **Nothing**, which indicates that it does not refer to any particular instance of an object.

Note In order to resize an array contained in a **Variant**, you must explicitly declare the **Variant** variable before attempting to resize its array.

See Also

Array Function, **Dim** Statement, **Private** Statement, **Public** Statement, **Option Base** Statement, **Static** Statement.

Example

This example uses the **ReDim** statement to declare dynamic-array variables and then allocate and reallocate storage space.

```
Dim MyArray() As Integer      ' Declare dynamic array.
ReDim MyArray(5)              ' Allocate 5 elements.
For I = 1 To 5               ' Loop 5 times.
    MyArray(I) = I           ' Initialize array.
Next I

' The next statement resizes the array and erases the elements.
ReDim MyArray(10)            ' Resize to 10 elements.
For I = 1 To 10              ' Loop 10 times.
    MyArray(I) = I           ' Initialize array.
Next I

' The next statement resizes the array but does not erase elements.
ReDim Preserve MyArray(15)   ' Resize to 15 elements.
```

ReferenceStyle Property

Applies To   Application.

Description   Returns or sets how Microsoft Excel displays cell references and row and column headings in A1 or R1C1 reference style (either **xlA1** or **xlR1C1**). Read-write.

Syntax   *object*.**ReferenceStyle**

Elements   *object*
                       Required. The Application object.

Example   This example alerts you that Microsoft Excel is using the R1C1 reference style.

```
If Application.ReferenceStyle = xlR1C1 Then
    MsgBox("Microsoft Excel is using R1C1 type references")
End If
```

RefersTo Property

Applies To   Name.

Description   Returns or sets a string containing the formula that the name is defined to refer to, in A1-style notation, in the language of the macro writer, beginning with an equal sign. Read-write.

Syntax   *object*.**RefersTo**

Elements   *object*
                       Required. The Application object.

See Also   **Formula** Property, **RefersToLocal** Property, **RefersToR1C1** Property, **RefersToR1C1Local** Property.

Example   This example creates a list of all the names in the active workbook, and shows their formulas in A1-style notation in the language of the macro.

```
i = 1
For Each nm In ActiveWorkbook.Names
    Cells(i,1).Value = nm.Name
    Cells(i,2).Value = nm.RefersTo
    i = i + 1
Next
```

RefersToLocal Property

Applies To   Name.

Description   Returns or sets a string containing the formula that the name is defined to refer to, in A1 notation, in the language of the user, beginning with an equal sign. Read-write.

Syntax   *object*.**RefersToLocal**

Elements   *object*
        Required. The Application object.

See Also   **RefersTo** Property, **RefersToR1C1** Property, **RefersToR1C1Local** Property.

Example   This example creates a list of all the names in the active workbook, and shows their formulas in A1-style notation in the language of the user.

```
i = 1
For Each nm In ActiveWorkbook.Names
    Cells(i,1).Value = nm.NameLocal
    Cells(i,2).Value = nm.RefersToLocal
    i = i + 1
Next
```

RefersToR1C1 Property

Applies To   Name.

Description   Returns or sets a string containing the formula that the name is defined to refer to, in R1C1-style notation, in the language of the macro writer, beginning with an equal sign. Read-write.

Syntax   *object*.**RefersToR1C1**

Elements   *object*
        Required. The Application object.

See Also   **RefersTo** Property, **RefersToR1C1** Property, **RefersToR1C1Local** Property.

Example	This example creates a list of all the names in the active workbook, and shows their formulas in R1C1-style notation in the language of the macro.

```
i = 1
For Each nm In ActiveWorkbook.Names
    Cells(i,1).Value = nm.Name
    Cells(i,2).Value = nm.RefersToR1C1
    i = i + 1
Next
```

RefersToR1C1Local Property

Applies To	Name.
Description	Returns or sets a string containing the formula that the name is defined to refer to, in R1C1-style notation, in the language of the user, beginning with an equal sign. Read-write.
Syntax	*object*.**RefersToR1C1Local**
Elements	*object* Required. The Application object.
See Also	**RefersTo** Property, **RefersToLocal** Property, **RefersToR1C1** Property.
Example	This example creates a list of all the names in the active workbook, and shows their formulas in R1C1-style notation in the language of the user.

```
i = 1
For Each nm In ActiveWorkbook.Names
    Cells(i,1).Value = nm.NameLocal
    Cells(i,2).Value = nm.RefersToR1C1Local
    i = i + 1
Next
```

RefreshDate Property

Applies To	PivotTable.
Description	Returns the date when the pivot table was last refreshed. Read-only.
Syntax	*object*.**RefreshDate**
Elements	*object* Required. The PivotTable object.

See Also	**RefreshName** Property, **RefreshTable** Method.
Example	This example displays a message box if the pivot table has not been refreshed since January 1, 1993.

```
If ActiveCell.PivotTable.RefreshDate < #1/1/93# Then
    MsgBox "Please update to this year's data."
End If
```

RefreshName Property

Applies To	PivotTable.
Description	Returns the name of the person who last refreshed the pivot table data. Read-only.
Syntax	*object*.**RefreshName**
Elements	*object* Required. The PivotTable object.
See Also	**RefreshDate** Property, **RefreshTable** Method.
Example	This example displays the name of the person who last refreshed the pivot table.

```
MsgBox(ActiveCell.PivotTable.RefreshName & _
    " was the last person to refresh this data.")
```

RefreshTable Method

Applies To	PivotTable.
Description	Refreshes the pivot table from the source data. Returns **True** if it is successful.
Syntax	*object*.**RefreshTable**
Elements	*object* Required. The PivotTable object.
See Also	**RefreshDate** Property,**RefreshName** Property.
Example	This example refreshes the active pivot table.

```
ActiveCell.PivotTable.RefreshTable
```

RegisteredFunctions Property

Applies To   Application.

Description   Returns an array containing a list of functions in dynamic-link libraries (DLLs) or code resources that were registered with the REGISTER or REGISTER.ID functions. Read-only. Each row in the array contains information about a single function, as shown in the following table.

Column	Contents
1	The name of the DLL or code resource.
2	The name of the procedure in the DLL or code resource.
3	Strings specifying the data types of the return values, and the number and data types of the arguments.

Syntax   *object*.**RegisteredFunctions**

Elements   *object*
       Required. The Application object.

Remark   If there are no registered functions, the property returns **Null**. Use the **IsNull** function to test the return value for **Null**.

Example   This example creates a list of the registered functions.

```
theArray = Application.RegisteredFunctions
If IsNull(theArray) Then
    MsgBox "No registered functions"
Else
    For i = 1 To UBound(theArray)
        For j = 1 To 3
            Cells(i, j).Formula = theArray(i, j)
        Next j
    Next i
End If
```

RegisterXLL Method

Applies To   Application.

Description   Loads an XLL code resource and automatically registers the functions and commands that the resource contains.

Syntax	*object*.**RegisterXLL**(*filename*)
Elements	The **RegisterXLL** method has the following object qualifier and named arguments:

object
> Required. The Application object.

filename
> Required. Specifies the name of the XLL to load.

Remarks	This method returns **True** if the code resource is successfully loaded. Otherwise, the method returns **False**.
See Also	**RegisteredFunctions** Property.
Example	This example loads an XLL file and registers the functions and commands in the file.

```
Application.RegisterXLL "XLMAPI.XLL"
```

Rem Statement

Description	Used to include explanatory remarks in a program.
Syntax 1	**Rem** *comment*
Syntax 2	' *comment*
Elements	The argument *comment* is the text of any comment you want to include. After the **Rem** keyword, a space before *comment* is required.
Remarks	If you use line numbers or line labels, you can branch from a **GoTo** or **GoSub** statement to a line containing a **Rem** statement. Execution continues with the first executable statement following the **Rem** statement.
	As shown in syntax 2, you can use a single quotation mark or apostrophe (') instead of the **Rem** keyword. If the **Rem** keyword follows other statements on a line, it must be separated from the statements by a colon. However, when you use a single quotation mark, the colon is not required after other statements.
Example	This example illustrates the various forms of the **Rem** statement, which is used to include explanatory remarks in a program.

```
Rem This is the first form of the syntax.
' This is the second form of the syntax.
MyStr1 = "Hello" : Rem Comment after a statement separated by a colon.
MyStr2 = "Goodbye"  ' This is also a comment.
```

RemoveAllItems Method

Applies To	DrawingObjects, DropDown, DropDowns, ListBox, ListBoxes.
Description	Removes all entries from a list box or drop-down list box.
Syntax	*object*.**RemoveAllItems**
Elements	*object*
	Required. The object to which this method applies.
See Also	**AddItem** Method, **List** Property, **RemoveItem** Method.
Example	This example removes all entries from list box one.

```
Application.DialogSheets(1).Listboxes(1).RemoveAllItems
```

RemoveItem Method

Applies To	DrawingObjects, DropDown, DropDowns, ListBox, ListBoxes.
Description	Removes one or more items from a list box or drop-down list box.
Syntax	*object*.**RemoveItem**(*index, count*)
Elements	The **RemoveItem** method has the following object qualifier and named arguments:

object
> Required. The object to which this method applies.

index
> Required. Specifies the number of the first item to remove. Valid values are from one to the number of items in the list (returned by the **ListCount** property).

count
> Optional. Specifies the number of items to remove starting at item *index*. If this argument is omitted, one item is removed. If *index* + *count* exceeds the number of items in the list, all items from *index* through the end of the list are removed without an error.

Remarks	This method fails if the object has a **ListFillRange** defined.
See Also	**AddItem** Method, **List** Property, **RemoveAllItems** Method.
Example	This example removes the first entry from list box one.

```
Application.DialogSheets(1).Listboxes(1).RemoveItem index:=1
```

RemoveSubtotal Method

Applies To   Range.

Description   Removes subtotals from a list.

Syntax   *object*.**RemoveSubtotal**

Elements   *object*
    Required. The Range object.

See Also   **Subtotal** Method.

Example   This example removes subtotals for the range A1:G37.

```
Range("A1", "G37").RemoveSubtotal
```

Repeat Method

Applies To   Application.

Description   Repeats the last user-interface action.

Syntax   *object*.**Repeat**

Elements   *object*
    Required. The Application object.

Remarks   This method can only be used to repeat the last action taken by the user before running the macro, and it must be the first line in the macro. It cannot be used to repeat Visual Basic commands.

Example   This example repeats the last user-interface command. It must be the first line in the macro.

```
Application.Repeat
```

Replace Method

Applies To   Range.

Description   Finds and replaces characters in cells within a range. Does not change the selection or active cell.

For help about using the **Replace** worksheet function in Visual Basic, see Using Worksheet Functions in Visual Basic.

Syntax	*object*.**Replace**(*what, replacement, lookAt, searchOrder, matchCase*)
Elements	The **Replace** method has the following object qualifier and named arguments:

object
  Required. Replace characters or cells in this range.

what
  Required. A string indicating the contents for which you want to search.

replacement
  Required. A string indicating the text with which you want to replace *what*.

lookAt
  Optional. If **xlWhole**, *what* must match the entire contents of a cell. If **xlPart** or omitted, *what* must contain part of the contents of a cell.

searchOrder
  Optional. Specifies whether to search by rows (**xlByRows**) or columns (**xlByColumns**). The default is **xlByRows**.

matchCase
  Optional. If **True**, search is case sensitive; if **False** or omitted, it is not.

Remarks	If the contents of the *what* argument are found in at least one cell of the sheet, the method returns **True**.
See Also	**Find** Method, **FindNext** Method.
Example	This example replaces the equal sign of a formula in cell A1 with the same equal sign, which forces Microsoft Excel to recalculate the formula without changing the formula.

```
Cells(1, 1).Replace what:="=", replacement:="="
```

Reply Method

Applies To	Workbook.
Description	Replies to the workbook by creating a copy of the workbook and pre-initializing the new workbook's mailer to send to the originator of the workbook. Valid only when the workbook has a received mailer attached (you can only reply to a workbook you have received). Available only in Microsoft Excel for the Apple Macintosh with the PowerTalk mail system extension installed.
Syntax	*object*.**Reply**
Elements	*object*

  Required. The Workbook object.

Remarks	To reply to a workbook, use this method to set up the mailer, use the **Mailer** property to adjust the mailer settings (if necessary), and then use the **SendMailer** method to send the reply.

This method generates an error if it is used in Microsoft Windows.

See Also   **Mailer** Property, **MailSystem** Property, **ReplyAll** Method, **SendMailer** Method.

Example   This example replies to the active workbook.

```
With ActiveWorkbook
    If .HasMailer Then
        .Reply
        .Mailer.Subject = "Here's my reply"
        .SendMailer
    End If
End With
```

ReplyAll Method

Applies To   Workbook.

Description   Replies to the workbook by creating a copy of the workbook and pre-initializing the new workbook's mailer to send to all recipients of the workbook. Valid only when the workbook has a received mailer attached (you can only reply to a workbook you have received). Available only in Microsoft Excel for the Apple Macintosh with the PowerTalk mail system extension installed.

Syntax   *object*.**ReplyAll**

Elements   *object*
     Required. The Workbook object.

Remarks   To reply to all recipients of a workbook, use this method to set up the mailer, use the **Mailer** property to adjust the mailer settings (if necessary), and then use the **SendMailer** method to send the reply.

This method generates an error if it is used in Microsoft Windows.

See Also   **Mailer** Property, **MailSystem** Property, **Reply** Method, **SendMailer** Method.

Example

This example replies to all recipients of the active workbook.

```
With ActiveWorkbook
    If .HasMailer Then
        .ReplyAll
        .Mailer.Subject = "Here's my reply"
        .SendMailer
    End If
End With
```

Reset Method

Applies To

MenuBar, RoutingSlip, Toolbar, ToolbarButton.

Description

Restores the built-in menu bar or toolbar to its original default configuration. Resets a toolbar button to its original face.

Resets the routing slip so that a new routing can be initiated with the same slip (using the same recipient list and delivery information). The routing must be completed before you use this method. Using this method at other times causes an error.

Syntax

object.**Reset**

Elements

object
    Required. The object to which this property applies.

Remarks

Be careful when you reset a menu bar or toolbar -- other macros may have added buttons or menu items, and resetting the bar will remove those as well. To avoid conflicting with other macros, remove the items or buttons your macro has added without resetting the menu bar or toolbar.

Example

This example resets the routing slip for the workbook if routing is complete.

```
With Workbooks("BOOK1.XLS").RoutingSlip
    If .Status = xlRoutingComplete Then
        .Reset
    Else
        MsgBox "Cannot reset routing; not yet complete"
    End If
End With
```

Reset Statement

Description

Closes all disk files opened using the **Open** statement.

Syntax	**Reset**
Remarks	The **Reset** statement syntax closes all active files opened by the **Open** statement and writes the contents of all file buffers to disk.
See Also	**Close** Statement, **End** Statement, **Open** Statement.
Example	This example uses the **Reset** statement to close all open files and write the contents of all file buffers to disk.

```
For FileNumber = 1 To 5                    ' Loop 5 times.
    ' Open file for output.
    Open "TEST" & FileNumber For Output As #FileNumber
    Write #FileNumber, "Hello World"      ' Write data to file.

Next FileNumber
Reset                              ' Close files and write contents to disk.
```

ResetTipWizard Method

Applies To	Application.
Description	Resets the TipWizard memory so that all tips will be shown. Normally tips that have been shown several times are disabled so that they do not become annoying.
Syntax	*object*.**ResetTipWizard**
Elements	*object* Required. The Application object.
See Also	**EnableTipWizard** Property.
Example	This example resets the TipWizard and enables it.

```
With Application
    .ResetTipWizard
    .EnableTipWizard = True
End With
```

Reshape Method

Applies To	Drawing, DrawingObjects, Drawings.
Description	Reshapes the drawing by inserting, moving, or deleting vertices.

Syntax	*object*.**Reshape**(*vertex, insert, left, top*)
Elements	The **Reshape** method has the following object qualifier and named arguments:

object
Required. The object to which this method applies.

vertex
Required. Specifies the vertex you want to insert, move, or delete.

insert
Required. If **True**, Microsoft Excel inserts a vertex between the vertices *vertex* and *vertex* - 1. The number of the new vertex then becomes *vertex*. The number of the vertex previously identified by *vertex* becomes *vertex* + 1, and so on. If *insert* is **False**, Microsoft Excel deletes the vertex (if *top* and *left* are omitted) or moves the vertex to the position specified by the *top* and *left* arguments.

left
Optional. The left position for the new or moved vertex, in points (1/72 inch) relative to the upper-left corner of cell A1 or the upper-left corner of the chart.

top
Optional. The top position for the new or moved vertex, in points relative to the upper-left corner of cell A1 or the upper-left corner of the chart.

Remarks	You cannot delete a vertex if only two vertices remain.
See Also	**AddVertex** Method, **Vertices** Property.
Example	This example reshapes drawing one by deleting vertex five.

```
ActiveSheet.Drawings(1).Reshape 5, False
```

Resize Method

Applies To	Range.
Description	Resizes the range.
Syntax	*object*.**Resize**(*rowSize, columnSize*)
Elements	The **Resize** method has the following object qualifier and named arguments:

object
Required. The Range object to resize.

rowSize
Optional. The number of rows in the new range. If omitted, the range will keep the same number of rows.

columnSize

Optional. The number of columns in the new range. If omitted, the range will keep the same number of columns.

Example

This example resizes the current selection to extend it by one row and one column.

```
numRows = Selection.Rows.Count
numColumns = Selection.Columns.Count
Selection.Resize(numRows + 1, numColumns + 1).Select
```

Resume Statement

Description

Resumes execution after an error-handling routine is finished.

Syntax

Resume [0]

Resume Next

Resume *line*

Elements

The **Resume** statement syntax can have any of the following forms:

Statement	Description
Resume [0]	If the error occurred in the same procedure as the error handler, execution resumes with the one that caused the error. If the error occurred in another procedure, execution resumes at the statement that last called out of the procedure containing the error-handling routine.
Resume Next	If the error occurred in the same procedure as the error handler, execution resumes with the statement immediately following the statement that caused the error. If the error occurred in another procedure, execution resumes with the statement immediately following the statement that last called out of the procedure containing the error-handling routine.
Resume *line*	Execution resumes at *line*, which is a line label or line number. The argument *line* must be in the same procedure as the error handler.

Remarks

If you use a **Resume** statement anywhere except in an error-handling routine, an error occurs.

When an error-handling routine is active and the end of the procedure (an **End Sub**, **End Function**, or **End Property** statement) is encountered before a **Resume** statement is encountered, an error occurs because a logical error is presumed to have been made inadvertently. However, if an **Exit Sub**, **Exit Function**, or **Exit Property** statement is encountered while an error handler is active, no error occurs because it is considered a deliberate redirection of execution.

See Also   **On Error** Statement, Trappable Errors.

Example   This example uses the **Resume** statement to end error handling in a procedure and
                     resume execution with the statement that caused the error. Error number 55 is
                     generated to illustrate its usage.

```
Sub ResumeStatementDemo()
    On Error GoTo ErrorHandler   ' Enable error-handling routine.
    Open "TESTFILE" For Output As #1 ' Open file for output.
    Kill "TESTFILE" '               Attempt to delete open file.
    Exit Sub' Exit Sub before error handler.
ErrorHandler:                        ' Error-handling routine.
    Select Case Err                  ' Evaluate Error Number.
        Case 55                      ' "File already open" error.
            Close #1                 ' Close open file.
        Case Else
                                     ' Handle other situations here...
    End Select
    Resume                           ' Resume execution at same line
                                     ' that caused the error.
End Sub
```

ReturnWhenDone Property

Applies To   RoutingSlip.

Description   **True** if the workbook is returned to the sender when the routing is finished. Read-
                     write before routing begins; read-only when routing is in progress.

Syntax   *object*.**ReturnWhenDone**

Elements   *object*
                     Required. The RoutingSlip object.

Example   This example sends BOOK1.XLS to three recipients, one after the other, and
                     returns the workbook to the sender when routing is complete.

```
Workbooks("BOOK1.XLS").HasRoutingSlip = True
With Workbooks("BOOK1.XLS").RoutingSlip
    .Delivery = xlOneAfterAnother
    .Recipients = Array("Adam Bendel", "Jean Selva", "Bernard Gabor")
    .Subject = "Here is BOOK1.XLS"
    .Message = "Here is the workbook. What do you think?"
    .ReturnWhenDone = True
End With
Workbooks("BOOK1.XLS").Route
```

ReversePlotOrder Property

Applies To   Axis.

Description   **True** if Microsoft Excel plots points from last to first. Read-write.

Syntax   *object*.**ReversePlotOrder**

Elements   *object*
                        Required. The Axis object.

Remarks   This property is not available for radar charts.

Example   This example sets Microsoft Excel to plot points on the value axis from last to first.

```
ActiveChart.Axes(xlValue).ReversePlotOrder = True
```

RGB Function

Description   Returns a whole number representing an RGB color value.

Syntax   **RGB (*red, green, blue*)**

Elements   The **RGB** function syntax has these named-argument parts:

Part	Description
red	Whole number in the range 0 to 255, inclusive, that represents the red component of the color.
green	Whole number in the range 0 to 255, inclusive, that represents the green component of the color.
blue	Whole number in the range 0 to 255, inclusive, that represents the blue component of the color.

Remarks   Application methods and properties that accept a color specification expect that specification to be a whole number representing an RGB color value. An RGB color value specifies the relative intensity of red, green, and blue, which combined cause a specific color to be displayed.

The value for any argument to **RGB** that exceeds 255 is assumed to be 255.

The following table lists some standard colors and the red, green and blue values they include:

Color	Red Value	Green Value	Blue Value
Black	0	0	0
Blue	0	0	255
Green	0	255	0
Cyan	0	255	255
Red	255	0	0
Magenta	255	0	255
Yellow	255	255	0
White	255	255	255

Note The RGB values returned by this function are incompatible with those used by the Macintosh operating system. They may be used within the context of Microsoft applications for the Macintosh, but should not be used when communicating color changes directly to the Macintosh operating system.

Example

This example shows how the **RGB** function is used to return a whole number representing an **RGB** color value. It is used for those application methods and properties that accept a color specification. The object MyObject and its property are used here for illustration purposes only.

```
Red = RGB(255, 0, 0)               ' Return the value for Red.
I = 75                             ' Initialize offset.
RGBValue = RGB(I, 64 + I, 128 + I) ' Same as RGB(75, 139, 203).
MyObject.Color = RGB(255, 0, 0)    ' Set the Color property of
                                   ' MyObject to Red.
```

Right Function

Description

Returns a specified number of characters from the right side of a string.

Syntax	**Right**(*string*,*length*)
Elements	The **Right** function syntax has these named-argument parts:

Part	Description
string	String expression from which the rightmost characters are returned. If *string* contains no valid data, **Null** is returned.
length	Numeric expression indicating how many characters to return. If 0, a zero-length string is returned. If greater than or equal to the number of characters in *string*, the entire string is returned.

Remarks   To determine the number of characters in *string*, use the **Len** function.

Note Another function (**RightB**) is provided for use with the double-byte character sets (DBCS) used in some Asian locales. Instead of specifying the number of characters to return, *length* specifies the number of bytes. In areas where DBCS is not used, **RightB** behaves the same as **Right**.

See Also   **Left** Function, **Len** Function, **Mid** Function.

Example   This example uses the **Right** function to return a specified number of characters from the right side of a string.

```
AnyString = "Hello World"        ' Define string.
MyStr = Right(AnyString, 1)      ' Returns "d".
MyStr = Right(AnyString, 6)      ' Returns " World".
MyStr = Right(AnyString, 20)     ' Returns "Hello World".
```

RightAngleAxes Property

Applies To   Chart.

Description   **True** if the chart axes are at right angles, independent of chart rotation or elevation. Applies only to 3-D line, column, and bar charts. Read-write.

Syntax   *object*.**RightAngleAxes**

Elements   *object*
　　　　　　Required. The Chart object.

Remarks   If this property is **True**, the **Perspective** property is ignored.

See Also   **Elevation** Property, **Perspective** Property, **Rotation** Property.

Example   This example sets the axes at right angles, independent of chart rotation or elevation.

```
Charts(1).RightAngleAxes = True
```

RightFooter Property

Applies To   PageSetup.

Description   Returns or sets the right part of the footer. Read-write.

Syntax   *object*.**RightFooter**

Elements   *object*
        Required. The PageSetup object (**ActiveSheet.PageSetup**, for example).

Remarks   Special format codes can be used in the footer text.

See Also   **CenterFooter** Property, **CenterHeader** Property, **LeftFooter** Property, **LeftHeader** Property, **RightHeader** Property.

Example   This example prints the page number at the lower-right corner of every page.

```
ActiveSheet.PageSetup.RightFooter = "&P"
```

RightHeader Property

Applies To   PageSetup.

Description   Returns or sets the right part of the header. Read-write.

Syntax   *object*.**RightHeader**

Elements   *object*
        Required. The PageSetup object (**ActiveSheet.PageSetup**, for example).

Remarks   Special format codes can be used in the header text.

See Also   **CenterFooter** Property, **CenterHeader** Property, **LeftFooter** Property, **LeftHeader** Property, **RightFooter** Property.

Example   This example prints the file name at the upper-right corner of every page.

```
ActiveSheet.PageSetup.RightHeader = "&F"
```

RightMargin Property

Applies To   PageSetup.

Description   Returns or sets the size of the right margin, in points (1/72 inch). Read-write.

Syntax   *object*.**RightMargin**

Elements   *object*
Required. The PageSetup object (**ActiveSheet.PageSetup**, for example).

Remarks   Margins are set or returned in points. Use the **Application.InchesToPoints** or **Application.CentimetersToPoints** function to convert.

SeeAlso   **BottomMargin** Property, **LeftMargin** Property, **TopMargin** Property.

Examples   This example sets the right margin to 1.5 inches.

```
ActiveSheet.Pag
eSetup.RightMargin = Application.InchesToPoints(1.5)
```

This example sets the right margin to 2 centimeters.

```
ActiveSheet.PageSetup.RightMargin = Application.CentimetersToPoints(2)
```

This example sets the variable `rightMarginInches` to the current right margin setting, in inches.

```
rightMarginInches = ActiveSheet.PageSetup.RightMargin / _
        Application.InchesToPoints(1)
```

RmDir Statement

Description   Removes an existing directory or folder.

Syntax   **RmDir** *path*

Elements   The *path* named argument is a string expression that identifies the directory or folder to be removed{bmc emdash.bmp}may include drive. If no drive is specified, **RmDir** removes the directory or folder on the current drive.

Remarks   An error occurs if you try to use **RmDir** on a directory or folder containing files. Use the **Kill** statement to delete all files before attempting to remove a directory or folder.

See Also   **ChDir** Statement, **CurDir** Function, **Kill** Statement, **MkDir** Statement.

This example uses the **RmDir** statement to remove an existing directory or folder.

```
' Assume that MYDIR is an empty directory or folder.
RmDir "MYDIR"   ' Remove MYDIR.
```

Rnd Function

Description   Returns a random number.

Syntax   **Rnd**[(*number*)]

Elements   The *number* named argument can be any valid numeric expression.

Remarks   The **Rnd** function returns a value less than 1 but greater than or equal to 0.

The value of *number* determines how **Rnd** generates a random number:

If *number* is:	Rnd generates:
Less than zero	The same number every time, using *number* as the seed.
Greater than zero	The next random number in the sequence.
Equal to zero	The most recently generated number.
Not supplied	The next random number in the sequence.

For any given initial seed, the same number sequence is generated because each successive call to the **Rnd** function uses the previous number as a seed for the next number in the sequence.

Use the **Randomize** statement without an argument to provide a random seed based on the system timer to initialize the random-number generator before **Rnd** is called.

To produce random integers in a given range, use this formula:

```
Int((upperbound - lowerbound + 1) * Rnd + lowerbound)
```

Here, *upperbound* is the highest number in the range, and *lowerbound* is the lowest number in the range.

See Also   **Randomize** Statement, **Timer** Function.

Example   This example uses the **Rnd** function to generate a random integer value from 1 to 6.

```
MyValue = Int((6 * Rnd) + 1)' Generate random value between 1 and 6.
```

Rotation Property

Applies To   Chart.

Description   Returns or sets the rotation of the 3-D chart view (the rotation of the plot area around the z-axis, in degrees). The value of this property must be between 0 and 360, except for 3-D Bar charts, where the value must be between 0 and 44. The default value is 20. Applies only to 3-D charts. Read-write.

Syntax   *object*.**Rotation**

Elements   *object*
          Required. The Chart object.

See Also   **Elevation** Property, **Perspective** Property, **RightAngleAxes** Property.

Example   This example sets the 3-D chart rotation to 30 degrees.

```
Charts(1).Rotation = 30
```

RoundedCorners Property

Applies To   ChartObject, ChartObjects, DrawingObjects, GroupObject, GroupObjects, Rectangle, Rectangles, TextBox, TextBoxes.

Description   **True** if the drawing object has rounded corners. Read-write.

Syntax   *object*.**RoundedCorners**

Elements   *object*
          Required. The object to which this property applies.

Example   This example adds rounded corners to rectangle one.

```
ActiveSheet.Rectangles(1).RoundedCorners = True
```

Route Method

Applies To   Workbook.

Description   Routes the workbook using the workbook's current routing slip.

Syntax   *object*.**Route**

Elements   *object*
          Required. The Workbook object.

Remarks	Routing a workbook forces the **Routed** property to **True**.
See Also	**Routed** Property, **RoutingSlip** Property, **SendMail** Method.
Example	This example creates a routing slip for BOOK1.XLS, and then sends the workbook to three recipients, one after the other.

```
Workbooks("BOOK1.XLS").HasRoutingSlip = True
With Workbooks("BOOK1.XLS").RoutingSlip
    .Delivery = xlOneAfterAnother
    .Recipients = Array("Adam Bendel", "Jean Selva", "Bernard Gabor")
    .Subject = "Here is BOOK1.XLS"
    .Message = "Here is the workbook. What do you think?"
End With
Workbooks("BOOK1.XLS").Route
```

Routed Property

Applies To	Workbook.
Description	**True** if the workbook has been routed to the next recipient; **False** if the workbook needs to be routed. Read-only.
Syntax	*object*.**Routed**
Elements	*object* 　　Required. The Workbook object.
Remarks	If the workbook was not routed to the current recipient, this property is always **False** (for example, if the document has no routing slip, or a routing slip was just created).
Example	This example sends the workbook to the next recipient.

```
If ActiveWorkbook.HasRoutingSlip And _
    Not ActiveWorkbook.Routed Then
        ActiveWorkbook.Route
End If
```

RoutingSlip Object

Description	The routing slip of a workbook.

RoutingSlip Property

Applies To	Workbook
Description	Returns the RoutingSlip for the workbook. Reading this property if there is no routing slip causes an error. Read-only.
Syntax	*object*.**RoutingSlip**
Elements	*object* 　　Required. The Workbook object.
See Also	**HasRoutingSlip** Property.
Examples	This example creates a routing slip for BOOK1.XLS, and then sends the workbook to three recipients, one after the other.

```
Workbooks("BOOK1.XLS").HasRoutingSlip = True
With Workbooks("BOOK1.XLS").RoutingSlip
    .Delivery = xlOneAfterAnother
    .Recipients = Array("Adam Bendel", "Jean Selva", "Bernard Gabor")
    .Subject = "Here is BOOK1.XLS"
    .Message = "Here is the workbook. What do you think?"
End With
Workbooks("BOOK1.XLS").Route
```

Row Property

Applies To	Range.
Description	Returns the number of the first row of the first area of the range. Read-only.
Syntax	*object*.**Row**
Elements	*object* 　　Required. The Range object.
See Also	**Column** Property, **EntireColumn** Property, **EntireRow** Property, **Rows** Method.
Examples	These examples show what the **Row** property returns for the given ranges:

```
MsgBox "Cells(1, 1).Row = " & Cells(1, 1).Row      ' 1
MsgBox "Range(""C5"", ""F9"").Row = " & Range("C5", "F9").Row      ' 5
```

RowDifferences Method

Applies To   Range.

Description   Returns a Range containing all the cells whose contents are different than the comparison cell in each of the rows. The comparison cell is a cell in the comparison column and is equal to the *comparison* argument.

Syntax   *object*.**RowDifferences(*comparison*)**

Elements   The **RowDifferences** method has the following object qualifier and named arguments:

object
Required. The object to which this method applies.

comparison
Required. A cell in the comparison column. Use the **ActiveCell** property if you are finding the differences between the active cell's column and all rows in the range.

See Also   **ColumnDifferences** Method.

Example   This example selects all cells in A1:C3 that are different in each of the rows to the comparison column B. The comparison cell is set as B2.

```
Range("A1", "C3").RowDifferences(Cells(2, 2)).Select
```

RowFields Method

Applies To   PivotTable.

Description   Returns a single pivot field (a PivotField object, Syntax 1) or a collection of the pivot fields (a PivotFields object, Syntax 2) that are currently showing as row fields. Read-only.

Syntax 1   *object*.**RowFields(*index*)**

Syntax 2   *object*.**RowFields**

Elements   The **RowFields** method has the following object qualifier and named arguments:

object
Required. The PivotTable object.

index
Required for Syntax 1. The name or number of the pivot field to return (can be an array to specify more than one).

See Also   **ColumnFields** Method, **DataFields** Method, **HiddenFields** Method, **PageFields** Method, **PivotFields** Method, **VisibleFields** Method.

Example   This example adds the active pivot table row field names to a list box.

```
For Each rwField In ActiveCell.PivotTable.RowFields
    rowFieldListBox.AddItem(rwField.Name)
Next rwField
```

RowGrand Property

Applies To   PivotTable.

Description   **True** if the pivot table shows row grand totals. Read-write.

Syntax   *object*.**RowGrand**

Elements   *object*
          Required. The PivotTable object.

See Also   **ColumnGrand** Property.

Example   This example sets the active pivot table to show row grand totals.

```
ActiveCell.PivotTable.RowGrand = True
```

RowHeight Property

Applies To   Range.

Description   Returns the height of all of the rows in the range specified, measured in points (1/72 inch). Read-write.

Syntax   *object*.**RowHeight**

Elements   *object*
          Required. The object to which this property applies.

See Also   **ColumnWidth** Property, **Height** Property, **StandardHeight** Property.

Remarks   For a single row, the value of the **Height** property is equal to the value of **RowHeight**. However, you can also use the **Height** property to return the total height of a range of cells.

Other differences between **RowHeight** and **Height** are:

- **Height** is read-only.

- If you return the **RowHeight** of several rows, you will either get the row height of each of the rows (if they are the same), or **Null** if they are different. If you return the **Height** property of several rows, you will get the total height of all the rows.

Examples   This example doubles the row height of rows 1 and 2.

```
With Range(Rows(1), Rows(2))
    .RowHeight = .RowHeight * 2
End With
```

This example restores row one to the standard row height.

```
Rows(1).RowHeight = Worksheets(1).StandardHeight
```

RowRange Property

Applies To   PivotTable.

Description   Returns the Range that includes the pivot table row area. Read-only.

Syntax   *object*.**RowRange**

Elements   *object*
     Required. The PivotTable object.

See Also   **ColumnRange** Property, **DataBodyRange** Property, **DataLabelRange** Property, **PageRange** Property.

Example   This example selects the active pivot table row headers.

```
ActiveCell.PivotTable.RowRange.Select
```

Rows Method

Applies To   Application, Range, Worksheet.

Description   Returns a single row (Syntax 1) or a collection of rows (Syntax 2). A row is a Range object.

Syntax 1	*object*.**Rows**(*index*)
Syntax 2	*object*.**Rows**

Elements   The **Rows** method has the following object qualifier and named arguments:

object
  Optional for Application, required for Range and Worksheet. The object to which this method applies.

index
  Required for Syntax 1. The name or number of the row.

Remarks   When applied to a Range object that is a multiple selection, this method returns rows from the first area of the range only. For example, if the Range object is a multiple selection with two areas, A1:B2 and C3:D4, **Selection.Rows.Count**, returns 2, not 4. To use this method on a range that may contain a multiple selection, test **Areas.Count** to determine if the range is a multiple selection, and if it is, then loop over each area in the range; see the second example.

See Also   **Columns** Method, **Range** Method.

Examples   This example deletes the third row in the active sheet.

```
Application.Rows(3).Delete
```

This example displays the number of rows in the selection. The code tests for a multiple selection and if one exists, loops on the areas of the multiple selection.

```
areaCount = Selection.Areas.Count
If areaCount <= 1 Then
    MsgBox "The selection contains " & _
        Selection.Rows.Count & " rows."
Else
    For i = 1 To areaCount
        MsgBox "Area " & i & " of the selection contains " & _
            Selection.Areas(i).Rows.Count & " rows."
    Next i
End If
```

RSet Statement

Description   Right aligns a string within a string variable.

Syntax	**RSet** *stringvar* = *string*
Elements	The **RSet** statement syntax has these parts:

Part	Description
stringvar	Name of a string variable.
string	String expression to be right aligned within *stringvar*.

Remarks   **RSet** replaces any leftover characters in *stringvar* with spaces, back to its beginning.

RSet can't be used with user-defined types.

See Also   **LSet** Statement.

Example   This example uses the **RSet** statement to right align a string within a string variable.

```
MyString = "0123456789" ' Initialize string.
RSet MyString = "Right->"    ' MyString contains "    Right->".
```

Run Method

Applies To   Application, Range.

Description   Syntax 1: Runs a macro or calls a function. This can be used to run a macro written in any language (Visual Basic, the Microsoft Excel 4.0 macro language, or a function in a DLL or XLL).

Syntax 2: Runs the Microsoft Excel 4.0 macro at this location. The range must be on a macro sheet.

Syntax 1   *object*.**Run(***macro, arg1, arg2, ...***)**

Syntax 2   *object*.**Run(***arg1, arg2, ...***)**

Elements   The **Run** method has the following object qualifier and named arguments.

object
Optional for Application, required for Range. The application that contains the macro, or a range on a macro sheet that contains an Microsoft Excel 4.0 macro.

macro
Required for Syntax 1 (not used with Syntax 2). The macro to run. This can be a string with the macro name, or a Range indicating where the function is, or a register ID for a registered DLL (XLL) function. If a string is used, the string will be evaluated in the context of the active sheet.

arg1, arg2, ...
    Optional. The arguments that should be passed to the function.

Remarks   The **Run** method returns whatever the called macro returns.

Example   This example shows how to call the function macro My_Func_Sum, which is defined on the macro sheet MYCUSTOM.XLM (the macro sheet must be open). The function takes two numeric arguments, 1 and 5 in this example.

```
mySum = Application.Run("MYCUSTOM.XLM!My_Func_Sum", 1, 5)
MsgBox "Macro result: " & mySum
```

RunAutoMacros Method

Applies To   Workbook.

Description   Runs the Auto_Open, Auto_Close, Auto_Activate, or Auto_Deactivate macros that are attached to the workbook.

These four auto macros do not run when workbooks are opened or closed (and when sheets are activated or deactivated) by a Visual Basic program. Use this method to run auto macros.

Syntax   *object*.**RunAutoMacros(*which*)**

Elements   The **RunAutoMacros** method has the following object qualifier and named arguments:

object
    Required. The Workbook object.

which
    Required. Specifies which macros to run, as shown in the following table.

Value	Meaning
xlAutoOpen	Auto_Open macros.
xlAutoClose	Auto_Close macros.
xlAutoActivate	Auto_Activate macros.
xlAutoDeactivate	Auto_Deactivate macros.

Remarks   The Auto_Activate and Auto_Deactivate macros are included for backward compatibility with the Microsoft Excel version 4.0 macro language. Use the **OnSheetActivate** and **OnSheetDeactivate** properties when you program in Visual Basic.

Examples

This example runs the Auto_Open macro for ANALYSIS.XLS.

```
Workbooks.Open "ANALYSIS.XLS"
ActiveWorkbook.RunAutoMacros xlAutoOpen
```

This example runs the Auto_Close macro for the active workbook, and then closes the workbook.

```
With ActiveWorkbook
    .RunAutoMacros xlAutoClose
    .Close
End With
```

Save Method

Applies To

Application, Workbook.

Description

Workbook object (Syntax 1): Saves changes to the specified workbook. Application object (Syntax 2): Saves the current workspace.

Syntax 1

object.**Save**

Syntax 2

object.**Save(*filename*)**

Elements

The **Save** method has the following object qualifier and named arguments:

object
Required. The Workbook object (Syntax 1) or Application object (Syntax 2).

filename
Optional. Specifies the name of the saved workspace file. If this argument is omitted, a default name is used.

Remarks

To open a workbook file, use the **Open** method.

To mark the workbook as saved without writing it to a disk, set its **Saved** property to **True**.

The first time you save a workbook, use the **SaveAs** method to specify a name for the file.

See Also

Open Method, **SaveAs** Method, **SaveCopyAs** Method, **Saved** Property.

Example

This example saves the active workbook.

```
ActiveWorkbook.Save
```

SaveAs Method

Applies To	Chart, DialogSheet, Module, Workbook, Worksheet.
Description	Saves changes to the sheet or workbook in a different file.
Syntax	*object*.**SaveAs**(*filename, fileFormat, password, writeResPassword, readOnlyRecommended, createBackup*)
Elements	The **SaveAs** method has the following object qualifier and named arguments:

object
Required. The object to which this method applies.

filename
Optional. A string indicating the name of the file to save. You can include a full path; if you do not, Microsoft Excel saves the file in the current directory or folder.

fileFormat
Optional. The file format to use when you save the file. See the **FileFormat** property for a list of valid choices.

password
Optional. A case-sensitive string indicating the protection password to be given to the file. Should be no more than 15 characters.

writeResPassword
Optional. A string indicating the write-reservation password for this file. If a file is saved with the password and the password is not supplied when the file is opened, the file is opened as read-only.

readOnlyRecommended
Optional. If **True**, when the file is opened, Microsoft Excel displays a message recommending that you open the file as read-only.

createBackup
Optional. If **True**, Microsoft Excel creates a backup file; if **False**, no backup file is created; if omitted, the status is unchanged.

Remarks	To mark the workbook as saved without writing it to a disk, set the **Saved** property of the workbook to **True**.

This method can only be used to save worksheets in a non-3D format.

Basic modules can only be saved in Text format.

See Also	**FileFormat** Property, **Save** Method, **SaveCopyAs** Method, **Saved** Property.

Example

In this example, if workbook BUDGET93.XLS is opened as read-only, the code saves it as TESTFILE.XLS.

```
If Workbooks("BUDGET93.XLS").ReadOnly Then
    Workbooks("BUDGET93.XLS").SaveAs fileName:="TESTFILE.XLS"
End If
```

SaveCopyAs Method

Applies To   Workbook.

Description   Saves a copy of the workbook to a file but does not modify the open workbook in memory.

Syntax   *object*.**SaveCopyAs(*filename*)**

Elements   The **SaveCopyAs** method has the following object qualifier and named arguments:

object
    Required. The Workbook object.

filename
    Required. Specifies the filename for the copy.

See Also   **Save** Method, **SaveAs** Method.

Example   This example saves a copy of the active workbook.

```
ActiveWorkbook.SaveCopyAs "C:\TEMP\XXXX.XLS"
```

Saved Property

Applies To   Workbook.

Description   **False** if changes have been made to a workbook since it was last saved. Read-write.

Syntax   *object*.**Saved**

Elements   *object*
    Required. The Workbook object.

Remarks   If a workbook has never been saved, its **Path** will return an empty string (" ").

You can set this property to **True** if you want to close a modified workbook without saving it or being prompted to save it.

See Also   **Save** Method, **SaveAs** Method, **SaveCopyAs** Method.

Example   This example displays a message reminding you to save the workbook before exiting if you have not done so.

```
If Not ActiveWorkbook.Saved Then
    MsgBox "Please remember to save this workbook " & _
        "before you exit."
End If
```

SaveData Property

Applies To   PivotTable.

Description   **True** if data for the pivot table is saved with the workbook; **False** if only the pivot table definition is saved. Read-write.

Syntax   *object*.**SaveData**

Elements   *object*
        Required. The PivotTable object.

Example   This example sets the active pivot table to save data with the workbook.

```
ActiveCell.PivotTable.SaveData = True
```

SaveLinkValues Property

Applies To   Workbook.

Description   **True** if Microsoft Excel will save external link values with this workbook. Read-write.

Syntax   *object*.**SaveLinkValues**

Elements   *object*
        Required. The Workbook object.

Example   This example causes Microsoft Excel to save external link values with the active workbook.

```
ActiveWorkbook.SaveLinkValues = True
```

ScaleType Property

Applies To   Axis.

Description   Returns or sets the value axis scale type (**xlLinear** or **xlLogarithmic**). Applies only to the value axis. Read-write.

Syntax   *object*.**ScaleType**

Elements   *object*
                   Required. The Axis object.

Remarks   A logarithmic scale uses base ten logarithms.

Example   This example sets the value axis to use a logarithmic scale.

```
ActiveChart.Axes(xlValue).ScaleType = xlLogarithmic
```

Scenario Object

Description   A scenario on a worksheet.

Scenarios Method

Applies To   Worksheet.

Description   Returns a single scenario (a Scenario object, Syntax 1) or a collection of scenarios (a Scenarios object, Syntax 2) on the worksheet.

Syntax 1   *object*.**Scenarios(*index*)**

Syntax 2   *object*.**Scenarios**

Elements   The **Scenarios** method has the following object qualifier and named arguments:

                   object
                   Required. The Worksheet object.

                   index
                   Required for Syntax 1. The name or number of the scenario (can be an array to specify more than one).

Example   This example sets the comment for the first scenario.

```
ActiveSheet.Scenarios(1).Comment = "Worst case July 1993 sales"
```

Scenarios Object

Description   A collection of Scenario objects.

ScreenUpdating Property

Applies To   Application.

Description   **True** if screen updating is on. Read-write.

Syntax   *object*.**ScreenUpdating**

Elements   *object*
    Required. The Application object.

Remarks   Turn screen updating off to speed up your macro code. You will not be able to see what the macro is doing, but it will run faster.

Example   This example turns screen updating off while Microsoft Excel calculates some formulas and assigns a format to cell A1, and then turns screen updating on. This makes the macro run faster.

```
Application.ScreenUpdating = False
Cells(3,3).Formula = Cells(1,1).Value + Cells(2,2).Value
Cells(1,1).Font.Bold = True
Application.ScreenUpdating = True
```

ScrollBar Object

Description   A scroll bar. Scroll bars do not support border or pattern formatting.

ScrollBars Method

Applies To   Chart, DialogSheet, Worksheet.

Description   Returns a single scroll bar control (a ScrollBar object, Syntax 1) or a collection of scroll bar controls on the chart or sheet (a ScrollBars object, Syntax 2).

Syntax 1	*object*.**ScrollBars(***index***)**
Syntax 2	*object*.**ScrollBars**
Elements	The **ScrollBars** method has the following object qualifier and named arguments:

object
   Required. The Chart, DialogSheet, or Worksheet object.

index
   Required for Syntax 1. Specifies the name or number of the scroll bar (can be an array to specify more than one).

See Also	**Max** Property, **Min** Property.
Example	This example sets the minimum and maximum values for scroll bar one.

```
With Application.DialogSheets(1).ScrollBars(1)
    .Min = 20
    .Max = 50
End With
```

ScrollBars Object

Description	A collection of ScrollBar objects.

ScrollColumn Property

Applies To	Pane, Window.
Description	Returns or sets the number of the column that appears at the left of the pane or window. Read-write.
Syntax	*object*.**ScrollColumn**
Elements	*object* Required. The Pane or Window object.
Remarks	If the window is split, **Window.ScrollColumn** refers to the top left pane. If panes are frozen, **Window.ScrollColumn** excludes the frozen areas.
See Also	**ScrollRow** Property.
Example	This example moves the third column to the left of the window.

```
ActiveWindow.ScrollColumn = 3
```

ScrollRow Property

Applies To   Pane, Window.

Description   Returns or sets the number of the row that appears at the top of the pane or window. Read-write.

Syntax   *object*.**ScrollRow**

Elements   *object*
    Required. The Window object.

Remarks   If the window is split, **Window.ScrollRow** refers to the top left pane. If panes are frozen, **Window.ScrollRow** excludes the frozen areas.

See Also   **ScrollColumn** Property.

Example   This example moves the tenth row to the top of the window.

```
ActiveWindow.ScrollRow = 10
```

ScrollWorkbookTabs Method

Applies To   Window.

Description   Scrolls the workbook tabs at the bottom of the window. Does not affect the active sheet in the workbook.

Syntax   *object*.**ScrollWorkbookTabs(*sheets, position*)**

Elements   The **ScrollWorkbookTabs** method has the following object qualifier and named arguments:

object
    Required. The Window object.

sheets
    Optional. The number of sheets to scroll. Positive means scroll forward, negative means scroll backward, zero means don't scroll. You must specify *sheets* if you do not specify *position*.

position
    Optional. **xlFirst** to scroll to the first sheet, or **xlLast** to scroll to the last sheet. You must specify *position* if you do not specify *sheets*.

Example   This example scrolls the workbook tabs to the last sheet.

```
ActiveWindow.ScrollWorkbookTabs position:=xlLast
```

Second Function

Description   Returns a whole number between 0 and 59, inclusive, representing the second of the minute.

Syntax   **Second(*time*)**

Elements   The *time* named argument is limited to a time or numbers and strings, in any combination, that can represent a time. If *time* contains no valid data, **Null** is returned.

See Also   **Day** Function, **Hour** Function, **Minute** Function, **Now** Function, **Time** Function, **Time** Statement.

Example   This example uses the **Second** function to obtain the second of the minute from a specified time.

```
' In the development environment, the time (date literal) will display
' in short format using the locale settings of your code.
MyTime = #4:35:17 PM#            ' Assign a time.
MySecond = Second(MyTime)        ' MySecond contains 17.
```

Seek Function

Description   Returns the current read/write position within a file opened using the **Open** statement.

Syntax   **Seek(*filenumber*)**

Elements   The *filenumber* named argument is any valid file number.

Remarks   **Seek** returns a value between 1 and 2,147,483,647 (equivalent to 2^31-1), inclusive. For files open in **Random** mode, **Seek** returns the number of the next record read or written. For files opened in **Binary**, **Output**, **Append**, or **Input** mode, **Seek** returns the byte position at which the next operation is to take place. The first byte in a file is at position 1, the second byte is at position 2, and so on.

See Also   **Get** Statement, **Open** Statement, **Put** Statement, **Seek** Statement.

Example

This example uses the **Seek** function to return the current file position.

```
' For files opened in random-file mode, Seek returns number of next
' record.  Assume TESTFILE is a file containing records of the
' user-defined type Record.
Type Record ' Define user-defined type.
    ID As Integer
    Name As String * 20
End Type
Dim MyRecord As Record   ' Declare variable.
' Open file in random-file mode.
Open "TESTFILE" For Random As #1 Len = Len(MyRecord)
Do While Not EOF(1) ' Loop until end of file.
    Get #1, , MyRecord   ' Read next record.
    Debug.Print Seek(1) ' Print record number to Debug
                ' window.
Loop
Close #1' Close file.

' For files opened in modes other than random mode, Seek returns the
' byte position at which the next operation will take place. Assume
' TESTFILE is a file containing a few lines of text.
Open "TESTFILE" For Input As #1  ' Open file for reading.
Do While Not EOF(1) ' Loop until end of file.
    MyChar = Input(1,#1)' Read next character of data.
    Debug.Print Seek(1) ' Print byte position to Debug
                ' window.
Loop
Close #1' Close file.
```

Seek Statement

Description

Sets the position for the next read or write within a file opened using the **Open** statement.

Syntax

Seek [#]*filenumber*,*position*

Elements

The **Seek** statement syntax has these parts:

Part	Description
filenumber	Any valid file number.
position	Number in the range 1 to 2,147,483,647, inclusive, that indicates where the next read or write should occur.

Remarks

Record numbers specified in **Get** and **Put** statements override file positioning done by **Seek**.

Performing a file write after doing a **Seek** operation beyond the end of a file extends the file. If you attempt a **Seek** operation to a negative or zero position, an error occurs.

See Also

Get Statement, **Open** Statement, **Put** Statement, **Seek** Function.

Example

This example uses the **Seek** statement to set the position for the next read or write within a file.

```
' For files opened in random-file mode, Seek sets the next
' record. Assume TESTFILE is a file containing records of the
' user-defined type Record.
Type Record                            ' Define user-defined type.
    ID As Integer
    Name As String * 20
End Type
Dim MyRecord As Record                 ' Declare variable.
' Open file in random-file mode.
Open "TESTFILE" For Random As #1 Len = Len(MyRecord)
MaxSize = LOF(1) \ Len(MyRecord)       ' Get number of records in file.
' The loop reads all records starting from the last.
For RecordNumber = MaxSize To 1 Step - 1
    Seek #1, RecordNumber              ' Set position.
    Get #1, , MyRecord                 ' Read record.
Next RecordNumber
Close #1' Close file.

' For files opened in modes other than random mode, Seek sets the
' byte position at which the next operation will take place. Assume
' TESTFILE is a file containing a few lines of text.
Open "TESTFILE" For Input As #1        ' Open file for input.
MaxSize = LOF(1)                       ' Get size of file in bytes.
' The loop reads all characters starting from the last.
For NextChar = MaxSize To 1 Step -1
    Seek #1, NextChar                  ' Set position.
    MyChar = Input(1,#1)               ' Read character.
Next NextChar
Close #1' Close file.
```

Select Case Statement

Description

Executes one of several groups of statements, depending on the value of an expression.

Syntax

Select Case *testexpression*
[**Case** *expressionlist-n*
    [*statements-n*]] . . .

[**Case Else**
   [*elsestatements*]]
End Select

Elements

The **Select Case** statement syntax has these parts:

Part	Description
testexpression	Any numeric or string expression.
expressionlist-n	Comma-delimited list of one or more of the following forms: *expression*, *expression* **To** *expression*, **Is** *comparisonoperator expression*. The **To** keyword specifies a range of values. If you use the **To** keyword, the smaller value must appear before **To**. Use the **Is** keyword with comparison operators (except **Is** and **Like**) to specify a range of values. If not supplied, the **Is** keyword is automatically inserted.
statements-n	One or more statements executed if *testexpression* matches any part of *expressionlist-n*.
elsestatements	One or more statements executed if *testexpression* doesn't match any of the **Case** clause.

Remarks

If *testexpression* matches any *expressionlist* expression associated with a **Case** clause, the *statements* following that **Case** clause are executed up to the next **Case** clause, or, for the last clause, up to the **End Select**. Control then passes to the statement following **End Select**. If *testexpression* matches an *expressionlist* expression in more than one **Case** clause, only the statements following the first match are executed.

The **Case Else** clause is used to indicate the *statements* to be executed if no match is found between the *testexpression* and an *expressionlist* in any of the other **Case** selections. When there is no **Case Else** statement and no expression listed in the **Case** clauses matches *testexpression*, execution continues at the statement following **End Select**.

Although not required, it is a good idea to have a **Case Else** statement in your **Select Case** block to handle unforeseen *testexpression* values.

You can use multiple expressions or ranges in each **Case** clause. For example, the following line is valid:

```
Case 1 To 4, 7 To 9, 11, 13, Is > MaxNumber
```

Note The **Is** comparison operator is not the same as the **Is** keyword used in the **Select Case** statement.

You also can specify ranges and multiple expressions for character strings. In the following example, **Case** matches strings that are exactly equal to everything, strings that fall between nuts and soup in alphabetical order, and the current value of TestItem:

```
Case "everything", "nuts" To "soup", TestItem
```

Select Case statements can be nested. Each **Select Case** statement must have a matching **End Select** statement.

See Also

If...Then...Else Statement, **On...GoTo** Statement, **On...GoSub** Statement, **Option Compare** Statement.

Example

This example uses the **Select Case** statement to evaluate the value of a variable. The second **Case** clause contains the value of the variable being evaluated and therefore only the statement associated with it is executed.

```
Number = 8              ' Initialize variable.
Select Case Number      ' Evaluate Number.
Case 1 To 5             ' Number between 1 and 5.
    MyString = "Between 1 and 5"
Case 6, 7, 8, 9, 10     ' Number between 6 and 10.
    ' This is the only Case clause that evaluates to True.
    MyString = "Between 6 and 10"
Case Else               ' Other values.
    MyString = "Not between 1 and 10"
End Select
```

Select Method

Applies To

Arc, Arcs, Axis, AxisTitle, Button, Buttons, Chart, ChartArea, ChartObject, ChartObjects, Charts, ChartTitle, CheckBox, CheckBoxes, Corners, DataLabel, DataLabels, DialogFrame, DialogSheet, DialogSheets, DownBars, Drawing, DrawingObjects, Drawings, DropDown, DropDowns, DropLines, EditBox, EditBoxes, ErrorBars, Floor, Gridlines, GroupBox, GroupBoxes, GroupObject, GroupObjects, HiLoLines, Label, Labels, Legend, LegendEntry, LegendKey, Line, Lines, ListBox, ListBoxes, Module, Modules, OLEObject, OLEObjects, OptionButton, OptionButtons, Oval, Ovals, Picture, Pictures, PlotArea, Point, Range, Rectangle, Rectangles, ScrollBar, ScrollBars, Series, SeriesLines, Sheets, Spinner, Spinners, TextBox, TextBoxes, TickLabels, Trendline, UpBars, Walls, Worksheet, Worksheets.

Description

Selects the object.

Syntax	*object*.**Select**(*replace*)
Elements	*object* Required. The object to be selected.
	replace Optional (used only with drawing objects and sheets). If **True** or omitted, the current selection is replaced with a new selection consisting of the specified object. If **False,** the current selection is extended to include any previously selected objects and the specified object.
Remarks	To select a cell or range of cells, use the **Select** method. To make a single cell the active cell, use the **Activate** method.
See Also	**Activate** Method, **Goto** Method.
Example	This example selects A1:B3 on the active sheet.

```
Range(Cells(1, 1), Cells(3, 2)).Select
```

Selected Property

Applies To	DropDown, DropDowns, ListBox, ListBoxes.
Description	Returns or sets an array of Boolean values indicating the selection state of items in the list box. Each entry in the array corresponds to an entry in the list box, and is **True** if the entry is selected or **False** if it is not selected. Use this property to obtain the selected items in a multi-select list box. Read-write.
Syntax	*object*.**Selected**
Elements	*object* Required. The object to which this property applies.
Remarks	For single-selection list boxes, it is easier to use the **Value** or **ListIndex** properties to get and set the selection.
See Also	**ListIndex** Property, **Selection** Property, **Value** Property.

Example   This example selects every other entry in the list box.

```
Dim items() as Boolean
Set lbox = ActiveSheet.ListBoxes(1)
ReDim items(1 to lbox.ListCount)
For i = 1 to lbox.ListCount
    If i Mod 2 = 1 Then
        items(i) = True
    Else
        items(i) = False
    End If
Next
lbox.Selected = items
```

SelectedSheets Method

Applies To   Window.

Description   Returns a collection of all the selected sheets in the window (a Sheets collection).

Syntax   *object*.**SelectedSheets**

Elements   *object*
Required. The Window object.

Example   This example sets the answer variable to **True** if Sheet1 is selected.

```
answer = False
For Each sheet In Windows(1).SelectedSheets
    If sheet.Name = "Sheet1" Then
        answer = True
        Exit For
    End If
Next
```

Selection Property

Applies To   Application, Window.

Description   Returns the object that is currently selected in the active window of the Application object, or the current selection in the given Window object. Read-only.

Syntax	*object*.**Selection**
Elements	*object* Optional for Application, required for Window. The object containing the selection.
Remarks	The object type returned by the **Selection** property depends on the type of selection (for example, if a text box is selected, this property returns a TextBox object.)
	The **Selection** property returns **Nothing** if nothing is selected.
See Also	**Activate** Method, **ActiveCell** Property, **Select** Method, **Selected** Property.
Example	This example deletes the current selection.

```
Selection.Delete
```

SendDateTime Property

Applies To	Mailer.
Description	Returns the date and time that the mailer was sent. The mailer must be sent before this property is valid. Read-only.
Syntax	*object*.**SendDateTime**
Elements	*object* Required. The Mailer object.
See Also	**BCCRecipients** Property, **CCRecipients** Property, **Enclosures** Property, **Mailer** Property, **Received** Property, **Sender** Property, **SendMailer** Method, **SendMailer** Property, **Subject** Property, **ToRecipients** Property.
Example	This example displays the sender and the date and time when the workbook was sent.

```
If ActiveWorkbook.HasMailer Then
    MsgBox "This workbook was sent by " & _
        ActiveWorkbook.Mailer.Sender & " at " & _
        ActiveWorkbook.Mailer.SendDateTime
End If
```

Sender Property

Applies To	Mailer.

Description	Returns the name of the user (as text) who sent this workbook mailer. Read-only.
Syntax	*object*.**Sender**
Elements	*object* Required. The Mailer object.
See Also	**BCCRecipients** Property, **CCRecipients** Property, **Enclosures** Property, **Mailer** Property, **Received** Property, **SendMailer** Method, **SendMailer** Property, **Subject** Property, **ToRecipients** Property.
Example	This example displays the sender and the date and time when the workbook was sent.

```
If ActiveWorkbook.HasMailer Then
    MsgBox "This workbook was sent by " & _
        ActiveWorkbook.Mailer.Sender & " at " & _
        ActiveWorkbook.Mailer.SendDateTime
End If
```

SendKeys Method

Applies To	Application.
Description	Sends keystrokes to the active application.
Syntax	*object*.**SendKeys(***keys, wait***)**
Elements	The **SendKeys** method has the following object qualifier and named arguments:

object
   Optional. The Application object.

keys
   Required. The key or key combination you want to send to the application, as text.

wait
   Optional. If **True**, Microsoft Excel waits for the keys to be processed before returning control to the macro. If **False** or omitted, the macro continues to run without waiting for the keys to be processed.

Remarks	This method places keystrokes into a key buffer. In some cases, you must call this method before you call the method that will use the keystrokes. For example, to send a password to a dialog box, you must call the **SendKeys** method before you display the dialog box.

The *keys* argument can specify any single key, or any key combined with ALT, CTRL, or SHIFT, or any combination of those keys (in Microsoft Excel for Windows) or COMMAND, CTRL, OPTION, or SHIFT or any combination of those keys (in Microsoft Excel for the Macintosh). Each key is represented by one or more characters, such as "a" for the character a, or "{ENTER}" for the ENTER key.

To specify characters that aren't displayed when you press the key, such as ENTER or TAB, use the codes shown in the following table. Each code in the table represents one key on the keyboard.

Key	Code
BACKSPACE	"{BACKSPACE}" or "{BS}"
BREAK	"{BREAK}"
CAPS LOCK	"{CAPSLOCK}"
CLEAR	"{CLEAR}"
DELETE or DEL	"{DELETE}" or "{DEL}"
DOWN ARROW	"{DOWN}"
END	"{END}"
ENTER (numeric keypad)	"{ENTER}"
ENTER	"~" (tilde)
ESC	"{ESCAPE} or {ESC}"
HELP	"{HELP}"
HOME	"{HOME}"
INS	"{INSERT}"
LEFT ARROW	"{LEFT}"
NUM LOCK	"{NUMLOCK}"
PAGE DOWN	"{PGDN}"
PAGE UP	"{PGUP}"
RETURN	"{RETURN}"
RIGHT ARROW	"{RIGHT}"
SCROLL LOCK	"{SCROLLLOCK}"
TAB	"{TAB}"
UP ARROW	"{UP}"
F1 through F15	"{F1}" through "{F15}"

In Microsoft Excel for Windows, you can also specify keys combined with SHIFT and/or CTRL and/or ALT. In Microsoft Excel for the Macintosh, you can also specify keys combined with SHIFT and/or CTRL and/or OPTION and/or COMMAND. To specify a key combined with another key or keys, use the following table.

To combine with	Precede the key code by
SHIFT	"+" (plus sign)
CTRL	"^" (caret)
ALT or OPTION	"%" (percent sign)
COMMAND	"*" (asterisk)

Example

This example uses the **SendKeys** method to quit Microsoft Excel.

```
Application.SendKeys("%fx")
```

SendKeys Statement

Description

Sends one or more keystrokes to the active window as if typed at the keyboard; not available on the Macintosh.

Syntax

SendKeys *string*[,*wait*]

Elements

The **SendKeys** statement syntax has these named-argument parts:

Part	Description
string	String expression specifying the keystroke(s) to send.
wait	Boolean value specifying the wait mode. If **False** (default), control is returned to the procedure immediately after the keys are sent. If **True**, keystrokes must be processed before control is returned to the procedure.

Remarks

Each key is represented by one or more characters. To specify a single keyboard character, use the character itself. For example, to represent the letter A, use "A" for *string*. If you want to represent more than one character, append each additional character to the one preceding it. To represent the letters A, B, and C, use "ABC" for *string*.

The plus sign (+), caret (^), percent sign (%), tilde (~), and parentheses ( ) have special meanings to **SendKeys**. To specify one of these characters, enclose it within braces. For example, to specify the plus sign, use {+}. Brackets ([ ]) have no special meaning to **SendKeys**, but you must enclose them in braces as well, because in other applications, brackets do have a special meaning that may be significant when dynamic data exchange (DDE) occurs. To send brace characters, use {{} and {}}.

To specify characters that aren't displayed when you press a key (such as ENTER or TAB) and keys that represent actions rather than characters, use the codes shown below:

Key	Code
BACKSPACE	{BACKSPACE}, {BS}, or {BKSP}
BREAK	{BREAK}
CAPS LOCK	{CAPSLOCK}
DEL	{DELETE} or {DEL}
DOWN ARROW	{DOWN}
END	{END}
ENTER	{ENTER}
ESC	{ESC}
HELP	{HELP}
HOME	{HOME}
INS	{INSERT}
LEFT ARROW	{LEFT}
NUM LOCK	{NUMLOCK}
PAGE DOWN	{PGDN}
PAGE UP	{PGUP}
PRINT SCREEN	{PRTSC}
RIGHT ARROW	{RIGHT}
SCROLL LOCK	{SCROLLLOCK}
TAB	{TAB}
UP ARROW	{UP}
F1 through F15	{F1} through {F15}

To specify keys combined with any combination of the SHIFT, CTRL, and ALT keys, precede the regular key code with one or more of the following codes:

Key	Code
SHIFT	+
CTRL (CONTROL)	^
ALT	%

To specify that any combination of SHIFT, CTRL, and ALT should be held down while several other keys are pressed, enclose the code for those keys in parentheses. For example, to specify to hold down SHIFT while E and C are pressed, use "+(EC)". To specify to hold down SHIFT while E is pressed, followed by C without SHIFT, use "+EC".

To specify repeating keys, use the form {key number}. You must put a space between key and number. For example, {LEFT 42} means press the LEFT ARROW key 42 times; {h 10} means press h 10 times.

Note **SendKeys** can't send keystrokes to an application that is not designed to run in Microsoft Windows. **Sendkeys** also can't send the PRINT SCREEN (PRTSC) key to any application.

See Also

AppActivate Statement, **DoEvents** Statement.

Example

This example uses the **Shell** function to run the Calculator application included with Microsoft Windows; it then uses the **SendKeys** statement to send keystrokes to add some numbers and then quit the Calculator. The **SendKeys** statement is not available on the Macintosh.

```
ReturnValue = Shell("Calc.exe", 1)      ' Run Calculator.
AppActivate ReturnValue                 ' Activate the Calculator.
For I = 1 To 100                        ' Set up counting loop.
    SendKeys I & "{+}", True ' Send keystrokes to Calculator
Next I                                   ' to add each value of I.
SendKeys "=", True                      ' Get grand total.
SendKeys "%{F4}", True       ' Send Alt+F4 to close Calculator.
```

SendMail Method

Applies To   Workbook.

Description   Sends the workbook using the installed mail system.

Syntax   *object*.**SendMail**(*recipients, subject, returnReceipt*)

Elements   The **SendMail** method has the following object qualifier and named arguments:

object
Required. The Workbook object.

recipients
Required. Specifies the name of the recipient as text, or an array of text strings if there are multiple recipients. At least one recipient must be specified, and all recipients are added as To recipients.

subject
Optional. Specifies the subject of the message. If omitted, the document name is used.

returnReceipt
Optional. If **True**, a return receipt is requested. If **False** or omitted, no return receipt is requested.

Remarks   Use the **SendMail** method on Microsoft Mail (MAPI or Microsoft Mail for the Apple Macintosh) email systems. Pass addressing information as parameters.

Use the **SendMailer** method on PowerTalk email systems on the Apple Macintosh. The **Mailer** object contains the addressing information for PowerTalk.

See Also   **Mailer** Object, **MailSystem** Property, **SendMailer** Method.

Example   This example sends the active workbook to a single recipient.

```
ActiveWorkbook.SendMail recipients:="Jean Selva"
```

SendMailer Method

Applies To   Workbook.

Description   Sends the workbook using the PowerTalk mailer. This method is available only on the Apple Macintosh with the PowerTalk system extension installed and can only be used on a workbook with a mailer attached.

Syntax	*object*.**SendMailer**(*fileFormat, priority*)
Elements	*object*
	Required. The Workbook object.

fileFormat
Optional. Specifies the file format to use for the workbook that is sent. See the **FileFormat** property for a list of valid types.

priority
Optional. Specifies the delivery priority of the message (one of **xlNormal**, **xlHigh**, or **xlLow**). The default value is **xlNormal**.

Remarks
Use the **SendMail** method on Microsoft Mail (MAPI or Microsoft Mail for the Apple Macintosh) email systems. Pass addressing information as parameters.

use the **SendMailer** method on PowerTalk email systems on the Apple Macintosh. The **Mailer** object contains the addressing information for PowerTalk.

See Also
BCCRecipients Property, **CCRecipients** Property, **Enclosures** Property, **FileFormat** Property, **Mailer** Property, **Received** Property, **SendDateTime** Property, **Sender** Property, **SendMail** Method, **Subject** Property, **ToRecipients** Property,

Example
This example sets up the Mailer object for workbook one, and then sends the workbook.

```
With Workbooks(1)
    .HasMailer = True
    With .Mailer
        .Subject = "Here is the workbook"
        .ToRecipients = Array("Jean")
        .CCRecipients = Array("Adam", "Bernard")
        .BCCRecipients = Array("Chris")
        .Enclosures = Array("TestFile")
    End With
    .SendMailer
End With
```

SendToBack Method

Applies To
Arc, Arcs, Button, Buttons, ChartObject, ChartObjects, CheckBox, CheckBoxes, Drawing, DrawingObjects, Drawings, DropDown, DropDowns, EditBox, EditBoxes, GroupBox, GroupBoxes, GroupObject, GroupObjects, Label, Labels, Line, Lines, ListBox, ListBoxes, OLEObject, OLEObjects, OptionButton, OptionButtons, Oval, Ovals, Picture, Pictures, Rectangle, Rectangles, ScrollBar, ScrollBars, Spinner, Spinners, TextBox, TextBoxes.

Description	Sends the object to the back of the z-order.
Syntax	*object*.**SendToBack**
Elements	*object* 　　Required. The object to which this method applies.
See Also	**BringToFront** Method, **ZOrder** Property.
Example	This example sends line one to the back of the z-order.

```
ActiveSheet.DrawingObjects("Line 1").SendToBack
```

Series Object

Description	A series on a chart.

SeriesCollection Method

Applies To	Chart, ChartGroup.
Description	Returns a single series (a Series object, Syntax 1) or a collection of all the series (a SeriesCollection object, Syntax 2) in the chart or chart group. Read-only.
Syntax 1	*object*.**SeriesCollection**(*index*)
Syntax 2	*object*.**SeriesCollection**
Elements	The **SeriesCollection** method has the following object qualifier and named arguments:
	object 　　Required. The Chart or ChartGroup object.
	index 　　Required for Syntax 1. The name or number of the series.
Example	This example turns on data labels for series one.

```
Charts(1).SeriesCollection(1).HasDataLabels = True
```

SeriesCollection Object

Description   A collection of Series objects.

SeriesLines Object

Description   Series lines on a bar or column chart.

SeriesLines Property

Applies To   ChartGroup

Description   Returns or sets the SeriesLines for a stacked bar or stacked column chart. Applies only to stacked bar and stacked column charts. Read-write.

Syntax   *object*.**SeriesLines**

Elements   *object*
    Required. The ChartGroup object.

See Also   **HasSeriesLines** Property

Examples   This example turns on series lines for the first chart group, and then sets their line style, weight, and color.

```
With ActiveChart.ChartGroups(1)
    .HasSeriesLines = True
    With .SeriesLines.Border
        .LineStyle = xlThin
        .Weight = xlMedium
        .Color = RGB(255, 0, 0)
    End With
End With
```

Set Statement

Description   Assigns an object reference to a variable or property.

Syntax	**Set** *objectvar* = {*objectexpression*	**Nothing**}
Elements	The **Set** statement syntax has these parts:

Part	Description
objectvar	Name of the variable or property; follows standard variable naming conventions.
objectexpression	Expression consisting of the name of an object, another declared variable of the same object type, or a function or method that returns an object of the same object type.
Nothing	Discontinues association of *objectvar* with any specific object. Assigning *objectvar* to **Nothing** releases all the resources associated with the previously referenced object when no other variable refers to it.

Remarks

To be valid, *objectvar* must be an object type consistent with the object being assigned to it.

The **Dim**, **Private**, **Public**, **Redim** and **Static** statements only declare a variable that refers to an object. No actual object is referred to until you use **Set** statement to assign a specific object.

Generally, when you use **Set** to assign an object reference to a variable, no copy of the object is created for that variable. Instead, a reference to the object is created. More than one object variable can refer to the same object. Because these variables are references to (rather than copies of) the object, any change is reflected in all variables that refer to it.

See Also

Dim Statement, **Let** Statement, **Private** Statement, **Public** Statement, **ReDim** Statement, **Static** Statement.

Example

This example uses the **Set** statement to assign object references to variables.

```
Set MyObject = YourObject           ' Assign object reference.
' MyObject and YourObject refer to the same object.
YourObject.Text = "Hello World"     ' Initialize property.
MyStr = MyObject.Text               ' Returns "Hello World".
' Discontinue association. MyObject no longer refers to YourObject.
Set MyObject = Nothing
```

SetAttr Statement

Description

Sets attribute information for a file.

Syntax

SetAttr *pathname* *,attributes*

Elements

The **SetAttr** statement syntax has these named-argument parts:

Part	Description
pathname	String expression that specifies a file name—may include directory or folder, and drive.
attributes	Constant or numeric expression, the sum of which specifies file attributes.

Constants and values for *attributes* are:

Constant	Value	File Attribute
vbNormal	0	Normal (default).
vbReadOnly	1	Read-only.
vbHidden	2	Hidden.
vbSystem	4	System—not available on the Macintosh.
vbArchive	32	File has changed since last backup—not available on the Macintosh.

Note These constants are specified by Visual Basic. As a result, the names can be used anywhere in your code in place of the actual values.

Remarks

A run-time error occurs if you try to set the attributes of an open file.

See Also

FileAttr Function, **GetAttr** Function.

Example

This example uses the **SetAttr** statement to set attributes for a file.

```
SetAttr "TESTFILE", vbHidden              ' Set hidden attribute.
SetAttr "TESTFILE", vbHidden + vbReadOnly
                                          ' Set hidden and Read-only
                                          ' attributes.
```

SetDefaultChart Method

Applies To

Application.

Description

Specifies the name of the chart template that Microsoft Excel will use when creating new charts.

| **Syntax** | *object*.**SetDefaultChart**(*formatName*) |

| **Elements** | The **SetDefaultChart** method has the following object qualifier and named arguments: |

object
Required. The Application object.

formatName
Required. Specifies the name of a custom autoformat. This name can be a custom autoformat, as a string, or the special constant **xlBuiltIn** to specify the built-in chart template.

| **Example** | This example sets the default chart template to the custom autoformat named "Monthly Sales." |

```
Application.SetDefaultChart formatName:="Monthly Sales"
```

SetInfoDisplay Method

| **Applies To** | Window. |

| **Description** | Sets the information displayed in the Info window (the specified window object must be the Info window). |

| **Syntax** | *object*.**SetInfoDisplay**(*cell, formula, value, format, protection, names, precedents, dependents, note*) |

| **Elements** | The **SetInfoDisplay** method has the following object qualifier and named arguments: |

object
Required. The Window object.

cell
Optional. **True** to display the cell reference text.

formula
Optional. **True** to display the cell formula.

value
Optional. **True** to display the cell value.

format
Optional. **True** to display cell formatting information.

protection
Optional. **True** to display cell protection information.

names
Optional. **True** to display cell name information.

precedents
Optional. Sets whether precedents are displayed (one of **xlNone**, **xlDirect**, or **xlAll**).

dependents
Optional. Sets whether dependents are displayed (one of **xlNone**, **xlDirect**, or **xlAll**).

note
Optional. **True** to display notes.

Remarks

If this method is applied to any window other than Info window, an error occurs.

Example

This example sets the Info window to display cell reference text and cell name information.

```
Windows(1).SetInfoDisplay cell:=True, names:=True
```

SetLinkOnData Method

Applies To

Workbook.

Description

Sets the name of a macro or procedure that runs whenever a link is updated.

Syntax

object.**SetLinkOnData**(*name, procedure*)

Elements

The **SetLinkOnData** method has the following object qualifier and named arguments:

object
Required. The Workbook object.

name
Required. Specifies the name of the Microsoft Excel or DDE/OLE link, as returned from the **LinkSources** method.

procedure
Optional. Specifies the name of the procedure to run when the link is updated. This can be either a Microsoft Excel version 4.0 macro or a Visual Basic procedure. Set this argument to an empty string ("") to indicate that no procedure should run when the link is updated.

Remarks

Use this method to set notification for a specific link. Use the **OnData** property if you wish to be notified when any link is updated.

See Also

OnData Property.

Example

This example sets the name of the procedure that runs whenever the link is updated.

```
ActiveWorkbook.SetLinkOnData "WinWord|'C:\MSGFILE.DOC'!DDE_LINK1", _
    "my_Link_Update_Macro"
```

Sgn Function

Description	Returns an integer indicating the sign of a number.
Syntax	**Sgn**(*number*)
Elements	The *number* argument can be any valid numeric expression.

Return Values

If number is	Sgn returns
Greater than zero	1
Equal to zero	0
Less than zero	-1

Remarks	The sign of the *number* argument determines the return value of the **Sgn** function.
See Also	**Abs** Function.
Example	This example uses the **Sgn** function to determine the sign of a number.

```
MyVar1 = 12: MyVar2 = -2.4: MyVar3 = 0
MySign = Sgn(MyVar1)         ' Returns 1.
MySign = Sgn(MyVar2)         ' Returns -1.
MySign = Sgn(MyVar3)         ' Returns 0.
```

Shadow Property

Applies To	AxisTitle, ChartArea, ChartObject, ChartObjects, ChartTitle, DataLabel, DataLabels, Drawing, DrawingObjects, Drawings, Font, GroupObject, GroupObjects, Legend, OLEObject, OLEObjects, Oval, Ovals, Picture, Pictures, Rectangle, Rectangles, TextBox, TextBoxes.
Description	**True** if the font is a shadow font or if the drawing object has a shadow. Read-write.
Syntax	*object*.**Shadow**
Elements	*object* Required. The object to which this property applies.
Remarks	For the Font object, this property has no effect in Microsoft Windows, but its value is retained (it can be set and returned).
Example	This example adds a shadow to the chart title.

```
Charts(1).ChartTitle.Shadow = True
```

Sheets Method

Applies To   Application, Workbook

Description   Returns a single sheet (Syntax 1) or a collection of sheets (Syntax 2) in the workbook. Read-only. A sheet can be a Chart, DialogSheet, Module, or Worksheet.

Syntax 1   *object*.**Sheets(*index*)**

Syntax 2   *object*.**Sheets**

Elements   The **Sheets** method has the following object qualifier and named arguments:

object
Optional for Application, required for Workbook. The object to which this method applies.

index
Required for Syntax 1. The name or number of the sheet to return.

Remarks   Using this method with no object qualifier is equivalent to **ActiveWorkbook.Sheets**.

See Also   **Charts** Method, **DialogSheets** Method, **Modules** Method, **Worksheets** Method.

Examples   This example deletes the third sheet in the active workbook.

```
ActiveWorkbook.Sheets(3).Delete
```

Sheets Object

Description   A collection of sheets in a workbook. The Sheets collection can contain Worksheet, Chart, Module, and DialogSheet objects.

SheetsInNewWorkbook Property

Applies To   Application.

Description   Returns or sets the number of sheets Microsoft Excel automatically inserts in new workbooks. Read-write.

Syntax	*object*.**SheetsInNewWorkbook**
Elements	*object* Required. The Application object.
Example	This example displays the number of sheets Microsoft Excel inserts in new workbooks.

```
MsgBox "Microsoft Excel inserts " & _
    Application.SheetsInNewWorkbook & _
    " sheet(s) in each new workbook"
```

Shell Function

Description	Runs an executable program.
Syntax	**Shell(***pathname*[,***windowstyle***])**
Elements	The **Shell** function syntax has these named-argument parts:

Part	Description
pathname	Name of the program to execute and any required arguments or command line switches; may include directory or folder and drive. May also be the name of a document that has been associated with an executable program.
	On the Macintosh, you can use the **MacID** function to specify an application's signature instead of its name. The following example uses the signature for Microsoft Word:
	`Shell MacID("MSWD")`
windowstyle	Number corresponding to the style of the window in which the program is to be run. In Microsoft Windows, if *windowstyle* is omitted, the program is started minimized with focus. On the Macintosh (System 7.0 or later), *windowstyle* only determines whether or not the application gets the focus when it is run.

The *windowstyle* named argument has these values:

Value	Window Style
1, 5, 9	Normal with focus.
2	Minimized with focus.
3	Maximized with focus.
4,8	Normal without focus.
6,7	Minimized without focus.

Remarks	If you use the **MacID** function with **Shell** in Microsoft Windows, an error occurs.

If the **Shell** function successfully executes the named file, it returns the task identification (ID) of the started program. The task ID is a unique number that identifies the running program. If the **Shell** function can't start the named program, an error occurs.

Note   The **Shell** function runs other programs asynchronously. This means you can't depend on a program started with **Shell** to be finished executing before the statements following the **Shell** function in your application are executed.

See Also   **AppActivate** Statement, **MacID** Function.

Example   This example uses the **Shell** function to run an application specified by the user. On the Macintosh, using the **MacID** function ensures that the application can be launched even if the file name of the application has been changed. The **Shell** function is not available on the Macintosh prior to System 7.0.

```
' In Microsoft Windows.
' Specifying 1 as the second argument runs the application normally and
' gives it the focus.
RetVal = Shell("C:\WINDOWS\CALC.EXE", 1) ' Run Calculator.

' On the Macintosh.
' Both statements launch Microsoft Excel.
RetVal = Shell("Microsoft Excel")    ' Specify file name.
RetVal = Shell(MacID("XCEL"))    ' Specify signature.
```

ShortcutKey Property

Applies To   Name.

Description   Returns or sets the shortcut key for a name defined as a custom Microsoft Excel version 4.0 macro command. Read-write.

Syntax   *object*.**ShortcutKey**

Elements   *object*
Required. The Name object.

Example   This example sets the shortcut key for name one.

```
ActiveWorkbook.Names(1).ShortcutKey = "K"
```

ShortcutMenus Method

Applies To   Application.

Description   Returns a single shortcut menu. Read-only.

Syntax   *object*.**ShortcutMenus(***index***)**

Elements   The **ShortcutMenus** method has the following object qualifier and named arguments:

object
>   Optional. The Application object.

index
>   Required. Specifies the shortcut menu, as shown in the following list.

Constant	Description
xlAxis	Chart Axis
xlButton	Button
xlChartSeries	Chart Series
xlChartTitles	Chart Titles
xlColumnHeader	Column
xlDebugCodePane	Debug Code Pane
xlDesktop	Desktop
xlDialogSheet	Dialog Sheet
xlDrawingObject	Drawing Object
xlEntireChart	Entire Chart
xlFloor	Chart Floor
xlGridline	Chart Gridline
xlImmediatePane	Immediate Pane
xlLegend	Chart Legend
xlMacrosheetCell	Macro Sheet Cell
xlModule	Module
xlPlotArea	Chart Plot Area
xlRowHeader	Row
xlTextBox	Text Box
xlTitleBar	Title Bar
xlToolbar	Toolbar
xlToolbarButton	Toolbar Button
xlWatchPane	Watch Pane

Constant	Description
xlWorkbookTab	Workbook Tab
xlWorksheetCell	Worksheet Cell

Example

This example adds a menu item to the column shortcut menu.

```
Application.ShortcutMenus(xlColumnHeader).MenuItems.Add _
    caption:="&More"
```

Show Method

Applies To

Dialog, DialogSheet, Range, Scenario.

Description

DialogSheet object (Syntax 1): Runs the dialog box. This method will not return to the calling procedure until the dialog box is closed or hidden, but event procedures assigned to the dialog box controls will run while the calling procedure is suspended.

Range object (Syntax 1): Scrolls the active window to move the range into view. The range must consist of a single cell which is a part of the currently active document

Scenario object (Syntax 1): Shows the scenario by inserting the scenario's values onto the worksheet. The affected cells are the changing cells of the scenario.

Dialog object (Syntax 2): Displays the dialog box and waits for the user to input data.

Syntax 1

object.**Show**

Syntax 2

object.**Show(***arg1, arg2, ..., arg30***)**

Elements

The **Show** method has the following object qualifier and named arguments:

object
Required. For Syntax 1, the DialogSheet, Range, or Scenario object. For Syntax 2, the Dialog object.

arg1, arg2, ..., arg30
Optional. For built-in dialog boxes only, provides the initial arguments for the command. For more information, see the following Remarks section.

Remarks

For built in dialog boxes, this method returns **True** if the user pressed OK, or **False** if the user pressed Cancel.

A single dialog box can change many properties at once. For example, the Format Cells dialog box can change all the properties of the Font object.

For some built-in dialog boxes (Open, for example), you can set initial values using *arg1, arg2, ..., arg30*. To find the arguments to set, search Microsoft Excel Macro Functions Help for the corresponding Microsoft Excel 4.0 macro function. For example, search for the **OPEN** function to find the arguments for the Open dialog box. For more information about built-in dialog boxes, see **Dialogs**.

Example

This example displays the Open dialog box and selects the Read-Only option in Microsoft Excel for Windows.

```
Application.Dialogs(xlDialogOpen).Show arg3:=True
```

ShowAllData Method

Applies To   Worksheet.

Description   Makes all rows visible for the currently filtered list. If the AutoFilter is in use, this method changes the arrows to "All".

Syntax   *object*.**ShowAllData**

Elements   *object*
            Required. The Worksheet object.

See Also   **AdvancedFilter** Method, **AutoFilter** Method, **FilterMode** Property.

Example   This example makes all data visible for the active worksheet.

```
ActiveSheet.ShowAllData
```

ShowDataForm Method

Applies To   Worksheet.

Description   Displays the data form associated with the worksheet.

Syntax   *object*.**ShowDataForm**

Elements   *object*
            Required. The Worksheet object.

Remarks   The macro pauses while you use the data form. When the user closes the data form, this macro will resume at the line following the **ShowDataForm** method.

The method will run the custom data form, if one exists.

Example	This example displays the data form for the first worksheet.

```
Worksheets(1).ShowDataForm
```

ShowDependents Method

Applies To	Range.
Description	Draws tracer arrows to the direct dependents of the range.
Syntax	*object*.**ShowDependents**(*remove*)
Elements	The **ShowDependents** method has the following object qualifier and named arguments:

object
  Required. The Range object. Must be a single cell.

remove
  Optional. If **True**, removes one level of tracer arrows to direct dependents. If **False** or omitted, expands one level of tracer arrows.

See Also	**ClearArrows** Method, **Dependents** Property, **ShowErrors** Method, **ShowPrecedents** Method.
Example	This example draws tracer arrows to dependents of the active cell.

```
ActiveCell.ShowDependents
```

ShowDetail Property

Applies To	PivotItem, Range.
Description	**True** if the outline is expanded for the specified range (the detail of the column or row is visible). The specified range must be a single summary column or row in an outline. Read-write.
	For the PivotItem object (or the Range object if the range is in a pivot table), this property is **True** if the pivot item is showing detail.
Syntax	*object*.**ShowDetail**
Elements	*object* Required. The PivotItem or Range object.

Remarks	If the specified range is not in a pivot table, the following comments apply:
	The range must be in a single summary row or column.
	This property returns **False** if *any* of the children of the row or column are hidden.
	Setting this property to **True** is equivalent to unhiding all the children on the summary row or column.
	Setting this property to **False** is equivalent to hiding all the children of the summary row or column.
	If the specified range is in a pivot table, it is possible to set this property for more than one cell at once if the range is contiguous. To return this property, the range must be a single cell.
Example	This example shows detail for column one.

```
Columns(1).ShowDetail = True
```

ShowErrors Method

Applies To	Range.
Description	Draws tracer arrows through the precedents tree to the cell that is the source of the error, and returns the range that contains the source of the error.
Syntax	*object*.**ShowErrors**
Elements	*object* Required. The Range object.
See Also	**ClearArrows** Method, **ShowDependents** Method, **ShowPrecedents** Method.
Example	This example displays a red tracer arrow if there is an error in the active cell.

```
If IsError(ActiveCell.Value) Then
    ActiveCell.ShowErrors
End If
```

ShowLegendKey Property

Applies To	DataLabel, DataLabels.
Description	**True** if the data label legend key is visible. Read-write.

Syntax	*object*.**ShowLegendKey**
Elements	*object*

Required. The DataLabel or DataLabels object.

Example   This example sets the data labels for series one to show values and the legend key.

```
With Charts(1).SeriesCollection(1).DataLabels
    .ShowLegendKey = True
    .Type = xlValue
End With
```

ShowLevels Method

Applies To	Outline.
Description	Displays the specified number of row and/or column levels of an outline.
Syntax	*object*.**ShowLevels** (*rowlevels, columnlevels*)
Elements	The **ShowLevels** method has the following object qualifier and named arguments:

object
> Required. The Outline object (**ActiveSheet.Outline**, for example).

rowLevels
> Optional. Specifies the number of row levels of an outline to display. If the outline has fewer levels than specified, Microsoft Excel shows all levels. If omitted or zero, no action is taken on rows.

columnLevels
> Optional. Specifies the number of column levels of an outline to display. If the outline has fewer levels than specified, Microsoft Excel shows all levels. If omitted or zero, no action is taken on columns.

Remarks	You must specify at least one argument.
Example	This example displays row levels one through three and column level one of the outline.

```
ActiveSheet.Outline.ShowLevels rowLevels:=3, columnLevels:=1
```

ShowPages Method

Applies To	PivotTable.

Description	Creates a new pivot table for each item in the page field. Each new pivot table is created on a new worksheet..
Syntax	*object*.**ShowPages**(*pageField*)
Elements	The **ShowPages** method has the following object qualifier and named arguments:

object
 Required. The PivotTable object.

pageField
 Required. A string that names a single page field in the pivot table.

Example	This example creates a new pivot table for the Year page of `pivotTable1`.

```
Set pivotTable1 = ActiveCell.PivotTable
pivotTable1.ShowPages("Year")
```

ShowPrecedents Method

Applies To	Range.
Description	Draws tracer arrows to the direct precedents of the range.
Syntax	*object*.**ShowPrecedents**(*remove*)
Elements	The **ShowPrecedents** method has the following object qualifier and named arguments:

object
 Required. The Range object. Must be a single cell.

remove
 Optional. If **True**, removes one level of tracer arrows to direct precedents. If **False** or omitted, expands one level of tracer arrows.

See Also	**ClearArrows** Method, **Precedents** Property, **ShowDependents** Method, **ShowErrors** Method.
Examples	This example draws tracer arrows to the precedents of the active cell.

```
ActiveCell.ShowPrecedents
```

This example removes the tracer arrow for one level of precedents of the active cell.

```
ActiveCell.ShowPrecedents remove := True
```

ShowToolTips Property

Applies To	Application.
Description	**True** if ToolTips are turned on. Read-write.
Syntax	*object*.**ShowToolTips**
Elements	*object* Required. The Application object.
Example	This example turns on ToolTips.

```
Application.ShowToolTips = True
```

Sin Function

Description	Returns the sine of an angle.
Syntax	**Sin(*number*)**
Elements	The ***number*** named argument can be any valid numeric expression that expresses an angle in radians.
Remarks	The **Sin** function takes an angle and returns the ratio of two sides of a right triangle. The ratio is the length of the side opposite the angle divided by the length of the hypotenuse.
	The result lies in the range -1 to 1.
	To convert degrees to radians, multiply degrees by pi/180. To convert radians to degrees, multiply radians by 180/pi.
See Also	**Atn** Function, **Cos** Function, **Tan** Function.
Example	This example uses the **Sin** function to return the sine of an angle.

```
MyAngle = 1.3                        ' Define angle in radians.
MyCosecant = 1 / Sin(MyAngle)        ' Calculate cosecant.
```

Single Data Type

Single (single-precision floating-point) variables are stored as 32-bit (4-byte) numbers, ranging in value from -3.402823E38 to -1.401298E-45 for negative values and from 1.401298E-45 to 3.402823E38 for positive values. The type-declaration character for **Single** is **!** (character code 33).

See Also   **CSng** Function, Data Type Summary , **Def**_type_ Statements, **Double** Data Type, **Variant** Data Type.

Size Property

Applies To   Font.

Description   Returns or sets the size of the font. Read-write.

Syntax   _object_.**Size**

Elements   _object_
        Required. The Font object.

Example   This example sets the font size for the active cell.

```
ActiveCell.Font.Size = 12
```

SizeWithWindow Property

Applies To   Chart.

Description   **True** if chart resizes to match the size of the chart sheet window. **False** if the chart size is not attached to the window size. Applies only to charts that are sheets in a workbook, not to embedded charts. Read-write.

Syntax   _object_.**SizeWithWindow**

Elements   _object_
        Required. The Chart object.

See Also   **ChartSize** Property.

Example   This example sets the active chart to match the size of the chart sheet window.

```
ActiveChart.SizeWithWindow = True
```

SmallChange Property

Applies To	DrawingObjects, ScrollBar, ScrollBars, Spinner, Spinners.
Description	Returns or sets the amount that the scroll bar or spinner increments or decrements for a line scroll (when the user clicks an arrow). Read-write.
Syntax	*object*.**SmallChange**
Elements	*object* Required. The object to which this property applies.
See Also	**LargeChange** Property.
Example	This example sets the scroll bar to move two units for each line scroll and 10 units for each page scroll.

```
With ActiveSheet.ScrollBars(1)
    .SmallChange = 2
    .LargeChange = 10
End With
```

SmallScroll Method

Applies To	Pane, Window.
Description	Scrolls the window by rows or columns.
Syntax	*object*.**SmallScroll**(*down, up, toRight, toLeft*)
Elements	The **SmallScroll** method has the following object qualifier and named arguments:

object
    Required. The window to scroll.

down
    Optional. The number of rows to scroll the window down.

up
    Optional. The number of rows to scroll the window up.

toRight
    Optional. The number of columns to scroll the window right.

toLeft
    Optional. The number of columns to scroll the window left.

Remarks	If *down* and *up* are both specified, the window is scrolled by the difference of the arguments. For example, if *down* is three and *up* is six, the window is scrolled up three rows.

If *toLeft* and *toRight* are both specified, the window is scrolled by the difference of the arguments. For example, if *toLeft* is three and *toRight* is six, the window is scrolled right three columns.

Any of the arguments can be a negative number.

See Also　　**LargeScroll** Method.

Example　　This example scrolls the active window down three rows.

```
ActiveWindow.SmallScroll down:=3
```

Smooth Property

Applies To　　LegendKey, Series.

Description　　**True** if the line or scatter chart has curve smoothing on. Applies only to line and scatter charts. Read-write.

Syntax　　*object*.**Smooth**

Elements　　*object*
　　　　Required. The LegendKey or Series object.

Example　　This example turns curve smoothing on.

```
ActiveChart.SeriesCollection(7).Smooth = True
```

Sort Method

Applies To　　Range.

Description　　Syntax 1: Sorts the range, or the current region if the range contains only one cell.

Syntax 2: Sorts a pivot table; see the argument list for more information.

Syntax 1　　*object*.**Sort(*key1, order1, key2, type, order2, key3, order3, header, orderCustom, matchCase, orientation*)**

Syntax 2　　*object*.**Sort(*key1, order1, type, orderCustom, orientation*)**

Elements　　The **Sort** method has the following object qualifier and named arguments:

object
　　　　Required. The Range object.

key1

Required (optional when sorting pivot tables). The first sort field, as text (a pivot field or range name) or a Range object ("Dept" or **Cells(1, 1)**, for example).

order1

Optional. If **xlAscending** or omitted, *key1* is sorted in ascending order. If **xlDescending**, *key1* is sorted in descending order.

key2

Optional. The second sort field, as text (a pivot field or range name) or a Range object. If omitted, there is no second sort field. Not used when sorting pivot tables.

type

Optional. Only used when sorting pivot tables. Specifies which elements are sorted, either **xlSortValues** or **xlSortLabels**.

order2

Optional. Sort order for *key2* (**xlAscending** or **xlDescending**); if omitted, **xlAscending** is assumed. Not used when sorting pivot tables.

key3

Optional. The third sort field, as text (a range name) or a Range object. If omitted, there is no third sort field. Not used when sorting pivot tables.

order3

Optional. Sort order for *key3* (**xlAscending** or **xlDescending**); if omitted, **xlAscending** is assumed. Not used when sorting pivot tables.

header

Optional. If **xlYes**, the first row contains headers (it is not sorted). If **xlNo** or omitted, no headers exist (the entire range is sorted). If **xlGuess**, Microsoft Excel guesses if there is a header, and where it is if there is one. Not used when sorting pivot tables.

orderCustom

Optional. One-based integer offset into the list of custom sort orders. If omitted, one (Normal) is used.

matchCase

Optional. If **True**, the sort is case sensitive. If **False**, the sort is not case sensitive. Not used when sorting pivot tables.

orientation

Optional. If **xlTopToBottom** or omitted, the sort is done from top to bottom (sort rows). If **xlLeftToRight**, the sort is done from left to right (sort columns).

Example

This example sorts the range A1:G37, using cell A1 as the first sort key and cell C1 as the second sort key. The sort is done in ascending order by rows, and there are no headers.

```
Range("A1", "G37").Sort key1:=Range("A1"), key2:=Range("C1")
```

SortSpecial Method

Applies To   Range.

Description   Syntax 1: Uses Far-East sorting methods to sort the range, or the current region if the range contains only one cell.

Syntax 2: Uses Far-East sorting methods to sort a pivot table; see the argument list for more information.

Syntax 1   *object*.**SortSpecial**(*key1, sortMethod, order1, key2, type, order2, key3, order3, header, orderCustom, matchCase, orientation*)

Syntax 2   *object*.**SortSpecial**(*key1, sortMethod, order1, type, orderCustom, orientation*)

Elements   The **Sort** method has the following object qualifier and named arguments:

object
   Required. The Range object.

key1
   Required (optional when sorting pivot tables). The first sort field, as text (a pivot field or range name) or a Range object ("Dept" or **Cells(1, 1)**, for example).

sortMethod
   Optional. Specifies how to sort (**xlSyllabary** to sort phonetically or **xlCodePage** to sort by code page). The default value is **xlSyllabary**.

order1
   Optional. If **xlAscending** or omitted, *key1* is sorted in ascending order. If **xlDescending**, *key1* is sorted in descending order.

key2
   Optional. The second sort field, as text (a pivot field or range name) or a Range object. If omitted, there is no second sort field. Not used when sorting pivot tables.

type
   Optional. Only used when sorting pivot tables. Specifies which elements are sorted, either **xlSortValues** or **xlSortLabels**.

order2
   Optional. Sort order for *key2* (**xlAscending** or **xlDescending**); if omitted, **xlAscending** is assumed. Not used when sorting pivot tables.

key3
   Optional. The third sort field, as text (a range name) or a Range object. If omitted, there is no third sort field. Not used when sorting pivot tables.

order3
> Optional. Sort order for *key3* (**xlAscending** or **xlDescending**); if omitted, **xlAscending** is assumed. Not used when sorting pivot tables.

header
> Optional. If **xlYes**, the first row contains headers (it is not sorted). If **xlNo** or omitted, no headers exist (the entire range is sorted). If **xlGuess**, Microsoft Excel guesses if there is a header, and where it is if there is one. Not used when sorting pivot tables.

orderCustom
> Optional. One-based integer offset into the list of custom sort orders. If omitted, one (Normal) is used.

matchCase
> Optional. If **True**, the sort is case sensitive. If **False**, the sort is not case sensitive. Not used when sorting pivot tables.

orientation
> Optional. If **xlTopToBottom** or omitted, the sort is done from top to bottom (sort rows). If **xlLeftToRight**, the sort is done from left to right (sort columns).

Example
> This example sorts the range A1:G37, using A1 as the first sort key and C1 as the second key. The sort is done in ascending code page order by rows, and there are no headers.

```
Range("A1", "G37").SortSpecial sortMethod:=xlCodePage, _
    key1:="A1", key2:="C1"
```

SoundNote Object

Description   A sound note in a cell.

SoundNote Property

Applies To   Range.

Description   Returns the SoundNote associated with the top left cell in the Range object. Read-only.

Syntax   *object*.**SoundNote**

Elements
object
> Required. The Range object that contains the cell with the sound note.

Remark   Your computer may require optional hardware to record and play sound notes.

See Also   **Import** Method, **Play** Method, **Record** Method.

Example   This example sets the `currentSoundNote` variable to the sound note in the top left cell of the current selection.

```
Set currentSoundNote = Selection.SoundNote
```

SourceData Property

Applies To   PivotTable.

Description   Returns the data source for the PivotTable, as shown in the following table.

Data Source	Return Value
Microsoft Excel list or database	The cell reference as text.
External data source	An array. Each row consists of a SQL connection string with the remaining elements as the query string broken down into 200-character segments.
Multiple Consolidation ranges	A two-dimensional array. Each row consists of a reference and associated page field items.
Another pivot table	One of the above three kinds of information.

Syntax   *object*.**SourceData**

Elements   *object*
          Required. The PivotTable object.

Example   This example sets the `dataSource` variable to the data source for the active pivot table.

```
dataSource = ActiveCell.PivotTable.SourceData
```

SourceName Property

Applies To   PivotField, PivotItem.

Description   Returns the object name (a string) as it appears in the original source data for the pivot table. This might be different from the current item name if the user renamed the item after creating the pivot table. Read-only.

Syntax	*object*.**SourceName**
Elements	*object*
	Required. The PivotField or PivotItem object.
Example	This example displays the original name of the active item..

```
MsgBox("The original item name is " & _
    ActiveCell.PivotItem.SourceName)
```

Space Function

Description	Returns a string consisting of the specified number of spaces.
Syntax	**Space(*number*)**
Elements	The *number* named argument is the number of spaces you want in the string.
Remarks	The **Space** function is useful for formatting output and clearing data in fixed-length strings.
See Also	**Spc** Function, **String** Function.
Example	This example uses the **Space** function to return a string consisting of a specified number of spaces.

```
' Returns a string with 10 spaces.
MyString = Space(10)
' Insert 10 spaces between 2 strings.
MyString = "Hello" & Space(10) & "World"
```

Spc Function

Description	Used with the **Print #** statement or the **Print** method to position output.
Syntax	**Spc(*n*)**
Elements	The *n* argument is the number of spaces to insert before displaying or printing the next expression in a list.
Remarks	If *n* is less than the output-line width, the next print position immediately follows the number of spaces printed. If *n* is greater than the output-line width, **Spc** calculates the next print position using the formula:

currentprintposition + (*n* **Mod** *width*)

For example, if the current print position is 24, the output-line width is 80 and you specify **Spc**(90), the next print will start at position 34 (current print position + the remainder of 90/80). If the difference between the current print position and the output-line width is less than *n* (or *n* **Mod** *width*), the **Spc** function skips to the beginning of the next line and generates a number of spaces equal to *n* - (*width* - *currentprintposition*).

Note Make sure your tabular columns are wide enough to accommodate wider letters.

When you use the **Print** method with a proportionally spaced font, the width of space characters printed using the **Spc** function is always an average of the width of all characters in the point size for the chosen font. However, there is no correlation between the number of characters printed and the number of fixed-width columns those characters occupy. For example, the uppercase letter W occupies more than one fixed-width column and the lowercase letter I occupies less.

See Also   **Print** Method, **Print #** Statement, **Space** Function, **Tab** Function, **Width #** Statement.

Example   This example uses the **Spc** function to position output in a file and in the Debug window.

```
' The Spc function can be used with the Print # statement.
Open "TESTFILE" For Output As #1        ' Open file for output.
Print #1, "10 spaces between here"; Spc(10); "and here."
Close #1                                ' Close file.
' The following statement causes the text to be printed in the Debug
' window, preceded by 30 spaces.
Debug.Print Spc(30); "Thirty spaces later..."
```

SpecialCells Method

Applies To   Range.

Description   Returns a range that refers to all the cells that match the specified type and value.

Syntax   *object*.**SpecialCells**(*type, value*)

Elements   The **SpecialCells** method has the following object qualifier and named arguments:

object
    Required. The Range object.

type
    Required. The types of cells to include, as shown in the following table.

Value	Meaning
xlNotes	Cells containing notes.
xlConstants	Cells containing constants.
xlFormulas	Cells containing formulas.
xlBlanks	Empty cells.
xlLastCell	Last cell of the used range.
xlVisible	All visible cells.

value

Optional. If *type* is **xlConstants** or **xlFormulas**, the *value* argument is used to determine which types of cells to include in the result. These values may be added together to return more than one type. The default is to select all constants or formulas, no matter what the type.

Value	Meaning
xlNumbers	Numbers
xlTextValues	Text
xlLogical	Logical values
xlErrors	Error values

Example

This example activates the last cell in the current selection.

```
Selection.SpecialCells(xlLastCell).Activate
```

Spinner Object

Description

A miniature scroll bar; often used next to edit boxes so that the user can select a numeric value without having to type in a number.

Remarks

A spinner is very similar to a scroll bar (ScrollBar object). Spinners do not have the **LargeChange** property, however.

Edit boxes do not have spinners by default. If you want an edit box to have a spinner, you must create a separate Spinner object and add the Visual Basic code to link the spinner value to the edit box.

Spinners Method

Applies To   Chart, DialogSheet, Worksheet.

Description   Returns a single spinner control (a Spinner object, Syntax 1) or a collection of spinner controls on the chart or sheet (a Spinners object, Syntax 2).

Syntax 1   *object*.**Spinners**(*index*)

Syntax 2   *object*.**Spinners**

Elements   The **Spinners** method has the following object qualifier and named arguments:

object
    Required. The Chart, DialogSheet, or Worksheet object.

index
    Required for Syntax 1. Specifies the name or number of the spinner (can be an array to specify more than one).

Example   This example displays the number of spinners on the active dialog sheet.

```
cSpinners = ActiveDialog.Spinners.Count
MsgBox "There are " & cSpinners & _
    " spinners on the active dialog sheet."
```

Spinners Object

Description   A collection of Spinner objects.

Split Property

Applies To   Window.

Description   **True** if the window is split. Read-write.

Syntax   *object*.**Split**

Elements   *object*
    Required. The Window object.

Remarks	It is possible for **FreezePanes** to be **True** and **Split** to be **False**, or vice versa.
	This property applies only to worksheets and macro sheets.
Examples	This example splits the active window at cell B2, without freezing panes. This causes the **Split** property to return **True.**

```
With ActiveWindow
    .SplitColumn = 2
    .SplitRow = 2
End With
```

There are two ways to remove the split.

```
ActiveWindow.Split = False              'method one

ActiveWindow.SplitColumn = 0            'method two
ActiveWindow.SplitRow = 0
```

This example removes the window split. You must set **FreezePanes** to **False** to remove frozen panes before you can remove the split.

```
With ActiveWindow
    .FreezePanes = False
    .Split = False
End With
```

SplitColumn Property

Applies To	Window.
Description	Returns or sets the column number where the window is split into panes (the number of columns to the left of the split line). Read-write.
Syntax	*object*.**SplitColumn**
Elements	*object* Required. The Window object.
See Also	**SplitHorizontal** Property, **SplitRow** Property, **SplitVertical** Property.
Example	This example splits the window and leaves 1.5 columns to the left of the split line.

```
ActiveWindow.SplitColumn = 1.5
```

SplitHorizontal Property

Applies To	Window.
Description	Returns or sets the location of the horizontal window split, in points (1/72 inch). Read-write.
Syntax	*object*.**SplitHorizontal**
Elements	*object* Required. The Window object.
See Also	**SplitColumn** Property, **SplitRow** Property, **SplitVertical** Property.
Example	This example sets the horizontal split for the active window to 216 points (3 inches).

```
ActiveWindow.SplitHorizontal = 216
```

SplitRow Property

Applies To	Window.
Description	Returns or sets the row number where the window is split into panes (the number of rows above the split). Read-write.
Syntax	*object*.**SplitRow**
Elements	*object* Required. The Window object.
See Also	**SplitColumn** Property, **SplitHorizontal** Property, **SplitVertical** Property.
Example	This example splits the active window so that there are 10 rows above the split line.

```
ActiveWindow.SplitRow = 10
```

SplitVertical Property

Applies To	Window.

Description	Returns or sets the location of the vertical window split, in points (1/72 inch). Read-write.
Syntax	*object*.**SplitVertical**
Elements	*object* Required. The Window object.
See Also	**SplitColumn** Property, **SplitHorizontal** Property, **SplitRow** Property.
Example	This example sets the vertical split for the active window to 216 points (3 inches).

```
ActiveWindow.SplitVertical = 216
```

SQLBind Function

Description	Specifies where results are placed when they are retrieved using the **SQLRetrieve** function.
	This function is designed to work exclusively with the **SQLClose**, **SQLError**, **SQLExecQuery**, **SQLGetSchema**, **SQLOpen**, and **SQLRetrieve** ODBC functions, to provide a way to create custom data access applications using Visual Basic.
	This function is contained in the XLODBC add-in. Before you use the function, you must establish a reference to the XLODBC add-in using the References command from the Tools menu. For more information, see "Calling Procedures in Another Workbook," in the *Visual Basic for Applications User's Guide*.
Syntax	**SQLBind**(*connection, column, ref*)
Elements	The **SQLBind** function has the following named arguments:

connection
Required. The unique connection ID of the data source, returned by **SQLOpen**, for which you want to define storage.

column
Optional. The number of the result set that you want bound. Columns in the result set are numbered from left to right starting with 1. If you omit *column*, all bindings for *connection* are removed.

Column number 0 contains row numbers for the result set. If column number 0 is bound, **SQLRetrieve** returns row numbers in the bound location.

ref
> Optional. The location of a single cell on a worksheet where you want the results bound, as a Range object. If *ref* is omitted, binding is removed for the column.

Return Value
This function returns an array listing the bound columns for the current connection by column number.

If **SQLBind** is unable to bind the column to the cell in the specified reference, it returns the #N/A error value.

If *connection* is not valid or if you try to bind a cell that is not available, **SQLBind** returns the #VALUE! error value.

If *ref* refers to more than a single cell, **SQLBind** returns the #REF! error value.

If **SQLRetrieve** does not have a destination parameter, **SQLBind** places the result set in the location indicated by reference.

Remarks
SQLBind tells the ODBC Control Panel Administrator where to place results when they are received using **SQLRetrieve** The results are placed in the reference cell and cells immediately below it.

Use **SQLBind** if you want the results from different columns to be placed in disjoint worksheet locations.

Use **SQLBind** for each column in the result set. A binding remains valid as long as the connection specified by *connection* is open.

SQLBind can be called any time there is a valid connection. Calls to **SQLBind** do not affect results that have already been retrieved.

See Also
SQLClose Function, **SQLError** Function, **SQLExecQuery** Function, **SQLGetSchema** Function, **SQLOpen** Function, **SQLRequest** Function, **SQLRetrieve** Function, **SQLRetrieveToFile** Function.

SQLClose Function

Description
Closes a connection to an external data source.

This function is designed to work exclusively with the **SQLBind**, **SQLError**, **SQLExecQuery**, **SQLGetSchema**, **SQLOpen**, **SQLRetrieve**, and **SQLRetrieveToFile** ODBC functions, to provide a way to create custom data access applications using Visual Basic.

This function is contained in the XLODBC add-in. Before you use the function, you must establish a reference to the XLODBC add-in using the References command from the Tools menu. For more information, see "Calling Procedures in Another Workbook," in the *Visual Basic for Applications User's Guide.*

Syntax   **SQLClose(*connection*)**

Elements   The **SQLClose** function has the following named argument:

connection
     Required. The unique connection ID of the data source from which you want to disconnect.

Return Value   If the connection is successfully closed, this function returns 0 (zero) and the connection ID is no longer valid.

If *connection* is not valid, this function returns the #VALUE! error value.

If **SQLClose** is unable to disconnect from the data source, it returns the #N/A error value.

See Also   **SQLBind** Function, **SQLError** Function, **SQLExecQuery** Function, **SQLGetSchema** Function, **SQLOpen** Function, **SQLRequest** Function, **SQLRetrieve** Function, **SQLRetrieveToFile** Function.

SQLError Function

Description   Returns detailed error information when called after one of the other ODBC functions fails. If **SQLError** itself fails, it cannot return error information.

Error information is defined and stored in memory whenever an ODBC function fails. To make the error information available, call the **SQLError** function.

SQLError provides detailed error information only about errors that occur when an ODBC function fails. It does not provide information about Microsoft Excel errors.

This function is designed to work exclusively with the **SQLBind**, **SQLClose**, **SQLExecQuery**, **SQLGetSchema**, **SQLOpen**, **SQLRetrieve**, and **SQLRetrieveToFile** ODBC functions, to provide a way to create custom data access applications using Visual Basic.

This function is contained in the XLODBC add-in. Before you use the function, you must establish a reference to the XLODBC add-in using the References command from the Tools menu. For more information, see "Calling Procedures in Another Workbook," in the *Visual Basic for Applications User's Guide.*

Syntax   **SQLError()**

Return Value   If there are errors, **SQLError** returns detailed error information in a two-dimensional array in which each row describes one error.

Each row has three fields for information obtained through the **SQLError** function call in ODBC. The fields are:

- A character string indicating the ODBC error class and subclass.
- A numeric value indicating the data source native error code.
- A text message describing the error.

If a function call generates multiple errors, **SQLError** creates a row for each error.

If there are no errors from a previous ODBC function call, this function returns only the #N/A error value.

See Also   **SQLBind** Function, **SQLClose** Function, **SQLExecQuery** Function, **SQLGetSchema** Function, **SQLOpen** Function, **SQLRequest** Function, **SQLRetrieve** Function, **SQLRetrieveToFile** Function.

SQLExecQuery Function

Description   Executes a query on a data source with a connection that has been established using **SQLOpen**.

SQLExecQuery executes only the query. Use **SQLRetrieve** or **SQLRetrieveToFile** to get the results.

This function is designed to work exclusively with the **SQLBind**, **SQLClose**, **SQLError**, **SQLGetSchema**, **SQLOpen**, **SQLRetrieve**, and **SQLRetrieveToFile** macro functions, to provide a way to create custom data access applications using Visual Basic.

This function is contained in the XLODBC add-in. Before you use the function, you must establish a reference to the XLODBC add-in using the References command from the Tools menu. For more information, see "Calling Procedures in Another Workbook," in the *Visual Basic for Applications User's Guide*.

Syntax   **SQLExecQuery(*connection, query*)**

Elements	The **SQLExecQuery** function has the following named arguments:

connection
> Required. The unique connection ID returned by **SQLOpen** that identifies the data source you want to query.

query
> Required. The query to be executed on the data source. The query must follow the SQL syntax guidelines for the specific driver.

Return Value

The value returned by **SQLExecQuery** depends on the type of SQL statement executed:

SQL statement executed	Return Value
SELECT	The number of columns in the result set.
UPDATE, INSERT or DELETE	The number of rows affected by the statement.
Any other valid SQL statement	0

If **SQLExecQuery** is unable to execute the query on the specified data source, it returns the #N/A error value.

If *connection* is not valid, **SQLExecQuery** returns the #VALUE! error.

Remarks

Before calling **SQLExecQuery** you must establish a connection to a data source using **SQLOpen** The unique connection ID returned by **SQLOpen** is used by **SQLExecQuery** to send queries to the data source.

If you call **SQLExecQuery** using a previously used connection ID, any pending results on that connection are replaced by the new results.

See Also

SQLBind Function, **SQLClose** Function, **SQLError** Function, **SQLExecQuery** Function, **SQLGetSchema** Function, **SQLOpen** Function, **SQLRequest** Function, **SQLRetrieve** Function, **SQLRetrieveToFile** Function.

SQLGetSchema Function

Description

Returns information about the structure of the data source on a particular connection.

This function is designed to work exclusively with the **SQLBind**, **SQLClose**, **SQLError**, **SQLExecQuery**, **SQLOpen**, **SQLRetrieve**, and **SQLRetrieveToFile** ODBC functions, to provide a way to create custom data access applications using Visual Basic.

This function is contained in the XLODBC add-in. Before you use the function, you must establish a reference to the XLODBC add-in using the References command from the Tools menu. For more information, see "Calling Procedures in Another Workbook," in the *Visual Basic for Applications User's Guide*.

Syntax

SQLGetSchema(*connection, action, qualifier*)

Elements

The **SQLGetSchema** function has the following named arguments:

connection
Required. The unique connection ID of the data source you connected to using **SQLOpen** and for which you want information.

action
Required. Specifies the type of information you want returned, as shown in the following list.

Value	Meaning
1	A list of available data sources.
2	A list of databases on the current connection.
3	A list of owners in a database on the current connection.
4	A list of tables for a given owner and database on the current connection.
5	A list of columns in a particular table and their ODBC SQL data types in a two-dimensional array. The first field contains the name of the column and the second field is the ODBC SQL data type of the column.
6	The user ID of the current user.
7	The name of the current database.
8	The name of the data source defined during setup or by using the ODBC Control Panel Administrator.
9	The name of the DBMS the data source uses, for example, ORACLE, or SQL Server.
10	The server name for the data source.
11	The terminology used by the data source to refer to the owners, for example "owner", "Authorization ID", or "Schema".

Value	Meaning
12	The terminology used by the data source to refer a table, for example, "table" or "file".
13	The terminology used by the data source to refer to a qualifier, for example, "database" or "directory".
14	The terminology used by the data source to refer to a procedure, for example, "database procedure", "stored procedure", or "procedure".

qualifier

Optional. Included only for *action* values of 3, 4 and 5. A string that qualifies the search, as shown in the following table:

action	qualifier
3	The name of the database in the current data source. **SQLGetSchema** returns the names of the table owners in that database.
4	Both a database name and an owner name. The syntax consists of the database name followed by the owner's name with a period separating the two; for example, "DatabaseName.OwnerName". This function returns an array of table names that are located in the given database and owned by the given owner.
5	The name of a table. **SQLGetSchema** returns information about the columns in the table.

Return Value

The return value from a successful call to **SQLGetSchema** depends on the type of information that is requested.

If **SQLGetSchema** cannot find the requested information, it returns the #N/A error value.

If *connection* is not valid, this function returns the #VALUE! error value.

Remarks

SQLGetSchema works with the ODBC functions **SQLGetInfo** and **SQLTables** to find the requested information.

See Also   **SQLBind** Function, **SQLClose** Function, **SQLError** Function, **SQLExecQuery** Function, **SQLOpen** Function, **SQLRequest** Function, **SQLRetrieve** Function, **SQLRetrieveToFile** Function.

SQLOpen Function

Description   Establishes a connection to a data source.

This function is designed to work exclusively with the **SQLBind**, **SQLClose**, **SQLError**, **SQLExecQuery**, **SQLGetSchema**, **SQLRetrieve**, and **SQLRetrieveToFile** ODBC functions, to provide a way to create custom data access applications using Visual Basic.

This function is contained in the XLODBC add-in. Before you use the function, you must establish a reference to the XLODBC add-in using the References command from the Tools menu. For more information, see "Calling Procedures in Another Workbook," in the *Visual Basic for Applications User's Guide.*

Syntax   **SQLOpen(***connectionStr, output, prompt***)**

Elements   The **SQLOpen** function has the following named arguments:

connectionStr
> Required. Supplies the information required by the driver being used to connect to a data source and must follow the driver's format.

> The *connectionStr* supplies the data source name and other information, such as user ID and passwords, that is required by the driver to make a connection.

> You must define the data source name (DSN) used in *connectionStr* before you try to connect to it.

output
> Optional. A single cell, as a Range object, that contains the completed connection string.

> Use *output* when you want **SQLOpen** to return the completed connection string to a worksheet.

prompt

Optional. Specifies when the driver dialog box is displayed and which options are available. Use one of the numbers described in the following table. If *prompt* is omitted, **SQLOpen** uses 2 as the default.

Value	Meaning
1	Driver dialog box is always displayed.
2	Driver dialog box is displayed only if information provided by the connection string and the data source specification are not sufficient to complete the connection. All dialog box options are available.
3	The same as 2 except that dialog box options that are not required are dimmed and unavailable.
4	Driver dialog box is not displayed. If the connection is not successful, **SQLOpen** returns an error.

Return Value

If successful, **SQLOpen** returns a unique connection ID number. Use the connection ID number with the other ODBC functions.

If **SQLOpen** is unable to connect using the information you provide, it returns the error value #N/A. Additional error information is placed in memory for use by **SQLError**.

See Also

SQLBind Function, **SQLClose** Function, **SQLError** Function, **SQLExecQuery** Function, **SQLGetSchema** Function, **SQLRequest** Function, **SQLRetrieve** Function, **SQLRetrieveToFile** Function.

SQLRequest Function

Description

Connects to an external data source and runs a query from a worksheet, and then returns the result as an array.

This function is designed to work exclusively with the **SQLBind**, **SQLClose**, **SQLError**, **SQLExecQuery**, **SQLGetSchema**, **SQLRetrieve**, and **SQLRetrieveToFile** ODBC functions, to provide a way to create custom data access applications using Visual Basic.

This function is contained in the XLODBC add-in. Before you use the function, you must establish a reference to the XLODBC add-in using the References command from the Tools menu. For more information, see "Calling Procedures in Another Workbook," in the *Visual Basic for Applications User's Guide*.

Syntax

SQLRequest(*connectionStr, query, output, prompt, columnNames***)**

Elements

The **SQLRequest** function has the following named arguments:

connectionStr

Required. Supplies information, such as the data source name, user ID, and passwords, required by the driver being used to connect to a data source and must follow the driver's format.

You must define the data source name (DSN) used in *connectionStr* before you try to connect to it.

If **SQLRequest** is unable to access the data source using *connectionStr*, it returns the #N/A error value.

query

Required. The SQL statement that you want to execute on the data source.

If **SQLRequest** is unable to execute *query* on the specified data source, it returns the #N/A error value.

output

Optional. A single cell, as a range object, where you want the completed connection string placed.

Use *output* when you want **SQLRequest** to return the completed connection string to a worksheet.

prompt

Optional. Specifies when the driver dialog box is displayed and which options are available. Use one of the numbers described in the following table. If *prompt* is omitted, **SQLRequest** uses 2 as the default.

Value	Meaning
1	Driver dialog box is always displayed.
2	Driver dialog box is displayed only if information provided by the connection string and the data source specification is not sufficient to complete the connection. All dialog box options are available.
3	Driver dialog box is displayed only if information provided by the connection string and the data source specification is not sufficient to complete the connection. Dialog box options are dimmed and unavailable if they are not required.
4	Dialog box is not displayed. If the connection is not successful, it returns an error.

columnNames

Optional. **True** if you want the column names to be returned as the first row of results. It should contain **False** if you do not want the column names returned. The default value, if *columnNames* is omitted, is **False**.

Return Value	If this function completes all of its actions, it returns an array of query results or the number of rows affected by the query.
	If **SQLRequest** is unable to complete all of its actions, it returns an error value and places the error information in memory for **SQLError**
	If **SQLRequest** is unable to access the data source using *connectionStr*, it returns the #N/A error value.
See Also	**SQLBind** Function, **SQLClose** Function, **SQLError** Function, **SQLExecQuery** Function, **SQLGetSchema** Function, **SQLOpen** Function, **SQLRetrieve** Function, **SQLRetrieveToFile** Function.

SQLRetrieve Function

Description	Retrieves all or part of the results from a previously executed query.
	Before using **SQLRetrieve**, you must establish a connection with **SQLOpen**, execute a query with **SQLExecQuery**, and have the results pending.
	This function is designed to work exclusively with the **SQLBind**, **SQLClose**, **SQLError**, **SQLExecQuery**, **SQLGetSchema**, and **SQLOpen** ODBC functions, to provide a way to create custom data access applications using Visual Basic.
	This function is contained in the XLODBC add-in. Before you use the function, you must establish a reference to the XLODBC add-in using the References command from the Tools menu. For more information, see "Calling Procedures in Another Workbook," in the *Visual Basic for Applications User's Guide*.
Syntax	**SQLRetrieve(***connection, destination, maxColumns, maxRows, columnNames, rowNumbers, namedRange, fetchFirst***)**
Elements	The **SQLRetrieve** function has the following named arguments:
	connection
	Required. The unique connection ID returned by **SQLOpen** and for which you have pending query results generated by **SQLExecQuery**.
	If *connection* is not valid, **SQLExecQuery** returns the #VALUE! error value.

destination

Optional. A Range object that specifies where the results should be placed. This function overwrites any values in the cells without confirmation.

If *destination* refers to a single cell, **SQLRetrieve** returns all of the pending results in that cell and in the cells to the right and below it.

If *destination* is omitted, the bindings established by previous calls to **SQLBind** are used to return results. If no bindings exist for the current connection, **SQLRetrieve** returns #REF! error value.

If a particular result column has not been bound and *destination* is omitted, the results are discarded.

maxColumns

Optional. The maximum number of columns returned to the worksheet starting at *destination*.

If *maxColumns* specifies more columns than are available in the result, **SQLRetrieve** places data in the columns for which data is available and clears the additional columns.

If *maxColumns* specifies fewer columns than are available in the result, **SQLRetrieve** discards the rightmost result columns until the results fit the specified size.

The order in which the data source returns the columns determines column position.

All of the results are returned if *maxColumns* is omitted.

maxRows

Optional. The maximum number of rows to be returned to the worksheet starting at *destination*.

If *maxRows* specifies more rows than are available in the results, **SQLRetrieve** places data in the rows for which data is available and clears the additional rows.

If *maxRows* specifies fewer rows than are available in the results, **SQLRetrieve** places data in the selected rows but does not discard the additional rows. Extra rows are retrieved by using **SQLRetrieve** again and by setting *fetchFirst* to **False**.

All of the rows in the results are returned if *maxRows* is omitted.

columnNames

Optional. **True** if you want the column names to be returned as the first row of results. **False** or omitted if you do not want the column names returned.

rowNumbers

Optional. Used only when *destination* is included in the function call. If *rowNumbers* is **True**, the first column in the result set contains row numbers. If *destination* is **False** or omitted, the row numbers are not returned. You can also retrieve row numbers by binding column number 0 with **SQLBind**.

namedRange

Optional. **True** if you want each column of the results to be declared as a named range on the worksheet. The name of each range is the result column name. The named range includes only the rows that are returned with **SQLRetrieve**. The default is **False**.

fetchFirst

Optional. Allows you to request results from the beginning of the result set. If *fetchFirst* is **False**, **SQLRetrieve** can be called repeatedly to return the next set of rows until all the result rows are returned. When there are no more rows in the result set, **SQLRequest** returns 0. If you want to retrieve results from the beginning of the result set, set *fetchFirst* to **True**. To retrieve additional rows from the result set, set *fetchFirst* to **False** in subsequent calls. The default is **False**.

Return Value

SQLRetrieve returns the number of rows in the result set.

If **SQLRetrieve** is unable to retrieve the results on the specified data source or if there are no results pending, it returns the #N/A error value. If no data is found, it returns 0.

Remarks

Before calling **SQLRetrieve**, you must:

1. Establish a connection with a data source using **SQLOpen**.
2. Use the connection ID returned in **SQLOpen** to send a query with **SQLExecQuery**.

See Also

SQLBind Function, **SQLClose** Function, **SQLError** Function, **SQLExecQuery** Function, **SQLGetSchema** Function, **SQLOpen** Function, **SQLRequest** Function, **SQLRetrieveToFile** Function.

SQLRetrieveToFile Function

Description

Retrieves all of the results from a previously executed query and places them in a file.

To use this function you must have established a connection with a data source using **SQLOpen**, executed a query using **SQLExecQuery**, and have the results of the query pending.

This function is designed to work exclusively with the **SQLClose**, **SQLError**, **SQLExecQuery**, **SQLGetSchema**, **SQLOpen** and **SQLRetrieve** ODBC functions, to provide a way to create custom data access applications using Visual Basic.

This function is contained in the XLODBC add-in. Before you use the function, you must establish a reference to the XLODBC add-in using the References command from the Tools menu. For more information, see "Calling Procedures in Another Workbook," in the *Visual Basic for Applications User's Guide.*

Syntax

SQLRetrieveToFile(*connection, destination, columnNames, columnDelimiter***)**

Elements

The **SQLRetrieveToFile** function has the following named arguments:

connection
   Required. The unique connection ID returned by **SQLOpen** and for which you have pending query results generated by **SQLExecQuery**.

   If *connection* is not valid, **SQLExecQuery** returns the #VALUE! error value.

destination
   Required. A string that specifies the name and path of the file where you want to place the results. If the file exists, its contents are replaced with the query results. If the file does not exist, **SQLRetrieveToFile** creates and opens the file and fills it with the results.

   The format of the data in the file is compatible with the Microsoft Excel .CSV (comma-separated value) file format.

   Columns are separated by the character specified by *columnDelimiter*, and the individual rows are separated by a carriage return.

   If the file specified by *destination* cannot be opened, **SQLRetrieveToFile** returns the #N/A error value.

columnNames
   Optional. **True** if you want the column names to be returned as the first row of data. **False** or omitted if you do not want the column names returned.

columnDelimiter
   Optional. A string that specifies the character used to separate the elements in each row. For example, use "","" to specify a comma delimiter or ";" to specify a semicolon delimiter. If you omit *columnDelimiter*, a TAB is used.

Return Value

If successful, **SQLRetrieveToFile** returns the query results, writes them to a file, and then returns the number of rows that were written to the file.

If **SQLRetrieveToFile** is unable to retrieve the results, it returns the #N/A error value, and does not write the file.

If there are no pending results on the connection, **SQLRetrieveToFile** returns the #N/A error value.

Remarks	Before calling **SQLRetrieveToFile**, you must:

1. Establish a connection with a data source using **SQLOpen**.
2. Use the connection ID returned by **SQLOpen** to send a query with **SQLExecQuery**.

See Also	**SQLBind** Function, **SQLClose** Function, **SQLError** Function, **SQLExecQuery** Function, **SQLGetSchema** Function, **SQLOpen** Function, **SQLRequest** Function, **SQLRetrieve** Function.

Sqr Function

Description	Returns the square root of a number.
Syntax	**Sqr(*number*)**
Elements	The *number* named argument can be any valid numeric expression greater than or equal to 0.
Example	This example uses the **Sqr** function to calculate the square root of a number.

```
MySqr = Sqr(4)   ' Returns 2.
MySqr = Sqr(23)  ' Returns 4.795832.
MySqr = Sqr(0)   ' Returns 0.
MySqr = Sqr(-4)  ' Generates run-time error.
```

StandardFont Property

Applies To	Application.
Description	Returns or sets the standard font name as a string. Read-write.
Syntax	*object*.**StandardFont**
Elements	*object* Required. The Application object.
Remark	If you change the standard font using this property, the change does not take effect until you restart Microsoft Excel.
See Also	**StandardFontSize** Property.

Example   This example sets the standard font to Arial.

```
Application.StandardFont = "Arial"
```

StandardFontSize Property

Applies To   Application.

Description   Returns or sets the standard font size in points (1/72 inch). Read-write.

Syntax   *object*.**StandardFontSize**

Elements   *object*
                       Required. The Application object.

Remark   If you change the standard font size using this property, the change does not take
                       effect until you restart Microsoft Excel.

See Also   **StandardFont** Property.

Example   This example sets the standard font size to 12 points.

```
Application.StandardFontSize = 12
```

StandardHeight Property

Applies To   Worksheet.

Description   Returns the standard (default) height of all the rows in the worksheet, measured in
                       points (1/72 inch). Read-only.

Syntax   *object*.**StandardHeight**

Elements   *object*
                       Required. The Worksheet object.

See Also   **Height** Property, **RowHeight** Property, **StandardWidth** Property.

Example   This example sets the height of the cells in row one to the standard height.

```
Worksheets(1).Rows(1).RowHeight = Worksheets(1).StandardHeight
```

StandardWidth Property

Applies To	Worksheet.
Description	Returns or sets the standard (default) width of all the columns in the worksheet, measured in characters of the normal font. Read-write.
Syntax	*object*.**StandardWidth**
Elements	*object* Required. The Worksheet object.
Remarks	If the normal font is a proportional font, this property returns the column width measured in characters of the zero (0) character in the normal font.
See Also	**ColumnWidth** Property, **StandardHeight** Property, **Width** Property.
Example	This example sets the width of the cells in column one to the standard width.

```
Worksheets(1).Columns(1).ColumnWidth = Worksheets(1).StandardWidth
```

StartupPath Property

Applies To	Application.
Description	Returns the complete path of the startup directory, not including the final separator. Read-only.
Syntax	*object*.**StartupPath**
Elements	*object* Required. The Application object.
Example	This example sets the variable currentStartupPath to the complete startup path in Microsoft Excel.

```
currentStartupPath = Application.StartupPath
```

Static Statement

Description   Used at the procedure level to declare variables and allocate storage space. Variables declared with the **Static** statement retain their value as long as the code is running.

Syntax   **Static** *varname*[([*subscripts*])][**As** *type*][,*varname*[([*subscripts*])][**As** *type*]] . . .

Elements   The **Static** statement syntax has these parts:

Part	Description
varname	Name of the variable; follows standard variable naming conventions.
subscripts	Dimensions of an array variable; up to 60 multiple dimensions may be declared. The *subscripts* argument uses the following syntax: [*lower* **To**] *upper* [,[*lower* **To**] *upper*] . . .
type	Data type of the variable; may be **Boolean**, **Integer**, **Long**, **Currency**, **Single**, **Double**, **Date**, **String** (for variable-length strings), **String** * *length* (for fixed-length strings), **Object**, **Variant**, a user-defined type, or an object type. Use a separate **As** *type* clause for each variable being defined.

Remarks   Once the module code is running, variables declared with the **Static** statement retain their value until the module is reset or restarted. Use the **Static** statement in nonstatic procedures to explicitly declare **Static** variables.

Use a **Static** statement within a procedure to declare the data type of a **Static** variable. For example, the following statement declares a fixed-size array of integers:

```
Static EmployeeNumber(200) As Integer
```

If you do not specify a data type or object type, and there is no **Def***type* statement in the module, the variable is **Variant** by default.

Note The **Static** statement and the **Static** keyword affect the lifetime of variables differently. If you declare a procedure using the **Static** keyword (as in `Static Sub CountSales ()`), the storage space for all local variables within the procedure is allocated once and the value of the variables is preserved for the entire time the code is running. For nonstatic procedures, storage space for variables is allocated each time the procedure is called and released when the procedure is exited. The **Static** statement is used to declare variables within nonstatic procedures to preserve their value as long as the program is running.

When variables are initialized, a numeric variable is initialized to 0, a variable-length string is initialized to a zero-length string, and a fixed-length string is filled with zeros. **Variant** variables are initialized to **Empty**. Each element of a user-defined type variable is initialized as if it was a separate variable. A variable that refers to an object must be assigned an existing object using the **Set** statement before it can be used. Until it is assigned an object, the declared object variable has the special value **Nothing**, which indicates that it does not refer to any particular instance of an object.

Tip When you use the **Static** statement in a procedure, it is a generally accepted programming practice to put the **Static** statement at the beginning of the procedure with any **Dim** statements.

See Also   **Array** Function, **Dim** Statement, **Function** Statement, **Option Base** Statement, **Private** Statement, **Public** Statement, **ReDim** Statement, **Sub** Statement.

Example   This example uses the **Static** statement to retain the value of a variable as long as module code is running.

```
' Function definition.
Function KeepTotal(Number)
    ' Only the variable Accumulate preserves its value between calls.
    Static Accumulate
    Accumulate = Accumulate + Number
    KeepTotal = Accumulate
End Function

' Static function definition.
Static Function MyFunction(Arg1, Arg2, Arg3)
    ' All local variables preserve value between function calls.
    Accumulate = Arg1 + Arg2 + Arg3
    Half = Accumulate / 2
    MyFunction = Half
End Function
```

Status Property

Applies To   RoutingSlip.

Description   Indicates the status of the routing slip (one of **xlNotYetRouted**, **xlRoutingInProgress**, or **xlRoutingComplete**). Read-only.

Syntax   *object*.**Status**

Elements   *object*
               Required. The RoutingSlip object.

Example   This example resets the routing slip for the workbook if routing is complete.

```
With Workbooks("BOOK1.XLS").RoutingSlip
    If .Status = xlRoutingComplete Then
        .Reset
    Else
        MsgBox "Cannot reset routing; not yet complete."
    End If
End With
```

StatusBar Property

Applies To   Application.

Description   Returns or sets the text in the status bar. Read-write.

Syntax   *object*.**StatusBar**

Elements   *object*
    Required. The Application object.

Remarks   This property returns **False** if Microsoft Excel has control of the status bar; set the property to **False** to restore the default status bar text. This works even if the status bar is hidden.

See Also   **DisplayStatusBar** Property.

Example   This example sets the status bar text to "Please be patient..." before it opens the workbook LARGE.XLS, and then restores the text to the default.

```
saveStatusBar = Application.DisplayStatusBar
Application.DisplayStatusBar = True
Application.StatusBar = "Please be patient..."
Workbooks.Open filename:="LARGE.XLS"
Application.StatusBar = False
Application.DisplayStatusBar = saveStatusBar
```

Stop Statement

Description   Suspends execution.

Syntax   **Stop**

Remarks   You can place **Stop** statements anywhere in procedures to suspend execution. Using the **Stop** statement is similar to setting a breakpoint in the code.

The **Stop** statement suspends execution, but unlike **End**, it doesn't close any files or clear variables.

See Also   **End** Statement.

Example   This example uses the **Stop** statement to suspend execution for each iteration through the **For...Next** loop.

```
For I = 1 To 10          ' Start For...Next loop.
    Debug.Print I          ' Print I to Debug window.
    Stop                 ' Stop each time through.
Next I
```

Str Function

Description   Returns a string representation of a number.

Syntax   **Str(*number*)**

Elements   The *number* named argument is any valid numeric_expression.

Remarks   When numbers are converted to strings, a leading space is always reserved for the sign of *number*. If *number* is positive, the returned string contains a leading space and the plus sign is implied.

Use the **Format** function to convert numeric values you want formatted as dates, times, or currency or in other user-defined formats. Unlike **Str**, the **Format** function doesn't include a leading space for the sign of *number*.

Note The **Str** function recognizes only the period (.) as a valid decimal separator. When a possibility exists that different decimal separators may be used (for example, in international applications), you should use **CStr** to convert a number to a string.

See Also   **CStr** Function, **Format** Function, Returning Strings From Functions, **Val** Function.

StrComp Function

Description   Returns a value indicating the result of a string comparison.

Syntax	**StrComp**(*string1*,*string2*[,*compare*])
Elements	The **StrComp** function syntax has these parts:

Part	Description
string1	Any valid string expression.
string2	Any valid string expression.
compare	Number specifying the type of string comparison. Specify a **1** to perform a textual comparison. Specify a **0** (default) to perform a binary comparison. If *compare* is **Null**, an error occurs. If *compare* is omitted, the setting of **Option Compare** is used to determine the type of comparison.

Return Values

Value	Description
-1	*string1* is less than *string2*.
0	*string1* is equal to *string2*.
1	*string1* is greater than *string2*.
Null	*string1* or *string2* is **Null**.

Remarks

Note When **Option Compare Text** is specified, comparisons are textual and case-insensitive. When **Option Compare Binary** is specified, comparisons are strictly binary.

See Also

Option Compare Statement.

Example

This example uses the **StrComp** function to return the results of a string comparison. If 1 is supplied as the third argument, a textual comparison is performed; whereas, if the third argument is 0 or omitted, a binary comparison is performed.

```
MyStr1 = "ABCD": MyStr2 = "abcd"        ' Define variables.
MyComp = StrComp(MyStr1, MyStr2, 1)     ' Returns 0.
MyComp = StrComp(MyStr1, MyStr2, 0)     ' Returns -1.
MyComp = StrComp(MyStr2, MyStr1)        ' Returns 1.
```

StrConv Constants

Constant	Value	Description
vbUpperCase	1	Uppercases the string.
vbLowerCase	2	Lowercases the string.

Constant	Value	Description
vbProperCase	3	Uppercases first letter of every word in string.
vbWide	4	Narrow (single-byte) characters in string converted to wide (double-byte) characters.
vbNarrow	8	Wide (double-byte) characters in string converted to narrow (single-byte) characters.
vbKatakana	16 *	Narrow Hiragana characters in string converted to wide Katakana characters.
vbHiragana	32 *	Wide Katakana characters in string converted to narrow Hiragana characters.

*Applies to Japan locales only.

See Also   **StrConv** Function.

StrConv Function

Description   Returns a converted string; available in Far East versions only.

Syntax   **StrConv**(*string,conversion*)

Elements   The **StrConv** function syntax has these named-argument parts:

Part	Description
string	The string expression to be converted.
conversion	The sum of values specifying the type of conversion to perform.

The *conversion* named argument has these constants and values:

Constant	Value	Description
vbUpperCase	1	Uppercases the string.
vbLowerCase	2	Lowercases the string.
vbProperCase	3	Uppercases first letter of every word in string.

Constant	Value	Description
vbWide	4	Narrow (single-byte) characters in string converted to wide (double-byte) characters.
vbNarrow	8	Wide (double-byte) characters in string converted to narrow (single-byte) characters.
vbKatakana	16 *	Wide Hiragana characters in string converted to wide Katakana characters.
vbHiragana	32 *	Wide Katakana characters in string converted to wide Hiragana characters.

*Applies to Japan locales only.

Note These constants are specified by Visual Basic. As a result, the names can be used anywhere in your code in place of the actual values.

Strikethrough Property

Applies To   Font.

Description   **True** if the font is struck through. Read-write.

Syntax   *object*.**Strikethrough**

Elements   *object*
                    Required. The Font object (**ActiveCell.Font**, for example).

Example   This example sets the font in the active cell to strikethrough.

```
ActiveCell.Font.Strikethrough = True
```

String Data Type

There are two kinds of strings:

- Variable-length strings, which can contain up to approximately 2 billion (2^{31}) characters (approximately 64K (2^{16}) characters for Microsoft Windows version 3.1 and earlier).

- Fixed-length strings, which contain a declared number of characters (less than 64K).

The type-declaration character for **String** is **$** (character code 36). The codes for **String** characters range from 0 to 255. The first 128 characters (0-127) of the character set correspond to the letters and symbols on a standard U.S. keyboard. These first 128 characters are the same as those defined by the ASCII character set. The second 128 characters (128-255) represent special characters, such as letters in international alphabets, accents, currency symbols, and fractions.

See Also   **CStr** Function, Data Type Summary, **Def***Type* Summary, **String** Function, **Variant** Data Type.

String Function

Description   Returns a repeating character string of the length specified.

Syntax   **String(***number,character***)**

Elements   The **String** function syntax has these named-argument parts:

Part	Description
number	Length of the returned string. If *number* contains no valid data, **Null** is returned.
character	Character code specifying the character or string expression whose first character is used to build the return string. If *character* contains no valid data, **Null** is returned.

Remarks   If you specify a number for *character* greater than 255, **String** converts the number to a valid character code using the formula:

character **Mod** 256

See Also   Character Set, **Space** Function, **String** Data Type.

Example   This example uses the **String** function to return repeating character strings of the length specified.

```
MyString = String(5, "*")       ' Returns "*****".
MyString = String(5, 42)        ' Returns "*****".
MyString = String(10, "ABC")    ' Returns "AAAAAAAAAA".
```

Style Object

Description   A style description. The Style object contains all style attributes (font, number format, alignment, and so on) as properties.

Style Property

Applies To   Range.

Description   Returns or sets the Style of the range. Read-write.

Syntax   *object*.**Style**

Elements   *object*
    Required. The Range object.

Examples   This example applies the Normal style to cell A1.

```
Cells(1, 1).Style = "Normal"
```

This example applies the Percent style to cell B4 if it currently has the Normal style.

```
If Cells(4, 2).Style.Name = "Normal" Then
    Cells(4, 2).Style = "Percent"
End If
```

This example changes the font size of the style attached to cell D72 from its current value to 24.

```
Cells(72, 4).Style.Font.Size = 24
```

Styles Method

Applies To   Workbook.

Description   Returns a single style (a Style object, Syntax 1) or a collection of all the styles (a Styles object, Syntax 2) in the workbook. Read-only.

Syntax 1   *object*.**Styles(*index*)**

Syntax 2   *object*.**Styles**

Elements   The **Styles** method has the following object qualifier and named arguments:

object
    Required. The Workbook object.

index
    Required for Syntax 1. The name or number of the style to return.

Example   This example deletes the user-defined style "Stock Quote Style" from the first workbook.

```
Workbooks(1).Styles("Stock Quote Style").Delete
```

Styles Object

Description   A collection of Style objects.

Sub Statement

Description   Declares the name, arguments, and code that form the body of a **Sub** procedure.

Syntax   [**Private** | **Public**][**Static**] **Sub** *name* [(*arglist*)]
          [*statements*]
          [**Exit Sub**]
          [*statements*]
          End Sub

Elements   The **Sub** statement syntax has these parts:

Part	Description
Public	Indicates that the **Sub** procedure is accessible to all other procedures in all modules. If used in a private module (one that contains an **Option Private** statement) the procedure is not available outside the project.
Private	Indicates that the **Sub** procedure is accessible only to other procedures in the module where it is declared.
Static	Indicates that the **Sub** procedure's local variables are preserved between calls. The **Static** attribute doesn't affect variables that are declared outside the **Sub**, even if they are used in the procedure.
name	Name of the **Sub**; follows standard variable naming conventions.
arglist	List of variables representing arguments that are passed to the **Sub** procedure when it is called. Multiple variables are separated by commas.
statements	Any group of statements to be executed within the body of the **Sub** procedure.

The *arglist* argument has the following syntax and parts:

[[**Optional**][**ByVal** | **ByRef**][**ParamArray**] *varname*[( )] **As** *type*]

Part	Description
Optional	Indicates that an argument is not required. If used, all subsequent arguments in *arglist* must also be optional and declared using the **Optional** keyword. All **Optional** arguments must be **Variant**. **Optional** can't be used for any argument if **ParamArray** is used.
ByVal	Indicates that the argument is passed by value.
ByRef	Indicates that the argument is passed by reference.
ParamArray	Used only as the last argument in *arglist* to indicate that the final argument is an **Optional** array of **Variant** elements. The **ParamArray** keyword allows you to provide an arbitrary number of arguments. May not be used with **ByVal**, **ByRef**, or **Optional**.
varname	Name of the variable representing the argument; follows standard variable naming conventions.
type	Data type of the argument passed to the procedure; may be **Boolean**, **Integer**, **Long**, **Currency**, **Single**, **Double**, **Date**, **String** (variable length only), **Object**, **Variant**, a user-defined type, or an object type.

Remarks

If not explicitly specified using either **Public** or **Private**, **Sub** procedures are **Public** by default. If **Static** is not used, the value of local variables is not preserved between calls.

All executable code must be in procedures. You can't define a **Sub** procedure inside another **Sub**, **Function**, or **Property** procedure.

The **Exit Sub** keyword causes an immediate exit from a **Sub** procedure. Program execution continues with the statement following the statement that called the **Sub** procedure. Any number of **Exit Sub** statements can appear anywhere in a **Sub** procedure.

Like a **Function** procedure, a **Sub** procedure is a separate procedure that can take arguments, perform a series of statements, and change the value of its arguments. However, unlike a **Function** procedure, which returns a value, a **Sub** procedure can't be used in an expression.

You call a **Sub** procedure using the procedure name followed by the argument list. See the **Call** statement for specific information on how to call **Sub** procedures.

Caution **Sub** procedures can be recursive; that is, they can call themselves to perform a given task. However, recursion can lead to stack overflow. The **Static** keyword usually is not used with recursive **Sub** procedures.

Variables used in **Sub** procedures fall into two categories: those that are explicitly declared within the procedure and those that are not. Variables that are explicitly declared in a procedure (using **Dim** or the equivalent) are always local to the procedure. Other variables used but not explicitly declared in a procedure are also local unless they are explicitly declared at some higher level outside the procedure.

Caution A procedure can use a variable that is not explicitly declared in the procedure, but a name conflict can occur if anything you have defined at the module level has the same name. If your procedure refers to an undeclared variable that has the same name as another procedure, constant or variable, it is assumed that your procedure is referring to that module-level name. Explicitly declare variables to avoid this kind of conflict. You can use an **Option Explicit** statement to force explicit declaration of variables.

Note You can't use **GoSub**, **GoTo**, or **Return** to enter or exit a **Sub** procedure.

See Also

Call Statement, **Dim** Statement, **Function** Statement, **Option Explicit** Statement, **Property Get** Statement, **Property Let** Statement, **Property Set** Statement, **Static** Statement.

Example

This example uses the **Sub** statement to declare the name, arguments and code that form the body of a **Sub** procedure.

```
' Sub procedure definition.
Sub SubComputeArea(Length, Width)              ' Sub with two arguments.
    Dim Area As Double    ' Declare local variable.
    If Length = 0 Or Width = 0 Then            ' If either argument = 0.
        Exit Sub' Exit Sub immediately.
    End If
    Area = Length * Width     ' Calculate area of rectangle.
    Debug.Print Area' Print Area to Debug window.
End Sub
```

Subject Property

Applies To

AddIn, Mailer, RoutingSlip, Workbook.

Description

Returns or sets the subject for an object, as a string. Read-only for AddIn, read-write for RoutingSlip and Workbook.

Syntax

object.**Subject**

Elements

object
Required. The object to which this property applies.

Remarks	The RoutingSlip subject is used as the subject of mail messages used to route the workbook.
	PowerTalk requires that a subject be present before the mailer can be sent.
See Also	**Author** Property, **Comments** Property, **KeyWord** Property, **Title** Property.
Example	This example sets the subject for the active workbook.

```
ActiveWorkbook.Subject = "Data for my presentation in April"
```

SubscribeTo Method

Applies To	Range.
Description	Apple Macintosh (running System 7 or later) only. Subscribes to a published edition.
Syntax	*object*.**SubscribeTo**(*edition, format*)
Elements	The **SubscribeTo** method has the following object qualifier and named arguments:

object
　　Required. The Range object.

edition
　　Required. The name of the edition, as a string, to which you want to subscribe.

format
　　Optional. **xlPicture** to subscribe to a picture, **xlText** to subscribe to text.

See Also	**CreatePublisher** Method.
Example	This example subscribes to an edition named Corporate Logo in the current folder.

```
Cells(3, 3).SubscribeTo edition:="Corporate Logo", format:=xlPicture
```

Subscript Property

Applies To	Font.
Description	**True** if the font is subscripted. Read-write.
Syntax	*object*.**Subscript**
Elements	*object*

　　Required. The Font object.

Remarks	This property is **False** by default.
See Also	**Characters** object, **Superscript** Property.
Example	This example makes the first character in the text box a subscript.

```
ActiveSheet.TextBoxes(1).Characters(1, 1).Font.Subscript = True
```

Subtotal Method

Applies To

Range

Description

Creates subtotals for the range (or current region if the range is a single cell).

For help about using the **Subtotal** worksheet function in Visual Basic, see Using Worksheet Functions in Visual Basic.

Syntax

object.**Subtotal**(*groupBy, function, totalList, replace, pageBreaks, summaryBelowData*)

Elements

The **Subtotal** method has the following object qualifier and named arguments:

object
Required. The Range object.

groupBy
Required. The field to group by, as a one-based integer offset. For more information, see the example.

function
Required. The subtotal function. Can be one of **xlAverage, xlCount, xlCountNums, xlMax, xlMin, xlProduct, xlStDev, xlStDevP, xlSum, xlVar,** or **xlVarP.**

totalList
Required. An array of one-based field offsets, indicating the fields to which the subtotals are added. For more information, see the example.

replace
Optional. If **True**, existing subtotals are replaced. If **False** or omitted, existing subtotals are not replaced.

pageBreaks
Optional. **True** to create page breaks after each group, **False** or omitted if no page breaks are created.

summaryBelowData
Optional. If **xlBelow** or omitted, the summary goes below detail. If **xlAbove**, the summary goes above detail.

See Also

RemoveSubtotal Method.

Example   This example creates subtotals for the selection. The subtotals are sums grouped by each change in field one, with the subtotals added to fields 2 and 3.

```
Selection.Subtotal groupBy:=1, function:=xlSum, _
    totalList:=Array(2, 3)
```

Subtotals Property

Applies To   PivotField.

Description   Returns or sets an array of Boolean values corresponding to the subtotals showing with the specified field. This property is valid only for non-data fields. Read-write.

Syntax   *object*.**Subtotals**

Elements   *object*
    Required. The PivotField object.

Remarks   This property returns an array of Boolean values, as shown in the following list.

Array Element	Meaning
1	Automatic
2	Sum
3	Count
4	Average
5	Max
6	Min
7	Product
8	Count Nums
9	StdDev
10	StdDevp
11	Var
12	Varp

If an array value is **True**, the field shows that subtotal. If automatic is **True**, all other values are set to **False.**

Example   This example sets the active field to show Sum subtotals.

```
ActiveCell.PivotField.Subtotals = _
    Array(False, True, False, False, False, False, _
        False, False, False, False, False, False)
```

SubType Property

Applies To   Chart, ChartGroup.

Description   Returns or sets the subtype for a single chart group or for all chart groups in the chart.

Syntax   *object*.**SubType**

Elements   *object*
          Required. The Chart or ChartGroup object.

Remarks   Set the **SubType** property *after* you set the **Type** property. Each type supports different subtypes (for example, a column chart type can have clustered, stacked, or percent subtypes). The easiest way to obtain the number of the subtype is to record the subtype formatting using the macro recorder.

Example   This example sets the subtype for the first radar chart group.

```
Charts(1).RadarGroups(1).SubType = 2
```

Summary Property

Applies To   Range.

Description   **True** if the range is an outlining summary row or column. The range should be a row or a column. Read-only.

Syntax   *object*.**Summary**

Elements   *object*
          Required. The row or column, as a Range object.

Example   This example formats a column as bold and italic if it is an outlining summary column.

```
If Columns("A").Summary = True Then
    Columns("A").Font.Bold = True
    Columns("A").Font.Italic = True
End If
```

SummaryColumn Property

Applies To   Outline.

Description	Returns or sets the location of the summary columns in the outline, as shown in the following table. Read-write.

Value	Meaning
xlLeft	The summary column will be to the left of the detail columns in the outline.
xlRight	The summary column will be to the right of the detail columns in the outline.

Syntax	*object*.**SummaryColumn**
Elements	*object* Required. The Outline object (**ActiveSheet.Outline**, for example).
Example	This example creates an outline with automatic styles, the summary row above the detail rows, and the summary column to the right of the detail columns.

```
Selection.AutoOutline
With ActiveSheet.Outline
    .SummaryRow = xlAbove
    .SummaryColumn = xlRight
    .AutomaticStyles = True
End With
```

SummaryRow Property

Applies To	Outline.
Description	Returns or sets the location of the summary rows in the outline, as shown in the following table. Read-write.

Value	Meaning
xlAbove	The summary row will be above the detail columns in the outline.
xlBelow	The summary row will be below the detail columns in the outline.

Syntax	*object*.**SummaryRow**
Elements	*object* Required. The Outline object (**ActiveSheet.Outline**, for example).
Remarks	Use **SummaryRow = xlAbove** for Microsoft Word-style outlines, where category headers are above the detail. Use **SummaryRow = xlBelow** for accounting-style outlines, where summations are below the detailed information.

Example   This example creates an outline with automatic styles, the summary row above the detail rows, and the summary column to the right of the detail columns.

```
Selection.AutoOutline
With ActiveSheet.Outline
    .SummaryRow = xlAbove
    .SummaryColumn = xlRight
    .AutomaticStyles = True
End With
```

Superscript Property

Applies To   Font.

Description   **True** if the font is superscripted. Read-write.

Syntax   *object*.**Superscript**

Elements   *object*
                 Required. The Font object.

Remarks   This property is **False** by default.

See Also   **Characters** object, **Subscript** Property.

Example   This example makes the last character in the text box a superscript.

```
c = ActiveSheet.TextBoxes(1).Characters.Count
ActiveSheet.TextBoxes(1).Characters(c).Font.Superscript = True
```

SurfaceGroup Property

Applies To   Chart.

Description   Returns the surface ChartGroup of a 3-D chart.

Syntax   *object*.**SurfaceGroup**

Elements   *object*
                 Required. The Chart object.

Example   This example makes the surface group an area group.

```
Charts(1).SurfaceGroup.Type = xlArea
```

Tab Function

Description   Used with the **Print #** statement or the **Print** method to position output.

Syntax   **Tab**[(*n*)]

Elements   The *n* argument is the column number to tab to before displaying or printing the next expression in a list. If omitted, **Tab** moves the cursor to the beginning of the next print zone. This allows **Tab** to be used instead of a comma in locales where the comma is used as a decimal separator.

Remarks   If the current print position on the current line is greater than *n*, **Tab** skips to the *n*th column on the next output line. If *n* is less than 1, **Tab** moves the print position to column 1. If *n* is greater than the output-line width, **Tab** calculates the next print position using the formula:

n **Mod** *width*

For example, if width is 80 and you specify **Tab**(90), the next print will start at column 10 (the remainder of 90/80). If *n* is less than the current print position, printing begins on the next line at the calculated print position. If the calculated print position is greater than the current print position, printing begins at the calculated print position on the same line.

The leftmost print position on an output line is always 1. When you use the **Print #** statement to print to files, the rightmost print position is the current width of the output file, which you can set using the **Width #** statement.

Note Make sure your tabular columns are wide enough to accommodate wider letters.

When you use the **Tab** function with the **Print** method, the print surface is divided into uniform, fixed-width columns. The width of each column is an average of the width of all characters in the point size for the chosen font. However, there is no correlation between the number of characters printed and the number of fixed-width columns those characters occupy. For example, the uppercase letter W occupies more than one fixed-width column and the lowercase letter I occupies less.

See Also   **Print** Method, **Print #** Statement, **Space** Function, **Spc** Function, **Width #** Statement.

Example

This example uses the **Tab** function to position output in a file or in the Debug window.

```
' The Tab function can be used with the Print # statement.
Open "TESTFILE" For Output As #1          ' Open file for output.
' The second word prints at column 20.
Print #1, "Hello"; Tab(20); "World."
' If the argument is omitted, cursor is moved to the next print zone.
Print #1, "Hello"; Tab ; "World"
Close #1                                   ' Close file.

' The Tab function can also be used with the Print method.
' The following statement prints text starting at column 10.
Debug.Print Tab(10); "10 columns from start."
```

Table Method

Applies To

Range.

Description

Creates a data table based on input values and formulas that you define on a worksheet.

Syntax

object.**Table**(*rowInput, columnInput*)

Elements

The **Table** method has the following object qualifier and named arguments:

object
Required. The object to which this method applies.

rowInput
Optional. A single cell to use as the row input for your table.

columnInput
Optional. A single cell to use as the column input for your table.

Remark

Use data tables to perform a what-if analysis by changing certain constant values on your worksheet to see how values in other cells are affected.

Example

This example creates a multiplication table in A1:K11.

```
Set dataTableRange = Range(Cells(1, 1), Cells(11, 11))
Set rowInputCell = Cells(12, 1)
Set columnInputCell = Cells(13, 1)

Cells(1, 1).Formula = "=A12*A13"
For i = 2 To 11
    Cells(i, 1) = i - 1
    Cells(1, i) = i - 1
Next i
dataTableRange.Table rowInputCell, columnInputCell
```

TableRange1 Property

Applies To   PivotTable.

Description   Returns the Range that contains the entire pivot table, but does not include page
                     fields. Read-only.

Syntax   *object*.**TableRange1**

Elements   *object*
                         Required. The PivotTable object.

Remarks   The **TableRange2** property includes page fields.

Example   This example selects the active pivot table, except for its page fields.

```
ActiveCell.PivotTable.TableRange1.Select
```

TableRange2 Property

Applies To   PivotTable.

Description   Returns the Range that includes the entire pivot table, including page fields. Read-
                     only.

Syntax   *object*.**TableRange2**

Elements   *object*
                         Required. The PivotTable object.

Remarks   The **TableRange1** property does not include page fields.

Example   This example selects the active pivot table, including page fields.

```
ActiveCell.PivotTable.TableRange2.Select
```

TabRatio Property

Applies To   Window.

Description   Returns or sets the ratio of the width of the window workbook tabs to the width of
                     the window horizontal scrollbar (as a number between zero and one; the default
                     value is 0.75). Read-write.

Syntax	*object*.**TabRatio**
Elements	*object* Required. The Window object.
Remarks	This property has no effect when **DisplayWorkbookTabs** is set to **False** (its value is retained, but it has no effect on the display).
See Also	**DisplayHorizontalScrollBar** Property, **DisplayWorkBookTabs** Property.
Example	This example makes the workbook tabs half the width of the horizontal scroll bar.

```
ActiveWindow.TabRatio = 0.5
```

Tan Function

Description	Returns the tangent of an angle.
Syntax	**Tan(*number*)**
Elements	The ***number*** named argument can be any valid numeric expression that expresses an angle in radians.
Remarks	**Tan** takes an angle and returns the ratio of two sides of a right triangle. The ratio is the length of the side opposite an angle divided by the length of the side adjacent to the angle.
	To convert degrees to radians, multiply degrees by pi/180. To convert radians to degrees, multiply radians by 180/pi.
See Also	**Atn** Function, **Cos** Function, **Sin** Function.
Example	This example uses the **Tan** function to return the tangent of an angle.

```
MyAngle = 1.3                        ' Define angle in radians.
MyCotangent = 1 / Tan(MyAngle)       ' Calculate cotangent.
```

Text Property

Applies To	AxisTitle, Button, Buttons, Characters, ChartTitle, CheckBox, CheckBoxes, DataLabel, DataLabels, DialogFrame, DrawingObjects, DropDown, DropDowns, EditBox, EditBoxes, GroupBox, GroupBoxes, Label, Labels, OptionButton, OptionButtons, Range, TextBox, TextBoxes.
Description	Returns or sets the text for the specified object, as shown in the following table. Read-write, except for the Range object, where this property is read-only.

Object	Text
AxisTitle, ChartTitle	The title text.
Button	The button text.
Characters	The text of this range of characters.
Controls	The control text (check box, dialog frame, drop down, edit box, group box, label, and option button).
DataLabel	The data label text.
Range	The actual text appearing in a cell, as a string. For example, if a cell is formatted to show dollar signs, returning the text of a cell will show the dollar sign. This can be used to create readable text representations of the values on a worksheet. Read-only.
TextBox	The text in the text box.

For help about using the **Text** worksheet function in Visual Basic, see Using Worksheet Functions in Visual Basic.

Syntax   *object*.**Text**

Elements   *object*
    Required. The object to which this property applies.

Example   This example changes the first three characters in the text box.

```
ActiveSheet.TextBoxes(1).Characters(1, 3).Text = "New"
```

TextBox Object

Description   A text box graphic object drawn on a chart or worksheet.

TextBoxes Method

Applies To   Chart, DialogSheet, Worksheet.

Description   Returns a single text box (a TextBox object, Syntax 1) or a collection of text boxes (a TextBoxes object, Syntax 2). Read-only.

Syntax 1	*object*.**TextBoxes**(*index*)
Syntax 2	*object*.**TextBoxes**
Elements	The **TextBoxes** method has the following object qualifier and named arguments:

object
> Required. The object containing the text boxes.

index
> Required for Syntax 1. The name or number of the text box.

Example	This example sets the caption in text box one.

```
ActiveSheet.TextBoxes(1).Caption = "Text Box One"
```

TextBoxes Object

Description	A collection of TextBox objects.

TextToColumns Method

Applies To	Range.
Description	Parses a column of cells containing text into several columns
Syntax	*object*.**TextToColumns**(*destination, dataType, textQualifier, consecutiveDelimiter, tab, semicolon, comma, space, other, otherChar, fieldInfo*)
Elements	The **TextToColumns** method has the following object qualifier and named arguments:

object
> Required. The Range object.

destination
> Optional. A range that specifies where Microsoft Excel will place the results. If the range is larger than a single cell, the top leftmost cell is used.

dataType
> Optional. Specifies the format of the text to split into columns. Can be either **xlDelimited** or **xlFixedWidth**. The default is **xlDelimited**.

textQualifier
> Optional. Specifies the text qualifier. Can be one of **xlDoubleQuote**, **xlSingleQuote**, or **xlNone**. The default is **xlDoubleQuote**.

consecutiveDelimiter
> Optional. **True** if consecutive delimiters should be considered as one delimiter. The default is **False**.

tab
> Optional. **True** if *dataType* is **xlDelimited** and the tab character is a delimiter. The default is **False**.

semicolon
> Optional. **True** if *dataType* is **xlDelimited** and the semicolon character is a delimiter. The default is **False**.

comma
> Optional. **True** if *dataType* is **xlDelimited** and the comma character is a delimiter. The default is **False**.

space
> Optional. **True** if *dataType* is **xlDelimited** and the space character is a delimiter. The default is **False**.

other
> Optional. **True** if *dataType* is **xlDelimited** and the character specified by the *otherChar* argument is a delimiter. The default is **False**.

otherChar
> Optional (required if *other* is **True**). Specifies the delimiter character when *other* is True. If more than one character is specified, only the first character of the string is used, remaining characters are ignored.

fieldInfo
> Optional. An array containing parse information for the individual columns of data. The interpretation depends on the value of *dataType*.
>
> When the data is delimited, this argument is an array of two-element arrays, with each two-element array specifying the conversion options for a particular column. The first element is the column number (one based), and the second element is one of the following numbers specifying how the column in parsed:
>
> 1   General
> 2   Text
> 3   MDY date
> 4   DMY date
> 5   YMD date
> 6   MYD date
> 7   DYM date

8 YDM date

9 Skip the column

The column specifiers may be in any order. If a column specifier is not present for a particular column in the input data, the column is parsed using the General setting. This example causes the third column to be skipped, the first column to be parsed as text, and the remaining columns in the source data to be parsed with the General setting:

```
Array(Array(3, 9), Array(1, 2))
```

If the source data has fixed-width columns, the first element of each two-element array specifies the starting character position in the column (as an integer; character zero is the first character). The second element of the two-element array specifies the parse option for the column as a number from one through nine, as listed above.

The following example parses two columns from a fixed-width file, with the first column starting at the beginning of the line and extending for 10 characters. The second column starts at position 15 and goes to the end of the line. To avoid including the characters between position 10 and position 15, a skipped column entry is added.

```
Array(Array(0, 1), Array(10, 9), Array(15, 1))
```

See Also   **OpenText** Method.

Example   This example parses the selection, which contains space-delimited text, into columns.

```
Selection.TextToColumns dataType:=xlDelimited, _
    consecutiveDelimiter:=True, space:=True
```

ThisWorkbook Property

Applies To   Application.

Description   Returns the Workbook where the current macro code is running. Read-only.

Syntax   **ThisWorkbook**

Note This property cannot be used with an object qualifier. Do not type anything to the left of **ThisWorkbook.**

Remarks   This property can be used only from inside Microsoft Excel. You cannot use this property to access a workbook from another application.

When you want to refer to anything located in the same workbook as your macro, it is a good idea to use **ThisWorkbook** instead of the **Workbooks(*index*)** method. When you use **ThisWorkbook,** your macro will still work if you change the name of the workbook.

ThisWorkbook and **ActiveWorkbook** may or may not have the same value:

- **ThisWorkbook** returns the workbook where the macro is stored.
- **ActiveWorkbook** returns the active workbook (which may or may not be the same workbook as the one where the macro is stored).

Example   This example saves the workbook that contains the example code.

```
ThisWorkbook.Save
```

TickLabelPosition Property

Applies To   Axis.

Description   Describes the position of tick labels on the specified axis (one of **xlNone**, **xlLow**, **xlHigh**, or **xlNextToAxis**). Read-write.

Syntax   *object*.**TickLabelPosition**

Elements   *object*
                    Required. The Axis object.

See Also   **MajorTickMark** Property, **MinorTickMark** Property, **TickLabels** Property, **TickLabelSpacing** Property, **TickMarkSpacing** Property.

Example   This example sets tick labels on the category (x) axis to the high position (above the chart).

```
ActiveChart.Axes(xlCategory).TickLabelPosition = xlHigh
```

TickLabels Object

Description   The text associated with tick marks on a chart axis.

TickLabels Property

Applies To	Axis.
Description	Returns the TickLabels for the specified axis. Read-only.
Syntax	*object*.**TickLabels**
Elements	*object* Required. The Axis object.
See Also	**MajorTickMark** Property, **MinorTickMark** Property, **TickLabelSpacing** Property, **TickMarkSpacing** Property, **TickPosition** Property.
Example	This example sets the color of the tick labels on the value axis.

```
ActiveChart.Axes(xlValue).TickLabels.Font.Color = RGB(0, 255, 0)
```

TickLabelSpacing Property

Applies To	Axis.
Description	Returns or sets the number of categories or series between tick labels. Applies only to category and series axes. Read-write.
Syntax	*object*.**TickLabelSpacing**
Elements	*object* Required. The Axis object.
Remarks	This property applies to the category and series axes only. Label spacing on the value axis is always calculated by Microsoft Excel.
See Also	**MajorTickMark** Property, **MinorTickMark** Property, **TickLabels** Property, **TickMarkSpacing** Property, **TickPosition** Property.
Example	This example sets the number of categories between tick labels on the category (x) axis.

```
ActiveChart.Axes(xlCategory).TickLabelSpacing = 10
```

TickMarkSpacing Property

Applies To	Axis.

Description	Returns or sets the number of categories or series between tick marks. Applies only to category and series axes. Read-write.
Syntax	*object*.**TickMarkSpacing**
Elements	*object* Required. The Axis object.
Remarks	This property applies to the category and series axes only. Use the **MajorUnit** and **MinorUnit** properties to set tick mark spacing on the value axis.
See Also	**MajorTickMark** Property, **MinorTickMark** Property, **TickLabels** Property, **TickLabelSpacing** Property, **TickPosition** Property.
Example	This example sets the sets the number of categories between tick marks on the category (x) axis.

```
ActiveChart.Axes(xlCategory).TickMarkSpacing = 10
```

Time Function

Description	Returns the current system time.
Syntax	**Time**
Remarks	To set the system time, use the **Time** statement.
See Also	**Date** Function, **Date** Statement, **Time** Statement, **Timer** Function.
Example	This example uses the **Time** function to return the current system time.

```
MyTime = Time    ' Return current system time.
```

Time Statement

Description	Sets the system time.
Syntax	**Time** = *time*
Elements	The *time* argument is limited to expressions that can represent a time. If *time* contains no valid data, **Null** is returned.

Remarks   If *time* is a string, **Time** attempts to convert it to a time using the time separators you specified for your system. If it can't be converted to a valid time, an error occurs.

Note If you use the **Time** statement to set the time on computers using versions of MS-DOS earlier than version 3.3, the change remains in effect only until you change it again or turn off your computer. Many computers have a battery-powered CMOS RAM that retains date and time information when the computer is turned off. However, to permanently change the time on computers running earlier versions of MS-DOS, you may have to use your Setup disk or perform some equivalent action. Refer to the documentation for your particular system.

See Also   **Date** Function, **Date** Statement, **Time** Function.

Example   This example uses the **Time** statement to set the computer system time to a user-defined time.

```
MyTime = #4:35:17 PM#        ' Assign a time.
Time = MyTime                ' Set system time to MyTime.
```

Timer Function

Description   Returns the number of seconds elapsed since midnight.

Syntax   **Timer**

Remarks   The return value of the **Timer** function is automatically used with the **Randomize** statement to generate a seed for the **Rnd** (random-number) function.

See Also   **Randomize** Statement, **Rnd** Function, **Time** Function.

Example   This example uses the **Timer** function to record the number of seconds taken to print output to the Debug window.

```
Start = Timer                    ' Set start time.
For I = 1 to 50                  ' Loop 50 times.
    Debug.Print I                ' Print to Debug window.
Next I
Finish = Timer                   ' Set end time.
TotalTime = Finish - Start       ' Calculate total time.
```

TimeSerial Function

Description   Returns a time containing the time for a specific hour, minute, and second.

Syntax   **TimeSerial(*hour,minute,second*)**

Elements   The **TimeSerial** function syntax has these named-argument parts:

Part	Description
hour	Number between 0 (12:00 A.M.) and 23 (11:00 P.M.), inclusive, or a numeric expression.
minute	Number between 0 and 59, inclusive, or a numeric expression.
second	Number between 0 and 59, inclusive, or a numeric expression.

Remarks   To specify a time, such as 11:59:59, the range of numbers for each **TimeSerial** argument should be in the normally accepted range for the unit; that is, 0-23 for hours and 0-59 for minutes and seconds. However, you can also specify relative times for each argument using any numeric expression that represents some number of hours, minutes, or seconds before or after a certain time. The following example uses expressions instead of absolute time numbers. The **TimeSerial** function returns a time for 15 minutes before (0 - 15) six hours before noon (12 - 6), or 5:45:00 A.M.

```
TimeSerial(12 - 6, 0 - 15, 0)
```

If the time specified by the three arguments, either directly or by expression, falls outside the acceptable range of times, an error occurs.

See Also   **DateSerial** Function, **DateValue** Function, **Hour** Function, **Minute** Function, **Now** Function, **Second** Function, **TimeValue** Function.

Example   This example uses the **TimeSerial** function to return a time for the specified hour, minute and second.

```
' MyTime contains the time for 4:35:17 PM
MyTime = TimeSerial(16, 35, 17)      ' Return time.
```

TimeValue Function

Description   Returns a time.

Syntax	**TimeValue**(*time*)
Elements	The *time* named argument is normally a string expression representing a time from 0:00:00 (12:00:00 A.M.) to 23:59:59 (11:59:59 P.M.), inclusive. However, *time* can also be any expression that represents a time in that range. If *time* contains no valid data, **Null** is returned.
Remarks	You can enter valid times using a 12- or 24-hour clock. For example, `"2:24PM"` and `"14:24"` are both valid time arguments.
	If the *time* argument contains date information, **TimeValue** doesn't return it. However, if *time* includes invalid date information, an error occurs.
See Also	**DateSerial** Function, **DateValue** Function, **Hour** Function, **Minute** Function, **Now** Function, **Second** Function, **TimeSerial** Function.
Example	This example uses the **TimeValue** function to convert a string to a time. In general, it is bad programming practice to hard code dates/ times as strings as shown in this example. Use date literals instead.

```
MyTime = TimeValue("4:35:17 PM")          ' Return time.
```

Title Property

Applies To	AddIn, Workbook.
Description	Returns or sets the long, descriptive title for the object, as a string. Read-only for AddIn, read-write for Workbook.
Syntax	*object*.**Title**
Elements	*object* Required. The AddIn or Workbook object.
See Also	**Author** Property, **AxisTitle** Property, **ChartTitle** Property, **Comments** Property, **Keywords** Property.
Example	This example checks to see that every open workbook has a title.

```
For Each wk in Workbooks
    If wk.Title = "" Then
        MsgBox "Workbook " & wk.Name & " needs a better " & _
            "title"
    End If
Next
```

Toolbar Object

Description   A toolbar, either built-in or custom.

ToolbarButton Object

Description   A button on a toolbar. Do not confuse the ToolbarButton object with the Button object, which is a custom button graphic object on a chart or worksheet.

ToolbarButtons Method

Applies To   Toolbar.

Description   Returns a single toolbar button (a ToolbarButton object, Syntax 1) or a collection of toolbar buttons (a ToolbarButtons object, Syntax 2) on the specified toolbar.

Syntax 1   *object*.**ToolbarButtons(*index*)**

Syntax 2   *object*.**ToolbarButtons**

Elements   The **ToolbarButtons** method has the following object qualifier and named arguments:

object
     Required. The Toolbar object.

index
     Required for Syntax 1. The name or number of the button.

Example   This example deletes the New Workbook button from toolbar one.

```
Application.Toolbars(1).ToolbarButtons(1).Delete
```

ToolbarButtons Object

Description   A collection of ToolbarButton objects.

Toolbars Method

Applies To   Application.

Description   Returns a single toolbar (a Toolbar object, Syntax 1) or a collection of toolbars (a Toolbars object, Syntax 2) in the current instance of Microsoft Excel. Read-only.

Syntax 1   *object*.**Toolbars**(*index*)

Syntax 2   *object*.**Toolbars**

Elements   The **Toolbars** method has the following object qualifier and named arguments:

object
    Optional. The Application containing the toolbars.

index
    Required for Syntax 1. The name or number of the toolbar.

Example   This example sets the variable `numberOfToolbars` to the number of toolbars in the current instance of Microsoft Excel.

```
numberOfToolbars = Application.Toolbars.Count
```

Toolbars Object

Description   A collection of Toolbar objects.

Top Property

Applies To   Application, Arc, Arcs, AxisTitle, Button, Buttons, ChartArea, ChartObject, ChartObjects, ChartTitle, CheckBox, CheckBoxes, DataLabel, DataLabels, DialogFrame, Drawing, DrawingObjects, Drawings, DropDown, DropDowns, EditBox, EditBoxes, GroupBox, GroupBoxes, GroupObject, GroupObjects, Label, Labels, Legend, Line, Lines, ListBox, ListBoxes, OLEObject, OLEObjects, OptionButton, OptionButtons, Oval, Ovals, Picture, Pictures, PlotArea, Range, Rectangle, Rectangles, ScrollBar, ScrollBars, Spinner, Spinners, TextBox, TextBoxes, Toolbar, Window.

Description   Returns or sets the position of the specified object, in points (1/72 inch). Read-write, except for the Range object.

Syntax	*object*.**Top**
Elements	*object* Required. The object to which this property applies.
Remarks	The **Top** property has several different meanings, depending on the object to which it is applied.

Object	Meaning
Application	The distance from the top edge of the physical screen to the top edge of the main Microsoft Excel window, in points. With Microsoft Windows, if the application window is minimized, this property controls the position of the icon (anywhere on the screen). On the Apple Macintosh the value is always zero; setting the value to something else will have no effect.
Button	The top position of the object, in points, measured from the top of row 1.
Range	The distance from the top edge of row one to the top edge of the range, in points. If the range is discontinuous, the first area is used. If the range is more than one row high, the top (lowest numbered) row in the range is used. Read-only.
Toolbar	If the toolbar is docked (the **Position** property of the Toolbar object is not **xlFloat**), the number of points from the top edge of the toolbar to the top edge of the toolbar docking area.If the toolbar is floating, the number of points from the top edge of the toolbar to the top edge of the Microsoft Excel workspace.
Window	The top position of the window, in points, measured from the top edge of the usable area (below the menus, top-docked toolbars, and/or the formula bar). You cannot set this property for a maximized window. Use the **WindowState** property to return or set the state of the window.
Arc, AxisTitle, ChartArea, ChartTitle, CheckBox, DataLabel, DialogFrame, Drawing, DrawingObjects, DropDown, EditBox, GroupBox, GroupObject, Label, Legend, Line, ListBox, OLEObject, OptionButton, Oval, Picture, PlotArea, Rectangle, ScrollBar, Spinner, TextBox, Title	The top position of the object, in points, measured from the top of row 1 (on a worksheet) or the top of the chart area (on a chart).

See Also	**Left** Property, **Height** Property, **Width** Property.
Example	This example expands the active window to the maximum size available (the window is not maximized).

```
With ActiveWindow
    .WindowState = xlNormal
    .Top = 1
    .Left = 1
    .Height = Application.UsableHeight
    .Width = Application.UsableWidth
End With
```

TopLeftCell Property

Applies To	Arc, Button, ChartObject, CheckBox, Drawing, DropDown, EditBox, GroupBox, GroupObject, Label, Line, ListBox, OLEObject, OptionButton, Oval, Picture, Rectangle, ScrollBar, Spinner, TextBox.
Description	Returns the cell that lies under the top left of this object. For drawing objects, this property applies only when the drawing object is on a worksheet. Read only.
Syntax	*object*.**TopLeftCell**
Elements	*object* Required. The object to which this property applies.
See Also	**BottomRightCell** Property.
Example	This example displays the reference for the cell under the top left corner of line one.

```
MsgBox "The top left corner is " & _
    Worksheets(1).Lines(1).TopLeftCell.Address
```

TopMargin Property

Applies To	PageSetup.
Description	Returns or sets the size of the top margin, in points (1/72 inch). Read-write.
Syntax	*object*.**TopMargin**
Elements	*object* Required. The PageSetup object (**ActiveSheet.PageSetup**, for example).

Remarks   Margins are set or returned in points. Use the **Application.InchesToPoints** or **Application.CentimetersToPoints** function to convert.

SeeAlso   **BottomMargin** Property, **LeftMargin** Property, **RightMargin** Property.

Examples   These examples set the top margin to 0.5 inch (36 points).

```
ActiveSheet.PageSetup.TopMargin = Application.InchesToPoints(0.5)
ActiveSheet.PageSetup.TopMargin = 36
```

This example displays the current top margin setting.

```
marginInches = ActiveSheet.PageSetup.TopMargin / _
    Application.InchesToPoints(1)
MsgBox "The current top margin is " & marginInches & " inches"
```

ToRecipients Property

Applies To   Mailer.

Description   Returns or sets the direct recipients of the mailer. Read-write.

Syntax   *object*.**ToRecipients**

Elements   *object*
    Required. The Mailer object.

Remarks   This property is an array of strings specifying the address, in one of the following formats:

- A record in the Preferred Personal Catalog. These names are one level deep ("Fred" or "June").

- A full path specifying either a record in a personal catalog ("HD:Excel Folder:My Catalog:Barney") or a plain record ("HD:Folder:Martin").

- A relative path from the current working directory specifying either a personal catalog record ("My Catalog:Barney") or a plain record ("Martin").

- A path in a PowerShare catalog tree of the form "CATALOG_NAME:<node>:RECORD_NAME" where <node> is a path to a PowerShare catalog. An example of a complete path is "AppleTalk:North Building Zone:George's Mac".

See Also   **BCCRecipient** Property, **CCRecipients** Property, **Enclosures** Property, **Mailer** Property, **Received** Property, **SendDateTime** Property, **Sender** Property, **SendMailer** Method, **SendMailer** Property, **Subject** Property.

Example   This example sets up the Mailer object for workbook one, and then sends the workbook.

```
With Workbooks(1)
    .HasMailer = True
    With .Mailer
        .Subject = "Here is the workbook"
        .ToRecipients = Array("Jean")
        .CCRecipients = Array("Adam", "Bernard")
        .BCCRecipients = Array("Chris")
        .Enclosures = Array("TestFile")
    End With
    .SendMailer
End With
```

TotalLevels Property

Applies To   PivotField.

Description   Returns the total number of fields in the current field grouping. If the field is not grouped, **TotalLevels** returns the value 1. Read-only.

Syntax   *object*.**TotalLevels**

Elements   *object*
        Required. The PivotField object.

Remarks   All fields in a set of grouped fields have the same **TotalLevels** value.

Example   This example displays the total number of fields in the current field grouping.

```
MsgBox "This group has " & _
    ActiveCell.PivotField.TotalLevels & " levels."
```

TrackStatus Property

Applies To   RoutingSlip.

Description   **True** if status tracking is enabled for the routing slip. Read-write before routing begins; read-only when routing is in progress.

Syntax   *object*.**TrackStatus**

Elements   *object*
        Required. The RoutingSlip object.

Example   This example sends BOOK1.XLS to three recipients with status tracking enabled.

```
Workbooks("BOOK1.XLS").HasRoutingSlip = True
With Workbooks("BOOK1.XLS").RoutingSlip
    .Delivery = xlOneAfterAnother
    .Recipients = Array("Adam Bendel", "Jean Selva", "Bernard Gabor")
    .Subject = "Here is BOOK1.XLS"
    .Message = "Here is the workbook. What do you think?"
    .ReturnWhenDone = True
    .TrackStatus = True
End With
Workbooks("BOOK1.XLS").Route
```

TransitionExpEval Property

Applies To   Worksheet.

Description   **True** if Microsoft Excel will use Lotus 1-2-3 expression evaluation rules for this worksheet. Read-write.

Syntax   *object*.**TransitionExpEval**

Elements   *object*
                      Required. The Worksheet object.

Example   This example sets Microsoft Excel to use Lotus 1-2-3 expression evaluation rules for the first worksheet.

```
Worksheets(1).TransitionExpEval = True
```

TransitionFormEntry Property

Applies To   Worksheet.

Description   **True** if Microsoft Excel will use Lotus 1-2-3 formula entry rules for this worksheet. Read-write.

Syntax   *object*.**TransitionFormEntry**

Elements   *object*
                      Required. The Worksheet object.

Remarks   This property is not available on the Apple Macintosh.

Example This example causes Microsoft Excel to use Lotus 1-2-3 formula entry rules for the first worksheet.

```
Worksheets(1).TransitionFormEntry = True
```

TransitionMenuKey Property

Applies To Application.

Description Returns or sets the alternate menu or help key, which is usually "/". Read-write.

Syntax *object*.**TransitionMenuKey**

Elements *object*
    Required. The Application object.

Example This example resets the alternate menu key to "/" if it is currently another character.

```
currentMenuKeyChar = Application.TransitionMenuKey
If (currentMenuKeyChar <> "/") Then
    Application.TransitionMenuKey = "/"
End If
```

TransitionMenuKeyAction Property

Applies To Application.

Description Returns or sets the action taken when the alternate menu key is pressed (one of **xlExcelMenus** or **xlLotusHelp**). Read-write.

Syntax *object*.**TransitionMenuKeyAction**

Elements *object*
    Required. The Application object.

Example This example sets the alternate menu key to run Lotus 1-2-3 help when it is pressed.

```
Application.TransitionMenuKeyAction = xlLotusHelp
```

TransitionNavigKeys Property

Applies To Application.

Description	**True** if alternate navigation keys are active. Read-write.
Syntax	*object*.**TransitionNavigKeys**
Elements	*object* Required. The Application object.
See Also	**TransitionMenuKey** Property,
Example	This example displays the current state of the Transition Navigation Keys option.

```
If  Application.TransitionNavigKeys Then
    keyState = "On"
Else
    keyState = "Off"
End If
MsgBox "The Transition Navigation Keys option is " & keyState
```

Trappable Errors

Trappable errors can occur while an application is running. Some of these can also occur during development or compile time. You can test and respond to trappable errors using the **On Error** statement and the **Err** function.

You can also work with Microsoft Excel cell error values in Visual Basic. For more information, see Cell Error Values.

Code	Message
3	Return without GoSub
5	Invalid procedure call
6	Overflow
7	Out of memory
9	Subscript out of range
10	Duplicate definition
11	Division by zero
13	Type mismatch
14	Out of string space
16	String formula too complex
17	Can't perform requested operation
18	User interrupt occurred
20	Resume without error

Code	Message
28	OUT OF STACK SPACE
35	Sub or Function not defined
48	Error in loading DLL
49	Bad DLL calling convention
51	Internal error
52	Bad file name or number
53	File not found
54	Bad file mode
55	File already open
57	Device I/O error
58	File already exists
59	Bad record length
61	Disk full
62	Input past end of file
63	Bad record number
67	Too many files
68	Device unavailable
70	Permission denied
71	Disk not ready
74	Can't rename with different drive
75	Path/File access error
76	Path not found
91	Object variable not set
92	For loop not initialized
93	Invalid pattern string
94	Invalid use of Null
95	User-defined error
323	Can't load module; invalid format
423	Property or method not found
424	Object required
430	Class does not support OLE Automation
438	Object doesn't support this property or method
440	OLE Automation error

Code	Message
445	Object doesn't support this action
446	Object doesn't support named arguments
447	Object doesn't support current locale setting
448	Named argument not found
449	Argument not optional
450	Wrong number of arguments
451	Object not a collection
452	Invalid ordinal
453	Specified DLL function not found
454	Code resource not found
455	Code resource lock error
1000	*Classname* does not have *propertyname* property
1001	*Classname* does not have *methodname* method
1002	Missing required argument *argumentname*
1003	Invalid number of arguments
1004	*Methodname* method of *classname* class failed
1005	Unable to set the *propertyname* property of the *classname* class
1006	Unable to get the *propertyname* property of the *classname* class

See Also   **CVErr** Function, **Err** Function, **Err** Statement, **Error** Statement, **Error** Function, **Resume** Statement.

Trendline Object

Description   A trend line on a chart.

Trendlines Method

Applies To	Series.
Description	Returns a single trendline (a Trendline object, Syntax 1) or a collection of all the trendlines (a Trendlines object, Syntax 2) for the series.
Syntax 1	*object*.**Trendlines**(*index*)
Syntax 2	*object*.**Trendlines**
Elements	*object* Required. The Series object. *index* Required for Syntax 1. The name or number of the trendline.
Example	This example sets the type of the first trendline.

```
ActiveChart.SeriesCollection(1).Trendlines(1).Type = xlLinear
```

Trendlines Object

Description	A collection of Trendline objects.

Type Property

Applies To	Axis, Chart, ChartGroup, DataLabel, DataLabels, Series, Trendline, Window, Worksheet.
Description	Returns the object type, as shown in the following table. Read-only.

Object	Type
Axis	Axis type. Can be one of **xlCategory**, **xlValue**, or **xlSeries** (only 3-D charts use **xlSeries**).
Chart	Chart type. Can be one of **xl3DArea**, **xl3DBar**, **xl3DColumn**, **xl3DLine**, **xl3DPie**, **xl3DSurface**, **xlArea**, **xlBar**, **xlColumn**, **xlDoughnut**, **xlLine**, **xlPie**, **xlRadar**, or **xlXYScatter**. If the chart has chart groups of more than one type, this property returns **Null**, but setting the property sets all the chart groups.

Object	Type
ChartGroup	ChartGroup type. Can be one of the values shown for the Chart object. If you set the chart group type to a type that is not on the chart, Microsoft Excel creates a new chart group.
DataLabel	DataLabel type (one of **xlNone**, **xlShowValue**, **xlShowLabel**, **xlShowPercent**, or **xlShowLabelAndPercent**)
Series	Series type. Can be one of the values shown for the Chart object. If you set the series type to a type that is not on the chart, Microsoft Excel creates a new chart group.
Trendline	Trendline type. Can be one of **xlLinear**, **xlLogarithmic**, **xlExponential**, **xlPolynomial**, **xlMovingAvg**, or **xlPower**.
Window	Window type. Can be one of **xlChartInPlace**, **xlChartAsWindow**, **xlWorkbook**, **xlInfo**, or **xlClipboard**.
Worksheet	Worksheet type. Can be one of **xlWorksheet**, **xlExcel4MacroSheet**, or **xlExcel4IntlMacroSheet**.

Syntax   *object*.**Type**

Elements   *object*
    Required. Return or set the type of this object.

See Also   **SubType** Property.

Example   This example makes the first group an area group.

```
Charts(1).ChartGroups(1).Type = xlArea
```

Type Statement

Description   Used at module level to define a user-defined data type containing one or more elements.

Syntax

[**Private** | **Public**] **Type** *varname*
  elementname [([*subscripts*])] **As** *type*
  [*elementname* [([*subscripts*])] **As** *type*]
  . . .
End Type

Elements

The **Type** statement syntax has these parts:

Part	Description
Public	Used to declare user-defined types that are available to all procedures in all modules in all projects.
Private	Used to declare user-defined types that are available only within the module where the declaration is made.
varname	Name of the user-defined type; follows standard variable naming conventions.
elementname	Name of an element of the user-defined type. Element names also follow standard variable naming conventions, except that reserved words can be used.
subscripts	Dimensions of an array element. Use only parentheses when declaring an array whose size can change.
type	Data type of the element; may be **Boolean**, **Integer**, **Long**, **Currency**, **Single**, **Double**, **Date**, **String**, **String** * *length* (for fixed-length strings), **Object**, **Variant**, another user-defined type, or an object type.

Remarks

The **Type** statement can be used only at module level. Once you have declared a user-defined type using the **Type** statement, you can declare a variable of that type anywhere within the scope of the declaration. Use **Dim**, **Private**, **Public**, **ReDim**, or **Static** to declare a variable of a user-defined type.

Line numbers and line labels aren't allowed in **Type...End Type** blocks.

User-defined types are often used with data records, which frequently consist of a number of related elements of different data types.

See Also

Date Type Summary, **Dim** Statement, **Private** Statement, **Public** Statement, **ReDim** Statement, **Static** Statement.

Example   The following example shows the use of fixed-size arrays in a user-defined type:

```
Type StateData
    CityCode (1 To 100) As Integer ' Declare a static array.
    County As String * 30
End Type

Dim Washington(1 To 100) As StateData
```

In the preceding example, StateData includes the CityCode static array, and the record Washington has the same structure as StateData.

When you declare a fixed-size array within a user-defined type, its dimensions must be declared with numeric literals or constants rather than variables.

The setting of the **Option Base** statement determines the lower bound for arrays within user-defined types.

TypeName Function

Description   Returns a string that provides information about a variable.

Syntax   **TypeName(*varname*)**

Elements   The *varname* named argument can be any variable except a variable of a user-defined type.

Remarks   The string returned by **TypeName** can be any one of the following:

String Returned	Variable contains
objecttype	An OLE Automation object whose type is *objecttype*.
Integer	An integer.
Long	A long integer.
Single	A single-precision floating point number.
Double	A double-precision floating point number.
Currency	A currency value.
Date	A date.
String	A string.
Boolean	A Boolean value.
Error	An error value.
Empty	Uninitialized.

String Returned	Variable contains
Null	No valid data.
Object	An object that doesn't support OLE Automation.
Unknown	An OLE Automation object whose type is unknown.
Nothing	An object variable that doesn't refer to an object.

If *varname* is an array, the returned string can be any one of the possible returned strings (or **Variant**) with empty parentheses appended. For example, if *varname* is an array of integers, **TypeName** returns "Integer()".

See Also

DataTypeSummary, **IsArray** Function, **IsDate** Function, **IsEmpty** Function, **IsError** Function, **IsMissing** Function, **IsNull** Function, **IsNumeric** Function, **IsObject** Function, **Variant** Data Type, **VarType** Function.

Example

This example uses the **TypeName** function to return information about a variable.

```
' Declare variables.
Dim StrVar As String, IntVar As Integer, CurVar As Currency
Dim ArrayVar (1 To 5) As Integer
NullVar = Null            ' Assign Null value.
MyType = TypeName(StrVar)    ' Returns "String".
MyType = TypeName(IntVar)    ' Returns "Integer".
MyType = TypeName(CurVar)    ' Returns "Currency".
MyType = TypeName(NullVar)   ' Returns "Null".
MyType = TypeName(ArrayVar)  ' Returns "Integer()".
```

UBound Function

Description

Returns the largest available subscript for the indicated dimension of an array.

Syntax

UBound(*arrayname*[,*dimension*])

Elements

The **UBound** function syntax has these parts:

Part	Description
arrayname	Name of the array variable; follows standard variable naming conventions.
dimension	Whole number indicating which dimension's upper bound is returned. Use 1 for the first dimension, 2 for the second, and so on. If *dimension* is omitted, 1 is assumed.

Remarks

The **UBound** function is used with the **LBound** function to determine the size of an array. Use the **LBound** function to find the lower limit of an array dimension.

UBound returns the values listed in the table below for an array with these dimensions:

```
Dim A(1 To 100, 0 To 3, -3 To 4)
```

Statement	Return Value
UBound(A, 1)	100
UBound(A, 2)	3
UBound(A, 3)	4

See Also

Dim Statement, **Public** Statement, **LBound** Function, **Option Base** Statement, **ReDim** Statement, **Static** Statement.

Example

This example uses the **UBound** function to determine the largest available subscript for the indicated dimension of an array.

```
Dim MyArray(1 To 10, 5 To 15, 10 To 20)' Declare array variables.
Dim AnyArray(10)
Upper = UBound(MyArray, 1)                    ' Returns 10.
Upper = UBound(MyArray, 3)                    ' Returns 20.
Upper = UBound(AnyArray)' Returns 10.
```

UCase Function

Description

Returns a string that has been converted to uppercase.

Syntax

UCase(*string*)

Elements

The ***string*** named argument is any valid string expression. If ***string*** contains no valid data, **Null** is returned.

Remarks

Only lowercase letters are converted to uppercase; all uppercase letters and nonletter characters remain unchanged.

See Also

LCase Function.

Example

This example uses the **UCase** function to return an uppercase version of a string.

```
LowerCase = "Hello World 1234"   ' String to convert.
UpperCase = UCase(LowerCase) ' Returns "HELLO WORLD 1234".
```

Underline Property

Applies To

Font.

Description	Returns or sets the type of underline applied to the font, as shown in the following table. Read-write.

Value	Meaning
xlNone	No underline.
xlSingle	Single underline.
xlDouble	Double underline.
xlSingleAccounting	Single accounting underline.
xlDoubleAccounting	Double accounting underline.

Syntax	*object*.**Underline**
Elements	*object* Required. The Font object (**ActiveCell.Font**, for example).
Example	This example sets the font in the active cell to single underline.

```
ActiveCell.Font.Underline = xlSingle
```

Undo Method

Applies To	Application.
Description	Cancels the last user-interface action.
Syntax	*object*.**Undo**
Elements	*object* Required. The Application object.
Remarks	This method can only be used to undo the last action taken by the user before running the macro, and it must be the first line in the macro. It cannot be used to undo Visual Basic commands.
Example	This example cancels the last user-interface action. It must be the first line in the macro.

```
Application.Undo
```

Ungroup Method

Applies To	DrawingObjects, GroupObject, GroupObjects, Range.

Description	Range object: Promotes a range in an outline level (in other words, decreases its outline level). The specified range must be a row or column, or a range of rows or columns. If the range is in a pivot table, ungroups the items contained in the range.
	GroupObject: Ungroups a group of drawing objects. Returns a DrawingObjects collection containing the objects in the group.
Syntax	*object*.**Ungroup**
Elements	*object*
	Required. The object to which this method applies.
Remarks	If the active cell is in a field header of a parent field, all the groups in that field are ungrouped and the field is removed from the pivot table. When the last group in a parent field is ungrouped, the entire field is removed from the pivot table.
See Also	**Group** Method, **OutlineLevel** Property.
Example	This example ungroups a group of drawing objects.

```
myGroup.Ungroup
```

Union Method

Applies To	Application.
Description	Returns the union of two or more ranges.
Syntax	*object*.**Union(*arg1, arg2, ...*)**
Elements	The **Union** method has the following object qualifier and named arguments:
	object
	Optional. The Application object.
	arg1, arg2, ...
	Required. Return the union of these ranges. At least two Range objects must be specified.
See Also	**Intersect** Method.
Example	This example sets the newConsolidatedRange object variable to the union of the current selection and the Totals range on SUMMARY.XLS.

```
Set newConsolidatedRange = _
    Application.Union(Selection, Range("SUMMARY.XLS!Totals"))
```

Unprotect Method

Applies To Chart, DialogSheet, Module, Workbook, Worksheet.

Description Removes protection from a sheet or workbook. This method has no effect if the sheet or workbook is not protected.

Syntax *object*.**Unprotect**(*password*)

Elements The **Unprotect** method has the following object qualifier and named arguments:

object
Required. The object to which this method applies.

password
Optional. A string giving the case-sensitive password to use to unprotect the sheet or workbook. If the sheet or workbook is not protected with a password, this argument is ignored. If this argument is omitted and the sheet or workbook has a password, you will be prompted for the password.

Remarks If you forget the password, you cannot unprotect the sheet or workbook. It's a good idea to keep a list of your passwords and their corresponding document names in a safe place.

See Also **Locked** Property, **Protect** Method, **ProtectContents** Property, **ProtectDrawingObjects** Property.

Example This example removes protection from the active workbook.

```
ActiveWorkbook.Unprotect
```

UpBars Object

Description An up bar on a chart.

UpBars Property

Applies To ChartGroup.

Description Returns the UpBars on a line chart. Applies only to line charts. Read-only.

Syntax	*object*.**UpBars**
Elements	*object* Required. The ChartGroup object.
See Also	**HasUpDownBars** Property, **DownBars** Property.
Example	This example turns on up and down bars for the first chart group, and then sets their colors.

```
With ActiveChart.ChartGroups(1)
    .HasUpDownBars = True
    .DownBars.Interior.Color = RGB(0, 255, 0)
    .UpBars.Interior.Color = RGB(255, 0, 0)
End With
```

Update Method

Applies To	OLEObject.
Description	Updates the link.
Syntax	*object*.**Update**
Elements	*object* Required. The OLEObject.
Example	This example updates every embedded Microsoft Word object on the active sheet.

```
For Each wordObj in ActiveSheet.OLEObjects
    If wordObj.OLEClass Like "*Word*" Then
        wordObj.Update
    End If
Next
```

UpdateFromFile Method

Applies To	Workbook.
Description	Updates a read-only workbook from the saved disk file version of the workbook if the disk version is more recent than the current copy of the workbook in memory. If the disk copy has not changed since the workbook was loaded, the in-memory copy of the workbook is not reloaded.

Syntax	*object*.**UpdateFromFile**
Elements	*object* Required. The Workbook object.
Remarks	This method is useful when a workbook is opened as read-only by user A and read-write by user B. If user B saves a newer version of the workbook to disk while user A still has the workbook open, user A cannot get the updated copy without closing and reopening the workbook and losing view settings. The **UpdateFromFile** method updates the in-memory copy of the workbook from the disk file.
See Also	**ChangeFileAccess** Method.
Example	This example updates the active workbook.

```
ActiveWorkbook.UpdateFromFile
```

UpdateLink Method

Applies To	Workbook.
Description	Updates a Microsoft Excel, DDE, or OLE link (or links).
Syntax	*object*.**UpdateLink**(*name, type*)
Elements	The **UpdateLink** method has the following object qualifier and named arguments:
	object Required. The Workbook object.
	name Required. Specifies the name of the Microsoft Excel or DDE/OLE link to update, as returned from the **LinkSources** method..
	type Optional. Specifies the link type. Can be either **xlExcelLinks** or **xlOLELinks** (also used for DDE links). **xlExcelLinks** if omitted.
Example	This example updates all links in the active workbook.

```
ActiveWorkbook.UpdateLink name:=ActiveWorkbook.LinkSources
```

UpdateRemoteReferences Property

Applies To	Workbook.
Description	**True** if remote references will be updated for the workbook. Read-write.

Syntax	*object*.**UpdateRemoteReferences**
Elements	*object*
	Required. The Workbook object.
Example	This example causes remote references to be updated on the active workbook.

```
ActiveWorkbook.UpdateRemoteReferences = True
```

UsableHeight Property

Applies To	Application, Window.
Description	Returns the height of the space that can be used by a window in the application window area (the window is not maximized). The height is returned in points (1/72 inch). Read-only.
Syntax	*object*.**UsableHeight**
Elements	*object*
	Required. The Application or Window object.
Remarks	Adding a toolbar reduces the usable height.
See Also	**UsableWidth** Property,
Example	This example expands the active window to the maximum size available.

```
With ActiveWindow
    .WindowState = xlNormal
    .Top = 1
    .Left = 1
    .Height = Application.UsableHeight
    .Width = Application.UsableWidth
End With
```

UsableWidth Property

Applies To	Application, Window.
Description	Returns the width of the space that can be used by a window in the application window area (the window is not maximized). The width is returned in points (1/72 inch). Read-only.

Syntax	*object*.**UsableWidth**
Elements	*object* Required. The Application or Window object.
See Also	**UsableHeight** Property.
Example	This example expands the active window to the maximum size available.

```
With ActiveWindow
    .WindowState = xlNormal
    .Top = 1
    .Left = 1
    .Height = Application.UsableHeight
    .Width = Application.UsableWidth
End With
```

UsedRange Property

Applies To	Worksheet.
Description	Returns the Range of the worksheet that is used. Read-only.
Syntax	*object*.**UsedRange**
Elements	*object* Required. The Worksheet object.
Example	This example selects the used range on the first worksheet.

```
Worksheets(1).UsedRange.Select
```

User-Defined Data Type

Any data type you define using the **Type** statement. User-defined data types can contain one or more elements of any data type, array, or a previously defined user-defined type. For example:

```
Type MyType
    MyName As String          ' String variable stores a name.
    MyBirthDate As Date       ' Date variable stores a birthdate.
    MySex as Integer          ' Integer variable stores sex (0 for
End Type                      ' female, 1 for male.
```

See Also	Data Type Summary, **Type** Statement.

UserName Property

Applies To	Application.
Description	Returns or sets the name of the current user (as a string). Read-write.
Syntax	*object*.**UserName**
Elements	*object*
	Required. The Application object.
Example	This example selects cell D3 if the current user's name is John Browne.

```
If Application.UserName = "John Browne" Then
    ActiveSheet.Cells(3, 4).Select
End If
```

UseStandardHeight Property

Applies To	Range.
Description	**True** if the row height of the Range object equals the standard height of the sheet. Read-write.
Syntax	*object*.**UseStandardHeight**
Elements	*object*
	Required. The Range object.
See Also	**RowHeight** Property, **StandardHeight** Property, **UseStandardWidth** Property.
Example	This example sets the height of row 1 of the active sheet to the standard height.

```
Rows("1").UseStandardHeight = True
```

UseStandardWidth Property

Applies To	Range.
Description	**True** if the column width of the Range object equals the standard width of the sheet. Read-write.
Syntax	*object*.**UseStandardWidth**
Elements	*object*
	Required. The Range object.

See Also **ColumnWidth** Property, **StandardWidth** Property, **UseStandardHeight**
Property.

Example   This example sets the width of column A of the active sheet to the standard width.

```
Columns("A").UseStandardWidth = True
```

Val Function

Description   Returns the numbers contained in a string.

Syntax   **Val**(*string*)

Elements   The *string* named argument is any valid string expression.

Remarks   The **Val** function stops reading the string at the first character it can't recognize as
part of a number. Symbols and characters that are often considered parts of
numeric values, such as dollar signs and commas, are not recognized. However, the
function recognizes radix prefixes &O (for octal) and &H (for hexadecimal).
Blanks, tabs, and linefeeds are stripped from the argument.

The following returns the value 1615198:

```
Val("    1615 198th Street N.E.")
```

In the code below, **Val** returns the decimal value -1 for the hexadecimal value
shown:

```
Val("&HFFFF")
```

Note The **Val** function recognizes only the period (**.**) as a valid decimal separator.
When a possibility exists that different decimal separators may be used (for
example, in international applications), you should use **CDbl** instead to convert a
string to a number.

See Also   **CDbl** Function, **Str** Function.

Example   This example uses the **Val** function to return the numbers contained in a string.

```
MyValue = Val("2457")        ' Returns 2457.
MyValue = Val(" 2 45 7")     ' Returns 2457.
MyValue = Val("24 and 57")   ' Returns 24.
```

Value Property

Applies To   Application, Borders, CheckBox, CheckBoxes, DrawingObjects, DropDown, DropDowns, ListBox, ListBoxes, Name, OptionButton, OptionButtons, PivotField, PivotItem, PivotTable, Range, ScrollBar, ScrollBars, Spinner, Spinners, Style.

Description   The meaning of the **Value** property depends on the object to which it is applied, as shown in the following table.

Object	Value
Application	Always returns "Microsoft Excel". Read-only.
Borders	Synonym for **Borders.LineStyle**.
CheckBox	Indicates check box status (**xlOn**, **xlOff**, or **xlMixed**).
DropDown, ListBox	Indicates the selected item in the list (the value is always between one and the number of items in the list). This method cannot be used with multi-select list boxes; use the **Selected** method instead.
Name	A string containing the formula that the name is defined to refer to, in A1-style notation, in the language of the macro, beginning with an equal sign. Read-write.
OptionButton	Indicates button status (one of **xlOn**, **xlOff**, or **xlMixed**).
PivotField	The name of the field in the pivot table.
PivotItem	The name of the item in the pivot table field.
PivotTable	The name of the pivot table.
Range	The value of a cell. If the cell is empty, returns the value **Empty**. Use the **IsEmpty** function to test for this case. If the Range object contains more than one cell, returns an array of values. Use the **IsArray** function to test for this case.
ScrollBar	The position of the scroll box.
Spinner	A value between the minimum and maximum range limit.
Style	The name of the style.

Syntax   *object*.**Value**

Elements   *object*
     Required. The object to which this property applies.

See Also   **LineStyle** Property, **MultiSelect** Property, **Selected** Property.

Example

This example replaces all values smaller than 1E-6 (0.000001) with zero, in the range named Extract.

```
For Each c In Range("Extract")
    If c.Value < 1e-6 Then
        c.Formula = 0
    End If
Next
```

Values Property

Applies To

Scenario, Series.

Description

Scenario object: Returns an array containing the current values for the scenario changing cells. Read-only.

Series object: Returns or sets a collection of all the values in the series. This can be a range on a worksheet or an array of constant values (but not a combination of both). See the examples for details. Read-write.

Syntax

*object.***Values**

Elements

object
    Required. The Scenario or Series object.

Examples

This example sets the series values from a range. This example uses the **Set** statement because the right hand side of the expression is an object, not a value.

```
Set ActiveChart.SeriesCollection(1).Values = _
    Worksheets(1).Range("C5:T5")
```

To set constant values for each individual data point, you must use an array. This example does not require the **Set** statement.

```
ActiveChart.SeriesCollection(1).Values = _
    Array(1.5,1.6,1.77,1.89,2.0001)
```

Variant Data Type

The **Variant** data type is the data type that all variables become if not explicitly declared as some other type (using statements such as **Dim**, **Private**, **Public**, or **Static**). The **Variant** data type has no type-declaration character.

The **Variant** is a special data type that can contain any kind of data as well as the special values **Empty**, **Error**, and **Null**. You can determine how the data in a **Variant** is treated using the **VarType** or **TypeName** function.

Numeric data can be any integer or real number value ranging from -1.797693134862315E308 to -4.94066E-324 for negative values and from 4.94066E-324 to 1.797693134862315E308 for positive values. Generally, numeric **Variant** data is maintained in its original data type within the **Variant**. For example, if you assign an **Integer** to a **Variant**, subsequent operations treat the **Variant** as if it were an **Integer**. However, if an arithmetic operation is performed on a **Variant** containing an **Integer**, a **Long**, or a **Single**, and the result exceeds the normal range for the original data type, the result is promoted within the **Variant** to the next larger data type. An **Integer** is promoted to a **Long**, and a **Long** and a **Single** are promoted to a **Double**. An error occurs when **Variant** variables containing **Currency** and **Double** values exceed their respective ranges.

You can use the **Variant** data type in place of any data type to work with data in a more flexible way. If the contents of a **Variant** variable are digits, they may be either the string representation of the digits or their actual value, depending on the context. For example:

```
Dim MyVar As Variant
MyVar = 98052
```

In the example shown above, MyVar contains a numeric representation{bmc emdash.bmp}the actual value 98052. Arithmetic operators work as expected on **Variant** variables that contain numeric values or string data that can be interpreted as numbers. If you use the + operator to add MyVar to another **Variant** containing a number or to a variable of a numeric data type, the result is an arithmetic sum. See the information about addition and concatenation operators for complete information on how to use them with **Variant** data.

The value **Empty** denotes a **Variant** variable that hasn't been initialized (assigned an initial value). A **Variant** containing **Empty** is 0 if it is used in a numeric context and a zero-length string ("") if it is used in a string context.

Don't confuse **Empty** with **Null**. **Null** indicates that the **Variant** variable intentionally contains no valid data.

In a **Variant**, **Error** is a special value used to indicate that an error condition has occurred in a procedure. However, unlike for other kinds of errors, normal application-level error handling does not occur. This allows the programmer, or the application itself, to take some alternative based on the error value. **Error** values are created by converting real numbers to error values using the **CVErr** function.

See Also   **CVar** Function, **CVErr** Function, Data Type Summary, **Def***type* Statements, **Dim** Statement, **Private** Statement, **Public** Statement, **Static** Statement, **TypeName** Function, **VarType** Function.

VarType Function

Description	Returns a value indicating the subtype of a variable.
Syntax	**VarType**(*varname*)
Elements	The ***varname*** named argument can be any variable except a variable of a user-defined type.

Return Values

Value Returned	Constant	Variable Type
0	vbEmpty	Empty (uninitialized).
1	vbNull	Null (no valid data).
2	vbInteger	Integer.
3	vbLong	Long integer.
4	vbSingle	Single-precision floating point number.
5	vbDouble	Double-precision floating point number.
6	vbCurrency	Currency.
7	vbDate	Date.
8	vbString	String.
9	vbObject	OLE Automation object.
10	vbError	Error.
11	vbBoolean	Boolean.
12	vbVariant	Variant (used only with arrays of Variants).
13	vbDataobject	Non-OLE Automation object.
8192	vbArray	Array.

Note These constants are specified by Visual Basic. As a result, the names can be used anywhere in your code in place of the actual values.

Remarks

The **VarType** function never returns the value for vbArray by itself. It is always added to some other value to indicate an array of a particular type. The constant vbVariant is only returned in conjunction with vbArray to indicate that the argument to the **VarType** function is an array of type **Variant**. For example, the value returned for an array of integers is calculated as vbInteger + vbArray, or 8194.

See Also

Data Type Summary, **IsArray** Function, **IsDate** Function, **IsEmpty** Function, **IsError** Function, **IsMissing** Function, **IsNull** Function, **IsNumeric** Function, **IsObject** Function, **TypeName** Function, **Variant** Data Type.

Example

This example uses **VarType** to determine the subtype of a variable.

```
' Initialize variables.
IntVar = 459: StrVar = "Hello World": DateVar = #2/12/69#
MyCheck = VarType(IntVar)    ' Returns 2.
MyCheck = VarType(DateVar)   ' Returns 7.
MyCheck = VarType(StrVar)    ' Returns 8.
```

VaryByCategories Property

Applies To   ChartGroup.

Description   If this property is **True**, Microsoft Excel assigns a different color or pattern to each data marker. The chart must contain only one series. Read-write.

Syntax   *object*.**VaryByCategories**

Elements   *object*
                    Required. The ChartGroup object.

Example   This example assigns a different color or pattern to each data marker in the first chart group.

```
ActiveChart.ChartGroups(1).VaryByCategories = True
```

Verb Method

Applies To   OLEObject.

Description   Sends a verb to the server of the specified OLE object.

Syntax   *object*.**Verb**(*verb*)

Elements   The **Verb** method has the following object qualifier and named arguments:

                    object
                    Required. The OLEObject.

                    verb
                    Optional. The verb that the server of the OLE Object should act upon. If this argument is omitted, the default verb is sent. The available verbs are determined by the object's source application. Typical verbs for an OLE 2 object are Open and Primary (represented by the **xlOpen** and **xlPrimary** constants).

Example   This example sends the default verb to the server.

```
ActiveSheet.OLEObjects(1).Verb
```

Version Property

Applies To	Application.
Description	Returns the version number of Microsoft Excel. Read-only.
Syntax	*object*.**Version**
Elements	*object* Required. The Application object.
See Also	**AddIndent** Property, **HorizontalAlignment** Property.
Example	This example shows a message box with the name and version of Microsoft Excel, and the name of the operating system.

```
MsgBox("Welcome to Microsoft Excel version " & _
    Application.Version & " running on " & _
    Application.OperatingSystem & "!")
```

VerticalAlignment Property

Applies To	AxisTitle, Button, Buttons, ChartTitle, DataLabel, DataLabels, DrawingObjects, GroupObject, GroupObjects, Range, Style, TextBox, TextBoxes.
Description	Returns or sets the vertical alignment of the object (can be one of **xlBottom**, **xlCenter**, **xlDistributed**, **xlJustify**, or **xlTop**). Read-write.
Syntax	*object*.**VerticalAlignment**
Elements	*object* Required. The object to which this property applies.
Remarks	The **xlDistributed** alignment style works only in Far East versions of Microsoft Excel.
See Also	**AddIndent** Property, **HorizontalAlignment** Property.
Example	This example sets the height of row 2 to twice the standard height, and then centers the vertical alignment.

```
Rows(2).RowHeight = 2 * ActiveSheet.StandardHeight
Rows(2).VerticalAlignment = xlCenter
```

Vertices Property

Applies To   Drawing, DrawingObjects.

Description   Returns or sets the vertices of a polygon or freehand drawing, as a two-dimensional array of vertex coordinates in points (1/72 inch) relative to the upper-left corner of cell A1. The x coordinate is in column one of the array, the y coordinate is in column two. Every drawing and polygon will have at least two vertices. Read-only.

Syntax   *object*.**Vertices**

Elements   *object*
                  Required. The object to which this property applies.

See Also   **AddVertex** Method, **Reshape** Method.

Examples   This example displays the vertex coordinates for drawing one.

```
allVertices = ActiveSheet.Drawings(1).Vertices
Range("A1:C1").HorizontalAlignment = True
Range("A1:C1").Font.Bold = True
Cells(1, 1) = "Vertex"
Cells(1, 2) = "X"
Cells(1, 3) = "Y"
for i = 1 to UBound(allVertices, 1)
    Cells(i + 1, 1) = i
    Cells(i + 1, 2) = allVertices(i, 1)
    Cells(i + 1, 3) = allVertices(i, 2)
Next i
```

This example reshapes the drawing by moving vertex five 12 points (1/6 inch) in the X direction.

```
With ActiveSheet.Drawings(1)
    vX = .Vertices(5,1)
    vY = .Vertices(5,2)
    .Reshape 5, FALSE, vX + 12, vY
End With
```

Visible Property

Applies To   Application, Arc, Arcs, Button, Buttons, Chart, ChartObject, ChartObjects, Charts, CheckBox, CheckBoxes, DialogSheet, DialogSheets, Drawing, DrawingObjects, Drawings, DropDown, DropDowns, EditBox, EditBoxes, GroupBox, GroupBoxes, GroupObject, GroupObjects, Label, Labels, Line, Lines, ListBox, ListBoxes, Module, Modules, Name, OLEObject, OLEObjects, OptionButton, OptionButtons,

Oval, Ovals, Picture, Pictures, PivotItem, Rectangle, Rectangles, ScrollBar, ScrollBars, Sheets, Spinner, Spinners, TextBox, TextBoxes, Toolbar, Window, Worksheet, Worksheets.

Description   **True** if the object is visible. For a chart, dialog sheet, module or worksheet, this property can be set to **xlVeryHidden**. This hides the object so that it can only be made visible by setting this property to **True** (the user cannot make the object visible). Read-write.

Syntax   *object*.**Visible**

Elements   *object*
　　Required. The object to which this property applies.

Remarks   The **Visible** property for a pivot item is **True** if the item is currently showing on the table.

If you set the **Visible** property for a name to **False**, the name will not appear in the Define Name dialog box.

Examples   This example hides worksheet one.

```
Application.Worksheets(1).Visible = False
```

This example makes worksheet one visible.

```
Application.Worksheets(1).Visible = True
```

VisibleFields Method

Applies To   PivotTable.

Description   Returns a single pivot field (a PivotField object, Syntax 1) or a collection of the visible pivot fields (a PivotFields object, Syntax 2). Visible pivot fields are showing as row, column, page or data fields. Read-only.

Syntax 1   *object*.**VisibleFields**(*index*)

Syntax 2   *object*.**VisibleFields**

Elements   The **VisibleFields** method has the following object qualifier and named arguments:

object
　　Required. The PivotTable object.

index
　　Required for Syntax 1. The name or number of the pivot field to return (can be an array to specify more than one).

See Also	**ColumnFields** Method, **DataFields** Method, **HiddenFields** Method, **PageFields** Method, **PivotFields** Method, **RowFields** Method.

Example

This example adds the active pivot table visible field names to a list box.

```
For Each vsbField In ActiveCell.PivotTable.VisibleFields
    visibleFieldListBox.AddItem(vsbField.Name)
Next vsbField
```

VisibleItems Method

Applies To

PivotField.

Description

Returns one visible pivot item (a PivotItem object, Syntax 1) or a collection of all the visible pivot items (a PivotItems object, Syntax 2) in the specified field. Read-only.

Syntax 1

object.**VisibleItems(*index*)**

Syntax 2

object.**VisibleItems**

Elements

The **VisibleItems** method has the following object qualifier and named arguments:

object
    Required. The PivotField object.

index
    Required for Syntax 1. The number or name of the pivot item to return (can be an array to specify more than one).

See Also

ChildItems Method, **HiddenItems** Method, **ParentItems** Method, **PivotItems** Method.

Example

This example adds the names of all the visible items in the active field to a list box.

```
For Each pvtItem in ActiveCell.PivotField.VisibleItems
    visibleItemListBox.AddItem pvtItem.Name
Next pvtItem
```

VisibleRange Property

Applies To

Pane, Window.

Description

Returns the Range of cells that are visible in the window or pane. If a column or row is partially visible, it is included in the range. Read-only.

Syntax	*object*.**VisibleRange**
Elements	*object*
	Required. The Pane or Window object.
Example	This example sets the font in all cells visible in pane one to bold.

```
ActiveWindow.Panes(1).VisibleRange.Font.Bold = True
```

Volatile Method

Applies To	Application.
Description	Marks a user-defined function as volatile. A volatile function must be recalculated whenever calculation occurs in any cells of the worksheet. A non-volatile function is recalculated only when the input variables change. This method has no effect if it is not inside a user-defined function used to calculate a worksheet cell.
Syntax	*object*.**Volatile**(*volatile*)
Elements	The **Volatile** method has the following object qualifier and named arguments:

object
Required. The Application object.

volatile
Optional. If **True** or omitted, the function is marked as volatile. If **False**, the function is marked as non-volatile.

Example	This example marks the user-defined function "My_Func" as volatile. The function will be recalculated whenever calculation occurs in any cells of the worksheet where this function is used.

```
Function My_Func()
    Application.Volatile
    '
    '    Remainder of the function
    '
End Function
```

Wait Method

Applies To	Application.

Description   Pauses a macro that is running until a specified time is reached.

> **Important**   The **Wait** method suspends all Microsoft Excel activity and may prevent you from performing other operations on your computer. Background processes, such as printing and recalculation, are continued.

Syntax   *object*.**Wait**(*time*)

Elements   The **Wait** method has the following object qualifier and named arguments:

object
    Required. The Application object.

time
    Required. The time you want the macro to resume, in Microsoft Excel date format.

Example   This example pauses a running macro until 6:23 P.M. today.

```
Application.Wait "18:23:00"
```

Walls Object

Description   The walls of a 3-D chart.

Walls Property

Applies To   Chart.

Description   Returns the Walls of the 3-D chart. Read-only.

Syntax   *object*.**Walls**

Elements   *object*
    Required. The Chart object.

Example   This example sets the wall color.

```
Charts(1).Walls.Border.Color = RGB(255,0,0)
```

WallsAndGridlines2D Property

Applies To   Chart.

Description   **True** if gridlines are drawn in 2-D on a 3-D chart. Read-write.

Syntax   *object*.**WallsAndGridlines2D**

Elements   *object*
       Required. The Chart object.

Example   This example causes Microsoft Excel to draw 2-D gridlines on chart one.

```
ActiveWorkbook.Charts(1).WallsAndGridlines2D = True
```

Weekday Function

Description   Returns a whole number representing the day of the week.

Syntax   **Weekday(*date*)**

Elements   The *date* named argument is limited to numbers or strings, in any combination, that can represent a date. If *date* contains no valid data, **Null** is returned.

Return Values

Value	Description
1	Sunday
2	Monday
3	Tuesday
4	Wednesday
5	Thursday
6	Friday
7	Saturday

See Also   **Date** Function, **Date** Statement, **Day** Function, **Month** Function, **Now** Function, **Year** Function.

Example   This example uses the **Weekday** function to obtain the day of the week from a specified date.

```
MyDate = #February 12, 1969#      ' Assign a date.
MyWeekDay = Weekday(MyDate)       ' MyWeekDay contains 4 since it
                                  ' was a Wednesday.
```

Weight Property

Applies To	Border, Borders.
Description	Returns or sets the the weight of the border (one of **xlHairline**, **xlThin**, **xlMedium**, or **xlThick**). Read-write.
Syntax	*object*.**Weight**
Elements	*object* Required. The Border or Borders object.
Example	This example sets the weight of the border for oval one.

```
ActiveSheet.Ovals(1).Border.Weight = xlMedium
```

While...Wend Statement

Description	Executes a series of statements as long as a given condition is **True**.
Syntax	**While** *condition* [*statements*] **Wend**
Elements	The **While...Wend** statement syntax has these parts:

Part	Description
condition	Numeric or string expression that evaluates to **True** or **False**.
statements	One or more statements executed while condition is **True**.

Remarks	If *condition* is **True**, all statements in *statements* are executed until the **Wend** statement is encountered. Control then returns to the **While** statement and *condition* is again checked. If *condition* is still **True**, the process is repeated. If it is not **True**, execution resumes with the statement following the **Wend** statement.

While...Wend loops can be nested to any level. Each **Wend** matches the most recent **While**.

Caution Do not branch into the body of a **While...Wend** loop without executing the **While** statement. Doing so may cause run-time errors or other problems that are difficult to locate.

Tip The **Do...Loop** statement provides a more structured and flexible way to perform looping.

See Also   **Do...Loop** Statement, **With** Statement.

Example   This example uses the **While...Wend** statement to increment a counter variable. The statements in the loop are executed as long as the condition evaluates to **True**.

```
Counter = 0                    ' Initialize variable.
While Counter < 20             ' Test value of Counter.
    Counter = Counter + 1      ' Increment Counter.
Wend
Debug.Print Counter            ' Prints 20 in Debug window.
```

Width Property

Applies To   Application, Arc, Arcs, Button, Buttons, ChartArea, ChartObject, ChartObjects, CheckBox, CheckBoxes, DialogFrame, Drawing, DrawingObjects, Drawings, DropDown, DropDowns, EditBox, EditBoxes, GroupBox, GroupBoxes, GroupObject, GroupObjects, Label, Labels, Legend, Line, Lines, ListBox, ListBoxes, OLEObject, OLEObjects, OptionButton, OptionButtons, Oval, Ovals, Picture, Pictures, PlotArea, Range, Rectangle, Rectangles, ScrollBar, ScrollBars, Spinner, Spinners, TextBox, TextBoxes, Toolbar, ToolbarButton, Window.

Description   Returns or sets an object's width in points (1/72 inch). Read-write for all objects, except Range, which is read-only.

Syntax   *object*.**Width**

Elements   *object*
                    Required. The object this property applies to.

Remarks   The **Width** property has several different meanings, depending on the object to which it is applied.

Object	Description
Application	The distance from the left edge of the application window to the right edge of the application window.
Range	The width of the range.
Toolbar	The width of the toolbar. When you set the width, Microsoft Excel snaps both the width and the height to match the nearest allowable size.
Window	The width of the window. Use the **UsableWidth** property to determine the maximum size for the window.
	You cannot set this property if the window is maximized or minimized. Use the **WindowState** property to determine the window state.
Arc, Button, ChartArea, CheckBox, DialogFrame, Drawing, DrawingObjects, DropDown, EditBox, GroupBox, GroupObject, Label, Legend, Line, ListBox, OLEObject, OptionButton, Oval, Picture, PlotArea, Rectangle, ScrollBar, Spinner, TextBox, ToolbarButton, Window	The width of the object

On the Apple Macintosh, **Application.Width** is always equal to the total width of the screen, in points. Setting this value to any other value will have no effect.

In Microsoft Windows, if the window is minimized, **Application.Width** is read-only and returns the width of the icon.

You can use negative numbers to set the **Height** and **Width** properties of the following drawing objects: Arc, Button, CheckBox, Drawing, DropDown, EditBox, GroupBox, GroupObject, Label, Line, ListBox, OLEObject, OptionButton, Oval, Picture, Rectangle, ScrollBar, Spinner, and TextBox. This causes the object to reflect or translate (the behavior depends on the object), after which the **Top** and **Left** properties change to describe the new position. The **Height** and **Width** properties always return positive numbers.

See Also   **Left** Property, **Height** Property, **Top** Property.

Example   This example expands the active window to the maximum size available (without maximizing it).

```
With ActiveWindow
    .WindowState = xlNormal
    .Top = 1
    .Left = 1
    .Height = Application.UsableHeight
    .Width = Application.UsableWidth
End With
```

Width # Statement

Description   Assigns an output-line width to a file opened using the **Open** statement.

Syntax   **Width #***filenumber***,***width*

Elements   The **Width** statement syntax has these parts:

Part	Description
filenumber	Any valid file number.
width	Numeric expression in the range 0 to 255, inclusive, that indicates how many characters appear on a line before a new line is started. If *width* equals 0, there is no limit to the length of a line. The default value for *width* is 0.

See Also   **Open** Statement, **Print #** Statement.

Example   This example uses the **Width** statement to set the output-line width for a file.

```
Open "TESTFILE" For Output As #1        ' Open file for output.
Width #1, 5                             ' Set output-line width to 5.
For I = 0 To 9  ' Loop 10 times.
    Print #1, Chr(48 + I);       ' This prints 5 characters per line.
Next I
Close #1                                ' Close file.
```

Window Object

Description   Any window in Microsoft Excel.

WindowNumber Property

Applies To   Window.

Description   Returns the window number. For example, a window entitled "BOOK1.XLS:2" has a window number of two. Most windows have a window number of one. Read-only.

Syntax   *object*.**WindowNumber**

Elements   *object*
                       Required. The Window object.

Remarks   The window number is not the same as the window **Index**, which is the position of the window within the **Windows** collection.

See Also   **Index** Property.

Windows Method

Applies To   Application, Workbook.

Description   Returns a single window (a Window object, Syntax 1) or a collection of windows (the Windows object, Syntax 2). Read-only.

Syntax 1   *object*.**Windows(***index***)**

Syntax 2   *object*.**Windows**

Elements   The **Windows** method has the following object qualifier and named arguments:

                       object
                           Optional. The Application or Workbook containing the windows.

                       index
                           Required for Syntax 1. The name or number of the window.

Remark   Syntax 2 returns a collection of both visible and hidden windows.

Example   This example closes the first open or hidden window in Microsoft Excel.

```
Application.Windows(1).Close
```

Windows Object

Description   A collection of Window objects.

WindowsForPens Property

Applies To	Application.
Description	**True** if the computer is running under Microsoft Windows for Pen Computing. Read-only.
Syntax	*object*.**WindowsForPens**
Elements	*object* Required. The Application object.
Example	This example shows how to limit handwriting recognition to numbers and punctuation only if the computer is running under Microsoft Windows for Pen Computing.

```
If Application.WindowsForPens Then
    Application.ConstrainNumeric = True
End If
```

WindowState Property

Applies To	Application, Window.
Description	Returns or sets the state of the window, as shown in the following table. Read-write.

Value	Meaning
xlNormal	Window is not maximized or minimized.
xlMaximized	Window is maximized (Microsoft Windows only). Maximizing a window maximizes all windows on the Microsoft Excel desktop.
xlMinimized	Window is minimized (Microsoft Windows only).

Syntax	*object*.**WindowState**
Elements	*object* Required. The Application or Window object.
Example	This example maximizes the application window.

```
Application.WindowState = xlMaximized
```

With Statement

Description   Executes a series of statements on a single object or a user-defined type.

Syntax   **With** *object*
              [*statements*]
              End With

Elements   The **With** statement syntax has these parts:

Part	Description
object	Name of an object or a user-defined type.
statements	One or more statements to be executed on *object*.

Remarks   The **With** statement allows you to perform a series of statements on a specified object without requalifying the name of the object. For example, if you have a number of different properties to change on a single object, it is more convenient to place the property assignment statements within the **With** control structure, referring to the object once instead of referring to it with each property assignment. The following example illustrates use of the **With** statement to assign values to several properties of the same object.

```
With MyLabel
    .Height = 2000
    .Width = 2000
    .Caption = "This is MyLabel"
End With
```

You can nest **With** statements by placing one **With** loop within another. Each *object* must be unique.

See Also   **Do...Loop** Statement, **While...Wend** Statement.

Example   This example uses the **With** statement to execute a series of statements on a single object. The object MyObject and its properties are generic names used for illustration purposes only.

```
With MyObject
    ' Same as MyObject.Height = 100
    .Height = 100
    .Caption = "Hello World"
    With .Font
        ' Same as MyObject.Font.Color = Red.
        .Color = Red
        .Bold = True
    End With
End With
```

Workbook Object

Description   A workbook in Microsoft Excel.

Workbooks Method

Applies To   Application.

Description   Returns a single workbook (a Workbook object, Syntax 1) or a collection of workbooks (the Workbooks object, Syntax 2). Read-only.

Syntax 1   *object*.**Workbooks(***index***)**

Syntax 2   *object*.**Workbooks**

Elements   The **Workbooks** method has the following object qualifier and named arguments:

object
   Optional. The Application containing the workbooks.

index
   Required for Syntax 1. The name or number of the workbook.

Remarks   The collection returned by syntax 2 of the **Workbooks** method does not include open add-ins, which are a special kind of hidden workbook.

You can, however, return a single open add-in if you know the filename. For example **Workbooks**("OSCAR.XLA") will return the open add-in named "OSCAR.XLA" as a Workbook object.

Example   This example displays the number of open workbooks in Microsoft Excel.

```
cWorkbooks = Application.Workbooks.Count
MsgBox cWorkbooks & " workbook(s) currently open"
```

Workbooks Object

Description   A collection of Workbook objects.

Worksheet Object

Description   A worksheet in a workbook. A worksheet can also be a Microsoft Excel version 4.0 macro sheet, or Microsoft Excel version 4.0 international macro sheet.

Worksheet Property

Applies To   Range.

Description   Returns the Worksheet containing the specified range. Read-only.

Syntax   *object*.**Worksheet**

Elements   *object*
     Required. Returns the worksheet containing this range.

Example   This example displays the name of the worksheet containing the active cell.

```
MsgBox ActiveCell.Worksheet.Name
```

Worksheets Method

Applies To   Application, Workbook.

Description   Returns a worksheet (a Worksheet object, Syntax 1) or a collection of all worksheets (a Worksheets object, Syntax 2) in the workbook. Read-only.

Syntax 1   *object*.**Worksheets(***index***)**

Syntax 2   *object*.**Worksheets**

Elements   The **Worksheets** method has the following object qualifier and named arguments:

     object
          Optional for Application, required for Workbook. The object that contains worksheets.

     index
          Required for Syntax 1. The name or number of the worksheet to return.

Remarks   This method returns worksheets with the **Type** property equal to **xlWorksheet**, not **xlExcel4MacroSheet** or **xlExcel4IntlMacroSheet**; use the **Excel4MacroSheets** method or the **Excel4IntlMacroSheets** method to return those types.

Using this method with no object qualifier is a shortcut for
ActiveWorkbook.Worksheets.

Example   This example displays the number of worksheets in the active workbook.

```
MsgBox "There are " & ActiveWorkbook.Worksheets.Count & _
    " worksheets in this workbook."
```

Worksheets Object

Description   A collection of Worksheet objects.

WrapText Property

Applies To   Range, Style.

Description   **True** if Microsoft Excel wraps the text in the object. Read-write.

Syntax   *object*.**WrapText**

Elements   *object*
                      Required. The Range or Style object.

Remark   Microsoft Excel will change the row height of the range, if necessary, to display the text in the range.

Example   This example formats cell B2 so that the text in it wraps.

```
Cells(2, 2).Value = "This is a phrase that should wrap."
Cells(2, 2).WrapText = True
```

Write # Statement

Description   Writes raw data to a sequential file.

Syntax	**Write** #*filenumber*[,*outputlist*]
Elements	The **Write** statement syntax has these parts:

Part	Description
filenumber	Any valid file number.
outputlist	One or more comma-delimited numeric or string expressions to write to a file.

Remarks

If you omit *outputlist* and include a comma after *filenumber*, a blank line prints to the file. Multiple expressions can be separated with a space, a semicolon, or a comma. A space has the same effect as a semicolon.

When **Write #** is used to output data to a file, several universal assumptions are followed so the data can always be read and correctly interpreted using **Input #**, regardless of locale:

- Numeric data is always output using the period (.) as the decimal separator.

- For Boolean data, either #TRUE# or #FALSE# is printed. The **True** and **False** keywords are not translated, regardless of locale.

- Date data is written to the file using the universal date format. When either the date or the time component is missing or zero, only the provided part gets written to the file.

- Nothing is written to the file if *outputlist* data is **Empty**. However, for **Null** data, #NULL# is output.

- For error data, the output appears as #ERROR errorcode#. The **Error** keyword is not translated, regardless of locale.

Unlike the **Print #** statement, the **Write #** statement inserts commas between items and quotation marks around strings as they are written to the file. You don't have to put explicit delimiters in the list. **Write #** inserts a newline character (carriage return or carriage return-linefeed) after it has written the final character in *outputlist* to the file.

See Also

Input # Statement, **Open** Statement, **Print #** Statement.

Example	This example uses the **Write #** statement to write raw data to a sequential file.

```
Open "TESTFILE" For Output As 1      ' Open file for output.
Write #1, "Hello World", 234 ' Written data is comma delimited.
Write #1,                            ' Write blank line.

' Assign Boolean, Date, Null and Error values.
MyBool = False : MyDate = #February 12, 1969# : MyNull = Null
MyError = CVErr(32767)
' Boolean data is written as #TRUE# or #FALSE#. Date literals are
' written in universal date format. Null data is written as #NULL#.
' Error data is written as #ERROR errorcode#.
Write #1, MyBool ; " is a Boolean value"
Write #1, MyDate ; " is a date"
Write #1, MyNull ; " is a null value"
Write #1, MyError ; " is an error value"
Close #1                             ' Close file.
```

WriteReserved Property

Applies To	Workbook.
Description	**True** if the workbook is write reserved. Read-only.
Syntax	*object*.**WriteReserved**
Elements	*object* 　　Required. The Workbook object.
Remarks	Use the **SaveAs** method to set this property.
Example	In this example, if the workbook BUDGET93.XLS is saved as write-reserved, the code saves it as TESTFILE.XLS.

```
If Workbooks("BUDGET93.XLS").WriteReserved Then
    Workbooks("BUDGET93.XLS").SaveAs fileName:="TESTFILE.XLS"
End If
```

WriteReservedBy Property

Applies To	Workbook.
Description	Returns a string that names the user with current write permission for the workbook. Read-only.

Syntax	*object*.**WriteReservedBy**
Elements	*object*
	Required. The Workbook object.
Example	This example displays a message reminding you to contact the user with the current write permission for the workbook PROFIT92.XLS if the **WriteReserved** property is **True**.

```
With Workbooks("PROFIT92.XLS")
    If .WriteReserved Then
        MsgBox "Please contact " & .WriteReservedBy & _
        " if you need to insert data in this workbook."
    End If
End With
```

Xor Operator

Description	Used to perform a logical exclusion on two expressions.
Syntax	*result* = *expression1* **Xor** *expression2*
Elements	The **Xor** operator syntax has these parts:

Part	Description
result	Any numeric variable.
expression1	Any expression.
expression2	Any expression.

Remarks	If one, and only one, of the expressions evaluates **True**, *result* is **True**. However, if either expression is a **Null**, *result* is also a **Null**. When neither expression is a **Null**, *result* is determined according to the following table:

If expression1 is	And expression2 is	The result is
True	True	False
True	False	True
False	True	True
False	False	False

The **Xor** operator also performs a bit-wise comparison of identically positioned bits in two numeric expressions and sets the corresponding bit in *result* according to the following truth table:

If bit in *expression1* is	And bit in *expression2* is	The *result* is
0	0	0
0	1	1
1	0	1
1	1	0

See Also

Operator Precedence.

Example

This example uses the **Xor** operator to perform logical exclusion on two expressions.

```
A = 10: B = 8: C = 6 : D = Null ' Initialize variables.
MyCheck = A > B Xor B > C    ' Returns False.
MyCheck = B > A Xor B > C    ' Returns True.
MyCheck = B > A Xor C > B    ' Returns False.
MyCheck = B > D Xor A > B    ' Returns Null.
MyCheck = A Xor B    ' Returns 2 (bit-wise comparison).
```

XValues Property

Applies To

Series.

Description

Returns or sets an array of the x values of the series on an XY scatter chart. The **XValues** property can be set to a range on a worksheet or an array of values, but it may not be a combination of both. Read-write.

Syntax

object.**XValues**

Elements

object
    Required. The Series object.

Example

This example sets the x values to the range B1:B5.

```
Set ActiveChart.SeriesCollection(1).XValues =
Worksheets(1).Range("B1:B5")
```

This example uses an array to set values for the individual points on the series.

```
ActiveChart.SeriesCollection(1).XValues = Array(5, 6.3, 8, 6.9, 10)
```

XYGroups Method

Applies To   Chart.

Description   On a 2-D chart, returns a single scatter chart group (a ChartGroup object, Syntax 1), or a collection of the scatter chart groups (a ChartGroups collection, Syntax 2).

Syntax 1   *object*.**XYGroups**(*index*)

Syntax 2   *object*.**XYGroups**

Elements   The **XYGroups** method has the following object qualifier and named arguments:

object
Required. The Chart object.

index
Required for Syntax 1. Specifies the chart group.

Example   This example makes the first scatter group an area group.

```
Charts(1).XYGroups(1).Type = xlArea
```

Year Function

Description   Returns a whole number representing the year.

Syntax   **Year**(*date*)

Elements   The *date* named argument is limited to a date or numbers and strings, in any combination, that can represent a date. If *date* contains no valid data, **Null** is returned.

See Also   **Date** Function, **Date** Statement, **Day** Function, **Month** Function, **Now** Function, **Weekday** Function.

Example   This example uses the **Year** function to obtain the year from a specified date.

```
' In the development environment, the date literal will display in short
' format using the locale settings of your code.
MyDate = #February 12, 1969# ' Assign a date.
MyYear = Year(MyDate)    ' MyYear contains 1969.
```

Zoom Property

Applies To   PageSetup, Window.

Description   **PageSetup object**:

Returns or sets a percentage to scale the worksheet for printing, between 10 and 400 percent. Read-write.

If this property is **False**, the **FitToPagesWide** and **FitToPagesTall** properties control how the worksheet is scaled.

Window object:

Returns or sets the display size of the window, in percent (100 means show at normal size; 200 means the window is double size, etc.).

The property can also be set to **True** to set the window size to fit the current selection.

Syntax   *object*.**Zoom**

Elements   *object*
Required. The PageSetup or Window object.

Remarks   **PageSetup object**:

This property applies only to worksheets.

All scaling retains the aspect ratio of the original document.

Window object:

This function will only affect the sheet that is currently active in the window. To use this property on other sheets, you must first activate them.

Example   This example scales the worksheet by 150 percent.

```
ActiveSheet.PageSetup.Zoom = 150
```

ZOrder Property

Applies To   Arc, Arcs, Button, Buttons, ChartObject, ChartObjects, CheckBox, CheckBoxes, Drawing, DrawingObjects, Drawings, DropDown, DropDowns, EditBox, EditBoxes, GroupBox, GroupBoxes, GroupObject, GroupObjects, Label, Labels, Line, Lines, ListBox, ListBoxes, OLEObject, OLEObjects, OptionButton, OptionButtons, Oval, Ovals, Picture, Pictures, Rectangle, Rectangles, ScrollBar, ScrollBars, Spinner, Spinners, TextBox, TextBoxes.

Description	Returns the z-order position of the object. Read only.
Syntax	*object*.**ZOrder**
Elements	*object* Required. The object to which this property applies.
Remarks	For any collection of objects, the object at the back of the z-order is *collection*(1), and the object at the front of the z-order is *collection*(*collection*.count). For example, if there are three ovals on the active sheet, the oval at the back of the z-order is **ActiveSheet.Ovals(1)**, and the oval at the front of the z-order is **ActiveSheet.Ovals(ActiveSheet.Ovals.Count)**.
See Also	**BringToFront** Method, **SendToBack** Method.
Example	This example displays the z-order position of oval one.

```
MsgBox "The oval position is " & _
    ActiveSheet.Ovals("Oval 1").ZOrder
```

Boost Your Word Processing Skills

Running Word 6 for Windows™
Russell Borland

Master the power and features of Microsoft Word 6 for Windows with this completely updated edition of the bestselling guide for intermediate to advanced users. This example-rich guide features in-depth, accessible coverage on Word's powerful new features and contains scores of insights and power tips not found in the documentation. To help you find information quickly and easily, this new edition offers an expanded, cross-referenced index, comprehensive tables of contents for each section and chapter, and icons that point out the new features of version 6.

832 pages, softcover $29.95 ($39.95 Canada)   ISBN 1-55165-574-3

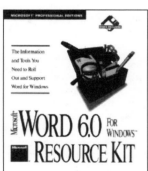

Microsoft® Word 6 for Windows™ Resource Kit
Microsoft Corporation

This is your one-stop guide to installing, customizing, and supporting Word 6 for Windows. It includes information on training new and migrating users, troubleshooting, preventing potential problems, and ensuring that users are taking full advantage of productivity-boosting features. The two accompanying disks include the Word 6 for Windows Converter, customizable self-paced training exercises, 250 tips and tricks, and a helpful file to make custom installation easier.

672 pages with two 3.5-inch disks
$39.95 ($53.95 Canada)   ISBN 1-55615-720-7

Microsoft® Word Developer's Kit
Microsoft Corporation

If you want to customize Microsoft Word 6 for Windows to work the way you do, create custom applications, or create macros that streamline routine tasks, the Microsoft Word Developer's Kit is your one-stop solution. You'll find all the technical information and tools you need, including detailed information on using WordBasic, using Workgroup MAPI and ODBC extensions, and using the Word API. The disk includes sample WordBasic macros and dynamic link libraries for putting MAPI and ODBC to work. Also includes source files and development tools for programming with the Word API.

1024 pages, softcover with one 3.5-inch disk
$39.95 ($53.95 Canada)   ISBN 1-55615-630-8

*Microsoft*Press

Microsoft Press® books are available wherever quality books are sold and through CompuServe's Electronic Mall—GO MSP.
*Call 1-800-MSPRESS for direct ordering information or for placing credit card orders.**
Please refer to BBK when placing your order. Prices subject to change.
*In Canada, contact Macmillan Canada, Attn: Microsoft Press Dept., 164 Commander Blvd., Agincourt, Ontario, Canada M1S 3C7, or call (416) 293-8464, ext. 340.
Outside the U.S. and Canada, write to International Sales, Microsoft Press, One Microsoft Way, Redmond, WA 98052-6399.

Build Your Spreadsheet Expertise

Microsoft® Excel Visual Basic® for Applications Step by Step
Reed Jacobson

Customize Microsoft Excel to work the way you do! Now you can learn the new macro language in Microsoft Excel version 5 for Windows the easy way—with self-paced lessons and disk-based practice files. Covers everything from automating everyday tasks to building a data-extraction utility.

350 pages, softcover with one 3.5-inch disk
$29.95 ($39.95 Canada)   ISBN 1-55615-589-1

Microsoft® Excel 5 Worksheet Function Reference
Covers version 5 for Windows™ and the Apple® Macintosh®
Microsoft Corporation

Tap into the number-crunching power of Microsoft Excel by using worksheet functions! You can solve nearly any type of numerical problem—on the job or at home! With worksheet functions, you don't have to be a genius at mathematics, statistics, or finance. Simply enter the right worksheet function with the required data, and Microsoft Excel does the rest. This reference provides complete information about each of the more than 300 worksheet functions built into Microsoft Excel 5 and is the hard-copy documentation for the Microsoft Excel 5 worksheet function online Help.

336 pages $12.95 ($16.95 Canada)   ISBN 1-55615-637-5

Running Microsoft® Excel 5 for Windows™
The Cobb Group with Mark Dodge,
Chris Kinata, and Craig Stinson

Here's the most accessible book that offers comprehensive and in-depth information for all levels of spreadsheet users. It includes hundreds of power tips and practical shortcuts for the powerful new features of Microsoft Excel 5 for Windows. In addition to the step-by-step tutorials, straightforward examples, and expert advice, this updated edition features a new and improved format designed to help you find answers faster!

1184 pages $29.95 ($39.95 Canada)   ISBN 1-55615-585-9

*Microsoft*Press

Register Today!

Return the
Microsoft® Excel Visual Basic®
for Applications Reference
registration card for:

✔ a Microsoft Press® catalog

✔ exclusive offers on specially
   priced books

U.S. and Canada addresses only. Fill in information below and mail postage-free. Please mail only the bottom half of this page.

Microsoft Excel Visual Basic for Applications Reference—Owner Registration Card

_____
NAME

_____
INSTITUTION OR COMPANY NAME

_____
ADDRESS

_____

_____
CITY   STATE   ZIP

Your feedback is important to us.

Include your daytime telephone number, and we may call to find out how you
use *Microsoft Excel Visual Basic for Applications Reference* and what we
can do to make future editions even more useful. If we call you, we'll send you
a **FREE GIFT** for your time!

(_____) _____
DAYTIME TELEPHONE NUMBER

1-55615-624-3A   W2E

It's a Jungle Out There!

Field Guide to Microsoft® Excel™ 5 for Windows™
Stephen L. Nelson
If you're new to Microsoft Excel for Windows, you
may at times find yourself lost in a spreadsheet jungle. If you
want quick answers about Microsoft Excel commands, this is
the guide for you. This handy guide is arranged by task and
organized in easy-to-use, easy-to-remember sections, with rich
cross-referencing for easy lookup. Look for the friendly guy
in the pith helmet, who leads you through from start to finish.
208 pages $9.95   ($12.95 Canada)   ISBN 1-55615-579-4

Microsoft Press

NO POSTAGE
NECESSARY
IF MAILED
IN THE
UNITED STATES

BUSINESS REPLY MAIL
FIRST-CLASS MAIL   PERMIT NO. 53   BOTHELL, WA

POSTAGE WILL BE PAID BY ADDRESSEE

MICROSOFT PRESS REGISTRATION
MICROSOFT EXCEL VISUAL BASIC
   FOR APPLICATIONS REFERENCE
PO BOX 3019
BOTHELL WA   98041-9910